THOMSON
COURSE TECHNOLOGY

Professional ■ Trade ■ Reference

SONAR™ 3

POWER!

By Scott R. Garrigus

MUSKA&LIPMAN
Publishing

SONAR™ 3 Power!

Senior Vice President, Retail and Strategic Market Group: Andy Shafran

Publisher: Stacy L. Hiquet

Credits: Senior Marketing Manager, Sarah O'Donnell; Marketing Manager, Heather Hurley; Manager of Editorial Services, Heather Talbot; Senior Acquisitions Editor, Kevin Harreld; Senior Editor, Mark Garvey; Associate Marketing Manager, Kristin Eisenzopf; Retail Market Coordinator, Sarah Dubois; Production Editor, Cathleen D. Snyder; Copy Editor, Cathleen D. Snyder; Technical Editor, Jim Healey, Technical Support Manager at Cakewalk; Proofreader, Gene Redding; Cover Designer, Course Design Team; Interior Design and Layout, Cathie Tibbetts; Indexer, Katherine Stimson.

Library of Congress Catalog Number: 2003113728

ISBN: 1-59200-339-7

5 4 3 2 1

Educational facilities, companies, and organizations interested in multiple copies or licensing of this book should contact the publisher for quantity discount information. Training manuals, CD-ROMs, and portions of this book are also available individually or can be tailored for specific needs.

MUSKA & LIPMAN

Muska & Lipman Publishing,
a Division of Course Technology
25 Thomson Place
Boston, MA 02210
www.muskalipman.com
publisher@muskalipman.com

About the Author

Scott R. Garrigus (http://www.garrigus.com) has been involved with music and computers since he was 12 years old. After graduating from high school, he went on to earn a B.A. in music performance with an emphasis in sound recording technology at UMass, Lowell. In 1993, he released his first instrumental album on cassette, entitled *Pieces Of Imagination*. In 1995, he began his professional writing career when his first article appeared in *Electronic Musician* magazine. In 2000, he authored his first book, *Cakewalk Power!* This was the first book to deal exclusively with the Cakewalk Pro Audio, Guitar Studio, and Home Studio software applications. In 2001, his second book, *Sound Forge Power!*, which was the first book to deal exclusively with Sony's Sound Forge audio editing software, was published. Also in 2001, his third book, *SONAR Power!*, which was the first book to deal exclusively with Cakewalk's SONAR software, was published. In 2002, his fourth and fifth books, *SONAR 2 Power!* and *Sound Forge 6 Power!*, were published. Today, Garrigus continues to contribute articles to a number of print and online publications. He also publishes his own music technology e-zine, called *DigiFreq* (http://www.digifreq.com), which provides free news, reviews, tips, and techniques for music technology users.

Dedication

For Greg Zaino and Ron Desjardins. We had some good times at UMass, Lowell. I never would have made it through college without you guys.

Acknowledgments

Thanks to all my music technology friends who take the time to visit my Web site and read my ramblings in the *DigiFreq* newsletter each month. The DigiFreq family is now over 14,000 strong!

Thanks to all the SONAR users whose dedication and support helped to make this book possible.

Thanks to all my friends over at Cakewalk (Steve Thomas, Carl Jacobson, Morten Saether, Jesse Jost, Tom Roussell, Russell Soule, and others).

Thanks to the Muska & Lipman publishing team.

Thanks also to my friend and neighbor, Ron LaMonica. I really appreciate all your help and support.

And as ever, thank you to my family and to God for the blessings you have bestowed upon my life.

Contents

14 Studio Control with StudioWare and Sysx 381

15 CAL 101 395

16 Advanced CAL Techniques 405

Introduction

This is the first book on the market that deals exclusively with Cakewalk's SONAR 3. You can find other Cakewalk-related and generic books about using computers to create and record music that might provide a small amount of information about SONAR 3, but none of them provides complete coverage of the product. Of course, SONAR 3 comes with an excellent manual, but like most other manuals, it is meant only as a feature guide.

Instead of simply describing the features of the program and how they work, I'm going to dig deep down into the software and show you exactly how to use the product with step-by-step examples and exercises that will help make your composing and recording sessions run more smoothly. I'll explain all of the features available, and I'll do it in a manner you can understand and use right away.

So why should you listen to me? Well, I've been using SONAR (and its predecessor, Pro Audio) for many years. I've written three Cakewalk-related books before this one—*Cakewalk Power!*, *Sonar Power!* and *Sonar 2 Power!*. I've also written about Cakewalk products in numerous review articles for magazines such as *Electronic Musician, Computer Music*, and *Future Music*. In addition, I've been working with the people at Cakewalk for quite some time now, learning all there is to know about SONAR 3, as well as testing the product during the beta process. And the people at Cakewalk have helped me develop much of the information in this book, making sure that everything is "officially" technically accurate. How's that for a seal of approval? Suffice it to say, I know my way around the product, and now I would like to share that knowledge with you.

I'm going to assume that SONAR 3 is installed on your computer and that you know how to start the program. In addition, you should have at least skimmed through the manual that comes with the software, and you should have all your external audio and MIDI gear set up already. I'm also going to assume you know how to use your mouse for clicking, dragging, double-clicking, right-clicking, and so on. You also should know how to work with basic Windows features such as Windows Explorer and the Windows Control Panel. And you should have access to the World Wide Web—or perhaps have a friend who does. Otherwise, all you need is a strong interest in learning how to get the most out of SONAR 3. Just leave the rest up to me, and I promise you'll be working with SONAR 3 like you never have before. You might even have some fun with it, too.

How This Book Is Organized

You'll find that although I've tried to avoid overlapping content between this book and the manual that comes with SONAR 3, in some instances this overlap just can't be avoided. I want to be sure to help you understand all the important features of the program, and doing so means including some basic explanations. For the most part, though, the information included in this book is more "how to" than "this feature does so-and-so."

Chapter 1, "MIDI and Digital Audio Basics," and Chapter 2, "Getting Started with SONAR 3," provide an introduction to computer music and the software. These chapters explain the importance of registration and how to find help, as well as the major features and more obscure parts of the software, and how they work together.

Chapter 3, "Customizing SONAR," shows you how to make SONAR 3 work the way you want it to. This chapter explains program preferences and workspace customization, as well as how to find the optimal settings for MIDI and audio functionality.

In Chapter 4, "Working with Projects," you'll learn how to work with projects. This chapter includes step-by-step instructions for opening, closing, and saving existing projects. You'll also learn how to create new projects and make your own project templates.

Chapter 5, "Getting Around in SONAR 3," and Chapter 6, "Recording and Playback," describe how to navigate within SONAR 3 and how to record and play back your projects. You'll find instructions on how to record and play MIDI as well as audio, and you'll learn about recording multiple tracks at once. I'll explain the importance of the Now time and show you how to use the Go menu, search, and markers, as well as the zoom features. After you read these chapters, you'll make your way through SONAR 3 like a pro.

In Chapter 7, "Editing Basics," and Chapter 8, "Exploring the Editing Tools," you're ready to dive into editing. First I'll explain the basics to you, including tracks and clips, the Event Editor, and Piano Roll. Then you can investigate the editing tools in more detail.

Chapter 9, "Composing with Loops," shows you how to use the looping features and Loop Construction view found in SONAR 3. Using these features, you can compose songs using nothing more than audio sample loops. The looping features add functionality to SONAR 3 similar to what you would find in Sony's ACID software.

Similar to the VST synth features that you find in Steinberg's Cubase software, SONAR 3 gives you access to virtual synthesizer plug-ins. These plug-ins let you compose music with MIDI using software-based synthesizers rather than the synth in your sound card or your external MIDI keyboard. Chapter 10, "Software Synthesis," explores these features.

Chapter 11, "Exploring Effects" explains one of my favorite parts of SONAR 3. The things you can do with these tools are amazing. I'll cover both the MIDI and audio effects, and I'll show you how to use them in offline and real-time situations. I'll even share some cool presets I've developed so you can use them in your own recording projects.

Chapter 12, "Mixing It Down," takes a look at mixing. I know that mixing music via software can be confusing sometimes. Nothing beats being able to just grab a fader on a hardware-based mixer, but after you read this chapter, you might find that with all the functionality SONAR 3 provides, mixing is actually easier, and you have more control when you're using an onscreen software mixer.

I've received many questions about SONAR's capabilities in terms of music notation, so that's the topic I'll cover in Chapter 13, "Making Sheet Music." I'll explain all the tools you have at your disposal, as well as what you can and cannot do. Although SONAR 3 doesn't provide full-fledged music notation features, you might be surprised at what you find here.

Chapter 14, "Studio Control with StudioWare and Sysx," Chapter 15, "CAL 101," and Chapter 16, "Advanced CAL Techniques," jump into some of the more complicated features that SONAR 3 offers. Don't worry if you think StudioWare and CAL are out of your reach as a beginning user. Actually, you can use these features in plenty of ways even if you decide not to explore them fully.

Finally, in Chapter 17, "Taking Your SONAR 3 Project to CD," I'll show you how to prepare your SONAR 3 project and burn it onto CD.

My hope is that by reading this book, you will learn how to master SONAR 3. If along the way you have a little fun while you're at it, that's all the better.

Conventions Used in This Book

As you begin to read, you'll see that most of the information in this book is solid and useful. It contains very little fluff. I won't bore you with unrelated anecdotes or repetitious data. But to help guide you through all this material, I'll use several different conventions that highlight specific types of information you should keep an eye out for.

TIP

Tips are extra information that you should know related to the topic being discussed. In some cases they include personal experiences and/or specific techniques not covered elsewhere.

CAUTION

Cautions highlight actions or commands that can make irreversible changes to your files or potentially cause problems in the future. Read them carefully because they might contain important information that can make the difference between keeping your files, software, and hardware safe and losing a huge amount of work.

NOTE

Sometimes you might like to know (but don't necessarily *need* to know) certain points about the current topic. Notes provide additional material to help you avoid problems or to shed light on a feature or technology, and they also offer related advice.

1

MIDI and Digital Audio Basics

If you're anything like me, you want to get started right away learning all about SONAR 3. But if you don't understand the basic concepts and terms associated with computer music, you might have a hard time working your way through this book. To give you a quick overview of the most significant aspects of music technology, this chapter will do the following:

▶ Define MIDI and explain how it works

▶ Define digital audio and explain how it works

▶ Explain the difference between MIDI and digital audio

Of course, this one chapter can't replace an entire book about the subject. If you want to learn more about MIDI and digital audio, plenty of extended resources are available. For example, there is an e-book called the *Desktop Music Handbook* available for free reading on the Web. You can find it at http://www.cakewalk.com/tips/desktop.asp.

What Is MIDI?

MIDI (*Musical Instrument Digital Interface*) is a special kind of computer language that lets electronic musical instruments (such as synthesizer keyboards) "talk" to computers. It works like this: Say you use a synthesizer keyboard as your musical instrument. Every key on the keyboard of your synthesizer has a corresponding electronic switch. When you press a key, its corresponding switch is activated and sends a signal to the computer chip inside your keyboard. The chip then sends the signal to the MIDI interface in your keyboard, which translates the signal into MIDI messages and sends those messages to the MIDI interface in your computer system.

MIDI INTERFACE

A *MIDI interface* is a device that is plugged into your computer, allowing it to understand the MIDI language. Basically, you can think of the interface as a translator. When your electronic musical instrument sends out MIDI messages to your computer, the MIDI interface takes those messages and converts them into signals that your computer can understand.

The MIDI messages contain information telling your computer that a key was pressed (called a *Note On message*), which key it was (the name of the note represented by a number), and how hard you hit the key (called the *MIDI velocity*). For example, if you press Middle C on your keyboard, a Note On message is sent to your computer, telling it that you pressed a key. Another message containing the number 60 is sent, telling the computer that you pressed Middle C. And a final message is sent containing a number from 1 to 127 (1 being very soft and 127 being very hard), which tells your computer how hard you hit the key.

Different MIDI messages represent all the performance controls on your keyboard. In addition to each key, MIDI messages represent the modulation wheel, pitch bend wheel, and other features. Your computer can store all the MIDI messages that are sent to it as you play your keyboard. The timing of your performance (how long it takes you to hit one key after another and how long you hold down each key) can be stored as well. Your computer can then send those MIDI messages back to your keyboard with the same timing, so that it seems like you are playing the music, but without touching the keys. The basic concept goes like this: You play a piece of music on your keyboard. Your performance is stored as instructions in your computer. Then those instructions are sent back to your keyboard from the computer, and you hear the piece of music played back exactly the same way you performed it, mistakes and all (see Figure 1.1).

Figure 1.1
This diagram shows how MIDI messages are recorded and played back with a computer.

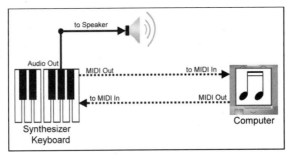

What Is Digital Audio?

Digital audio is the representation of sound as numbers. Recording sound as digital audio is similar to recording sound using a tape recorder, but slightly different. Suppose you have a microphone connected to your computer system. When you make a sound (such as singing a tune, playing a musical instrument, or even simply clapping your hands), the microphone "hears" it and converts the sound to an electronic signal. The microphone then sends the signal to the sound card in your computer, which translates the signal into numbers. These numbers are called *samples*.

SOUND CARD
A *sound card* is a device that is plugged into your computer, allowing it to understand the electronic signals of any audio device. Basically, you can think of the sound card as a translator. When an audio device (such as a microphone, electronic musical instrument, CD player, or anything else that can output an audio signal) sends out signals to your computer, the sound card takes those signals and converts them into numbers that your computer can understand.

The samples contain information that tells your computer how the recorded signal sounded at certain instances in time. The more samples used to represent the signal, the better the quality of the recorded sound. For example, to make a digital audio recording that has the same quality as audio on a CD, the computer needs to receive 44,100 samples for every second of sound that's recorded. The number of samples received per second is called the *sampling rate*.

The size of each individual sample also makes a difference in the quality of the recorded sound. This size is called the *bit depth*. The more bits used to represent a sample, the better the sound quality. For example, to make a digital audio recording with the same quality as audio on a CD, each sample has to be 16 bits in size.

BINARY NUMERALS

Computers use binary numerals to represent numbers. These binary numerals are called *bits*, and each bit can represent one of two numbers: 1 or 0. By combining more than one bit, computers can represent larger numbers. For instance, any number from 0 to 255 can be represented with 8 bits. With 16 bits, the range becomes 0 to 65,535.

Your computer can store all the samples that are sent to it. The timing of each sample is stored as well. Your computer can then send those samples back to the sound card with the same timing so what you hear sounds exactly the same as what was recorded. The basic concept goes like this: Your sound card records an electronic signal from an audio device (such as a microphone or CD player). The sound card converts the signal into numbers called *samples*, which are stored in your computer. Then those samples are sent back to the sound card, which converts them back into an electronic signal. The signal is sent to your speakers (or other audio device), and you hear the sound exactly as it was recorded (see Figure 1.2).

Figure 1.2
This diagram shows how audio is converted into numbers so it can be recorded and played back with a computer.

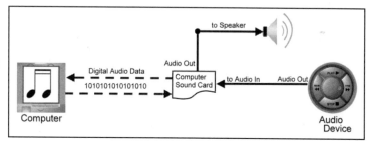

So What's Really the Difference?

After reading the explanations of MIDI and digital audio, you might still be wondering what the difference is between them. Both processes involve signals being sent to the computer to be recorded, and then the computer sending those signals back out to be played, right? Well, you have to keep in mind that when you're recording MIDI data, you're not recording actual sound; you are recording only performance instructions. This concept is similar to a musician reading sheet music, with the sheet music representing MIDI data and the musician representing a computer. The musician (or computer) reads the sheet music (or MIDI data) and then stores it in memory. The musician then plays the music back via a musical instrument. Now what if the musician uses a different instrument to play back the music? The musical performance remains the same, but the sound changes. The same thing happens with MIDI data. A synthesizer keyboard can make all kinds of different sounds, but playing the same MIDI data back with the keyboard yields the exact same performance, no matter what.

When you're recording digital audio, you *are* recording actual sound. If you record a musical performance as digital audio, you cannot change the sound of that performance, as described earlier. Because of these differences, MIDI and digital audio have their advantages and disadvantages. Because MIDI is recorded as performance data and not actual sound, you can manipulate it much more easily than you can manipulate digital audio. For example, you can easily fix mistakes in your performance by simply changing the pitch of a note. And MIDI data can be translated into standard musical notation, but digital audio can't. On the other hand, MIDI can't be used to record anything that requires actual audio, such as sound effects or vocals. With digital audio, you can record any kind of sound, and you can always be sure that your recording will sound exactly the same every time you play it back. With MIDI, you can't be sure of that because although the MIDI data remains the same, the playback device or sound can be changed.

I hope this description clears up some of the confusion you might have about MIDI and digital audio. You need to be familiar with a number of other related terms, but I will cover them in different areas of the book as I go along. For now, as long as you understand the difference between MIDI and digital audio, I can begin talking about the real reason you bought this book—to learn how to use SONAR 3.

2

Getting Started with SONAR 3

Now that you have a basic understanding of the technology involved in making music with computers, I think you'll find working with SONAR 3 more enjoyable. Ready to get started? This chapter will do the following:

▶ Tell you how to obtain the latest product update

▶ Explain the importance of registering your software

▶ Give you a quick tour of SONAR's major features

▶ Briefly cover the new features in SONAR 3

▶ Describe a basic studio environment

▶ Let you know where to look for help if problems arise

What Version of SONAR Do You Have?

Even though you're using SONAR 3, it might not be latest version. Cakewalk is constantly fixing and improving the software. Any problems you experience might easily be remedied with an update. To find out exactly what version you're using, start SONAR, and click on Help > About SONAR. A dialog box similar to Figure 2.1 will appear, displaying your exact version number. You should then check to see whether a more recent update is available.

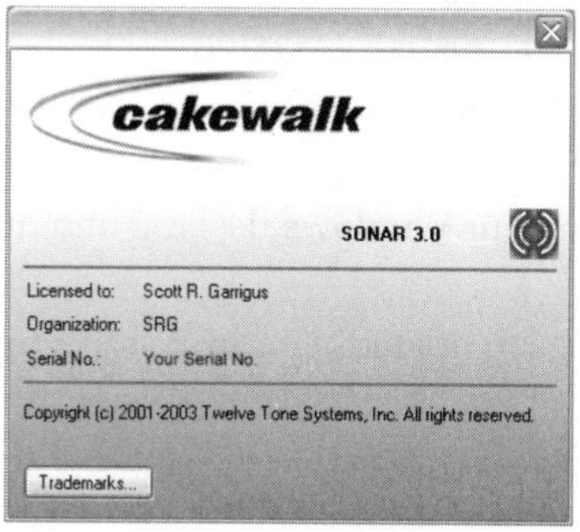

Figure 2.1
The About SONAR dialog box shows the program's current version number.

Getting the Latest Product Update

Although automatically receiving new product updates would be nice, most companies can't afford to send CDs to all their users every time they update their product. That's one of the reasons why the Internet has become such a wonderful tool. Sometimes the answer to your problem is just a download away. Cakewalk provides a support area on its Web site where you can get the latest updates for SONAR. Just follow these steps to get the updates:

1. Log on to the Internet.
2. Start SONAR and choose Help > SONAR on the Web. This will automatically open your Web browser and take you to the SONAR Owner's Page, as shown in Figure 2.2.

Figure 2.2
You can download SONAR updates from the SONAR Owner's Page.

3. In the section labeled Updates and Patches, click on the name of the update you need. If more than one update is available, simply compare your current version to the updates listed and select the appropriate one. For instance, if you have SONAR 3.0, you'll want the update that upgrades version 3.0 to the current version.
4. Click on the Download link for the update, and then follow the instructions to download the update patch.
5. Create a temporary folder on your Windows desktop and download the update file to that folder.
6. Run the file. That's all there is to upgrading—your software is now updated.

FOUND A BUG?

Think you've found a bug? Just because a software product is released to the public doesn't mean it's perfect. Improvements are always being made; that's why updates become available. If you have a problem with SONAR on a regular basis and you can reproduce that problem by performing the same steps each time, you might have found a bug in the software. Before you go spreading any rumors, though, first tell some friends about it and see whether they can reproduce the problem on their computer systems. If so, then after the bug has occurred in SONAR, choose Help > Cakewalk Problem Report to create a report about your PC and current SONAR project. You should then e-mail that report, along with a detailed description of the problem, to Cakewalk at support@cakewalk.com. The staff might already be aware of the bug and be working on a fix for it. Then again, they might not be aware of it, and although your diligence won't make you famous, you'll feel good to know that you might have saved your fellow SONAR users a lot of frustration.

Registering Your Software

Do you think registering your software is important? If not, think again. First and foremost, if you don't register your software, Cakewalk won't provide you with technical support. You'll be sorry if you run into a problem that causes you to lose some of your precious work, and the only thing between you and your sanity is the people at Cakewalk. If you're a techno-wizard and this situation doesn't worry you, that's great. But there's something else you might not have considered. What if your hard drive crashes and you need to reinstall all your software applications, including SONAR? And what if you can't find the jewel case for your SONAR CD? Yes, the jewel case—not the CD. Why is it significant? Because the jewel case has a little sticker with a very important number printed on it—your serial number. Without that number, you can't install SONAR. So now who ya gonna call? Remember to send in that registration card! And just to be safe, you might want to check with Cakewalk to make sure your information is on file. Just do the following:

1. Find your CD jewel case and look on the back to make sure your serial number is printed there.

2. You can also find your product serial number by looking on the detachable part of your registration card or by starting SONAR and choosing Help > About SONAR.

3. Log on to the Internet and start SONAR (if you haven't already).

4. Choose Help > Register Online. This will automatically open your Web browser and take you to the Cakewalk Registration Form page.

5. Fill in the form and click on the Register button.

Now you can rest easy, knowing that help is just a phone call or e-mail away.

STORING YOUR SERIAL NUMBERS

To avoid losing your serial number, you might want to write it on your SONAR CD. Be sure to use an indelible pen and write the numbers on the top (the side with the printed material) of the CD. Don't write on the shiny side. You also might want to write down the number in a second location, just in case. I like to keep track of all the serial numbers for my software applications in a simple text file. I have a list containing the names and serial numbers of all the important software installed on my computer system. I also include the current version number and company contact information for each product. Then, if I ever run into a problem, I just refer to the list. By the way, you might also want to print the text file each time you update it. If your hard drive crashes, the text file won't do you any good because you won't be able to access it.

Taking a Quick Tour of SONAR

Because SONAR is such a powerful application, you can use it for a variety of different tasks including composing music, developing computer game music and sounds, producing compact discs, creating audio for the Web, and even scoring films and videos. SONAR provides a number of features to support all these endeavors and more. As a matter of fact, you can use SONAR as the central piece of equipment in your studio because it allows you to control all your music gear from your computer via onscreen control panels. However you decide to use SONAR, you'll find plenty of flexibility and power in the tools provided.

Projects

In SONAR, all your music data for a single body of work is organized as a *project*. A project can be anything from a Top 40 song or a 30-second radio spot to a full-length symphonic score, such as a movie soundtrack. Along with the music data, all of SONAR's settings for a single work are stored in the project as well. A project is saved on disk as a single file with a .CWP or .CWB file extension. The difference between the two file types is that a work (.CWP) file stores only MIDI data and project settings, whereas a bundle (.CWB) file also includes any audio data within a project. (For more information, see Chapter 4, "Working with Projects.")

Tracks, Clips, and Events

The music data within a project is organized into units called *tracks*, *clips*, and *events*. Events, which are the smallest units, consist of single pieces of data, such as one note played on a MIDI keyboard. Clips are groups of events. They can be anything from a simple MIDI melody to an entire vocal performance recorded as audio. Tracks are used to store clips. For example, a pop song project might contain seven tracks of music data—six for the instruments and one for the vocal performance. Each track can contain any number of clips that might represent one long performance or different parts of a performance. SONAR gives you unlimited tracks. The only limitations are the speed of your CPU and hard drive and the amount of memory (RAM) you have in your computer. I'll talk more about tracks, clips, and events in Chapter 7, "Editing Basics."

Track View

To work with the data in a project, you have to use the *views* in SONAR. Views are like windows that let you see and manipulate the data in a project in a variety of ways. The most important is the Track view, shown in Figure 2.3.

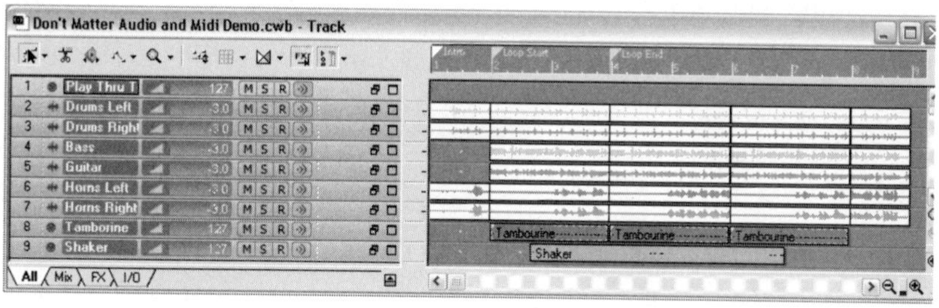

Figure 2.3
The Track view is the main window used to work with a project in SONAR.

In this window, you can see all the tracks that are available in a project. You also can view and edit all the basic track settings, as well as all the clips contained in each track. I'll talk about the Track view extensively in a number of different chapters in the book.

Staff View

In the Staff view, you can work with the MIDI data in your project as standard music notation. By selecting one or more MIDI tracks in the Track view and opening the Staff view, you can see your music just as if it were notes on a printed page, as in Figure 2.4.

Figure 2.4
In the Staff view, you can see and edit your MIDI data as standard music notation.

Using the Staff view, you also can edit your music notation by adding, changing, or deleting notes. Special notation functions such as dynamics markings, percussion parts, and guitar chord symbols are included, too. You can notate anything from a single one-staff melody to an entire 24-part musical score. I'll talk about using the Staff view in Chapter 13, "Making Sheet Music."

Piano Roll View

Although the Staff view is great for traditional music editing, it doesn't allow you to access expressive MIDI data, such as note velocity or pitch bend controller messages. For that data, you can use the Piano Roll view. This view displays notes as they might appear on a player-piano roll, as shown in Figure 2.5.

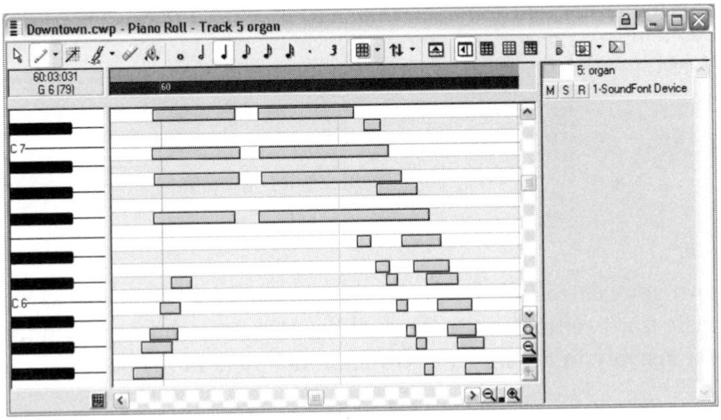

Figure 2.5

The Piano Roll view gives you access to both note and MIDI controller messages.

You can change note pitch and duration by simply dragging the rectangular representations. But more important, you can view and edit MIDI controller messages graphically with the mouse instead of having to deal with raw numbers. For more details about the Piano Roll view, see Chapter 7.

Event List View

If you really want precise control over the data in your project, the Event List view is the tool for the job. The Event List view shows individual events in a track (or the entire project) as special keywords and numbers in a list, as shown in Figure 2.6.

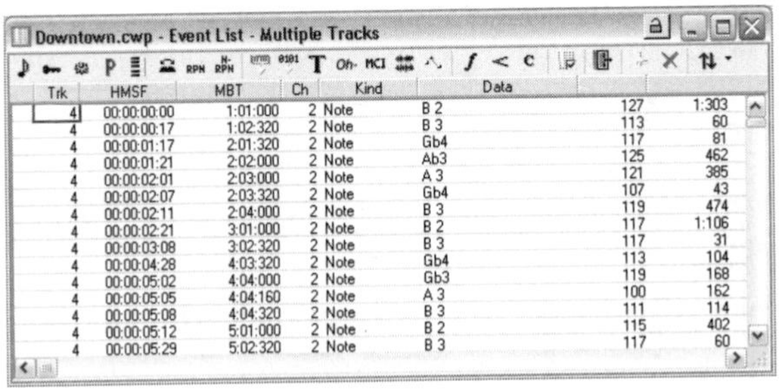

Figure 2.6

For really precise editing tasks, the Event List view gives you access to the individual events in a project.

Using this view is similar to looking at the raw MIDI data that is recorded from your MIDI keyboard or controller. You can edit the characteristics of single notes and MIDI controller messages by typing in data. You'll probably use the Piano Roll view more often, but it's nice to know the Event List view is available if you need it. I'll talk more about the Event List view in Chapter 7.

Loop Construction View

The Loop Construction view gives you an easy way to create your own sample loops. You can use these loops, which are digital audio clips designed to be played over and over, to construct entire songs. When you're working with the Loop Construction view, you see the sound wave of your loop, as in Figure 2.7.

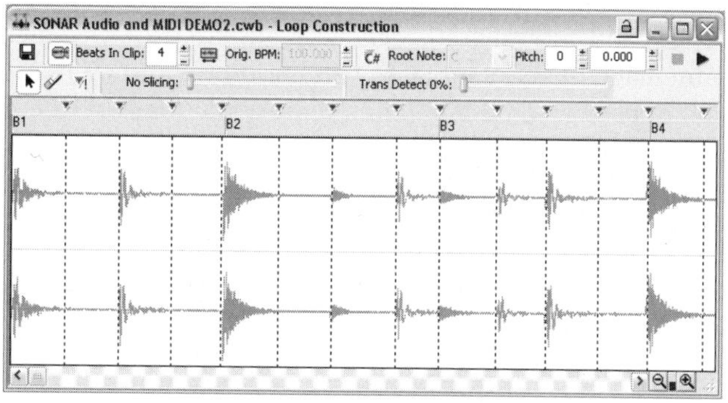

Figure 2.7
The Loop Construction view is a special editing tool for creating sample loops.

Not only does the Loop Construction view allow you to create your own sample loops, you can even use ACID-compatible loops, like the loops found in Sony's ACID software. In Chapter 9, "Composing with Loops," I'll get into more detail about the Loop Construction view.

Console View

When you're ready to mix all your MIDI and audio tracks down to a single stereo file, you can use the Console view. This tool is made to look and function like a real recording studio mixing console, as you can see in Figure 2.8.

Figure 2.8
The Console view looks and functions similar to a real recording studio mixing console.

You can use the Console view to adjust the panning and volume for each track in a project. As a matter of fact, you can use the Console view in place of the Track view for adjusting track settings and recording new tracks. And just like on a real mixing console, you can monitor volume levels via onscreen meters, as well as mute and solo individual tracks or groups of tracks. I'll talk more about the Console view in Chapter 6, "Recording and Playback," Chapter 11, "Exploring Effects," and Chapter 12, "Mixing It Down."

CHAPTER 2

StudioWare and CAL

Two of the most advanced features provided by SONAR are StudioWare and CAL (*Cakewalk Application Language*). Even though these features seem complicated, they're actually quite easy to use. Sure, if you really want to dive in and master these features they can get complex, but for the most part they are accessible to even the most timid user. What's more, when you start using StudioWare and CAL, you won't want to stop. StudioWare allows you to design onscreen panels to manipulate MIDI data and control your MIDI gear, and CAL allows you to create macros or small programs to automate the different tasks you perform within SONAR. These two features alone have quite a bit of power, so I'll talk much more about them in Chapters 14 through 17.

What's New in SONAR 3?

SONAR has changed a bit from version 2.0. In the interim, Cakewalk provided two free updates (versions 2.1 and 2.2), which included bug fixes and alterations in terms of features. Here's a brief list of the changes:

▶ **Open Media Format (OMF).** SONAR now supports the new Open Media Format. This allows you to save your project in a standard file format that can be loaded into other sequencing applications. I'll cover this topic in Chapter 4.

▶ **Windows Media Advanced Streaming 9 export.** SONAR has added support for the new Windows Media 9 streaming file format. You can export your audio to this new format for posting on the Internet. Check out Appendix C, "Producing for Multimedia and the Web," for more information.

▶ **Event Properties Inspector toolbar.** This is a new toolbar that makes it easier for you to edit the characteristics of single notes in a MIDI clip or track. I'll cover this topic in Chapter 7.

▶ **New video features.** SONAR allows you to set a video offset and trim for all video media types instead of just AVI files. The new Render Quality property page in the Video Properties dialog box lets you specify preview mode, frame rate, and video size. Check Appendix C to learn about these features.

▶ **Import Audio multi-selection.** The Import Audio feature supports multi-selection, which allows you to import multiple audio files simultaneously. Chapter 6 provides more detailed information.

▶ **ASIO support.** SONAR now supports the ASIO (*Audio Stream Input Output*) sound card driver specification. If your sound card provides ASIO drivers, you can now access them. I'll talk more about this in Chapter 3, "Customizing SONAR."

SONAR 3 also introduces many changes in terms of features, some of which were suggested by users. These features include:

▶ **Unmerged MIDI input.** SONAR no longer merges input from all MIDI ports and is not limited to echoing only the active track. MIDI echo is now controlled on a per-track basis by a button on the track header. I'll go into detail on this topic in Chapter 6.

▶ **Per-track input monitoring.** Audio input monitoring has been changed to operate on a per-track basis, and has also been functionally separated from the Record Arm button. I'll tell you more about this in Chapter 6.

▶ **MTC and MIDI sync to multiple ports.** SONAR will now generate MIDI timecode and send it to any port. Also, it will send MIDI sync to multiple user-defined ports. See Chapter 6 for more information on these features.

▶ **MIDI Groove clips.** MIDI Groove clips, as the name implies, are much like audio groove clips. You can roll them out to create a looping pattern, and they can follow tempo changes and pitch markers. Check out Chapter 9 for more information.

▶ **New audio bussing.** SONAR now provides much more flexible audio bussing. Basically, this means that any track or bus can be routed to any bus or directly to the hardware ports. I'll tell you all about it in Chapter 12.

▶ **New Console view.** A definite oversight of version 2, SONAR 3's new Console view is completely reconfigured. It's divided into three panes. The left pane contains all tracks, the center pane contains all buses, and the right pane contains the mains. The strip at the far left contains controls for the modules on the various track and bus strips. I'll show you how to use this view in Chapter 12.

▶ **VST/VSTi support.** In addition to DirectX and DXi plug-ins, SONAR now supports the standard VST and VSTi plug-ins. This means you get access to literally thousands of free effects and software synths available on the Internet. I'll give you the scoop on this in Chapters 10, "Software Synthesis," and 11, "Exploring Effects."

Like version 2, SONAR 3 comes in two flavors: SONAR 3 Studio and SONAR 3 Producer. The only difference between the two is that SONAR 3 Producer includes the following extras:

▶ **Enhanced Console view.** In addition to the new design I mentioned earlier, the Console view also includes assignable channel effect controls and integrated audio channel EQ. I'll talk about this in Chapter 12.

▶ **VSampler 3.0 DXi.** This is a high-quality, software-based sampler with new audio engine, effects, and mixer features. There's also support for multiple sample file formats (AKAI 1000/3000, DLS, SF2, VC3, HALion FXP, and Tascam .GIG). I'll cover this in Chapter 10.

▶ **Ultrafunk Sonitus:fx.** This is a very high-quality audio effects plug-in package that includes the following effects: compressor, delay, parametric EQ, gate, modulator, multi-band compressor, phase, reverb, surround, and wahwah. I'll talk about this in Chapter 11.

A Basic Studio Setup

Over the years, I've built up quite an arsenal of tools that currently reside in my home studio. But you don't need a ton of gizmos and gadgets to produce great music. If I were to scale down my setup to include only the basics, I'd be left with everything I need to compose and record my tunes with SONAR.

CHAPTER 2

Computer

Other than SONAR itself, a basic studio revolves around one main component—your PC. If you already have a PC, be sure to check it against Cakewalk's system requirements for SONAR. Your best bet is to check it against the recommended system requirements rather than the minimum because the minimum requirements won't give you very high-quality performance.

SYSTEM REQUIREMENTS

Cakewalk's system requirements for SONAR are as follows:

Minimum system requirements

- ▶ Windows 2000/XP operating system
- ▶ 500 MHz processor speed
- ▶ 64 MB of RAM
- ▶ 100 MB of hard disk space for full program installation
- ▶ Any type of hard disk
- ▶ 800×600 resolution, 256 color depth
- ▶ *Windows-compatible MIDI interface
- ▶ **Windows-compatible, ***WDM-compatible sound card

Recommended system requirements

- ▶ Windows 2000/XP operating system
- ▶ 1.2 GHz processor speed
- ▶ 256 MB of RAM
- ▶ 100 MB of hard disk space for full program installation
- ▶ EIDE/Ultra DMA (7200 RPM) or SCSI hard drive
- ▶ 1024×768 resolution, 24-bit color depth
- ▶ *Windows-compatible MIDI interface
- ▶ **Windows-compatible, ***WDM-compatible sound card

* Required to connect to external MIDI devices
** Required for audio playback
*** Requires Windows Me/2000/XP

If your system matches (or exceeds) the recommended system requirements, you should be all set to run SONAR. If not, then you should seriously consider either upgrading or purchasing a new system. If you decide to go with a new system, you might want to think about building it yourself or picking out the components and having it built for you. It's not that a generic Gateway or Dell PC won't do, but they are not really optimized for audio work, which is the main reason I decided to put together my own system. I cheated a little, though—I had a company called Aberdeen, Inc. (http://www.aberdeeninc.com) build the base system for me. I actually went with a bare-bones system called a Shuttle PC, and then added the necessary additional components. The specifications for my current system are as follows:

- ▶ Shuttle PC SS51G Bare-Bone system
- ▶ Intel Pentium 4 2.4B GHz/533FSB processor
- ▶ 1.0 GB DDR333 SDRAM memory

► Teac 3.5 1.44 MB floppy drive

► Two Seagate 80GB 9.5ms 7200 RPM ATA/100 2MB hard drives

► Integrated SIS 651 graphic engine for video

► Onboard 10/100 Fast Ethernet LAN

► Toshiba CD-R/RW and DVD-ROM combo drive

► NEC AccuSync 75F monitor

► Echo Mona audio interface (sound card)

► Windows XP Professional

THE NEW DIGIFREQ AUDIO PC

The reason I went with a Shuttle PC system wasn't just because I needed a better PC with more power; I also chose it because it is one of the quietest systems on the market and it gives off much less heat than a typical PC. If you'd like to hear more about the Shuttle PC, check out my feature article entitled "The New DigiFreq Audio PC" in Issue 18 of *DigiFreq*. You can download the issue for free at

http://www.digifreq.com/digifreq/issues.asp.

As you can tell, my current PC can easily run SONAR and then some, but you don't need a top-of-the-line system to get good performance. As long as the specifications for your computer land somewhere between SONAR's minimum and recommended system requirements, you shouldn't have any trouble running the software. But if you have the money and decide to get a new PC, by all means get the most powerful system you can afford. You won't be sorry.

OPTIMIZE YOUR AUDIO PC

One of the reasons many people can get away with using a less powerful system is that they have optimized it for audio work. There are a number of things you can do to your PC that will make it run more efficiently for the purposes of making music. These include making adjustments to the system itself, as well as to the Windows OS. If you'd like more information about how to optimize your audio PC, check out my feature article entitled "Optimize Your Audio PC" in Issue 14 of *DigiFreq*. You can download the issue for free at

http://www.digifreq.com/digifreq/issues.asp.

Sound Card

The most important thing to consider when purchasing a sound card for use with SONAR is whether there are WDM or ASIO drivers available for the card. You'll need to get in touch with the manufacturer of the card to verify this. Why is it so important? Because SONAR supports a Microsoft technology called WDM (*Windows Driver Model*) and a Steinberg technology called ASIO (*Audio Stream Input Output*). If you have a sound card that has WDM or ASIO drivers, SONAR will give you much better performance in terms of audio *latency*. Basically, latency is a form of audio delay that occurs when a software program such as SONAR can't communicate with your sound card fast enough while processing audio data, which results in an audible delay. This is usually only noticeable with features that use real-time processing. In SONAR, these include input monitoring and real-time DXi and VSTi performance. I'll talk more about latency in Chapter 3, input monitoring in Chapter 6, and DXi and VSTi in Chapter 10.

You should also be aware that Windows 2000 and Windows XP are the only operating systems that are truly compatible with WDM drivers, which is why 2000 and XP are listed in the recommended system requirements. Windows 98 SE also provides limited support for WDM drivers, but most manufacturers are not supporting it. As far as Windows Me is concerned…well, let's just say it's more trouble than it's worth. Some people use Windows Me without any problems, but I've heard from too many people who've had trouble with the OS to recommend it. Luckily, SONAR only supports Windows 2000 and XP, so you shouldn't have any trouble with regard to the version of Windows you are using.

RECOMMENDED SOUND CARDS

For a list of audio cards recommended by Cakewalk, go to

http://www.cakewalk.com/tips/audiohw.asp.

Of course, there are many other things to consider when choosing a particular card. You should look for a PCI-based sound card (one that is installed inside your computer) rather than a USB-based sound card. USB audio interfaces don't really provide enough bandwidth to transfer audio data fast enough for sufficient use. However, with the new USB 2.0 spec, that shouldn't present a problem once manufacturers update their products in the near future. You might also want to consider using a FireWire-based sound card; those are beginning to hit the market. They still aren't as good as a PCI-based card, but they're definitely better than USB 1.0. You should also be aware of the types of connections that sound cards supply. The typical sound card provides a number of different audio inputs and outputs including line level, microphone level, and speaker. Line-level inputs and outputs are used to transfer sound from cassette decks, radios, electronic keyboards, or any other standard audio device. Microphones generate a very low audio level by themselves, so they need a special input of their own, which is connected to an internal preamplifier on the sound card. Speakers also need their own special connector with a built-in amplifier to produce a decent amount of volume. Some high-end sound cards also offer digital inputs and outputs. These special connectors let you attach the sound card directly to compatible devices such as some CD players and DAT (*Digital Audio Tape*) decks. Using these connections gives you the best possible sound because audio signals stay in the digital domain and don't need to be converted into analog signals. In addition, connectors come in a variety of forms. Low-cost cards usually provide the same 1/8-inch jacks used for headphones on boom boxes. For better quality, there are 1/4-inch, RCA, or XLR jacks. Connections can also be *balanced* or *unbalanced*. Balanced connections provide shielding to protect the audio signal against RFI (*Radio Frequency Interference*). Unbalanced connections don't provide any type of protection.

If you want to be able to record more than one audio track at once, you'll need a card with multiple audio connections. Most average sound cards internally mix all of their audio sources down to one stereo signal, but higher-end (more expensive) cards let you record each device separately on its own discreet stereo channel. This capability is much more desirable in a music-recording studio, but not everyone needs it.

A good-quality audio signal is something that everybody desires. During recording, the sampling rate (which I talked about in Chapter 1) plays a big part in the quality of the audio signal. Suffice it to say, the higher the sampling rate that a sound card can handle, the better the sound quality. The sampling rate of a CD is 44.1 kHz (44,100 samples per second); all sound cards on the market support this. Professional cards can hit 48 kHz or higher.

Bit resolution (which I also talked about in Chapter 1) is a factor in determining digital sound quality as well. The more bits you have to represent your signal, the better it will sound. The CD standard is 16 bits, which is supported by all sound cards. Some cards (again, mostly high-end) go up to 20, 22, or even 24 bits.

Two other measurements you need to look out for are signal-to-noise ratio and frequency response. As with the other measurements mentioned earlier, the higher the better. Since all electronic devices produce some amount of noise, the signal-to-noise ratio of a sound card tells you how much higher the signal strength is compared to the amount of internal noise made by the sound card. The greater the number, the quieter the card. A good signal-to-noise measurement is about 90 dB or higher. Frequency response is actually a range of numbers, which is based on the capabilities of human hearing. The frequency response of human hearing is approximately 20 Hz to 20 kHz. A good sound card will encompass at least that range, maybe even more.

What do I use? I decided to go with the Mona from Echo Audio. You'll notice that it is on Cakewalk's recommended list, and for good reason. The Mona provides a wide variety of professional features, and the sound quality is great. My main reasons for choosing it, however, were good WDM drivers, built-in preamps, and multiple connections. If you get a card with built-in preamps, you can eliminate the need for yet another component in the signal chain, which can potentially add noise. And if you get a card with multiple connections, you can usually do away with having to use a mixing board, which can also be a source of additional noise. I love being able to just plug my microphone and instruments directly into my sound card, knowing that I'm getting the cleanest signal possible. Unfortunately, the Mona was discontinued and is no longer sold by the company, but you can find other cards with similar features. I usually recommend checking out the products available from Echo Audio (http://www.echoaudio.com), M-Audio (http://www.m-audio.com), and Aardvark (http://www.aardvark-pro.com).

MIDI Interface

If you have any external MIDI devices (like a MIDI keyboard), then you'll need a MIDI interface for your computer. I explained MIDI interfaces back in Chapter 1, but I didn't really go into what you should know when you're looking to buy one. If you have a simple setup with only one MIDI keyboard, then you can easily get away with a simple single- or double-port MIDI interface. The best way to go here is to get a USB-based interface. It will be easy to install (just plug it in) and it won't take up an IRQ or PCI slot inside your computer. Also be sure that the interface has Windows 2000 or Windows XP compatible drivers (depending on what OS you are using). Bad drivers can cause problems. Other than that, the only major differences between interfaces are the number of ports they provide. If you have many external MIDI devices, it's best to connect each device to its own dedicated MIDI port. I'm currently using an M-Audio Midisport 2x2 USB interface under Windows XP. It works great and does just what I need it to. I usually recommend checking out the products available from Midiman (http://www.midiman.com) when people ask me about MIDI interfaces.

CHAPTER 2

Microphone

If you plan to do any acoustic recording (vocals, acoustic guitar, and so on), you'll need a good microphone. There are literally hundreds of microphones on the market, and entire books have been written on the subject, so I won't go into great detail here. Basically, the microphone you choose depends on the application. I needed a good vocal mic, but not something that was going to put me in the poor house. While I would love to get a Neumann U87 (one of the best), there's no way I could afford one. So luckily, Shure came to my rescue with their KSM27. It's a great vocal mic that isn't too expensive. You can find more information about it at http://www.shure.com/ microphones/models/ksm27.asp?PN=Selection%20Guides. I like that it can also be used for other applications in a pinch. But what's right for me might not be right for you, so I've rounded up a number of online resources that will allow you to educate yourself on the subject of microphones.

▶ **Microphone University:** http://www.dpamicrophones.com/eng_pub/index.html

▶ **Shure Performance and Recording Microphone Selection Guide:** http://www.shure.com/selectionguides/sel-perfrecmics.html

▶ **The Microphone FAQ:** http://www.harmony-central.com/Other/mic-faq.txt

▶ **Harmony Central Microphone Manufacturers List:** http://www.harmony-central.com/Recording/manufact.html#mic

Speakers

Of course you also need to be able to hear the music you're recording, so you'll need a good set of speakers (or monitors, as they're called in the professional audio world). Like microphones, there are literally hundreds of different monitors on the market. For home studio purposes, you'll probably want to get yourself a good pair of active, nearfield monitors. They're called *active* because they come with a built-in amplifier, which saves you from having to buy an external amp and match it up to your monitors. They're called *nearfield* because you listen to them at a fairly close distance (about four feet). This lets you set up your home studio in just about any space you can find because you don't have to acoustically treat the room, at least not professionally.

CREATE THE RIGHT RECORDING ENVIRONMENT

For some tips about how to set up your home studio space for better recording, check out my feature article entitled "Creating the Right Recording Environment" in Issue 15 of *DigiFreq*. You can download the issue for free at

http://www.digifreq.com/digifreq/issues.asp.

There is a wide variety of monitors available, but I'm currently having fun with the V4s from KRK Systems (http://www.krksys.com). These are a pair of active, nearfield monitors that really deliver great sound. I also love that they've been designed for small workstation areas and they're shielded, which means you can sit them close to your computer screen without problems. Of course, as with microphones, what I like might not be what you like, so I've compiled a number of online resources that will help you learn about and choose the right monitors for you.

▶ **Ten Powered Nearfields Reviewed:** http://www.prorec.com/prorec/articles.nsf/ files/0B7FAE7ED3205D3C86256AE100044F41

▶ **Audio FAQ (Speakers):** http://www.tm.tue.nl/vakgr/ok/vos/audio-faq/faq-09.htm

▶ **eCoustics.com Speaker Articles:** http://www.ecoustics.com/Home/Home_Audio/
Speakers/Speaker_Articles/

▶ **Harmony Central Speakers Manufacturer List:** http://www.harmony-central.com/
Recording/manufact.html#speak

Finding Help When You Need It

Cakewalk provides a number of ways for you to find help when you're having a problem with
SONAR. The two most obvious places to look are the user's guide and the SONAR Help file.
Actually, these two sources contain basically the same information, but with the Help file, you can
perform a search to find something really specific. At the first sign of trouble, you should go
through the included troubleshooting information. If you can't find an answer to your problem
there, you can pay a visit to the Cakewalk Web site.

The support page of the Cakewalk Web site (http://www.cakewalk.com/Support) contains a ton of
helpful information, including FAQs and technical documents that provide details on a number of
Cakewalk-related topics. You should check them first. If you still can't find an answer to your
problem, the next place to look is either in the Cakewalk newsgroups
(http://www.cakewalk.com/Support/newsgroups.asp) or the DigiFreq discussion area
(http://www.digifreq.com/digifreq/discuss.asp). In the newsgroups and discussion area, you can
trade tips, advice, and information with other Cakewalk product users. Many times, you'll find
that someone has had the same problem you're having, and he or she has already found a solution.
Isn't sharing great? For even more helpful information, check out Appendix D, "SONAR Resources
on the Web," at the end of this book.

FREE MUSIC TECHNOLOGY NEWSLETTER

Also be sure to sign up for a free subscription to my *DigiFreq* music technology
newsletter. *DigiFreq* is a monthly e-mail newsletter that helps you learn more about
music technology. It provides free news, reviews, tips, and techniques for music
technology users. By applying for your own free subscription, you can learn all
about the latest music product releases, read straightforward reviews, explore
related Web resources, and have a chance to win free products from brand-name
manufacturers. To get your free subscription, go to
http://www.digifreq.com/digifreq.

Of course, you can also contact Cakewalk Technical Support directly. You can either e-mail your
questions to support@cakewalk.com or you can call 617-423-9021 (USA). Currently, the hours are
Monday through Friday from 10 a.m. to 6 p.m. Eastern time. But remember, to receive technical
support you have to be a registered user. If you call or send e-mail, you'll be asked for your serial
number. As I said before, remember to send in that registration card! You'll be a much happier
camper…er, Cakewalker.

3

Customizing SONAR

Although we all may be SONAR users, that doesn't mean we like to work with the product in exactly the same way. I have my way of doing things, and you probably have your own way. Luckily, SONAR provides a number of settings so you can make the program conform to your way of working. This chapter will do the following:

▶ Tell you how to organize all the different files associated with SONAR

▶ Teach you to customize the program's workspace, including colors, toolbars, window layouts, and key bindings

▶ Explain how you can set up all the MIDI parameters

▶ Tell you how to find the optimal audio settings

Organizing Files

As you work with SONAR, you'll deal with many different types of files. These include project files, audio files, StudioWare files, CAL files, and so on. To keep things organized, SONAR allows you to specify different disk locations for storing each file type. Initially, SONAR stores most of the files in the C:\Program Files\Cakewalk\SONAR 3\Sample Content folder on your hard drive, but that doesn't mean they have to stay there.

Changing File Locations

To specify your own file locations, follow these steps.

1. In SONAR, choose Options > Global to open the Global Options dialog box, and then click on the Folders tab (see Figure 3.1).

Figure 3.1
Use the Global Options
dialog box to specify your
file storage locations.

Global Options
General   Timecode   MIDI   Folders   Editing   Audio Data

Project Files: C:\Cakewalk Projects

Templates: C:\Program Files\Cakewalk\SONAR 3\Sample C

CAL Files: C:\Program Files\Cakewalk\SONAR 3\Sample C

Window Layouts: C:\Program Files\Cakewalk\SONAR 3\Sample C

Wave Files: C:\Program Files\Cakewalk\SONAR 3\Sample C

Video Files: C:\Program Files\Cakewalk\SONAR 3\Sample C

Sysx Files: C:\Program Files\Cakewalk\SONAR 3\Sample C

Groove Quantize: C:\Program Files\Cakewalk\SONAR 3\Sample C

StudioWare: C:\Program Files\Cakewalk\SONAR 3\Sample C

Patterns: C:\Program Files\Cakewalk\SONAR 3\Pattern Br

Drum Maps: C:\Program Files\Cakewalk\SONAR 3\Drum Map

OK   Cancel   Help

2.   In the Project Files field, specify where you would like to store all your SONAR projects by typing in a new folder location. This includes .CWP (Work), .CWB (Bundle), and .MID (MIDI) files. When you specify a folder location for this parameter, it affects the location to which the File > Open and File > Save As dialog boxes will initially open. I'll talk more about working with project files in Chapter 4, "Working with Projects."

BROWSE FOR FOLDERS

An easier way to specify a folder location is to click on the ellipsis button located to the right of each field. This will open the Browse for Folder dialog box, which will let you specify a folder location by navigating through your computer's file directory using your mouse.

Also, if your computer is connected to a network, you can specify a folder location on the network rather than on your computer's hard drive. This can be useful if you want to share your project data with other musicians in your studio.

After you have selected a new file location, click on OK.

3.   In the Templates field, specify where you would like to store all your SONAR project templates by typing in a new folder location. This includes .CWT files. I'll talk more about project templates in Chapter 4, "Working with Projects."

4.   In the CAL Files field, specify where you would like to store all your CAL files by typing in a new folder location. This includes .CAL files. I'll talk more about CAL files in Chapters 16, "Advanced CAL Techniques," and 17, "Taking Your SONAR Project to CD."

5.   In the Window Layouts parameter, specify where you would like to store all your window layouts by typing in a new folder location. This includes .CakewalkWindowLayout files. I'll talk more about window layouts later in this chapter, in the section called "Working with Window Layouts."

6.   In the Wave Files parameter, specify where you would like SONAR to look for any external audio files (such as sample loops) for importing into your projects. This

includes .WAV, Apple .AIFF, .MPEG, Windows Media, and Next/Sun files. When you specify a folder location for this parameter, it affects the location to which the File > Import Audio dialog box will initially open. I'll talk more about importing audio files in Chapter 6, "Recording and Playback," and sample loops in Chapter 9, "Composing with Loops."

COPY YOUR LOOPS TO YOUR HARD DRIVE

If you have a large sample loop collection that spans a number of different CDs, it can be cumbersome to try to find the right loop when you have to keep loading and unloading different discs from your CD-ROM drive. Instead, you might want to consider copying all your loops to a folder on your hard drive, and then specify that folder location for the Wave Files parameter. From then on, whenever you need to import an audio loop into a project, you have instant access to all the loops in your collection.

7. In the Video Files parameter, specify where you would like SONAR to look for any external video files to import into your projects. This includes .AVI, .MPG, and .MOV files. When you specify a folder location for this parameter, it affects the location to which the File > Import Video File dialog box will initially open. I'll talk more about importing video files in Appendix C, "Producing for Multimedia and the Web."

8. In the Sysx Files parameter, specify where you would like to store all your system-exclusive files by typing in a new folder location. This includes .SYX files. When you specify a folder location for this parameter, it affects the location to which the Load Bank from File and Save Bank to File dialog boxes in the Sysx view will initially open. I'll talk more about system exclusive files and the Sysx view in Chapter 14, "Studio Control with StudioWare and Sysx."

9. In the Groove Quantize parameter, specify where you would like to store all your Groove Quantize files by typing in a new folder location. This includes .GRV files. When you specify a folder location for this parameter, it affects the location to which the Open Groove File dialog box from the Groove Quantize function will initially open. I'll talk more about the Groove Quantize function in Chapter 8, "Exploring the Editing Tools."

10. In the StudioWare parameter, specify where you would like to store all your StudioWare files by typing in a new folder location. This includes .CakewalkStudioWare files. I'll talk more about StudioWare in Chapter 14 and Chapter 15, "CAL 101."

11. In the Patterns parameter, specify where you would like SONAR to look for any pattern files for the Pattern Brush feature by typing in a new folder location. This includes .MID (MIDI) files. When you specify a folder location for this parameter, it affects the patterns that will appear in the Pattern Brush menu in the Piano Roll view. I'll talk more about the Pattern Brush feature and the Piano Roll view in Chapter 7, "Editing Basics."

CHAPTER 3

12. In the Drum Maps parameter, specify where you would like to store all your Drum Map files by typing in a new folder location. This includes .MAP files. I'll talk more about drum maps in Chapter 7.

13. When you're finished assigning new folder locations for your files, click on OK.

Putting Everything in Its Place

If you've decided to change the location of any of the file types mentioned earlier, be sure to move all your existing files to their new locations as well, including all the files that ship with SONAR.

1. Open Windows Explorer, and then locate and open the C:\Program Files\Cakewalk\SONAR 3\Sample Content folder on your hard drive.

2. SONAR ships with a few sample project files whose filenames end in .CWP and .CWB. Move those files to the same folder you specified in the Project Files parameter of the Global Options > Folders dialog box.

3. A large number of templates are included with SONAR as well; their names end in .CWT. Move those files to the same folder you specified in the Templates parameter.

4. There are 13 CAL files shipped with SONAR whose names end in .CAL. Move those files to the same folder you specified in the CAL Files parameter.

5. SONAR doesn't provide any default window layouts, so there are no files to move in this case. But if you've created some of your own, look for files whose names end in .CakewalkWindowLayout and move them to the same folder you specified in the Window Layouts parameter.

6. Although no audio sample loops are installed when you install SONAR on your hard drive, SONAR still includes a collection of loops for you to use; they are located on the SONAR CD. Pop the CD into your drive and choose Explore CD from the menu that appears. Then navigate to the Audio Loops folder. Copy the contents of the Audio Loops folder to the same folder you specified in the Wave Files parameter of the Global Options > Folders dialog box. This will take up space on your hard drive, but it will also give you quick and easy access to your loops if you ever want to import them into a project.

7. SONAR doesn't include any sample video files, so there are no files to move in this case. But if you have a collection of your own, look for files whose names end in .AVI, .MPG, or .MOV and move them to the same folder you specified in the Video Files parameter.

8. SONAR includes three sample system exclusive files: GMSYSTEM.SYX, GS-RESET.SYX, and XG-RESET.SYX. These are located in the C:\Program Files\Cakewalk\SONAR 3 folder. Move those files to the same folder you specified in the Sysx Files parameter of the Global Options > Folders dialog box.

9. SONAR includes one sample Groove Quantize file: CAKEWALK DNA GROOVES.GRV. This file is located in the C:\Program Files\Cakewalk\SONAR 3\Sample Content folder. Move this file to the same folder you specified in the Groove Quantize parameter.

10. The Sample Content folder also contains a large number of StudioWare files that ship with SONAR. These files have names that end in .CakewalkStudioWare. Move these files to the same folder you specified in the StudioWare parameter.

11. SONAR also ships with a number of Pattern Brush files. These files are located in the C:\Program Files\Cakewalk\SONAR 3\Pattern Brush Patterns folder. Move these files to the same folder you specified in the Patterns parameter.

12. Finally, SONAR ships with a number of sample Drum Map files. These files are located in the C:\Program Files\Cakewalk\SONAR 3\Drum Maps folder. Move these files to the same folder you specified in the Drum Maps parameter.

That's it—any other files you see in the folder locations I mentioned should be left alone. Do not move them; only move files that have the file extensions I discussed. Of course, you don't really have to move all of SONAR's included sample files, but personally, I really enjoy having all my files properly organized. It makes finding what I need easier, and it makes working with SONAR much more efficient.

Customizing Audio Folders

Although I've already talked about sample loops and audio files that you can import into your projects, SONAR has to deal with additional audio files that represent the audio tracks that you record directly into SONAR. SONAR stores the data for these audio tracks in a special folder on your hard drive. By default, this folder is located at C:\Cakewalk Projects\Audio Data. However, like the other folders I mentioned earlier, you can change the location of this folder if you'd like. One of the main reasons you might want to do so would be if you are using two hard drives in your computer—one for installing all your software and another for storing only your SONAR audio data. This improves SONAR's efficiency during playback and recording tremendously, and I highly recommend it.

If you'd like to change the location of your audio data folder, follow these steps:

1. In SONAR, choose Options > Global > Audio Data to open the Global Options dialog box with the Audio Data tab selected (see Figure 3.2).

Figure 3.2
Use the Audio Data tab in the Global Options dialog box to change your audio data folder location.

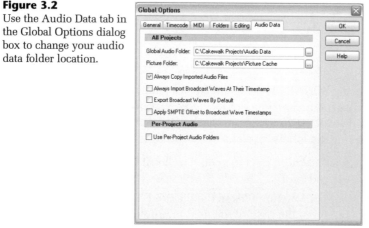

2. In the Global Audio Folder parameter, type the new location for your audio data folder. You can also click the ellipsis button to the right of the parameter to browse for a new location instead of typing one.

3. By default, whenever you import an audio file into a project, SONAR will automatically make a copy of that file and place it in your audio data folder. If you don't want SONAR to do this, then deactivate the Always Copy Imported Audio Files option.

ALWAYS COPY IMPORTED AUDIO FILES

If your audio folder is located on the same hard drive as the audio you are importing, you can save drive space by deactivating the Always Copy Imported Audio Files option. But if your audio folder is located on a different drive (perhaps a second drive, as I mentioned earlier), then you should keep this option activated. I recommend this because if you are using a second hard drive to store your audio data, you don't want SONAR to have to look for your imported audio in a different location on a different drive. This will decrease playback and recording efficiency.

4. Click on OK.

Per-Project Audio Folders

Instead of storing all the audio data from all your projects in the same folder, you can use a different folder for each project, if you'd like. These folders are called *per-project audio folders*. The advantage of using per-project audio folders is that all the data for each project is stored in its own separate location, which makes it easy to find if you want to access the audio files associated with a project (perhaps for editing in a different software application). To set up SONAR for per-project audio folders, follow these steps:

1. Choose Options > Global > Audio Data to open the Global Options dialog box with the Audio Data tab selected.

2. Activate the Use Per-Project Audio Folders option.

3. Click on OK.

Now when you create a new project, you will be able to specify a folder name for it. I'll talk more about creating projects in Chapter 4, "Working with Projects."

The Picture Folder

Whenever you record audio data using SONAR, the program creates temporary picture files for the audio data in your project. These files hold "drawings" of the audio waveforms. Initially, these picture files are stored in the C:\Cakewalk Projects\Picture Cache folder on your hard drive. You can change this location by completing the following steps.

1. Choose Options > Global > Audio Data to open the Global Options dialog box with the Audio Data tab selected.

2. Type a new location for your picture files in the Picture Folder field. You can also click on the ellipsis button to the right of the field to browse for a new location instead of typing one.

DON'T MOVE THE PICTURE FOLDER

If you are using a second hard drive for your audio data, do *not* put your picture folder on the second hard drive with the audio data. This can decrease SONAR's performance. Instead, keep the picture folder on the same hard drive on which the SONAR software is installed.

3. Click on OK.

Now SONAR will look for your picture files in the new picture folder location. Don't worry about moving any existing picture files; SONAR will automatically create new ones when you open your projects again. You can just delete the old picture folder and all the files in it.

Customizing the Workspace

Not only can you change the way SONAR handles files, but you also can change the way SONAR looks and the way it responds to your commands. By customizing the SONAR workspace, you can increase your efficiency with the program and make it more comfortable to use. You can adjust the colors, toolbars, window layouts, and key bindings.

Changing Colors

SONAR allows you to change the colors of almost every element on the program screen. Personally, I haven't found much use for making color changes, though. The default colors that the program ships with work just fine for me. However, you might find a different set of colors more pleasant to work with, or maybe you can see some colors better than others. Changing the colors SONAR uses is simple—just follow these steps:

1. In SONAR, choose Options > Colors. The Configure Colors dialog box will appear, as shown in Figure 3.3.

Figure 3.3
In the Configure Colors dialog box, you can change the appearance of SONAR to your liking.

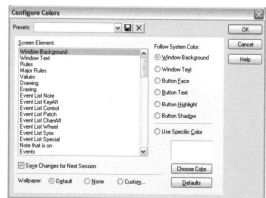

2. The left side of the dialog box contains a list of all the screen elements you can change. To change the color of an element, select it.

3. Next select how you want that screen element to look by choosing a color from the right side of the dialog box. You can have the color of the element follow the color of some of the default Windows element colors, or you can use a specific color.

4. You also can change the background wallpaper of the SONAR workspace by choosing one of the options at the bottom of the dialog box. If you choose the Custom option, you can even load your own Windows bitmap (.BMP) file for display. Loading your own file is not particularly useful, but it can be fun.

5. If you want SONAR to use the same color settings every time you run the program, make sure the Save Changes for Next Session option is activated.

6. If you'd like to set up a number of different color schemes, you can save your settings as a preset. Just type a name for the current color settings in the Presets field, and then click on the Save button (the button with the picture of a floppy disk). You can then quickly change color schemes by simply choosing a preset.

7. When you've finished making your changes, just click on the OK button.

Using Toolbars

To increase your productivity, SONAR provides a number of toolbars for quick access to many of its major functions. Instead of having to hunt through a series of menus, you can simply click on a single toolbar button. Toolbars are available for standard file access functions, recording and playback controls, and so on.

SONAR allows you to change the look and position of its toolbars, as well as determine whether they are visible. Why wouldn't you want to have all the toolbars on the screen all the time? Because they can clutter up the workspace and get in the way while you're working on a project.

Changing Toolbar Position

Just as with most toolbars in other Windows programs, you can dock the SONAR toolbars to the top, bottom, or sides of the workspace by dragging and dropping them. If you drop a toolbar anywhere within the workspace, it will become a floating window, as shown in Figure 3.4.

Figure 3.4
You can dock toolbars at the top or bottom of the SONAR workspace. They can also reside anywhere else within the workspace as small floating windows.

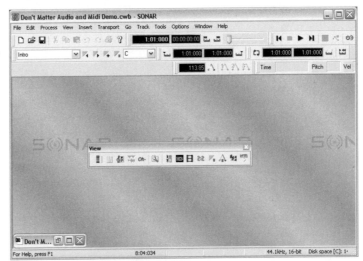

Changing Toolbar Appearance

To change the appearance of the toolbars, you need to access the Toolbars dialog box. Just choose View > Toolbars, and the Toolbars dialog box will appear, as shown in Figure 3.5.

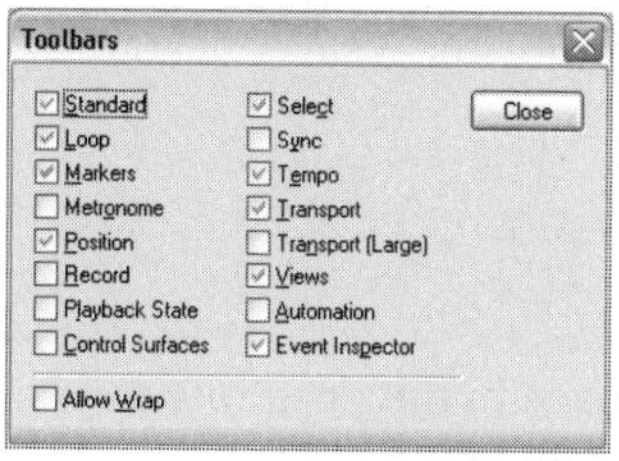

Figure 3.5
Using the Toolbars dialog box, you can change the appearance of SONAR's toolbars.

You can select or deselect each toolbar to determine whether it will be visible. For example, if you remove the checkmark in the box next to the Standard selection, the Standard File Functions toolbar will disappear.

Working with Window Layouts

When you're working on a project in SONAR, you need to use many of the views described in Chapter 2. When you save the project, the size and position of the view windows are saved along with it. This capability is nice because you can pick up exactly where you left off the next time you open the project. As you get more experienced with SONAR, you'll probably find that having the views set up in certain configurations helps your recording sessions go more smoothly. For instance, you might like having the Track view positioned at the top of the workspace and the Staff view and the Piano Roll view positioned underneath it, as shown in Figure 3.6.

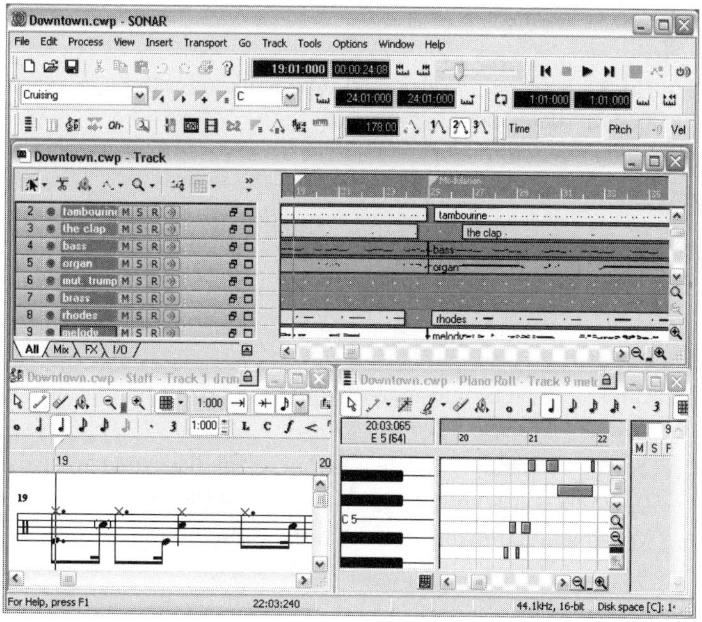

Figure 3.6
The size and position of all views are saved along with a project.

What if you come up with a few favorite configurations that you like to use during different stages of the same project? Or what if you want to use those configurations in a different project? That's where window layouts come in handy. Using window layouts, you can save the current size and position of the view windows as a layout file. Later, you can load the saved layout and apply it to any open project. You can also update, delete, or rename a saved layout by using the Window Layouts dialog box.

Creating a Layout

Follow these steps to create a window layout:

1. Arrange the views in the workspace in the positions and sizes in which you would like them saved. You also must decide whether you want certain views to be open.

2. Choose View > Layouts to open the Window Layouts dialog box, as shown in Figure 3.7.

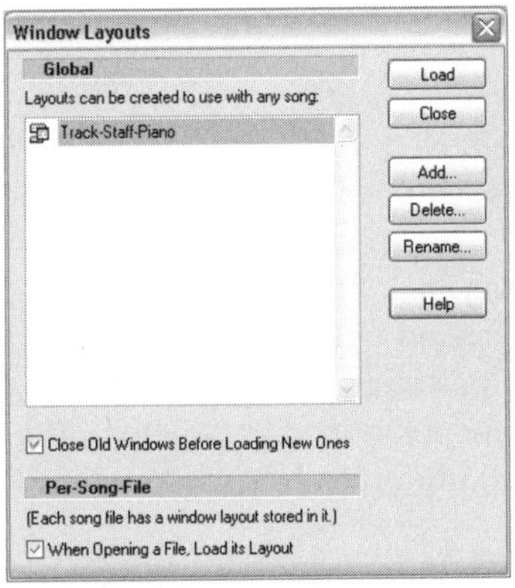

Figure 3.7
You can create new layouts by using the Window Layouts dialog box.

3. Click on the Add button and type a name for the new layout in the New Global Layout dialog box that appears.

USE A DESCRIPTIVE NAME
I've found that giving a descriptive name to each layout helps me when I want to load them. For example, I include the names of each open view in the name of the layout. If I have the Track, Staff, and Piano Roll views open in the layout, I name it Track-Staff-Piano.

4. Click on the OK button, and your new layout will be listed in the Window Layouts dialog box.

5. You can rename or delete a layout in the list. You can also load a layout by selecting it from the list and clicking on the Load button.

6. When you're finished, click on the Close button.

Using Layout Options

The Window Layouts dialog box contains two optional settings that let you control how layouts are loaded. The Close Old Windows Before Loading New Ones option determines whether any views you have currently open in the workspace will be closed when you load a new layout. The When Opening a File, Load Its Layout option determines whether SONAR will load the accompanying layout when a project is opened. I like to keep both of these options activated.

Using Key Bindings

Key bindings are one of the most useful customization features that SONAR provides. Like toolbars, they give you quick access to most of SONAR's features. Instead of having to click through a series of menus, you can simply press a key combination on your computer's keyboard. Initially, SONAR ships with a few default key bindings, such as for opening and saving a project. These bindings are displayed next to their assigned menu functions, as in the File menu shown in Figure 3.8.

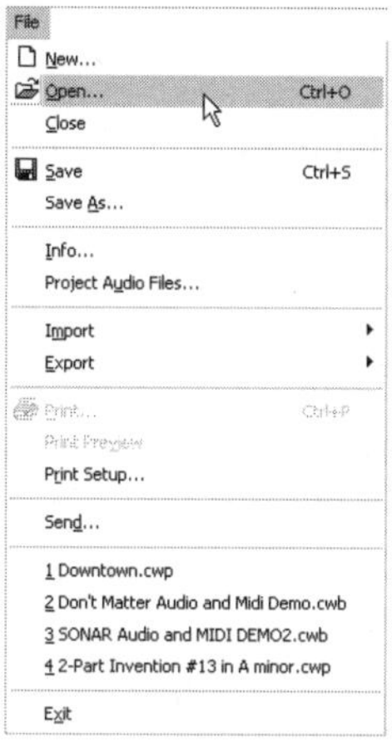

Figure 3.8
Initially, the key binding for opening a project is Ctrl+O.

The wonderful thing about key bindings is that if you don't like them, you can change them. You can also create new ones for functions that don't already have preassigned key bindings. There's only one limitation: You can have a maximum of 134 key bindings. You can work around this limitation, however; I'll talk about that later in this chapter, in the "Using MIDI Key Bindings" section. The available computer keyboard combinations include the following:

▶ The Ctrl key in combination with any letter of the alphabet, any number, or any function key (except F10)

▶ The Shift key in combination with any function key (except F10)

▶ Any function key (except F1 and F10)

▶ The Ctrl+Shift keys in combination with any letter of the alphabet, any number, or any function key (except F10)

▶ The Ctrl+Alt keys in combination with any letter of the alphabet, any number, or any function key (except F10)

Creating Your Own Key Bindings

You can easily create your own key bindings and change existing ones. Here's how:

1. Choose Options > Key Bindings to open the Key Bindings dialog box, as shown in Figure 3.9.

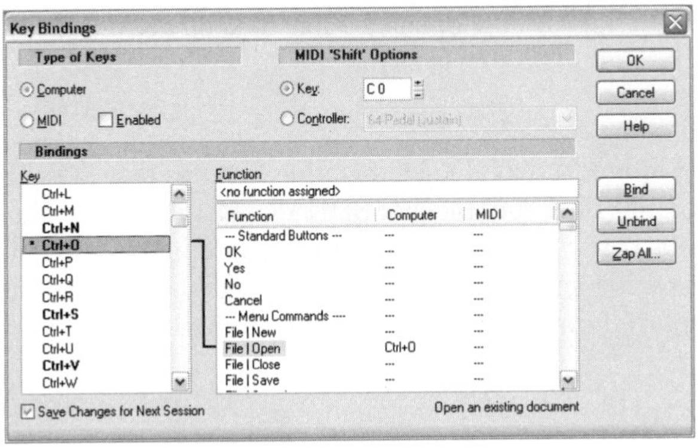

Figure 3.9

You can set key combinations in the Key Bindings dialog box.

2. In the Key list under the Bindings section of the dialog box, select the key combination that you want to bind to a function.

3. In the Function list, select the SONAR function that you want to bind to the selected key combination.

4. Click on the Bind button. You will see a connection created.

5. As I mentioned before, you can create up to 134 key bindings. You can also remove single key bindings using the Unbind button. If you want to get rid of all key bindings, just click on the Zap All button.

6. When you're done, click on the OK button.

SAVE CHANGES FOR NEXT SESSION

Near the bottom of the Key Bindings dialog box is the Save Changes for Next Session option. When you select it, any key bindings you create will be saved so you can use them every time you run SONAR. If this option is not selected, you will lose any changes you've made when you exit the program. This option is selected by default. I suggest you keep it that way, unless for some reason you just need a few temporary key bindings during a recording session.

After you've created (or changed) some key bindings, you'll notice the changes in SONAR's menus. As I mentioned earlier, the key bindings are displayed next to their assigned menu functions.

Using MIDI Key Bindings

Remember when I mentioned that you can get around the limit of the 134 available key bindings? This is how: You use MIDI key bindings. You can assign the keys on your MIDI keyboard synthesizer or controller as key bindings to execute functions within SONAR. (Cool, huh?)

For example, you could assign the File > New function in SONAR to the Middle C key on your keyboard. Then, when you press Middle C, SONAR would open the New Project File dialog box.

 **REMOTE MIDI KEY BINDINGS**

If your studio is set up so that your computer isn't located next to your MIDI keyboard or controller, using MIDI key bindings is a great way to still have access to SONAR. For example, if you want to be able to start and stop SONAR recording via your MIDI keyboard, you can just assign one MIDI key binding along with the shift key or controller to the Transport > Play function and another MIDI key binding along with the shift key or controller to the Transport > Stop function.

You create MIDI key bindings the same way you create computer keyboard bindings. The only difference is that you have to select MIDI as the Type of Keys option in the Key Bindings dialog box and make sure to activate MIDI key bindings by selecting the Enabled option, as shown in Figure 3.10. Also, when you select a key combination in the Key list, you select musical keys rather than computer keyboard keys.

Figure 3.10
You select MIDI as the Type of Keys option to activate MIDI key bindings.

In addition, to prevent the MIDI key bindings from activating while you're performing, you need to set up a shift key or controller to turn on and off the MIDI key bindings. Under MIDI Shift Options in the Key Bindings dialog box, you can assign a MIDI key or controller message to act as a sort of on/off switch. When you want to use a MIDI key binding, activate the shift key or controller first to tell SONAR you're about to use a MIDI key binding.

 **WINDOW LAYOUT KEY BINDINGS**

Remember earlier when I talked about window layouts? Normally, you need to choose View > Layouts, select a layout, and click on Load just to call up a window layout. For a much quicker way to do this, you can assign key bindings to any or all of the layout files you create. After you've created your window layouts, you will find them listed under the Global Layout Files section of the Function list in the Key Bindings dialog box. Just assign key bindings as described earlier, and then you can switch instantly between window layouts at the press of a computer key.

CHAPTER 3

Customizing MIDI Settings

Even though SONAR does a good job of setting up all its MIDI options during installation, it's still a good idea to go through them to make sure everything is the way you want it to be. You might be surprised at how much control you have over how SONAR handles MIDI data. Not only can you designate which MIDI devices the program will use, you can also determine what types of MIDI data will be recorded and optimize MIDI playback.

Working with MIDI Devices

The first time you run SONAR, it scans your computer system to see whether you have a MIDI interface installed. SONAR prompts you to select the available MIDI ports that you want to use, but you can always change your selections later.

MIDI PORTS

As explained in Chapter 1, a *MIDI interface* is a device that is plugged into your computer, allowing it to understand the MIDI language. Every MIDI interface has at least two connections on it, called *MIDI ports*. One is the MIDI In port, which is used to receive MIDI data; the other is the MIDI Out port, which is used to send MIDI data. Some of the more sophisticated MIDI interfaces on the market have multiple pairs of MIDI ports, which allow you to connect more than one MIDI instrument to your computer.

To see what MIDI ports SONAR is using and to designate the ports you want to use, follow these steps:

1. Choose Options > MIDI Devices to open the MIDI Devices dialog box. This dialog box lists all the input and output MIDI ports you have available. For an example, see Figure 3.11.

Figure 3.11
The MIDI Devices dialog box lists all the available input and output MIDI ports.

2. Simply select the input and output ports that you want to be able to access for use within SONAR.

3. When you're finished, click on the OK button.

All the ports selected here will be available in the Track Properties dialog box, which I'll talk about in Chapter 4.

Setting Global MIDI Options

SONAR provides a number of different MIDI options, some of which are global and some of which are project-oriented. The project-oriented options (which I'll talk about in Chapter 4) are saved and loaded along with project files. The global options remain the same no matter which project is currently open.

Filtering Out MIDI Messages

MIDI MESSAGES

There are seven types of MIDI messages, and each one provides different kinds of functionality within the MIDI language. These categories include notes, key aftertouch, channel aftertouch, controllers, program changes, pitch bend, and system exclusive.

The notes category pertains to MIDI Note On and MIDI Note Off messages. Whenever you press a key on your MIDI keyboard, a MIDI Note On message is sent. When you release the key, a MIDI Note Off message is sent.

On some MIDI keyboards, in addition to hitting the keys, you can press and hold them down to apply varying degrees of pressure. This pressure is called *aftertouch*. Depending on how the synthesizer is programmed, aftertouch lets you control how loud the synth is or even how it sounds. Aftertouch comes in both key and channel varieties. *Key aftertouch* allows you to have different pressure levels for each individual key on the keyboard. *Channel aftertouch* restricts you to a single pressure level over the entire range of the keyboard.

There is a wide range of controller MIDI messages available. Basically, these messages give you control over different aspects of your MIDI synthesizer or device. Some controller messages let you control volume, whereas others let you control the position of a synthesizer sound in the stereo field. However, far too many are available to discuss them all here.

Program changes (also called patch changes) let you select from the many different sounds available in a MIDI synthesizer. For example, a program change #1 MIDI message might activate a piano sound in your synthesizer, and a program change #10 might activate a glockenspiel sound.

Pitch bend messages allow you to temporarily alter the tuning of your MIDI instrument. Many MIDI keyboards have a lever or a wheel that lets you control pitch bend. Moving this wheel makes the instrument send out pitch bend (also called pitch wheel) messages.

System exclusive messages pertain to special MIDI data that is (as the name implies) exclusive to the instrument sending and receiving it. For instance, the manufacturer of a MIDI synthesizer might include special functions in the product that can't be controlled via standard MIDI messages. By using system exclusive messages, the manufacturer gives you access to these special functions but still keeps the product compatible with the MIDI language.

For more in-depth information about MIDI and the different types of messages available, check out the *Desktop Music Handbook*, which is available for free on the Cakewalk Web site at http://www.cakewalk.com/tips/desktop.asp. Also read the section of the SONAR Help file entitled *Beginner's Guide to Cakewalk Software*.

The global MIDI options allow you to select the types of MIDI messages you want to record in SONAR. Sometimes you might not want certain MIDI data to be included in your recordings. For example, if your MIDI keyboard sends channel aftertouch messages or key aftertouch messages, you might want to filter them out. These types of messages are very resource-intensive and can sometimes bog down your synthesizer with too much data.

By default, SONAR has notes, controllers, program changes, pitch bend, and system exclusive messages activated, and it has key aftertouch and channel aftertouch deactivated. If you want to change these settings, though, you can follow these steps:

1.   Choose Options > Global to open the Global Options dialog box.

2.   Click on the MIDI tab at the top of the dialog box.

3.   Under the Record section, select the types of MIDI messages you want to allow SONAR to record, as shown in Figure 3.12.

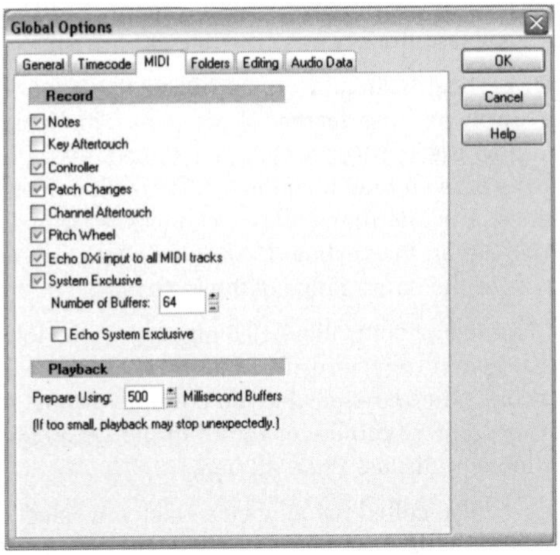

Figure 3.12
You can determine the types of MIDI messages SONAR will be allowed to record.

4.   Click on the OK button when you're finished.

Optimizing MIDI Playback

To get smooth and consistent playback of MIDI data, SONAR uses a buffer (a temporary storage area) to hold the data before it gets sent out through the MIDI interface. This buffer keeps the data from getting backed up, which can cause erratic playback or even stop playback altogether. The buffer also helps to control playback latency. Whenever you change a parameter in SONAR while a project is playing, a slight delay occurs between the time you make the adjustment and when you hear the results. That's called *latency*.

The Global Options dialog box contains a setting that allows you to adjust the size of SONAR's MIDI playback buffer. If the buffer is set too low, it can cause erratic playback, and if it is set too high, it can cause noticeable latency. By default, the buffer size is set to 500 milliseconds. This setting should be fine in most cases. However, you might want to experiment to find an even better setting. The trick is to find the lowest setting that doesn't affect playback. I've been able to get away with a setting of 100 at most times unless I have a lot of MIDI data being played in a project. You can change the buffer size by following these steps:

1. Choose Options > Global to open the Global Options dialog box.
2. Click on the MIDI tab at the top of the dialog box.
3. Under the Playback section, type the new buffer size.
4. Click on the OK button when you're finished.

Understanding Instrument Definitions

Most MIDI instruments today provide a bank of sounds compatible with the General MIDI standard. At the same time, most instruments also provide additional sounds as well as other features that aren't defined by General MIDI. Some older MIDI instruments don't support General MIDI at all. To let you work more efficiently with these instruments, SONAR provides instrument definitions.

GENERAL MIDI

Sounds in a MIDI instrument are stored as groups of parameter settings called *patches*, and patches are stored in groups called *banks*. A MIDI instrument can have up to 16,384 banks of 128 patches each. This means that a MIDI instrument can theoretically contain up to 2,097,152 different sounds, although most don't.

With such a great potential for diversity, MIDI instruments from one manufacturer usually don't provide the same functionality as instruments from another manufacturer. This point is important because MIDI data is ambiguous. The same data can be played back using any MIDI instrument, but that doesn't mean it will sound the same. Different instruments contain different sounds, and they interpret MIDI differently as well.

To remedy the problem, GM (*General MIDI*) was created. GM is a set of rules applied to the MIDI language that standardizes the types of sounds contained in a MIDI instrument (along with their patch numbers) and how different MIDI controller messages are interpreted. Most modern MIDI instruments provide a special bank of GM sounds and a GM operating mode. When you are running in GM mode, different MIDI instruments respond to the same MIDI data in the same way. MIDI data played back on one instrument is guaranteed to sound the same when played on any other instrument.

Using instrument definitions, you can "tell" SONAR all about the features and capabilities provided by each of the MIDI instruments in your studio. This information includes the name of each patch, the range of notes supported by each patch, the supported MIDI controller messages, the supported registered parameter numbers (RPNs) and non-registered parameter numbers (NRPNs), and the bank select method used. Basically, instrument definitions allow you to refer to the patches in your MIDI instruments by name rather than number when you're assigning sounds to tracks in SONAR. (I'll talk more about this subject in Chapter 4.) The same applies for musical note names and MIDI controller message names.

Setting Up Your Instruments

SONAR includes a number of predefined instrument definitions so you can simply assign them without having to go through the process of creating your own. You can assign instrument definitions to each of the MIDI ports on your MIDI interface. You can also assign them to the individual MIDI channels (1 through 16).

CHAPTER 3

MIDI CHANNELS

The MIDI language provides 16 different channels of performance data over a single MIDI port connection. MIDI instruments can be set to receive MIDI data on a single channel if need be. This means you can control up to 16 different MIDI instruments (each with its own unique sound), even if they are all connected to the same MIDI port on your MIDI interface. In addition, most MIDI instruments are capable of playing more than one sound at a time. This means the instrument is *multi-timbral*. If you assign a different sound to each of the 16 MIDI channels, a single MIDI instrument can play 16 different sounds simultaneously.

To assign instrument definitions to each of the MIDI ports and channels in your setup, follow these steps:

1. Choose Options > Instruments to open the Assign Instruments dialog box, as shown in Figure 3.13.

Figure 3.13
You can assign instrument definitions in the Assign Instruments dialog box.

2. From the Output/Channel list, select the MIDI port(s) and/or MIDI channel(s) to which you want to assign definitions.

3. From the Uses Instrument list, select the instrument definition you want to use. For example, if you're going to use the MIDI instrument that's connected to the selected port in General MIDI mode, choose the General MIDI instrument definition.

SAVE CHANGES FOR NEXT SESSION

Near the bottom of the Assign Instruments dialog box is the Save Changes for Next Session option. When you select it, any assignments you create will be saved so you can use them every time you run SONAR. If this option is not selected, you will lose any changes you make when you exit the program. I suggest you select this option, unless for some reason you change the configuration of your studio for each new recording session.

4. Click on the OK button when you're finished.

Now SONAR will know the capabilities of your MIDI instrument(s) and will act appropriately when you access different features, such as editing MIDI controller messages (which I'll talk about in Chapter 7).

Taking the Easy Way Out

If you don't see a specific instrument definition for your MIDI instrument listed in the Assign Instruments dialog box, SONAR allows you to import more definitions. The program ships with a large collection of additional instrument definitions that cover many of the MIDI instruments on the market from manufacturers such as Alesis, E-mu, Ensoniq, General Music, Korg, Kurzweil, Roland, and Yamaha. The instrument definitions are stored in files with .INS extensions. For example, the Yamaha instrument definitions are stored in the file YAMAHA.INS. Importing these files is simple; just follow these steps:

1. Choose Options > Instruments to open the Assign Instruments dialog box.
2. Click on the Define button to open the Define Instruments and Names dialog box, as shown in Figure 3.14.

Figure 3.14
The Define Instruments and Names dialog box allows you to import additional instrument definitions.

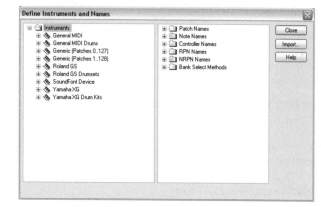

3. Click on the Import button to open the Import Instrument Definitions dialog box, and then select the .INS file you want to import. For example, if Roland manufactures your MIDI instrument, select the ROLAND.INS file, and then click on Open.
4. When SONAR displays a list of the instrument definitions contained in that file, select the one(s) you want and click on the OK button. Your selections will be listed under Instruments in the Define Instruments and Names dialog box.
5. Click on the Close button, and you will see your selections listed under Uses Instrument in the Assign Instruments dialog box. From here you can assign the instrument definitions as described earlier.
6. Click on the OK button when you're finished.

If you still can't find an instrument definition for your MIDI instrument from the extensive collection included with SONAR, you can download even more from the Internet. Cakewalk provides a download section on its Web site (http://www.cakewalk.com/download) where you can pick up additional instrument definition files. Other sites on the Web supply them, too. For more details, take a look at Appendix D, "SONAR Resources on the Web."

Creating Your Own Instrument Definitions

More than likely, you'll find instrument definitions for all your MIDI equipment either included with SONAR or available for download from the Internet. On the off chance that you don't, though, SONAR allows you to create your own definitions. This can be a bit complicated because you must have a good knowledge of the MIDI language and you need to be able to read the MIDI implementation charts that come with your instruments.

MIDI IMPLEMENTATION CHARTS

The MIDI language contains more than 100 different messages to convey musical information, and a MIDI instrument isn't required to send or recognize all of them. A MIDI instrument needs to transmit and receive only the messages that are relevant to the features it provides; it can ignore all the other messages. Therefore, manufacturers include MIDI implementation charts with all their products.

A MIDI implementation chart lists all the types of MIDI messages that are transmitted and recognized by its accompanying MIDI instrument. The chart includes the note range of the instrument, the MIDI controller messages it supports, whether it supports system exclusive messages, and more.

To give you an idea of how to read a simple MIDI implementation chart and how to create a basic instrument definition, I want to go through the process step by step.

1. Choose Options > Instruments to open the Assign Instruments dialog box.

2. Click on the Define button to open the Define Instruments and Names dialog box.

3. Take a look at Table 3.1, which shows the MIDI implementation chart for an E-mu PROformance Plus Stereo Piano MIDI instrument.

Table 3.1
E-mu PROformance Plus MIDI Implementation Chart

MIDI Command	Transmitted	Received	Comments
Note On	No	Yes	
Note Off	No	Yes	
Pitch Wheel	No	Yes	
Program Change	No	Yes	0–31
Overflow Mode	Yes	Yes	
Channel Pressure	No	No	
Poly Key Pressure	No	No	
Control Change	No	Yes	PWH, #1, #7
Sustain Footswitch	No	Yes	#64
Sostenuto Footswitch	No	Yes	#66

MIDI Command	Transmitted	Received	Comments
Soft Footswitch	No	Yes	#67
Split Footswitch	No	Yes	#70
All Notes Off	No	Yes	
Omni Mode	No	No	
Poly Mode	No	No	
Mono Mode	No	No	
System Exclusives	No	No	

4.   Right-click on Instruments on the left side of the Define Instruments and Names dialog box, and select Add Instrument from the menu that appears.

5.   Type a name for the new instrument. For this example, type **E-mu PROformance Plus**.

6.   Open the new instrument by double-clicking on it to display its data, as shown in Figure 3.15.

Figure 3.15
This dialog box shows a new instrument definition.

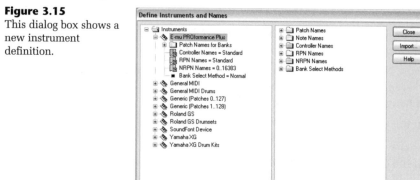

7.   Take a look at what the new instrument contains. SONAR automatically creates the standard settings needed. Because the E-mu PROformance Plus doesn't support bank select messages, RPNs, or NRPNs, you don't need to change them. The PROformance supports the standard MIDI controllers, too, so you don't have to change them either. You do need to change the patch names, though.

8.   Open the Patch Names for Banks folder in the E-mu PROformance Plus instrument by double-clicking it. You should see General MIDI listed there. Because this instrument doesn't support GM, you need to change that name.

9.   To change the General MIDI patch names list, you first need to create a new patch names list specifically for the PROformance by right-clicking on the Patch Names folder on the right side of the Define Instruments and Names dialog box.

CHAPTER 3

10. Select Add Patch Names List from the menu that appears and type a name for the new list. In this case, type **E-mu PROformance Plus**.

11. The PROformance manual shows all the patch names for the instrument (numbers 0 to 31). To add those names to the new patch name list, right-click on the list and select Add Patch Name from the menu that appears.

12. Type a name for the first patch (in this case, **Dark Grand**) and press the Enter key on your computer keyboard. Because this is just an example you can leave the list as is, but if you were to add more names to the list, it would look something like Figure 3.16.

Figure 3.16
This dialog box shows a patch name list for the E-mu PROformance Plus.

13. Drag and drop the E-mu PROformance Plus patch names list into the General MIDI list in the E-mu PROformance Plus instrument definition.

14. In the Bank Number dialog box, enter the number of the bank that you want to use for this set of patch names. Click on OK. The patch names list for the instrument will be changed.

15. Click on the Close button, and then click on the OK button to finish.

This set of steps was actually a very simplified demonstration of how to create your own instrument definition. If the controller names need to be changed or if the instrument supports RPNs or NRPNs, you would create and edit those lists in the same way you do a patch name list. It's doubtful that you'll ever need to create your own instrument definitions because SONAR comes with a large number of them and you can download even more from the Internet, but just in case, you can find more details in the SONAR user's guide.

Optimal Audio Settings

When SONAR plays back digital audio on your computer, it puts a lot of stress on the system. Remember when I talked about digital audio in Chapter 1? A CD-quality digital audio recording requires 44,100 numbers (samples) to be processed every second. During playback, most of your computer's processing power is used solely for that purpose. Depending on the power of your system, this processing can make the response of some of SONAR's controls a bit sluggish, particularly the Console view controls. For example, if you adjust the volume of a digital audio track in the Console view during playback, you might experience a slight delay between the time you make the adjustment and the time you hear the results. As I mentioned earlier, this period is called latency, and you'll want as little of it as possible to occur during your sessions.

SONAR provides a number of different advanced settings that enable you to reduce latency. The first time you start the program, it attempts to make some educated guesses about what these settings should be, and although these settings usually work just fine, you still might be able to squeeze better performance out of your computer system. However, adjusting these settings can be tricky and unfortunately, there are no set rules. There are, however, some general guidelines you can follow to optimize your audio settings for the best possible performance.

Adjusting the Latency Slider

One of the most important adjustments you can make is to the Latency slider, and it's pretty simple to do. The lower you set the slider, the lower the latency; the higher you set it, the higher the latency. It can't be that simple, can it? No, I'm afraid not. By lowering the Latency slider, you also run the risk of making your playback unstable. If you set the Latency slider too low, you might hear dropouts or glitches, or playback might even stop altogether. And the lower you set the Latency slider, the fewer digital audio tracks you can play at the same time.

To find the right setting, you have to experiment with a number of different projects. For projects with only a few digital audio tracks, you might be able to get away with a very low Latency slider setting. For projects with many digital audio tracks, you might have to raise the Latency slider and put up with a bit of latency while you work. The required level for the Latency slider also depends on whether you are using ASIO or WDM drivers for your sound card, which I talked about in Chapter 2. If you are using ASIO or WDM drivers, then SONAR will run much more efficiently and you should be able to set the Latency slider to a very low value. To set the Latency slider, follow these steps:

1. Choose Options > Audio to open the Audio Options dialog box.
2. Click on the General tab. The Latency slider (or Buffer Size slider) is located in the Mixing Latency section, as shown in Figure 3.17.

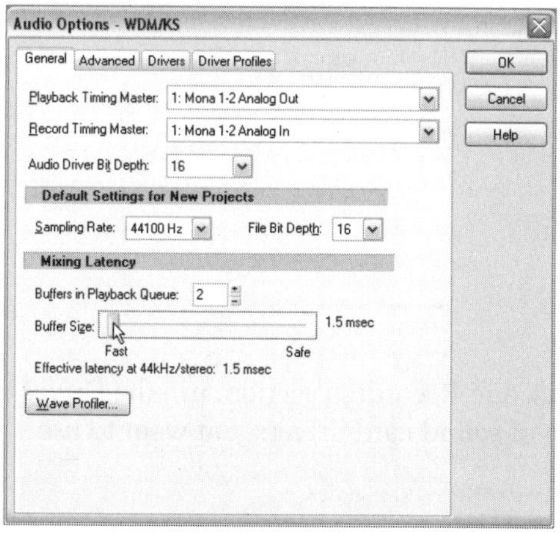

Figure 3.17
In the Audio Options dialog box, you can adjust the Latency slider.

3. Click and drag the Latency slider to the left to lower latency. Drag it to the right to increase latency.

PRACTICAL LATENCY SLIDER SETTINGS

A good rule of thumb for setting the Latency slider is this: If you are recording using input monitoring (see Chapter 6) or playing DX instruments live via your MIDI keyboard, set your latency to a low value—maybe as low as two to four milliseconds when using WDM sound card drivers. If you are playing many audio tracks and using a lot of real-time effects (see Chapter 11, "Exploring Effects") while mixing down (see Chapter 12, "Mixing It Down"), set your latency to a higher value to relieve the strain on your computer system—maybe a value of around 20 milliseconds (or higher if needed) when you are using WDM sound card drivers.

4. Click on the OK button when you're finished.

Setting Driver Mode

As with MIDI settings, the first time you run SONAR, it scans your computer system to see whether you have a sound card installed. SONAR then automatically chooses the drivers that will be used with your card, but you might get better performance using different drivers. To choose the type of drivers you want to use with SONAR, follow these steps:

1. Choose Options > Audio > Advanced to open the Audio Options dialog box, as shown in Figure 3.18.

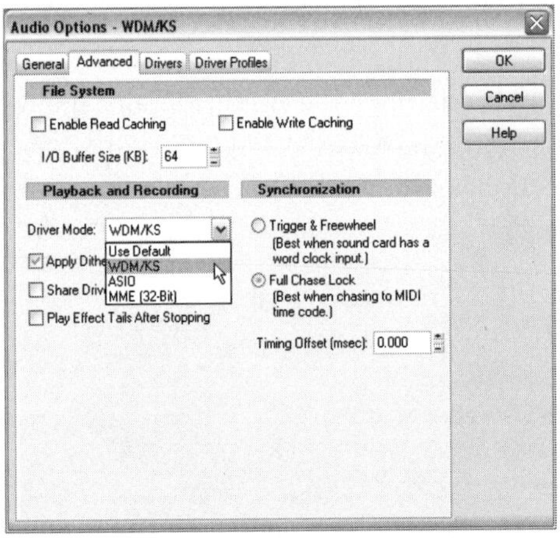

Figure 3.18
Use the Audio Options dialog box to choose your sound card drivers.

2. Under the Playback and Recording section, use the Driver Mode drop-down menu to choose the type of sound card drivers you want to use.

SOUND CARD DRIVERS

I talked about sound card drivers in Chapter 2, but just to recap a bit, MME drivers are an old variety of Windows sound card drivers and are provided for the support of older sound cards that might still be in existence. If at all possible, do not choose the MME option for your sound card output because it will provide very poor playback performance. Instead, you will want to choose either WDM or ASIO, depending on the type of drivers you have available. As to whether WDM or ASIO is better, that's a tough call. It really depends on the quality of the driver and how well it was programmed, so if you have both available, you'll have to try both to see which provides you with better performance.

3. Click on OK.

You need to close SONAR and restart it for your Driver Mode setting to take effect.

ASIO Drivers

If you are using ASIO drivers, you need to open the Audio Options dialog box again and click on the ASIO Panel button to make further adjustments after you have restarted SONAR. You might have noticed that the Latency slider might not work in this situation. With ASIO drivers, instead of using the Latency slider to adjust latency, you have to use the ASIO control panel for your sound card. My current sound card is the Echo Mona from Echo Audio (http://www.echoaudio.com). The ASIO control panel for the Mona looks like Figure 3.19.

Figure 3.19
Use the ASIO control panel to adjust latency when you are using ASIO drivers.

ASIO Echo WDM

Buffer size
- ○ 128 samples
- ○ 256 samples
- ◉ 512 samples
- ○ 1,024 samples
- ○ 2,048 samples
- ○ 4,096 samples
- ○ 8,192 samples
- ○ 16,384 samples

Configuration
- ☑ Enable ASIO 2.0 Direct Monitoring
- ☑ Show 96 kHz-capable cards only
- ☐ Short channel names

echo
digital audio

OK
Cancel

When you use the ASIO drivers for the Mona, the Latency slider in the Audio Options dialog box doesn't work. Instead, you have to choose a buffer size using the ASIO control panel. To do so, you simply click on the ASIO Panel button in the Audio Options dialog box, and then choose one of the available options in the Buffer Size section of the ASIO control panel. The lower the buffer size setting, the lower the latency; the higher the setting, the higher the latency. It works just like the Latency slider except there are set options to choose from instead of an adjustable slider.

Setting Queue Buffers and I/O Buffer Size

Two other settings that affect latency and audio performance are the number of buffers in the playback queue and the I/O (input/output) buffer size. Like the Latency slider, if they are set too low you can experience dropouts or glitches during playback. Higher settings mean more latency. Again, you need to experiment with the settings. I've found that values between two and four for the number of buffers in the playback queue and around 64 for the I/O buffer size work quite well. If you want to change them, you can follow these steps:

1. Choose Options > Audio to open the Audio Options dialog box.

2. Click on the General tab. The Buffers in Playback Queue setting is located in the Mixing Latency section, as shown in Figure 3.20.

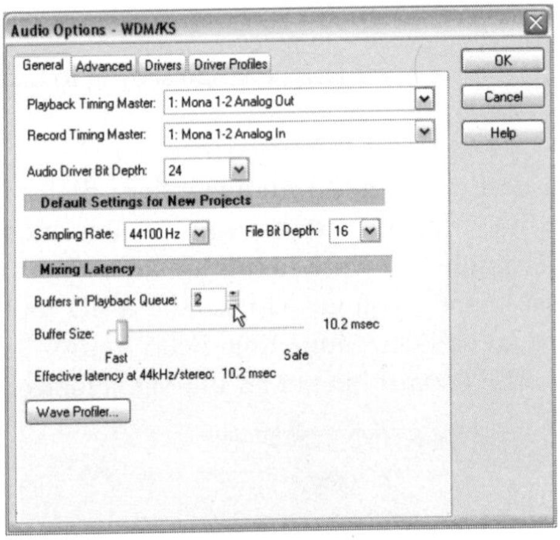

Figure 3.20
In this dialog box, you can adjust the Buffers in Playback Queue setting.

3. Type the new value.

4. Click on the Advanced tab. The I/O Buffer Size setting is located in the File System section, as shown in Figure 3.21.

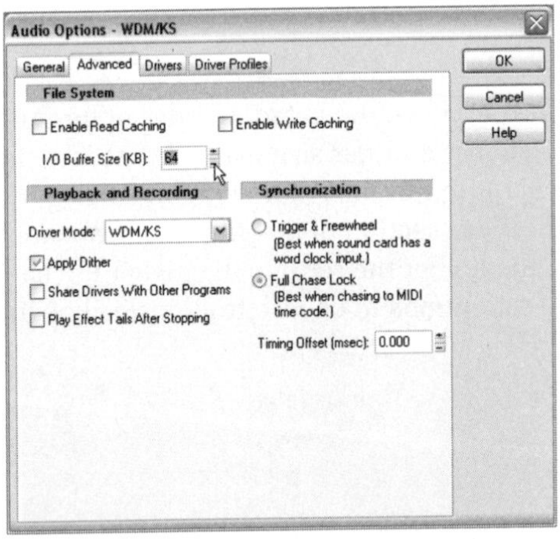

Figure 3.21
In this dialog box, you can adjust the I/O Buffer Size setting.

5. Type the new value.

6. Click on the OK button when you're finished.

Read and Write Caching

When your computer sets aside a part of its memory to hold recently read or written information from a disk drive, the process is known as *disk caching*. Windows uses disk caching to help speed up read and write operations to your disk drives. When data is read or written to disk as a continuous stream (as with digital audio), disk caching can actually slow things down.

SONAR has two options that let you enable or disable disk caching while the program is running. By default, SONAR keeps disk caching disabled. If you have a large amount of memory in your computer (such as 128 MB or more), disk caching may actually improve performance. If you want to see whether enabling this option makes any difference with your computer system, follow these steps:

1. Choose Options > Audio to open the Audio Options dialog box.

2. Click on the Advanced tab. The Enable Read Caching and Enable Write Caching settings are located in the File System section, as shown in Figure 3.22.

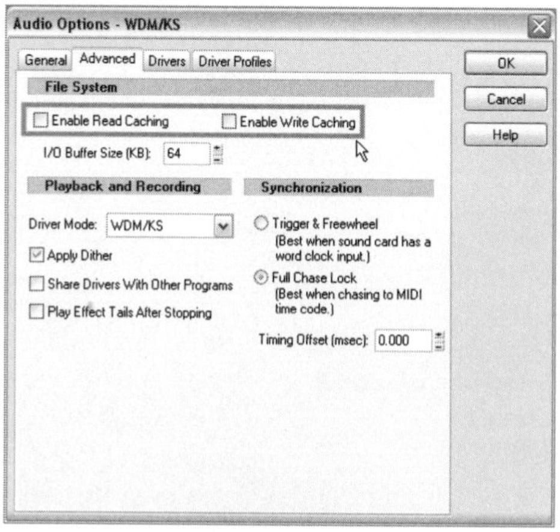

Figure 3.22
In this dialog box, you can adjust the Enable Read Caching and Enable Write Caching settings.

3. Click on each setting to activate it.

4. Click on the OK button when you're finished.

Understanding DMA and the Wave Profiler

A device that can read your computer's memory directly (without involving the CPU) is said to support DMA (*Direct Memory Access*). A sound card is such a device. SONAR uses the DMA settings of your sound card to ensure that MIDI and digital audio tracks within a project play in synchronization with one another. When you first run SONAR, it scans your sound card to automatically determine the DMA settings. These settings are listed in the Audio Options dialog box under the Driver Profiles tab. Leave these settings alone! In all but the most extreme cases, it won't do you any good to change them. If you're having excessive problems with MIDI and audio playback, you should contact Cakewalk Technical Support.

If you accidentally change the DMA settings (or if you just can't help yourself from seeing what will happen if you do), you can easily have SONAR scan your sound card again to bring back the original settings.

1. Choose Options > Audio to open the Audio Options dialog box.

2. Click on the General tab.

3. Click on the Wave Profiler button at the bottom of the dialog box. SONAR will scan your sound card and reset its DMA settings.

4. Click on the OK button to close the Audio Options dialog box.

IMPROVING AUDIO PERFORMANCE

For more information about optimizing SONAR, be sure to read the SONAR Help file section entitled Improving Audio Performance. Also, if you'd like more information about how to optimize your audio PC, check out my feature article in Issue 14 of *DigiFreq*. You can download the issue for free at

http://www.digifreq.com/digifreq/issues.asp.

4

Working with Projects

As I mentioned in Chapter 2, a project is SONAR's way of representing a song or any other musical body of work. A project holds all your music data, including MIDI and/or audio, along with a number of program settings. You can't do anything in SONAR without first creating a new project or opening an existing one. In this chapter, I'm going to talk all about projects. This chapter will do the following:

▶ Teach you to open an existing project

▶ Explain how to create a new project

▶ Show you how to create your own templates

▶ Tell you how to save a project

Opening Projects

Every time you start SONAR, it presents you with the SONAR Quick Start dialog box (see Figure 4.1). In this dialog box, you can open an existing project or a project you recently worked with, or you can create a new one.

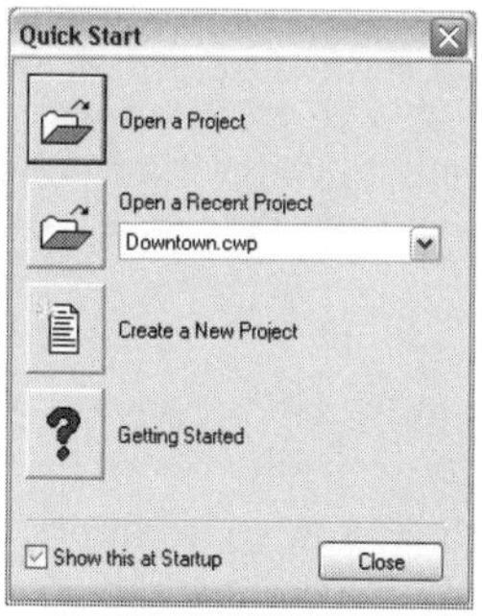

Figure 4.1
The SONAR Quick Start dialog box appears when you start SONAR.

If you choose to open an existing project, SONAR displays a standard file selection dialog box so you can select the project you want to load. If you changed the disk location of your project files (as described in Chapter 3), the dialog box will initially display the contents of the folder specified in the Project Files field of the Global Options > Folders dialog box. Of course, you can examine other disk locations just as you would when you are loading a file in any other Windows application.

By choosing the Open a Recent Project option in the SONAR Quick Start dialog box, you can open a project you've worked with previously. You simply select the project from the drop-down list and then click on the folder button next to the list. SONAR keeps track of the last eight projects you've used. When you open a ninth, the project on the bottom of the list is bumped off—not killed or deleted, just removed from the list.

You can also open an existing or recent project using SONAR's standard menu functions. To open an existing project, just choose File > Open. To open a recent project, select the File menu and then click on the name of the project you want to open in the list on the bottom half of the menu (see Figure 4.2).

Figure 4.2
You can use the File
menu to open an existing
or recent project.

File	
New...	
Open...	Ctrl+O
Close	
Save	Ctrl+S
Save As...	
Info...	
Project Audio Files...	
Import	▶
Export	▶
Print...	Ctrl+P
Print Preview	
Print Setup...	
Send...	
1 Downtown.cwp	
2 Don't Matter Audio and Midi Demo.cwb	
3 SONAR Audio and MIDI DEMO2.cwb	
4 2-Part Invention #13 in A minor.cwp	
Exit	

SHOW THIS AT STARTUP

Personally, I find it easier to use the standard menu functions to open a project. To keep the SONAR Quick Start dialog box from appearing every time you start SONAR, make sure the Show This at Startup check box at the bottom of the box is not selected (refer to Figure 4.1). You can do the same thing with the Tip of the Day dialog box.

Opening in Safe Mode

If you've used Microsoft Windows for any length of time, you've no doubt come across its notorious Safe Mode, which allows you to start the OS in a somewhat crippled state if you're having trouble booting up your PC. Basically, Safe Mode lets you start Windows with only the bare essentials needed to run the OS. For instance, all unnecessary device drivers are disabled. This allows you to troubleshoot Windows and attempt to find the source of your faulty startup.

SONAR provides a similar feature (also called Safe Mode) for use when opening project files. Like any computer data, project files can become corrupt occasionally, preventing you from opening them. This can be caused by computer resource limitations or bad DirectX (audio effect), MFX (MIDI effect), or DXi (DirectX Instrument) plug-ins. (I'll talk more about these plug-ins in Chapter 11, "Exploring Effects.") Using Safe Mode, SONAR allows you to load a project file with only the

Track view (in its default layout) open. If you had any other open views in the project, they will not open in Safe Mode. You are also prompted for each and every plug-in that you have assigned to your tracks in the project. This lets you determine whether a particular plug-in is preventing you from opening your project. Here is how Safe Mode works:

1. When opening a project using one of the methods described earlier, hold down the Shift key on your computer keyboard. This tells SONAR to open the project in Safe Mode and displays the File Open - Safe Mode dialog box (see Figure 4.3).

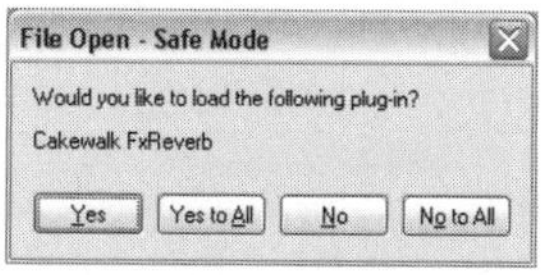

Figure 4.3
Use SONAR's Safe Mode
to open corrupt project
files.

2. If your project contains any plug-ins assigned to your tracks, the Safe Mode dialog box will ask you whether you want to load the plug-ins. You have four choices: Yes, Yes to All, No, and No to All. Choosing Yes will load the currently displayed plug-in. Choosing No will not load the currently displayed plug-in. Choosing Yes to All will close the dialog box and load all plug-ins. Choosing No to All will close the dialog box and open the project without any plug-ins.

3. If you don't choose either Yes to All or No to All, the Safe Mode dialog box will ask you about each individual plug-in contained in the project, and you will have to answer either Yes or No to each one. This method allows you to determine whether a certain plug-in is causing trouble, and which plug-in it is.

SAFE SAVING

If you load a project in Safe Mode with some or all of the plug-ins disabled, be careful when you save the project to disk. You should save the project using a different name so the original file remains intact. If you save the file using the same name, the original file will be overwritten and all your plug-in assignments will be lost.

Personally, I've found the best way to use Safe Mode is to load a project and individually determine whether or not each plug-in should be loaded. This lets me narrow down the problem to a specific plug-in. I may lose the settings for that troublesome plug-in, but I can keep all the settings for any other plug-ins I have assigned to my tracks in the project.

Finding Missing Audio Files

Another problem that can occur when you are opening projects that contain audio data is that SONAR might be unable to determine the location of the data for that project on your disk. This can happen if you move the location of your audio data folder (discussed in Chapter 3) and you forget to specify the new location in the SONAR folder settings. You can also run into this problem if you use individual folders for each project (described in Chapter 3). But if your data gets misplaced, you can use SONAR's Find Missing Audio function.

1. When you open a project in which SONAR cannot find the associated audio data for the audio tracks, the Find Missing Audio dialog box is displayed (see Figure 4.4).

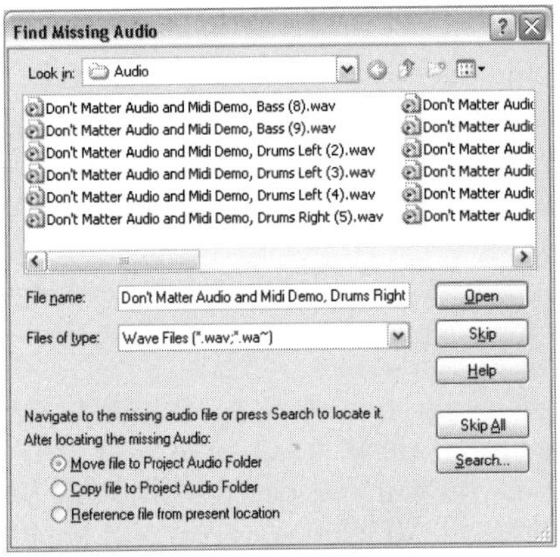

Figure 4.4
Use the Find Missing Audio function to locate misplaced audio data.

2. To locate the missing audio data, you can navigate manually through the folders on your hard drive using the Look In drop-down menu or you can use the Search feature. The Look In drop-down menu is self-explanatory. To use Search, click on the Search button. SONAR will automatically search your entire hard drive for the audio file currently displayed in the File Name field of the Find Missing Audio dialog box. During the search, the Search for Missing Audio dialog box is shown (see Figure 4.5). If the file is found, select it and click on OK. If the file isn't found, click on Cancel and search for it manually.

Figure 4.5
Use Search to automatically locate audio files.

3. After you've found the missing file, you can move it to your project's audio data folder, copy it to your project's audio data folder (which also leaves a copy of the file in its current location), or have the project point to the file in its current location. You accomplish these tasks by choosing one of the options in the After Locating the Missing Audio section of the Find Missing Audio dialog box (Move File to Project Audio Folder, Copy File to Project Audio Folder, or Reference File from Present Location, respectively).

4. To finish the operation, click on the Open button. If you no longer want to use the file in your project, you can click on the Skip button. To discard all audio data for a project, click on Skip All.

5. If your project contains data from more than one audio file, you need to repeat steps 2 through 4 for each missing file.

Any files that you couldn't find or just skipped over will be replaced with silence in your project. The clips will still appear in the tracks, but the clips will be empty.

Creating a New Project

To create a new project, you can select the appropriate option in the SONAR Quick Start dialog box or you can choose File > New from SONAR's menu. Whichever method you use, SONAR displays the New Project File dialog box (see Figure 4.6).

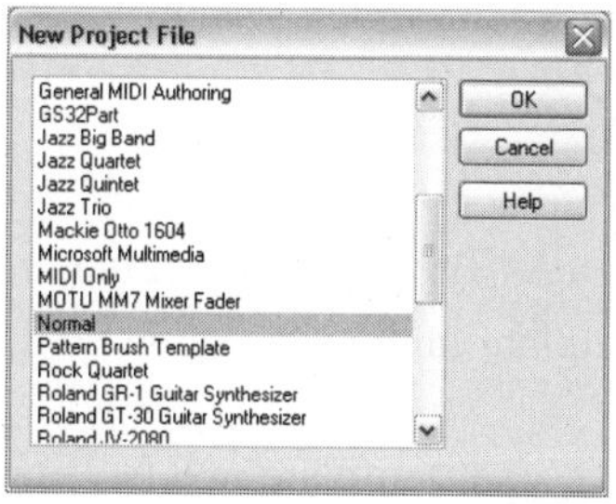

Figure 4.6
Start a new project by selecting an option from the New Project File dialog box.

In the dialog box, you need to choose a template upon which to base your new project. After you make your selection, SONAR creates a new project complete with predefined settings that reflect the template you selected.

What's a Template?

A *template* is a special type of file upon which new projects are based. You can think of templates as sort of like predefined projects. Templates contain the settings for all the parameters in a project. They enable you to set up a new project quickly and easily for a particular type of musical session. For example, if you need to record a rock song with guitar, organ, bass, and drums, you could get a head start on your project by using SONAR's Rock Quartet template. You can also use templates to set up SONAR for different kinds of studio configurations or to work with a particular MIDI instrument.

SONAR ships with more than 30 different templates that represent a wide range of recording situations. You can use a template called Normal to start a new project totally from scratch. And if you don't find what you need in the templates included with SONAR, you can always create your own.

Creating Your Own Template

Any parameters that are saved in a project can also be saved as a template. To create your own template, you simply follow these steps:

1. Choose File > New, and then choose the Blank (No Tracks) template. Choosing this template creates a new, blank project, ready to be filled.

2. Set SONAR's parameters to reflect the type of template you want to create. This includes track configurations.

3. Choose File > Save As to display the Save As dialog box (see Figure 4.7).

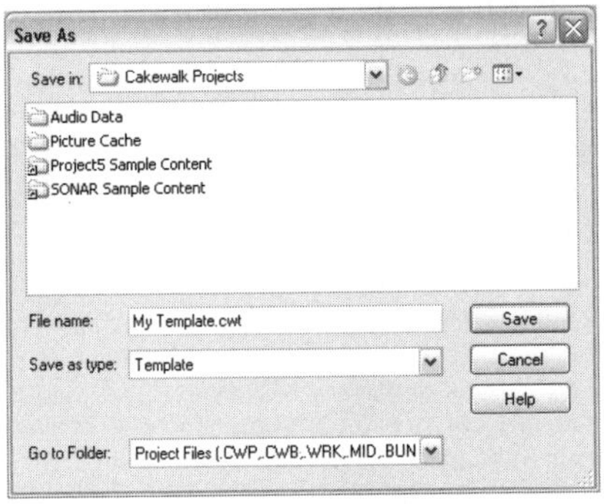

Figure 4.7
You can name your new template in the Save As dialog box.

4. Choose Template from the Save As Type drop-down menu.

5. Enter a name for your new template in the File Name field, and then click on the Save button.

The next time you want to create a new project, your template will be listed along with the other templates in the New Project File dialog box.

AUTOMATIC TEMPLATE

If you bypass the SONAR Quick Start dialog box—either by disabling it (as I mentioned earlier) or by clicking on its close button—SONAR will create a new project automatically every time you start the program. This project is based on the Normal template, which is saved as the NORMAL.CWT file. If you want to have SONAR configured in a particular way every time you run the program, simply create a new template and save it as the NORMAL.CWT file. SONAR will load your special template automatically during startup.

But what parameters do you need to set when you're creating a new template? I'll go through them one at a time.

Track Configuration and Parameters

Before you start recording any MIDI or audio data in SONAR, you have to set up your tracks in the Track view. You need to add tracks and tell SONAR their types (MIDI or audio) by right-clicking in the Track pane of the Track view and choosing either Insert Audio Track or Insert MIDI Track from the menu that appears (see Figure 4.8). Continue doing this until you have all the tracks you need for your template.

Figure 4.8
Add new tracks to your template using the Track pane of the Track view.

In addition to adding new tracks, you also need to set up the accompanying parameters for each track. These parameters include the name, channel, bank, patch, volume, pan, key offset, velocity offset, time offset, input, and output.

ADDITIONAL PARAMETERS

When you look in the Track view, you'll notice there are some additional parameters available for adjustment. These parameters are not usually set up when you create a template, so I will cover them later in the book.

You can change all of these parameters directly in the Track view (see Figure 4.9), but you can also access some of them via the Track Properties dialog box (see Figure 4.10). Because you can change all of the parameters in the Track view, most of the time just using that method is easiest. The only time you might need to use the Track Properties dialog box is if you want to add a descriptive comment to a track or you want to access the Patch browser. (I'll talk more about the Patch browser in a few minutes.) To access the Track Properties dialog box, right-click on the number of the track you want to change and choose Track Properties from the menu that appears.

Figure 4.9
You can change all track parameters in the Track view.

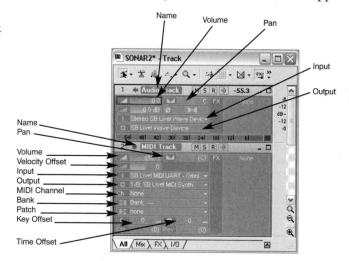

CHAPTER 4

Figure 4.10
Some track parameters
are available in the Track
Properties dialog box.

Name

To name a track, double-click in its Name field in the Track view, and then type the name. Press the Enter key on your computer keyboard when you're done; that's all there is to it. A track name can be anything from a short, simple word like *Drums* to a longer, descriptive phrase such as *Background Vocals (Left Channel)*.

MIDI Channel (Ch)

This parameter is for MIDI tracks only. It tells SONAR what MIDI channel you want it to use to play back the data in a track. To change this parameter, just click on the Ch drop-down list and choose a channel.

Bank (Bank)

Also for MIDI tracks only, the Bank parameter tells SONAR which bank of sounds you want to use in your MIDI instrument. To change this parameter, just click on the Bank drop-down list and choose a bank.

Patch (Patch)

Also for MIDI tracks only, the Patch parameter tells SONAR which patch (or sound) you want to use from the bank in your MIDI instrument. To choose a patch, click on the Patch drop-down list. If you set up your instrument definitions as described in Chapter 3, you should see the names of the patches for your MIDI instrument in the Patch drop-down list.

THE PATCH BROWSER

You also can choose patches for a track using the Patch browser. Just right-click on the number of a MIDI track and choose Track Properties to open the Track Properties dialog box. Then click on the Browse Patches button to open the Patch Browser dialog box (see Figure 4.11). You will see a list of all the patches available from the instrument definitions you set up earlier. To search for a particular patch, type some text in the Show Patches Containing the Text field. To choose a patch, select it from the list. Then click on OK.

Figure 4.11
Use the Patch browser as
an alternative for
assigning patches to a
track.

Volume (Vol)

The Volume parameter sets the initial loudness of a track. That's basically all there is to it. You can set the volume by clicking and dragging in the Vol parameter. Drag to the left to lower the volume; drag to the right to increase the volume. You can also change the volume numerically by clicking the Vol parameter to highlight it, pressing F2 on your computer keyboard, typing in a new value, and pressing Enter. The value can range from 0 (off) to 127 (maximum) for MIDI tracks and −INF to +6 dB for audio tracks. To quickly set the volume to its default value (0 dB), double-click on it.

Pan (Pan)

The Pan parameter determines where the sound of a track will be heard in the sound field between two stereo speakers. You can make the sound play out of the left speaker, the right speaker, or anywhere in between. That is called *panning*. You can set the pan by clicking and dragging in the Pan parameter. Drag to the left to pan the track to the left; drag to the right to pan the track to the right. You can also change the pan numerically by clicking the Pan parameter to highlight it, pressing F2 on your computer keyboard, typing in a new value, and pressing Enter. The value can range from 100% L (100 percent left) to 100% R (100 percent right). A value of C is dead center. To quickly set the panning to its default value (C), double-click on it. Pan works on both MIDI and audio tracks.

Key Offset (Key+)

The Key Offset parameter (which works only with MIDI tracks) lets you transpose the MIDI notes in a track during playback. It doesn't change the data that's actually recorded in the track. If you know you're going to want the notes in a track transposed after they've been recorded, setting up this parameter in your template can be useful. To set the key offset, double-click the Key+ parameter to activate it, and then type in a new value and press Enter. The Key+ value can range from −127 to +127, with each number representing a semitone (or half-step). For example, a value of −12 would transpose the notes down an octave; a value of +12 would transpose them up an octave. A value of 0 means no transposition will be applied.

Velocity Offset (Velocity Trim)

The Velocity Offset parameter (which works only with MIDI tracks) is similar to the Key Offset parameter, except instead of transposing MIDI notes during playback, it raises or lowers the MIDI velocity of each note in a track by adding or subtracting a number from -127 to $+127$. Again, the data that's actually recorded in the track isn't changed. You can set the Velocity Offset by clicking and dragging in the Velocity Trim parameter. Drag left to decrease the value; drag right to increase the value. You can also change the Velocity Offset numerically by clicking on the Velocity Trim parameter to highlight it, pressing F2 on your computer keyboard, typing in a new value, and pressing Enter.

Time Offset (Time+)

When you record a MIDI performance in SONAR, the timing of your performance is recorded along with the notes, and so on. Each MIDI event is "stamped" with an exact start time, which is measured in measures, beats, and clock ticks. The Time Offset parameter is similar to Key Offset and Velocity Offset, except that it adds or subtracts an offset value to the start time of the events in a MIDI track. Just as with Key Offset and Velocity Offset, the data that's actually recorded in the track isn't changed. The offset occurs only during playback, and you can set it back to zero to hear your original performance.

The Time Offset is useful if you want to make a track play a little faster or slower than the rest of the tracks, in case the performance is rushed or late. To change it, just double-click on the Time+ parameter to activate it. Then type in the number of clock ticks by which you want the events in the track to be offset and press Enter.

Input (Input)

The Input parameter lets SONAR know where the data for that track will be recorded from—an audio track or a MIDI track. To set the Input for an audio track, choose one of the inputs from your sound card from the Input drop-down menu. For example, if you have a Sound Blaster Live! card, your choices would be Left SB Live Wave In, Right SB Live Wave In, or Stereo SB Live Wave In. If you pick either the left or right choices, the track will record audio from either the left or right input on your sound card. If you pick the stereo choice, the track will record audio from both inputs at the same time, making it a stereo audio track.

Setting the Input parameter for a MIDI track is a bit different. Because MIDI can have multiple ports, and each port has 16 different channels, you can choose to record data using any one of those ports/channels. Just make sure your MIDI instrument is set to the same port/channel that you choose as your input, or your performance won't be recorded. You can also use the MIDI Omni setting, which allows SONAR to record data on all 16 channels at the same time. This way, the data from your MIDI instrument will be recorded regardless of the channel to which it is set. But if you're using multiple instruments, each one set to a different channel, you're better off just setting the correct channel in each of the tracks from the start.

Output (Output)

The Output parameter tells SONAR which MIDI port or sound card output you want to use to play back the data in a track. If the track is MIDI, you can select a MIDI port from the Output drop-down menu. If the track is audio, you can select a sound card output or audio bus from the Output drop-down menu. I'll talk more about audio buses in Chapter 12, "Mixing It Down."

CHANGE MULTIPLE PROPERTIES
You can also change the properties for multiple tracks simultaneously. Just select the tracks you want to adjust by Ctrl-clicking or Shift-clicking on the appropriate track numbers in the Track view. Then choose Track > Property > and the property you would like to change.

MIDI Input Presets

When you choose an input for a MIDI track, you might notice a couple of selections in the drop-down menu that I didn't mention earlier—the Presets and Manage Presets selections. Normally, when you choose an input for a MIDI track, you are limited to a single port and single channel selection. Using MIDI input presets, you can set up a MIDI track so it records data from multiple ports and specific multiple channels of your choice. This type of flexibility can come in handy if you have a number of outboard MIDI devices sending MIDI data to SONAR that you would like recorded on the same MIDI track, for example.

To set up a MIDI input preset, follow these steps:

1. Click on the Input parameter of the MIDI track and choose Manage Presets from the drop-down menu to open the MIDI Input Presets dialog box (see Figure 4.12).

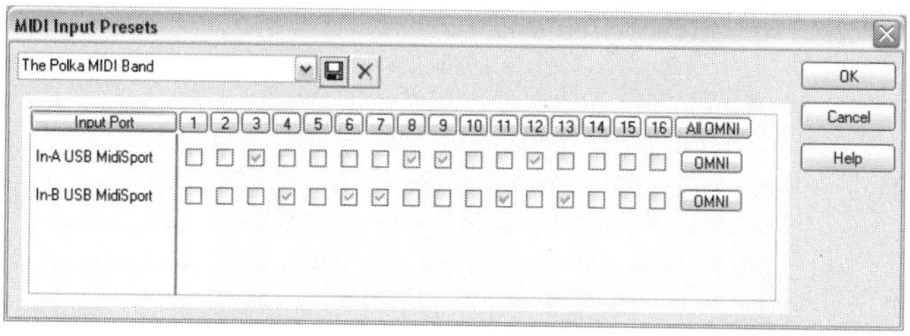

Figure 4.12
Use the MIDI Input Presets dialog box to create your own MIDI port/channel presets.

2. You'll see two lists in the box. In the left list, you will see all the MIDI ports provided by your MIDI interface. In the right list, you will see all the MIDI channels available for each port. To allow MIDI input on a port/channel, put a checkmark under that port/channel. You can activate as many port/channel combinations as you'd like.

3. If you want to allow MIDI input on all the channels of a port, click on the OMNI button at the end of the channel list for that port.

4. When you're finished activating ports and channels, type a name for your new preset in the Preset list at the top of the dialog box.

5. Click on the Save button (the floppy disk icon) to save your preset.

6. Click on OK to close the MIDI Input Presets dialog box.

After you have created your preset(s), they will be listed under the Preset selection in the Input drop-down menu for your MIDI track(s).

Timebase

Just like all sequencing software, SONAR uses clock ticks to keep track of the timing of your MIDI performance. Most of the time you see the clock ticks as measures and beats because the program translates them automatically. Hundreds of clock ticks occur for each measure or beat.

The number of clock ticks that happen within a beat are called *pulses per quarter note* (*PPQ*) or the *timebase*. The timebase determines the resolution or accuracy of your MIDI timing data. For example, if you want to use eighth-note septuplets (seven eighth notes per quarter note) in your performance, you have to use a timebase that is divisible by seven (such as 168 PPQ); otherwise, SONAR cannot record the septuplets accurately. By default, SONAR uses a timebase of 960 PPQ, which means every quarter note is represented by 960 clock ticks. You can set the timebase anywhere from 48 to 960 PPQ. To set the timebase, follow these steps:

1. Choose Options > Project to open the Project Options dialog box (see Figure 4.13).

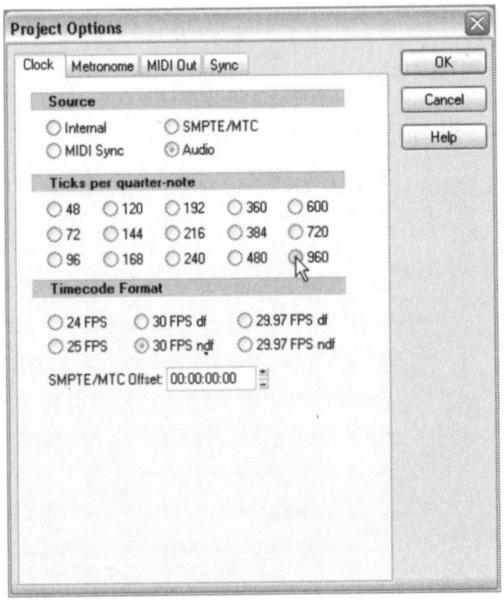

Figure 4.13
You can set the timebase in the Project Options dialog box.

2. Click on the Clock tab.
3. Choose the timebase you want to use from the options in the Ticks Per Quarter-Note section.
4. Click on the OK button.

System Exclusive Banks

SONAR includes a System Exclusive (Sysx) librarian, which lets you store MIDI System Exclusive messages in up to 256 banks (or storage areas). All the data in the librarian is saved along with a project, which means that each project can hold its own unique library of Sysx data. This capability can be very useful when you're putting together templates for special MIDI recording situations. Because the Sysx librarian is a significant part of SONAR, I will talk about it in more detail in Chapter 14, "Studio Control with StudioWare and Sysx." I just wanted to mention it here so you know that data contained in the librarian is saved along with your template.

File Information and Comments

SONAR allows you to save description information in a project, including title, subtitle, instructions, author, copyright, keywords, and comments. This information can be useful to remind yourself exactly what the file contains, especially when you're creating a template. To add information to a project, follow these steps:

1. Choose File > Info to open the File Info dialog box (see Figure 4.14).

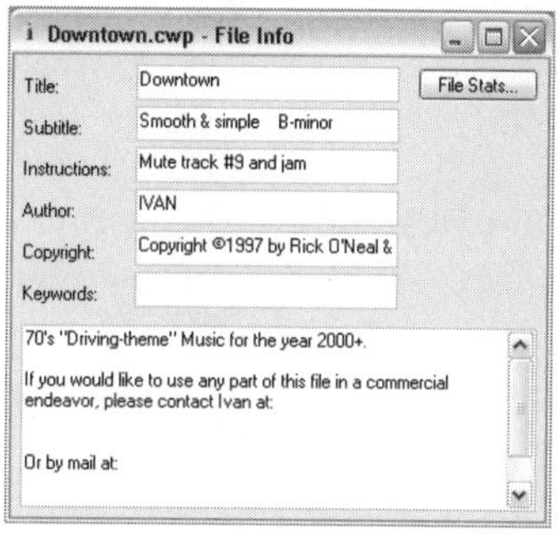

Figure 4.14
You can use the File Info dialog box to add a description to your project or template.

2. Type the appropriate information in each of the fields. By the way, the information you enter in the Title, Subtitle, Instructions, Author, and Copyright fields will appear in the Staff view and on your music notation printouts (see Chapter 13, "Making Sheet Music").

3. Close the File Info dialog box when you're finished.

The information you entered will be included in the project or template file when you save it.

AUTOMATIC FILE INFO

If you plan to share your project or template files with others, and you want them to follow special instructions you've included in the File Info dialog box (or you just want to be sure they see your copyright notice), you can display the File Info dialog box automatically when the file is opened. Just save the project or template while the File Info dialog box is still open.

Tempo, Meter, and Key

Every piece of music needs to have a tempo, meter (time signature), and key, so of course SONAR allows you to set and save these parameters within a project or template.

Setting the Tempo

You can set the tempo for your piece by following these steps:

1. Choose View > Toolbars to make sure the Tempo toolbar is visible (see Figure 4.15).

Figure 4.15
To set the tempo for a project, you need to use the Tempo toolbar.

2. Click on the Tempo display in the Tempo toolbar. The tempo will be highlighted.

3. Type a new value between 8.00 and 250.00 for the tempo. You can also use the + and − spin controls to adjust the tempo with your mouse.

4. Press the Enter key on your computer keyboard to set the tempo.

MORE TEMPO INFORMATION

For more information about changing the tempo in an existing project, see Chapter 7, "Editing Basics."

Setting the Meter (Time Signature) and Key (Key Signature)

Because a piece of music can have multiple time signatures and key signatures, SONAR allows you to add multiple meters and keys to a project. For the purpose of creating a template, more than likely you'll want to set only the initial meter and key. To do so, follow these steps:

1. Choose View > Meter/Key to open the Meter/Key view (see Figure 4.16).

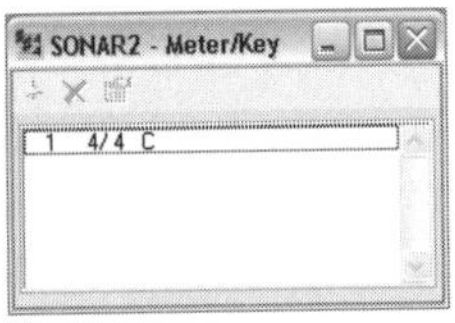

Figure 4.16
You can add multiple time and key signatures to a project in the Meter/Key view.

2. Double-click on the first meter/key change in the list to open the Meter/Key Signature dialog box (see Figure 4.17). (For this example, there should be only one meter/key change in the dialog box.)

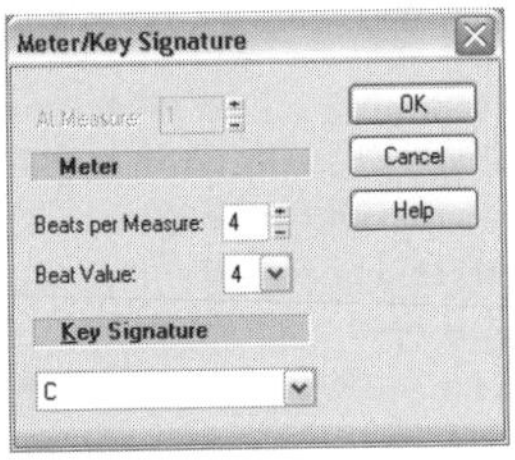

Figure 4.17
In the Meter/Key Signature dialog box, you can edit individual meter/key changes.

3. Enter the Beats Per Measure and the Beat Value you want to use. For example, if your song were in 6/8 time, you would change the Beats Per Measure to 6 and the Beat Value to 8.

4. Choose a key from the Key Signature drop-down menu. For example, if your song is in the key of A, choose 3 Sharps (A).

5. Click on OK, and then close the Meter/Key view.

Other Parameters

A few other parameters are saved along with projects and templates, including synchronization settings, MIDI echo, metronome, record mode, and Punch In/Out Times. You'll usually set these parameters while you're working on a project (not beforehand), so I'll talk more about them in Chapter 6, "Recording and Playback." For the purpose of creating a template, you can just let these parameters be saved at their default values.

ADDITIONAL TEMPLATE MATERIAL

A template can also contain MIDI and audio data, which can be useful if you have some favorite drum grooves or melodic phrases that you like to use frequently in your projects, for example. Simply store these tidbits as clips in one of the tracks, and the MIDI and/or audio data will be saved along with it when you save the template. Then, whenever you create a new project with that template, the MIDI and/or audio data will be ready and waiting for you to use.

THE ULTIMATE TEMPLATE

When inspiration hits, you don't want to waste your time fiddling with sequencer setup parameters; you want to be able to start your software and get right to work. If you create a template file that contains everything set just the way you like it, you'll have a much better chance of getting that cool lick down before you forget it. For instructions on how to set up the ultimate template, check out my "Sequencer Techniques" feature article in Issue 11 of *DigiFreq*. You can download the issue for free at http://www.digifreq.com/digifreq/issues.asp.

Saving Your Project

When it comes time to save your SONAR project, follow these steps:

1. Choose File > Save As to open the Save As dialog box.
2. Choose the type of project file you want to save from the Save As Type drop-down menu.
3. Enter a name for the file and click on the Save button.

Other than the name of the file, the only thing you really have to decide is the file type.

Project File Types

You can save projects as four different types of files: MIDI (.MID), Open Media Format (.OMF), work (.CWP), and bundle (.CWB).

MIDI Files

If you ever need to collaborate on a project with someone who owns a sequencing application other than SONAR, you should save your project as a MIDI (.MID) file. A MIDI file is a standard type of file that you can use to transfer musical data between different music software applications. Most music programs on the market today can load and save MIDI files. The problem with MIDI files, however, is that they can store only MIDI data; they can't hold audio data. None of SONAR's settings are saved within a MIDI file either, so if you're working on a project alone or everyone else in your songwriting group uses SONAR, you don't need to deal with MIDI files. Of course, MIDI files can be useful in other circumstances, such as when you're composing music for multimedia or sharing your music with others via the Internet.

Open Media Format

As with MIDI files, if you ever need to collaborate on a project with someone who owns a sequencing application other than SONAR, you can save your file in the Open Media Format (.OMF). Instead of MIDI data, the Open Media Format only saves the audio data from a project. Why would you need this format? Well, you might want to bring your project into another studio where they don't have SONAR available and hire a recording engineer to mix or master your project. To export your project to OMF, follow these steps:

1. Choose File > Export > OMF to open the Export OMF dialog box (see Figure 4.18).

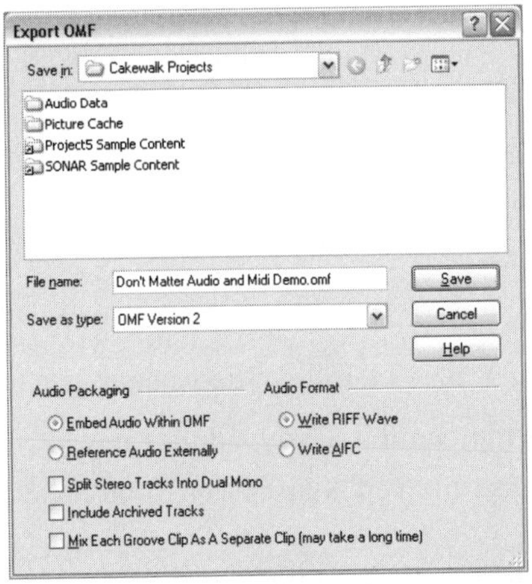

Figure 4.18
Use the Export OMF
dialog box to export your
project to an OMF file.

2. From the Save In menu, select the folder to which you want to save your OMF file. Then type a name for the file in the File Name box.

3. Choose a file type from the Save As Type menu. Choose OMF Version 1 if you will be importing the OMF file into an application that supports this version. Choose OMF Version 2 if you will be importing the file into an application that supports this version. (Usually newer applications support Version 2.)

4. In the Audio Format section, choose whether you want the audio data from your project saved in Wave format or AIFF format. Usually, if you are using a Windows-based PC, you should use Wave format. For Macs, AIFF format is the norm.

5. In the Audio Packaging section, choose whether you want to embed the audio data from your project into the OMF file or whether you want the audio data saved as separate audio files. Choose the Embed Audio within OMF or Reference Audio Externally option, respectively.

6. If you want the stereo tracks in your project to be converted into two separate mono tracks, activate the Split Stereo Tracks into Dual Mono option. This option can come in handy if the application you'll use to open the OMF file only supports stereo tracks as two separate mono tracks.

7. If you have any archived tracks in your SONAR project, you can include them in the exported OMF file by activating the Include Archived Tracks option. See Chapter 6 for more information on SONAR's track archive feature.

8. In SONAR, Groove clips contain multiple repetitions of the same audio data over a number of different measures in a track. Normally when you export a project, the Groove clips are simply exported as one clip that contains the Groove clip information. However, some applications might not support this type of clip, so you might need to save each repetition of each Groove clip as a separate audio clip. To do so, activate the Mix Each Groove Clip as a Separate Clip option. You should know that this process can take a long time depending on the size of your project.

9. Click on Save.

If you choose to embed the audio data in the OMF file, you will export only one file. If you chose to reference the audio data externally, you will have one OMF file along with all the audio files representing the tracks from your original project.

Work Files

If you're working on a project that contains only MIDI data and no audio data, you should save the project as a work (.CWP) file. Work files store all the MIDI data in a project, plus all the parameter settings (which you learned about earlier in this chapter) for the project. Work files do not store audio data.

MORE TEMPO INFORMATION

For more information about changing the tempo in an existing project, see Chapter 7, "Editing Basics."

MANAGE PROJECTS MANUALLY

If you decide to manage your project audio files manually (as mentioned in Chapter 3), you should save your audio projects as work files. In this case the audio data is stored separately from the project file.

Bundle Files

You can save projects that contain both MIDI and audio data as bundle (.CWB) files, although I recommend saving them as work (.CWP) files and using the Per-Project Audio Folders feature mentioned in Chapter 3. If you use a bundle file, you can store all the data in a project (MIDI data, audio data, and project parameter settings) in a single file, but this format is best used for archiving completed projects. A single file makes it very easy to keep track of all the data in a project and make a backup of the project for easy recovery in case something goes wrong. I'll talk more about backing up your project files in Appendix B, "Backing Up Your Project Files."

AUTO SAVE FEATURE

SONAR has an Auto Save feature that automatically saves your data to a special backup file at fixed time intervals or every time a certain number of changes have been made to the project. Using this feature is a great way to keep your data safe in case a power outage occurs or you make a huge mistake that you can't undo. To activate Auto Save, follow these steps:

1. Select Options > Global to open the Global Options dialog box. Click on the General tab.

2. For the option Auto-Save Every 0 Minutes or 0 Changes, set either the number of minutes or the number of changes to occur for SONAR to automatically save your project.

3. If you want to disable Auto Save, set both the minute and changes values back to zero.

4. Click on the OK button.

During an automatic save, SONAR saves your project in a special file with a different name. If your project is named myproject.cwp, for example, SONAR automatically saves to a file named "auto save version of myproject.cwp." If you ever need to recover your project, you can just open the special Auto Save file and then save it under the original filename.

5

Getting Around in SONAR

To record, play, and edit your music in SONAR, you have to know how to navigate through the data in your project. As you learned in Chapter 2, SONAR includes a number of tools that allow you to examine and manipulate your data: They are the Track, Piano Roll, Staff, and Event views. Although each of these views provides a different way to edit your data, they all share some common means of control. In other words, even though your data appears (and is edited) differently in each view, you access the data in a similar manner no matter which view you use. A little confused? Don't worry, you'll understand exactly what I mean after you finish reading this chapter. This chapter will do the following:

▶ Explain how to use the Now time

▶ Show you how to use the Go menu

▶ Describe how to set place marks in your project

▶ Teach you how to search for specific music data in your project

The Now Time

You learned a little about timing in Chapters 1 and 3. Essentially, you learned that in addition to the musical data itself, the timing of your performance is stored during recording. This means that SONAR keeps track of exactly when you play each note on your MIDI keyboard during a performance, and it stores those notes along with a *timestamp* (a timing value) containing the measure, beat, and clock tick when each note occurred.

To give you access to your data in a project, SONAR provides a feature known as the *Now time*. The Now time is essentially a pointer that indicates your current time location within a project. For example, the beginning of a project has a Now time of 1:01:000 (designating measure, beat, and tick), which is the first beat of the first measure. If you want to view the data at the second beat of the tenth measure, for example, you have to set the Now time to 10:02:000. Of course, you can get more precise by specifying clock ticks, such as in a Now time of 5:03:045, which would be the forty-fifth clock tick of the third beat in the fifth measure.

The Now time is also updated in real time, which means it changes constantly during recording or playback of a project. For example, when you play your project, the Now time counts along and shows you the current measure, beat, and tick while you listen to your music.

Show Me the Now Time

You can view the Now time in several different ways. The Now time is displayed numerically in the Position toolbar (see Figure 5.1).

Figure 5.1
You can view the Now time in the Position toolbar.

You can also use the Transport toolbar to view the Now time (see Figure 5.2). For more information about toolbars, refer to Chapter 3.

Figure 5.2
The Now time is displayed in the Transport toolbar as well.

On either toolbar, you'll notice that the Now time is shown as measures, beats, and ticks. But each toolbar has an additional numeric display that also displays the Now time—shown as hours, minutes, seconds, and frames (known as SMPTE).

THE BIG TIME VIEW

If you're like me, and you have some of your MIDI instruments set up in your home studio a fair distance away from your computer, you might have trouble reading the very tiny Now time display on the Position or Transport toolbars. To remedy this situation, Cakewalk has included the Big Time view in SONAR. Basically, it displays the Now time in large numbers on your computer screen (see Figure 5.3). The Big Time view has its own window so you can position it anywhere within the SONAR workspace. You can change the size of the Big Time view by dragging any of its corners, just like you would any window. To toggle the time format between measures, beats, and ticks and SMPTE, just click inside the Big Time view window. You can also change the font and color of the display by right-clicking in the window and then making your selections in the standard Windows Font dialog box.

Figure 5.3
You can use the Big Time view to display the Now time in varying fonts and sizes on your computer screen.

WHAT IS SMPTE?

SMPTE (*Society of Motion Picture and Television Engineers*) is a special timing code used for synchronizing audio and video data, although it can be used for other purposes too. NASA originally developed the technology because they needed an accurate way to keep track of space mission data. In SONAR, you can use SMPTE to keep track of the timing of your project. SONAR automatically converts the measures, beats, and ticks in a project to the hours, minutes, seconds, and frames format used by SMPTE. The frames parameter comes from the fact that SMPTE is used extensively with video, film, and television. Video is created by recording a series of still picture frames very quickly. When these frames are played back, you see them as a moving picture. You can use SMPTE to time video data accurately, down to a single frame. Every second of video data usually has 30 frames, but the number depends on the data format. You'll learn more details about using SMPTE in Chapter 6, "Recording and Playback." For now, just know that you can view and set the Now time of your project either in measures, beats, and ticks or hours, minutes, seconds, and frames.

In addition to being displayed numerically, the Now time is displayed graphically in any of SONAR's view windows. In the Track, Piano Roll, and Staff views, the Now time is displayed as a vertical line cursor that extends from the top to the bottom of the view. As the Now time changes (from being set manually or in real time during playback or recording), the cursor in each of the views follows along in perfect sync and indicates graphically the place in the project at which the Now time is pointing currently. To see what I mean, try the following steps:

1. Choose File > Open and load one of the sample project files that comes included with SONAR. For this example, choose Latin.cwp (see Figure 5.4).

Figure 5.4
This screen shows the layout of the Latin.cwp sample project.

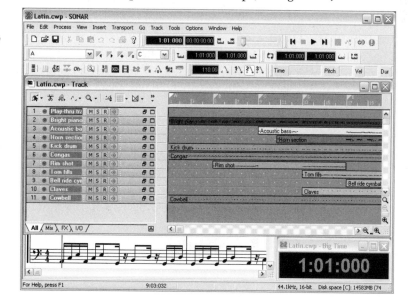

2. Close all the windows except for the Track view, and then choose Transport > Play or just click on the Play button in the Transport toolbar to start playing the project.

3. Look at the Track view. See the Now time cursor moving across the track display as the music plays?

4. Click on the track number for track 2 to select it, and then choose View > Piano Roll and look at the Piano Roll view. The same thing is happening, right? Notice the row of numbers just above the place where the Now time cursor is moving. This is the Time Ruler, and every view has one (except the Event view, which I'll talk about in Chapter 7, "Editing Basics"). The Time Ruler displays the measure numbers in the current project. By lining up the top of the Now time cursor with the Time Ruler in any of the views, you can get a quick estimate of the current Now time.

TIME RULER FORMAT

If you right-click on the Time Ruler in Track view and choose Time Ruler Format, you can change the format of the measurements shown. So instead of keeping track of the Now time in measures, beats, and ticks, you can use hours, minutes, seconds, and frames. The sample's measurement setting comes in handy when you are editing audio data, which I'll discuss in Chapter 7, "Editing Basics" and Chapter 8, "Exploring the Editing Tools."

5. Choose View > Event List and look at the Event view. It's different from all the other views because it shows the data as one long list instead of displaying it from left to right. And instead of a vertical line, it shows the Now time cursor as a small red box. While a project plays, the Now time cursor in the Event view moves down the list, and it marks the same place in the project that all the other view cursors do. Everything is synchronized to the Now time.

Setting the Now Time

As you just saw, the Now time changes automatically as a project is played, but you can also set it manually when a project isn't playing. SONAR gives you this capability so you can access different parts of your project for editing, which I'll talk about in Chapter 7.

Numerically

Changing the Now time is easy. If you want to set the Now time to a precise numerical value, you can simply type it in the display on the Position toolbar.

1. If you want to set the Now time using measures, beats, and ticks, click on the measures, beats, and ticks display in the Position toolbar. The display will be highlighted, and + and − spin controls will appear next to it (see Figure 5.5).

Figure 5.5
You can change the Now time by clicking on the display to highlight it.

Position

`1:01:000` `00:00:00:00`

2. Type the measures, beats, and ticks value you want to use and press Enter on your computer keyboard. You can also click on the spin controls to change the value.

NOW TIME SHORTCUTS

If you want to set the Now time quickly to a particular measure or beat, you don't have to enter all the numerical values. For example, to set the Now time to measure two, type 2. That's it. Or to set the Now time to measure five, beat three, type 5:3 or 5 spacebar 3. To specify ticks, you must enter something for all the values.

3. If you want to set the Now time using hours, minutes, seconds, and frames, click on the SMPTE display in the Position toolbar. The display will be highlighted, and + and − spin controls will appear next to it (see Figure 5.6).

Figure 5.6
You can change the Now time by specifying SMPTE time code values too.

4. Type the hours, minutes, seconds, and frames values you want to use and press Enter on your computer keyboard. You can also click on the spin controls to change the values.

SMPTE SHORTCUTS

Just as with the measures, beats, and ticks, if you want to set the Now time quickly to a particular hour, minute, or second, you don't have to enter all the numerical values. For example, to set the Now time to two minutes, type 0:2. To set the Now time to five minutes, three seconds, type 0:5:3. To specify frames, you must enter something for all the values.

Graphically

Remember when I described the Time Rulers in each of the views? Well, you can change the Now time quickly by simply clicking on any of the Time Rulers.

1. As you did earlier, choose File > Open and load one of the sample project files that comes included with SONAR. For this example, choose Latin.cwp.

2. Click on the Time Ruler in Track view. See how the Now time changes?

3. Click on the Time Ruler in Piano Roll view. Same result, right? Depending on where you click on the Time Ruler, the Now time changes to the appropriate value within the measure that you click.

SNAP TO GRID

You might notice that when you click on the Time Ruler in any of the views, the Now time is automatically set to the first beat of the nearest measure. This is due to SONAR's Snap to Grid feature. Snap to Grid automatically snaps the Now time cursor to the nearest predefined value when you try to set it via a Time Ruler. This feature makes it easy to specify quick and precise settings. Without Snap to Grid, setting the Now time accurately using a Time Ruler can be difficult.

Each view (except Event view) in SONAR has its own separate Snap to Grid, but the feature is set in the same manner no matter which view you're using. To activate or deactivate Snap to Grid in a view, just click on the Snap to Grid button (see Figure 5.7). To set a Snap to Grid interval, right-click on the Snap to Grid button (or in Track view, click on the down arrow next to the Snap to Grid button) to display the Snap to Grid dialog box (see Figure 5.8). Then select a resolution by choosing a note duration from the list, typing a time value to use, or selecting a standard resolution such as Events, Markers, or Clip Boundaries. After you're finished setting the Snap to Grid options, click on the Time Ruler, and you'll notice that the Now time cursor will snap to the resolution you've chosen.

Figure 5.7
The Snap to Grid button controls whether the Snap to Grid feature is on or off.

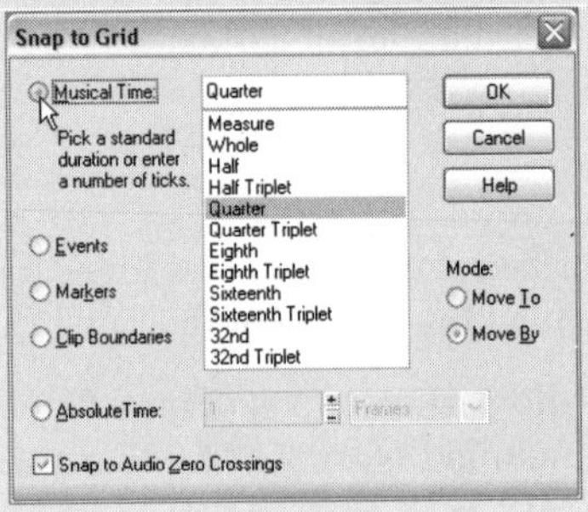

Figure 5.8
You can set the Snap to Grid options in the Snap to Grid dialog box.

4. As before, the Event view works a little differently. Here, you can click on any event in the list, and the Now time will change to the exact timing value of that event.

The Position Slider

Another quick way to set the Now time graphically is to use the Position slider. The slider is part of the Position toolbar (see Figure 5.9). To use the slider, just click and drag it. If you click to the left or right of the slider, the Now time will update one measure at a time.

Figure 5.9
You can drag the Position slider left or right to decrease or increase the Now time, respectively.

Sticky Now Time

As you were clicking around in the Time Rulers of the various views, you might have noticed the white flag attached to the top of the Now time cursor. This flag is the Now time marker. It adds a special functionality to the Now time cursor. By clicking and dragging the Now time marker, you can set a place in your project to which the Now time cursor will return every time you stop playback.

In earlier versions of SONAR, the Now time cursor would always return to the beginning of a project when playback was stopped. Now you can have it return to the Now time marker instead. Why is this useful? Well, suppose you're editing data in a certain section of a project and you want to hear how your changes sound. Just set the Now time marker to the edit spot and start playback. When you stop playback, you'll be returned to the edit spot you designated with the marker.

REWIND TO NOW MARKER
If you would rather not have the Now time cursor return to the Now time marker when you stop playback, choose Options > Global > General, and then deactivate the On Stop, Rewind to Now Marker option.

The Go Menu

In addition to allowing you to set the Now time numerically and graphically, SONAR provides a few special functions that let you quickly change the Now time to some musically related points in a project. All these functions are a part of the Go menu. To activate them, simply click on the Go menu and choose the appropriate function. The following sections provide explanations for the functions on the Go menu.

Go-Time

Go-Time allows you to change the Now time numerically by entering measure, beat, and tick values. It works in exactly the same way as the measure, beat, and tick display in the Position toolbar; the only difference is that Go-Time opens a dialog box.

Go-From and Go-Thru

When you're editing data in SONAR, you first need to select the data you want to use. This process is the same as in any computer program that lets you work with data. For instance, if you want to delete some text in a word processor, you first select the data to highlight it, and then you delete it.

CHAPTER 5

If you have some data currently selected in your project, you can quickly set the Now time to the time that corresponds to the beginning (called the From time) or the end (called the Thru time) of the selection using the Go-From and Go-Thru functions, respectively. You'll learn more details about selecting data in Chapter 7.

Go-Beginning and Go-End

The Go-Beginning and Go-End functions are pretty self-explanatory. Simply put, they allow you to set the Now time to correspond to the beginning or the end of a project, respectively.

Go-Previous Measure and Go-Next Measure

As with Go-Beginning and Go-End, Go-Previous Measure and Go-Next Measure are self-explanatory. They let you quickly set the Now time to correspond to the first beat of the previous measure or the first beat of the next measure relative to the current Now time. In other words, if the Now time is set at 5:01:000 (beat one of measure five), selecting Go-Previous Measure changes it to 4:01:000 (beat one of measure four), and selecting Go-Next Measure changes it to 6:01:000 (beat one of measure six).

GO-PREVIOUS MEASURE QUIRK
If the Now time is set to something like 5:01:050, Go-Previous Measure actually changes it to the first beat of the current measure, which in this case would be 5:01:000. I'm not sure why, but that's how it works.

Go-Previous Marker and Go-Next Marker

The Go-Previous Marker and Go-Next Marker functions work in a similar manner to the Go-Previous Measure and Go-Next Measure functions. Go-Previous Marker and Go-Next Marker let you quickly set the Now time to correspond to the closest previous marker or next marker relative to the current Now time. Of course, because I haven't told you about markers yet, you're probably wondering what I mean. So, let's talk about markers, shall we?

Markers, Oh My!

All the methods for setting the Now time that I've described so far have been based on numbers or predefined musical designations such as measures, beats, or the beginning and ending of a project. These methods are all fine when you already have the music for your project written out so you know exactly where everything occurs ahead of time, but what if you're creating a song from scratch simply by recording the parts on the fly? In a case like that, being able to put names on certain locations within a project would be very helpful, and that's exactly what markers allow you to do.

Using markers, you can assign a name to any exact point in time (in either measures, beats, and ticks or SMPTE) in a project. They're great for designating the places where the verses and choruses start and end within a song. And they make it very easy for you to jump to any point in a project that you specify simply by name.

Make Your Mark(ers)

Creating markers is a simple process. Essentially, you just need to set the Now time to the measure, beat, and tick at which you want to place the marker in the project, activate the Marker dialog box, and type in a name. Activating the Marker dialog box is the key here because you can do so in a number of different ways. To create a marker, just follow these steps:

1. Set the Now time to the measure, beat, and tick or the SMPTE time at which you want to place the marker in the project. As you learned earlier, you can set the Now time either numerically or graphically.

2. Choose Insert > Marker to open the Marker dialog box (see Figure 5.10). You can also open the Marker dialog box by pressing F11 on your computer keyboard; holding the Ctrl key on your computer keyboard and clicking just above the Time Ruler (the Marker section) in the Track, Staff, or Piano Roll views; right-clicking on a Time Ruler; clicking on the Insert Marker button on the Markers toolbar; or clicking on the Insert Marker button in the Markers view. (I'll describe the Markers toolbar and view later in this chapter.)

Figure 5.10
You can create a marker using the Marker dialog box.

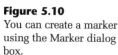

3. Type a name for the marker in the Name field.

4. If you want the marker to be assigned to a measure/beat/tick value, you don't need to do anything more. The measure/beat/tick time of the marker is shown in the Time field in the middle of the Marker dialog box.

5. If you want the marker to be assigned to an SMPTE time, activate the Lock to SMPTE (Real World) Time option.

LOCK TO SMPTE TIME

If you use the Lock to SMPTE (Real World) Time value, your marker will be assigned an exact hour/minute/second/frame value. It will retain that value no matter what. Even if you change the tempo of the project, the marker will keep the same time value, although its measure/beat/tick location might change because of the tempo. This feature is especially handy when you're putting music and sound to video because you need to have cues that always happen at an exact moment in the project. By leaving a marker assigned to a measure/beat/tick value, you can be sure that it will always occur at that measure, beat, and tick even if you change the tempo of the project.

6. Click on OK.

When you're finished, your marker (with its name) will be added to the Marker section, just above the Time Ruler in the Track, Staff, and Piano Roll views.

REAL-TIME MARKERS

Usually, you add markers to a project while no real-time activity is going on, but you can also add them while a project is playing. Simply press the F11 key on your computer keyboard, and SONAR will create a marker at the current Now time. The new marker be assigned a temporary name automatically; you can change this name later.

Editing the Markers

Editing existing markers is just as easy as creating new ones. You can change their names and times, make copies of them, and delete them.

Changing Marker Names

To change the name of a marker, follow these steps:

1. Right-click on the marker in the Marker section of the Time Ruler in one of the views to open the Marker dialog box. Alternatively, choose View > Markers to open the Markers view (see Figure 5.11) and double-click on the marker in the list to open the Marker dialog box.

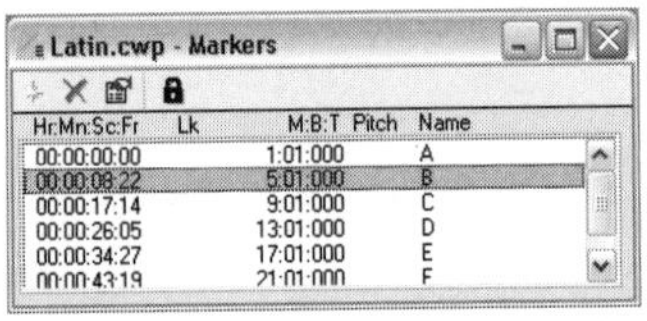

Figure 5.11
The Markers view displays a list of all the markers in a project.

2. Type a new name for the marker.
3. Click on OK.

Changing Marker Time

Follow these steps to change the time value of a marker numerically:

1. Right-click on the marker in the Marker section of the Time Ruler in one of the views to open the Marker dialog box. Alternatively, choose View > Markers to open the Markers view and double-click on the marker in the list to open the Marker dialog box.
2. Type a new measure/beat/tick value for the marker. If you want to use an SMPTE value, activate the Lock to SMPTE (Real World) Time option and then type a new hour/minute/second/frame value for the marker.
3. Click on OK.

You can also change the time value of a marker graphically by simply dragging the marker within the Marker section of the Time Ruler in one of the views. Drag the marker to the left to decrease its time value or drag it to the right to increase its time value. Simple, no?

Making a Copy of a Marker

To make a copy of a marker, follow these steps:

1. Hold down the Ctrl key on your computer keyboard.
2. Click and drag a marker in the Marker section of the Time Ruler in one of the views to a new time location.
3. Release the Ctrl key and mouse button. SONAR will display the Marker dialog box.
4. Enter a name for the marker. You can also change the time by typing a new value, if you want. The time value is initially set to the time for the location on the Time Ruler to which you dragged the marker.
5. Click on OK.

Deleting a Marker

You can delete a marker in one of two ways—either directly in the Track, Staff, or Piano Roll views or via the Markers view. Here's the exact procedure:

1a. If you want to use the Track, Staff, or Piano Roll view, click and hold the left mouse button on the marker you want to delete.

or

1b. If you want to use the Markers view, choose View > Markers to open the Markers view. Then select the marker you want to delete from the list.

2. Press the Delete key on your computer keyboard.

Navigating with Markers

Of course, what good would creating markers do if you couldn't use them to navigate through the data in your project? What's more, all you need to do is select the name of a marker, and the Now time will be set automatically to the exact time of that marker. You can jump to a specific marker in a project in two different ways—either by using the Markers view or the Markers toolbar.

Using the Markers View

To jump to a specific marker using the Markers view, follow these steps:

1. Choose View > Markers to open the Markers view.
2. Select the marker to which you want to jump from the list. SONAR will set the Now time to correspond to that marker, and the Track, Staff, Piano Roll, and Event views will jump to that time.

Using the Markers Toolbar

To jump to a specific marker using the Markers toolbar, just select the marker from the drop-down list (see Figure 5.12).

Figure 5.12
Using the Markers toolbar, you can set the Now time to any marker by simply selecting a name from the list.

SONAR will set the Now time to correspond to that marker, and the Track, Staff, Piano Roll, and Event views will jump to that time.

QUICK MARKER LIST

One other quick way to jump to a specific marker in a project is to select the Now time in the Position toolbar and then press the F5 key on your computer keyboard to bring up a list of all the markers in the current project. Select a marker from the list and click on OK. The Now time will be set automatically to the time corresponding to that marker.

Where, Oh Where?

Until now, I have been describing how to navigate through the data in a project by somehow specifying the Now time, with the result being that you go to a specific point in the project. Well, what happens when you don't know the exact position to which you want to move in a project? For instance, out of all the data in all the tracks in your project, suppose you need to set the Now time to the first occurrence of the note Middle C? Instead of playing the project and trying to listen for the note or looking through each and every track manually, you can use SONAR's Go-Search function.

Go-Search allows you to examine automatically all the data in your project and find any MIDI events that have certain attributes that you specify. Upon finding the first event of the specified type, Go-Search sets the Now time to correspond to that event. This function is very useful for finding significant points within a project and placing markers there or for precision editing tasks, which you'll learn more about in Chapter 8, "Exploring the Editing Tools." In the meantime, you can find specific MIDI events using the Go-Search function.

1. Choose Go > Beginning to set the Now time to the beginning of the project. If you don't take this step, Go-Search will start looking at your data at the current Now time, not at the beginning of the project. This means if the Now time is currently set to 10:01:000, Go-Search does not look at any of the data contained in the first nine measures.

2. Choose Go > Search to open the Event Filter - Search dialog box (see Figure 5.13).

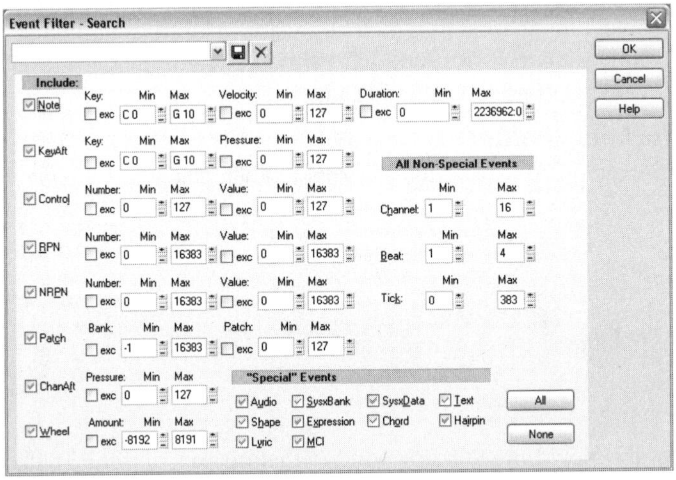

Figure 5.13
In the Event Filter - Search dialog box, you specify the criteria for your search.

3. Select the criteria for your search. Don't let all the settings in the Event Filter - Search dialog box intimidate you; they aren't very complicated to use. Basically, all you need to do is select the types of MIDI events you want to include in your search. For instance, if you want to look for MIDI note and pitch wheel events (but nothing else), deselect all the event types except for Note and Wheel.

DESELECT ALL EVENT TYPES

By the way, whenever you open the Event Filter - Search dialog box, it automatically has all event types selected. To quickly deselect all event types, click on the None button. The All button performs the exact opposite operation.

After you select all your event types, you need to set the ranges for each of the parameters. For example, suppose you want to look for any MIDI note events between the pitches of C5 and G7 and with a velocity between 50 and 80. To do so, simply set the Note Key Minimum parameter to C5, the Note Key Maximum parameter to G7, the Note Velocity Minimum parameter to 50, and the Note Velocity Maximum parameter to 80. You can also specify a range of durations (note length) if you want. Each event type has its own unique set of parameter ranges: Key Aftertouch has key and pressure parameters, Patch Change has bank and patch number parameters, and so on. You can also set up searches that are a little more complicated by excluding ranges of parameters. If you select the Exclude (exc) option next to any of the parameter range settings, the search excludes event types with that specific parameter range. For example, if you want to search for MIDI note events that do not fall within the range of C5 and G7, you set up the Minimum and Maximum parameters, as in the earlier example, and you activate the Key Exclude option.

Using the Event Filter - Search dialog box, you can specify special events too, such as Audio, SysxData, Text, and Chord events. These special events don't include any additional parameter settings, though, so Go-Search simply finds any events of that kind within the data of your project. Last, you can choose to set a range of MIDI channels, beats, or ticks to search. These are called non-special events.

SAVE PRESETS

Because setting these search criteria every time you need to find specific data in a project can be tedious, it would be nice if you could save the settings for future use, wouldn't it? Well, you can. Just type a name in the Preset box at the top of the Event Filter - Search dialog box and click on the Save button (the button with the little disk icon on it). All your current search criteria settings will be saved under that name. The next time you use Go-Search, you can simply select the name from the Preset drop-down list, and all your previous settings will be loaded. You can save as many presets as you want, and if you ever want to delete one, just select it from the list and click on the Delete button (the button with the red X on it).

4. Click on OK.

SONAR will search through the data in your project, find the first event that falls under the search parameters that you specified, and then set the Now time to correspond to that event. If you want to apply that same search again to find the next event with the same criteria, choose Go > Search Next. SONAR will continue the search (beginning at the current Now time), find the next event that falls under the search parameters you specified, set the Now time to correspond to that event, and so on. Here's another fact you should be aware of: If you first select some of the data in your project, the search will be conducted only on that selected data, not all the data in the project.

The Go-Search Challenge

So do you think you now have a good understanding of how the Go-Search function works? To test you on what you've learned, I put together a little search challenge. First read the challenge, and then see whether you can set up the Event Filter - Search dialog box options appropriately. When you think you've got it, take a look at the answer to see how you did.

A Simple Search

Find the first MIDI note event in the project that falls between the pitches of F4 and D7 and that has a velocity between 40 and 70. Also, restrict the search to MIDI Channel 2 only.

Here's the answer:

1. Choose Go > Beginning to set the Now time to the beginning of the project.
2. Choose Go > Search to open the Event Filter - Search dialog box.
3. Click on the None button to clear all settings.
4. Select the MIDI note event type.
5. Set the Note Key Minimum parameter to F4.
6. Set the Note Key Maximum parameter to D7.
7. Set the Note Velocity Minimum parameter to 40.
8. Set the Note Velocity Maximum parameter to 70.
9. Set the Non-Special Event Channel Minimum parameter to 2.
10. Set the Non-Special Event Channel Maximum parameter to 2.
11. Click on OK.

Did you get it right? If so, congratulations! I threw that MIDI channel restriction in there to make it a little more confusing. Setting both the minimum and maximum Channel parameters to the same number restricts the search to that MIDI channel. In this case, it was 2. If you didn't get the settings quite right, don't worry. With a little practice, you'll easily master this feature.

6

Recording and Playback

Being able to record and play your music with SONAR turns your computer into a full-fledged recording studio. Without these features, SONAR would just be a glorified music data editor/processor. If you're going to memorize one chapter in the book, this should be it. You'll probably use the recording and playback features of SONAR most often. Therefore, I'm going to devote separate sections of the chapter to each way you can possibly record data in SONAR. This chapter will do the following:

▶ Review the parameters that need to be set prior to recording

▶ Show you how to record and play MIDI tracks

▶ Show you how to record and play audio tracks

▶ Demonstrate how you can record multiple tracks at once

▶ Demonstrate recording new tracks automatically using looping

▶ Show you how to correct mistakes using punch in and punch out

▶ Explain how to record MIDI one note at a time

▶ Show you how to use importing instead of recording

▶ Explain what synchronization is and how you can use it

Preliminary Parameters

In Chapter 4, you learned about a number of parameters you can save to define a project template. Some of those parameters are related to recording, including track parameters, timebase, tempo, meter, and key. I'll mention those parameters throughout this chapter, but I won't go into detail about how to change them. If you need to refresh your memory, take a look at Chapter 4 again.

The Track Inspector

Setting the parameters for individual tracks can be cumbersome sometimes because you have to widen the track parameter display before you can access the parameters for a track. To make setting track parameters easier, SONAR provides the Track Inspector. You can use the Track Inspector for both audio and MIDI tracks. Basically, the Track Inspector is a replica of the track modules provided in the Console view. (I'll talk more about the Console view in Chapter 12, "Mixing It Down.") To activate the Track Inspector in the Track view, press the I key on your computer keyboard.

When you make a MIDI track active in the Track view, the Track Inspector displays the parameters for a MIDI track as they pertain to the active track (see Figure 6.1).

Figure 6.1
Access MIDI track parameters easily with the Track Inspector.

When you make an audio track active in the Track view, the Track Inspector displays the parameters for an audio track as they pertain to the active track (see Figure 6.2).

Figure 6.2
Access audio track parameters easily with the Track Inspector.

This means you can keep the track parameters in the Track pane hidden but still have easy access to them simply by making the appropriate track active. I'll talk more about the Track Inspector and track modules in Chapter 12.

In the meantime, in addition to these track parameters, you need to be aware of a few other parameters before you do any recording in SONAR. I didn't describe them in Chapter 4 because you usually set these parameters while you're working on a project, not before, when you're creating a template.

Metronome

If you've ever taken music lessons, you know what a *metronome* is. It's a device that makes a sound for each beat in each measure of a piece of music. You simply set the tempo you want, and the metronome sounds each beat accurately and precisely. You use this device to help you play in time with the correct rhythm. In SONAR, the metronome feature helps you keep the right time so your music data is stored at the right measure and beat within the project.

The metronome feature in SONAR is electronic (of course), and it's a bit more sophisticated than what you might find in a handheld unit. First of all, the tempo for the metronome is the same as the tempo setting for the project, so when you set the project tempo, you're also setting the metronome tempo. Normally, you would just have to turn the metronome on and off, but in SONAR, you need to set several other parameters before you use the metronome feature. You can access these parameters by selecting Options > Project to open the Project Options dialog box, and then clicking on the Metronome tab (see Figure 6.3).

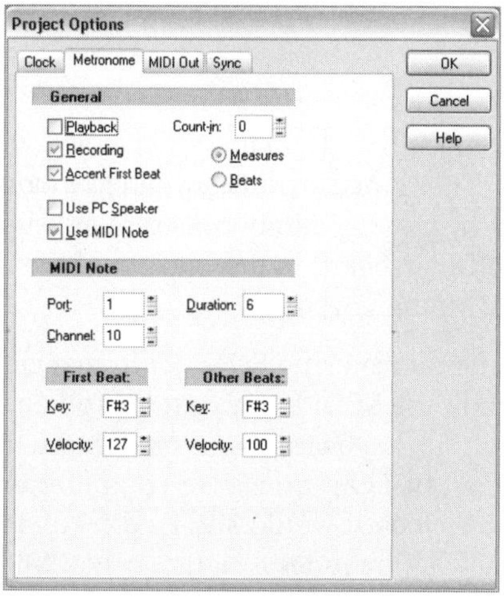

Figure 6.3
In the Project Options dialog box, you can access the metronome parameters.

General

In the General section of the Project Options dialog box, you can determine whether the metronome will sound during playback, recording, or both by activating the Playback and Recording options. The Accent First Beat option determines whether the metronome will sound the first beat of each measure a little louder than the others. You also can select whether the metronome will use your computer's built-in speakers or one of your MIDI instruments to make its sound by activating the Use PC Speaker or Use MIDI Note options. (I'll talk more about this last option shortly.) You have to activate one of them; otherwise, the metronome won't make any sound at all.

Count-In

Using the Count-In option in the General section, you can get the feel of the tempo before SONAR starts recording your performance. Depending on how you set it, the metronome will sound a number of beats or measures before recording begins. For example, if your project is set for a 4/4 meter, and you set the Count-In option to 1 Measures, the metronome will sound four beats before SONAR begins recording.

MIDI Note

If you select the Use MIDI Note option in the General section of the Project Options dialog box, the settings in the MIDI Note section determine which MIDI instrument is used to make the metronome sound and which note is used for the first beat and remaining beats of each measure. The settings are reasonably self-explanatory. In the Port and Channel fields, you can set the MIDI port and channel that your MIDI instrument uses. Duration determines how long each metronome "beep" will sound. The duration is measured in ticks, so if you use the default timebase of 120 ticks per quarter note, a duration of 15 would be equivalent to a thirty-second note.

You can set the pitch (key) and loudness (velocity) of the first beat and remaining beats in each measure by using the First Beat and Other Beats options. If you want the first beat of each measure to be accented, you should set the velocity a little higher in the First Beat Velocity option. For example, you could set it to 127 and set the Other Beats Velocity to 110. Also, if your MIDI instrument is General MIDI-compatible and you set the Channel option to 10, you can use a percussion instrument for the metronome sound. I like to use a rimshot sound.

MIDI Echo

Some MIDI instruments (such as a built-in keyboard) do not provide any way for you to play them except by sending them MIDI messages. These instruments are called *modules*. To play a module, you need to trigger the module's sounds by playing another instrument, such as a MIDI keyboard. If you connect the MIDI Out from the MIDI keyboard to the MIDI In of the module, you can play the sounds in the module by performing on the keyboard.

But what if you want to record your performance using SONAR? In that case, you would have to connect the MIDI Out from the keyboard to the MIDI In on your computer. This means you would no longer be sending MIDI messages from the keyboard to the module, so how would you hear your performance? You could connect the MIDI Out from your computer to the MIDI In of the module, but the MIDI messages from the keyboard would still go directly to the computer and not the module. To remedy this situation, SONAR includes a feature called MIDI echo.

Basically, MIDI echo takes the MIDI messages from your computer's MIDI input(s) and sends them back out to your computer's MIDI output(s). You can control the MIDI channels from which the data is echoed and the ports and channels to which it is echoed.

The Input Echo Button

Each MIDI track in a project provides an Input Echo button. This button is located right next to the Mute, Solo, and Record buttons on a track's property bar (see Figure 6.4).

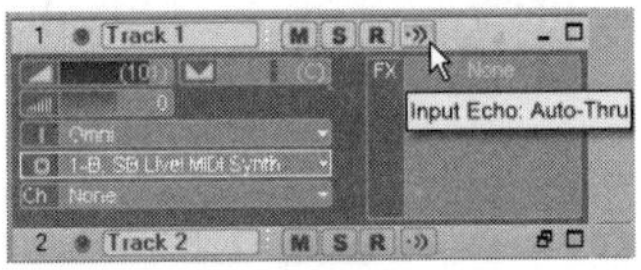

Figure 6.4
The Input Echo button controls MIDI echo for a MIDI track.

The Input Echo button provides three states—On, Off, and Auto-Thru. By default, the Input Echo button is set to Off. When Input Echo is set to Off, MIDI data coming into a MIDI track (via the MIDI port/channel that is set using its Input parameter) is not echoed to the MIDI port that is set using its Output parameter. However, if you make a MIDI track the active track (by clicking on its number), Input Echo is set automatically to Auto-Thru, which means that any MIDI data coming into the MIDI port/channel set in that track's Input parameter is echoed automatically to the MIDI port set in that track's Output parameter.

DISABLE AUTO-THRU

If you would rather not have Auto-Thru active so your MIDI track doesn't enable MIDI echo automatically when the track is activated, you can disable the Auto-Thru feature by choosing Options > Global and deactivating the Always Echo Current MIDI Track option.

By clicking on the Input Echo button, you can change its state. If you click on the button to turn it on, it will become highlighted. When the Input Echo for a MIDI track is turned on, it means any MIDI data coming into the MIDI port/channel set in that track's Input parameter is echoed to the MIDI port set in that track's Output parameter.

Echo Applications

So what can you do with MIDI input echoing? The most basic application allows you to hear the sounds you are playing on your MIDI module or software synth, as I described earlier. But you can also use input echoing for some more sophisticated applications such as recording multiple MIDI performances at the same time or layering sounds of multiple synths from one MIDI performance.

Recording Multiple Performances

Suppose you're in a situation where you need to record the performances of more than one MIDI musician at the same time, and each musician is using a different synth. This means each one will want to hear his or her individual performance during recording. Accomplishing this is actually quite easy with SONAR's Input Echo feature.

Depending on the number of musicians you need to record, you would create a MIDI track in your project to represent each musician. Then set the Input parameter for each MIDI track to correspond to the MIDI port/channel each musician is using for his or her MIDI device. Next, you would set the Output parameter for each MIDI track to the MIDI port that is being used for each musician's synthesizer. Finally, you would set the Input Echo button to On for each of the MIDI tracks. Each musician's individual performance would be recorded to a separate MIDI track and during recording, each musician would be able to hear his or her performance in real-time.

Layering Multiple Synths

Creating new synthesizer sounds requires knowledge of synth programming, and not everyone has the time or patience to try programming their own sounds. But there's an easier way to experiment with new synth sounds; you can combine (or layer) the sounds from multiple synths to create an entirely new sound. SONAR's Input Echo feature makes this very easy to do; here's an example of how you can accomplish it:

1. Choose File > New and select the Normal template from the New Project File dialog box.
2. Press Ctrl+A on your computer keyboard to select all the current tracks.
3. Choose Track > Delete to remove the existing tracks.
4. Choose Insert > DXi Synth > DreamStation.
5. In the Insert DXi Synth Options dialog box, activate the MIDI Source Track, First Synth Output, and Synth Property Page options. Leave all the other options deactivated.
6. Assign a sound to the DreamStation synth using the Preset drop-down list at the top of the DreamStation window.
7. Repeat steps 4, 5, and 6 to set up one more soft synth.
8. Set the Input parameters for both of the MIDI tracks you just created to the same MIDI port and channel that you are using for your MIDI keyboard.
9. Set the Input Echo buttons on both MIDI tracks to On.
10. Play your MIDI keyboard.

Isn't that cool? When you play on your MIDI keyboard, you should hear the sounds from both of the software synths playing at the same time. They are effectively layered together, creating a new sound from the combination of both. Of course, you can take this even further and continue to layer more synths, creating a huge ensemble of sound. I'll talk more about software synthesis in Chapter 10, "Software Synthesis." In the meantime, experiment and have fun.

Sampling Rate and Bit Depth

You learned about the meaning of the terms *sampling rate* and *bit depth* in Chapter 1. SONAR lets you set the sampling rate and bit depth used for the audio data that you record. Depending on the sophistication of your sound card, you can set the sampling rate up to 96,000 Hz and the bit depth up to 24-bit.

So what settings should you use? Well, the higher the sampling rate and bit depth, the better the quality of your recorded audio. Higher settings also put more strain on your computer system, however, and the data takes up more memory and hard disk space. Plus, if your input signal is already bad (if you use a low-end microphone to record your vocals, for instance), higher settings won't make it sound any better.

In my opinion, if your computer has enough power, memory, and hard disk space, you should use the highest settings your sound card will support. Using these settings will ensure that you get the best-quality recording. The only problem to watch out for is if you plan to put your music on CD. In that case, the audio needs to have a sampling rate of 44,100 Hz and a bit depth of 16-bit.

CHANGE THE AUDIO FORMAT

To store music on a CD, the audio data must have a sampling rate of 44,100 Hz and a bit depth of 16. These values cannot be higher or lower; they must be exact. Of course, you can start by recording your audio with different settings. For example, if your computer has a limited amount of memory or hard disk space, you might want to use smaller values. However, I wouldn't recommend this unless it's absolutely necessary because lower values mean lower-quality audio. You also can record using higher values, which actually improves the quality of your audio data. When it comes time to put the audio on CD, however, you must convert the sampling rate and bit depth to the values I mentioned.

Using SONAR's Change Audio Format feature, you can convert the bit depth of the audio in your project. Simply select Tools > Change Audio Format to access it. Unfortunately, the Change Audio Format feature only lets you convert between 16- and 24-bit. For any other bit-depth values (and to convert the sampling rate) you need to use a separate digital audio editing application, such as Sony's Sound Forge (http://mediasoftware.sonypictures.com/), Adobe's Audition (http://www.adobe.com), or Steinberg's WaveLab (http://www.steinberg.net).

To access these parameters, select Options > Audio to open the Audio Options dialog box, and then click on the General tab (see Figure 6.5).

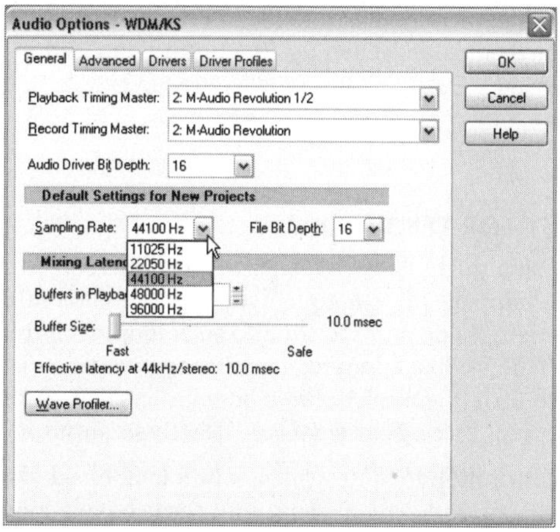

Figure 6.5
In the Audio Options dialog box, you can access the sampling rate and file bit-depth parameters.

In the Default Settings for New Projects section, you can make your selections from the Sampling Rate and File Bit Depth drop-down lists.

Input Monitoring

When you record an audio track, you usually want to listen to your performance as it's being recorded. In the past, due to the limitations of sound card drivers, you could listen only to the "dry" version of your performance. This meant you would have to listen to your performance without any effects applied. With the input monitoring feature, however, SONAR allows you to listen to your performance with effects applied as it's recorded. This can be especially useful, for example, when you are recording vocals, when it's customary to let the singer hear a little echo or reverberation during his or her performance. If you're not sure what I'm talking about, don't worry. I'll cover effects in more detail in Chapter 11, "Exploring Effects."

Similar to MIDI tracks, audio tracks provide an Input Echo button. This button can be turned on or off, and it activates or deactivates the input monitoring feature (see Figure 6.6).

Figure 6.6
Use the Input Echo button to turn input monitoring on or off for an audio track.

⚡ **MONITOR ON ALL TRACKS**
You can easily activate or deactivate input monitoring on all audio tracks at once using the Playback State toolbar. Make the toolbar visible by choosing View > Toolbars > Playback State. Then use the Input Echo button on the toolbar to adjust input monitoring.

✋ **WATCH OUT FOR FEEDBACK**
Input monitoring might cause a feedback loop between your sound card inputs and outputs. This happens, for example, when the signal coming out of a speaker is fed back into a microphone and the sound keeps looping and building up into a very loud signal. This feedback looping can damage your speakers. To be safe, you might want to turn down the volume on your speaker system before you activate input monitoring. If you hear feedback, deactivate input monitoring.

For a possible solution to your feedback problem, check the Windows Mixer settings for your sound card. Some sound cards have a monitoring feature that should be turned off when you are using input monitoring. For instance, if you have a Sound Blaster Live! card, open the Record Controls in the Windows Mixer and make sure you are not using the What U Hear option as your recording input.

Record Mode

When you record MIDI or audio data into an empty track, SONAR simply places that data into the track within a new clip. (In Chapter 2, you learned how SONAR stores data as events, which are stored within clips, which in turn are stored within tracks.) When you record data in a track that already contains data, what happens to that existing data?

SONAR provides two different recording modes. (Actually there are three, but I'll talk about Auto Punch later in the "Punch Recording" section of this chapter.) Both of these modes provide a different means of dealing with existing data. The Sound on Sound mode mixes the new data with the existing data. For example, if you record a vocal part into a track that already contains music, you hear both the vocal and the music when you play back that track. The Overwrite mode replaces the existing data with the new data. So in this example, the music is erased, and the vocal takes its place. When you try to play the track, you hear only the vocal.

Keep in mind that you need to deal with recording modes only when you're recording data into a track that already contains data. More than likely, you won't be doing that very often because SONAR allows you to record an unlimited number of tracks, and you can easily place each part of your song on a separate track. If you do need to set the recording mode, however, just select Transport > Record Options to open the Record Options dialog box (see Figure 6.7).

Figure 6.7
In the Record Options dialog box, you can set the recording mode.

In the Recording Mode section, select either Sound on Sound or Overwrite and click on OK.

MIDI Track Recording and Playback

Believe it or not, you now have the knowledge you need to start recording in SONAR. Nothing is very complicated about the process, but you should follow a number of steps to make sure everything occurs smoothly. Here and in the following sections, I'll show you step by step how to record MIDI tracks, audio tracks, and multiple tracks at once. First you'll tackle MIDI tracks. To get started, follow these steps:

1. Create a new project or open an existing one. If you use a template to create a new project, you might be able to skip some of the following steps, but you probably should run through them anyway, just in case.

2. Set the meter and key signature for the project. The default settings are 4/4 and the key of C Major.

3. Set the metronome and tempo parameters. The default tempo for a new project is 100 beats per minute.

4. Set the timebase for the project. The default setting is 960 PPQ (pulses per quarter note). More often than not, you won't have to change this setting.

5. Set the recording mode. Unless you plan to record data to a track that already contains data, you can skip this step. The default recording mode is Sound on Sound.

6.   Add a new MIDI track to the Track view and adjust the track's properties. For more information about track properties and how to set them, refer to Chapter 4.

7.   Arm the track for recording to let SONAR know that you want to record data on the track. Right after the name parameter in the Track view, you'll see three buttons labeled M, S, and R. Click on the R button to arm the track for recording (see Figure 6.8).

Figure 6.8

You arm a track for recording by clicking on its associated R button in the Track view.

8.   Set the Now time to the point in the project where you would like the recording to begin. Most of the time it will be the very beginning of the project, but SONAR provides flexibility to let you record data to a track starting at any measure, beat, or tick within a project.

9.   Select Transport > Record to start recording. (You can also press the R key on your computer keyboard or click on the Record button on the Transport toolbar.) If you set a Count-In, the metronome will first count the number of beats you entered, and then SONAR will begin recording.

10.   Perform the material you want to record.

11.   After you finish performing, select Transport > Stop to stop recording. (You also can press the spacebar on your computer keyboard or click on the Stop button in the Transport toolbar.) SONAR will create a new clip in the track containing the MIDI data you just recorded (see Figure 6.9).

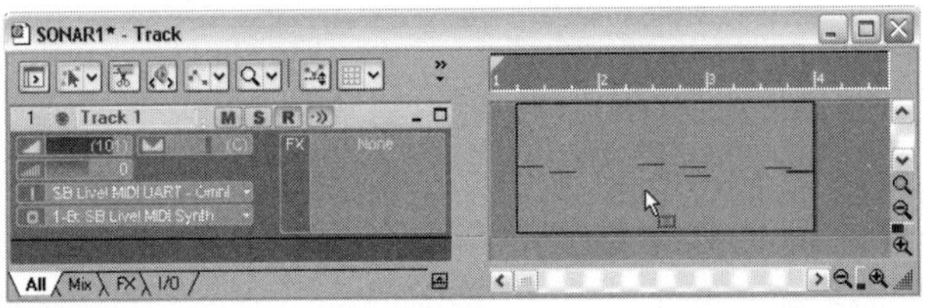

Figure 6.9

After you've finished recording, SONAR will create a new clip in the track representing the MIDI data.

12.   Listen to your performance by setting the Now time back to its original position and selecting Transport > Play. (Alternatively, you can press the spacebar on your computer keyboard or click on the Play button on the Transport toolbar.) If you don't like the performance, you can erase it by selecting Edit > Undo Recording. Then go back to Step 8 and try recording again.

UNDO HISTORY

SONAR provides an Undo feature that allows you to reverse any action you take while working on a project. You're probably familiar with this feature because it is included in most applications that allow you to manipulate data, such as word processing software and so on. SONAR goes a bit further, however, by providing an Undo History feature. This feature logs every step you take while working on a project and allows you to undo each step all the way back to the beginning of your current session. The Undo History is not saved, though, so as soon as you close a project, you lose the ability to undo any changes.

To access the Undo History feature, select Edit > History to open the Undo History dialog box (see Figure 6.10). You will see a list of all the tasks you've done during the current session. To go back to a certain point in the session, select a task in the list and click on OK. SONAR will undo any tasks performed after the task you selected. SONAR can keep track of as many as 2,147,483,647 tasks; this is the maximum number you can set in the Maximum Undo Levels parameter of the Undo History dialog box. Remember, though, the more tasks SONAR keeps track of, the more memory and hard disk space it needs.

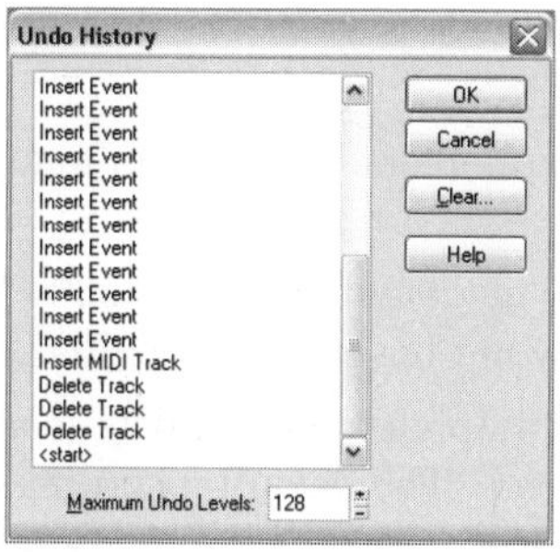

Figure 6.10
Using the Undo History dialog box, you can reverse your actions.

EDIT MIDI DATA

If you find that your performance is good for the most part, except for a few trouble spots, you might want to try fixing the mistakes by editing the MIDI notes rather than using Undo and then performing the entire thing all over again. You'll learn how to edit MIDI data in Chapter 7, "Editing Basics."

13. After you've recorded a performance you like, disarm the track by clicking on its R button again. By disarming the track, you won't accidentally record over the data while you're recording any additional tracks.

14. Go back to Step 6, and record any additional tracks you want to add to the project. While you're recording the new tracks, you will hear the previously recorded tracks being played back. Because you can hear these tracks, you might want to turn off the metronome and just follow the music of the previous tracks as you perform the material for the new ones.

SAVE YOUR PROJECT
Be sure to save your project after each successful track recording. This step isn't mandatory, but it's a good precautionary measure because you never know when your computer might decide to crash on you. Rather than lose that really great performance you just recorded, quickly select File > Save (or press Ctrl+S on your computer keyboard) so you can rest easy in knowing that your data is safe.

Audio Track Recording and Playback

Recording audio tracks in SONAR is very similar to recording MIDI tracks, but because the nature of the data is different, you need to take a few additional steps. Here's the step-by-step process for recording audio tracks:

1. Create a new project or open an existing one. If you use a template to create a new project, you might be able to skip some of the following steps, but you should probably run through them anyway, just in case.

2. Set the meter and key signature for the project. The default settings are 4/4 and the key of C Major.

3. Set the metronome and tempo parameters. The default tempo for a new project is 100 beats per minute.

4. Set the timebase for the project. The default setting is 960 PPQ (pulses per quarter note). More often than not, you won't have to change this setting.

5. Set the recording mode. Unless you plan to record data to a track that already contains data, you can skip this step. The default recording mode is Sound on Sound.

6. Set the sampling rate and the file bit depth for the project.

7. Add a new audio track to the Track view and adjust the track's properties. For more information about these properties and how to set them, refer to Chapter 4.

8. If you want to hear effects added to your performance while you're recording, activate input monitoring for the audio track. Then add effects to your track by right-clicking on the Fx bin (located in the Track pane along with all the other track parameters) and choosing Audio Effects > Cakewalk > [*the effect you would like to add*]. I'll talk more about effects in Chapter 11.

9. Arm the track for recording to let SONAR know you want to record data on the track. Right after the name parameter in the Track view, you'll see three buttons labeled M, S, and R. Click on the R button to arm the track for recording.

10. After you arm the track, you'll notice the meter (shown to the right of the Fx bin) light up (see Figure 6.11). This meter displays the level of the audio input for your sound card in decibels.

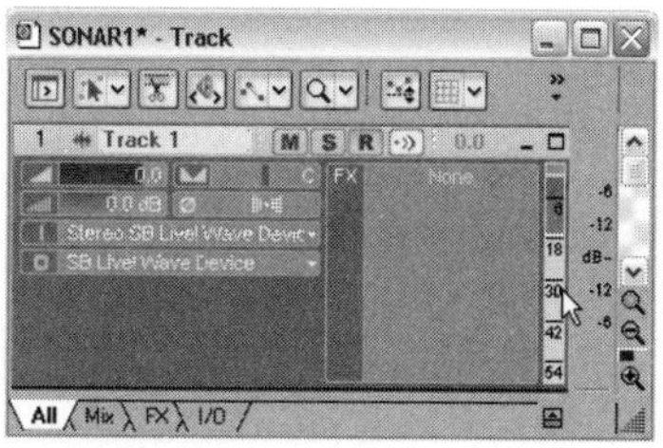

Figure 6.11
Each audio track has a
meter showing its input
signal level in decibels.

THE DECIBEL

Decibel is a very complicated term to describe. The most basic explanation would
be that a decibel is a unit of measurement used to determine the loudness of
sound. In SONAR, the audio meters can range from − 90 dB (soft) to 0 dB (loud).
To change the display range of a meter, right-click on it and choose a new setting
from the drop-down menu. For a more detailed explanation, see the following
topic in the SONAR Help file: Editing Audio > Digital Audio Fundamentals > The
Decibel Scale.

11. Set the audio input level for your sound card so it's not too loud but also not too
soft. To do so, you have to use the software mixer that came with your sound card.
On the Windows taskbar, you should see a small speaker icon. Double-click on the
speaker icon to open your sound card mixer. Then select Options > Properties to
open the sound card mixer's Properties dialog box. In the Adjust Volume For
section, select Recording, make sure all boxes below it are checked, and click on
OK to display the recording controls for your sound card mixer (see Figure 6.12).

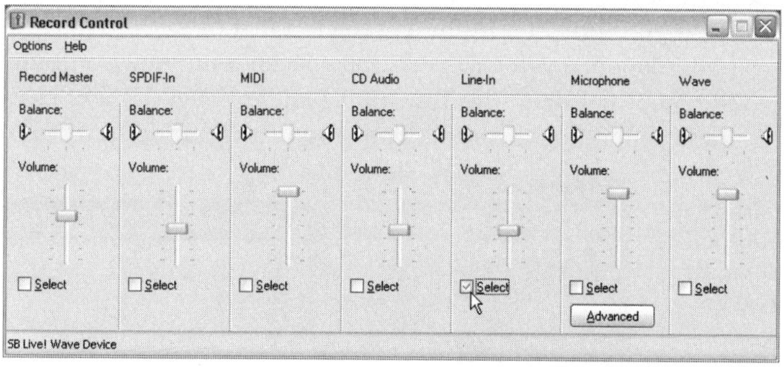

Figure 6.12
You use your sound card
mixer to adjust the input
levels for your sound
card.

12. For the set of controls labeled Line-In, either activate the Select option or
deactivate the Mute option (depending on your mixer configuration). This option
tells your sound card that you want to record audio using its line-input
connection. If you want to use a different connection (such as a microphone or
internal CD player), you need to use the set of controls associated with that
connection.

YOUR SOUND CARD MIXER

These steps show you how to use a standard Windows sound card for recording. You might have a sound card that uses a different method for setting audio input levels. In that case, you need to read the documentation for your sound card to find out how to use it correctly.

13. When you have access to the input level controls for your sound card, begin your performance, playing at the loudest level at which you plan to record. As you play, the meter for the track will light up, displaying the sound level of your performance. You should adjust the input level so that when you play the loudest part of your performance, the meter does *not* turn red. If it turns red, you have overloaded the input, and if you record at that level your audio signal will be distorted. When you play the loudest part of your performance, if the meter lights up anywhere between −6dB and −3dB, then you have a good input level setting.

14. After you finish setting your input level, close the sound card mixer. Next, set the Now time to the point in the project where you would like the recording to begin. Most of the time, it will be the very beginning of the project, but SONAR provides flexibility to let you record data to a track starting at any measure, beat, or tick in a project.

15. Select Transport > Record to start recording. (Alternatively, you can press the R key on your computer keyboard or click on the Record button on the Transport toolbar.) If you set a Count-In, the metronome will count the number of beats you entered, and then SONAR will begin recording.

16. Perform the material you want to record.

17. After you finish performing, select Transport > Stop to stop recording. (Alternatively, you can press the spacebar on your computer keyboard or click on the Stop button on the Transport toolbar.) SONAR will create a new clip in the track containing the audio data you just recorded (see Figure 6.13).

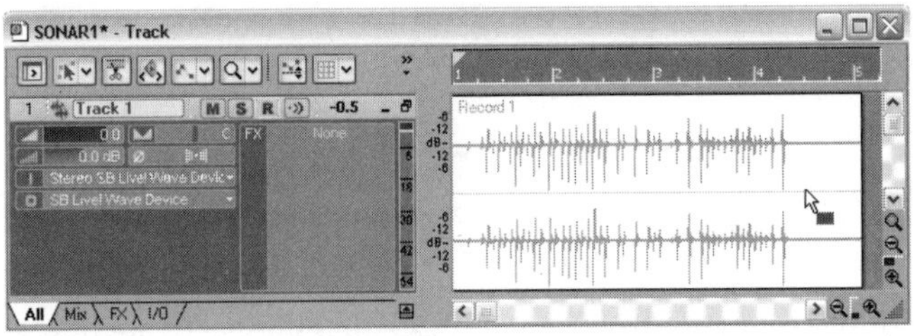

Figure 6.13
After you've finished recording, SONAR will create a new clip in the track representing the audio data.

18. Listen to your performance by setting the Now time back to its original position and selecting Transport > Play to start playback. (Alternatively, you can press the spacebar on your computer keyboard or click on the Play button on the Transport toolbar.) If you don't like the performance, erase it by selecting Edit > Undo Recording. Then go back to Step 14 and try recording again.

19. After you've recorded a performance you like, disarm the track by clicking on its R button again. By disarming the track, you won't accidentally record over the data while you're recording any additional tracks.

20. Go back to Step 7 and record any additional tracks you want to add to the project. While you're recording the new tracks, you will hear the previously recorded tracks playing back. Therefore, you might want to turn off the metronome and just follow the music of the previous tracks as you perform the material for the new ones.

RECORDING ROOM

If you have your home studio set up in a single room containing all your equipment (including your computer) and you are recording audio tracks using a microphone, the microphone will pick up the background noise made by your electronic devices (including the fan inside your computer). To remedy this situation, you might want to set up your microphone and one of your MIDI instruments in a different room, while keeping them connected to your computer via longer cables. Then you can set up some MIDI key bindings (which you learned about in Chapter 3) so you can control SONAR remotely. That way, when you record the audio from your microphone, it won't pick up all that background noise.

Multiple Track Recording and Playback

If you have more than one MIDI input on your MIDI interface or more than one audio input on your sound card, you can record to multiple tracks simultaneously. Recording multiple tracks works well when you need to record an entire band of musicians. Instead of having each musician play individually (which can sometimes ruin the "groove"), you can record everyone's part at once (which usually makes the song flow much better).

To record multiple tracks, just follow the same instructions I outlined earlier for recording MIDI and audio tracks. The only difference is that you must set up and arm more than one track. When you start recording, the MIDI or audio data for each musician will be recorded to separate tracks simultaneously.

BASIC SOUND CARD

Even if you're using a basic sound card to record audio, you can still record two different audio tracks at once because your sound card has a stereo input. This means you can use the left and right audio channels separately to record two individual tracks. When you set up the tracks prior to recording, just select the input for one track to be the left audio channel of your sound card and the input for the other track to be the right audio channel of your sound card. You also might need a special audio cable. Most basic sound cards provide only one stereo input connection at a 1/8-inch size. The cable you will need is called a Y-adapter audio cable with a stereo 1/8-inch mini plug to phono plugs (or connections). You should be able to find the cable at your local Radio Shack.

Loop Recording

If you plan to add a vocal track or an instrumental track (such as a guitar solo) to your project—
something that might require more than one try to get right—you might want to use *loop recording*
instead of recording and undoing a single track over and over again manually. Loop recording
allows you to record several tracks, one right after the other, without having to stop between each
one. Here's how it works:

1. If you want to record MIDI tracks, follow steps 1 through 7 in the "MIDI Track
    Recording and Playback" section presented earlier in this chapter. If you want to
    record audio tracks, follow steps 1 through 13 in the "Audio Track Recording and
    Playback" section earlier in this chapter.

2. Set the Now time to the point in the project at which you want looping to begin.
    Then select Transport > Loop and Auto Shuttle to open the Loop/Auto Shuttle
    dialog box (see Figure 6.14). Press F5 on your computer keyboard to bring up the
    Markers dialog box. Select the marker named <Now> from the list and click on OK
    to set the start time at which the looping will begin.

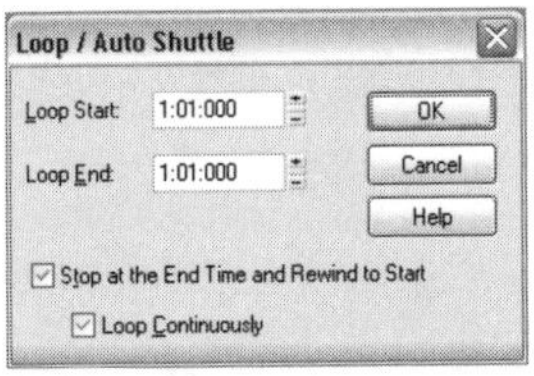

Figure 6.14
In the Loop/Auto Shuttle
dialog box, you can set
the loop recording
parameters for SONAR.

3. Type an end time for the loop using measure, beat, and tick values. Then activate
    the Stop at the End Time and Rewind to Start and Loop Continuously options and
    click on OK. Setting these options tells SONAR that when you start recording, it
    will begin at the loop start time, continue to the loop end time, and then loop back
    to the start time to cycle through the loop over and over again, until you stop it.

SET LOOP POINTS QUICKLY

For a quick way to set the start and end times, just click and drag in the Time
Ruler of the Track view to make a data selection, and then right-click on the Time
Ruler and choose Set Loop Points from the drop-down menu. For more
information on selecting data, read Chapters 7 and 8.

THE LOOP TOOLBAR

You also can use the Loop toolbar to set the parameters for looping. Refer to
Chapter 3 for more information about toolbars.

4. Select Transport > Record Options to open the Record Options dialog box. In the Loop Recording section, select either Store Takes in a Single Track or Store Takes in Separate Tracks. The first option stores each performance in the same track but in different clips stacked on top of each other. The second option stores each performance in a different track, automatically setting the same track parameters as the one you began with. I like to use the second option because it's more flexible, especially when I want to edit the data I just recorded. For this example, choose the Store Takes in Separate Tracks option. You can experiment with the other option later if you want.

5. Select Transport > Record to start recording. (Alternatively, you can press the R key on your computer keyboard or click on the Record button on the Transport toolbar.) If you set a Count-In, the metronome will count the number of beats you entered, and then SONAR will begin recording.

6. Perform the material you want to record until you get a good take.

7. After you finish performing, select Transport > Stop to stop recording. (Alternatively, you can press the spacebar on your computer keyboard or click on the Stop button in the Transport toolbar.) SONAR will create a new track containing the data you just recorded for every loop you cycled through (see Figure 6.15).

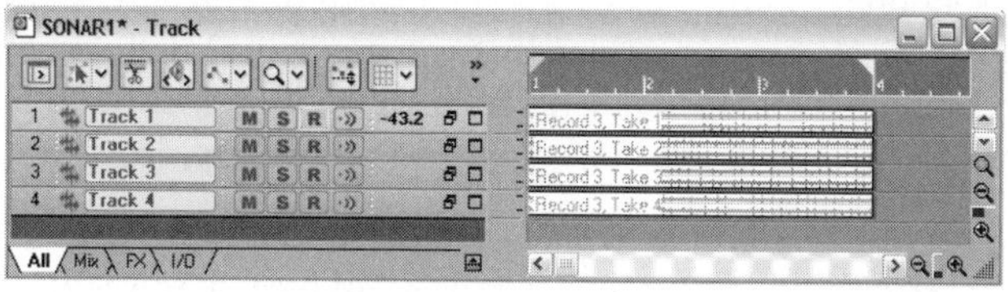

Figure 6.15
For every loop you record, SONAR creates a new track containing each individual performance.

8. Each track (except for the original one) is disarmed. To listen to any of your performances, turn off looping by selecting Transport > Loop and Auto Shuttle to open the Loop/Auto Shuttle dialog box. Deactivate the Stop at the End Time option and click on OK. Set the Now time back to its original position and select Transport > Play to start playback. (Alternatively, you can press the spacebar on your computer keyboard or click on the Play button on the Transport toolbar.) To listen to one of the recorded tracks, solo it by clicking on the S button next to its name parameter in the Track view.

9. After you've found a performance that you like and want to keep, delete the others by clicking on the appropriate track number on the left side of the Track view to select a track, and then selecting Track > Delete. If you want to select more than one track, just hold down the Ctrl key on your computer keyboard while you're selecting track numbers.

CHAPTER 6

ARCHIVE TRACKS

Instead of deleting all the extra tracks you created during looping, you might want to keep them for use later. You can do so by using SONAR's Archive feature. By archiving tracks, you store them within the current project, but they become invisible to SONAR. This means when you play your project, the archived tracks will not play. As a matter of fact, archiving tracks helps increase SONAR's performance because it doesn't process the tracks at all when they are archived. To archive a track, just right-click on its track number and select Archive from the drop-down menu. You'll notice that the track's Mute button turns into an A (Archive) button. This change in the button name shows that the track is archived. You can still make changes to the track (and the data in it), but SONAR will not play it.

Punch Recording

When you make a mistake while recording MIDI data, it's usually no big deal because you can make corrections easily (such as changing the pitch of a note) with SONAR's various editing tools (see Chapter 7). But what about when you're recording audio? Sure, you can edit the data by cutting and pasting sections or processing it with effects, but you can't edit the pitch of a single note or make any other precision corrections like you can with MIDI data. With audio, you have to record your performance all over again. Using SONAR's punch recording feature, however, you have to rerecord only the part of the performance you messed up, leaving the good parts alone.

Using punch recording, you can set up SONAR to start and stop recording automatically at precise times during a project. You therefore can record over certain parts of your performance without having to redo the entire thing. Punching is very similar to regular audio track recording, but with a few differences. Here's the step-by-step procedure:

1. Suppose you want to correct some mistakes on an audio track you just recorded. To get started, make sure the track is still armed for recording (its R button is red).

2. Activate punch recording by selecting Transport > Record Options to open the Record Options dialog box (see Figure 6.16). In the Recording Mode section, select Auto Punch (Replace). Then, in the Punch In Time field, type the measure, beat, and tick at which you want SONAR to begin recording. In the Punch Out Time field, type the measure, beat, and tick at which you want SONAR to stop recording. The section of the track that falls between the Punch In Time and the Punch Out Time should contain the part of your performance in which you made the mistakes.

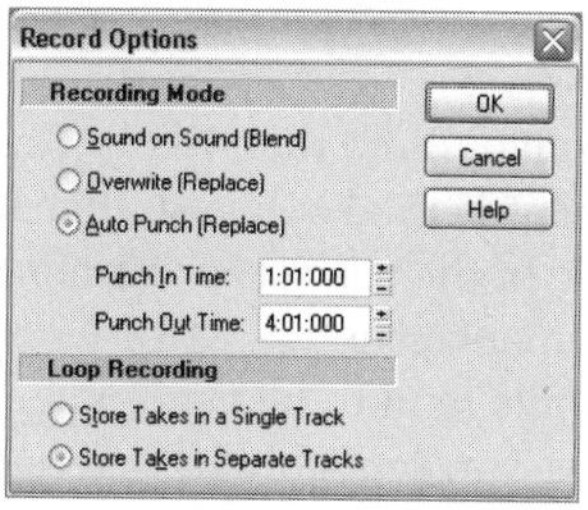

Figure 6.16
You use the Record Options dialog box to set the recording mode to Auto Punch and to set the Punch In and Punch Out Times.

SET PUNCH POINTS QUICKLY

For a quick way to set the Punch In and Out Times, just click and drag in the Time Ruler of the Track view to make a data selection, then right-click on the Time Ruler and choose Set Punch Points from the drop-down menu. For more information on selecting data, read Chapters 7 and 8.

3. Set the Now time to the point in the project before the Punch In Time where you want playback to begin. You might want to start from the very beginning of the project or just a few measures before the Punch In Time. However long it takes you to get into the groove of the performance is how far ahead of the Punch In Time you should set the Now time.

4. Select Transport > Record to start recording. (Alternatively, you can press the R key on your computer keyboard or click on the Record button on the Transport toolbar.) If you set a Count-In, the metronome will count the number of beats you entered, and then SONAR will begin playback.

5. Play along with the existing material, exactly as you did before when you first recorded the track. When SONAR reaches the Punch In Time, it will automatically start recording the new part of your performance.

6. When the Now time has passed the Punch Out Time, SONAR will stop recording, and you can select Transport > Stop to stop SONAR. (Alternatively, you can press the spacebar on your computer keyboard or click on the Stop button on the Transport toolbar.) SONAR will replace any existing material between the Punch In Time and the Punch Out Time with the new material you just played. As long as you didn't make any mistakes this time, your track will be fixed.

7. Listen to your performance by setting the Now time back to its original position and selecting Transport > Play to start playback. (Alternatively, you can press the spacebar on your computer keyboard or click on the Play button on the Transport toolbar.) If you don't like the performance, you can erase it by selecting Edit > Undo Recording. Then go back to Step 3 and try recording again.

Step Recording

Even though you might be an accomplished musician, more than likely you have one main instrument you're good at playing. If that instrument is the keyboard, that skill puts you ahead of some other musicians because the keyboard is one of the easiest instruments to use to record a MIDI performance. You can use other MIDI instruments, such as MIDI woodwind instruments, MIDI drums, and MIDI guitars, but those instruments tend to be very expensive. And if you learn to play a wind instrument or the drums or a guitar, you probably have a real instrument of that kind, not a MIDI one. This puts you at a bit of a disadvantage when you're trying to record MIDI tracks. However, SONAR provides a feature called step recording that allows you to record a MIDI track one note at a time without having to worry about the timing of your performance.

In other words, you select the type of note you want to enter (such as a quarter note or a sixteenth note), and then you press one or more keys on your MIDI keyboard. SONAR then records those notes into the track with the timing you selected. You can also enter the measure, beat, and tick at which you want the notes to occur. Here's how the step recording feature works:

1. Follow steps 1 through 8 in the "MIDI Track Recording and Playback" section earlier in this chapter.

2. Select Transport > Step Record to open the Step Record dialog box (see Figure 6.17).

Figure 6.17
Using the Step Record dialog box, you can record MIDI data to a track without having to worry about the timing of your performance.

3. In the Step Size section, enter the size of the note you want to record. For example, if you want to record a quarter note, select Quarter.

4. In the Duration section, you can set the length of the note independent of the step size. More often than not, though, you'll want the duration to be the same as the step size. To make things easier, you can set the Duration to Follow Step Size so both values will be the same and you won't have to bother selecting a duration.

5. To record the note, press a key on your MIDI instrument. For example, if you want to record a Middle C to the track, press Middle C on your MIDI instrument. By the way, you can press more than one key at a time if you want to record a chord. For example, if you want to record a C Major chord, press the C, E, and G keys on your MIDI instrument at the same time.

6. SONAR will record the data to the track and (if the Auto Advance option is activated, which it is by default) will move the Now time forward by the step size amount (which is a quarter note in this example). If the Auto Advance option isn't activated, you have to click on the Advance button to move the Now time manually. Also, if you want to record a rest instead of a note, you have to click on the Advance button. This way, SONAR will move the Now time ahead by the step size amount without recording anything.

7. To change the Now time manually, just enter a new value into the field below the Auto Advance option. To move forward or backward by a step, click on the arrows on the scroll bar next to the Now time. Also, if you want to delete the most recent step, click on the Delete button.

RECORD PATTERNS

If you need to record many repeating patterns, you might want to use the Pattern option in the Step Record dialog box. In the Pattern box, you can enter a pattern of beats that SONAR will follow automatically so you don't have to click on the Advance button at all, even for rests. For example, if you need to record a pattern with notes on the first two beats, a rest on the third beat, and another note on the fourth beat, you enter 12R4 in the Pattern box. Now when you start to record the pattern, you simply press keys on your MIDI instrument for beats 1 and 2, SONAR advances past beat 3 because it is a rest, and then you press another key for beat 4. Then you keep repeating the same routine over and over again until you get to the point in your music where you no longer need to repeat the same rhythmic pattern. I know this process sounds a bit complicated, but if you play with it for a while, you'll get the hang of it.

8. When you're finished recording, click on the Keep button to keep the data and have SONAR add it to the track. Alternatively, you can click on the Close button to discard the data you just recorded.

9. Listen to your performance by setting the Now time back to its original position and selecting Transport > Play to start playback. (Alternatively, you can press the spacebar on your computer keyboard or click on the Play button on the Transport toolbar.) If you don't like the performance, you can erase it by selecting Edit > Undo Recording. Then go back to Step 2 and try recording again.

TRY THE STAFF VIEW

As an alternative to the step recording feature, you might want to try using the Staff view. With the Staff view, you still can enter your MIDI data one note at a time without worrying about performance timing. Plus, the Staff view allows you to enter and edit your data using standard music notation. I'll describe this feature in more detail in Chapter 13, "Making Sheet Music."

Importing

One other way you can get MIDI and audio data into a project is to import it rather than record it. SONAR allows you to import data from audio files, MIDI files, and other project files. Why would you want to import files? Well, you might have a great drum track in a project or a MIDI file that you want to use in another project. You also might want to use sample loops for some of the material in your audio tracks. (I'll talk about sample loops in Chapter 9, "Composing with Loops.") Importing material is actually very easy.

Importing from Project and MIDI Files

Importing data from a project or a MIDI file into another project is just a matter of copying and pasting, as shown in the following steps. To get started, just follow these steps:

1. Open the project or MIDI file from which you want to copy data.

2. In the Track view, select the clips you want to copy. You also can select an entire track or a number of whole tracks to copy.

3. Select Edit > Copy to open the Copy dialog box (see Figure 6.18). Make sure the Events in Tracks option is activated, and then click on OK.

Figure 6.18
Using the Copy dialog box, you can copy data within a project or from one project into another.

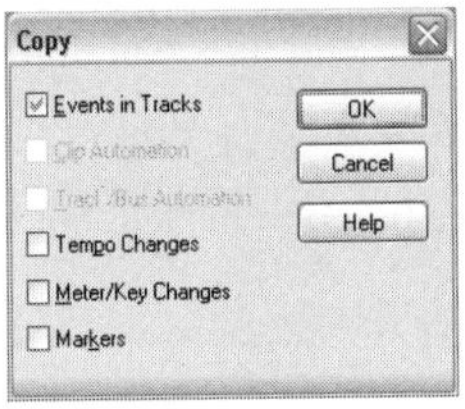

4. Open the project into which you want to paste the data.

5. In the Track view, select the track where you want to start pasting the data. If you copied more than one track, the first copied track will be pasted to the selected track, and the other copied tracks will be pasted to consecutive tracks after the selected one.

6. Set the Now time to the point in the track at which you want the data to be pasted.

7. Select Edit > Paste to open the Paste dialog box (see Figure 6.19). You don't have to change any of the parameters here. (I'll go over them in more detail in Chapter 8, "Exploring the Editing Tools.") Click on OK.

Figure 6.19
The Paste dialog box takes any previously copied data and places it where you specify.

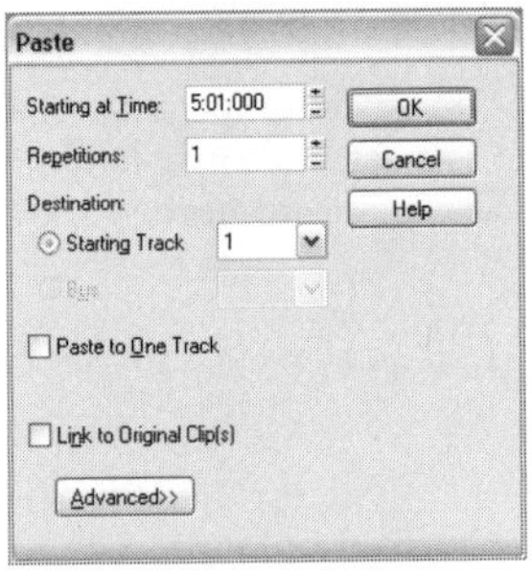

SONAR will copy the data you selected from the first project or MIDI file and place a copy of it into the second project in the tracks and at the Now time you specify. In addition to reusing your own material, you can share material with a friend this way.

Importing Audio Files

You learned about audio files in Chapter 3. SONAR allows you to import WAV, Apple AIFF, MPEG, Windows Media, and Next/Sun audio files. This is important because at some time you might record some audio using another program, and you might want to use that data in one of your SONAR projects. Doing so is really simple; just follow these steps:

1. Select the track into which you want to import the audio file.

2. Set the Now time to the point in the track that the file should be placed.

3. Select File > Import Audio to open the Import Audio dialog box.

4. Choose the audio files you want to import.

IMPORT MULTIPLE FILES

You can import more than one audio file at a time. To select more than one file in the Import Audio dialog box, just hold down the Ctrl key on your computer keyboard while selecting your files.

5. If you want to listen to the file before you import it, click on the Play button. This function will not work if you select multiple files.

6. If the file is a stereo audio file, you can have the left and right channels merged into one track or you can split between two different tracks (starting with the one you selected). To have the file split, activate the Stereo Split option.

7. Click on Open.

SONAR will import the files and insert them into the tracks you selected at the Now time you specified.

SAMPLE RATE CONVERSION

If the sampling rate of the audio file you are importing is different from your project's sampling rate, SONAR will convert the sampling rate of the audio file to match the sampling rate of the project.

Synchronization

One other aspect related to recording that you should know about is *synchronization*. This subject is fairly complicated and a bit beyond the scope of this book, but you might need to utilize synchronization in two somewhat popular situations. I'll cover a few of the basics and explain how to use synchronization in those two particular situations.

Synchronization Basics

All music is based on time. Without time, there is no music. To record and play music data, SONAR needs a timing reference. It uses this reference to determine the exact measure, beat, and tick at which an event should be stored during recording or at which it should be played. When you work with SONAR alone, it uses one of two different clock sources as its reference—either the clock built into your computer (internal) or the clock built into your sound card (audio). By default, SONAR uses the internal clock as its timing reference. Because the internal clock cannot be used if you have audio data in your project, SONAR automatically changes the clock to audio when a track's source is set to an audio input or when an audio file is inserted into the project. So the built-in clock on your sound card provides the timing for all the data you record into a project, and it allows SONAR to keep all the tracks synchronized during playback. This is internal synchronization.

Sometimes, though, you might need to synchronize SONAR externally with another piece of equipment. For example, if you have a drum machine (a special type of MIDI instrument that plays only drum sounds) containing some special songs that you programmed into it, you might want to have the data in your current SONAR project play along with the data contained in the drum machine. You would have to synchronize SONAR to the drum machine. In this situation, the drum machine would be known as the *master device*, and SONAR would be the *slave device*. The master would send messages to the slave, telling it when to start and stop playback and what tempo to use so that they can stay in sync with one another. To accomplish this, you need to use what is called MIDI Sync.

MIDI Sync

MIDI Sync is a special set of MIDI messages that allow you to synchronize MIDI devices to one another. These messages include Start (which tells a slave device to start playback at the beginning of the song), Stop (which tells a slave device to stop playback), Continue (which tells a slave device to continue playback from the current location in the song—the Now time in SONAR), Song Position Pointer or SPP (which tells a slave device to jump to a specific time position in the song—the Now time in SONAR), and Clock (a steady pulse of ticks sent to the slave device, telling it the speed of the current tempo of the song).

To synchronize SONAR with an external MIDI device using MIDI Sync, follow these steps:

1. Configure your drum machine (or other MIDI device you want to use as the master) to transmit MIDI Sync messages. You'll have to refer to the user guide for your device for information on how to do so.

2. In SONAR, open the project you want to synchronize. Select Options > Project to open the Project Options dialog box, and then click on the Clock tab (see Figure 6.20).

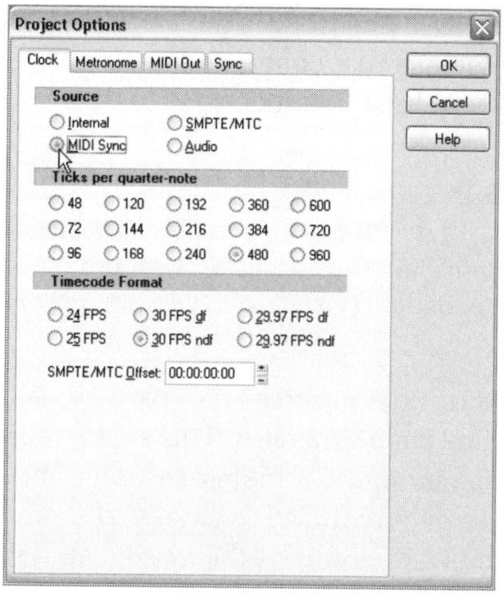

Figure 6.20
Using the Project Options dialog box, you can configure SONAR for synchronization.

Project Options

Clock | Metronome | MIDI Out | Sync

OK
Cancel
Help

Source
○ Internal   ○ SMPTE/MTC
◉ MIDI Sync   ○ Audio

Ticks per quarter-note
○ 48   ○ 120   ○ 192   ○ 360   ○ 600
○ 72   ○ 144   ○ 216   ○ 384   ○ 720
○ 96   ○ 168   ○ 240   ◉ 480   ○ 960

Timecode Format
○ 24 FPS   ○ 30 FPS df   ○ 29.97 FPS df
○ 25 FPS   ◉ 30 FPS ndf   ○ 29.97 FPS ndf

SMPTE/MTC Offset: 00:00:00:00

3. In the Source section, click on the MIDI Sync option, and then click on OK.

4. Follow the steps outlined earlier for recording or playing MIDI tracks. However, when you activate recording or playback, SONAR won't respond right away. Instead, it will display a message that says "Waiting for MIDI Sync."

5. After you see this message, start playback on your master device. It will send a Start message to SONAR, and both the device and SONAR will play through the song in sync with one another. In the case of the drum machine, you will hear it play its sounds in time with the music being played by SONAR.

6. To stop playback, don't use the commands in SONAR; instead, stop playback from the master device. It will send SONAR a Stop message, and SONAR will stop at the same time automatically.

While working with SONAR via MIDI Sync, just remember to start, stop, and navigate through the project using the master device instead of SONAR. Otherwise, all the other steps for recording and playback are the same.

NO AUDIO WITH MIDI SYNC
You cannot record or play audio tracks in SONAR while using MIDI Sync. If you have some previously recorded MIDI data stored in a drum machine (or other MIDI device) that you want to use in your SONAR project, first use MIDI Sync to transfer that data into SONAR. Then use the drum machine (or other MIDI device) as a playback device.

CHAPTER 6

SMPTE/MIDI Time Code

You might need to use synchronization when you're composing music to video. Here, though, the synchronization method is different because a VCR is not a MIDI device, so MIDI Sync won't work. Instead, you have to use SMPTE/MIDI Time Code. You learned a little about SMPTE in Chapter 5, so you know it is a timing reference that counts hours, minutes, seconds, and frames (as in video frames). But you really didn't learn how it works.

SYNC TO A TAPE DECK

In addition to video, SMPTE/MIDI Time Code is used often to synchronize a sequencer to an external multitrack tape recorder or DAT (*Digital Audio Tape*) deck. The procedure for doing so (explained in just a moment) is the same.

SMPTE is a complex audio signal that is recorded onto a tape track (or, in the case of video, onto one of the stereo audio tracks) using a time code generator. This signal represents the absolute amount of time over the length of the tape in hours, minutes, seconds, and frames. A sequencer (such as SONAR) reading the code can be synchronized to any exact moment along the length of the entire tape recording. In this case, the VCR would be the master, and SONAR would be the slave. When you play the tape in the VCR, SONAR will play the current project in sync to the exact hour, minute, second, and frame.

Reading the time code from tape requires an SMPTE converter, which translates the SMPTE code into MTC (*MIDI Time Code*). The MIDI Time Code is read by the MIDI interface and sent to the sequencer (SONAR). MIDI Time Code is the equivalent of SMPTE, except it exists as special MIDI messages rather than an audio signal. As SONAR receives MTC, it calculates the exact measure, beat, and tick that correspond to the exact time reading. This means you can start playback anywhere along the tape, and SONAR will begin playing or recording MIDI or audio data at precisely the right point in the current project in perfect sync.

As an example, suppose you need to compose some music to video. This video could be your own or a video from a client. To synchronize SONAR to the video, you need to follow these steps:

1. If the video is your own, you need to add SMPTE Time Code to it using an SMPTE generator. This process is called *striping*. I won't go into the details of doing that here. You'll need to purchase a SMPTE generator and read the instructions in the included manual on how to stripe SMPTE to tape. If the video is from a client, he or she will probably stripe the tape before sending it to you.

SMPTE CONVERTER

You also need an SMPTE converter to read the time code from the tape. If you have a professional MIDI interface attached to your computer, it might provide SMPTE generating and converting capabilities. Check the user manual to make sure. You might be able to save yourself some money.

2. In SONAR, open the project you want to synchronize. Then select Options > Project to open the Project Options dialog box, and click on the Clock tab.

3. In the SMPTE/MTC Format section, you need to select a frame rate for the time code. If you're composing music to your own video, just use the default selection, 30 FPS ndf (Frames Per Second - Non-Drop Frame). If you're composing music for a client, he or she should let you know the frame rate you need to use.

FRAME RATES

Different types of video material use different tape speeds for recording. The frame rate corresponds to the number of frames per second used to record the video to tape. For film, 24 frames per second are used. For video, several different rates are used depending on whether the video is recorded in color or black-and-white, and so on. For more information about frame rates, you should consult the user guide for your SMPTE generating/reading device.

4. You might also need to enter an SMPTE/MTC Offset in hours, minutes, seconds, and frames. Whether you need to enter an offset depends on whether the video material starts at the very beginning of the time code stripe, which is a value of 00:00:00:00.

SMPTE OFFSET

When you stripe a tape with SMPTE, the time code always starts with a value of 00 hours, 00 minutes, 00 seconds, and 00 frames. However, the actual video material on the tape may start a bit later, say at 00 hours, 01 minutes, 20 seconds, 00 frames. If that's the case (your client should let you know this fact), you need to enter an offset of 00:01:20:00 into SONAR so SONAR will begin playing the project at that time rather than at the initial time code value.

5. After you finish entering the settings, click on OK.

6. Now you can follow the steps outlined earlier for recording or playing MIDI tracks. However, when you activate recording or playback, SONAR won't respond right away. Instead, it will display a message saying "Waiting for 30 Frame" (or whatever frame rate you selected).

7. After you see this message, start playback on your master device. (In this case, start the tape playing in the VCR.) It will then send SMPTE code to SONAR, and both the device and SONAR will play through the song in sync. In the case of the VCR, you will see it play the video in time with the music that is being played by SONAR.

8. To stop playback, don't use the commands in SONAR; instead, stop playback from the master device.

CONTROL PLAYBACK FROM THE DEVICE

If you would rather control playback from the master device (the VCR) entirely, without having to first start it in SONAR, select Transport > Loop and Auto Shuttle to display the Loop/Auto Shuttle dialog box. Then activate the Loop Continuously option and click on OK.

A little confused? Well, as I said, synchronization is a complicated subject. You'll find a little more information in the SONAR user guide and the Help files, but it isn't any easier to understand than the information I've provided here. Your best bet is to experiment as much as possible with synchronization and get a good beginner book on audio recording. Knowing how to utilize synchronization is worthwhile in case a situation that requires it ever arises.

7

Editing Basics

After you've finished recording all your tracks, it's time to do some editing. Actually, if you're like me, you might end up doing some editing during the recording process. This is especially true for MIDI tracks because it's so easy to fix the pitch or timing of a note quickly if you happen to make a mistake or two. You'll do most of your editing after the fact, though, and SONAR provides a number of different tools to get the job done. I briefly described these features in Chapter 2, but this chapter will do the following:

▶ Show you how to deal with tracks and clips in the Track view

▶ Describe editing MIDI note and controller messages in the Piano Roll view

▶ Explain creating and editing drum tracks in the Piano Roll view

▶ Teach you how to edit audio data in the Track view

▶ Describe editing individual events in the Event List view

▶ Show you how to change the tempo via the Tempo view

BACK UP YOUR PROJECT

Before you do any kind of editing to your recently recorded material, I suggest you make a backup of your project file. That way, if you totally mess things up during the editing process, you'll still have your raw recorded tracks. Take a look at Appendix B, "Backing Up Your Project Files," for more information.

Arranging with the Track View

The first part of the editing process deals with arranging the material in your project. Of course, you can do any kind of editing at any time you like. You don't have to follow exactly what I say, but it's logical to start with arranging. Basically, this step involves rearranging the tracks and clips in your project so they provide a better representation of the song you're trying to create. For example, after listening to the project a few times, you might find that the guitar part in the second verse sounds better in the first verse, or you might want the vocal to come in a little earlier during the chorus. You can accomplish these (and many other) feats by manipulating your tracks and clips.

Dealing with Tracks

You already learned how to work with the Track view in terms of setting up track properties, navigating within SONAR, and recording new tracks. However, I haven't talked about actually manipulating the tracks themselves and the data they contain. Manipulating includes selecting, sorting, inserting, and otherwise changing your original data.

Scrolling

As you already know, the Track view consists of two areas. The Track pane (on the left) shows the track properties and the Clips pane (on the right) shows the track data. The Clips pane contains scroll bars (see Figure 7.1). These scroll bars work the same as scroll bars in any standard Windows application. You either click on the arrows to move the display, or you click and drag the scroll bars to move the display.

Figure 7.1
Using the scroll bars, you can access additional information that doesn't fit on the screen.

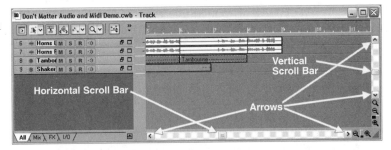

The horizontal scroll bar allows you to display all the data in all the tracks. As you scroll to the right, the measure numbers on the Time Ruler increase. Scrolling doesn't change the Now time, though (as you learned in Chapter 5). The vertical scroll bar affects both the Track and Clips pane areas. As you move the bar up or down, the different tracks in the project are displayed, starting from 1 (at the top of the list).

In addition to the Track view, scroll bars are available in all the other views. In the Piano Roll view, you can scroll horizontally to display the data in a track similar to the clips in the Track view. You also can scroll vertically to display different MIDI note ranges. The Event List view is the oddball because it only lets you scroll vertically to display all the events in a track as one long list. I'll describe the different views later in this chapter.

Zooming

The Track view (as well as other views, except the Event List view) also provides zooming functions. Using these functions, you can magnify the data in a track in case you want to do some really precise editing. If you take a look at the bottom-right corner of the Track view (see Figure 7.2), you'll notice two sets of buttons (one along the bottom and one along the side) that have little pictures of magnifying glasses on them.

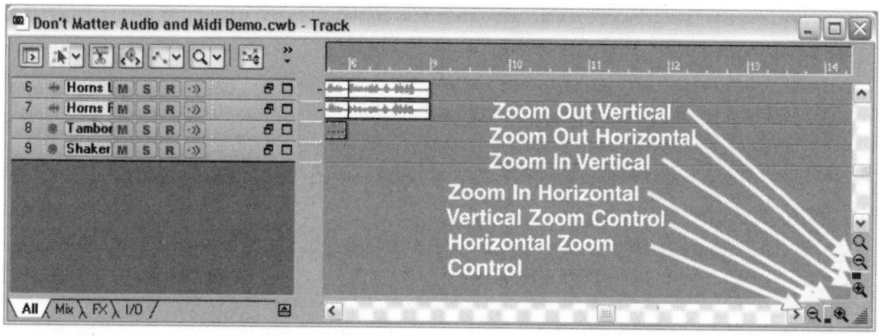

Figure 7.2
The zoom features reside in the bottom-right corner of the view.

Using the buttons along the bottom, you can magnify the track data horizontally. When you click on the Zoom In button (the button with the magnifying glass with a + sign on it), the clips will grow larger horizontally and give you a more detailed look at the data they contain. Clicking on the Zoom Out button, of course, does the opposite. The same buttons along the side of the Track view perform the same functions, except they affect the display vertically. You'll also notice that as you zoom in vertically, the track parameters will be shown beneath each track in the Track pane. In addition, you'll notice a little control between each set of zoom buttons. These controls show you the current level of magnification.

ZOOM METER

Click and hold the mouse on either zoom control, and a zoom meter will pop up. You can use the meter to quickly set the zoom level by dragging your mouse (see Figure 7.3).

Figure 7.3
You can also change the zoom level via the zoom meters.

In addition to the Zoom In and Zoom Out buttons on the right side of the view, you'll find another button with an empty magnifying glass on it. This button activates the Zoom tool. You can also click on the Zoom tool button in the Track view toolbar to activate the Zoom tool (see Figure 7.4).

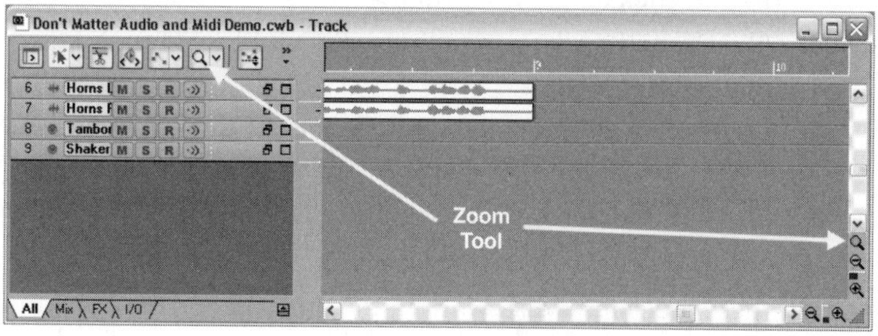

Figure 7.4
Activate the Zoom tool using either of the Zoom tool buttons.

You can use this tool to select a range of data and zoom in on that selection. To use it, simply follow these steps:

1.   Click on one of the Zoom tool buttons.

2.   Move your mouse pointer within the Clips pane, and it will turn into a magnifying glass.

3.   Click and drag anywhere within the area to select some data (see Figure 7.5).

Figure 7.5
You simply click and drag to make a selection with the Zoom tool.

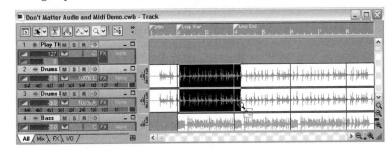

4.   Release the mouse button. SONAR will zoom in on the selection (both horizontally and vertically, depending on how you drag the mouse), and your mouse pointer will return to normal.

You have to click on the Zoom tool button every time you want to use it.

Selecting

To manipulate your tracks for editing in a project, you have to be able to select them. In Chapter 6, I mentioned how to select a single track: You simply click on the track number of the track you want to select. But sometimes you might want to have multiple tracks selected at one time. You also might need a quick way to select all the tracks in your project. Or after going through the trouble of selecting a number of tracks, you might want to deselect one or two while keeping the others selected. You accomplish these tasks as follows:

▶   To select more than one track, hold down the Ctrl key on your computer keyboard as you click on the track numbers.

▶   To select all tracks in a project, select Edit > Select > All or press Ctrl+A on your computer keyboard.

▶   To deselect all tracks in a project, select Edit > Select > None or press Ctrl+Shift+A on your computer keyboard.

▶   To deselect a track while keeping others selected, hold down the Ctrl key on your computer keyboard as you click on the track number.

By the way, all these procedures also work in the other views; the only difference is the items being selected. Just remember that to select a single item, you simply click on it. To select more than one item, you hold down the Ctrl key on your computer keyboard as you click. To select all or none of the items, you choose Edit > Select. Some special selection features are also available, but I'll talk about them later in this chapter and in Chapter 8, "Exploring the Editing Tools."

Sorting Tracks

You can change the order in which the tracks appear in a couple of different ways. Being able to sort the tracks can be useful if you want to keep related tracks together in the track list. For instance, you might want to keep all the percussion tracks or all the vocal tracks together. It's easier to work on your song when the tracks are grouped together in this way—at least, it is for me.

Clicking and Dragging

The easiest way to move a track within a list is simply to drag it to a new location. Just move your mouse pointer over the little icon next to the name of the track you want to move (see Figure 7.6), and then click and drag it up or down anywhere in the list. When you release your mouse button, the track will move to the new location and take on a new track number.

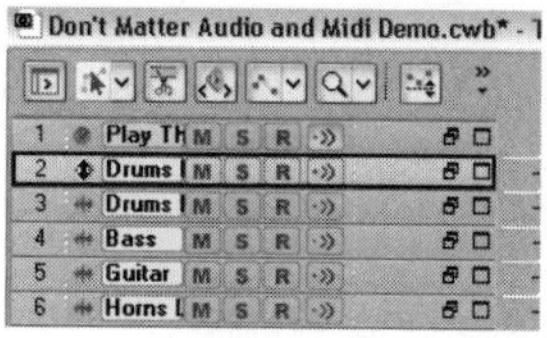

Figure 7.6
Click and drag a track icon to move the track within the track list.

Using the Track Sort Function

You also can use the Track Sort function to sort tracks in the list based on the track properties. You use this function as follows:

1. Choose Track > Sort to open the Sort Tracks dialog box (see Figure 7.7).

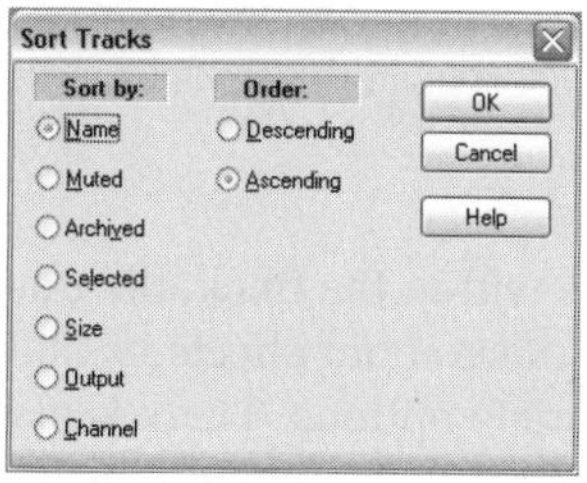

Figure 7.7
Using the Sort Tracks dialog box, you can rearrange the tracks in the Track view.

2. In the Sort By section, select the track property by which you want to sort the tracks.

3. In the Order section, select whether you want the tracks to be sorted in ascending or descending order.

4. Click on OK.

SONAR will sort the tracks according to the settings you specified. Remember, the track numbers for the tracks will be changed as well because the tracks have moved to new locations in the list. Each track maintains its parameter settings and data, though.

Inserting Tracks

If you ever need to insert a new track between two existing tracks in the list, you can do so by following these steps:

1. Right-click on the track number of the track above which you want to insert a new track.

2. From the drop-down menu, select Insert Audio Track or Insert MIDI Track, depending on the type of track you need.

SONAR will move the current track down one location in the list and insert a new track at the location on which you clicked. For example, if you right-click on track 2 and select Insert MIDI Track, SONAR will move track 2 (and all the tracks below it) down by one and insert a new MIDI track at number 2 in the list.

Cloning Tracks

If you ever need to make a copy of a track, you can do the following:

1. Select the track you want to copy.

2. Choose Track > Clone to open the Track Clone dialog box (see Figure 7.8).

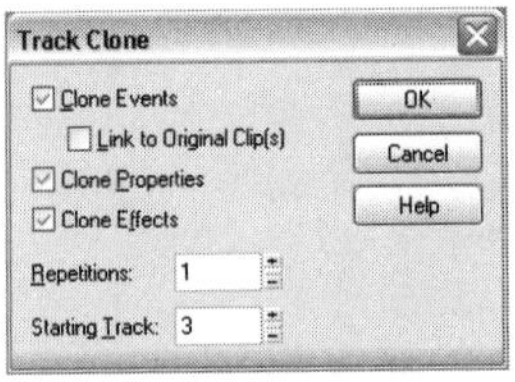

Figure 7.8
You can make a copy of a track by using the Track Clone dialog box.

Track Clone	
☑ Clone Events	OK
☐ Link to Original Clip(s)	Cancel
☑ Clone Properties	Help
☑ Clone Effects	
Repetitions: 1	
Starting Track: 3	

CLONE A TRACK

For a quicker method, just right-click on the track you want to copy and choose Clone from the drop-down menu to open the Track Clone dialog box.

3. You can choose to copy the events within the track, the track properties, the effects (Fx) assigned to the track (I'll talk more about effects in Chapter 11), or all of the above. Simply activate the appropriate options. There is also an option for preserving linked clips. (I'll talk more about linked clips later in this chapter, in the "Linked Clips" section.)

4. You can also choose how many copies of the track you want to make by entering a number in the Repetitions field.

5. To designate the number of the first copied track, enter a number in the Starting Track field. Your first copied track will use this number, and all other copies will be consecutively numbered after this one.

6. Click on OK.

SONAR will make a copy (or copies) of the tracks you selected according to the parameter settings you specified. If you want to move the tracks to a new location in the list, you can do so using the methods explained earlier.

Erasing Tracks

Getting rid of tracks you no longer need is very easy. Simply select the track and choose Track > Delete. Alternatively, you can right-click on the track and choose Delete Track from the drop-down menu. But SONAR also provides another erasing function that's a little more flexible. Instead of erasing the track entirely, it allows you to delete all the data in the track while keeping the track properties intact. To do so, just select the track, and then choose Track > Wipe. Nothing could be easier.

Hiding Tracks

If you open the View Options menu (which I'll explain shortly, in the "The View Options Menu" section) and click on the Track Manager selection (see Figure 7.9), you can access the Track Manager. Using the Track Manager, you can hide tracks in the Track view. To hide tracks, follow these steps:

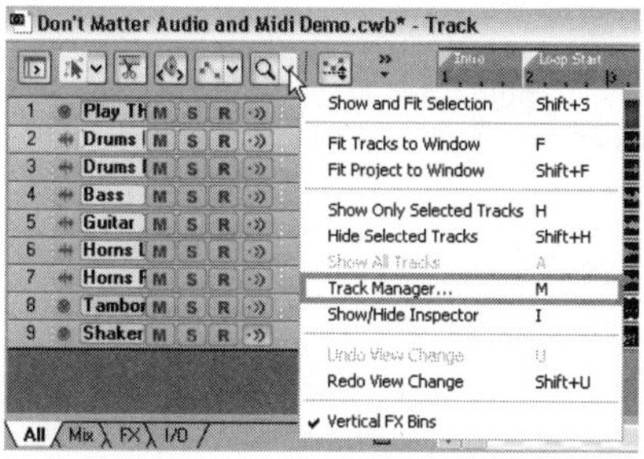

Figure 7.9
Use the View Options menu to open the Track Manager.

1. Choose the Track Manager selection in the View Options menu to open the Track Manager (see Figure 7.10). You will see a list of all the tracks in the Track view. You also will see some other items (aux bus, mains, etc.). Don't worry about those for now. I'll talk more about them in Chapter 12, "Mixing It Down."

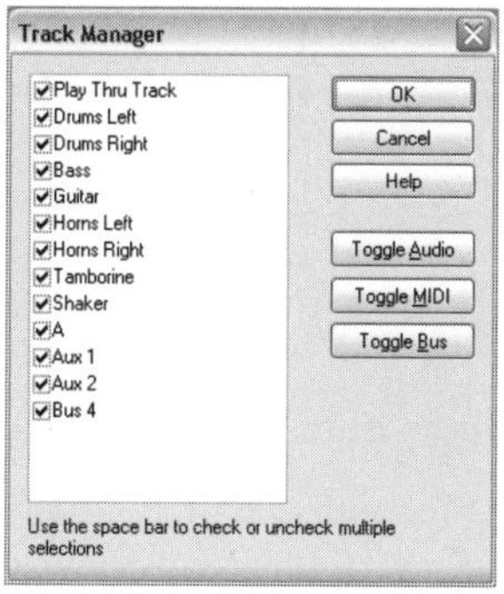

Figure 7.10
Use the Track Manager to hide tracks in the Track view.

PRESS THE M KEY

You can also open the Track Manager by pressing the M key on your computer keyboard while you are using the Track view.

2. To hide an individual track, click to remove the check mark next to that track in the list, and then click on OK.

3. To hide a group of tracks (such as all the audio tracks or all the MIDI tracks), click on the appropriate button—Toggle Audio or Toggle MIDI—to select the appropriate group. Then press the spacebar on your computer keyboard to remove the check marks. Finally, click on OK.

Of course, you can make tracks reappear by doing the opposite of the preceding procedures. These changes to the Track view are in appearance only; they don't affect what you hear during playback. For example, if you hide an audio track that outputs data during playback, you'll hear that data even if you hide the track. Hiding tracks can come in handy when you want to work only on a certain group of tracks and you don't want to be distracted or overwhelmed by the number of controls being displayed.

HIDE TRACK

You can quickly hide a single track by right-clicking on its track number and choosing Hide Track from the drop-down menu. To make the track visible again, however, you need to use the Track Manager.

The View Options Menu

In addition to all of the features I've already described, SONAR provides some predefined options for zooming and the appearance of tracks. These options are available from the View Options menu, which you can access by clicking on the small down arrow button located to the right of the Zoom tool button in the Track view toolbar (see Figure 7.11).

Figure 7.11
Use the View Options menu for additional zooming and track appearance options.

Each of the selections in the View Options menu has a different function. They work as follows:

▶ **Show and Fit Selection.** Choosing this option will make the data in the selected tracks fit within the current dimensions of the Track view and will show only the selected tracks. All other tracks will be hidden. This also works if you simply select some data within a track (or tracks), which I'll explain in the "Dealing with Clips" section of this chapter.

▶ **Fit Tracks to Window.** Choosing this option will set the vertical zoom to make all the tracks fill the current dimensions of the Track view vertically.

▶ **Fit Project to Window.** Choosing this option will set both the vertical and horizontal zoom functions to make all the tracks fill the current dimensions of the Track view both vertically and horizontally.

▶ **Show Only Selected Tracks.** Choosing this option will keep all currently selected tracks visible and will hide any unselected tracks.

▶ **Hide Selected Tracks.** The opposite of the Show Only Selected Tracks option, choosing this option will hide all currently selected tracks and keep all unselected tracks visible.

▶ **Show All Tracks.** Choosing this option will make all tracks in the project visible.

▶ **Track Manager.** As I mentioned earlier, choosing this option will give you access to the Track Manager dialog box.

▶ **Show/Hide Inspector.** Choosing this option will toggle the visibility of the Track Inspector, which I talked about in Chapter 6.

▶ **Undo View Change.** Choosing this option will undo the last view change you made to the Track view.

▶ **Redo View Change.** Choosing this option will redo the last view change you undid using the Undo View Change option.

▶ **Vertical FX Bins.** Choosing this option toggles whether or not the FX parameter for each track is displayed vertically or horizontally.

Dealing with Clips

Unless you insert, copy, or erase tracks in your project, you're not actually doing any kind of data manipulation. If you move a track in the track list or sort the tracks, that doesn't change the data within them. To make changes to the data in your project, you have to manipulate the clips within the tracks.

Clip Properties

For organizational purposes, SONAR allows you to change the way clips are displayed. To change the properties, you can right-click on a clip and select Clip Properties from the drop-down menu to open the Clip Properties dialog box (see Figure 7.12). Here you can assign a name to the clip (which doesn't have to be the same name as the track in which the clip resides) and set the color of the clip.

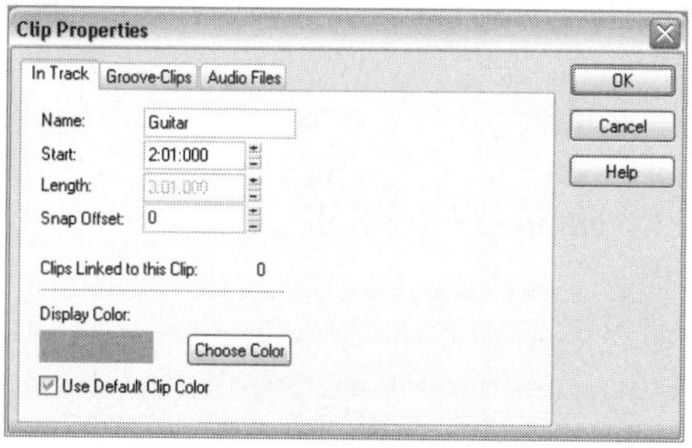

Figure 7.12
To change the name or color of a clip, you use the Clip Properties dialog box.

The name and the color of a clip don't affect the data within your project, but you also can change the start time of the clip in this dialog box. The start time is the position within the project at which the clip begins. If you enter a new start time for the clip, the clip is moved to the new time within the track and, during playback, SONAR will play the clip at the new time. This move *does* change the data in your project.

View Options

You also can change whether the names you assign to clips will be displayed and whether clips will be displayed with a graphical representation of the data they contain. In other words, if a clip contains audio data, it shows a drawing of what the sound wave for the audio data might look like. For MIDI data, the clip shows a mini piano roll display.

To change these options, just right-click anywhere in the Clips pane and select View Options from the drop-down menu to display the Track View Options dialog box (see Figure 7.13). Activate the appropriate options (Display Clip Names and Display Clip Contents) and click on OK.

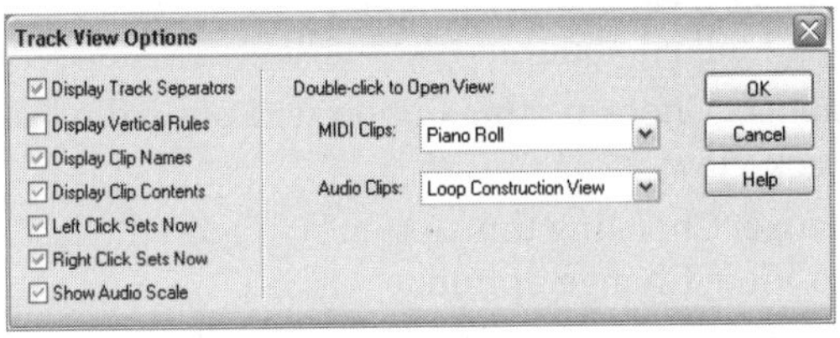

Figure 7.13
Using the Track View Options dialog box, you can show or hide clip names and contents.

Using the Track View Options dialog box, you also can specify whether left-clicking or right-clicking will change the Now time (using the Left Click Sets Now or Right Click Sets Now option), whether to display vertical rule lines for the Time Ruler (using the Display Vertical Rules option), and which views open automatically when you double-click on a MIDI or audio clip. Another option allows you to choose whether or not to display the Audio Scale, which I'll talk about later in this chapter.

Selecting Clips

You select clips the same way you select tracks. To select a single clip, click on it. To select more than one clip, hold down the Ctrl key on your computer keyboard while you click on the clips you want to select. You know the rest.

There is one additional selection method that doesn't apply to tracks—selecting only a portion of a clip. This procedure is known as working with partial clips. This capability is useful when you want to split a clip into smaller clips or combine one clip with another clip to make a larger clip. I'll describe this topic in more detail later in this chapter, in the "Splitting and Combining Clips" section.

To select only part of a clip, hold down the Alt key on your computer keyboard and drag your mouse pointer across the clip to select a part of it. You also can drag across several clips (or even over several tracks) to make a partial selection of multiple clips.

SNAP TO GRID
When you're making selections or moving data, the start and end times of your selections or data are affected by the Snap to Grid. You learned how to use the Snap to Grid feature in Chapter 5.

Splitting and Combining Clips

Using partial selections, you can combine and split clips into new smaller or larger clips. Combining clips is very easy. Just select the clips you want to combine and choose Edit > Bounce to Clip(s). SONAR will create one new clip from the old selected ones.

The Bounce to Track(s) Function

The problem with the Bounce to Clip(s) function is that it works only on clips that are on the same track. If you want to combine clips from different tracks, you have to use the Bounce to Track(s) function as follows:

ONLY AUDIO TRACKS

The Bounce to Track(s) function also has a limitation: It works only with audio tracks, unless you are using software synthesizers. In that case, it will also work with MIDI tracks. I'll talk more about software synthesizers in Chapter 10, "Software Synthesis."

1. Select the clips you want to combine.
2. Choose Edit > Bounce to Track(s) to open the Bounce to Track(s) dialog box (see Figure 7.14).

Figure 7.14
Use the Bounce to Track(s) function to combine clips from multiple tracks.

```
Bounce to Track(s) - [Selected 1:1:0 - 9:1:0]                    ☒

Destination:  <10> New Track                                  ▼

Format:       Mix to Single Track Stereo Event(s)        ▼

Source Bus(es):                        Mix Enables
A                                      ☑ Track Mute/Solo
                                       ☑ Bus Mute/Solo
                                       ☑ Track Automation
                                       ☑ Clip Automation
                                       ☑ Bus Automation
                                       ☑ FX Automation
                                       ☑ Track FX
Separation:  Each Bus To Separate Submix  ▼   ☑ Bus FX

                             OK      Cancel      Help
```

3. Because you are combining clips from multiple tracks into one clip, the new clip has to reside on a single track. In the Destination drop-down list, choose the track on which you want your new combined clip to reside.
4. The Bounce to Track(s) function lets you determine the format of your new clip. In the Format drop-down list, choose the format you want to use. Choose Mix to Single Track Stereo Event(s) to create a single stereo track from your combined clips. Choose Mix to Separate Left and Right Tracks to create two new tracks, each holding the left and right stereo channels of your new audio data respectively. Choose Mix Stereo Content to Mono to create a single mono track from your combined clips.
5. In the Source Bus(es) section, select the buses that you want SONAR to use when combining your clips.

CHAPTER 7

6. In the Separation field, choose how you want SONAR to deal with the output from each bus. Select the Each Bus to Separate Submix option for situations in which you have each track assigned to a different output bus and you want the combined clips from each track to be put on a separate new track. Choose the Each Main Out to Separate Submix option for situations in which you have each track assigned to a different physical sound card output and you want the combined clips from each track to be put on a separate new track. Choose the All Main Outs to Single Mix option to combine all the clips from the selected tracks onto one new track. I'll talk more about buses and mains in Chapter 12.

7. In the Mix Enables section, activate the automation and effects options you want to include in the new clip from the clips being combined. Usually you should keep all these options activated. I'll talk more about effects and automation in Chapters 11 and 12.

8. Click on OK.

SONAR will combine all your clips into one new clip and put it in the track you specified.

The Split Function

SONAR enables you to split clips using its Split function. It works like this:

1. Select the clips that you want to split.

2. Choose Edit > Split to open the Split Clips dialog box (see Figure 7.15).

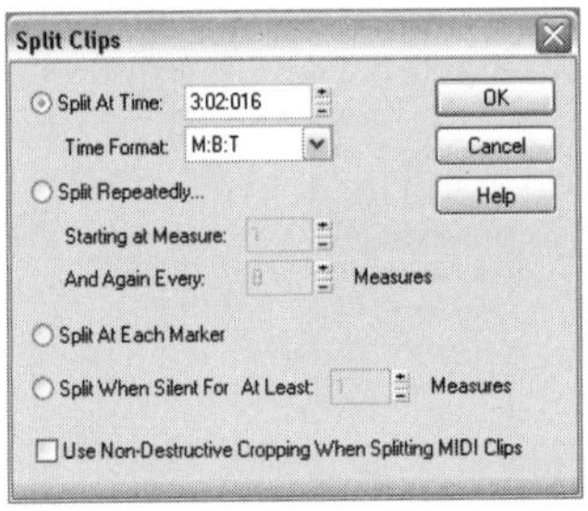

Figure 7.15
Using the Split Clips dialog box, you can split clips into new, smaller clips in a variety of ways.

3. Choose the split option you want to use. The Split at Time option lets you split a clip at a certain measure, beat, or tick. The Split Repeatedly option lets you split a clip into a bunch of smaller clips instead of just two new smaller ones. Just enter the measure at which you want the first split to occur and the number of measures at which you want each consecutive split to occur after that. For example, if you have a clip that begins at measure 2 and ends at measure 7, and you want to create three two-bar clips out of it, enter 2 for the starting measure and 2 for the split interval. The Split at Each Marker option lets you split clips according to the markers you set up in the Track view. You learned about markers in Chapter 5. Finally, the Split When Silent for at Least option lets you split clips at any place within them where silence occurs. You can set the interval of silence that SONAR has to look for by entering a number of measures.

4. If you are splitting MIDI clips, you have the option of having them split non-destructively, which means that any data (such as note durations) that extends

beyond the split point isn't deleted; only the appearance of the clips is changed. To do this, activate the Use Non-Destructive Cropping When Splitting MIDI Clips option. More than likely you usually will want to have this option activated.

5. Click on OK.

The Split Tool

In addition to the Split function, you can split clips graphically with your mouse by using the Split tool. You access this tool via the Split tool button on the Track view toolbar (see Figure 7.16).

Figure 7.16
Access the Split tool using the Split tool button on the Track view toolbar.

Using the Split tool, you can split long audio and MIDI clips into shorter ones by clicking and dragging with your mouse. To use the Split tool, simply follow these steps:

1. Click on the Split tool button in the Track view toolbar.

2. Move your mouse pointer within the Clips pane, and it will turn into a pointer with a pair of scissors attached to it.

3. Click and drag anywhere within the Clips pane to select some data (see Figure 7.17). You can make a selection over multiple clips and multiple tracks simultaneously if you want.

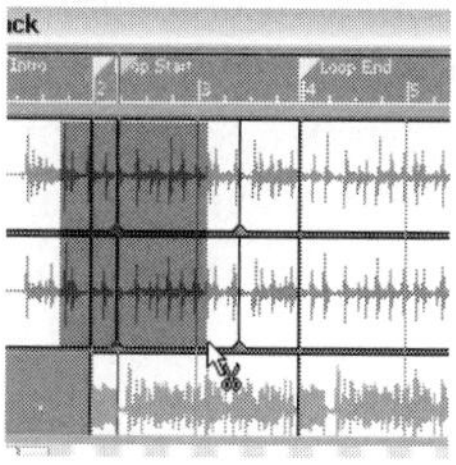

Figure 7.17
You just click and drag to make a selection with the Split tool.

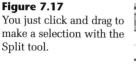

4. Release the mouse button. SONAR will split all the selected clips according to the boundaries of the selection.

5. When you are finished using the Split tool, be sure to activate the Select tool (press T on your computer keyboard) so you don't accidentally split some clips by mistake when you're just trying to make a selection.

Moving and Copying Clips

You also can change the arrangement of your data by moving and copying clips to new locations, either within the same tracks or into other tracks. One way to move a clip is to use the Clip Properties dialog box and enter a new start time for the clip. You also can move a clip by simply clicking and dragging it to a new location with your mouse. As long as the track you're dragging the clip into doesn't contain any other existing clips, you don't have to worry; SONAR simply will move the clip to its new location.

However, if the track contains existing data, SONAR will ask how you want the data to be handled by displaying the Drag and Drop Options dialog box (see Figure 7.18). You then have to choose one of three options: Blend Old and New, Replace Old with New, or Slide Over Old to Make Room.

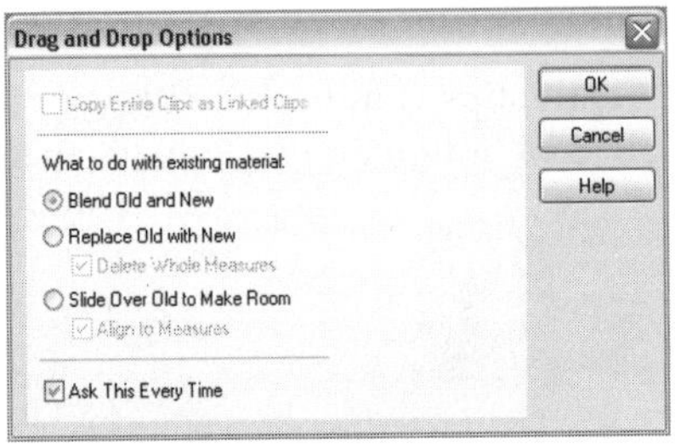

Figure 7.18
If you move a clip within a track that contains existing material, SONAR will display the Drag and Drop Options dialog box.

ASK THIS EVERY TIME
If you have the Ask This Every Time option activated in the Drag and Drop Options dialog box, SONAR will open the box every time you drag data, even if there is no existing data in the track to which you're dragging. If you don't want this to happen, deactivate the Ask This Every Time option.

If you choose the Blend Old and New option, the clip you're moving simply will overlap any existing clips. This means that the clips remain separate, but they overlap so that during playback the data in the overlapping sections will play simultaneously. If you choose the Replace Old with New option, the overlapping portion of the clip you are moving will replace (which means it will erase and take the place of) the portion of the clip being overlapped. If you choose the Slide Over Old to Make Room option, the start times of any existing clips will be changed to make room for the new clip. During playback, the new clip will play at the time it was placed at, and the existing clips will play a little later, depending on how much their start times had to be changed.

If you would rather copy a clip instead of moving it, you can use SONAR's Copy, Cut, and Paste functions. Actually, using the Cut function is the same as moving a clip. If you use the Copy function, though, you can keep the original clip in its place and put a copy of it in the new location. This procedure works as follows:

1. Select the clips you want to copy.
2. Choose Edit > Copy (or press Ctrl+C on your computer keyboard) to open the Copy dialog box (see Figure 7.19).

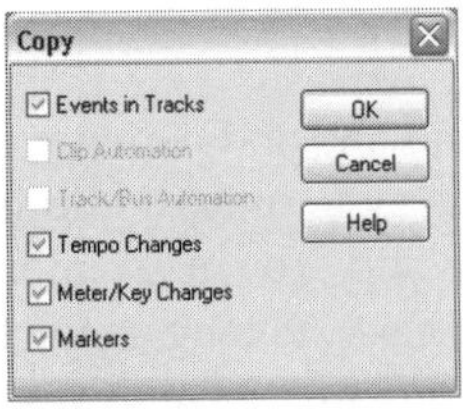

Figure 7.19
To copy clips, you use the Copy dialog box.

3. Choose the type(s) of data you want to copy. Usually, you should choose the Events in Tracks option.

4. Click on OK.

5. Click on the number of the track into which you want to copy the clips.

6. Set the Now time to the point in the track at which you want to place the clips.

7. Choose Edit > Paste (or press Ctrl+V on your computer keyboard) to open the Paste dialog box, and then click on the Advanced button to open the advanced Paste dialog box (see Figure 7.20).

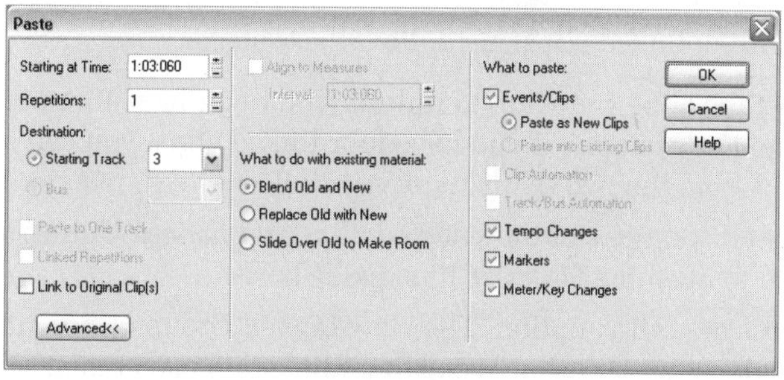

Figure 7.20
The advanced Paste dialog box provides many different options for copying data in SONAR.

8. Choose the options you want to use. Most of these options are self-explanatory. Setting the Starting at Time option is the same as setting the Now time in Step 6. Setting the Destination: Starting Track option is the same as setting the track in Step 5. The Repetitions option simply lets you create more than one copy of the clip if you want. I've already talked about the What to Do with Existing Material options. The only new options are Paste as New Clips and Paste into Existing Clips. The Paste as New Clips option creates a new clip and then follows the overlapping rules that you chose with the What to Do with Existing Material options. The Paste into Existing Clips option, however, merges the clip that you are copying with any existing clips that it overlaps. You end up with material from both clips merged into one.

9. Click on OK.

If some of these options sound a little confusing, just experiment with them a bit. Make an extra backup of your project, and then use it to go wild with the copying and pasting functions. Try every possible combination, and soon you'll get the hang of using them.

QUICK CLIP COPY
You can copy a clip quickly by holding down the Ctrl key on your computer keyboard and clicking and dragging the clip to a new location. A copy of the clip will be made and placed at the new location.

Linked Clips

You might have noticed a few other options in the Paste dialog boxes, namely the Linked Repetitions and Link to Original Clip(s) options. These options deal with a special feature in SONAR called *linked clips*. Using this feature, you can link copies of a clip to each other so that any changes you make to one clip will affect the other clips that are linked to it. This way, you can easily create repeating patterns and later make changes to the patterns.

For example, you might have a cool drum pattern in a clip that takes up one measure and you want to repeat that pattern through the first eight measures of your song. You can copy the clip and then paste it (setting the Repetitions to 7 and activating the Linked Repetitions and Link to Original Clips options). SONAR will copy your clip and paste seven identical, linked copies of it. If you make any changes to one of the clips, these changes affect them all. For instance, you can change the snare drum from sounding on beat 2 to sounding on beat 3 in one of the clips, and the change will happen in all of them. Linked clips are a fun, cool, and timesaving feature.

If you ever want to unlink linked clips, just follow these steps:

1. Select the clips you want to unlink. You don't have to unlink all linked clips in a group. For example, if you have four linked clips, you can select two of them to unlink, and the two that you leave unselected will remain linked.

2. Right-click on one of the selected clips and choose Unlink from the drop-down menu to open the Unlink Clips dialog box.

3. Choose an unlink option. The New Linked Group option unlinks the selected clips from the other clips but keeps them linked to each other. The Independent, Not Linked at All option totally unlinks the clips from any others.

4. Click on OK.

Linked clips are shown with dotted outlines in the Clips pane of the Track view. When you unlink them, they appear as normal clips again.

Erasing Clips

Deleting any clips that you no longer need is an easy process. Simply follow these steps:

1. Select the clips you want to delete.

2. Choose Edit > Delete to open the Delete dialog box (see Figure 7.21).

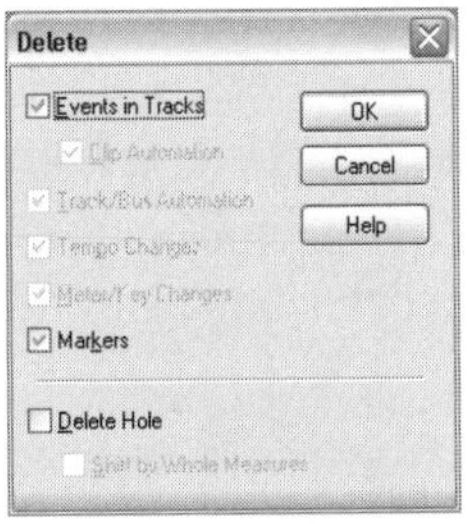

Figure 7.21
In the Delete dialog box, you can determine the type of data you want to erase.

3. Make sure the Events in Tracks option is activated.

4. If you want SONAR to remove the space that's created when you delete the clips, activate the Delete Hole option. SONAR will move any other existing clips in the track backward (toward the beginning of the project) by the amount of time opened when you delete the clips. Just give it a try, and you'll see what I mean.

5. If you activate the Shift by Whole Measures option as well, the existing clips will be moved back only to the nearest whole measure.

6. Click on OK.

Inserting Space

Instead of manipulating existing data, you sometimes might need to introduce silent parts into your project. You can do so by using SONAR's Insert > Time/Measures feature. This feature allows you to insert blank space in the form of measures, ticks, seconds, or frames. You can insert the space either into the whole project or into selected tracks. It works like this:

1. Choose Edit > Select > None (or press Ctrl+Shift+A on your computer keyboard) to clear any currently selected data in the project.

2. If you want to insert space into the whole project, skip to Step 3. Otherwise, select the tracks into which you want to insert space.

3. Set the Now time to the point in the tracks or project at which you want the space inserted.

4. Choose Insert > Time/Measures to open the Insert Time/Measures dialog box (see Figure 7.22).

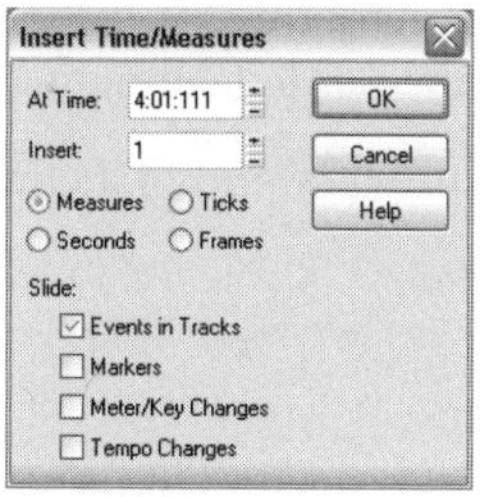

Figure 7.22
Using the Insert Time/Measures dialog box, you can insert blank space into selected tracks or the entire project.

5. The At Time field reflects the current Now time. Type a new time here, or make adjustments if you want.

6. For the Insert field, type the number of units of blank space you want inserted.

7. Select the type of unit you want inserted. You can choose to insert measures, ticks, seconds, or frames.

8. In the Slide section, choose the types of data that will be affected by the insert process. The types of data you select will be moved to make room for the new blank space. Of course, you'll almost always want to have the Events in Tracks option activated. When you're inserting space into selected tracks, the Events in Tracks option is usually the only one you want to have activated. When you're inserting space into the entire project, on the other hand, more than likely you'll want to have all the options activated.

9. Click on OK.

SONAR will insert the number of measures, ticks, seconds, or frames you typed into the Insert parameter at the Now time you specified. It also will move the types of data you selected by sliding the data forward in time (toward the end of the project). For instance, if you inserted a measure of blank space in the entire project at measure 2, then all the data in all the tracks starting at measure 2 will be shifted forward by one measure. Whatever data was in measure 2 will be in measure 3, any data that was in measure 3 will be in measure 4, and so on.

Slip Editing

Up until now, all of the editing functions I've described in this chapter work by making permanent changes to the MIDI and audio data in your clips and tracks. This is called *destructive processing* because it "destroys" the original data by modifying (or overwriting) it according to any editing you apply.

UNDO FUNCTION

As you know, you can remove any destructive processing done to your data by using SONAR's Undo function. You also can load a saved copy of your project containing the original data. However, neither of these restoration methods is as convenient as using non-destructive processing.

In contrast to destructive processing, SONAR also includes some editing functions (called *slip editing* functions) that provide *non-destructive* processing. The slip editing functions are non-destructive because they don't apply any permanent changes to your data. Instead, they are applied only during playback and let you hear the results while leaving your original data intact.

You can use the slip editing functions to crop the beginning or end of a clip, shift the contents of a clip, or shift-crop the beginning or end of a clip.

Cropping a Clip

To crop the beginning or end of a clip, follow these steps:

1. If you want to crop the beginning of a clip, position your mouse over the left end of the clip until the cursor turns into a square (see Figure 7.23).

Figure 7.23
Position your mouse over the left end of the clip to crop the beginning.

2. Click and drag your mouse to the right so that the clip changes length, as shown in Figure 7.24.

Figure 7.24
Click and drag to the right to shorten the clip from the beginning.

3. If you want to crop the end of a clip, follow steps 1 and 2 but adjust the right end of the clip rather than the left end, so it looks like Figure 7.25.

Figure 7.25
Click and drag the right end of the clip to crop the end.

When you crop a clip, the data that is cropped is not deleted. Instead, the data is masked so you will not hear it during playback. So if you crop the first two beats in a one-measure clip, those first two beats will not sound during playback. And if you crop the last two beats in a one-measure clip, those last two beats will not sound during playback.

REPOSITION YOUR CLIPS

When you crop a clip, the length of the clip is altered. The space where the cropped data used to be will be filled with silence during playback. You might need to make some adjustments to the positions of your clips within your tracks.

PERMANENT CHANGES

If you ever want to apply your cropping changes to a clip permanently, choose Edit > Apply Trimming.

Shifting a Clip

Instead of cropping a clip (and thus changing its length), you can shift the data inside the clip without changing the clip's length. To shift a clip, follow these steps:

1. Press and hold the Alt+Shift keys on your computer keyboard.
2. Position your mouse over the middle of the clip until the cursor turns into a square (see Figure 7.26).

Figure 7.26
To shift a clip, position your mouse in the middle of it.

3. Click and drag to the left to shift the data in the clip toward the beginning of the clip.
4. Click and drag to the right to shift the data in the clip toward the end of the clip.

When you shift a clip, the data in the beginning or end of the clip is cropped, but the length of the clip is not altered, as shown in Figure 7.27.

Figure 7.27
Shifting a clip crops the data but doesn't alter the length of the clip.

Shift-Cropping a Clip

Shift-cropping is a combination of the aforementioned functions. When you shift-crop a clip, the data in the clip is shifted and the length of the clip is altered. To shift-crop a clip, follow these steps:

1. Press and hold the Alt+Shift keys on your computer keyboard.
2. Position your mouse over the left or right end of the clip (depending on whether you want to shift-crop the beginning or end of the clip) until the cursor turns into a square.
3. Click and drag to the left or right to alter the length of the clip and shift the data inside the clip at the same time.

The slip editing functions can be a very powerful alternative to cutting and pasting. Since the data from the clips isn't deleted, you can edit the clips at any time to specify the portions of their data that will sound during playback. For example, if you have a clip that contains a vocal phrase, and the first word in the phrase isn't quite right, you can crop it. But later on, if you decide that the word actually sounded good, just uncrop it, and your data will restored, just like magic.

ENVELOPES

SONAR provides some additional non-destructive editing functions called *envelopes*. I'll talk more about envelopes in Chapter 12.

Audio Editing

Although SONAR provides separate views for precise editing of MIDI data, it doesn't provide a dedicated view for editing audio data. Instead, the Track view doubles as an audio editor. To edit audio in the Track view, you simply use all of the functions described previously in this chapter to edit any audio clips in your tracks. There are some other more sophisticated functions available for editing audio data that I'll describe in Chapter 8, "Exploring the Editing Tools."

There are, however, a few things you should keep in mind while editing audio in the Track view. The following sections will describe these things.

Audio Waveforms

When examining audio clips, you'll notice that they display the audio waveforms corresponding to the audio data inside them.

AUDIO WAVEFORMS

An *audio waveform* is a graphical representation of sound. Let me try to explain using the cup and string analogy. Remember when you were a kid, and you set up your own intercom system between your bedroom and your tree house using nothing but a couple of paper cups and a long piece of string? You poked a hole in the bottom of each cup and then tied one end of the string to one cup and the other end of the string to the other cup. Your friend would be in the tree house with one of the cups, and you would be in your bedroom with the other. As you talked into your cup, your friend could hear you by putting his cup to his ear, and vice versa.

Why did it work? Well, when you talked into the cup, the sound of your voice vibrated the bottom of the cup, making it act like a microphone. This movement, in turn, vibrated the string up and down, and the string carried the vibrations to the other cup. This movement made the bottom of that cup vibrate so it acted like a speaker, thus letting your friend hear what you said. If it were possible for you to freeze the string while it was in motion and then zoom in on it so you could see the vibrations, it would look similar to the audio waveform shown in Figure 7.28.

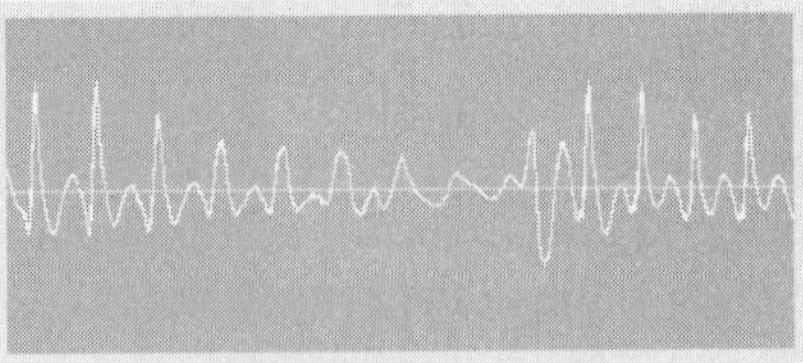

Figure 7.28
An audio waveform is similar to a vibrating string if you could freeze and zoom in on the string to observe the vibrations.

As you can see, a waveform shows up and down movements just like a vibrating string. A line, called the *zero axis,* runs horizontally through the center of the waveform. The zero axis represents the point in a waveform at which there are no vibrations or there is no sound, so the value of the audio data at the zero axis is the number zero (also known as *zero amplitude*). When a waveform moves above or below the zero axis, vibrations occur, and thus there is sound. The amplitude value of a waveform in these places depends on how high above or how low below the zero axis the waveform is at a certain point in time (shown on the Time Ruler).

Snap to Zero Crossing

Another thing to keep in mind is that you need to make sure to edit your audio data at zero crossings in the waveform to avoid noisy pops or clicks. You can do so by activating the Snap to Audio Zero Crossings feature, which you access via the Snap to Grid dialog box. Just open the Snap to Grid dialog box by clicking on the Snap to Grid Options button in the Track view toolbar (see Figure 7.29). Then put a check mark next to the Snap to Audio Zero Crossings option.

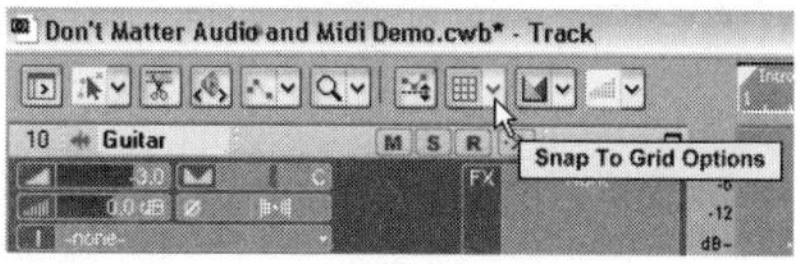

Figure 7.29
Use the Snap to Grid Options button to access the Snap to Grid dialog box.

The Snap to Audio Zero Crossings feature (when activated) makes sure that, when you make a selection or perform an edit, your selections or edits fall on zero crossings in the audio waveform.

ZERO CROSSING
Remember the description of the zero axis? Well, any point in an audio waveform that lands on the zero axis is called a *zero crossing*. It's called that because as the waveform moves up and down, it crosses over the zero axis.

Why is it important that your selections and edits line up with zero crossings? A zero crossing is a point in the audio waveform at which no sound is being made, so it provides a perfect spot at which to edit the waveform—for example, when you're cutting and pasting pieces of audio. If you edit an audio waveform at a point where it's either above or below the zero axis, you might introduce glitches, which can come in the form of audible pops and clicks. You get these glitches because you cut at a moment when sound is being produced. You also get them because when you're pasting pieces of audio together, you cannot guarantee that the ends of each waveform will line up perfectly (except, of course, if they both are at zero crossings).

Audio Scaling

Lastly, SONAR provides some special zooming features when you are working with audio tracks. These are the *audio scaling* features, and they allow you to zoom in on the audio waveforms shown inside the clips in your audio tracks. Audio scaling allows you to measure the amplitude of your audio data, and it comes in handy for doing very precise audio editing.

When you are working with audio tracks, you'll notice some numbers displayed along the left side of the Clips pane in the Track view (see Figure 7.30). These are the Audio Scale, which displays a measurement of the amplitude of the audio data in your audio tracks.

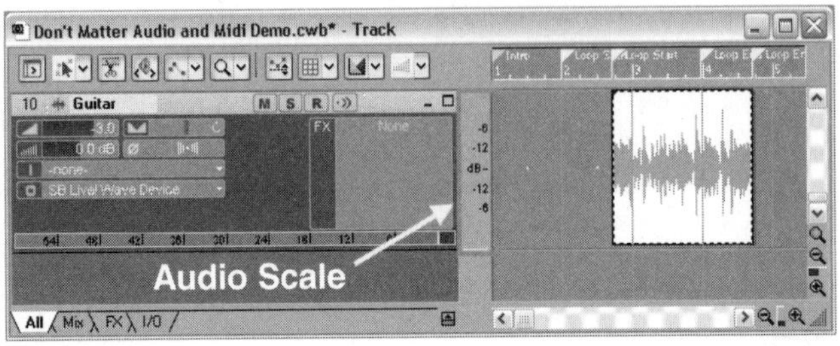

Figure 7.30
Use the Audio Scale to measure the amplitude of your audio.

Audio Scale

The measurement can be shown in decibels, as a percentage, or as a zoom factor. To change the measurement display, right-click anywhere in the Audio Scale area and choose an option (see Figure 7.31).

Figure 7.31
Change the Audio Scale measurement display by right-clicking on it.

To change the Audio Scale factor for a single audio track, just left-click and hold your mouse on the Audio Scale of the track. Then drag your mouse up or down to change the Audio Scale factor. You'll notice that the audio waveform display for the track changes as you move your mouse. This allows you to zoom in and out of the audio waveform, but it doesn't affect the Track view zooming that I talked about earlier in the chapter.

You also can change the audio scaling factor for all audio tracks at once using the Zoom Out Vertical, Zoom In Vertical, and Vertical Zoom Control functions I talked about earlier in the chapter. To use them for audio scaling, just hold down the Ctrl key on your computer keyboard while you manipulate the functions with your mouse.

Using the Piano Roll View

By manipulating the tracks and clips in your project you can change the overall structure, but to fix single-note mistakes and make smaller changes, you need to do some precision editing. You do so by selecting individual or multiple tracks or clips in the Track view and then using the View menu to open the data within one of the other available views. For editing MIDI data, that would be the Piano Roll view. (You also can edit MIDI data as standard music notation in the Staff view, which I'll talk about in Chapter 13, "Making Sheet Music.")

Using the Piano Roll view (see Figure 7.32), you can add, edit, and delete MIDI note and controller data within your MIDI tracks. Looking somewhat like a player-piano roll, the Piano Roll view represents notes as colored shapes on a grid display with the pitches of the notes designated by an onscreen music keyboard.

Figure 7.32
The Piano Roll view resembles the old player-piano rolls used in the late 1800s and early 1900s.

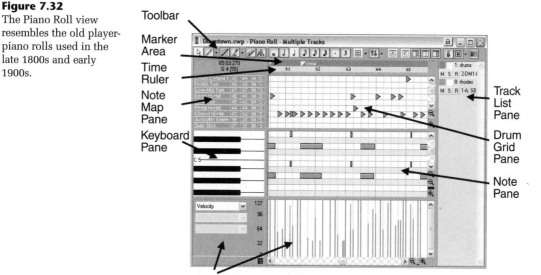

More precisely, the Piano Roll view consists of seven major sections: the toolbar (containing all the view's related controls), the Drum Grid pane (displaying the drum notes in the currently selected track), the Note Map pane (displaying the drum instruments represented by the note shown in the Drum Grid pane), the Note pane (displaying the melodic notes in the currently selected track), the Keyboard pane (displaying the pitch values of the notes shown in the Note pane), the Controllers pane (displaying the MIDI controller data in the currently selected track), and the Track List pane (showing a list of all the tracks currently being displayed; the Piano Roll view can display the data from more than one track at one time).

You'll also notice that the Piano Roll view has scroll bars and zoom tools just like the Track view. These tools work the same way as they do in the Track view. In addition, a Snap to Grid function is represented by the Snap to Grid button in the toolbar (see Figure 7.33). Other similarities are the Marker area and the Time Ruler, which are located just above the Drum Grid pane. Basically, you can use the Piano Roll view to edit and view the data in the MIDI tracks of your project in more detail.

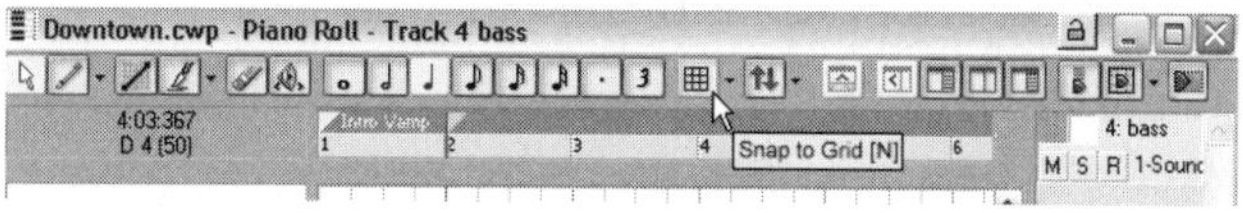

Figure 7.33
Use the Snap to Grid button to access the Piano Roll view's Snap to Grid function.

You can open the Piano Roll view in three different ways.

▶ In the Track view, select the tracks you want to edit and then choose View > Piano Roll or press Alt+5 on your computer keyboard.

▶ In the Track view, right-click on a track or clip and choose View > Piano Roll from the drop-down menu.

▶ In the Track view, double-click on a MIDI clip in the Clips pane.

Whichever method you choose, SONAR will open the Piano Roll view and display the data from the tracks you selected.

Working with Multiple Tracks

If you select more than one track to be displayed at one time, the Piano Roll view will show the data from each track using a unique color. For example, the notes and controllers from one track might be shown as yellow, and the data from another track might be shown as blue.

CHANGE TRACK COLORS

The one exception to the use of track colors is that tracks with numbers ending in the same digit (that is, 1, 11, 21, and so on) must all share the same color. There's no way around this. You can change the color used by each number group, however, by using the Colors dialog box, which you access by selecting Options > Colors. You learned how to customize SONAR's colors in Chapter 3.

Each track also is listed in the Track pane with a set of individual controls (see Figure 7.34).

Figure 7.34
The data from multiple tracks is shown with different colors, and each track is listed in the Track pane.

The Track Pane

When you open the Piano Roll view, the names and numbers of the tracks you selected are listed in the Track pane. For convenience, the associated Mute, Solo, and Record buttons for each track are provided as well. Plus, you'll notice two other controls available for each track in the list.

▶ **Enable/Disable Track Editing.** The white button next to each track in the Track pane is the Enable/Disable Track Editing button. This button determines whether the notes for its associated track can be edited. When the button is white, the notes appear in color in the Drum Grid and Note panes, and they can be edited. When the button is gray, the notes appear gray in the Drum Grid and Note panes, and they cannot be edited. Clicking on the button toggles it on and off.

▶ **Show/Hide Track.** The button to the left of the Track Editing button is the Show/Hide Track button. This button determines whether the notes for its associated track will be displayed in the Drum Grid and Note panes. When the button is in color (the same color as the notes for that track), the notes are shown in the Drum Grid and Note panes. When the button is white, the notes are not shown in the Drum Grid and Note panes. Clicking on the Show/Hide Track button toggles it on and off.

The Track Tools

In addition to the Track pane controls, six other track-related controls are located on the toolbar (see Figure 7.35):

Figure 7.35
Use the track controls via the Piano Roll toolbar to manipulate your displayed tracks.

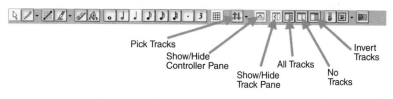

Pick Tracks

Show/Hide
Controller Pane

Show/Hide
Track Pane

All Tracks

No
Tracks

Invert
Tracks

▶ **Invert Tracks.** Clicking on this button toggles the Show/Hide Track buttons for each of the tracks in the Track pane. If one track has its Show/Hide Track button on and another track has its button off, clicking on the Invert Tracks button turns off the first track's Show/Hide button and turns on the second track's Show/Hide button. It toggles the current state of each Show/Hide Track button.

▶ **No Tracks.** Clicking on this button turns off the Show/Hide Track buttons for each track in the Track List pane. No matter what state each Show/Hide Track button is in (either on or off), the No Track button turns them all off.

▶ **All Tracks.** This button is the exact opposite of the No Tracks button. Clicking on the All Tracks button turns on the Show/Hide Track buttons for each track in the Track List pane.

▶ **Show/Hide Track Pane.** Clicking on this button simply toggles between having the Track pane open or closed.

▶ **Show/Hide Controllers Pane.** Clicking on this button simply toggles between having the Controllers pane open or closed. I'll talk more about the Controllers pane later in this chapter, in the "Dealing with Controllers" section.

▶ **Pick Tracks.** While you have the Piano Roll view open, you might want to add or remove some of the tracks in the Track pane. Instead of having to close the Piano Roll view, select other tracks in the Track view, and then open the Piano Roll view again, you can use the Pick Tracks feature.

Clicking on the Pick Tracks button opens the Pick Tracks dialog box. This box displays a list of all the tracks in your project. You can select one or more tracks from the list. (Hold down the Ctrl key on your computer keyboard to select multiple tracks.) After you click on the OK button, the tracks that you selected will be listed in the Track pane.

CHANGE TRACK ORDER

If you have two or more tracks that contain the same exact notes, those notes overlap one another in the Drum Grid and Note panes. The order of the tracks in the track List pane determines which track's notes are on top. For example, if track 4 is listed above track 2 in the Track List pane, the data from track 4 overlaps the data from track 2 in the Note pane. If you want to change this order (meaning you want the data from track 2 to overlap the data from track 4), you can click and drag the track listing in the Track List pane to a new position in the list.

Dealing with Notes

When you open a melodic MIDI track in the Piano Roll view, the notes in that track are displayed in the Note pane. Each note is represented by a colored rectangle. The horizontal location of a note designates its start time when you line up the left side of the rectangle with the numbers in the Time Ruler, and the vertical location of a note designates its pitch when you line up the whole rectangle with the keys in the Keyboard pane. The length of the rectangle designates the duration of the note (for instance, quarter note, eighth note, and so on).

You can add new notes to a track or edit the existing ones using the tools represented by the first six buttons in the toolbar, from left to right on the left side of the Piano Roll view (see Figure 7.36).

Figure 7.36
Add and edit notes using the tools represented by the first six toolbar buttons.

Selecting Notes

Using the Select tool, you can select notes for further manipulation, such as deleting, copying, moving, and so on. Essentially, you select notes the same way you select clips in the Track view. To select a single note, click on it. To select more than one note, hold down the Ctrl key on your computer keyboard while clicking on the notes you want to select. You know the rest.

One additional selection method involves the Keyboard pane. To select all the notes of a certain pitch, you can click on one of the keys in the Keyboard pane. You can also drag your mouse pointer across several keys to select the notes of a number of different pitches.

Editing

After you've made a selection, you can copy, cut, paste, move, and delete the notes the same way you do with clips in the Track view. You can also edit notes individually by using the Draw tool. Using this tool, you can add (which I'll describe shortly) and edit the notes in the Note pane.

To change the start time of a note, simply drag the left edge of its rectangle left or right. This action moves it to a different horizontal location along the Time Ruler. To change the pitch of a note, simply drag the middle of its rectangle up or down. This action moves it to a different vertical location along the Keyboard pane. To change the duration of a note, simply drag the right edge of its rectangle left or right. This action changes the length of the rectangle and thus the duration of the note.

Of course, sometimes you might want to make more precise changes to a note. There are two ways to do this. The first method is to use the Select tool to select the note and then use the Time, Pitch, Vel (Velocity), Dur (Duration), and Chn (MIDI Channel) parameters in the Event Inspector toolbar to change those characteristics of the note.

EVENT INSPECTOR

The Event Inspector toolbar is no longer a part of the Piano Roll view as it was in Sonar 2. In Sonar 3, the Event Inspector is a global toolbar that can be accessed from any view. It acts just like any other toolbar. If it is not active, choose View > Toolbars to make the Event Inspector visible. For more information about toolbars, you can review Chapter 3.

You can also use the Note Properties dialog box to edit a note. Just right-click on a note to open the Note Properties dialog box (see Figure 7.37).

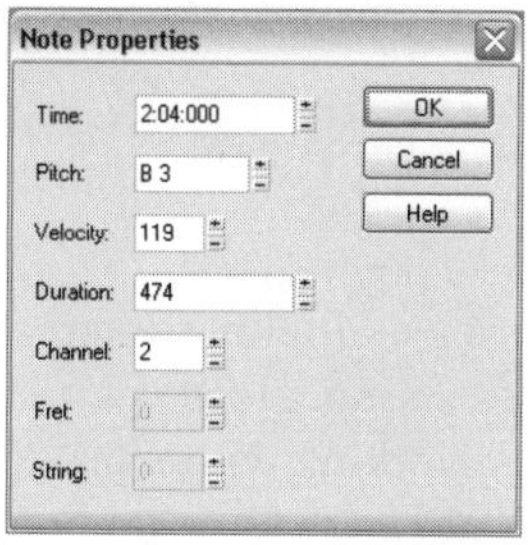

Figure 7.37
In the Note Properties dialog box, you can make precise changes to a note in the Piano Roll view.

In the Note Properties dialog box, you can make precise changes to the start time, pitch, velocity, duration, and MIDI channel of an individual note by typing numerical values. If you're wondering about the fret and string parameters, I'll describe them in Chapter 13, "Making Sheet Music."

Drawing (or Adding) Notes

In addition to editing, the Draw tool allows you to add notes to a track by literally drawing them in. To do so, just follow these steps:

1. Select the Draw tool by clicking on its toolbar button.

2. Select a duration for the new notes. If you look a little further over in the toolbar, you'll notice a number of buttons with note values shown on them (see Figure 7.38). Clicking on these buttons determines the duration for your new notes. For example, if you click on the Quarter Note button, the duration will be set to a quarter note. You'll also see two additional buttons—one representing a dotted note and another representing a triplet note. So if you want your notes to be dotted or triplets, click on one of those buttons as well.

Figure 7.38
Use the duration toolbar buttons to choose a duration for your new notes.

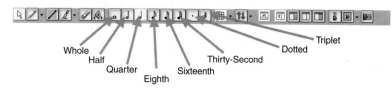

Whole · Half · Quarter · Eighth · Sixteenth · Thirty-Second · Dotted · Triplet

3. Click on the Note pane at the point at which you want to place the new notes. Remember, the horizontal position of the note determines its start time, and the vertical position of the note determines its pitch.

Erasing Notes

Although you can select and delete notes (as I described earlier), the Piano Roll view also includes an Erase tool for added convenience. To use it, just select the Erase tool and then click on any notes in the Note pane that you want to delete. You can also click and drag the Erase tool over a number of notes to erase them all at once.

AUTO-ERASE OPTION

You also can use the Draw tool to erase notes if you activate the Auto-Erase feature. Just click the down arrow to the right of the Draw tool button in the toolbar and choose the Auto-Erase option from the menu. Then when you click on an existing note, it will be erased. But if you click anywhere there isn't on an existing note, a new note will be drawn.

Scrubbing

When you're editing the data in a track, the procedure usually involves making your edits and then playing back the project to hear how the changes sound. However, playing back very small sections can be a bit difficult, especially when you're working with a fast tempo. To remedy this situation, SONAR provides a Scrub tool.

Using the Scrub tool, you can drag your mouse pointer over the data in the Piano Roll view and hear what it sounds like. To use the Scrub tool, simply select it by clicking on its button on the toolbar. Then click and drag your mouse pointer over the data in the Drum Grid and/or Note panes. Dragging left to right plays the data forward (what would normally happen during playback), and dragging right to left enables you to hear the data played in reverse. This capability can be useful for testing very short (one or two measure) sections.

EDIT DATA WHILE LOOPING

Instead of using the Scrub tool, you might want to try a more useful technique for hearing what your changes sound like. Did you know you can edit the data in your project as it's being played back? Of course, it's a bit difficult to edit anything while SONAR is scrolling the display as the project plays. I like to work on a small section of a project at a time. I set up a section of the project to loop over and over, and as SONAR is playing the data, I make any changes I think might be needed. Because the data is being played back while I edit, I can instantly hear what the changes sound like. This procedure is much easier than going back and forth, making changes and manually starting and stopping playback. You learned about looping in Chapter 6. By the way, you can use any of the views to edit your data while SONAR is playing a project. This tip is not just for the Piano Roll view.

DRAW LINE AND PATTERN BRUSH

I'm sure you noticed that I didn't talk about the Draw Line tool or the Pattern Brush tool. I'll cover those later on in this chapter, in the "Drawing" and "The Pattern Brush" sections, respectively.

Dealing with Drum Tracks

Because drum tracks are a bit different from regular MIDI tracks, SONAR provides some special features for dealing with drum tracks. What do I mean by different? Well, notes in a drum track usually represent a number of different percussion instruments grouped in the same track. Each note pitch in a drum track represents a different instrument. It used to be that if you wanted to work easily with each specific instrument, you had to split a drum track into many different tracks—one track for each note pitch. This allowed you to mute and solo different instruments, as well as do other things that you couldn't do when all the drum notes where grouped together on the same track.

With SONAR's new drum-specific features, you no longer have to go through the trouble of creating separate tracks for each drum instrument. You also have the flexibility of specifying different MIDI channels and MIDI ports for each instrument (among other things) using *drum maps*.

Using Drum Maps

A drum map allows you to define your drum instruments for SONAR, thus "telling" SONAR how each note pitch in a drum track should be handled. Each note pitch defined in a drum map can have its own instrument name, MIDI channel, MIDI port, velocity offset, and velocity scale. I know this sounds a little confusing, but hang in there with me for a moment.

Assigning Drum Maps

The easiest way to explain drum maps is to show you how to assign a drum map to a MIDI track and explain the results. I'll use an example to help clarify things a bit:

1. Choose File > Open and select the demo project file included with SONAR named Downtown.cwp. Then click on Open to load the project.

2. Close the Auto-Send Sysx, File Info, Big Time, and Staff view windows. You won't need them.

3. Select track 1 (drums) by clicking on its number, and then choose View > Piano Roll to open the track in the Piano Roll view. This is what a drum track looks like without a drum map assigned to it. You can see the notes in the track, but you don't know what percussion instruments they represent. And you can't easily work with each individual instrument because there is no way to mute or solo a specific group of note pitches. In addition, all the notes in the track have to share the same MIDI port and channel specified by the parameters in track 1. To get beyond these limitations, you need to assign a drum map to track 1.

4. Close the Piano Roll view, and in the Track view expand track 1 (drums) so you have access to its Output parameter. Then click on the Output parameter to display the Output menu (see Figure 7.39).

Figure 7.39
Use a track's Output parameter to assign a drum map to the track.

5. Highlight the New Drum Map option, and then choose GM Drums (Complete Kit) from the extended menu. This assigns the GM Drums (Complete Kit) drum map to track 1. SONAR ships with a number of predefined drum maps, as you can see from the list.

6. Select track 1 by clicking on its number, and then choose View > Piano Roll to open the track in the Piano Roll view again. Also, choose Edit > Select > None to get rid of the selection.

This time the track data looks a bit different, right? Instead of the Note pane, the Drum Grid pane is shown, and instead of rectangles there are triangles representing the notes, even though these are the same notes as before.

More important is what is shown in the Note Map pane. Each row in the Note Map pane represents a different percussion instrument. By lining up the notes in the Drum Grid pane with the rows in the Note Map pane, you can see what instrument the notes represent. And even though all these note pitches (instruments) reside on the same MIDI track, each instrument can be muted or soloed individually using the M and S buttons next to each instrument name in the Note Map pane. This makes working with drum tracks much easier.

Creating Drum Maps

Of course, there might be times when the predefined drum maps included with SONAR don't provide what you need. In that case, you'll need to create a drum map of your own. To do that, you need to use the Drum Map Manager (see Figure 7.40), which you can access by choosing Options > Drum Map Manager.

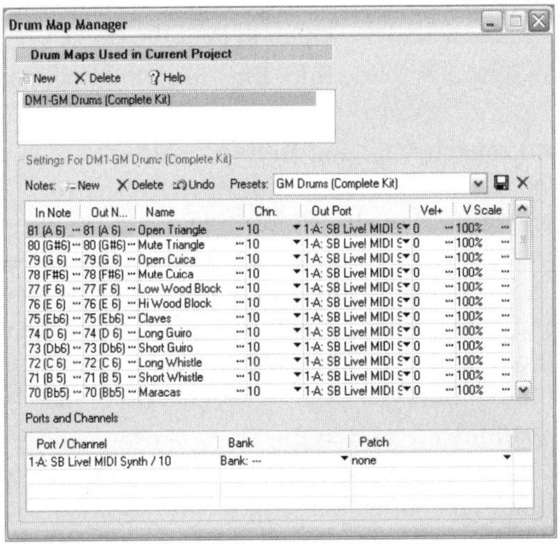

Figure 7.40
Use the Drum Map Manager to create and manage your drum maps.

The Drum Map Manager is divided into three sections. The first section (Drum Maps Used in Current Project) lists all the drum maps being used in the current project. It also allows you to delete existing drum maps or create new ones. The second section (Map Settings) shows all the parameter settings for the selected drum map. It also allows you to define each instrument in the drum map by specifying note pitches, instrument names, MIDI channels, MIDI out ports, velocity offsets, and velocity scales. And the third section lists all the MIDI output port and channel pairs that are used by the selected drum map. It also allows you to specify a MIDI bank and patch for each port/channel combination.

To create a drum map of your own, follow these steps:

1. With a project already open in SONAR, choose Options > Drum Map Manager to open the Drum Map Manager.

2. Click on the New button in the first section (Drum Maps Used in Current Project) of the window to create a blank drum map. Don't worry about naming or saving it yet; you'll do that later.

3. Click on the New button in the second section (Map Settings) of the window to create a new instrument mapping complete with default parameter settings, as shown in Figure 7.41.

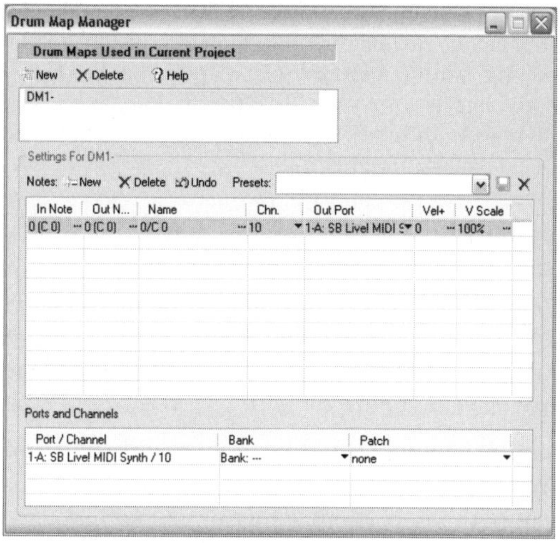

Figure 7.41
New instrument mappings initially contain default parameter settings.

Drum Map Manager
Drum Maps Used in Current Project
⌐ New   ✕ Delete   ? Help
DM1-

Settings For DM1-
Notes: ⌐ New   ✕ Delete   ↻ Undo   Presets:

In Note	Out N...	Name	Chn.	Out Port	Vel+	V Scale
0 (C 0)	⋯ 0 (C 0)	⋯ 0/C 0	⋯ 10	▾ 1-A: SB Level MIDI S ▾ 0	⋯ 100%	⋯

Ports and Channels

Port / Channel	Bank	Patch
1-A: SB Level MIDI Synth / 10	Bank: ⋯	▾ none	▾

4. Double-click on the In Note parameter for the new instrument mapping and enter a number (from 0 to 127) to specify the source pitch for this instrument. I'll explain what I mean by source pitch in a moment.

NOTE PITCHES

Note pitches in MIDI are represented by a range of numbers (0 to 127). These numbers represent the note pitches C0 (pitch/octave) to C8, with the number 60 (C4) being middle C. Unfortunately, you have to enter numbers for note values in the Drum Map Manager. There is no way to enter the pitch/octave of a note directly. However, after you enter a number, the pitch/octave of the note is displayed.

5. Double-click on the Out Note parameter for the new instrument mapping and enter a number (from 0 to 127) to specify the destination pitch for this instrument.

HOW DRUM MAPS WORK

A drum map is sort of like a MIDI data processor. After you assign a drum map to a MIDI track, SONAR passes all the data in that MIDI track through the drum map for processing during playback. As SONAR reads each note from the MIDI track, it compares the pitch of the note to all of the source pitches (In Note parameters) in the drum map. If it finds a match, it converts the incoming note to the destination pitch (Out Note parameter) of the matching source pitch. For example, if you set up an instrument mapping in your drum map with an In Note pitch of C4 and an Out Note pitch of D5, any incoming notes that have a pitch of C4 will be converted to a pitch of D5.

Why is this useful? Well, more often than not the In Note and Out Note parameters for an instrument mapping will be the same. But there might be times when you have a MIDI drum track that was recorded using a MIDI percussion synth other than what you have in your studio. This means that the drum sounds in your MIDI percussion device will be different and are probably triggered with different pitches. Using a drum map, you can map the pitches from the MIDI track to the different pitches used by your MIDI percussion device. This saves you the work of having to rewrite all the note pitches in the MIDI track.

6. Double-click on the Name parameter for the new instrument mapping and enter a name for the instrument. For example, if you are creating your own General MIDI drum map and you enter 56 for both the In Note and Out Note parameters, that means you are creating an instrument mapping for a cowbell sound because the number 56 represents a cowbell in General MIDI. So for the name, you would enter something like Cowbell.

7. Double-click on the Chn (channel) parameter and enter a MIDI channel for the instrument. This should be the same MIDI channel that your MIDI percussion synth is using to play the particular instrument sound.

8. Double-click on the Out Port parameter and choose a MIDI output port for the instrument. This should be the same MIDI output port that your MIDI percussion synth is using to play the particular instrument sound.

9. If you find that this instrument sound in your MIDI track is too loud or soft, you can add an offset to the MIDI velocity of the notes for that instrument sound. Just double-click on the Vel+ parameter and enter a number from −127 to +127. This number will be subtracted or added to the MIDI velocity value of each incoming note for that instrument sound.

10. You also can adjust the loudness of an instrument sound using the V Scale parameter. Instead of having to designate a set value to be added to or subtracted from the MIDI velocity values of the incoming notes, you can apply a velocity scale. Just double-click on the V Scale parameter and enter a value from 10% to 200%. A value of 100% means there is no change. A value less than 100% means the velocity values will be decreased. A value greater than 100% means the velocity values will be increased.

11. Repeat steps 3 through 10 to create as many instrument mappings in the drum map as you need. If you make a mistake, you can use the Undo button to remove your last change. To delete an instrument mapping, just click on the Delete button.

12. In the third section (Ports and Channels) of the window, you can set the bank and patch parameters for each MIDI port/channel combination used in the drum map. Basically, this is where you designate the drum set sounds that each MIDI percussion synth connected to your computer system should use. Your MIDI percussion synths should allow you to choose from a number of different drum sets.

13. To save your drum map, type a name in the Presets parameter and click on the Save button (located just to the right of the Presets parameter, showing a picture of a computer disk).

When you go to assign a drum map to a MIDI track, you'll see your new drum map listed there along with all the others.

Composing Drum Tracks

After you've assigned a drum map to a MIDI track, you can start composing the percussion parts for your project. By opening the track in the Piano Roll view, you can use the Note Map pane and the Drum Grid pane to add, edit, and delete drum notes. Most of the procedures that I described earlier in the "Dealing with Notes" section of this chapter (for selecting, editing, drawing, and erasing notes) can be applied here. But there are a few differences of which you need to be aware. Instead of just describing these differences, I'd like to walk you through the procedure I use to compose my own drum patterns. Here is how it goes:

1. Choose File > New and select the Normal template to create a new project. Assuming you haven't changed the Normal template, you'll be presented with four blank tracks. Select the first three tracks and choose Track > Delete, leaving you with one MIDI track as your new drum track.

2. Assign a drum map to the MIDI track. For this example, use the GM Drums (Complete Kit) drum map. You'll need to use a synth that has a General MIDI-compatible mode. Most modern synths have this capability.

3. If you need to set a bank and patch for your synth, choose Options > Drum Map Manager. In the third section (Ports and Channels) of the window, set a bank and patch for single port/channel listing there. Close the Drum Map Manager.

TIP

You can also use a DXi synth to play the sounds for your drum track. I'll talk more about DXis in Chapter 10, "Software Synthesis," but for now, follow these directions to set up one:

1. Choose Insert > DXi Synth > Edirol VSC.

2. In the Insert DXi Synth Options dialog box, deactivate the MIDI Source Track option, and then click on OK.

3. The VSC DXi window will open. Close it.

4. Choose Options > Drum Map Manager to open the Drum Map Manager.

5. While holding down the Ctrl+Shift keys on your computer keyboard, double-click on one of the Out Port parameters in the Map Settings list and choose Edirol VSC 1 from the menu.

6. Close the Drum Map Manager.

Now the Edirol VSC DXi will play any notes you add to your MIDI drum track. If you need to change the sound card output for the DXi, expand track 2 in the Track view and change its Output parameter.

4. I like to create my drum tracks by composing small sections at a time, and I also like to hear my music as I'm composing it. SONAR allows me to do this using its playback looping features. Suppose you want to create a one-measure drum pattern starting at the very beginning of the project and going to the beginning of measure 2. To set up a playback loop for this example, just choose Transport > Loop and Auto Shuttle. Set the Loop Start parameter to 1:01:000 and the Loop End parameter to 2:01:000. Activate the Stop at the End Time and Loop Continuously options, and then click on OK.

5. To continue with your drum composing exercise, choose View > Piano Roll to open the MIDI drum track in the Piano Roll view. You'll be presented with the Note Map pane filled with all the instruments available in the drum map you assigned to track 1, as well as a blank Drum Grid pane. Scroll down the window vertically until you can see the last instrument (Acoustic Bass Drum) in the Note Map pane. You might also want to increase the horizontal zoom of the window a bit so the first measure of the track fills the window.

6. The best way to start composing a drum pattern is to lay down a solid beat foundation. That means creating a kick drum part. You'll see in the list that you've got two kick drum sounds available to you—Bass Drum 1 and Acoustic Bass Drum. To audition an instrument, just click on its name in the list. Personally, I like the Acoustic Bass Drum, so I'll use that for this exercise. For the kick drum part of the pattern, lay down a basic four–quarter note beat. To do that, activate the Draw tool and choose the quarter–note duration using the Quarter Note button on the toolbar. Then place a note at each of the four beats in the first measure of the track, as shown in Figure 7.42.

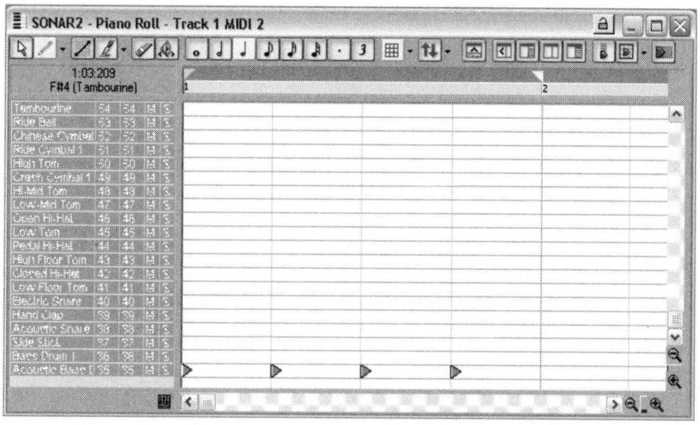

Figure 7.42
Start a drum pattern with
a solid kick drum beat
foundation.

🗲 **SNAP TO GRID**

If have a hard time placing the notes exactly on the beats, activate the Snap to Grid
function by clicking on the Snap to Grid button (see Figure 7.43). Then right-click
on the Snap to Grid button to set the function to a musical time interval that you
want to use (in this case, a quarter note).

Figure 7.43
Use Snap to Grid to
help you place the
notes in your drum
pattern.

You can have SONAR display a visual grid over the Drum Grid pane to help you
place notes by clicking on the Show/Hide Grid button (see Figure 7.44). I also
like to click on the down arrow button to the right of the Show/Hide Grid button
and choose the Follow Snap Settings option. This makes the visual grid use the
same resolution settings as the Snap to Grid function, so if you change the Snap
to Grid resolution, the visual grid will change along with it.

Figure 7.44
Use the Show/Hide
Grid button to display
a visual grid to help
with note placement.

7. Choose Transport > Play (or press the spacebar on your computer keyboard) to
start playback and listen to the drum pattern so far. It sounds good, but now you
need to add accompanying instruments to emphasize the beat, like a snare drum
part. There are two snare drum instruments available in the list—Electric Snare
and Acoustic Snare. I think you should go with the Acoustic Snare sound for this
example, so place a quarter note at beats 2 and 4 in the pattern for the Acoustic
Snare instrument, as shown in Figure 7.45. You should hear both the kick and
snare instruments playing.

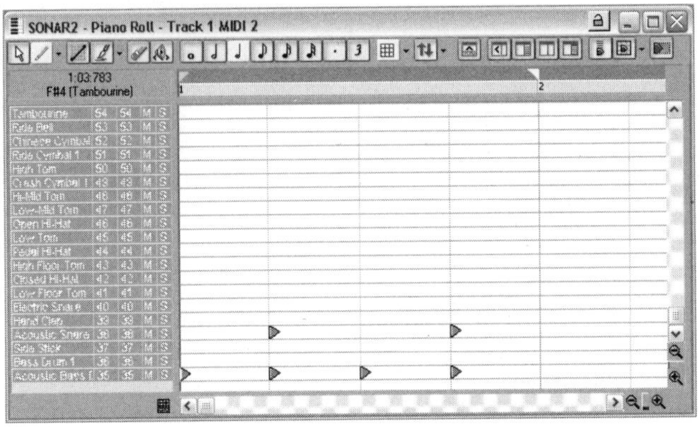

Figure 7.45
Add some acoustic snare
to the drum pattern.

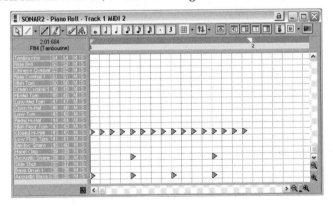

FIX MISTAKES

Remember that if you make any mistakes, you can use the same editing techniques
I talked about earlier in the chapter to fix things. If you need to delete a note, you
can use the Erase tool or the Auto-Erase feature of the Draw tool. If you place a
note on the wrong beat, just use the Select tool to click and drag the note right or
left along the grid. Or if you place a note in the wrong instrument row, just use the
Select tool to click and drag the note up or down to the correct instrument row.

Also, if the Drag and Drop Options dialog box keeps popping up and you don't
want it to, just deactivate the Ask This Every Time option in the box.

8. Now let's spice up the pattern a bit with a closed hi-hat rhythm. Instead of quarter
    notes, however, use sixteenth notes. Change the Snap to Grid to a sixteenth-note
    resolution, and then place notes at every sixteenth note line on the grid using the
    Closed Hi-Hat instrument, as shown in Figure 7.46.

Figure 7.46
Add a rhythmic closed
hi-hat part to the drum
pattern.

9. The closed hi-hat part is missing something. Usually a part like this will
    emphasize each beat in a pattern by playing each sixteenth note that falls on a beat
    a little louder than the rest. To make this happen, you need to adjust the velocity
    of these four notes using the Show Velocity Tails feature. To activate the feature,
    click on the Show Velocity Tails button (see Figure 7.47).

Figure 7.47
Use the Show Velocity
Tails feature to adjust
note velocities.

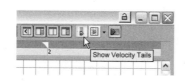

CHAPTER 7

10. You'll notice some vertical lines attached to each of the notes in the pattern. These lines represent the MIDI velocity for each note. To adjust the velocity of a note, use the Draw tool and just hover your mouse over the lines of a note until your mouse turns into a pointer with some vertical lines attached to it. Then click and drag your mouse up to increase the note's velocity or down to decrease the note's velocity. For this example, increase the velocity of the four closed hi-hat notes that reside right on each beat of the pattern to 127 (see Figure 7.48).

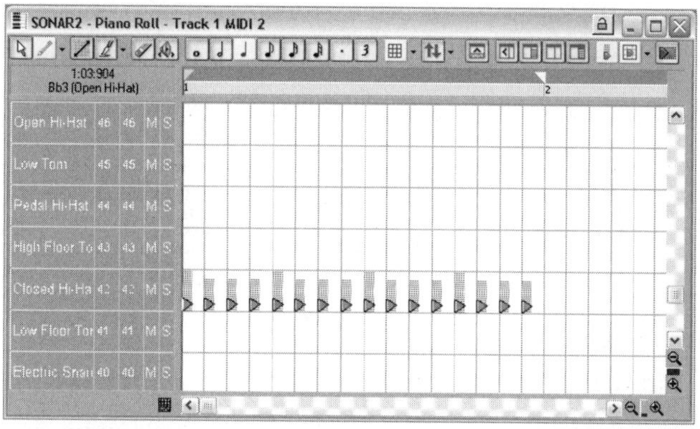

Figure 7.48
Increase the velocity of
the four closed hi-hat
notes that sit right on
each beat.

EVENT INSPECTOR

Instead of using the Show Velocity Tails feature to change the velocity of each note graphically, you can make changes more precisely by selecting notes with the Select tool and then entering a new value in the Vel parameter of the Event Inspector toolbar.

11. Your new drum pattern sounds pretty good, no? I know it's basic, but I mainly want to show you how to use all the tools at your disposal. To create more patterns, just repeat steps 4 through 10. In Step 4, just change the loop points to cover the next measure in the track (or several measures if you want to create longer drum patterns).

AUDITION DRUM INSTRUMENTS

If you ever want to audition the entire drum track, you'll need to disable looping playback and then enable it again to continue working on your current drum pattern. A quick way to do this is to set up a key binding for the Loop On/Off function.

Also remember that as you're listening to your drum patterns, you can mute and solo individual instruments by using the M and S buttons next to each instrument in the Note Map pane. And for quick access to the drum map parameter settings for an individual instrument, just double-click on the instrument.

The Pattern Brush

If you're not inclined to compose your own drum parts, then you'll really enjoy SONAR's Pattern Brush tool. Also found in the Piano Roll view (see Figure 7.49), the Pattern Brush tool allows you to create drum parts by "painting" in whole drum patterns that have already been composed for you.

Figure 7.49

Access the Pattern Brush tool in the Piano Roll view.

Composing with the Pattern Brush

To compose drum parts using the Pattern Brush tool, follow these steps:

1.   Set up a MIDI drum track as I explained in the "Composing Drum Tracks" section of this chapter.

2.   Click on the down arrow to the right of the Pattern Brush button in the Piano Roll view toolbar. The first four options in the menu allow you to adjust how the Pattern Brush will work. The Velocity option allows you to specify an exact MIDI velocity to which all your notes will be set. The Note Duration option makes all your notes use the duration specified in the Piano Roll view toolbar. Personally, I don't use those settings very much because you can achieve the same thing using the Draw tool, as I described earlier in the chapter. The Use Pattern Velocities and Use Pattern Polyphony options tell SONAR to use the MIDI velocities and rhythms from the predefined patterns, which you can choose from the remaining menu selections. So basically, you'll almost always want to have the Use Pattern Velocities and Use Pattern Polyphony options activated. Activate them now for this example.

3.   The lower part of the Pattern Brush menu allows you to choose predefined drum patterns you can use to compose your drum tracks. In this example, choose Kick+Snare Patterns (D-F) > Funky 1 for your first pattern.

4.   Choose the Pattern Brush tool by clicking on the Pattern Brush button on the toolbar. Then click and drag your mouse from left to right over the first measure in your drum track. It doesn't matter at what vertical location you drag; the drum

notes are placed automatically with the correct instruments at the correct rhythmic locations (see Figure 7.50). Is that cool or what?

Figure 7.50
Just click and drag the Pattern Brush to create a drum part automatically.

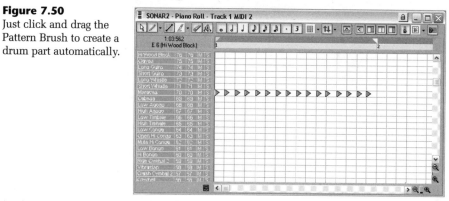

5. Now add another instrument to the drum part by choosing a different Pattern Brush pattern. This time try the Dumbec, Egg Shaker, Finger Bongos, and Guiro Patterns > Egg Shaker 1 pattern. Click and drag the Pattern Brush. You'll notice that this adds a Maracas instrument to the drum part.

6. Let's add one more final touch. Choose Conga Patterns > Congas 1 for the Pattern Brush pattern, and "paint" the instrument into the drum part (see Figure 7.51).

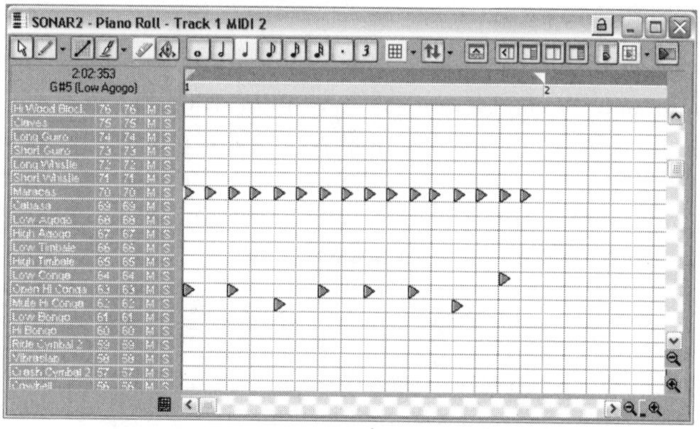

Figure 7.51
Add a conga instrument to the drum part.

7. The drum part sounds pretty good, but it could use a few adjustments. The Open Hi Conga and Mute Hi Conga instruments are a bit low in volume. Double-click on each instrument and set the Vel+ parameters to 36 and 45, respectively. You see; this is where the Vel+ and V Scale settings can come in handy.

8. You can't really hear the Mute Hi Conga instrument because it sounds at the same time as the snare drum. To fix this, activate the Select tool and then drag both notes for that instrument to the left by one sixteenth note (see Figure 7.52). Just because you are using predefined patterns, that doesn't mean you can't make changes to them. Many times you'll find that you come up with something even better.

CHAPTER 7

Figure 7.52

Fix the Mute Hi Conga with some small adjustments.

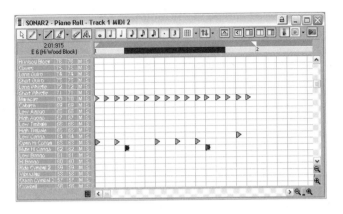

You can keep going to add more instruments to the drum part or add more drum parts (measures) to the drum track. The process is really intuitive. Don't be afraid to experiment. If something doesn't sound good, just change it. Choose Edit > Undo and try a different pattern. Or make small adjustments like I showed you earlier. I guarantee you'll have a lot of fun with the Pattern Brush while creating your own drum tracks.

Creating Pattern Brush Patterns

After you've created some of your own drum patterns, you might want to save them for future use in other projects. You can do this by converting them into patterns that can be used with the Pattern Brush. Follow these steps to do so:

1. After you've finished creating a drum pattern as I described in the previous sections, close the Piano Roll view and switch to the Track view.

2. You'll notice a clip in the Clips pane of the Track view that represents the drum pattern you just created (see Figure 7.53). Click on the clip to select it, and then choose Edit > Copy. Make sure the Events in Tracks option is activated in the Copy dialog box, and then click on OK.

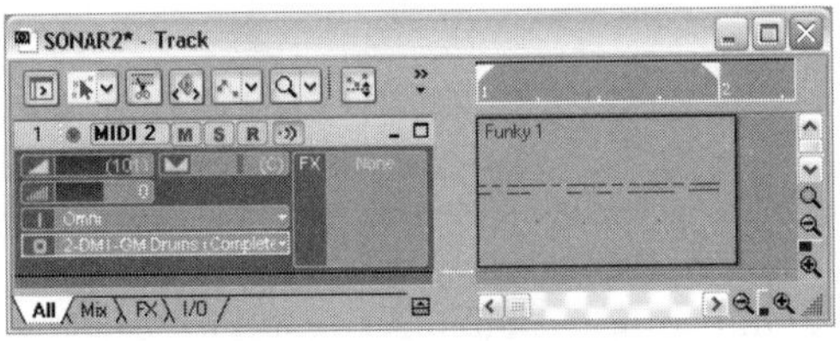

Figure 7.53

A clip in the Track view represents your newly created drum pattern.

3. Choose File > New. Then select the Pattern Brush Template and click on OK. Also, close the File Info window. In the Track view of this new project, you'll see a single MIDI track with a bunch of markers placed in it. Each marker is there to represent a different pattern. You can put as many patterns in a Pattern Brush file as you'd like, but the last marker in the file always has to be an END marker.

4. Set the Now time to the beginning of the project.

5. Choose Edit > Paste, leave the Paste dialog box settings as they are, and click on OK. Your drum pattern will be pasted in the place of the first pattern in the project.

6. You can add more patterns if you want, but for now just delete the rest of the pattern markers and move the END marker to the beginning of measure 2 (2:01:000), as shown in Figure 7.54. You can also change the name of the first pattern marker to something that describes the pattern. This name will be displayed later in the Pattern Brush menu.

Figure 7.54

Paste your drum patterns in a new file with markers.

7. Choose File > Save As. Set the Save as Type parameter to MIDI Format 0. Type a name for the file. Also be sure to save the file in the same folder location as specified in the Patterns parameter of the Global Options > Folders dialog box. Initially, SONAR has this location set to the C:\Program Files\Cakewalk\SONAR 3\Pattern Brush Patterns folder. Click on Save.

Now your new Pattern Brush patterns will be displayed in the Pattern Brush menu for you to use in future projects.

Dealing with Controllers

When you open a MIDI track in the Piano Roll view, in addition to the notes in the Drum Grid and Note panes, SONAR will display the MIDI controller data for that track in the Controllers pane (see Figure 7.55). Because there are many different types of MIDI controller messages, the Piano Roll view displays only one type at a time to help you avoid confusion. You can tell the type of MIDI controller that's being displayed by looking at the Control Type drop-down lists located to the left of the Controllers pane. The first list shows the type of controller being displayed. The second list shows the number of the controller being displayed. The third list shows the MIDI channel being used for that controller. You can change the values for any of these lists by simply clicking on them and selecting a new value from the list that appears. Initially, MIDI Note Velocity is shown when you open the Piano Roll view.

Figure 7.55

MIDI controller data for a track is displayed in the Controllers pane when you open the Piano Roll view.

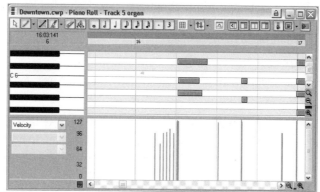

Each controller is represented by a colored line that runs from the bottom of the Controllers pane toward the top. The height of the line designates the value of the controller according to the ruler on the left side of the Controllers pane. This ruler gives you a reference for determining the value of a controller; it usually runs from 0 to 127, starting at the bottom of the Controllers pane and going all the way to the top. The values can be different according to the type of controller being edited. The horizontal location of a controller designates its start time according to the Time Ruler at the top of the Piano Roll view.

PITCH WHEEL

In one instance, the controllers in the Controllers pane and the ruler values appear differently. If you select the pitch wheel event type for editing, you'll notice that, instead of originating at the bottom of the Controllers pane, the controllers start at the center and extend either up or down (see Figure 7.56). They do so because values for the pitch wheel range from −8192 to 0 to +8191, which you can see in the ruler values. Other than that, pitch wheel events are handled exactly the same as any other types.

Figure 7.56

The pitch wheel is the one exception to the way controllers are displayed in the Controllers pane.

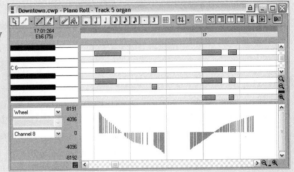

Editing Controllers

You edit controllers exactly the same way as you do notes in terms of selecting, copying, cutting, deleting, pasting, and so on. Unfortunately, no precision editing is available like with the Note Properties dialog box, although you can edit the numerical values of controllers via the Event List view (which you'll learn about later in this chapter, in the "Using the Event List View" section). One other exception is that you can't move controllers simply by dragging them, as you can with notes. You have to cut and paste them instead.

Erasing and Scrubbing

The Erase and Scrub tools work with controllers exactly the same as they do with notes.

Drawing Controllers

You add controllers pretty much the same way you add notes, but with a couple of exceptions. When you're using the Draw tool, in addition to clicking in the pane to add a single controller, you can click and drag within the pane to add a series of controllers.

In addition, you can use another tool, called the Draw Line tool (its button is located right next to the Draw tool button on the toolbar) to create a smooth series of controllers starting at one value and smoothly increasing or decreasing to another value. Without this tool, it's a bit difficult to achieve the same effect by drawing freely with the Draw tool. To use the Draw Line tool, you just click anywhere in the Controllers pane at the controller value you want to begin with, and then drag either to the left or right within the pane to draw a line that ends at a different time and a different value. When you release the mouse button, SONAR will add a smooth series of controller values from the first point to the second point in the pane.

Inserting Controllers

SONAR provides one other way to add a smooth series of controller values to your tracks—the Insert Series of Controllers function. I find using the Draw Line tool in the Piano Roll view much more intuitive, but if you need to add controllers over a very long span of time, the Insert Series of Controllers function can be useful. To use it, just follow these steps:

1. Select the track to which you want to add the controller values. You can do so either in the Piano Roll view or the Track view.

2. Select Insert > Series of Controllers to open the Insert Series of Controllers dialog box (see Figure 7.57).

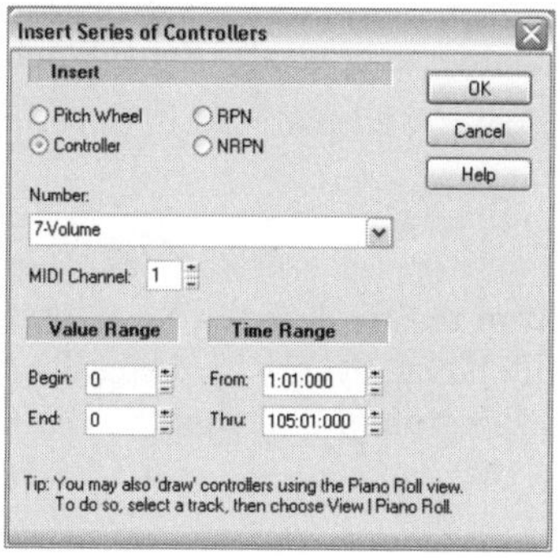

Figure 7.57
Using the Insert Series of Controllers dialog box, you can add a series of controllers that change smoothly from one value to another.

3. In the Insert section, choose the type of controller you want to add, the number of the controller (if appropriate), and the MIDI channel you want the controller to use.

4. In the Value Range section, type numbers for the Begin and End parameters. These numbers determine the values of the controller over the range of the series. For example, if you're using a volume controller type, you can have an instrument get louder over time by typing a small value for Begin and a larger value for End. If you want the instrument to get softer over time, you type a larger value for Begin and a smaller value for End.

5. In the Time Range section, type the measure, beat, and tick values for the location in the project where you want the series of controllers to be inserted.

TIME RANGE SELECTION

You also can set the Time Range parameters before you open the Insert Series of Controllers dialog box by dragging your mouse pointer over the Time Ruler in either the Piano Roll view or the Track view. This action sets up a selection within the project that is used automatically to set the From and Thru values of the Time Range parameters.

Bank/Patch Change

The one type of data that the Piano Roll view doesn't allow you to manipulate is the bank/patch change. This type of event is useful when you want the sound of your MIDI instrument to change automatically during playback of your project. SONAR provides an Insert Bank/Patch Change function that you can use if you need it.

Using the Insert Bank/Patch Change function is very simple. You just follow these steps:

1. Click on the number of the track in the Track pane into which you want to insert the bank/patch change.

2. Set the Now time to the measure, beat, and tick at which you want the bank/patch change to occur.

3. Choose Insert > Bank/Patch Change to open the Bank/Patch Change dialog box.

4. Choose a bank select method, bank, and patch from the appropriate drop-down lists.

5. Click on OK.

SONAR will insert a bank/patch change event in the track at the Now time you specified. By the way, you can insert (and also edit) bank/patch change events by using the Event List view; I'll describe that task later in the "Editing Events" section of this chapter.

Using the Event List View

For the most precise data editing (meaning individual events and their properties), you have to use the Event List view (see Figure 7.58). Using this view, you can add, edit, and delete any kind of event in any track within the entire project. The Event List view doesn't resemble any of the other views; instead of providing a graphical representation of your data, it provides a numerical representation, which you can edit and view. The Event List view displays events as one long list of columns and rows (similar to a spreadsheet). Each row holds the data for a single event, and columns separate the event's different properties.

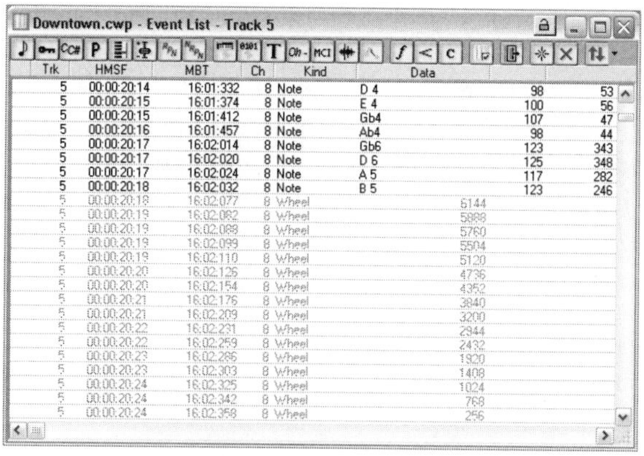

Figure 7.58

You can use the Event List view to edit events numerically using a spreadsheet-like format.

You can use the first column in the list to select events (which I'll describe later, in the "Selecting Events" section). The second column (titled Trk) shows the track number in which an event is stored. The third column (titled HMSF) shows the start time of an event in hours, minutes, seconds, and frames. The fourth column (titled MBT) also shows the start time of an event, but as measures, beats, and ticks. If an event is a MIDI event, the fifth column (titled Ch) shows the MIDI channel to which that event is assigned. The sixth column (titled Kind) shows the type of data an event holds (for example, a MIDI note event). The seventh column (titled Data) actually spans the seventh, eighth, and ninth columns (the last three), and these columns hold the data values associated with each event. For instance, for a MIDI note event, the seventh column would hold the pitch, the eighth column would hold the velocity, and the ninth column would hold the duration for the note.

Because the Event List view doesn't have any graphical data to contend with, it doesn't provide any Snap to Grid, Zoom, Time Ruler, or Marker features. It does allow you to scroll the list up and down and left and right so you can access all the events shown. It also provides a toolbar full of buttons (which I'll describe in the "Filtering Events" section). One button that you'll recognize, though, is the Pick Tracks button. Just as with the other views, the Event List view allows you to display the data from multiple tracks at once.

Opening the View

You open the Event List view via the Track view. You simply select one or more tracks and then select View > Event List or right-click on one of the selected tracks and choose View > Event List from the drop-down menu. That's all there is to it.

Filtering Events

There are many different types of events available in SONAR, and sometimes having to wade through them all in the Event List view can get a bit confusing, especially when you're displaying the data from multiple tracks. To help you deal with the problem, the Event List view allows you to filter each of the event types from being displayed. This filtering does not affect the data at all; it just helps unclutter the list display if that's what you need.

The first 18 buttons on the toolbar represent different event types. Initially, all these buttons are set so that all event types are shown in the list when you open the Event List view. By clicking on a button, you can filter out its associated event type from the list. You can click on as many of the buttons as you want to filter out multiple types of events. Clicking on a button again turns off its associated event type filter so the events can be shown in the list again. To see the type of event with which each button is associated, just hover your mouse pointer over a button until the pop-up text appears, showing the name of the event type.

The Event Manager

If you find it easier to deal with the event types by name rather than by using the buttons, you can use the Event Manager. Just press V on your computer keyboard to open the Event Manager dialog box (see Figure 7.59).

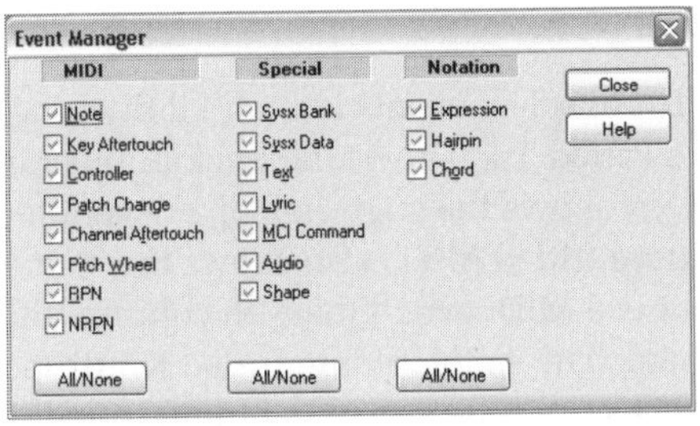

Figure 7.59
You can use the Event Manager dialog box to filter event types by name.

Initially, all the event types are activated so they will be displayed in the list. To filter out a certain type, just click on it to remove its check mark. You can also use the All/None buttons to quickly activate or deactivate groups of event types. Click on the Close button when you're done.

EVENT TYPE LIST
You can also filter out event types by simply right-clicking anywhere in the Event List and then selecting an event type from the drop-down list.

Editing Events

If you've ever used a spreadsheet application, you'll be right at home with editing events in the Event List view. To navigate through the list, you use the arrow keys on your computer keyboard. These keys move a small rectangular cursor through the list. This cursor represents the Now time. As you move the cursor up and down through the list, the Now time changes to reflect the time of the event upon which the cursor is positioned. You also can move the cursor (which I'll call the Now time cursor from this point on) left and right to access the different event parameters.

Changing Event Parameters

To change an event parameter, just position the Now time cursor over the parameter, type a new value, and then press the Enter key on your computer keyboard to accept the new value.

MOUSE EDITING

You also can increase or decrease the value of an event parameter by double-clicking on it and then clicking on the little plus or minus buttons, respectively.

You can change the start time in the HMSF or MBT columns, the MIDI channel, the type of event, and most or all of the values in the data columns, depending on the type of event you're editing. The only thing you can't change is the track number of an event.

Changing the type of an event via the parameter in the Kind column is a bit different from changing the values of the other parameters. Instead of typing a new value, you either must press the Enter key on your computer keyboard or double-click on the parameter. This action opens the Kind of Event dialog box (see Figure 7.60). The Kind of Event dialog box displays a list of all the event types available. Select the type of event you want to use and then click on OK.

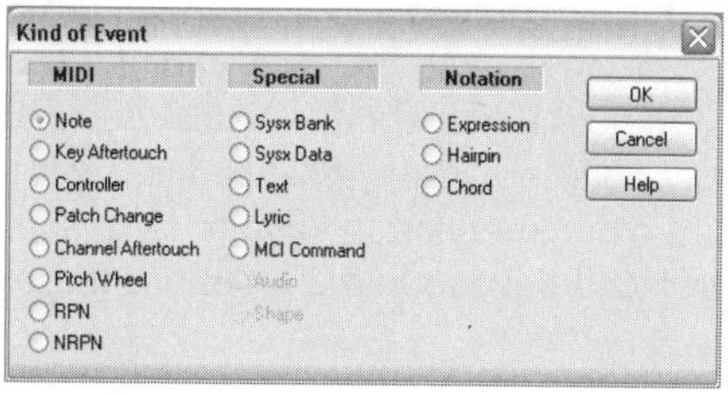

Figure 7.60
You use the Kind of Event dialog box to change the type of an event.

Selecting Events

If you ever need to copy, cut, or paste events in the Event List view, you have to select them first. To select a single event, just click in the first column of the row representing the event. You also can select more than one event by dragging your mouse pointer in the first column of the list. If you want to remove a selection, click or drag a second time.

Inserting Events

You can add new events to the list by using the Insert function. It works as follows:

1. Position the Now time cursor at the point in the list at which you want to insert a new event.

POSITION THE NOW TIME CURSOR

Setting the position of the Now time cursor in the Event List view isn't very intuitive. Because the list gives you such a specific close-up look at your data, it's sometimes hard to tell where in your project the Now time cursor is pointing. You might find it easier to use one of the other views (such as the Track view or the Piano Roll view) to position the Now time cursor. That way, you get a graphical representation of your project and a better feel for the placement of the cursor. Then you can simply switch to the Event view, and the cursor will be positioned exactly at the point where you want to insert the new event (or at least very close to it).

2. Press the Insert key on your computer keyboard or click on the Insert Event button in the toolbar (the one with the star shown on it). SONAR will create a new event in the list using the same parameter values as the event upon which the Now time was positioned.

3. Edit the event parameters.

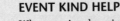

EVENT KIND HELP

When you're changing the type of event using the Kind parameter, the values in the Data columns change according to the type of event you choose. For a list of all the types of events available, along with all their associated parameters, look in the SONAR Help file under Editing MIDI Events And Controllers > The Event List View > Event List Buttons And Overview.

Special Events

There are two types of events in SONAR that you can access only via the Event List view. You can't manipulate them in any of the other views. The first one, called a *text event*, allows you to add notes to the data in your project. I'm not talking about musical notes; I'm talking about text notes. (You know, like those little sticky notes you have plastered all over your studio.) Text events can act as little reminders to yourself in case you need to keep track of some kind of special information in certain parts of your project. I haven't had a lot of use for text events, but it's nice to know they're available if I need them.

The other type of special event is called the *MCI Command event*, or the *Windows Media Control Interface (MCI) command event.* You can use the MCI Command event to control the multimedia-related hardware and software in your computer system. For example, by setting the type of an event to MCI Command and setting the event's Data parameter to PLAY CDAUDIO, you can make the audio CD inside your CD-ROM drive start to play. You also can use MCI Command events to play audio files, video files, and more. But the problem is that you can't synchronize any of these files to the music in your project, so you can't really use these events for too many things. In addition, the subject of MCI commands can be complex and is well beyond the scope of this chapter. If you want to find more information, take a look at http://msdn.microsoft.com and do a search for the term *MCI.*

Deleting Events

Erasing events from the list is as easy as it gets. Just move the Now time cursor to the row of the event you want to remove and then click on the Delete Event button on the toolbar (the one with the big red X on it). Alternatively, you can press the Delete key on your computer keyboard.

If you want to delete more than one event, select the events you want to remove and then select Edit > Delete to open the Delete dialog box. The parameters in this dialog box work the same way I described them in the Track view section of this chapter.

Playing

If you want to quickly preview the event you're currently editing, you can have SONAR play back that single event by holding down the Shift key on your computer keyboard and then pressing the spacebar. If you continue holding the Shift key, each press of the spacebar will scroll down through the list and play each event. This capability is especially useful for testing MIDI note events.

CHAPTER 7

PRINT THE EVENT LIST
You can print a hard copy reference of the Event List if you have a printer connected to your computer system. While the Event List view is open, just select File > Print to print a copy of the list. You also can preview the list before you print it by choosing File > Print Preview.

Using the Tempo View

You learned how to set the initial tempo for a project by using the Tempo toolbar in Chapter 4. But in addition to the initial project tempo, you also can have the tempo change automatically during playback. To allow you to specify tempo changes in a project, SONAR provides the Tempo view (see Figure 7.61). The Tempo view has some similarities to the Piano Roll view in that it displays a graphical representation of the data you need to manipulate—in this case, tempo. The Tempo view shows the tempo as a line graph with the horizontal axis denoting time (via the Time Ruler) and the vertical axis denoting tempo value.

Figure 7.61
The Tempo view displays the tempo in a project as a line graph.

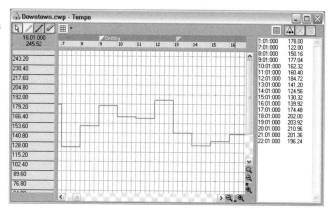

More precisely, the Tempo view consists of three major sections—the toolbar (located at the top of the view, containing all the view's related controls), the Tempo pane (located in the main part of the view, displaying all the tempo changes in the project as a line graph), and the Tempo Change pane (located at the right of the view, showing a list of all the tempo changes within the project). Because tempo affects the entire project, no track selection tools are available here.

Because the Tempo view shows tempo changes graphically, it has scroll bars and zoom tools just like in the Piano Roll view. And, of course, these tools work the same here. In addition, this view provides a Snap to Grid function, which is represented by the Grid button on the toolbar. The Tempo view also contains a marker area and a Time Ruler located just above the Tempo pane. Along the left of the Tempo pane are the tempo measurements, which show the value of the tempo changes displayed in the line graph.

Opening the View

To open the Tempo view, simply choose View > Tempo. You don't need to select a track, clip, or anything else. For a new project (or a project that doesn't contain any tempo changes), the Tempo view will display a straight horizontal line located vertically on the graph at the tempo measurement value that corresponds to the current tempo setting for the project. For instance, if your project has a main tempo of 100, then the line is shown at a tempo measurement of 100 on the graph. In addition to the horizontal line, a single entry in the Tempo Change pane shows the measure, beat, and tick at which the tempo event occurs, along with the tempo value itself. In this example, it is 1:01:000 for the measure, beat, and tick, and 100 for the tempo value.

Editing Tempo Changes

Just as you can edit controller messages graphically in the Piano Roll view, you can use the Tempo view to edit tempo changes. Also, just as in the Piano Roll view, the Tempo view provides Select, Draw, Draw Line, and Erase tools. All these tools work the same way they do in the Piano Roll view. You can use the Select tool to select individual changes and groups of tempo changes by clicking and dragging. Using the Draw tool, you can literally draw in tempo changes on the line graph in the Tempo pane. The Draw Line tool enables you to create smooth tempo changes from one value to another by clicking and dragging. And using the Erase tool, you can erase single and multiple tempo changes by clicking and dragging. As you draw and erase within the Tempo pane, the line graph will change its shape accordingly to display how the tempo will change over time as the project plays. An increase in the tempo (*accelerando*, in musical terms) is shown as an incline in the line graph, and a decrease in tempo (*diminuendo*, in musical terms) is shown as a decline in the line graph.

The Tempo Change Pane

As I mentioned earlier, tempo changes also are listed numerically in the Tempo Change pane. Luckily, you can edit them there too. I find it easier and more accurate to add and edit tempo changes via the Tempo Change pane than to draw them in.

Inserting Tempo Changes

To add a new tempo change to the list, follow these steps:

1. Set the Now time to the measure, beat, and tick at which you want the tempo change to occur.

2. Click on the Insert Tempo button on the toolbar (the one with the plus sign on it) or press the Insert key on your computer keyboard to open the Tempo dialog box (see Figure 7.62).

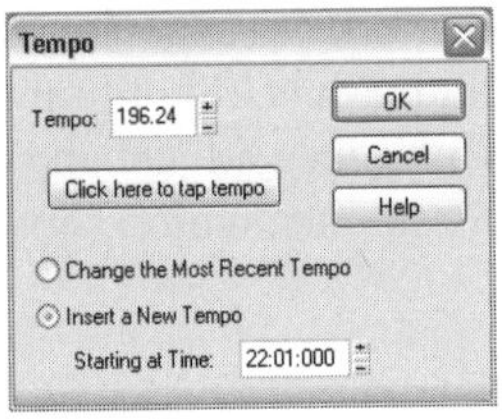

Figure 7.62
In the Tempo dialog box, you can add and edit tempo events.

3. Enter a value for the Tempo parameter. You can also tap out a tempo by clicking on the Click Here to Tap Tempo button. When you click repeatedly on the button, SONAR will measure the time between each click and calculate the tempo at which you're clicking. It will then enter the value into the Tempo parameter automatically.

TAP THE SPACEBAR

Instead of using your mouse to click on the Click Here to Tap Tempo button, you might find it easier (and more accurate) to use the spacebar on your computer keyboard. Click on the button with your mouse once to highlight it, and then use your spacebar to tap out a tempo value.

4. Make sure the Insert a New Tempo option is activated.

5. You shouldn't have to enter a value for the Starting at Time parameter because you set the Now time earlier. However, you can change it here if you want.

6. Click on OK.

SONAR will add the new tempo change and display it in the Tempo Change pane as well as on the graph in the Tempo pane.

Deleting and Editing Tempo Changes

You can edit or remove a tempo change from the list by using the appropriate toolbar buttons. First, select the tempo change you want to edit or delete by clicking on it in the list. If you want to delete the tempo change, click on the Delete Tempo button on the toolbar (the one with the big red X on it) or press the Delete key on your computer keyboard. If you want to edit the tempo change, click on the Tempo Properties button on the toolbar (the very last button at the right end of the toolbar) or press P on your computer keyboard. This action will open the Tempo dialog box. Make any changes necessary, as per the same settings I described for inserting a new tempo change.

Using the Tempo Commands

In addition to the Tempo view (and the Tempo toolbar), SONAR provides two other tempo-related functions. The Insert Tempo Change function works the same as adding a new tempo change in the Tempo Change pane in the Tempo view. However, you can use this function from any of the other views. To access it, just choose Insert > Tempo Change to open the Tempo dialog box (which you learned about earlier).

SONAR also provides a function that allows you to insert a series of tempos so you can have the tempo change smoothly from one value to another over time. Using it is similar to using the Draw Line tool in the Tempo view, but here you specify your values numerically. You use this function as follows:

1. Choose Insert > Series of Tempos to open the Insert Series of Tempos dialog box (see Figure 7.63).

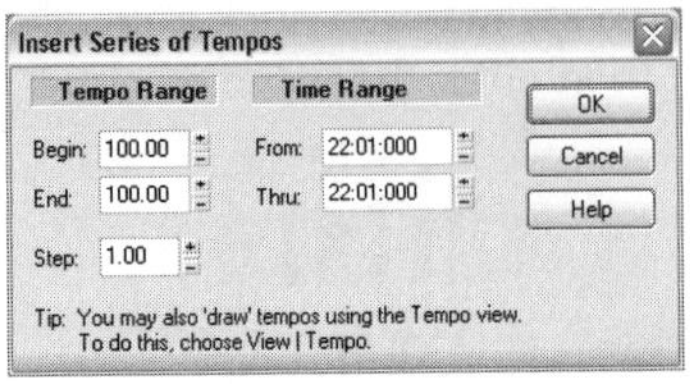

Figure 7.63
You can change the tempo smoothly from one value to another by using the Insert Series of Tempos dialog box.

2. In the Tempo Range section, enter a beginning and an ending value for the range of tempos to be inserted.

3. In the Time Range section, enter a beginning and an ending value for the range of time in your project in which you want the tempo changes to occur.

TIME RANGE SELECTION

If you make a selection by dragging your mouse pointer in the Time Ruler of the Track view, for instance, before you select Insert > Series of Tempos, the Time Range values in the Insert Series of Tempos dialog box will be set according to your selection. This shortcut makes it easier to see where in your project the tempo changes will be inserted.

4. For the Step parameter, enter a beat and tick value for how often you want a tempo change to be inserted within the time range you specified. For example, if you enter a value of 1.00, then the Insert Series of Tempos function will insert a new tempo change at every beat within the time range you specified.

5. Click on OK.

SONAR will insert a smooth series of tempo changes starting and ending with the Tempo Range values you specified within the time range you specified. Any existing tempo changes will be overwritten.

8

Exploring the Editing Tools

In Chapter 7, you learned about some of the essential editing features found in SONAR, including all the views (and the tools they provide), as well as how to manipulate your data via copy, cut, paste, move, delete, and other functions. Although these features provide a lot of power, you might be asking yourself, "Is that all there is?" Not likely! In addition to its fundamental tools, SONAR provides a full arsenal of sophisticated editing features. Some can be used to process audio data, some to process MIDI data, and some to process both kinds of data. One aspect they all have in common, however, is that they can be accessed in more than one view (similar to the copy, cut, and paste functions). Of course, as you learned previously, for MIDI data you'll use the Track, Piano Roll, Staff, and Event views, and for audio data you'll use the Track view.

This chapter will do the following:

▶ Explain advanced data selection

▶ Show you how to change the loudness of audio clips

▶ Describe equalization

▶ Explain quantization

▶ Cover transposition

▶ Show you how to use various advanced timing features

Advanced Data Selection

As you learned in the preceding chapter, you can select the data in your project in each of the views by using some basic clicking and dragging techniques. SONAR also provides some more sophisticated data selection features that enable you to use time as well as individual event properties for more precise editing.

Selecting a Range of Data by Time

If you ever need to select a range of data in a project that is based on time rather than data that is neatly tucked away in individual clips, you can choose Edit > Select > By Time to do so. For example, suppose you need to copy the data in track 8 that falls between the range of 4:2:010 (measure, beat, tick) and 13:3:050. But what if that data is stored in multiple clips within that range, and the clips don't neatly start and end at the beginning and ending times you specified? That's the kind of situation for which this feature is useful. It works like this:

1.   Choose Edit > Select > By Time to open the Select by Time dialog box (see Figure 8.1).

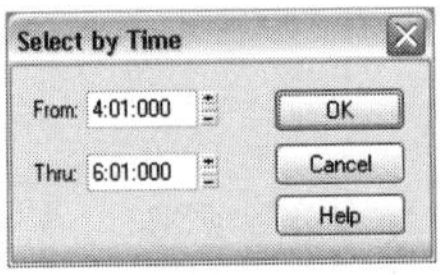

Figure 8.1
You can use the Select by Time dialog box to define a time range within your project in which data will be selected for editing.

2.   Type the beginning (From) and ending (Thru) measure, beat, and tick values to define the range of time you want to select. Then click on OK. You use this dialog box to select a range of time within your project, but it doesn't select any actual data. For that, you need to select the tracks you want to edit.

3.   In the Track view, select the tracks that contain the data you want to edit.

SONAR selects the data in the clips within the tracks in the time range you specified so you can edit it by using copy, cut, and the other features that you'll learn about in this chapter.

USE THE TIME RULER
You also can make time selections in any of the views by simply clicking and dragging on the Time Ruler or by Alt-dragging within a clip (you learned about this approach in Chapter 7). However, by choosing Edit > Select > By Time, you can make more precise selections because you can enter the exact numerical values for the measures, beats, and ticks that define the range.

Selecting a Range of Data by Filter

For really precise editing tasks, you can choose Edit > Select > By Filter. Using this approach, you can refine a selection that you've already made with any of the other methods discussed previously. For instance, if you select some clips or tracks in the Track view, you can choose Edit > Select > By Filter to zero in (so to speak) your selection even further on the individual events within those clips and tracks based on their event properties.

Suppose you have a MIDI track in which you want to change all the notes with a pitch of C4 to C5. You can easily select only those notes by choosing Edit > Select > By Filter, and then you can change their pitch by using the Transpose feature (which you'll learn about later). All the C4 pitches are then changed to C5, but none of the other notes in the track are affected. This feature works as follows:

1.   Select the clips, tracks, or set of events you want to use as your initial selection. You can select clips and tracks in the Track view or a group of events in the Piano Roll view, Event view, or Staff view.

2.   Choose Edit > Select > By Filter to open the Event Filter - Select Some dialog box (see Figure 8.2).

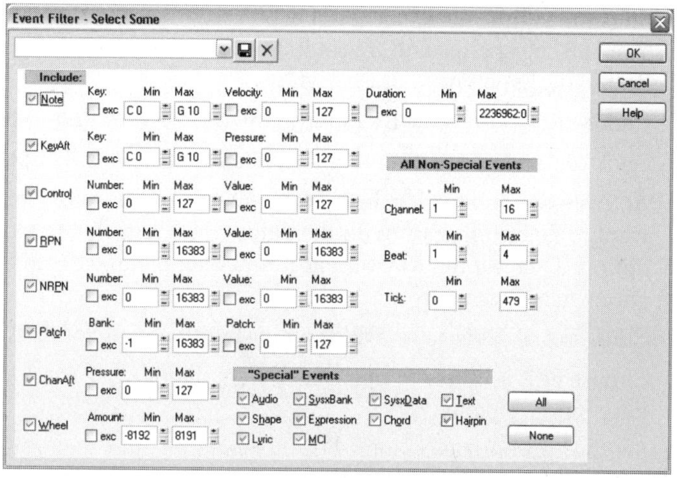

Figure 8.2
You can use the Event Filter - Select Some dialog box to set the criteria for the type of data you want to have selected.

3. Does this dialog box look familiar? The Event Filter - Select Some dialog box is the same as the Event Filter - Search dialog box, which you learned about in Chapter 5. The same information about how to use all the options applies here, so go ahead and set the options as you want.

SAVE A SELECT PRESET

As with the Event Filter - Search dialog box, the Event Filter - Select Some dialog box enables you to save presets for instant access to your favorite settings. By the way, presets are also available in many of the features that you'll learn about later in this chapter. I described how to use them in Chapter 5.

4. Click on OK.

SONAR will search through the data in your initial selection, find the events that fall under the filter parameters you specified, and then select those events while leaving any other events alone. If you want to refine your selection even further, just choose Edit > Select > By Filter again on the previous selection results.

Some Selection Applications

Of course, just describing the selection features at your disposal doesn't always convey the types of things you can accomplish with them. The following section provides a small sample of what you can do with the advanced data selection features in SONAR.

Specific Deletions

I've had many people ask me how to go about deleting specific notes or data within a MIDI track, while at the same time leaving other data in the track alone. Here's an example of how you can do that:

1. Select the clips, tracks, or set of events you want to use as your initial selection. You can select clips and tracks in the Track view or a group of events in the Piano Roll view, Event view, or Staff view.

2. Choose Edit > Select > By Filter to open the Event Filter - Select Some dialog box.

3. Click on the None button to deactivate all the available options.

4. Activate the options for the type of data you want to delete. For example, if you want to delete all notes with the value of C5 within a track, activate the Note option. Then set the Key Min and Key Max parameters to C5. Leave all the other parameters as they are.

5. Click on OK. This selects all the notes with a value of C5 in your initial selection.

6. Choose Edit > Delete to open the Delete dialog box. You learned about this function in Chapter 7.

7. Set the appropriate options. For this example, just make sure the Events in Tracks option is activated so the selected notes will be deleted.

8. Click on OK.

SONAR will delete all the selected data from your initial selection. In this case, all the notes with a value of C5 have been deleted. You can use this procedure for any other kinds of specific data deletions as well. You also can use it to manipulate selected data in other ways. For example, instead of deleting all the C5 notes, maybe you want to transpose them. In that case, instead of using the Delete function, you would use the Transpose function by choosing Process > Transpose in Step 6 of the preceding steps. I'll talk more about the Transpose function later on in this chapter, in the "Transpose" section.

Advanced Audio Editing

Using the cut, copy, paste, and slip editing tools in the Track view, you can manipulate the data in your audio tracks in a variety of ways. SONAR also provides a number of advanced features you can use to adjust the volume, apply equalization, and even reverse the data within audio clips. You access all these features by choosing Process > Audio.

Adjusting Audio Volume

If you ever need to adjust the volume of an audio clip, you can use a number of different SONAR features to increase or decrease the volume of your data.

The 3dB Louder Feature

Using the 3dB Louder feature, you can increase the volume of audio data by 3 dB each time you apply it. So if you want to increase the volume of your data by 6 dB, you can apply the 3dB Louder feature to it twice. To use it, simply select the audio data you want to change and choose Process > Audio > 3dB Louder. SONAR will process the data and you will be able to see the results via the higher amplitude values in the audio waveforms.

CLIPPING AND DISTORTION

Remember the description of setting your input level during the recording process in Chapter 6? I mentioned that you have to be careful not to set the level too high because it could overload the input and cause your audio to be distorted. Well, when you're raising the volume of audio data, you also have to be careful not to raise it too high because it can cause *clipping*. Clipping occurs when SONAR attempts to raise the amplitude of audio data higher than 100 percent. The top and bottom of the waveform become clipped, and the audio sounds distorted when you play it. So be careful when using the 3dB Louder feature. Be sure to keep an eye on the amplitude levels of your audio waveforms, and also be sure to listen to your audio data right after you increase its volume to see whether it sounds okay. If you hear distortion, use Undo to remove the volume change.

The 3dB Quieter Feature

The 3dB Quieter feature works the same way as the 3dB Louder feature except it decreases the volume of audio data by 3 dB.

AUDIO DEGRADATION

You also have to be careful when using the 3dB Quieter feature—not because you might introduce distortion into the audio, but because every time you use it, it degrades the audio slightly. For instance, if you use the 3dB Quieter feature to lower the volume of audio data and then you use the 3dB Louder feature to raise the volume, the quality of the audio will not be the same as it was originally. This difference is due to the limitations of processing digital audio signals, a subject that is a bit complex to explain here. More than likely, though, you won't be able to hear the difference in quality because it really is only a slight degradation, so you don't need to worry about this too much.

The Normalize Feature

Like the 3dB Louder feature, the Normalize feature also raises the volume of audio, but in a different way. Instead of simply increasing the volume, Normalize first scans the audio waveform to find its highest amplitude level. It subtracts that amplitude level from the maximum level, which is 100 percent. Normalize then takes that value and uses it to increase the volume of the audio data. So when all is said and done, the highest amplitude in the waveform is 100 percent, and all the other amplitude values are increased.

In other words, if an audio waveform has its highest amplitude value at 80 percent, Normalize subtracts that value from 100 percent to get 20 percent. It then increases the volume of the audio data by 20 percent so the highest amplitude value is 100 percent and all the other amplitude values are 20 percent higher. Basically, you can use Normalize to raise the volume of audio data to the highest it can be without causing any clipping.

To use Normalize, simply select the audio data and choose Process > Audio > Normalize.

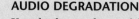

NORMALIZE AFTER PROCESSING

You knew this caution was coming, didn't you? When you use the Normalize feature you have to be careful, just like with the 3dB Louder and 3dB Quieter features. If you increase the volume of the audio data to its maximum, you can easily introduce clipping to the signal if you process it later with some of the other editing or effects features in SONAR. Usually you should use the Normalize feature only after you know you're not going to do any more processing on that particular audio data. Then again, you probably shouldn't use the Normalize feature at all. (See the Tip at the end of the "Crossfades" section.)

The Fade Feature

If you want to get a little more creative with your volume changes, you can build much more complex volume changes by using the Fade/Envelope feature as follows:

FADE-IN AND FADE-OUT

A *fade-in* is a gradual and smooth increase from a low volume (loudness) to a higher volume. This increase in volume is also called a *crescendo* in musical terms. A *fade-out* is the exact opposite—a gradual and smooth decrease from a higher volume to a lower volume. In musical terms, this decrease in volume is called a *decrescendo*.

1. Select the audio data to which you want to apply the fade. Then choose Process > Audio > Fade/Envelope to open the Fade/Envelope dialog box (see Figure 8.3). The dialog box displays a graph. The left side of the graph displays amplitude values, 0 to 100 percent from bottom to top. Inside the graph is a line, which represents the fade that will be applied to your selected audio data. If you look at the line from left to right, the left end of the line represents the beginning of your audio data selection, and the right end of the line represents the end of your audio data selection. When you open the dialog box, the line runs from the bottom left to the top right of the graph. If you leave it this way, a straight linear fade-in will be applied to your audio data because, as you look at the graph, the left end of the line is set at 0 percent, and the right end of the line is set at 100 percent. Therefore, the volume of the audio data would begin at 0 percent and fade all the way up to 100 percent. See how it works?

Figure 8.3
You can use the Fade/Envelope dialog box to apply fades to your audio data.

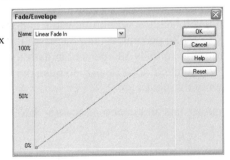

2. You can change the shape of the fade line in one of two ways. You can select one of the six available presets from the drop-down list at the top of the dialog box. Alternatively, you can change the fade line graphically by clicking and dragging the small squares at the ends of the line. These squares are called *nodes*.

3. If you want to create some really complex fades, you can add more nodes by clicking anywhere on the fade line. The more nodes you add, the more flexibility you have in changing the shape of the line (see Figure 8.4).

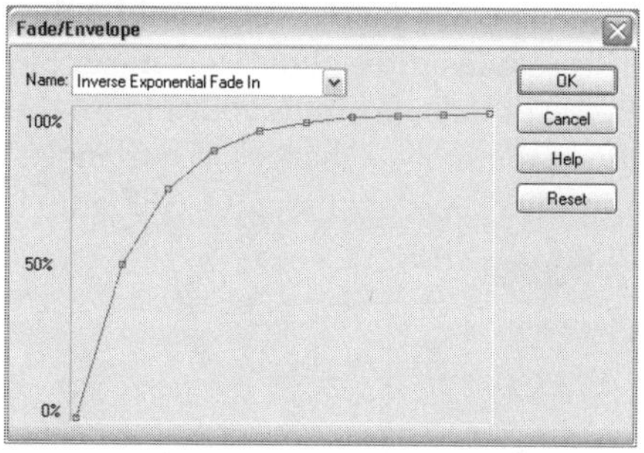

Figure 8.4
You can create some really complex fades by adding more nodes.

4. After you've finished setting up the graph the way you want it, click on OK.

SONAR will change the volume of your audio data selection according to the fade you defined in the Fade/Envelope dialog box.

In addition to the Fade/Envelope feature (which allows you to apply destructive fades to your data), SONAR allows you to apply non-destructive fades. To apply a fade non-destructively, follow these steps:

1. If you want to create a fade-in for an audio clip, position your mouse in the upper-left corner of the clip until the shape of the mouse changes to a triangle. Then click and drag the mouse toward the right end of the clip to define the fade, as shown in Figure 8.5.

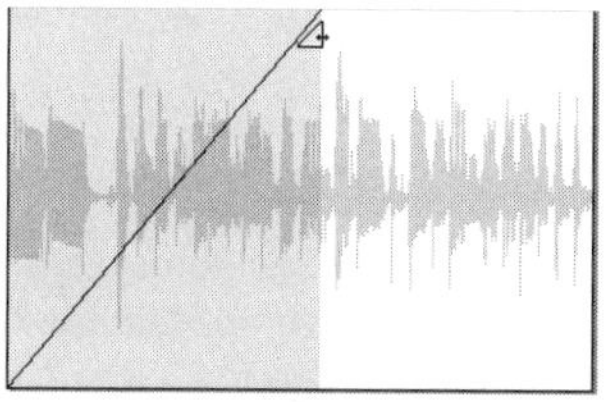

Figure 8.5
Apply a non-destructive fade-in to a clip by clicking in the upper-left corner of the clip and dragging toward the right.

2. If you want to create a fade-out for an audio clip, position your mouse in the upper-right corner of the clip until the shape of the mouse changes to a triangle. Then click and drag the mouse toward the left end of the clip to define the fade, as shown in Figure 8.6.

CHAPTER 8

Figure 8.6
Apply a non-destructive fade-out to a clip by clicking in the upper-right corner of the clip and dragging toward the left.

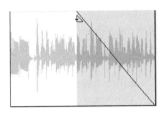

3. You also can define the shape of a fade if you would rather not use the straight linear process. SONAR provides three choices—Linear, Slow Curve, and Fast Curve. To change the type of fade, position your mouse on the fade line at the top of the clip so the shape of the mouse changes to a triangle. Then right-click and choose a fade type from the drop-down menu (see Figure 8.7).

Figure 8.7
Change the fade type by right-clicking at the top of the fade line.

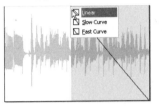

SET THE DEFAULT FADE TYPE

If you use a particular type of fade most often, you can set the default fade types. Just click on the small down arrow next to the Enable/Disable Automatic Crossfades button to reveal a menu, which will let you choose the default types for fade-in, fade-out, and crossfades (see Figure 8.8). I'll talk about crossfades in the next section of this chapter.

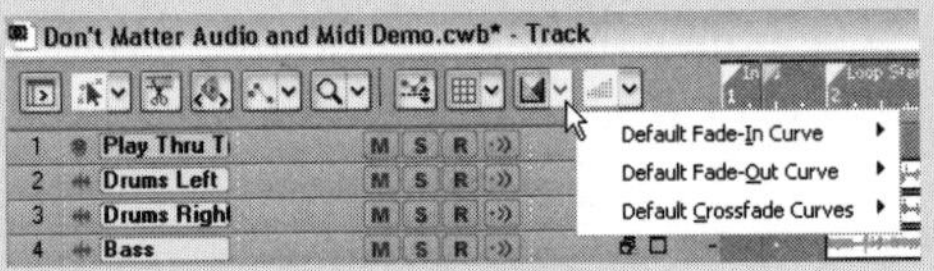

Figure 8.8
Set the default fade type using the Enable/Disable Automatic Crossfades menu.

COMPLEX FADES WITH ENVELOPES

The non-destructive fade feature doesn't allow you to define complex fades by adding nodes as you can with the Fade/Envelope feature, but you can apply non-destructive complex fades or volume changes to a clip (or an entire track) using envelopes. I'll talk more about envelopes in Chapter 12, "Mixing It Down."

Crossfades

A *crossfade* is a special kind of fade that you can apply only to overlapping audio clips. This kind of fade can come in handy when you want to make a smooth transition from one style of music to another or from one instrument to another. It is especially useful when you're composing to video; you can change smoothly from one type of background music to another as the scene changes. Of course, it has many other types of creative uses as well.

When you apply a crossfade to two overlapping audio clips, it works like this: During playback, as the Now time reaches the point at which the two audio clips overlap, the first audio clip fades out and the second audio clip fades in at the same time. You can apply a crossfade as follows:

1. Select the two overlapping audio clips to which you want to apply the crossfade.

DIFFERENT TRACKS

The two audio clips you select don't have to reside on the same track; they only have to overlap in time.

2. Choose Process > Audio > Crossfade to open the Crossfade dialog box (see Figure 8.9).

Figure 8.9
You can apply a crossfade to two overlapping audio clips by using the Crossfade dialog box.

3. Notice that the Crossfade dialog box looks almost exactly the same as the Fade/Envelope dialog box. It works almost exactly the same, too. You can choose from three preset fades, and you can manipulate the fade line with your mouse by adding, clicking, and dragging nodes. The only difference here is that an additional line appears on the graph. The gray line represents the second selected audio clip, and you can't manipulate it directly. As you make changes to the purple line, the gray line mimics it. This feature ensures that the volumes of both audio clips are synchronized, and it provides a perfectly smooth crossfade. So go ahead and make your changes as discussed earlier.

4. Click on OK.

SONAR will apply the crossfade to the parts of the two audio clips that are overlapping. When you play back the audio, you will hear the data from the first clip gradually fade out at the same time the data from the second audio clip gradually fades in.

CHAPTER 8

In addition to the Crossfade feature (which allows you to apply destructive crossfades to your data), SONAR allows you to apply non-destructive crossfades. To apply a crossfade non-destructively, follow these steps:

1. Activate the Enable/Disable Automatic Crossfades button located in the Track view toolbar, which I mentioned earlier. You also can just hit the X key on your computer keyboard for a much quicker method.

2. Click and drag one audio clip so it overlaps another audio clip. Both clips must reside on the same track.

3. In the Drag and Drop Options dialog box, choose the Blend Old and New option.

4. Click on OK. SONAR will overlap the clips and automatically apply a perfect crossfade to the overlapping sections, as shown in Figure 8.10.

Figure 8.10
SONAR automatically applies a crossfade to the overlapping sections of the clips.

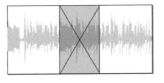

5. As with fades, you can define the shape of a crossfade if you would rather not use the straight linear process. SONAR provides nine different choices. To change the type of crossfade, position your mouse in the crossfade area, and then right-click and choose a crossfade type from the drop-down menu (see Figure 8.11).

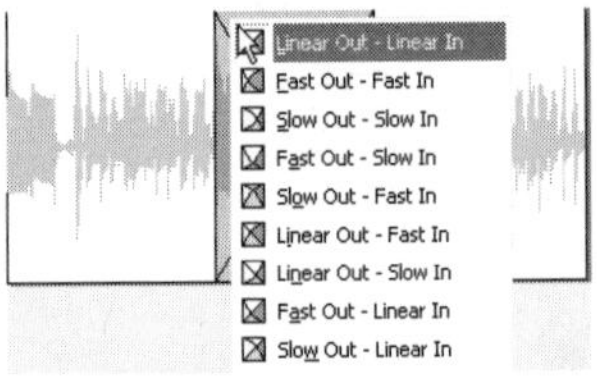

Figure 8.11
Change the crossfade type by right-clicking in the crossfade area.

SET THE DEFAULT CROSSFADE

If you use a particular type of crossfade most often, you can set the default crossfade type. Just click on the small down arrow next to the Enable/Disable Automatic Crossfades button in the Track view toolbar to reveal a menu, which will let you choose the default crossfade type. As I mentioned earlier, this is also how you define the default fade-in and fade-out types.

Equalization (EQ)

You have a radio in your car, right? Maybe even a cassette or CD player, too? If so, then you've probably used equalization without even knowing it. Adjusting the bass and treble controls on your car radio is a form of equalization. Equalization (EQ) enables you to adjust the tonal characteristics of an audio signal by increasing (boosting) or decreasing (cutting) the amplitude of different frequencies in the audio spectrum.

THE AUDIO SPECTRUM

When a musical object (such as a string) vibrates, it emits a sound. The speed at which the object vibrates is called the *frequency*, which is measured in vibrations (or cycles) per second. This measurement is also called *Hertz* (Hz). If an object vibrates 60 times per second, the frequency would be 60 Hz. The tricky point to remember here, though, is that most objects vibrate at a number of different frequencies at the same time. The combination of all these different vibrations makes up the distinct sound (or *timbre*) of a vibrating object. That's why a bell sounds like a bell, a horn sounds like a horn, and so on with all other types of sounds.

Of course, we humans can't perceive some very slow and very fast vibrations. Technically, the range of human hearing resides between the frequencies of 20 Hz and 20 kHz (1 kHz is equal to 1,000 Hz). This range is known as the *audio spectrum*.

Equalization enables you to manipulate the frequencies of the audio spectrum, and because sounds contain many of these frequencies, you can change their tonal characteristics (or timbre).

In other words, using EQ, you can bump up the bass, add more presence, reduce rumble, and sometimes eliminate noise in your audio material. Not only that, but you also can use EQ as an effect. You know how in some of the modern dance tunes, the vocals sound like they're coming out of a telephone receiver or an old radio? That's an effect done with EQ.

SONAR provides two different types of EQ features—Graphic EQ and Parametric EQ. (Actually, five different EQ features are available, but I'll describe the others in Chapter 11, "Exploring Effects.") Both have their strengths and weaknesses.

Graphic EQ

You might already be familiar with graphic equalizers because they are sometimes included on boom boxes and home stereo systems. SONAR's Graphic EQ feature simulates a hardware-based graphic equalizer. It even looks similar (see Figure 8.12).

Figure 8.12
The Graphic EQ feature resembles a real graphic equalizer.

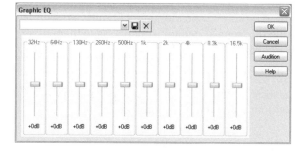

The Graphic EQ feature provides 10 different frequencies (called *bands*) you can adjust. Each band can be boosted or cut by 12 dB. You simply drag the appropriate slider up (boost) or down (cut) to increase or decrease the amplitude of that frequency. But herein lies the weakness of Graphic EQ. Although it's very easy to use, you are limited by the frequencies you can manipulate. You can't change any of the frequencies below, above, or in between the ones provided. Still, Graphic EQ is very useful if you want to make quick equalization changes, and the frequencies provided are the most common ones. It works like this:

1. Select the audio data you want to change.

2. Choose Process > Audio > Graphic EQ to open the Graphic EQ dialog box.

3. Adjust the sliders for the frequencies you want to cut or boost.

WATCH OUT FOR CLIPPING

Be careful when you're boosting frequencies, because doing so also increases the overall volume of the audio data. If you raise the volume too high, you could introduce clipping into the data.

4. Click on the Audition button to hear the first few seconds of the processed audio before you accept the settings. That way, you can decide whether you like the way it sounds. By listening to a few seconds of the audio, you can test whether any clipping occurs. When you're finished listening, click on Stop. By the way, SONAR includes the Audition button in many of its other features too, and it always works in exactly the same way.

CANCEL CLIPPING WITH 3DB QUIETER

If clipping does occur, but you really want to boost some of the frequencies in your audio data, click on Cancel to exit the Graphic EQ dialog box without making any changes. Then lower the volume of the audio data by using the 3dB Quieter feature. Finally, go back and try to apply the EQ again. By lowering the volume of the audio first, you can make enough room to allow more frequency boosting.

5. If you want to be able to use the same EQ settings again later without having to keep making the same slider adjustments, save them as a preset. You learned about presets in Chapter 5.

6. Click on OK.

SONAR will process the selected audio data, and when you play it back it should sound the same as it did when you listened to it using the Audition feature.

ADJUST AUDITION TIME

By default, the Audition feature plays only the first few seconds of the selected data. You can adjust the Audition time by selecting Options > Global to open the Global Options dialog box. Under the General tab, set the Audition Commands For option to the number of seconds you want to use for the Audition feature. I usually like to keep this set anywhere between 5 and 10 seconds.

Parametric EQ

Parametric equalization, on the other hand, is much more powerful and flexible, but it's also a lot more complex and difficult to understand. With the Parametric EQ feature, you're not limited to specific frequencies. You can specify an exact frequency to adjust, and you can cut or boost by much larger amounts. You also can process a range of frequencies at the same time, such as cutting all frequencies above 10 kHz by 20 dB (which would reduce all the frequencies between 10 kHz and 20 kHz but leave the frequencies between 20 Hz and 10 kHz alone). I can explain the Parametric EQ feature a little better by showing you how it works.

1. Select the audio data you want to change.

2. Choose Process > Audio > Parametric EQ to open the Parametric EQ dialog box (see Figure 8.13).

Figure 8.13
The Parametric EQ
feature provides much
more power, but it's also
more difficult to use.

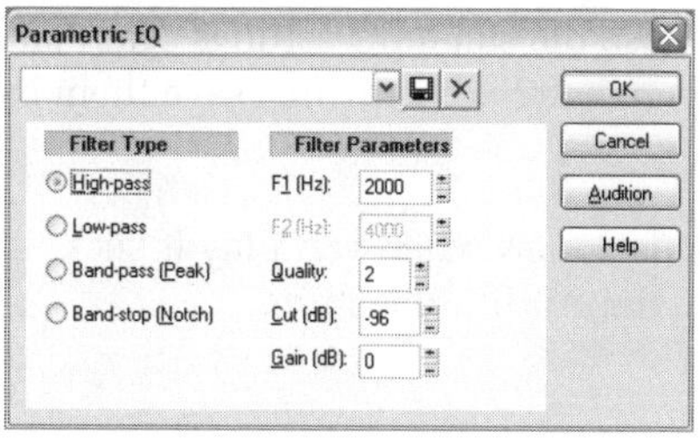

3. Choose one of the options in the Filter Type section—High-Pass, Low-Pass, Band-Pass (Peak), or Band-Stop (Notch). Then set the appropriate parameters in the Filter Parameters section. You can use the F1 and F2 parameters to set the frequencies you want to adjust. They work differently depending on the type of filter you choose. (I'll talk more about this in a minute.)

    The Cut parameter enables you to reduce the volume of the frequencies. To change this setting, just enter a negative number (such as −20) to cut by that number of decibels. The Gain parameter allows you to boost the volume of the frequencies. To change this setting, just enter a positive number (such as +20) to boost by that number of decibels. You can set the Quality parameter to determine how precise the Parameter EQ feature will be when processing your audio.

    If you really want to zero in on a frequency or range of frequencies, use a higher value for the Quality parameter (200 being the highest). This setting gives you a sharper (for lack of a better word) sound. A low value (such as 2) allows the Parametric EQ feature to slightly process the other frequencies not defined specifically or outside the range, which gives you a smoother sound. It's a bit difficult to describe. Experiment with it a little, and you'll be able to hear the difference.

    If you select the High-Pass filter type, all the frequencies below the frequency that you set in the F1 parameter will be cut, and all the frequencies above it will be boosted, depending on how you set the Cut and Gain parameters. If you select the Low-Pass filter type, all the frequencies above the frequency that you set in the F1 parameter will be cut, and all the frequencies below it will be boosted, depending on how you set the Cut and Gain parameters.

CHAPTER 8

If you select either the Band-Pass (Peak) or Band-Stop (Notch) filter type, you have to set up a range of frequencies using both the F1 and F2 parameters. Use the F1 parameter to mark the beginning of the range and the F2 parameter to mark the end of the range. For the Band-Pass (Peak) filter type, any frequencies outside the range are cut, and frequencies within the range are boosted, depending on how you set the Cut and Gain parameters. For the Band-Stop (Notch) filter type, any frequencies outside the range are boosted and frequencies within the range are cut, depending on how you set the Cut and Gain parameters.

4.   Click on the Audition button to hear the first few seconds of the processed audio before you accept the settings. That way, you can decide whether you like the way it sounds. By listening to a few seconds of the audio, you can test whether any clipping occurs. When you're finished listening, click on Stop.

5.   If you want to be able to use the same EQ settings again later without having to keep making the same parameter adjustments, save them as a preset.

6.   Click on OK.

SONAR will process the selected audio data, and when you play it back, it should sound the same way it did when you listened to it using the Audition feature.

Applications

Right about now, you might be saying to yourself, "Okay, EQ sounds pretty cool, but what can I do with it?" Well, you can use EQ in many different ways to process your audio. To begin with, you might want to try some of the presets that come included with SONAR. Not very many are provided for the Graphic EQ and Parametric EQ features, but you can find enough to give you a taste of what EQ can do. After that, you might want to try experimenting with some of the settings described in the following sections.

Fullness

To make your audio sound a little fuller, try boosting the range of frequencies between 100 and 300 Hz by 6 dB. To do so, use the Parametric EQ feature with the Band-Pass (Peak) filter type and set the filter parameters to the following: F1 = 100, F2 = 300, Quality = 2, Cut = 0, and Gain = 6.

Punch

To add a little more punch to your audio, try boosting the range of frequencies between 800 Hz and 2 kHz by 6 dB. To do so, use the Parametric EQ feature with the Band-Pass (Peak) filter type and set the filter parameters to the following: F1 = 800, F2 = 2000, Quality = 2, Cut = 0, and Gain = 6.

Noise Reduction

You can use EQ as a simple means of reducing noise in your audio as well. This is especially true for high-frequency hiss. Use the Parametric EQ feature with the Low-Pass filter type and set the filter parameters to the following: F1 = 18000, Quality = 2, Cut = −96, and Gain = 0.

To get rid of buzzing or humming noises with EQ, use the Parametric EQ feature with the Band-Stop (Notch) filter type and set the filter parameters to the following: F1 = 60, F2 = 60, Quality = 100, Cut = −96, and Gain = 0.

Specific Sounds

EQ is handy for molding specific types of sounds, such as stringed instruments like guitar and bass. For example, to give a bit of a different sound to an acoustic or electric guitar, try using the Graphic EQ feature with the following settings: 32 Hz = −12, 64 Hz = 0, 130 Hz = +4, 260 Hz = +7, 500 Hz = +6, 1 k = +3, 2 k = 0, 4 k = +4, 8.3 k = +7, and 16.5 k = 0.

For a bass guitar, trying using the Graphic EQ feature with the following settings: 32 Hz = −12, 64 Hz = 0, 130 Hz = +6, 260 Hz = +7, 500 Hz = +5, 1 k = +1, 2 k = 0, 4 k =0, 8.3 k = +6, and 16.5 k = +12.

And So On

Don't be afraid to experiment. The more you practice using the EQ features, the more skilled you will become at applying them. Keep one point in mind, though: With just the right amount of spices, a meal tastes great. Too many spices, and the taste takes a turn for the worse. The same goes for applying EQ to your audio. Too much EQ will make your projects sound amateurish.

Getting Rid of Silence

When you record an audio track in SONAR, even though there might be pauses in your performance (such as between musical phrases), your sound card still picks up a signal from your microphone or instrument, and that data is recorded. Although you might think that the data is just recorded silence, in actuality it contains a very minute amount of noise that might come from your sound card itself or the microphone or instrument connected there. More often than not, you can't really hear this noise because it's masked by the other music data in your project. And even during quiet passages, if you have only one or two audio tracks playing, the noise is probably still inaudible. With a large number of audio tracks, however, the noise can add up.

In addition, during playback SONAR still processes those silent passages even though they don't contain any actual music. These passages take up valuable computer processing power and disk space. To remedy this problem, SONAR provides the Remove Silence feature. This feature automatically detects sections of silence in audio clips according to a loudness threshold that you set. Then, by first splitting long audio clips into shorter ones, it removes the resulting clips containing only silence. Thus, SONAR doesn't process that extra data during playback, and it doesn't save it to disk when you save your project.

To detect silent passages in audio, the Remove Silence feature uses a digital noise gate. Depending on the parameter settings you specify, this noise gate opens up when the Remove Silence feature comes upon a section in your audio that has an amplitude level greater than the one you set. It identifies this part of the audio as acceptable sound and lets it pass through. When the level of audio dips below a certain amplitude level that you set, the noise gate identifies that part of the audio as silence, and it closes to stop it from passing through. At that point, the Remove Silence feature splits the audio clip with one new clip containing just the music and another new clip containing just the noise. This process happens over and over until the entire initial audio clip is finished being scanned.

You use this feature by following these steps:

1. Select the audio data you want to scan for silence.

2. Choose Process > Audio > Remove Silence to open the Remove Silence dialog box (see Figure 8.14).

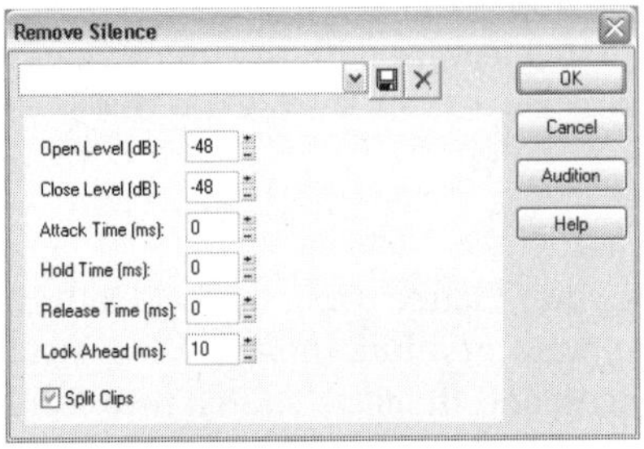

Figure 8.14

You can use the Remove Silence feature to clean up your audio tracks and make them more manageable.

3. Type a value in the Open Level field. This parameter determines how loud the audio data has to be to make the noise gate open, thus identifying the data as acceptable sound.

4. Type a value in the Close Level field. This parameter determines how soft the data has to be to make the noise gate close, thus identifying the data as silence.

5. Type a value in the Attack Time field. This parameter determines how quickly (in milliseconds) the noise gate will open to the amplitude set in the Open Level parameter. If the beginning of your audio data starts off soft (such as with a fade-in) and its amplitude is below the Open Level setting, it could get cut off by the noise gate. For example, the beginnings of the words in a vocal part might be cut. To prevent this problem, you can set the Attack Time parameter so the noise gate takes this kind of situation into consideration.

6. Type a value in the Hold Time field. This parameter determines how long the noise gate will remain open even when the amplitude level of the audio dips below the close level. This parameter is useful when the level of your audio goes up and down very quickly, which could make the noise gate react when it's not supposed to (such as during quick percussion parts). By setting a Hold Time, you can make sure that musical passages containing quick sounds don't get cut by mistake.

7. Type a value in the Release Time field. This parameter is the same as the Attack Time parameter but in reverse. It determines how quickly the noise gate will close after the amplitude of the audio reaches the close level. This feature is useful if your audio data gradually gets softer at the end, such as with a fade-out.

8. Type a value in the Look Ahead field. This parameter determines how long (in milliseconds) the amplitude of the audio must stay above the Open Level before the noise gate will open. Basically, this setting lets you finetune the way the noise gate determines whether the audio being scanned is acceptable sound or silence.

9. If you want SONAR to delete the audio clips that contain only silence, activate the Split Clips option. Otherwise, the silent portions of the audio won't be deleted—they will be reduced to vacant space, but your clips will remain as they are.

10. You can save your settings as a preset, and you can use the Audition feature to hear the results of your settings if you want.

11. Click on OK.

SONAR will scan the selected audio clip and then split it up into pieces (and also remove the clips containing only silence) according to the settings you specified.

SPLIT THE AUDIO CLIPS

Unless the musical passages and silent passages of your audio are separated pretty neatly, it can be difficult to get the right settings for the Release Time feature to perform accurately. You might find it easier and more precise if you simply split the audio clips by hand using the Split function. The process is a bit more time-consuming, though.

Audio to MIDI Conversion

In Chapter 1, you learned about the differences between MIDI and audio data. MIDI data represents recorded performance instructions, and audio data represents actual sound. Because audio data is actual sound, SONAR really doesn't know what's being recorded in an audio track except that it's a bunch of numbers that represent sound. It can't tell whether the sound is notes being played on an instrument, a voice singing lyrics, or even the sound of birds chirping on a sunny summer afternoon.

With recent advances in digital audio-processing technology, however, you can scan audio data for rhythmic values under certain circumstances. This means that a program can scan audio data and determine the rhythm of the instruments being played. Then it can convert that data into MIDI notes. SONAR provides the Extract Timing feature to give you this capability.

Extract Timing

Using the Extract Timing feature, SONAR can scan audio data for quick percussive changes in volume and thus determine the rhythm of the music. Then it can convert those rhythmic values into MIDI notes and velocity messages. The Extract Timing feature works best with single-note melodies and percussion performances.

You might want to use this feature in a number of different situations. One of the most obvious is when you are converting melodies (such as a melody played on a piano) into MIDI notes. The Extract Timing feature will pick up only the rhythm of the notes, but you can easily add the pitches by hand.

To take this example one step further, you can create a new MIDI melody by scanning a percussion track. The new melody will play in sync with the rhythm track, emphasizing the same notes, beats, and so on. Using this feature is a great way to sync a bass line to a percussion part. Another situation might arise in which you already have a bunch of MIDI tracks recorded, and you have some existing percussion audio sample beats that you want to use in your project. Using the Extract Timing feature, you can convert the audio rhythm pulses into tempo changes for your song so the MIDI tracks play at the same tempo as the audio samples. You also can use the Extract Timing feature to create your own templates for the Groove Quantize feature (which you'll learn about later in this chapter, in the "Groove Quantize Feature " section). Here's how Extract Timing works:

1. Select the audio data you want to scan for rhythmic values.

2. Choose Process > Audio > Extract Timing to open the Extract Timing dialog box (see Figure 8.15).

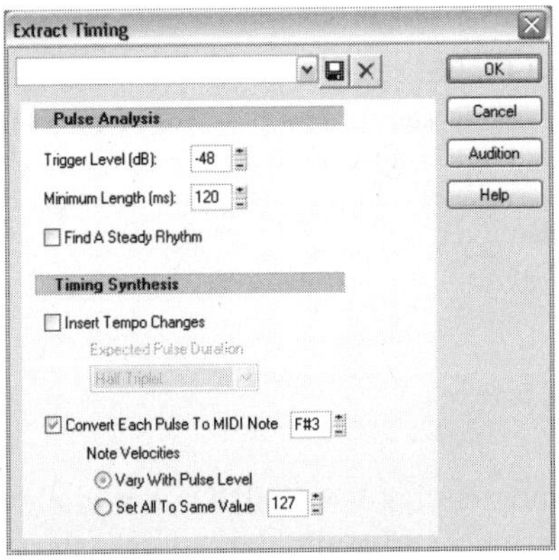

Figure 8.15
You can detect the rhythm of audio recordings using the Extract Timing feature, and then apply that rhythm to your MIDI data.

3. In the Pulse Analysis section, set the Trigger Level parameter. This parameter (set in decibels) tells SONAR how loud the audio data being scanned has to be in order to be considered a rhythmic value. For example, if you have a snare drum track, and each snare drum hit has a volume of −50dB, you have to set the Trigger Level to at least −50dB for the snare drum to be picked up. If you have audio data with many varied volume levels, you have to experiment with the Trigger Level to be sure all the rhythmic values are picked up.

4. Set the Minimum Length parameter. This parameter (set in milliseconds) tells SONAR how much time should be allowed between rhythmic values. If you set the Minimum Length parameter too low, many extraneous values (that aren't really rhythmic values) might be picked up. If you set it too high, not all the legitimate rhythmic values will be picked up. As you do with the Trigger Level parameter, you have to experiment with Minimum Length parameter to find the right setting for the audio material being scanned.

5. Activate or deactivate the Find a Steady Rhythm option. This option tells SONAR to look for a steady rhythm within the audio material being scanned. For example, if you have a snare drum track that has even hits on each beat but also has some syncopated hits between the beats, activating the Find a Steady Rhythm option will weed out the syncopated hits and just pick up the rhythm values that are steady.

6. Set the appropriate parameters in the Timing Synthesis section. The options and values set here depend on what you want to do with the Extract Timing feature. If you want to match the tempo of some existing MIDI tracks to the tempo of some existing audio material, activate the Insert Tempo Changes option. Then set the Expected Pulse Duration parameter to the length of rhythmic values in your audio material. For example, if you are scanning some percussion material that has a

snare drum being played as steady quarter notes, you can set the Expected Pulse Duration parameter to Quarter. If you want to convert the rhythmic values from your audio material into MIDI notes so you can use the data in some of the situations described earlier, you can activate the Convert Each Pulse to MIDI Note option. Then enter the pitch at which you want all the MIDI notes to be set. If you want the velocity values of the MIDI notes to match the volume levels of the rhythmic values being scanned, activate the Vary with Pulse Level option under Note Velocities. Otherwise, you can set all the MIDI notes to the same velocity by activating the Set All to Same Value option and then entering a value for the velocity you want to use.

7. Click on the Audition button. In this case, the button works a bit differently from any of the other editing and effects features in SONAR. Instead of hearing anything, you'll see some red marks placed over the audio material you selected in the Track view (see Figure 8.16). These marks represent the rhythmic values that will be picked up by the Extract Timing feature. You need to see whether they match up to the rhythmic values in the audio material. If they do, you can move on to the next step; otherwise, you might need to adjust some of the parameters a little more to make everything line up correctly.

Figure 8.16
Before you leave the Extract Timing dialog box, you should use the Audition feature to make sure the correct rhythmic values from the audio material are being picked up.

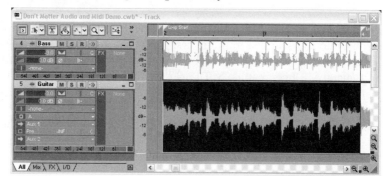

8. Click on OK.

Depending on the parameter settings you chose, SONAR will scan the selected audio data and attempt to detect the rhythmic values of the material. If you activated the Insert Tempo Changes option, SONAR will insert tempo changes into your project so the MIDI tracks will play along at the same tempo as the audio material. If you activated the Convert Each Pulse to MIDI Note option, SONAR will store the MIDI note data temporarily on the clipboard. From there, you can paste the data into a clip or track using the Track or Piano Roll views, and then use it to create a new melody or bass line that plays along with the audio material.

Extract Timing Example

The Extract Timing feature is a bit complicated, and it might be difficult to understand why you need it. Take a look at a sample application to make it a bit clearer.

1. Open the sample project called Don't Matter Audio and MIDI Demo.cwb that is included with SONAR.

2. Close the File Info window and the Staff view. You won't need them.

3. Select the first clip in track 5 (Guitar).

4. Choose Process > Audio > Extract Timing to open the Extract Timing dialog box.

5. Set the Trigger Level parameter to −17dB.

6. Set the Minimum Length parameter to 50 milliseconds.

7. Because the audio material you're scanning has an irregular rhythm, make sure the Find a Steady Rhythm option is deactivated.

8. Activate the Convert Each Pulse to MIDI Note option, and set the note value to G#4.

9. Under Note Velocities, activate the Vary with Pulse Level option.

10. Click on OK. SONAR will scan the audio material, convert the rhythmic values to MIDI note and velocity data, and store the data on the clipboard.

11. Choose Edit > Paste to open the Paste dialog box.

12. Set the Starting at Time parameter to 2:01:000 (in measures, beats, and ticks).

13. Set the Repetitions parameter to 3.

14. Set the Starting at Track parameter to New.

15. Click on OK.

SONAR will create a new track (track 10) containing three clips, each of which contains the rhythmic data that was scanned from the first clip of the guitar track. Before you play the project back to hear how it sounds, be sure to set the Output and Channel for track 10. Set it so the track uses your General MIDI-compatible MIDI instrument and MIDI channel 10 (the standard channel for drums). When you play the project, you'll hear a cowbell sound playing along in time with the rest of the tracks. In particular, it should have almost the same rhythm as the audio material in the guitar track. Some of the MIDI notes might be slightly off, but you can fix their timing in the Piano Roll view. In any case, this example illustrates just one of the many applications for which you can use the Extract Timing feature.

Playing It Backward

Assuming you're old enough to remember vinyl recordings, did you ever take a record and play it backward to see whether your favorite band had left some satanic messages in their songs or perhaps a recipe for their favorite lentil soup? Well, guess what? You can do the same thing with your audio data. SONAR lets you flip the data in an audio clip so that it plays in reverse.

This feature doesn't have much practical use, but combined with some other processing, it can render some cool effects. To use it, simply select the audio clip you want to change and choose Process > Audio > Reverse. Now the data in that clip will play backward.

REVERSE A TRACK

If you want to reverse the data in an entire track, make sure to combine all the audio clips in the track into one large audio clip first. If you don't, the data in each separate clip will be reversed, which is not the same as reversing the entire track. Try it, and you'll hear what I mean.

AUDIO EDITING SOFTWARE

With the combination of the audio editing features discussed so far in this chapter and the audio effects features described in Chapter 11, "Exploring Effects," there's no doubt that SONAR packs a lot of audio data editing power. But there might be times when you still want to use your favorite dedicated audio editing application, such as Sony's Sound Forge (http://mediasoftware.sonypictures.com), Adobe's Audition (http://www.adobe.com), or Steinberg's WaveLab (http://www.steinberg.net). The people at Cakewalk included a little-known feature that enables you to access your favorite audio editing applications from within SONAR. I've tested the previously mentioned products, but there might be others that can use the feature as well.

To use your audio editing software from within SONAR, simply select the audio data that you want to edit, and then select the Tools menu. You should see your software listed at the bottom of the menu. (SONAR automatically detects it during installation.) Choose the program that you want to run. Your audio editing software will open with the audio data you selected, ready to be processed. Make any changes you want and then close the audio editing software. Before closing, the program will ask whether you want to save the changes you made. Click on Yes. The program will close, and you will return to SONAR. Then SONAR will tell you that the audio data has changed and ask whether you want to reload it. Click on Yes. That's all there is to it, and now you have easy access to all the power of your audio editing software as well as SONAR. Isn't that cool?

If your audio editing software doesn't show up in the Tools menu automatically, you can add it to the menu manually by manipulating the Windows Registry. For more information on how to do this, check out my article "Adjusting the Cakewalk Tools Menu" in Issue 2 of the *DigiFreq* newsletter. You can download the issue for free at http://www.digifreq.com/digifreq/issues.asp.

CHAPTER 8

The Edit Menu

Up until now, I've talked about editing features that pertain strictly to audio data. The rest of SONAR's editing features are more diverse in their uses, meaning some can be used with MIDI data, some with audio data, and some with both. The one aspect they all have in common is that they are accessed via the Process menu. Because of their diversity, I'll go through each feature, explaining what it does and how and why you would want to use it. Of course, I'll also let you know the kinds of data with which each feature works.

Deglitch

Occasionally, you might find that while you're playing your MIDI instrument, some unintended notes get recorded along with the legitimate musical material. This is especially true for people who play a MIDI guitar. The strings on a MIDI guitar can easily trigger notes when they're not supposed to. To help with this problem, SONAR provides the Deglitch feature. Using this feature, you can filter out any notes from your MIDI data that don't fall within the correct pitch, velocity, and duration range for the music you're recording. It works like this:

1.   Select the MIDI data from which you want to filter any unwanted notes.

2. Choose Process > Deglitch to open the Deglitch dialog box (see Figure 8.17).

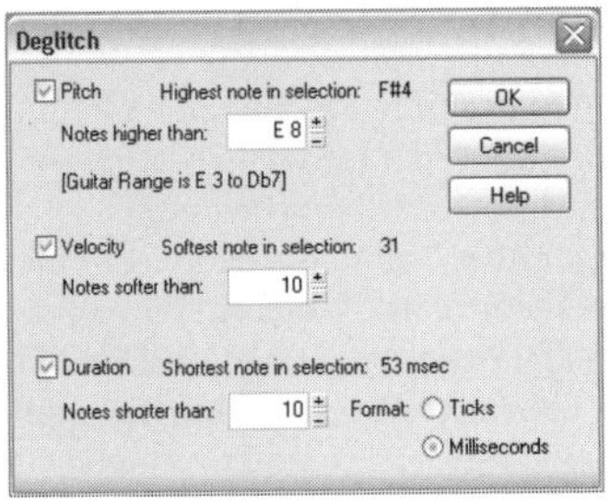

Figure 8.17
Using the Deglitch
feature, you can filter out
any unintended notes
from your MIDI data by
specifying acceptable
pitch, velocity, and
duration ranges.

3. If you want to filter out notes by pitch, activate the Pitch option. In the Notes Higher Than field, type the maximum note value allowed in your material. For example, if the highest note in your MIDI data should be C5, then you should set the Notes Higher Than parameter to C5. If the Deglitch feature finds any notes in the data that have a pitch higher than C5, it will delete them.

4. If you want to filter out notes by velocity, activate the Velocity option. In the Notes Softer Than field, type the minimum velocity value allowed in your material. For example, if the lowest velocity in your MIDI data should be 15, then you should set the Notes Softer Than parameter to 15. If the Deglitch feature finds any notes in the data that have a velocity lower than 15, it will delete them.

5. If you want to filter out notes by duration, activate the Duration option. In the Notes Shorter Than field, type the minimum duration value allowed in your material. Also, be sure to specify whether the duration should be measured in ticks or milliseconds by choosing either the Ticks option or the Milliseconds option for the Format parameter. For example, if the lowest duration in your MIDI data should be 20 ticks, then you should set the Notes Shorter Than parameter to 20 and the Format parameter to Ticks. If the Deglitch feature finds any notes in the data that have durations lower than 20 ticks, it will delete them.

6. Click on OK.

SONAR will scan the selected MIDI data and remove any notes that fall within the criteria you set. By the way, you can scan for pitch, velocity, and duration all at once by having all the options activated if you want.

Slide

Remember back in Chapter 7, when I described how to move clips in the Track view by dragging and dropping them or by using the Clip Properties dialog box to change their start times? Well, the Slide feature performs the same function. You can use it to move clips backward or forward within a track. So why does SONAR provide the same functionality more than once? Because the Slide feature has a few differences. Instead of just working with clips, you can use it with any kind of selected data, from a group of MIDI notes to single events. And instead of having to specify an exact start time (as in the Clip Properties dialog box), you can move data by any number of measures, ticks, seconds, or frames. In addition, the Slide feature doesn't give you the option of blending with, replacing, or sliding over existing events in a track. It simply moves the selected data so it overlaps with any existing data. You use it as follows:

1.   Using the appropriate view, select the MIDI data or audio clips you want to move.

2.   Choose Process > Slide to open the Slide dialog box (see Figure 8.18).

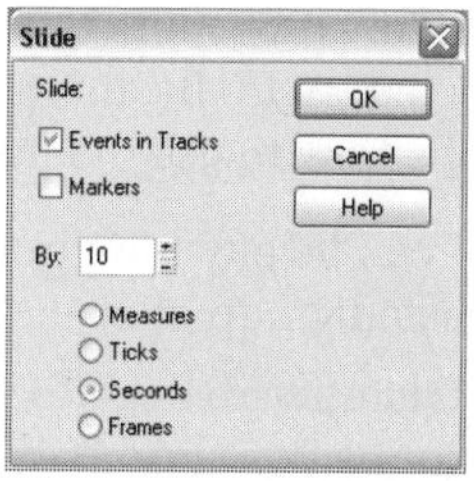

Figure 8.18
You can use the Slide feature to move any kind of data, not just clips.

3.   If you want to move events, be sure the Events in Tracks option under the Slide parameter is activated. If you want to move any markers that happen to fall within the same time range as the selected data, activate the Markers option.

4.   For the By parameter, type the number of units by which you want to move the selected data. If you want to move the data backward in time, enter a negative number. If you want to move the data forward in time, enter a positive number.

5.   Choose the type of unit by which you want to move the selected data by activating the appropriate option. You can select Measures, Ticks, Seconds, or Frames.

6.   Click on OK.

SONAR will move the selected data backward or forward in time by the amount you specified and the unit type you chose.

Quantize

Even though you might be a great musician, you're bound to occasionally make mistakes when playing your instrument, especially when it comes to timing. No one I know can play in perfect time during every performance, and having to listen to a metronome while you play can be distracting sometimes. Instead of playing notes at the exact same time as the metronome sounds, you'll more than likely play some of them either a little ahead or a little behind the beat. You might even hold some notes a little longer than you're supposed to. Usually, if these timing errors are slight enough, they'll make your performance sound more human than anything else. But if the mistakes are obvious enough to stand out, they can make your performance sound sloppy. At this point, the Quantize feature comes in handy. It can help you correct some of the timing mistakes you make.

To understand how to use the Quantize feature, you first have to know how it works. The Quantize feature scans the MIDI events in your selected data one by one, and it changes the start time of each event so it is equal to the nearest rhythmic value you specify (using the Resolution parameter). If you want all the events in your data to be moved to the nearest sixteenth note, you can set the Resolution parameter to Sixteenth. The Quantize feature uses this value to set up an imaginary (for lack of a better word) time grid over your data. In this case, the grid is divided into sixteenth notes.

During the scanning process, the Quantize feature moves an imaginary pointer along the grid one division at a time. Centered around the pointer is an imaginary window, for which you can set the size using the Window parameter. As the Quantize feature moves its pointer and window along the grid, it looks to see whether any of your events are in the vicinity. Any events that fall within the window have their start times changed so they line up with the current position of the pointer. Any events that fall outside the window are left alone. This procedure continues until the Quantize feature comes to the end of the data you selected. Actually, there's a little more to the procedure than that, but I'll explain the rest as I describe how to use the feature.

1. Select the data you want to quantize. It can be anything from all the data in your project to a single track or clip or a selected group of events.

2. Select Process > Quantize to open the Quantize dialog box (see Figure 8.19).

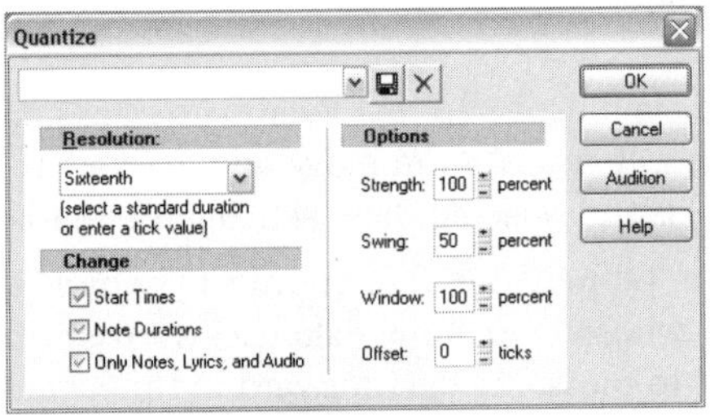

Figure 8.19
The Quantize dialog box provides a number of parameters you can set to determine exactly how you want your data to be corrected.

3. In the Resolution section, set the Resolution parameter. This parameter determines the rhythmic value that will be used to set up the imaginary grid and the nearest rhythmic value to which the events in your data will be aligned. It's best to set this parameter to the smallest note value found in your data. For instance, your data might contain quarter notes, eighth notes, and sixteenth notes. Because the smallest note value in your data is the sixteenth note, you would set the Resolution parameter to Sixteenth.

4. In the Change section, activate the appropriate options for the types of events and the event properties you want to have quantized. You'll almost always want to activate the Start Times option. Along with the start times of events, you can also quantize the durations of MIDI note events by activating the Note Durations option. You'll almost always want to activate this option as well. If you don't, the ends of some notes may overlap the beginnings of others, which might not sound very good. You might not want to quantize the start times of events, but only the durations if you want to create a staccato (separated notes) feel to your music. When activated, the Only Notes, Lyrics, and Audio option quantizes only MIDI note, lyric, and audio events and leaves any other events (such as MIDI controller events) alone. Usually you'll want to keep this option activated; otherwise, the Quantize feature will move controller events to the nearest grid point, which can actually screw up their timing.

QUANTIZE AUDIO

Even though the Quantize feature can change the start times of audio clips, don't be confused and think that it can correct the timing of your audio data. It can't. Remember, audio data is different from MIDI data. The Quantize feature can move an entire audio clip to the nearest rhythmic value. However, if you record a sloppy performance as audio data, you cannot correct it except by doing the recording over again.

You can use one trick, however, to quantize a monophonic (one note at a time) melody or percussion part that was recorded as an audio clip. If you split the clip into smaller clips, each containing one note of the melody, then each note will have its own start time, and you can use the Quantize feature to change the timing of each note.

5. In the Options section, set the Strength parameter. Quantizing your data so that all the events are aligned in perfect time with the grid can make your performance sound mechanical (as if it is being played by a machine). So instead of having the Quantize feature move an event to the exact current pointer position on the grid during the scanning process, you can have it move the event only slightly toward the pointer, thus taking the sloppiness out of the performance but keeping the "human" feel. You can do so by setting a percentage for the Strength parameter. A value of 100 percent means that all events will be moved to the exact grid point. A value of 50 percent means that the events will be moved only halfway toward the grid point. You'll have to experiment with this parameter to find the best-sounding setting.

6. Set the Window parameter. This parameter tells SONAR how close to the current grid point an event has to be in order to be quantized. If the event falls inside the window, it is quantized. If it falls outside the window, it isn't. You set the Window parameter by using a percentage. A value of 100 percent means the window extends halfway before and halfway after the current pointer position on the grid. Basically all events get moved; if they don't fall inside the window at the current pointer position, they will fall inside at the next position. A value of 50 percent means the window extends only one-quarter of the way before and after the current pointer position, meaning only half of the events in your selection will be processed.

7. Set the Offset parameter. This parameter is an extra setting thrown in to make the Quantize feature even more flexible (and complicated) than it already is. When the Quantize feature sets up its imaginary grid over your selected data, the grid is perfectly aligned to the measures and beats in your project. So if your data selection started at the beginning of your project, the grid would be set up starting at 1:01:000 (measure, beat, and tick). If you enter a value for the Offset parameter (in ticks), the grid will be offset by the number of ticks you enter. For example, if you enter an Offset of +3, the grid will be set up starting at 1:01:003 instead of 1:01:000. This means that if the current event being scanned was initially supposed to be moved to 1:01:000, it would be moved to 1:01:003 instead. Basically, you can use this parameter to offset the selected data from the other data in your project, in case you want to create some slight timing variations, and so on.

It works similarly to the Time Offset parameter in the Track view, which you learned about in Chapter 4.

8. Set the Swing parameter, which is yet another parameter that makes the Quantize feature more flexible (and more difficult to understand). You might use it to work on a song that has a "swing" feel to it, similar to a waltz, where the first in a pair of notes is played longer than the second. It's difficult to explain, but essentially the Swing parameter distorts the grid by making the space between the grid points uneven. If you leave the parameter set at 50 percent, it doesn't have any effect. If you set it to something like 66 percent, the space between the first two points in the grid becomes twice as much as the space between the second and third points. This pattern of long space, short space is repeated throughout the length of the grid, and your data is aligned according to the uneven grid points. You'll need to experiment with this parameter a bit to hear the effect it has on your data.

9. Click on the Audition button to hear how the quantized data will sound. Go back and make any parameter changes you think might be necessary.

10. If you want to use the same settings again later, save them as a preset.

11. Click on OK.

SONAR will quantize the selected data, and when you play it back, it should sound the same way it did when you listened to it using the Audition feature.

THE QUANTIZE MIDI EFFECT
SONAR provides additional quantizing features with the Quantize MIDI effect. See Chapter 11 for more information.

The Groove Quantize Feature

Not only can you use quantizing to correct the timing of your performances, but you can use it to add a bit of a creative flair as well. The Groove Quantize feature works almost the same as the Quantize feature, but it's slightly more sophisticated. Instead of using a fixed grid (meaning you can set the grid to use only straight rhythmic values, such as sixteenth notes), it uses a grid with rhythmic values that are based on an existing rhythmic pattern called a *groove pattern*. This groove pattern can contain any kind of musical rhythm, even one taken from an existing piece of music.

Basically, the Groove Quantize feature works by imposing the timing, duration, and velocity values of one set of events onto another set. For example, suppose you record a melody that comes out sounding a bit too mechanical, but your friend slams out this really kickin' MIDI bass line that has the exact feel you want. You can copy the bass clip data and use it as a groove pattern to groove quantize the melody clip data. By doing so, you impose the timing, duration, and velocity values (depending on your parameter settings) from the bass line on to the melody. Thus, the melody will have the same rhythm as the bass line but keep its original pitches.

The preceding example is just one of the many uses for the Groove Quantize feature. Just like the Quantize feature, the Groove Quantize feature provides Strength parameters to give you control of how much influence a groove pattern has over the data you're quantizing. You can define via percentages how much the timing, duration, and velocity values of the events will be affected, so you can use this feature for all kinds of editing tasks. You can correct off-tempo tracks, add complex beat accents to each measure of a tune, synchronize rhythm and solo tracks, align tracks with bad timing to one with good timing, and steal the feeling from tracks, as I explained in the preceding example.

As a matter of fact, groove quantizing has become so popular that companies now sell groove pattern files so you can steal the feeling from tracks that have been recorded by professional keyboard, drum, and guitar players. It's almost like having Steve Vai play on your latest tune! Just look in any copy of *Electronic Musician* or *Keyboard* magazine, and you'll see advertisements for these types of products. Of course, you need to know how to use the Groove Quantize feature before you can use these groove pattern files, so let me tell you how.

1. If you want to grab the timing, duration, and velocity values from existing data, first select and copy that data so it is placed onto the clipboard. Otherwise, you can use one of the groove patterns that comes included with SONAR (which I'll show you how to choose later).

2. Select the data you want to groove quantize.

3. Choose Process > Groove Quantize to open the Groove Quantize dialog box (see Figure 8.20).

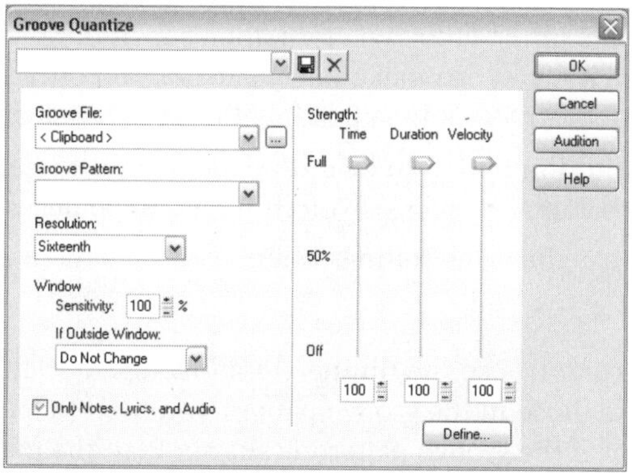

Figure 8.20
The Groove Quantize dialog box provides a number of parameters you can set to determine exactly how you want your data to be groove quantized.

4. Set the Groove File parameter. If you're grabbing the values from existing data, as explained previously, then select Clipboard from the drop-down list and skip to Step 6. Otherwise, choose an existing groove file. SONAR ships with only one groove file (Cakewalk DNA Grooves.grv), so unless you've created your own groove files, choose the Cakewalk DNA Grooves.grv file. If you have other groove files available, you can load them by clicking on the small button to the right of the Groove File parameter to bring up the Open Groove File dialog box. Just select a file and then click on Open.

5. Set the Groove Pattern parameter. Each groove file can contain any number of groove patterns. For example the groove file that comes with SONAR contains 12 different groove patterns. Choose the groove pattern you want to use.

6. The rest of the parameters for the Groove Quantize feature are the same as for the Quantize feature. You need to set the Resolution parameter; the Only Notes, Lyrics, and Audio option; and the Window parameter. The Window Sensitivity parameter is the same as the Window parameter for the Quantize feature, but one additional Window parameter is available here. You can choose the If Outside Window parameter to have Groove Quantize change events even if they fall outside the window. If you select Do Not Change, then events outside the window are left alone (just as with the Quantize feature). If you select Quantize to Resolution, any events outside the window are moved to the nearest grid point, as specified by the Resolution parameter. If you select Move to Nearest, then the Window Sensitivity parameter is ignored, and all events outside the window are moved to the nearest grid point, as defined by the groove pattern. If you select Scale Time, SONAR looks at the events located right before and after the current event being scanned (as long as they are within the window), and it sets their relative timing so that they're the same. The Scale Time parameter is very difficult to explain, so you should try it out to hear what kind of effect it has on your music.

7. You also need to set the Strength parameters. They work the same as with the Quantize feature, but instead of just having one parameter to affect the timing of events, three Strength parameters are provided to give you control over how the Groove Quantize feature will affect the time, duration, and velocity of each event. If you want the events to have the exact same timing, duration, and velocity as their counterparts in the groove pattern, then set all these parameters to 100 percent. Otherwise, you can make the events take on only some of the feel of the events in the groove pattern by adjusting the percentages of these parameters.

8. Click on the Audition button to hear how the quantized data will sound. Go back and make any parameter changes you think might be necessary.

9. If you want to use the same settings again later, save them as a preset.

10. Click on OK.

SONAR will quantize the selected data so the timing, duration, and velocity of the events will sound exactly or somewhat like those in the groove pattern you used (depending on your parameter settings). By the way, if the groove pattern is shorter than the material you are quantizing, the Groove Quantize feature will loop through the groove pattern as many times as necessary to get to the end of your selected data. For example, if you use a groove pattern that is only one measure long, but your selected data is three measures, then the timing, duration, and velocity values of the groove pattern will be repeated over each of those three measures.

Saving Groove Patterns

If you create your own groove pattern by grabbing the timing, duration, and velocity values from existing data, you can save it for later use as follows:

1. After you've gone through steps 1 through 4 in the preceding example on how to use the Groove Quantize feature and you've set the Groove File parameter to Clipboard, click on the Define button at the bottom of the Groove Quantize dialog box to open the Define Groove dialog box (see Figure 8.21).

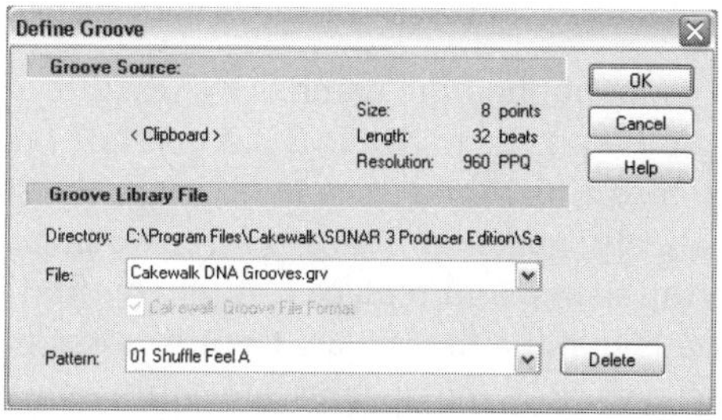

Figure 8.21
Using the Define Groove
dialog box, you can save
your own groove patterns
and groove files.

2. In the Groove Library File section, select an existing groove file via the File
    parameter. You can also type a new name to create your own new groove file.

GROOVE FILE FORMATS

SONAR supports two types of groove files. One type is the DNA groove files,
which contain only timing data but are compatible with other sequencing software.
The groove files being sold by other companies are usually in this file format.
SONAR also has its own proprietary groove file format that stores timing, duration,
and velocity data. Unless you really need to share your groove files with others
who don't own SONAR, I suggest you save your files in the SONAR format
because it provides more flexibility. To do so, be sure to activate the Cakewalk
Groove File Format option in the Define Groove dialog box.

3. If you want to replace an existing groove pattern in the current groove file, just
    select one from the Pattern drop-down list. If you want to save your groove pattern
    under a new name, type the name in the Pattern parameter.

DELETE EXISTING PATTERNS

You can delete existing groove patterns in the current groove file. Just select the
groove pattern you want to delete from the Pattern drop-down list, and then click
on the Delete button. SONAR will ask you to confirm the deletion process.

4. Click on OK. If you're replacing an existing groove pattern, SONAR will ask you to
    confirm the replacement process.

SONAR will save your new groove pattern inside the groove file you selected (or created) under
the name you specified.

GROOVE QUANTIZE APPLICATIONS

For examples of some cool applications for the Groove Quantize feature, look at
the SONAR Help in the Editing MIDI Events and Controllers > Changing the Time
of a Recording > Quantizing section.

CHAPTER 8

The Interpolate Feature

Throughout the text of this book, I've mentioned the name SONAR quite a few times. What if I want to change all those instances of the phrase to SONAR 3.0 instead? Luckily, I'm using a word processing program on my computer, so all I would have to do is use the search and replace feature to have the program automatically make the changes for me. I mention this point because the Interpolate feature is similar to the search and replace feature you find in most word processing programs. The difference is that the Interpolate feature works with event properties, and in addition to simply searching and replacing, it can scale entire ranges of event properties from one set of values to another. This means you can easily transpose notes, change key signatures, convert one type of controller message into another, and so on. It works like this:

1. Select the data you want to change.

2. Choose Process > Interpolate to open the Event Filter - Search dialog box. You learned about this dialog box and its parameters in Chapter 5.

3. Set all the available parameters so that SONAR can select the exact events you want to process.

4. Click on OK to open the Event Filter - Replace dialog box (see Figure 8.22). This dialog box is almost the same as the Event Filter - Search dialog box. It has most of the same settings, except some of the settings are not available because here you need to enter only the values to which you want to change the original selected data. So, enter the replacement values in the appropriate parameters.

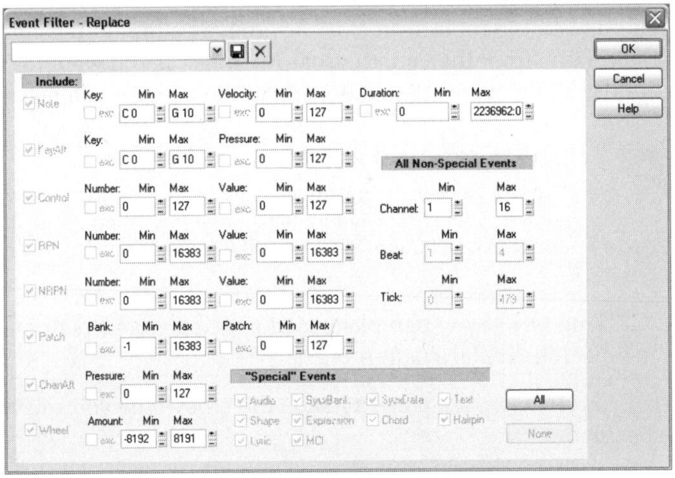

Figure 8.22
In the Event Filter - Replace dialog box, you can enter the replacement values only for the data you're trying to change.

5. Click on OK.

SONAR will select all the events in your initial selection according to the parameters you set in the Event Filter - Search dialog box. Then it will change the values of those events according to the parameters you set in the Event Filter - Replace dialog box.

Interpolation Applications

You didn't think I was going to leave you high and dry, trying to figure out such a complicated feature, did you? Actually, when you get the hang of it, using the Interpolate feature isn't too difficult, especially if you're just trying to make straight replacements of data. Anyway, the following sections describe some of the changes you can accomplish with this feature.

Straight Replacement

If all you want to do is replace one value with another, setting up the parameters in both dialog boxes is fairly easy. Suppose you want to change all the notes with a pitch of C#2 to notes with a pitch of D#7. To do so, set up the Event Filter - Search dialog box so only the Note option is activated in the Include section. Then type C#2 for both the Key Min and Key Max parameters and click on OK. In the Event Filter - Replace dialog box, type D#7 for the Key Min and Key Max parameters and click on OK. All the C#2 notes will be changed to D#7 notes. Pretty easy, no? And you can use this approach with any of the data. Earlier, I mentioned changing one type of controller message to another. Just use the Control option along with the Number Min and Number Max parameters, as you did with the Note option and the Key Min and Key Max parameters.

USING WILDCARDS

You can also use wildcards when you're designating an octave number for the pitch of a note. With regard to the preceding example, suppose you want to change all the C# notes to D notes, not just the ones in octave 2 to octave 7. Instead of using C#2, you can use C#?, and instead of using D#7, you can use D#?. The ? is the wildcard, which stands for any octave.

Scaling Values

When you're working with ranges of values, you can use the Interpolate feature to scale them from one range to another. This capability is useful for limiting certain values to keep them within a set of boundaries. For example, some of the note velocities in one of your MIDI tracks might be a bit high, and you might want to quiet them down a bit. Usually, quieting them would mean having to use the Piano Roll view to change them all one by one. Using the Interpolate feature, you can compress their range down in a couple of easy steps. To do so, set up the Event Filter - Search dialog box so only the Note option is activated in the Include section. Then type 0 for Velocity Min and 127 for Velocity Max and click on OK. In the Event Filter - Replace dialog box, type 0 for Velocity Min and 100 for Velocity Max and click on OK. All the note velocities will be scaled down from a range of 0 to 127 to a range of 0 to 100. See how it works? You can use this approach with any of the other value ranges, too.

Inverting Values

You also can invert any of the value ranges by reversing the Min and Max parameters. For example, what if you want to make all the loud volume controller messages soft and the soft volume controller messages loud? To do so, set up the Event Filter - Search dialog box so only the Control option is activated in the Include section. Then type 7 (the number for volume controller messages) for both the Number Min and Number Max parameters. Also, type 0 for Value Min and 127 for Value Max and click on OK. In the Event Filter - Replace dialog box, type 7 for both the Number Min and Number Max parameters. Also, type 127 for Value Min and 0 for Value Max and click on OK. All the loud sections of your selected data will become soft and vice versa. Again, you can use this technique for any of the other value ranges.

CHAPTER 8

As a matter of fact, you can change a whole bunch of different parameters at once by activating the appropriate parameters in the Event Filter - Search dialog box. (You can even mix straight replacement, scaling, and inverting.) For instance, you could easily set up all three of the preceding examples so that you would have to use the Interpolate feature only one time to process the same data. This feature is very powerful. You should experiment with it as much as possible because it can save you a lot of editing time in the long run.

OTHER INTERPOLATE APPLICATIONS
You can find some other Interpolate application ideas in the SONAR Help file under the Editing MIDI Events and Controllers > Searching for Events > Event Filters section.

The Length Feature

The Length feature is one of the very simple but also very useful features provided in SONAR. Using it, you can change the size of a clip or a group of selected data by specifying a percentage. It works like this:

1. Select the data you want to change.

2. Choose Process > Length to open the Length dialog box (see Figure 8.23).

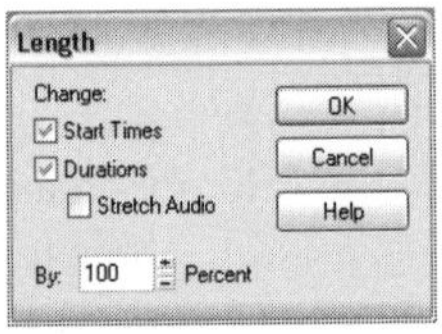

Figure 8.23
You can change the size of clips or selected groups of events by using the Length feature.

3. Activate the Start Times, Durations, and/or Stretch Audio options. Activating the Start Times option makes the Length feature change the start times of the selected events so the entire selection will change in size. Activating the Durations option makes the Length feature change the durations of the selected events. If you activate the Durations option without the Start Times option, the Length feature will change only the durations of the selected events. This feature can be useful if you want to create a staccato effect for your notes. And if you want the length of your audio data to be changed, you can activate the Stretch Audio option.

4. Enter a value for the By Percent parameter. A value of 100 percent doesn't make any changes at all. A value of 50 percent changes the selection to half its original length. A value of 200 percent changes the selection to twice its original length.

5. Click on OK.

SONAR will change the size of the clips or the entire selection of events according to your parameter specifications.

FIT TO TIME

For a more intuitive way to change the length of your data (meaning you can enter a length using an actual time value instead of a percentage), use the Fit to Time feature, which you'll learn about later in this chapter, in the "Fit to Time" section.

The Retrograde Feature

The Retrograde feature works similarly to the Reverse feature that you learned about earlier in this chapter. Instead of reversing the data in audio clips, however, the Retrograde feature reverses MIDI data. This means you can have your MIDI data play backward if you apply this feature. Just select the data you want to reverse and then select Process > Retrograde. SONAR will reverse the order of the selected events. In other words, if you were looking at the data via the Event view, the data would be changed so this list essentially is flipped upside down. That's about it.

The Transpose Feature

Transposition is a common occurrence when you're composing music, and SONAR's Transpose feature enables you to transpose quickly and easily. It works like this:

1. Select the data that you want to transpose.

2. Choose Process > Transpose to open the Transpose dialog box (see Figure 8.24).

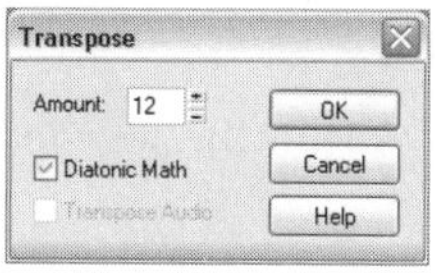

Figure 8.24
By entering a number of steps, you can transpose the pitches of note events up or down using the Transpose feature.

3. You can use the Transpose feature to transpose the pitches of your note events either chromatically (so they can be changed by half steps) or diatonically (so they remain in the current key signature of your project). If you want to transpose chromatically, leave the Diatonic Math option deactivated. If you want to transpose diatonically, activate the Diatonic Math option.

4. If you have selected any audio data, you can opt to have its pitch changed as well. To do so, activate the Transpose Audio option.

5. Enter a value for the Amount parameter. A positive value transposes up, and a negative value transposes down. If you are transposing chromatically, this value corresponds to half steps. If you are transposing diatonically, the Transpose feature changes the pitches of your notes according the major scale of the current key signature. For example, if you enter a value of +1 and the key signature is D major, a D becomes an E, an E becomes an F#, and so on.

6. Click on OK.

SONAR will transposes the pitches of the notes (or audio) in the selected data according to your parameter settings.

The Scale Velocity Feature

You learned about scaling the velocity values of events earlier in the description of the Interpolate feature. Using the Scale Velocity feature, you can do the same thing, but this feature has an extra option that enables you to scale the velocities by a percentage rather than enter exact values or a range of values. It works like this:

1. Select the data you want to change.

2. Choose Process > Scale Velocity to open the Scale Velocity dialog box (see Figure 8.25).

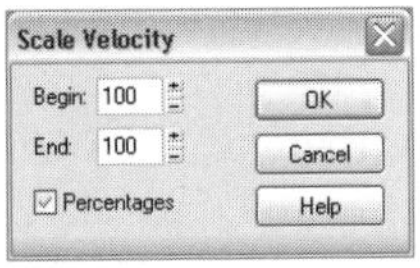

Figure 8.25
You can scale the velocities of note events by percentages if you use the Scale Velocity feature.

3. If you want to scale the velocities by percentages, activate the Percentages option. Otherwise, the values that you enter will be exact velocity values.

4. Enter values for the Begin and End parameters. For example, you can use the Scale Velocity feature to create crescendos and decrescendos. To create a crescendo, enter a small value (such as 0 or 50 percent) for the Begin parameter and a larger value (such as 127 or 150 percent) for the End parameter. Do the opposite for a decrescendo.

5. Click on OK.

SONAR will scale the velocity values of the note events within the selected data according to your parameter settings.

> **THE DRAW LINE TOOL**
> You can create crescendos and decrescendos with more precise control by drawing them with the Draw Line tool in the Controllers pane of the Piano Roll view. You learned how to use this tool in Chapter 7.

Fit to Time

As I mentioned earlier, the Fit to Time feature works similarly to the Length feature. Using it, you can change the size of clips and selected groups of data. But instead of having to use a percentage, you can specify an actual time (according to the Time Ruler) at which the data will end. For example, if you have a clip that begins at 1:01:000 and ends at 4:02:000, the start time of the clip will remain the same, but you can change the end time of the clip so it stops playing at the exact moment you specify. This feature is great when you need to compose music to a precise length, such as for a radio commercial or a video. It works like this:

1. Select the data you want to change.

2. Choose Process > Fit to Time to open the Fit to Time dialog box (see Figure 8.26).

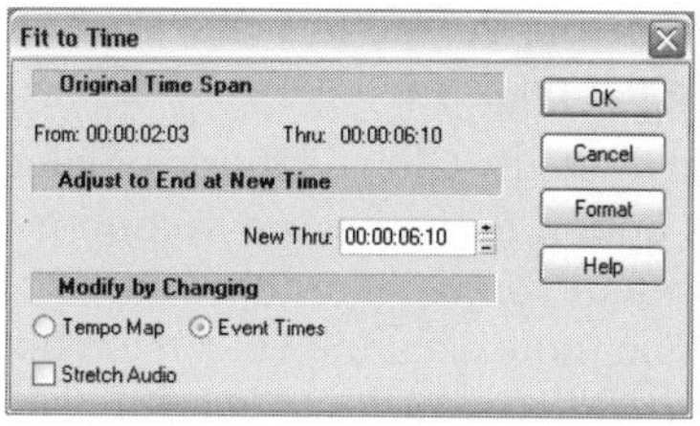

Figure 8.26
You can specify the exact
length of clips or selected
groups of events by using
the Fit to Time feature.

3. The Original Time Span section shows the beginning and end times for the selected data. In the Adjust to End at New Time section, enter a new end time for the selected data. You can enter either hours, minutes, seconds, and frames or measures, beats, and ticks. To change the format, click on the Format button.

4. In the Modify by Changing section, activate either the Tempo Map option or the Event Times option. If you want the actual data to be changed (meaning the start times of every event in the selection will be adjusted to accommodate the new end time), activate the Event Times option. If you would rather leave the data as it is and just have SONAR insert tempo changes into the project to accommodate the new end time, activate the Tempo Map option. The key difference here is that using the Tempo Map option affects the entire project, and all the data in all the tracks during the selected time will play at a different rate. If you want the data in only one track to be affected, you must use the Event Times option.

5. If you want to change the length of audio clips, you have to activate the Stretch Audio option.

6. Click on OK.

SONAR will change the length of the selected data or insert tempo changes into the project (depending on your parameter settings) to accommodate the new end time that you specified.

Fit Improvisation

Having to play along with a metronome while recording in SONAR can be a nuisance sometimes. Depending on the type of music you are performing, using the metronome might not be conducive to your mood during the performance, which means you might end up with a less than acceptable recording. Some people just can't stand using a metronome. The problem is that if you don't use the metronome while recording in SONAR, your data will not line up correctly to the measure, beat, and tick values along the Time Ruler. Therefore, editing your music can be a lot more difficult.

If you are one of those people who hates metronomes, then you're in luck. SONAR allows you to record your MIDI tracks without using the metronome, but still line up your data correctly after the fact by using the Fit Improvisation feature. This feature works by adding tempo changes to your project according to an additional reference track that you must record. This reference track gives SONAR an idea of the tempo at which you were playing when you were recording your MIDI track without the metronome. Following is a more detailed version of how this feature works:

1. Record a MIDI track without using the metronome. For the most accurate results, try to play using as steady a tempo as possible.

2. Choose Options > Global to open the Global Options dialog box. Click on the MIDI tab. Be sure only the Notes option in the Record section is activated. This filters out any extraneous events when you're recording your reference track so they don't mess up the timing. The more accurate your reference track, the better. After you're done recording your reference track, you can go back to the Global Options dialog box and change the options back to the way they were.

3. Record a reference MIDI track. To do so, simply tap out the tempo of your initial MIDI recording by hitting a key on your MIDI instrument for every beat. So if you recorded a track in 4/4 time, you would have to hit the key four times for every measure of music you recorded. Also, be sure the first note in your reference track has a start time of 1:01:000 so it starts at the very beginning of the project. You can adjust it manually by using the Event view or Piano Roll view if you have to.

4. Select the reference track.

5. Choose Process > Fit Improvisation.

SONAR will scan your reference track, analyzing where the beats fall, and add tempo changes to your project so the data in your recorded track lines up with the measure, beat, and tick values on the Time Ruler. Now you can edit your data just as you would any other data that was recorded along with the metronome.

9

Composing with Loops

In addition to creating music by recording and editing your MIDI and audio performances, SONAR allows you to compose music with *sample loops*. Sample loops are usually (though not always) short audio recordings that you can piece together to create entire musical performances. Using them is a great way to add some acoustic audio tracks to your project without actually having to do any recording or know how to play an instrument. For example, you can buy a CD full of sample loops that contain nothing but acoustic drum beats. Not only can you buy drum loops, but you can also get real guitar solos, vocal chorus recordings, orchestral recordings, and more. You can create an entire project just by using sample loops, and SONAR even provides you with the tools to create your own loops. In this chapter, I'll tell you about all the loop-based features that SONAR provides, and the chapter will also do the following:

▶ Explain Groove clips

▶ Show you how to create and save Groove clips

▶ Describe the Loop Construction view

▶ Demonstrate how to work with Groove clips

▶ Describe the Loop Explorer view

▶ Explain project pitch and pitch markers

Groove Clips

In SONAR, sample loops are known as *Groove clips*. If you're familiar with Sony's ACID software (formerly owned by Sonic Foundry), you won't have any trouble with Groove clips because they are Cakewalk's equivalent to the loops for ACID. Like loops for ACID, Groove clips automatically take care of the sometimes tedious chore of matching the playback tempo and pitch of each loop you use in a song. This is because Groove clips contain extra information that lets SONAR know their basic tempo, pitch, and playback properties. SONAR can accurately shift the tempo and pitch of the Groove clips so they match the tempo and pitch of the current project. Why is this important? Because not all sample loops are recorded at the same tempo and pitch, and in order to use them in the same song, they have to "groove" with one another, so to speak. Before loops for ACID or Groove clips came along, a musician would have to match the tempo and pitch of multiple loops manually. Let me tell you, it's not a fun task.

Of course, not all sample loops contain the extra information I mentioned earlier. Plain sample loops need to be converted into Groove clips before you can use them in a SONAR project. But don't worry—it's not nearly as difficult as you might think.

Creating Groove Clips

With the introduction of SONAR 3, there are now two types of Groove clips—audio Groove clips and MIDI Groove clips. For the most part, both types of Groove clips are handled in the same way, but there are some subtle differences, which I will describe throughout this chapter.

Creating Audio Groove Clips

You can easily convert any audio clip in SONAR into a Groove clip with a few clicks of your mouse. To convert a regular audio clip into a Groove clip, follow these steps:

1. Right-click on an audio clip in the Clips pane of the Track view and choose Clip Properties from the drop-down menu to open the Clip Properties dialog box.

2. Click on the Groove-Clips tab to display the Groove clip's parameters (see Figure 9.1).

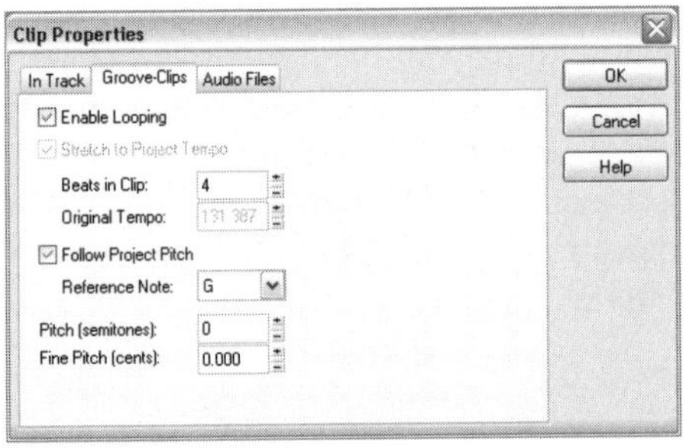

Figure 9.1
Use the Clip Properties dialog box to convert an audio clip into a Groove clip.

3. Activate the Enable Looping option. That's basically all you need to do, but there are some extra parameters that you need to deal with if you want some extra control over how SONAR will handle your new Groove clip.

QUICK GROOVE CLIP CREATION

Instead of opening the Clip Properties dialog box to enable looping for an audio clip, you can right-click on the clip and choose Groove-Clip Looping from the drop-down menu. You also can select the clip (or multiple clips) and press Ctrl+L on your computer keyboard. These methods are quicker, but they don't give you access to the extra parameters.

4. When you activate the Enable Looping option for a clip, SONAR automatically activates the Stretch to Project Tempo parameter and makes a guess as to how many rhythmic beats are in the clip, as well as the original tempo of the clip. If the beats are inaccurate, you can change the number of beats for the clip by entering a new number in the Beats in Clip field. These parameters must be accurate for SONAR to be able to change the playback tempo of the clip to follow the tempo of your project.

5. In addition to changing the tempo of the clip, SONAR can change the pitch of the clip to follow the pitch of the project. This ensures that Groove clips stay in tune with one another in the same project. If you want SONAR to control the pitch of the clip, activate the Follow Project Pitch option.

PERCUSSION GROOVE CLIPS

Not all Groove clips should follow the pitch of the project. Why? Well, if you have a Groove clip that contains percussive data like a drum instrument performance, you don't want the pitch of that clip to change because it will make the drum performance sound strange. For these types of Groove clips, only the Stretch to Project Tempo option should be activated. The Follow Project Pitch option should be activated only for clips containing pitch-related performances such as guitar, bass, woodwinds, horns, strings, vocals, and the like.

6. When you activate the Follow Project Pitch option, you have to tell SONAR the original pitch of the material in the clip. SONAR doesn't determine the pitch automatically for you. Choose a pitch from the Reference Note drop-down list. For example, if the notes played in the clip are based on a C chord, choose C in the Reference Note drop-down list. How do you know the original pitch of the clip? You have to figure it out by listening to it.

7. If you want to transpose the pitch of the clip so that it plays differently from the project pitch, you can enter a value (measured in semitones) for the Pitch parameter. This parameter can come in handy if you are composing with orchestral instrument loops that need to be played in a different key.

8. If the pitch of the clip is slightly out of tune, you can adjust it by entering a value (measured in cents) for the Fine Pitch parameter.

9. Click on OK.

SONAR will now treat your original audio clip as a Groove clip. If the tempo or pitch of the project changes (I'll talk more about this later, in the "Working with Groove Clips" section), the Groove clip will be stretched and transposed accordingly. In addition, you'll notice that in the Track view, a regular audio clip is shown as a rectangle, but when a clip is converted into a Groove clip, it is shown as a rectangle with rounded corners (see Figure 9.2).

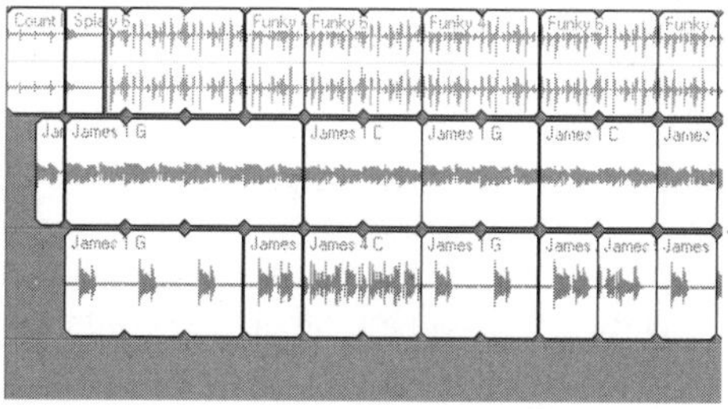

Figure 9.2
A Groove clip is indicated by a rectangle with rounded corners.

Creating MIDI Groove Clips

To create a MIDI Groove clip, you can follow the same procedures for creating audio Groove clips. The only difference is that MIDI Groove clips provide fewer parameters in the Clip Properties dialog box (see Figure 9.3).

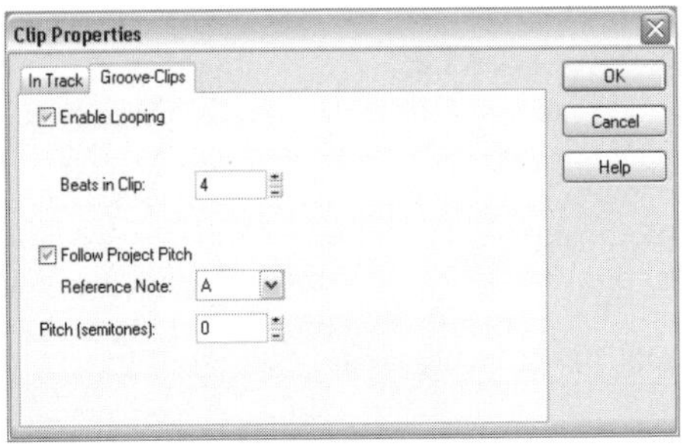

Figure 9.3
MIDI Groove clips
provide fewer parameters
in the Clip Properties
dialog box.

The Clip Properties dialog box for a MIDI Groove clip only provides the Enable Looping option, the Beats in Clip parameter, the Follow Project Pitch option, and the Reference Note and Pitch parameters. These options and parameters, however, work just like they do for audio Groove clips.

The Loop Construction View

There might be times when SONAR doesn't seem to stretch your audio Groove clips accurately. If this occurs, you'll hear slight anomalies in the audio when you change the tempo of your project. To correct this, you can try using the Loop Construction view to convert your audio clip. To use the Loop Construction view, follow these steps:

1. Right-click on the audio clip in the Clips pane of the Track view and choose View > Loop Construction (or double-click on the clip) to open the Loop Construction view (see Figure 9.4).

Figure 9.4
Instead of the Clip
Properties dialog box, use
the Loop Construction
view to convert your
clips.

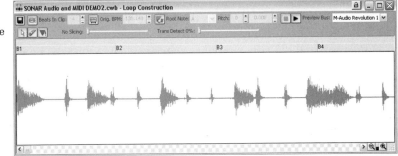

2. Along the top of the view, you'll see a toolbar that contains all of the same parameters found in the Clip Properties dialog box. From left to right, the options are the Save Loop to WAV File function (more about this later in the "Saving Groove Clips" section); the Enable Looping option; the Beats in Clip parameter; the Enable Stretching option (which is the same as the Stretch to Project Tempo option); the Orig. BPM parameter (which is the same as the Original Tempo parameter); the Follow Project Pitch option; the Root Note parameter (which is the same as the Reference Note parameter); and the Pitch parameters (which are the same as the Pitch and Fine Pitch parameters). You can set these parameters as I explained in the previous section.

3. The last three toolbar parameters are Stop Preview, Preview Loop, and Preview Bus. The Preview Loop and Stop Preview parameters let you listen to the loop currently displayed in the Loop Construction view. The Preview Bus parameter lets you choose which bus (audio channel or sound card output) will be used to play the loop. I'll talk more about buses in Chapter 12, "Mixing It Down."

4. You'll also notice a second toolbar, as well as the audio waveform of the loop currently displayed in the Loop Construction view. I'll talk more about the second toolbar in a minute. For now, notice that when you activate the Enable Looping option, SONAR automatically adjusts two of the parameters in the second toolbar and adds vertical lines to the audio waveform (see Figure 9.5). These lines are *slicing markers*, which designate a specific place in a loop where the timing data needs to be preserved when the timing of the loop is being stretched to fit the project tempo. The slicing markers make it so that a loop can be stretched without having its pitch change at the same time.

Figure 9.5
SONAR uses slicing markers to maintain the audio quality of a loop when it is stretched.

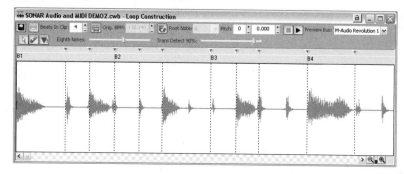

EXPLANATION OF SLICING

Normally when you stretch (in other words, change the length of) audio data, the pitch is changed as well. Make the data shorter, and the pitch is raised. Make the data longer, and the pitch is lowered. By slicing the data into smaller pieces, you can stretch the data very accurately, preserving its original quality without changing its pitch. This slicing happens in real-time during playback, and it's non-destructive (meaning the original data is not changed).

5. To control the way SONAR automatically adds slicing markers to your loop, you need to adjust the Basic Slicing and Trans Detect (short for *Transient Detection*) sliders, which are located on the second toolbar. The Basic Slicing slider places slicing markers at specific rhythmic locations in the loop according to the Beats in Clip parameter (which I mentioned earlier). For example, if you set the Basic Slicing slider to Eighth Notes, slicing markers will be placed at every eighth note location in your loop. If your loop contains four beats, it will have seven slicing markers. You would think there should be eight slicing markers (since there are two eighth notes to every beat, and two multiplied by four is eight), but the beginning of a loop never needs a slicing marker, so there is one fewer than expected. When you adjust the Basic Slicing slider, it's usually best to go with a note value equal to the smallest rhythmic value in your audio data performance.

For example, if your loop contains sixteenth notes, try setting the Basic Slicing slider to 16th Notes. You also can try a setting that is one value lower, which in this case would be eighth notes. Just be aware that too few or too many slicing markers will introduce unwanted artifacts into the audio when your loops are being stretched.

6. When you adjust the Trans Detect slider, slicing markers are placed at the beginning of detected transients in the audio data of the loop. Transients are large spikes (big changes in volume) in the audio waveform. Because of this, the Trans Detect slider works best with percussive material. A setting of about 90 percent usually works well. Usually you'll want to use a combination of the Basic Slicing and Trans Detect sliders to get the optimum number of slicing markers set up in your loop.

7. If the Basic Slicing and Trans Detect sliders don't provide enough slicing markers or if they provide the wrong placement, you can use the Select, Erase Marker, and Default All Markers tools to create, erase, and adjust the slicing markers manually. The first three buttons in the second toolbar correspond to the Select, Erase Marker, and Default All Markers tools, respectively. Use the Select tool to move existing slicing markers by clicking and dragging the marker triangles in the marker area above the audio waveform display (see Figure 9.6). You also can use the Select tool to create your own slicing markers by simply double-clicking in the marker area. Manually created or changed markers are shown with a blue triangle.

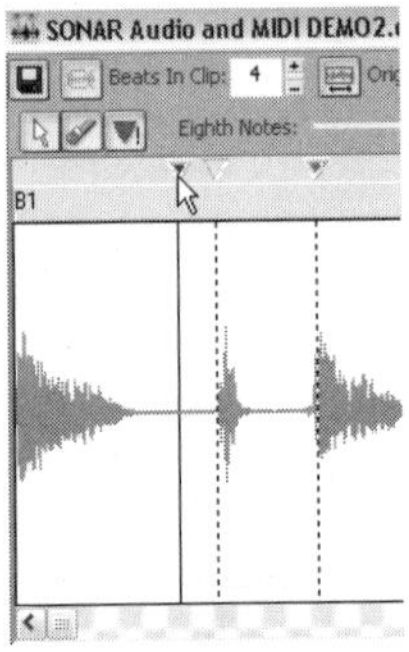

Figure 9.6
Use the Select tool to create or move slicing markers.

8. To erase a slicing marker, just choose the Erase Marker tool and click on the triangle of the slicing marker that you want to erase.

9. If you moved any of the automatically created slicing markers and you want to put them back in their original positions, just click on the Default All Markers button. If you created any slicing markers manually, those markers will remain untouched.

10. After you are finished adjusting all the parameters for your new Groove clip, close the Loop Construction view.

Usually you can rely on the automatic settings that SONAR provides, but just in case, it's good to know that you have total control over how your Groove clips are handled.

EDIT MIDI GROOVE CLIPS

MIDI Groove clips don't rely on slicing, so you can't edit them with the Loop Construction view. Instead, you edit the data in MIDI Groove clips in the Piano Roll view, just like a regular MIDI clip. However, there are a couple unique aspects to editing MIDI Groove clips. First, you can edit data in any of the clip repetitions without affecting other repetitions. For example, if you delete a note in the first clip repetition, that note is not also deleted in the other repetitions. Also, if you slip edit a MIDI Groove clip to make it shorter, any edits you performed will be lost.

Saving Groove Clips

When you create Groove clips in a SONAR project, those clips are saved along with the project. But what if you want to use your Groove clips in another project? Or maybe you'd like to share the clips with your friends. This is where the Save Loop to WAV File function (which I mentioned earlier) comes in handy. The Save Loop to WAV File function lets you save your Groove clips to disk as a special WAV file. Unlike most ordinary WAV files, which just contain audio data, the Groove clip WAV files contain all the special looping information I talked about earlier. Here's how it works:

1. With your Groove clip still open in the Loop Construction view, click on the Save Loop to WAV File button to open the Save As dialog box.

2. Use the Save In drop-down list to navigate to the location on your disk drive to which you want to save the file.

3. Type a name for the file in the File Name field.

4. Click on Save.

Your Groove clip will be saved to disk as a WAV file that contains the audio data for the clip plus all the looping information that you set, such as the Beats in Clip, Root Note, Pitch, and slicing markers. The next time you open the clip, this information will be loaded automatically as well.

Exporting MIDI Groove Clips

In addition to saving audio Groove clips, you can save (or export) MIDI Groove clips for later use in other projects. MIDI Groove clips are exported as standard MIDI files that can later be imported. To export a MIDI Groove clip, follow these steps:

1. Select the MIDI Groove clip and choose File > Export > MIDI Groove Clip to open the Export MIDI Groove Clip dialog box. (You can export only one clip at a time.)

2. Use the Save In drop-down list to navigate to the location on your disk drive to which you want to save the file.

3. Type a name for the file in the File Name field.

4. Click on Save.

Your MIDI Groove clip will be saved as a MIDI (MID) file that contains the MIDI data for the clip plus all the looping information you set, such as the Beats in Clip, Follow Project Pitch, and Reference Note parameters.

CHAPTER 9

Working with Groove Clips

After you've created your Groove clips, you can use them to compose music in a current project or to create an entirely new project. Composing with Groove clips involves a combination of dragging and dropping to add clips to a project and slip editing to make the clips conform to the music you are trying to create.

The Loop Explorer View

If you have some Groove clips stored on disk, you can use the Loop Explorer view to add them to your project. The Loop Explorer view lets you examine and preview your stored Groove clips, as well as add them to your project by dragging and dropping with your mouse. To use the Loop Explorer view, follow these steps:

1. Choose View > Loop Explorer to open the Loop Explorer view (see Figure 9.7). The Loop Explorer view is very similar to Windows Explorer.

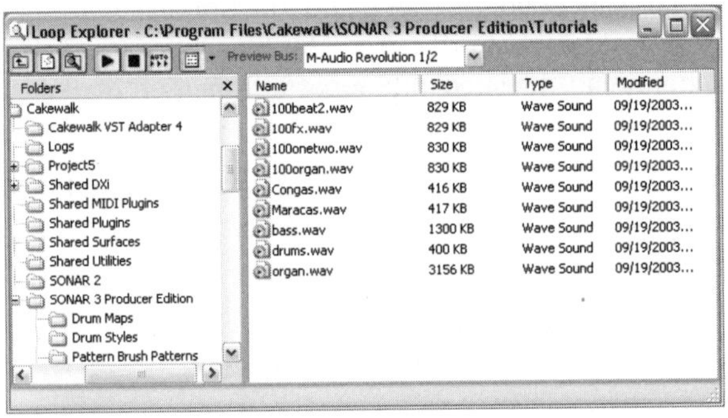

Figure 9.7
Use the Loop Explorer view to add existing Groove clips to your project.

2. In the Folders pane, navigate to the folder on your disk drive that contains your Groove clip files, and then select the folder. Its contents will be displayed in the File pane.

3. You can display your Groove clip files as large or small icons, a list of file names, or a detailed list of file names. Just use the Views drop-down list to choose your option (see Figure 9.8).

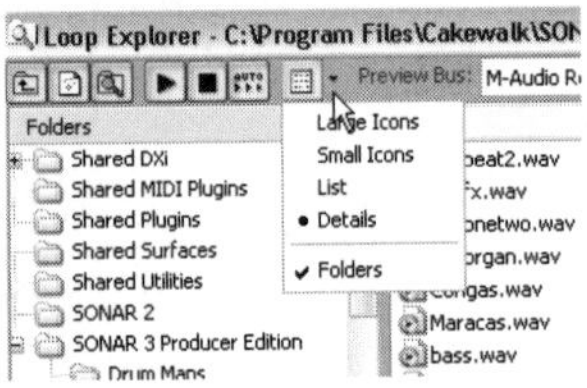

Figure 9.8
Use the Views drop-down list to choose the Groove clip file display option.

4. To preview a Groove clip, select its file in the File pane and then click on the Play button on the Loop Explorer view toolbar. To stop playback, click on the Stop button. If you want a file to start playing automatically as soon as you select it, activate the Auto-Preview option (see Figure 9.9). As in the Loop Construction view, you can choose which bus to use for the loop playback. I'll talk more about buses in Chapter 12.

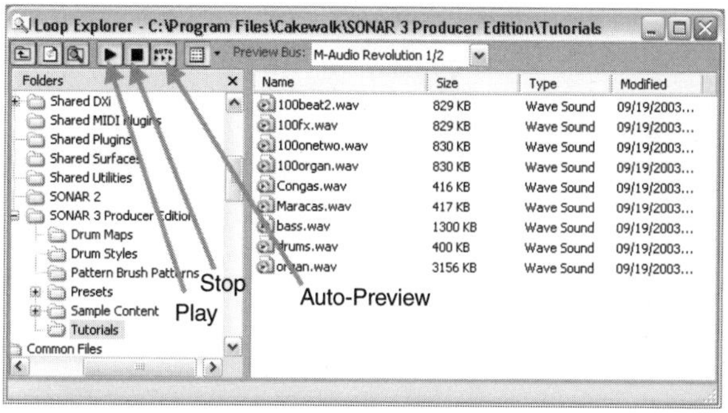

Figure 9.9
Use the Play, Stop, and
Auto-Preview options
to preview a Groove
clip file.

5. To add a Groove clip to a project, just drag and drop the clip from the Loop
    Explorer view into the Clips pane of the Track view. If you drag the clip onto an
    existing track, the clip will be added to that track. If you drag the clip onto a blank
    area of the Clips pane, a new track containing the clip will be created for you.
    Also, depending on the horizontal position to which you drag and drop, the clip
    will be added to the track at the closest measure position in the track. For example,
    if you drag and drop the clip anywhere inside measure 2 in the track, the clip will
    be added to the track with its beginning at the beginning of measure 2.

6. You can keep the Loop Explorer view open for as long as you need to continue
    dragging and dropping Groove clips into your project.

After you've added your Groove clips, you can slip edit them to make them conform to the music
you are trying to create. I talked about slip editing back in Chapter 7, but later in this chapter (in
the "A Groove Clip Exercise" section), I'll give you an example of how to use the technique with
Groove clips.

IMPORT AUDIO
You also can add Groove clips to a project by using the Import Audio feature. I
talked about this feature back in Chapter 6.

Controlling Project Pitch

Controlling the pitch of the Groove clips in your project is extremely easy. The first thing you need
to do is set the default pitch for the entire project. This is called the *project pitch*. To set the
project pitch, follow these steps:

1. Make sure the Markers toolbar is visible by choosing View > Toolbars. Activate the
    Markers option and click on Close.

2. On the Markers toolbar, use the Default Groove-Clip Pitch drop-down list to set the
    initial pitch for your project (see Figure 9.10). For example, if you want the music
    in your project to start using a C chord, choose C in the Default Groove-Clip Pitch
    drop-down list.

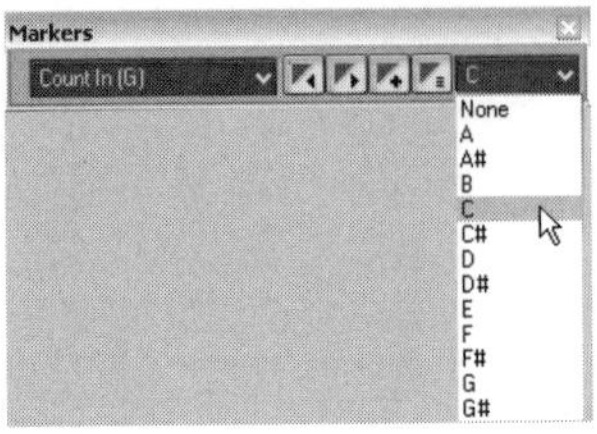

Figure 9.10
Use the Default Groove-
Clip Pitch drop-down list
to set the initial pitch of
your project.

Pitch Markers

After you've set the initial pitch for your project, all the Groove clips automatically will be transposed to play using that pitch until you change it. To change the project pitch at specified points in your project, you need to use pitch markers. I talked about markers back in Chapter 5, and although pitch markers work almost the same as regular markers, they do have a slight difference.

Creating Pitch Markers

Creating pitch markers is essentially the same as creating regular markers. You simply set the Now time to the measure, beat, and tick at which you want to place the marker in the project, activate the Marker dialog box, and type in a name. But you also have to designate a pitch setting for that marker, which tells SONAR to change the project pitch at that point in the project. To create a pitch marker, just follow these steps:

1. Set the Now time to the measure, beat, and tick or the SMPTE time at which you want to place the marker in the object.

2. Choose Insert > Marker to open the Marker dialog box (see Figure 9.11). You can also open the Marker dialog box by pressing F11 on your computer keyboard; holding the Ctrl key on your computer keyboard and clicking just above the Time Ruler (the Marker section) in the Track, Staff, or Piano Roll views; right-clicking in a Time Ruler; clicking on the Insert Marker button in the Markers toolbar; or clicking on the Insert Marker button in the Markers view.

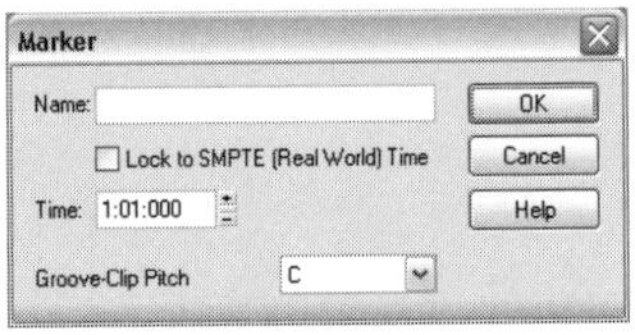

Figure 9.11
Using the Marker dialog
box, you can create a
pitch marker.

3. Type a name for the marker.

4. If you want the marker to be assigned to a measure/beat/tick value, you don't need to do anything more.

5. If you want the marker to be assigned to an SMPTE time, activate the Lock to SMPTE (Real World) Time option.

LOCK TO SMPTE TIME

If you use the Lock to SMPTE (Real World) Time value, your marker is assigned an exact hour/minute/second and frame value. It retains that value no matter what. Even if you change the tempo of the project, the marker keeps the same time value, although its measure/beat/tick location might change because of the tempo. This feature is especially handy when you're putting music and sound to video and you need to have cues that always happen at an exact moment within the project.

By leaving a marker assigned to a measure/beat/tick value, however, you can be sure that it will always occur at that measure, beat, and tick even if you change the tempo of the project.

6.   Assign a pitch to the marker using the Groove-Clip Pitch drop-down list.

7.   Click on OK.

When you're finished, your pitch marker (and its pitch) will be added to the Marker section (just above the Time Ruler) in the Track, Staff, and Piano Roll views.

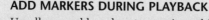

ADD MARKERS DURING PLAYBACK

Usually you add markers to a project while no real-time activity is going on, but you also can add markers while a project is playing. Simply press the F11 key on your computer keyboard, and SONAR will create a marker at the current Now time. The new marker will be assigned a temporary name automatically, which you can change later. You also need to add a pitch to each marker after you stop playback because SONAR will not assign pitches to markers automatically.

Changing Pitch Marker Names

To change the name of a pitch marker, follow these steps:

1.   Right-click on the marker in the Marker section of the Time Ruler in one of the views to open the Marker dialog box. Alternatively, select View > Markers to open the Markers view, and double-click on the marker in the list to open the Marker dialog box.

2.   Type a new name for the marker.

3.   Click on OK.

Changing Pitch Marker Time

Follow these steps to change the time value of a pitch marker numerically:

1.   Right-click on the marker in the Marker section of the Time Ruler in one of the views to open the Marker dialog box. Alternatively, select View > Markers to open the Markers view, and then double-click on the marker in the list to open the Marker dialog box.

2.   Type a new measure/beat/tick value for the marker. If you want to use an SMPTE value, activate the Lock to SMPTE (Real World) Time option, and then type a new hour/minute/second/frame value for the marker.

3.   Click on OK.

You also can change the time value of a pitch marker graphically by simply dragging the marker in the Marker section of the Time Ruler in one of the views. Drag the marker to the left to decrease its time value or drag it to the right to increase its time value. Simple, no?

Making a Copy of a Pitch Marker

To make a copy of a pitch marker, follow these steps:

1. Hold down the Ctrl key on your computer keyboard.
2. Click and drag a pitch marker to a new time location in the Marker section of the Time Ruler in one of the views.
3. Release the Ctrl key and mouse button. SONAR will display the Marker dialog box.
4. Enter a name for the marker. You can change the time by typing a new value if you want. The time value is initially set to the time corresponding to the location on the Time Ruler to which you dragged the marker.
5. Click on OK.

Deleting a Pitch Marker

You can delete a marker in one of two ways—directly in the Track, Staff, or Piano Roll view or via the Markers view. Here's the exact procedure:

1. If you want to use the Track, Staff, or Piano Roll view, click and hold the left mouse button on the marker you want to delete.
2. If you want to use the Markers view, select View > Markers to open the Markers view. Then select the marker you want to delete from the list.
3. Press the Delete key on your computer keyboard.

A Groove Clip Exercise

Now that I've talked about how to create Groove clips and how to use them in a project, you can put that knowledge to practical use by working through a detailed exercise so you can actually see Groove clips in action. Are you ready? Let's go:

1. Start SONAR. A blank new project should open automatically. If not, then choose File > New and choose the Normal template from the New Project File dialog box to create one.
2. If there are any tracks in the project, delete them. You should now have a totally blank Track view.
3. Set the Default Project Pitch to C and set the tempo for the project to 114 bpm. Also activate the Snap to Grid feature and, in the Snap to Grid dialog box, choose the Musical Time: Measure options and Move To mode.
4. Choose File > Open and open the demo project called SONAR Audio and MIDI Demo2.cwb.
5. If the File Info window appears, close it. Then choose Window > Tile in Rows to adjust the view layout so you can see the Track views from both projects.

6. Drag and drop the first clip in track 1 from the demo project into your new project. If the Drag and Drop Options dialog box appears, click on OK. SONAR will create a new track for the clip automatically. Make sure the clip is positioned at the very beginning of the track (see Figure 9.12). Zoom in a bit so you can see the data in the clip.

Figure 9.12
Drag and drop the clip to the beginning of the new track.

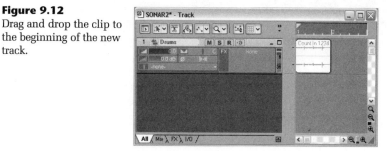

7. Drag and drop the clip in track 1 at measure 6 from the demo project into track 1 of your new project. Position the start of this clip at measure 2 and slip edit the clip so its end extends to the beginning of measure 12 (see Figure 9.13). If the Drag and Drop Options dialog box appears, choose the Slide Over Old to Make Room option and activate Align to Measures. Then click on OK.

Figure 9.13
Slip edit the clip in track 1 to extend its end to measure 12.

8. Drag and drop the clip in track 1 at measure 13 from the demo project into track 1 of your new project. Position the start of this clip at measure 12. If the Drag and Drop Options dialog box appears, choose the Slide Over Old to Make Room option and activate Align to Measures. Then click on OK.

9. Drag and drop the clip (named Kick and Crash) in track 1 at measure 37 from the demo project into track 1 of your new project. Position the start of this clip at measure 13. If the Drag and Drop Options dialog box appears, choose the Slide Over Old to Make Room option and activate Align to Measures. Then click on OK. track 1 in your new project will now contain all the drum parts (see Figure 9.14). Play the project to hear what it sounds like so far.

CHAPTER 9

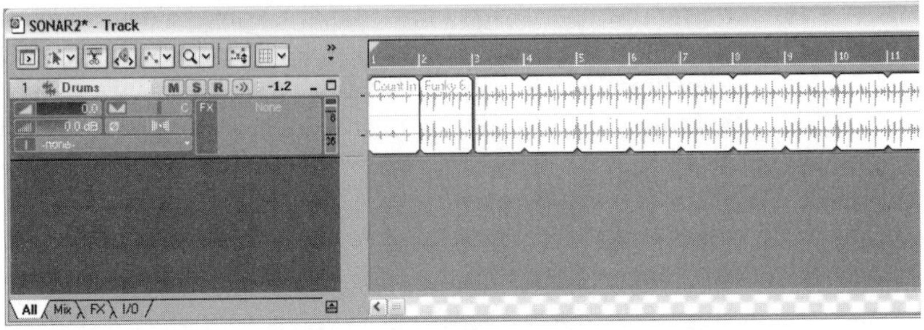

Figure 9.14
Track 1 contains all the
drum parts for the
project.

10. Close the SONAR Audio and MIDI Demo2 project. Then pop your Sonar CD into
your CD-ROM drive and open the Loop Explorer. Navigate to the Audio
Loops\Smart Loops\Electric Guitars\Mid Tempo loops folder.

11. Drag and drop the Shorty 1 C maj.wav file from the Loop Explorer into your new
project. Drop the clip somewhere underneath track 1 in the new project so that
SONAR will create a new track (Track 2, Shorty 1). Position the start of the clip at
measure 2. Widen the track so you can see the data in the clip.

12. Slip edit the clip in track 2 so its end goes to the beginning of measure 13. Play the
song. Sounds kind of dull, huh? Okay, let's add some pitch markers.

13. Place pitch markers at the beginning of measures 2, 6, 8, 10, 11, and 12. Give these
markers the following pitches, respectively: C, F, C, G, F, C. Your project should
now look like what is shown in Figure 9.15.

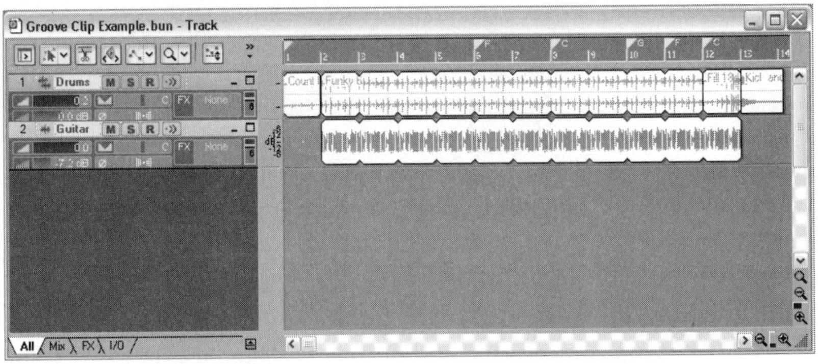

Figure 9.15
Place some pitch markers
to make the project more
interesting.

14. Play the project. Sounds better, right? The guitar doesn't sound quite right when
it's transposed to G in measure 10, though, does it? SONAR seems to be
transposing down instead of up. Normally there's no way around this by just using
pitch markers. Instead, you need to create a Groove clip that is independent of the
project pitch. Slip edit the clip in track 2 so its end goes to the beginning of
measure 10 rather than 13. Drag another copy of the Shorty 1 C maj.wav file from
the Loop Explorer into track 2, and position the start of the clip at measure 10.
Now right-click on the clip and choose Clip Properties > Groove-Clips. Deactivate
the Follow Project Pitch option and enter a value of 7 for the Pitch parameter. This
will transpose the clip up 7 semitones to G, and the project pitch won't affect it.
Click on OK.

15. Drag another copy of the Shorty 1 C maj.wav file from the Loop Explorer into track 2, and position the start of the clip at measure 11. Then slip edit the clip so its end goes to the beginning of measure 13. Ah, now that sounds better.

16. Add a bass track by navigating to the Audio Loops\Smart Loops\Bass Guitars\ Mid Tempo Loops folder in the Loop Explorer. Now drag the Straight Slap 2 D.wav file into your new project. Drop the clip somewhere underneath track 2 so SONAR will create a new track (track 3, Straight Slap). Position the start of the clip at measure 2. Widen the track so you can see the data in the clip.

17. Slip edit the clip in track 3 so its end goes to the beginning of measure 13. Play the song. Cool! Now it's starting to sound like a real song. There's still one thing missing, though.

18. Close the Loop Explorer. Then open another sample project that comes with SONAR called Don't Matter Audio and MIDI Demo.cwb. Close the File Info window, as well as the Staff view. Also, choose Window > Tile in Rows to reposition the Track views.

19. Drag and drop the first clip in track 6 (Horns Left) from the demo project into your new project. Drop the clip somewhere underneath track 3 in the new project so that SONAR will create a new track (track 4, Horns Left). Position the start of the clip at measure 3. Widen the track so you can see the data in the clip. Also, make sure the panning for the track is set to 100 percent left.

20. Right-click on the new clip in track 4 and choose Clip Properties to open the Clip Properties dialog box. Click on the Groove-Clips tab. Activate the Enable Looping option. Activate the Follow Project Pitch option. Choose D in the Reference Note drop-down list. Click on OK.

21. Select the Horns Left clip and choose View > Loop Construction to open the clip in the Loop Construction view. Adjust the Trans Detect slider to a value of 90 percent. Then adjust the Basic Slicing slider to a value of 16th Notes. Close the Loop Construction view.

22. Copy the Horns Left clip (using the Edit > Copy feature) and then paste (using the Edit > Paste feature) copies of the clip at measures 6, 8, and 10. Now slip edit the clip in measure 10 so its end extends to measure 12. The Horns Left track should look like what is shown in Figure 9.16.

Figure 9.16
Copy and paste the clips in the Horns Left track.

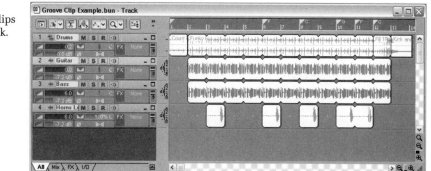

23. Drag and drop the first clip in track 7 (Horns Right) from the demo project into your new project. Drop the clip somewhere underneath track 4 in the new project so SONAR will create a new track (track 5, Horns Right). Position the start of the clip at measure 3. Widen the track so you can see the data in the clip. Also, make sure the panning for the track is set to 100 percent right.

24. Right-click on the new clip in track 5 and choose Clip Properties to open the Clip Properties dialog box. Click on the Groove-Clips tab. Activate the Enable Looping option. Activate the Follow Project Pitch option. Choose D in the Reference Note drop-down list. Click on OK.

25. Select the Horns Right Clip and choose View > Loop Construction to open the clip in the Loop Construction view. Adjust the Trans Detect slider to a value of 90 percent. Then adjust the Basic Slicing slider to a value of 16th Notes. Close the Loop Construction view.

26. Copy the Horns Right clip (using the Edit > Copy feature), and then paste (using the Edit > Paste feature) copies of the clip at measures 6, 8, and 10. Now slip edit the clip in measure 10 so its end extends to measure 12.

27. The final version of your new project should look like what is shown in Figure 9.17.

Figure 9.17
The final version of your example project should look like this.

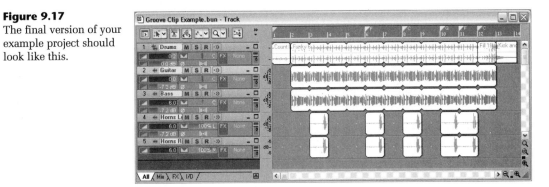

28. Play the project. Sounds cool, no?

Now you have a good working knowledge of how to use Groove clips. You can add to this exercise by creating more tracks and inserting more clips. Don't forget that you can also change the mix by adjusting the Volume and Pan Parameters for each track. Plus, because these are audio tracks, you can apply real-time effects as well. For more information on effects, read Chapter 11, "Exploring Effects."

ADJUST THE TEMPO

Change the tempo of the example project to 120 bpm. Play the project. Isn't that great? SONAR automatically adjusts the Groove clips so they will play at the correct speed whenever you change the tempo of the project.

10
Software Synthesis

In Chapter 1, I talked about the differences between MIDI and digital audio. MIDI is simply performance data. MIDI data alone does not produce any sound. In order to have sound produced from your MIDI data, you need a MIDI instrument. Usually, a MIDI instrument comes in the form of a MIDI synthesizer keyboard or module. These are hardware-based synthesizers. Today, however, personal computers have become so powerful that it is now possible to simulate a MIDI synthesizer via a computer software program. This process is known as *software synthesis*, and basically it has the power to turn your computer into a full-fledged MIDI synthesizer module. SONAR has built-in software synthesis features. In this chapter, I'll tell you all about the software synthesis features that SONAR provides. This chapter will do the following:

▶ Explain DX and VST instruments

▶ Show you how to set up and play DX and VST instruments

▶ Explain the Virtual Sound Canvas

▶ Demystify the DreamStation

▶ Explain the Cyclone

▶ Discuss the VSampler 3

▶ Discuss the ReValver

▶ Introduce SoundFonts and LiveSynth Pro

▶ Explain the ReWire technology

DX instruments (DXis for short) are a technology developed by Cakewalk that is based on Microsoft's DirectX technology. VST instruments (VSTis for short) are a technology developed by Steinberg. DXis and VSTis come in the form of plug-ins that can simulate any kind of hardware-based synthesizer module. As a matter of fact, many DXis and VSTis have interfaces that look like onscreen versions of a hardware-based synth, with all kinds of knobs and switches that you can tweak with your mouse. Because DXis and VSTis are plug-ins, you can use them interchangeably within SONAR, just like effects plug-ins. (See Chapter 11, "Exploring Effects," for more information about effects.)

WHAT IS A PLUG-IN?

In basic terms, a *plug-in* is a small computer program that by itself does nothing but when used with a larger application provides added functionality to the larger program. Therefore, you can use plug-ins to add new features easily to a program. In SONAR's case, plug-ins provide you with additional ways to produce music through the use of DXis and VSTis.

Using DX and VST Instruments

Using a DXi or VSTi to generate music is just like using a hardware-based synth, except that because a DXi or VSTi is software-based, it is run on your computer as an application from within SONAR. You control the settings of a DXi or VSTi by tweaking onscreen parameters. You can generate sound with a DXi or VSTi either in real time, as you perform on your MIDI keyboard, or by using data from a pre-existing MIDI track. To use a DXi or VSTi in your SONAR project, follow these steps:

1. Create a new project or open a pre-existing project.

2. Right-click in the Track pane of the Track view and choose Insert Audio Track to create a new audio track. Then widen the track to display its parameters.

3. Set the Input parameter to None, and set the Output parameter to one of your sound card outputs.

4. Right-click in the Fx bin of the audio track and choose DXi Synth > [*name of the DXi or VSTi you want to use*] to set up a DXi or VSTi for that track (see Figure 10.1). If you ever want to remove a DXi or VSTi, just right-click on its name in the Fx bin and choose Delete from the drop-down menu.

Figure 10.1
To use a DXi or VSTi, add it to the Fx bin of an audio track.

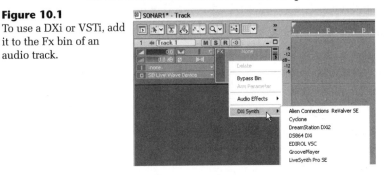

GENERATE SOUND

Even though DXis and VSTis are software-based, they still need to use a sound card output (which is hardware) to generate sound. Adding a DXi or VSTi to an audio track allows the synth to use the output of the track to generate sound. You can also add DXis to the audio bus Fx bins. For more information about buses, read Chapter 12, "Mixing It Down."

5. After you add a DXi or VSTi to the Fx bin of the audio track, the window for that DXi will appear, showing the Property page (or control interface) of the DXi (see Figure 10.2). Using those controls, you can set up the DXi's parameters, such as the sounds it will produce, and so on. After you've finished setting the DXi's parameters, you can close the window to get it out of the way. If you need to access the DXi's controls again, just double-click on the name of the DXi in the Fx bin of the audio track.

Figure 10.2
When a DXi is added to the Fx bin, a window appears, showing all the controls available for the DXi that you chose.

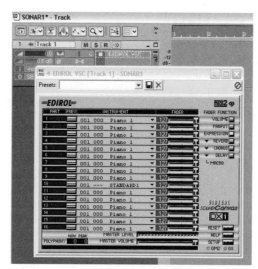

6. If you opened a pre-existing project that already contains MIDI tracks, you can skip this step. Otherwise, right-click in the Track pane of the Track view and choose Insert MIDI Track to create a new MIDI track. Then widen the track to display its parameters.

7. Set the Input parameter to the MIDI port and channel being used to receive data from your MIDI keyboard. Then click on the Output parameter to display a list of available outputs. In addition to your MIDI interface outputs, the list will also show any DXis you previously set up (see Figure 10.3). Choose the DXi you want to use.

Figure 10.3
After you set up a DXi, it will be displayed in the Output parameter list of your MIDI track.

8. Set the Channel, Bank, and Patch parameters for the MIDI track. The settings you choose for these parameters will depend on the DXi you are using. For the Channel parameter, choose the same channel to which the DXi is set. The Bank and Patch parameters automatically display different settings depending on the DXi. The parameters will show the sound presets available for the DXi. Choose the bank and patch that correspond to the sound you want to use.

9. Either start performing some music on your MIDI keyboard or start playback of the project. Whichever action you choose, you should hear sound coming from the DXi.

REAL-TIME PERFORMANCE

When you use a DXi in real time by performing on your MIDI keyboard, you might hear a delay between the time you press a key on your keyboard and the time it takes for the DXi to produce sound. This is caused by sound card latency. To prevent this delay, you need to use ASIO or WDM drivers for your sound card, and you also need to adjust the Latency slider to its lowest possible setting. I talked about ASIO and WDM drivers and latency in Chapters 2 and 3.

Those are the basic steps you need to take to use DXis and VSTis in your projects.

The Insert DXi Synth Function

There is actually an easier way to add a DXi or VSTi to a project, but I wanted to be sure you knew everything that was needed to add one manually. And it allowed me to explain the process in more detail as well. More often than not, however, you'll probably use the Insert DXi Synth function. This function allows you to automatically add a DXi to a project, along with the accompanying audio and MIDI tracks needed for the DXi. Here is how the Insert DXi Synth function works:

1. Create a new project or open a pre-existing project.

2. Choose Insert > DXi Synth > [*name of the DXi or VSTi you want to use*] to open the Insert DXi Synth Options dialog box (see Figure 10.4).

Figure 10.4
Use the Insert DXi Synth function as a quick way to add a DXi or VSTi to a project.

Insert DXi Synth Options		
Insert DXi into project, and:		OK
Create These Tracks:	Open These Windows:	Cancel
☑ MIDI Source Track	☑ Synth Property Page	Help
☑ First Synth Output (Audio)	☐ Synth Rack View	
☐ All Synth Outputs (Audio)		
☑ Ask This Every Time		

3. In the Create These Tracks section, activate the MIDI Source Track option if you want a MIDI track to be created automatically for your DXi.

4. In the Create These Tracks section, activate either the First Synth Output (Audio) option or the All Synth Outputs (Audio) option if you want the audio tracks for your DXi to be created automatically.

MULTIPLE AUDIO OUTPUTS

Some DXis provide multiple audio outputs, similar to some hardware-based synthesizers. This gives you more control over how the sounds of the DXi are processed and routed. For example, if a DXi can produce 16 different instrument sounds at the same time and has four outputs (like the Virtual Sound Canvas DXi, which I will talk about later), you can group those 16 instruments into four different sections and send them to their own outputs. This means you could send all drum sounds to one output, all guitar sounds to another output, and so on. You could then apply different effects to each output (or group of sounds). Each output of a DXi requires its own audio track. If you choose the All Synth Outputs (Audio) option in the Insert DXi Synth Options dialog box, and the DXi provides four outputs, then four separate audio tracks will be created.

5. In the Open These Windows section, activate the Synth Property page option if you want the DXi's Property page (or control interface) to be opened after the DXi is added to the project.

6. In the Open These Windows section, activate the Synth Rack View option if you want the Synth Rack view (which I will talk about shortly) to be opened after the DXi is added to the project.

7. Click on OK. The DXi you chose will be added to the project along with the MIDI track and audio tracks, depending on the options you activated in the Insert DXi Synth Options dialog box.

8. If you chose to have a MIDI track automatically created for you, you still need to set the track parameters. Set the Channel, Bank, and Patch parameters for the MIDI track as I described in the previous section of this chapter.

9. Either start performing some music on your MIDI keyboard or start playback of the project. Whichever action you choose, you should hear sound coming from the DXi.

Don't worry if the instructions in the last two sections seem a bit generic. I'll provide some more specific examples on how to use the DXis that are included with SONAR a little later. Before we get to that, let me tell you about the Synth Rack view.

The Synth Rack View

When you add a DXi or a VSTi to a project, the DXi is listed as an entry in SONAR's Synth Rack view (see Figure 10.5).The Synth Rack view allows you to manage all the DXis in a project by letting you add, remove, and change DXis, as well as manipulate their properties.

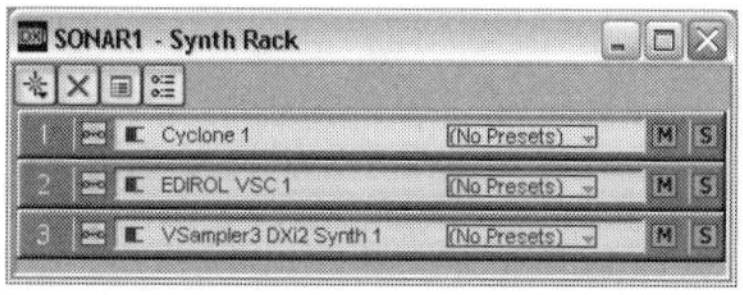

Figure 10.5
All DXis and VSTis in a project are listed in the Synth Rack view.

Adding a DXi or VSTi

To add a DXi to a project using the Synth Rack view, just click on the Insert DXi Instruments and ReWire Devices button (see Figure 10.6). Then choose a DXi from the drop-down menu. This will open the Insert DXi Synth Options dialog box. From there, you can follow the same steps as shown in the previous section of this chapter.

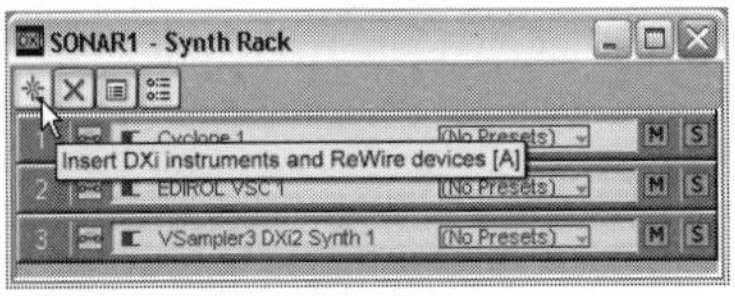

Figure 10.6
Use the Insert DXi
Instruments and ReWire
Devices button to add a
DXi to a project via the
Synth Rack.

Removing a DXi or VSTi

To remove a DXi from a project using the Synth Rack view, select the DXi you want to remove by clicking on its number in the Synth Rack. Then click on the Delete button (see Figure 10.7).

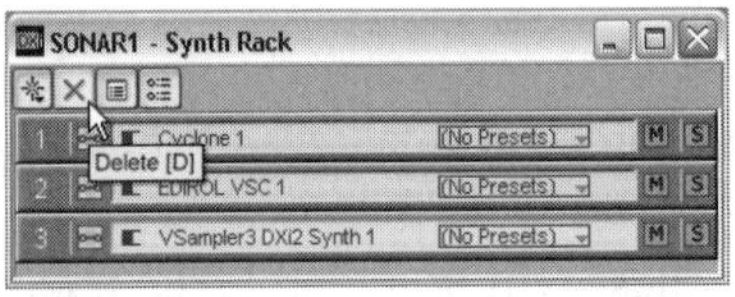

Figure 10.7
Use the Delete button to
remove a DXi from a
project via the Synth
Rack.

DELETE ASSOCIATED TRACKS

If there are any MIDI or audio tracks associated with the deleted DXi, they will not be removed from the project. You have to delete those tracks manually if you no longer want them in the project.

Setting DXi Properties

To access the Property page (or control interface) of a DXi or VSTi via the Synth Rack view, select the DXi by clicking on its number, and then click on the Properties button (see Figure 10.8).

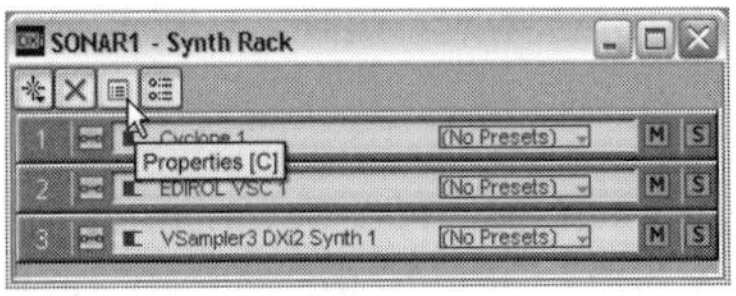

Figure 10.8
Use the Properties button
to access a DXi's Property
page via the Synth Rack.

DOUBLE-CLICK TO OPEN

You can also just double-click on the number of a DXi in the Synth Rack to open the DXi's Property page.

Synth Rack Parameters

When a DXi is listed in the Synth Rack, it is shown using a graphical representation that has a number of control parameters you can use to manipulate certain aspects of the DXi. These include turning the DXi on or off, showing its patch point, showing its name, displaying its current preset, and muting and/or soloing the DXi (see Figure 10.9).

Figure 10.9
Use the Synth Rack control parameters to manipulate a selected DXi.

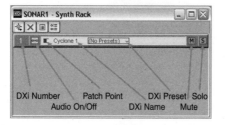

DXi Audio Connection

Just like a hardware-based synth, you can turn on or off a DXi. To do so, just click on the Audio On/Off parameter of the DXi in the Synth Rack. Internally, this changes the DXi's connection to SONAR's audio engine. When the DXi is on, it is connected to the audio engine, which means it produces sound and also takes up some of your computer's processing power. When the DXi is off, it is not connected to the audio engine, which means it does not produce sound and it doesn't use any of your computer's processing power. Using the Audio On/Off parameter is an easy way to disable/enable a DXi without having to keep adding or removing it (and its associated tracks) from a project.

CONNECTION METHODS

Sometimes you might notice that the Audio On/Off button doesn't work. This is because DXis are "connected" to a project in two different ways. When you add a DXi manually to a project by inserting it into the Fx bin of an audio track, the DXi is treated like an effect, and it can't be disconnected from the SONAR audio engine without being removed completely from the project. When you add a DXi via the Insert DXi Synth function, it is inserted into the input of the audio track, which means it can be disconnected from the SONAR audio engine without having to be removed from the project.

Why two connection methods? Because while most DXis are software synthesizers, there are some that must be used as effects (like the Alien Connections ReValver SE included with SONAR, which I'll talk about later in "The ReValver" section of this chapter). The DXis that provide effects processing must be treated like effects; otherwise, they won't work. You'll need to refer to the documentation for your DXi to determine whether it is a software synth or an effect.

DXi Patch Point

You can tell how a DXi is "connected" to a project by hovering your mouse over the Patch Point parameter of the DXi in the Synth Rack. One symbol designates that the DXi is connected to the input of an audio track (see Figure 10.10).

Figure 10.10
This DXi is connected to the In (input) of an audio track.

Another symbol designates that the DXi is connected to the Fx bin of an audio track (see Figure 10.11).

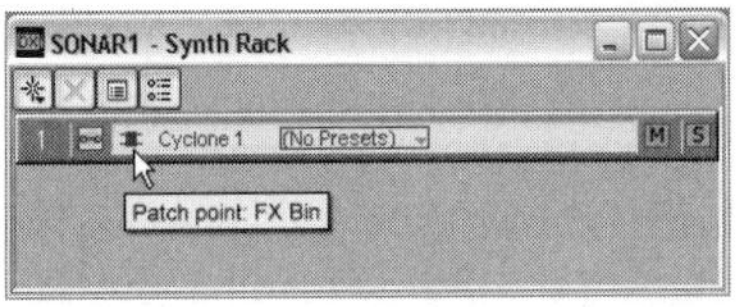

Figure 10.11
This DXi is connected to the Fx bin of an audio track.

DXi Presets

You can change the current synth preset (sound) of a DXi in the Synth Rack by clicking on the DXi's Preset parameter. This displays a menu that allows you to choose the preset you want to use. Unfortunately, this only works with SONAR presets, meaning the presets listed in the Presets drop-down list of the Property page of a DXi. Some DXis have their own method of storing presets, and some DXis are multi-timbral (they can produce more than one sound at the same time). For these DXis, you need to access their Property pages to change their presets.

DXi Mute and Solo

You also can mute and solo DXis in the Synth Rack by clicking on their Mute and Solo buttons. This is just like muting and soloing tracks in the Track view. And just like muting a track, when you mute a DXi it no longer produces any sound, but it is still processed by your computer. Muting a DXi doesn't disconnect it from the SONAR audio engine. If you want to mute and disconnect a DXi, use the Audio On/Off parameter instead.

The Virtual Sound Canvas

SONAR ships with a number of DXis, one of which is the Virtual Sound Canvas DXi (or VSC DXi for short). The VSC DXi simulates the Roland Sound Canvas, which is a hardware-based MIDI playback module. The VSC DXi is multi-timbral (meaning it can play more than one different sound at a time—up to 16 different sounds), has a polyphony of 128 voices (meaning it can play up to 128 notes at a time), and comes with 902 built-in sounds as well as 26 different drum sets. You can't change the sounds in the VSC DXi or create your own sounds, but the selection is quite varied so I don't think you'll run out any time soon.

VSC DXi Basics

If you examine the main interface for the VSC DXi (see Figure 10.12), you'll notice that it provides 16 parts—one part for each of the 16 available MIDI channels. Part 1 corresponds to MIDI channel 1, Part 2 to MIDI channel 2, and so on. Each part provides a number of adjustable parameters. These parameters include the instrument, volume, panpot, expression, reverb, chorus, and delay.

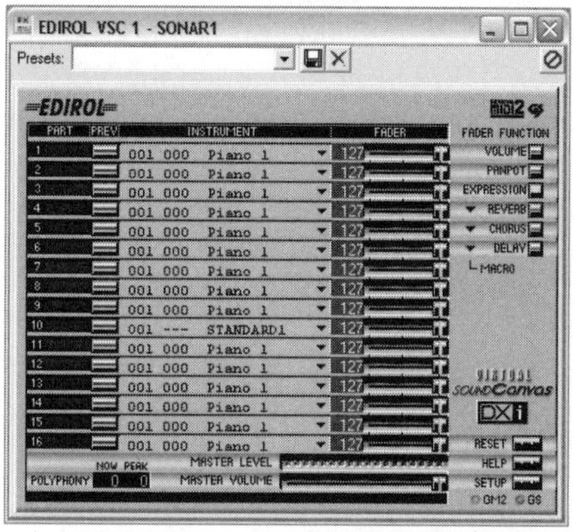

Figure 10.12
You can adjust the VSC DXi parameter settings using its main interface.

Selecting Instruments

Instruments refers to the sounds, programs, or patches the VSC DXi provides. To assign an instrument to a part, just click on the Instrument drop-down list that corresponds to the part and choose an instrument from the menu (see Figure 10.13).

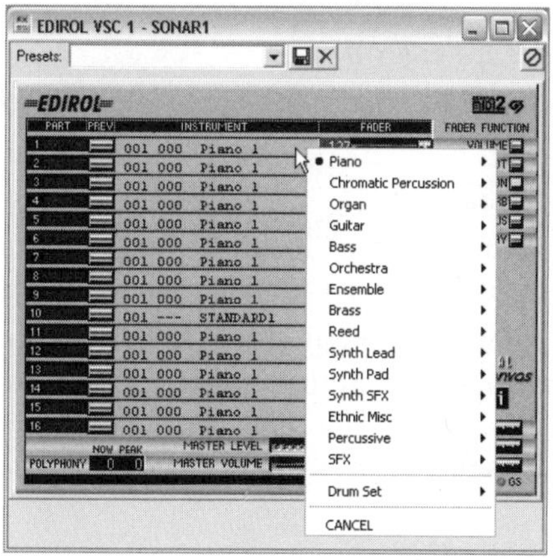

Figure 10.13
Use the Instrument drop-down list to choose an instrument for a part.

Previewing the Instrument

To test the instrument and hear what it sounds like, click on the Prev (preview) button for the part (see Figure 10.14).

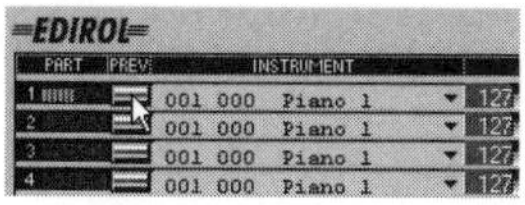

Figure 10.14
To test the sound of the instrument, click the part's Prev button.

Additional Instruments

The VSC DXi provides two different categories of instruments. One category is a set of GM (General MIDI)-compatible instruments. The other category is a set of GS (Roland GS format)-compatible instruments. The GS format is similar to GM in that it provides a standardized set of rules for MIDI synths, but they usually pertain only to Roland MIDI devices. The GS format provides an expanded set of rules to include many more instruments, as well as additional features not covered by GM. To switch between the GM and GS modes for the VSC DXi, click on the Setup button at the bottom of the VSC DXi window to open the VSC Setup dialog box (see Figure 10.15). Under the Performance tab, choose the GM2 or GS option for the Generator Mode parameter and click on OK.

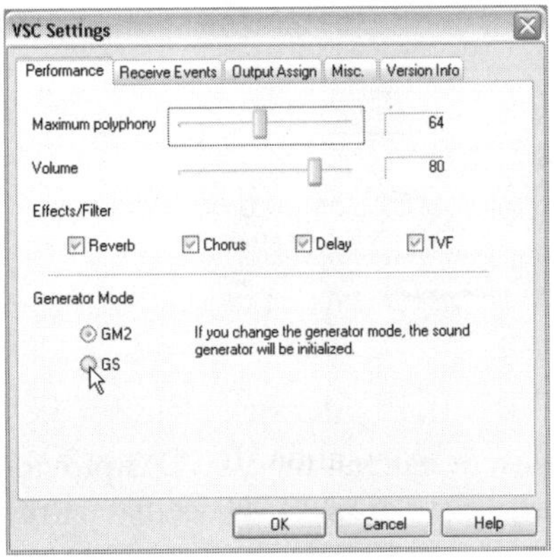

Figure 10.15
Choose between two sets of instruments using the Generator Mode parameter.

Adjusting Volume, Panpot, and Expression

To adjust the Volume, Panpot (panning), and Expression parameters for each part, follow these steps:

1. In the Fader Function section, choose the parameter you want to adjust. To adjust Volume, click on the Volume button. To adjust Panpot, click on the Panpot button. To adjust Expression (velocity depth), click on the Expression button.

2. When you click on a parameter button, it will light up with a green color (see Figure 10.16). This indicates that all the sliders in the Fader sections for each part now correspond to the parameter you selected. For example, if you chose the Volume parameter, each slider would control the volume of its corresponding part.

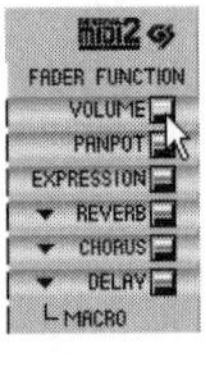

Figure 10.16
Activating a parameter makes it light up with a green color.

3. Click and drag the sliders in the Fader sections for each part to adjust the selected parameter (see Figure 10.17).

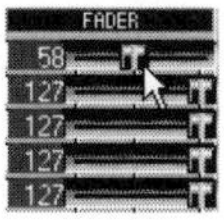

Figure 10.17
Click and drag the Fader
sliders to adjust the
chosen parameter for
each part.

Applying Effects

In addition, the VSC DXi provides effects that you can apply to each part individually. This gives
you much more flexibility than if you were to apply SONAR's effects because with the VSC DXi
effects, you can apply a different amount of effect to each part. With SONAR's effects you would
have to apply them to all the parts in the same amount because you would be assigning the effects
to the audio track to which the VSC DXi is assigned. For more information about effects, read
Chapter 11.

Assigning effects to parts works in exactly the same way as adjusting the Volume, Panpot, and
Expression parameters. Just click on the appropriate effect parameter button in the Fader Function
section, and then adjust the Fader sliders for each part. The Fader sliders determine the amount of
the effect that will be applied to each part. For example, you could have a large amount of reverb
on one part and a small amount of reverb on another part.

The only difference is that each effect provides a number of variations. Each part cannot have its
own effect variation; all parts use the same effect variation. To change the variation of an effect,
just click on the Macro down arrow next to the effect and choose a variation from the drop-down
menu (see Figure 10.18).

Figure 10.18
Choose effect variations
using the Macro arrows.

⚡ **SAVE INSTRUMENTATION PRESETS**

You can set some of the VSC DXi parameters by simply setting the corresponding
MIDI track parameters. For instance, by changing the Volume, Pan, Bank, Patch,
Chorus, and Reverb parameters of the MIDI track driving one of the VSC DXi parts,
you can control the Volume, Panpot, Instrument, Chorus Effect, and Reverb Effect
parameters for that part. When you save your project, those parameters are stored
along with it. But there is an advantage to adjusting parameters within the VSC
DXi itself. You can save all the VSC DXi parameters as a preset using the Preset
drop-down list and Preset Save and Delete buttons located at the top of the
window. By saving a number of parameter configurations as presets, you can
switch quickly between configurations to test out different instrumentation for the
project on which you are working.

Multiple Outputs

In the previous section, I mentioned that when you apply SONAR's effects to the VSC DXi, you have to apply the same effect to all the parts because they share the same audio track. This isn't entirely true. The VSC DXi provides four separate audio outputs to which you can assign any of the 16 available parts. Each VSC DXi output gets its own audio track, so you could essentially separate the 16 parts into four different groups, each of which can use its own set of SONAR effects. This can come in handy if you want to apply one type of effect to your drum instruments, another type of effect to your guitar instruments, and so on.

Earlier I talked about how to set up a DXi to use multiple outputs in a project, but you still need to set up the internal parameters of the DXi, and this procedure is different for each DXi. To designate the parts that are assigned to the four available outputs in the VSC DXi, follow these steps:

1. In the VSC DXi, click on the Setup button to open the VSC Settings dialog box. Then click the Output Assign tab (see Figure 10.19).

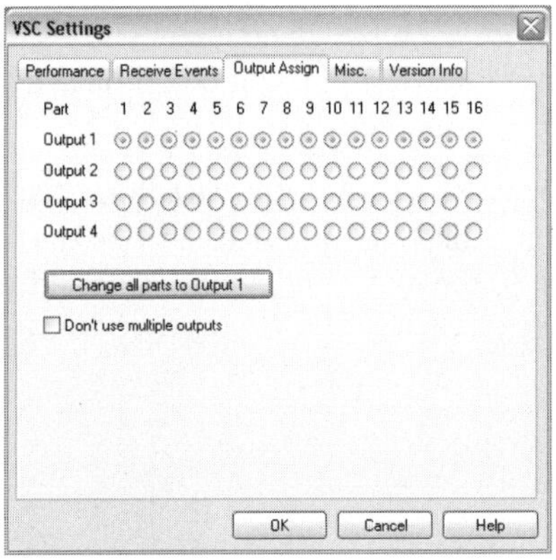

Figure 10.19
Use the VSC Settings dialog box to assign parts to different outputs.

2. In the displayed grid, you'll see the part numbers shown along the top and the output numbers shown along the left. To assign a part to a specific output, line up your mouse with the part number along the top and the output along the left, and then click at that grid point to make the assignment.

3. If you want to reset all part assignments to output 1, click on the Change All Parts to Output 1 button.

4. You can turn off multiple outputs using the Don't Use Multiple Outputs option. This keeps your grid assignments intact if you want to send all parts to output 1 temporarily.

5. Click on OK.

VSC DXi Exercise

Now that I've covered all the boring parameter basics for the VSC DXi, what do you say we kick it up a notch? How about working through an exercise so you can hear what the VSC DXi is really capable of doing?

To give you an idea of the amount of power the VSC DXi provides, try this:

1. Choose File > Open and select the sample project called Latin.cwp that is included with SONAR. Click on Open.
2. Click on Cancel in the Auto-Send Sysx dialog box.
3. Close the File Info window, the Staff view, and the Big Time view, and then delete track 1. You won't need them.
4. Choose Insert > DXi Synth > Edirol VSC.
5. In the Insert DXi Synth Options dialog box, activate the All Synth Outputs and Synth Property page options. Make sure all the other options are deactivated and then click on OK.
6. In the Track view, change the names of tracks 11, 12, 13, and 14 to Drums, Bass, Piano, and Brass, respectively.
7. Select tracks 1 through 10. Then choose Track > Property > Outputs, and choose Edirol VSC in the MIDI Outputs drop-down list. Click on OK.

CHANGE MULTIPLE TRACK PARAMETERS

If you ever need to change the parameters for more than one track at a time, just select the tracks that you want to adjust, then use the Track > Property menu to change the properties for all of those tracks simultaneously.

8. Press the spacebar on your computer keyboard to start playback of the project. Notice that in the VSC DXi window, all the MIDI tracks are being played by only four different parts—2, 3, 4, and 10. This works perfectly because the VSC DXi provides up to four separate audio outputs. You've already set up our audio tracks, but now you need to assign the VSC DXi parts to the different outputs.
9. In the VSC DXi window, click on the Setup button to open the VSC Settings dialog box, and then click the Output Assign tab. In the grid, assign Part 2 to Output 2 (Bass audio track), Part 3 to Output 3 (Piano audio track), Part 4 to Output 4 (Brass audio track), and Part 10 to Output 1 (Drums audio track), as shown in Figure 10.20. Then click on OK.

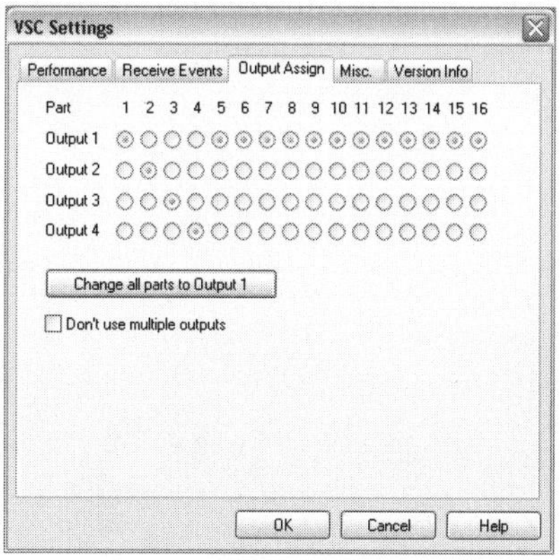

Figure 10.20
Assign Parts 2, 3, 4, and 10 to Outputs 2, 3, 4, and 1, respectively.

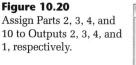

10. Expand the four audio tracks in the Track view so you can see their playback meters, and then play the project again. You should notice that the drum, bass, piano, and brass instruments are now playing through tracks 11, 12, 13, and 14, respectively (see Figure 10.21). This allows you to apply different SONAR audio effects to each separate group of instruments.

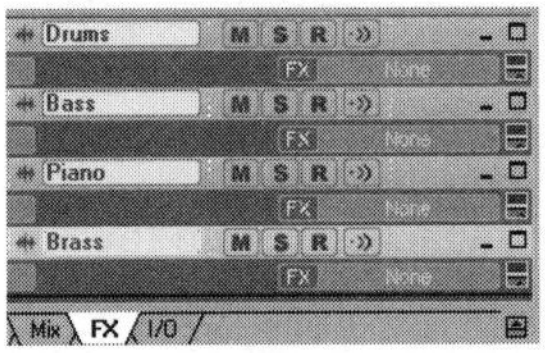

Figure 10.21
Each group of instruments is now assigned to its own audio track.

11. I'll talk more about effects in Chapter 11, but in the meantime you can add some effects to each group of instruments. Right-click on the Fx bin of track 11 (Drums) and choose Audio Effects > Cakewalk > FxReverb. In the Cakewalk FxReverb window, choose the Drum Room – Small, Warm preset, and then close the window. Now do the same for track 13 (Piano).

12. Right-click on the Fx bin for track 14 (Brass) and choose Audio Effects > Cakewalk > FxChorus. In Cakewalk FxChorus window, choose the Big Stereo Spread preset, and then close the window.

13. Play the project one last time, and then just sit back and listen.

Can you believe all of that sound is coming from one little software synthesizer? Of course, you can always try out different effects. Don't be afraid to experiment. For the full scoop on effects, read Chapter 11.

SCRATCH-PAD SYNTH

One more thing about the VSC DXi is that even though some of the sounds aren't the greatest, this DXi works wonderfully as a scratch-pad synth—meaning you can use it to work out your musical ideas and then use some more professional equipment for the final production. In addition, if you have a songwriting partner (or team) and everyone is using SONAR, then everyone has access to the VSC DXi. This means you can use the VSC DXi to work out your song ideas, and you can be sure that the project will sound exactly the same whether it is played on your computer or someone else's.

The DreamStation

Another of the DXis included with SONAR is the DreamStation. The DreamStation DXi simulates an analog modular synth (see Figure 10.22).

Figure 10.22
The DreamStation DXi puts the power of analog synthesis in your hands.

The DreamStation DXi provides three oscillator modules, an amplifier module, a filter module, an LFO (*low frequency oscillator*) module, an envelope module, vibrato and portamento features, and controls pertaining to synth output, such as volume and panning. By adjusting the controls provided by each of the modules, you can create your own unique synthesizer sounds just like you would with a hardware-based analog synth.

In this section, I'll show you how to load and save pre-existing sounds (called *instruments*) in the DreamStation DXi, and I'll provide an example of how you can use the DreamStation DXi in your SONAR projects.

INTRODUCTORY SYNTHESIS

Although I won't be going into the subjects of analog synthesis or how to create your own sounds with the DreamStation DXi, you can find some good introductory synthesis information at http://tyala.freeyellow.com and http://nmc.uoregon.edu/emi/emp_win/main.html. And for more specific information about the DreamStation DXi (as well as some free downloadable instruments), check out http://www.audio-simulation.de.

RANDOM SOUND CREATION

There is one way you can create your own sounds with the DreamStation DXi automatically, and without having to know anything about analog synthesis. Just hold down the Shift key on your computer keyboard, and then click on the CLR button at the top of the DreamStation DXi window. This makes the DreamStation DXi randomly set all of its parameters, thus automatically creating a new sound. Many of the sounds may not be usable, but click enough times and you could come up with something very cool.

Loading and Saving Instruments

The DreamStation DXi sounds are called instruments. You can save and load instruments for your own use, and you also can share instruments with others. To load and save instruments for your own use, follow these procedures:

▶ To load an instrument, choose an instrument name from the Preset drop-down list at the top of the DreamStation DXi window. The DreamStation DXi comes with 95 pre-existing instruments.

▶ To save an instrument, type a name for the instrument in the Preset parameter, and then click on the Save button (the one with the picture of a floppy disk on it). Your new instrument will appear in the Preset drop-down list.

▶ To delete an instrument from the Preset drop-down list, select the instrument from the list and then click on the Delete button (the one with the large red X on it).

In addition to saving and loading instruments for your own use, you can save and load instruments as DSI files to share with other SONAR and DreamStation users. To use DSI files, follow these procedures:

▶ To load a DSI file, click on the Load button at the top of the DreamStation DXi window. Choose your DSI file in the Open dialog box and then click on Open.

▶ To save the current instrument as a DSI file, click on the Save button. In the Save As dialog box, type a name for the DSI file and then click on Save.

A DreamStation DXi Exercise

Okay, now let's have some fun. To hear the DreamStation DXi in action, try the following exercise:

1. Choose File > Open and select the sample project file that comes included with SONAR called Downtown.cwp. Click on Open.

2. Click on Cancel in the Auto-Send Sysx dialog box.

3. Close the File Info window, as well as Staff and Big Time views. You won't need them.

4. You'll use the VSC DXi to play your drum tracks. Choose Insert > DXi Synth > Edirol VSC. In the Insert DXi Synth Options dialog box, activate the First Synth Output option and make sure the other options are deactivated.

5. Select tracks 1, 2, and 3. Then choose Track > Property > Outputs and select Edirol VSC in the MIDI Outputs drop-down menu of the Track Outputs dialog box. Click on OK.

6. Choose Insert > DXi Synth > DreamStation DXi2. In the Insert DXi Synth Options dialog box, activate the First Synth Output and Synth Property page options. Click on OK.

7. In the DreamStation DXi window, choose Bass: 01-Soft Bass in the Preset drop-down list. Then close the window.

8. In the Track view, assign the Out of track 4 to DreamStation DXi2 1. Also adjust the Vol of track 4 to 75.

MULTIPLE INSTANCES

One drawback to the DreamStation DXi is that it's single-timbral rather than multi-timbral. This means that it can play only one kind of sound at a time. In addition, the DreamStation DXi only provides one audio output. It doesn't have multiple outputs like the VSC DXi. Luckily, the DreamStation DXi doesn't take up much computer processing power, so you can set up multiple instances, each playing a unique sound.

9. Set up another instance of the DreamStation DXi using the steps covered earlier. In the DreamStation DXi window, choose Organ: 02-Jazz in the Preset drop-down list and then close the window. Then set the Out of track 5 to DreamStation DXi2 2 and the Vol to 50.

10. Set up another instance of the DreamStation DXi. In the DXi window, choose Synth: 09-Brass in the Preset list and then close the window. Then set the Out parameters of tracks 6 and 7 to DreamStation DXi2 3 and the Vol parameters to 40.

11. Set up another instance of the DreamStation DXi. In the DXi window, choose Synth: 21-Analogic 2 in the Preset list and then close the window. Then set the Out of track 8 to DreamStation DXi2 4 and the Vol to 50.

12. Set up one last instance of the DreamStation DXi. In the DXi window, choose Synth: 16-Rhodes in the Preset list and then close the window. Then set the Out of track 9 to DreamStation DXi2 5 and the Vol to 80.

13. Play the project.

That's a cool sound, isn't it? Of course, you can liven things up even more by applying some effects. The nice thing about using multiple instances of the DreamStation DXi is that each instance can have different effects applied to it.

The Cyclone

The Cyclone DXi is the equivalent of a very powerful MIDI sample playback device. Like the VSC DXi, the Cyclone is multi-timbral (meaning it can play more than one different sound at a time—up to 16), but instead of having built-in sounds, the Cyclone allows you to load in your own sounds in the form of audio sample loops in the WAV file format. The music-making possibilities of this DXi are astonishing to say the least.

Cyclone Basics

If you examine the main interface for the Cyclone (see Figure 10.23), you'll notice that it provides 16 parts (called Pad Groups)—one Pad Group for each of the 16 available MIDI channels. Pad Group 1 for MIDI channel 1, Pad Group 2 for MIDI channel 2, and so on (although you can assign any MIDI channel to any Pad Group if you want).

Figure 10.23
You can adjust the
Cyclone parameters using
its main interface.

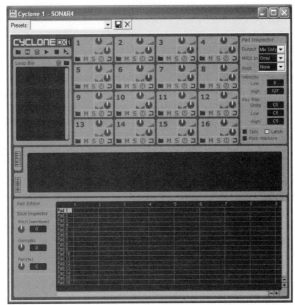

Each Pad Group provides a number of adjustable parameters, which include Sample File Load, Volume, Pan, Sync, Loop, Mute, and Solo (see Figure 10.24).

Figure 10.24
Each Pad Group provides
some adjustable
parameters.

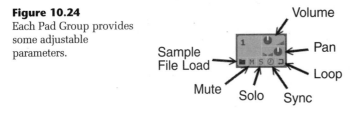

Loading Sample Files

To load a sample file into a Pad Group, click on the Load button. Then select a WAV file in the Open dialog box and click on Open. If you later want to remove a file from a Pad Group, right-click on the Pad Group and choose Clear Pad from the drop-down menu.

Loop Bin Loading

When you load a sample file into a Pad Group, the sample file is listed in the Loop Bin as well (see Figure 10.25).

Figure 10.25
Sample files loaded into
Pad Groups are also listed
in the Loop Bin.

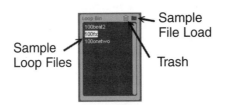

The Loop Bin lists all the sample files in the current Cyclone Sound Bank. You can load sample files into the Loop Bin separately and then apply them to Pad Groups later on if you want. Just click on the Loop Bin Load button, choose a sample file in the Open dialog box, and click on Open. To apply a sample file from the Loop Bin to a Pad Group, just drag and drop the file from the Loop Bin onto the Pad Group.

USE THE LOOP EXPLORER

You also can use the Loop Explorer view to apply sample files to Pad Groups. Just drag and drop files from the Loop Explorer onto the appropriate Pad Groups. I talked about the Loop Explorer view in Chapter 9.

If you want to delete a file from the Loop Bin, select the file and click on the Trash button.

DELETED FILES

If you delete a file that is being used by any of the Pad Groups from the Loop Bin, that file will be deleted from those Pad Groups as well.

Previewing Sample Files

To preview a sample file listed in the Loop Bin, just select the file and then click on the Preview button on the Cyclone toolbar (see Figure 10.26).

Figure 10.26
Preview sample files using the Preview button on the Cyclone toolbar.

Preview   Stop

To stop the sample file preview, click on the Stop button. You also can preview a sample file that's already loaded into a Pad Group by clicking on the number of the Pad Group. Click on the number of the Pad Group a second time to stop playback.

Adjusting Pad Group Parameters

To adjust the Volume, Pan, Mute, Solo, Sync, and Loop parameters for each Pad Group, do the following:

▶ **Volume and Pan.** Click and hold your mouse on the onscreen knob, then drag your mouse up or down to raise or lower the value. If you want to reset the parameter to its default value, just double-click on it.

▶ **Mute and Solo.** To mute or solo a Pad Group, just click on the Mute or Solo button.

> ▶ **Sync.** Activating the Sync parameter will synchronize the playback tempo of the sample file loaded into the Pad Group with the playback tempo of the current SONAR project.

> ▶ **Loop.** Activating the Loop parameter will loop the playback of the sample file loaded into the Pad Group so that the file keeps repeating over and over again.

The Pad Inspector

Each Pad Group also provides a number of other adjustable parameters, which are accessed via the Pad Inspector (see Figure 10.27). To see the Pad Inspector parameter values for a Pad Group, just click on the number of the Pad Group.

Figure 10.27
Use the Pad Inspector to adjust additional Pad Group parameters.

Output

Like the VSC DXi, the Cyclone provides multiple audio outputs (up to 17–16 individual outputs and one mix output). Each Pad Group can be assigned to its own separate output using the Output parameter. If you choose the Mix Only option, the sound from the Pad Group will be sent only to the mix output, which contains a mix of all the sound coming from all the Pad Groups in Cyclone.

MIDI In

As I mentioned earlier, Cyclone can play up to 16 different sounds at once, each one assigned to its own MIDI channel. Use the MIDI In parameter to assign a MIDI input channel to a Pad Group. Then any MIDI data coming into that channel will be used to trigger playback of that Pad Group. If you choose the MIDI Omni option, then the Pad Group will receive MIDI data from all 16 MIDI channels.

Root

The Root parameter determines the original pitch of the sample file loaded into a Pad Group. If you load an ACID-compatible WAV file or a SONAR Groove clip WAV file into a Pad Group, the Root parameter will be set for you automatically. If you load a regular WAV file into a Pad Group, you will have to determine the pitch of the file yourself and set the Root parameter manually.

Velocity and Key Map

When a Pad Group receives MIDI note messages via its assigned MIDI channel, those MIDI note messages trigger the playback of the sample file loaded into the Pad Group. You can limit the range of notes and their velocities that can be used to trigger the Pad Group by setting the Velocity and Key Map parameters as follows:

▶ **Velocity Low.** Set this to the lowest note velocity value you want to trigger the Pad Group.

▶ **Velocity High.** Set this to the highest note velocity value you want to trigger the Pad Group.

▶ **Key Map Unity.** Set this to the note value that will be used to play the sample file in the Pad Group at its Root pitch. Most of the time, you'll probably set this parameter to the same pitch value as the Root parameter.

▶ **Key Map Low.** Set this to the lowest note value you want to trigger the Pad Group.

▶ **Key Map High.** Set this to the highest note value you want to trigger the Pad Group.

Pitch Markers

I talked about pitch markers back in Chapter 9. They are used to change the pitch of Groove clips in a project. You also can use them to change the pitch of Pad Groups throughout a project. If your project uses pitch markers, and you want your Pad Groups to change pitch along with the markers, activate the Pitch Markers option for the Pad Groups in the Pad Inspector.

The Loop View

When you select a sample file listed in the Loop Bin, its audio waveform is displayed in the Loop view section of the Cyclone main interface (see Figure 10.28).

Figure 10.28
The Loop view displays sample file audio waveforms.

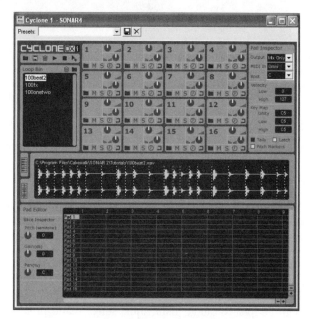

If the selected sample file is an ACID-compatible loop or a SONAR Groove clip, then the Loop view will display any slices contained in the file as well; these slices are designated by vertical dotted lines shown on the audio waveform.

SLICES IN CYCLONE

In Chapter 9 I talked about Groove clips and the Loop Construction view. When you open a Groove clip in the Loop Construction view, you'll notice that SONAR breaks the clip down into small sections. These sections are called *slices*. Slices are based on the beat values and audio waveform spikes (transients) in a clip. They allow SONAR to accurately change the tempo and pitch of a Groove clip. In Cyclone, however, you can use slices to break sample files apart and create new sample files by combining the slices from several different files. This is where the Pad Editor comes into play.

The Pad Editor

When you load a sample file into a Pad Group, a track for that Pad Group is created in the Pad Editor (see Figure 10.29). This track contains green blocks, with each separate block representing a different slice in the sample file. At the end of the track is a white *track handle* that marks the point in the track at which the track will loop back to the beginning.

Figure 10.29
Examine and manipulate Pad Group sample file slices with the Pad Editor.

Using the Pad Editor, you can select, change, and edit slices to create entire compositions out of nothing but sample file slices if you want.

Selecting a Slice

To select a slice, just click on its associated green block. If you want to select more than one slice, hold down the Shift key on your computer keyboard as you click on the blocks. Also, to select all the slices in a track, double-click on the track number.

The Slice Inspector

You can edit the parameters of a slice using the Slice Inspector. Each slice has adjustable pitch, gain (volume), and panning. Just select the slice you want to change and then click and drag your mouse over the parameter knobs. You also can change the settings by double-clicking on the numerical values and typing in new values.

Changing Slices

You also can change slices in a track by deleting them, moving them, or swapping them with slices from a different sample file. To delete a slice, just select it and press the Delete key on your computer keyboard.

You can move slices by clicking and dragging them with your mouse. To move a slice within the same track, click and drag the slice left or right. To move a slice to a different track, click and drag the slice up or down.

To swap a slice with another slice from a different file, first select a sample file in the Loop Bin so its audio waveform is shown in the Loop view. Then click and drag a slice from the Loop view into the Pad Editor (see Figure 10.30).

Figure 10.30
Click and drag slices from the Loop view to the Pad Editor to swap slices.

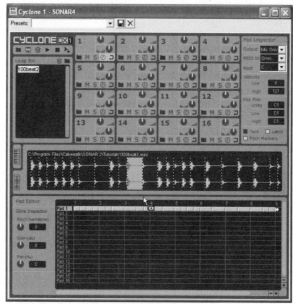

Cyclone DXi Exercise

With the boring basics out of the way, let's have some fun and give the Cyclone a whirl. To hear what the Cyclone can do, try the following exercise:

1. Choose File > New and select the Normal template in the New Project File dialog box to create a new project. If any preconfigured tracks appear in the Track view, delete them.

2. Choose Insert > DXi Synth > Cyclone to add an instance of the Cyclone to the project. In the Insert DXi Synth Options dialog box, activate the First Synth Output and Synth Property page options while leaving the other options deactivated.

3. Put your SONAR CD in your CD-ROM drive.

4. Choose View > Loop Explorer to open the Loop Explorer view.

5. Load the following file into Pad Group 1: D:\Audio Loops\Smart Loops\Dry Studio Kit (sample loops)\Funky 2.wav.

6. Load the following file into Pad Group 2: D:\Audio Loops\Smart Loops\Bass Guitars (sample loops)\Mid Tempo loops\Eight G.wav.

7. Load the following file into Pad Group 3: D:\Audio Loops\Smart Loops\Electric Guitars (sample loops)\Mid Tempo loops\Funk Junk 13 G.wav.

8. Load the following file into Pad Group 4: D:\Audio Loops\Smart Loops\Percussion Kit (sample loops)\Claves 1.wav.

9. Click on the numbers of Pad Groups 1 through 4 to start them playing. Sounds pretty good, huh? But it's also a little boring. I think we need to spice up this groove a bit.

10. Load the following file into the Loop Bin: D:\Audio Loops\Smart Loops\Dry Studio Kit (sample loops)\DSK (with Power Snare)\Funky 2.wav. The file will be selected and shown in the Loop view.

11. Drag and drop the fifth slice in the Loop view onto the fifth slice in the Pad 1 track of the Pad Editor (see Figure 10.31).

Figure 10.31
Drag and drop slices from the Loop view to the Pad Editor to replace slices (sounds) in a track.

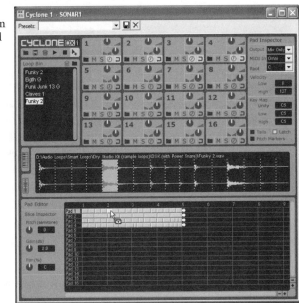

12. Drag and drop the thirteenth slice in the Loop view onto the thirteenth slice in the Pad 1 track. Then click on the Pad Group 1 number to hear it play. Click on it again to stop playback.

CHAPTER 10

TAIL OPTION

You might have noticed when listening to Pad Group 1 that the new snare drum sound gets cut off. This can happen when you replace slices in a sample file because not all slices are exactly the same length. To remedy this, you can choose to have cut slices play through as if they weren't being cut off by having Cyclone allow the tail ends of the slices to play. To do this, select the Pad Group (by clicking on its number) in which the slice resides, and then activate the Tail option for that Pad Group, which is located at the bottom of the Pad Inspector.

13. Okay, the drums in Pad Group 1 sound pretty good, but the bass in Pad Group 2 is extremely boring. Load the following file into the Loop Bin: D:\Audio Loops\Smart Loops\ Bass Guitars (sample loops)\Mid Tempo loops\Marmalade 4 G.wav.

14. Drag and drop the first three slices from the Loop view onto the last three slices in the Pad 2 track of the Pad Editor. You'll notice that the track handle for that track has been moved out of position. You need to drag the track handle to the left so it lines up with the other track handles (see Figure 10.32). This will ensure that all the tracks loop at the same time. Play both Pad Groups 1 and 2 to hear what the groove sounds like so far.

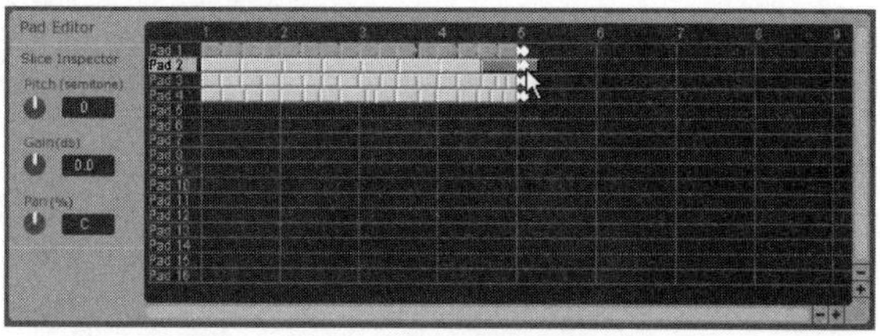

Figure 10.32
Move the Pad 2 track handle in the Pad Editor.

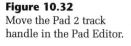

15. I think we'll leave the guitar in Pad Group 3 alone, but the percussion in Pad Group 4 needs some tweaking. Load the following file into the Loop Bin: D:\Audio Loops\Smart Loops\ Percussion Kit (sample loops)\Bongos Roll 1 (2 beats).wav.

16. Drag and drop the last four slices from the Loop view onto the last four slices in the Pad 4 track of the Pad Editor. Adjust the track handle so it lines up with the other track handles.

17. Click on the numbers of Pad Groups 1 through 4 to hear the entire groove. Cool, no?

18. To save your current Cyclone setup as a file for later editing, click on the Export Sound Bank button on the Cyclone toolbar (see Figure 10.33).

Figure 10.33
Use the Export Sound Bank function to save your current Cyclone setup as a Cyclone file.

That was just a small taste of what you can accomplish with the Cyclone. This is one very powerful tool. In addition to creating entire compositions out of audio slices, you can use it for sample playback via MIDI tracks in a project, live sample triggering via a MIDI keyboard, and to create entirely new sample files. I'm sure you'll get a lot of creative use out of the Cyclone DXi.

MORE CYCLONE INFORMATION

For more information and tutorials concerning the Cyclone DXi, be sure to read through the Cyclone DXi section of the SONAR Help file.

I'll also provide additional Cyclone coverage in future issues of my *DigiFreq* music technology newsletter. You can sign up for a free subscription at

http://www.digifreq.com/digifreq.

VSampler 3 (SONAR Producer)

If you purchased the Producer edition of SONAR, you also received a copy of the VSampler 3 DXi. Like the Cyclone DXi, the VSampler DXi is a sample playback synth, but rather than focusing on sample loops and slices, the VSampler provides advanced sample playback and synthesis (see Figure 10.34).

Figure 10.34
The VSampler 3 DXi is a very advanced sample playback synthesizer.

VSampler 3 provides 16 different outputs, each of which can be assigned an instrument for playback. These outputs represent playback modules that can be triggered via MIDI note messages from your MIDI tracks in SONAR. With 16 pads at your disposal, this means you can have an extremely large instrument ensemble at your disposal, all playing from a single DXi.

VSampler 3 is very complex so I'll show you how to load and save settings, and I'll provide instructions on how to set up instruments in VSampler so you can use it in your SONAR projects.

MORE VSAMPLER INFORMATION

Although I won't be going into detail on how to use VSampler 3, you can find a lot of good information in the Help file that comes included with the DXi. Just click on Help > Help on the VSampler 3 menu bar. In addition, you can find even more information about VSampler 3 at http://www.vsampler3.com.

Libraries, Instruments, Banks, and Programs

VSampler 3 stores sounds as libraries. A library contains (and is divided into) 128 banks, and each bank can contain up to 128 instruments (sounds). A single library can contain up to 16,384 instruments. To get any sound out of VSampler 3, you must have a library open containing at least one bank with at least one instrument in it.

Opening a Library

To open a library in VSampler 3, follow these steps:

1. Choose File > Open from the menu at the top of the VSampler 3 window to access the Open a Library dialog box.

2. Use the Look In drop-down list to access the folder in which your VSampler libraries are stored.

FILE FORMATS

VSampler 3 can load a number of different sample file formats including VSampler libraries, SoundFont banks, Downloadable Sounds, Akai AKP and PRG files, Gigasampler banks, HALion banks and programs, as well as LM4/LM9 banks. Suffice it to say, VSampler is very versatile when it comes to the formats supported, so you should have no trouble finding sample files to use with it.

3. Select a file to open by clicking on it.

VSAMPLER CDS

In addition to VSampler 3 itself, SONAR 3 Producer edition also includes two CD-ROMs filled with a large collection of files that can be used with this DXi.

4. Click on Open to load the library.

VSampler 3 will open the library file and make its banks/instruments available to you. From here you need to assign instruments to any or all of the 16 available playback outputs so you can trigger the instruments from your SONAR MIDI tracks.

Assigning Instruments

To assign an instrument to a playback output, follow these steps:

1. Double-click on one of the playback outputs (see Figure 10.35).

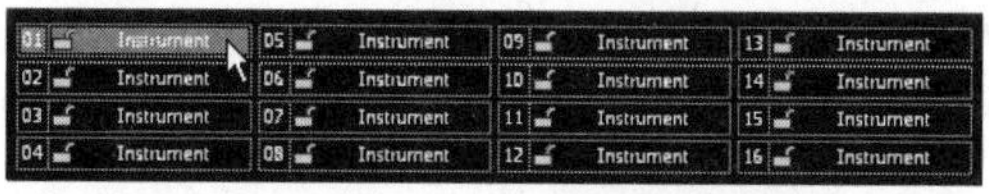

Figure 10.35
Double-click on a playback output to begin assigning an instrument.

2. In the Assign Instrument to MIDI Channel dialog box, double-click on an instrument listed under one of the available banks.

3. Repeat steps 1 and 2 for each of the playback outputs you want to use. If you assign instruments to all 16 outputs, it will look something like Figure 10.36.

Figure 10.36
You can assign
instruments to all 16
playback outputs.

After you've assigned instruments to your playback outputs you can play the sounds using the data from your MIDI tracks in SONAR. Each playback output has a designated number, which corresponds to the MIDI channel it uses. For example, to use the instrument you assigned to playback output 1, you need to play MIDI data using MIDI channel 1.

Saving a Library

After you make your instrument assignments, you can save the current library and VSampler configuration for future use. To save the current VSampler library, follow these steps:

1. Choose File > Save As from the menu at the top of the VSampler window to open the Save a Library dialog box.

2. Use the Save In drop-down list to choose a folder location for your saved file.

3. In the File Name parameter, type a name for the new library and give it a .VS3 extension.

4. Click on Save to save the new library.

These are just some basic instructions on how to get up and running with VSampler 3. Be sure to read through the Help file and experiment with all the different library files included with the DXi.

The ReValver

Unlike all the other DXis included with SONAR, the ReValver DXi is actually an audio effect. You use it to apply amplifier simulation effects to your audio tracks.

MORE AMPLIFIER EFFECTS
For more information about amplifier simulation effects and audio effects in general, read Chapter 11, "Exploring Effects."

The best way to describe the ReValver DXi is to actually show it to you in action. To use the ReValver in a project, follow these steps:

1. Choose File > Open and select the sample project file that comes included with SONAR called Don't Matter Audio and Midi Demo.cwb. Click on Open.

2. Close the File Info window and the Staff view. Then delete all the tracks in the projects except for the Guitar track. You won't need the others for this demonstration.

3. Right-click on the Fx bin of the Guitar track and choose DXi Synth > Alien Connections ReValver SE to apply the ReValver DXi to the track.

APPLY TO FX BIN

As I mentioned earlier in the chapter, the ReValver DXi must be added to a project via the Fx bin of an audio track rather than through the Insert DXi Synth Options dialog box. Because the ReValver DXi is an audio effect rather than a regular DXi, it will not work if you apply it using the dialog box.

4. In the ReValver DXi window, you'll see a virtual rack mount bay containing virtual rack mount modules used to virtually emulate preamplifiers, power amplifiers, speakers, and effects (see Figure 10.37). The first module in the rack is permanent and controls the ReValver DXi. In the first module, adjust the In and Out parameters to control the input and output levels of the ReValver.

Figure 10.37
The main ReValver interface looks like a virtual rack mount bay.

5. Click on Bypass to temporarily turn off and on ReValver processing. This allows you to compare the audio signal with the ReValver applied and without it applied.

6. Click on Clear to delete the current configuration of modules in the rack.

7. Click on Save to save the current configuration of modules in the rack as a ReValver preset file.

8. Click on Load to open a ReValver preset file.

REVALVER PRESETS

The ReValver DXi includes a selection of preset files, which are located in the following folder on your hard drive: C:\Program Files\Cakewalk\Shared DXi\ReValver SE\presets.

9. By clicking on a module, you can move, remove, replace, bypass, reset, as well as load and save individual presets for a module by choosing the appropriate option from the drop-down menu.

10. To add a new module to the rack, click in an empty rack space and choose Insert Module Here from the drop-down menu to open the Choose Module dialog box (see Figure 10.38).

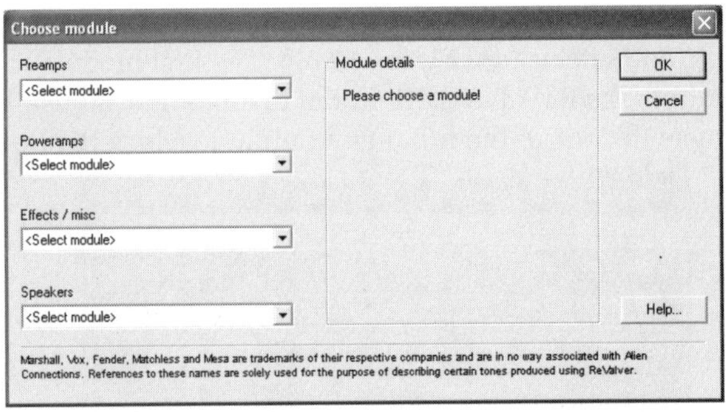

Figure 10.38

Use the Choose Module dialog box to insert a new module into the rack mount space.

11. To add a preamplifier module, choose one from the Preamps list. To add a power amplifier, choose one from the Poweramps list. To add an effect, choose one from the Effects / Misc list. To choose a speaker simulator, choose one from the Speakers list. Then click on OK.

12. If you play the project, you should hear the Guitar track being processed by the ReValver. The audio signal is processed starting with the first module in the rack and ending with the last module in the rack. This means that the order in which the modules appear in the rack makes a different as to how the audio is processed and how it sounds.

13. You also can adjust the individual parameters of some of the modules to affect processing. Each module is different.

Those are the basic steps required for using the ReValver DXi. For more in-depth information about how the ReValver works and how to adjust the parameters of each individual module, you should read the ReValver manual by clicking on the Help button in the first ReValver module.

ReWire

In addition to DX instruments, there are software-based synthesizers that run as separate applications. This means that normally, they cannot be connected in any way to a sequencing application such as SONAR. If, however, the software synth application supports a technology called ReWire, the synth can be used within SONAR, almost exactly like a DX instrument.

ReWire is a virtual connection technology that allows two different music applications to connect to one another and share audio data, synchronize their internal clocks, and share transport control. For example, Cakewalk's Project5 software synthesizer studio supports ReWire. Project5 provides built-in synthesis and sequencing features. When ReWired with SONAR, you can stream audio from Project5 to SONAR just like you would with a DX instrument. In addition, the sequencer aspects in both Project5 and SONAR are completely synchronized, meaning that the Now time in SONAR would correspond to the exact same sequencer time in Project5. And both applications share common transport functions, meaning that using the Play, Stop, Rewind, and so on functions in one application triggers that same function in the other application. The ReWire technology is very powerful and allows you to use SONAR with any other ReWire-compatible application on the market.

MORE PROJECT5 INFO

For more information about Project5, visit http://www.cakewalk.com/Products/Project5/default.asp.

As far as using the ReWire functions in SONAR—to be honest, there really isn't much more I can say that isn't already covered in the SONAR user guide. Instead of just rehashing the same information, I recommend that you read through the ReWire information in the guide. If you have questions, don't be afraid to post them in the discussion area of my DigiFreq music technology Web site at http://www.digifreq.com/digifreq.

MORE REWIRE INFO

For more information about the ReWire technology in general, be sure to visit http://www.propellerheads.se/products/rewire/frame.html.

SoundFonts

Last and somewhat least (I'll explain in a moment), SONAR includes the LiveSynth Pro DXi. This DXi allows you to use SoundFonts even if you don't have a SoundFont-compatible sound card. Unfortunately, the version of LiveSynth Pro DXi included with SONAR is only a trial version. You get full use of the DXi for 30 days, but after that you are limited to using SoundFonts that are 1 MB or less in size. Most good SoundFonts are larger than that.

LIVESYNTH PRO REVIEW

For a review of the full shipping version of the LiveSynth Pro DXi product, go to http://www.digifreq.com/digifreq/reviewdetails.asp?ProdReviewID=8.

SOUNDFONTS

Most modern MIDI instruments and sound cards use sample playback to produce sounds. Sample playback can produce some very realistic sounds. The reason for this realism lies in the fact that a sample-playback device plays samples, which are actually audio recordings of real-life instruments and sounds. When the sample-playback device receives a MIDI Note On message, instead of creating a sound electronically from scratch, it plays a digital sample, which can be anything from the sound of a piano note to the sound of a coyote howling.

A SoundFont is a special type of digital sample format that works only with a SoundFont-compatible sound card. Creative Labs, the makers of the ever-popular Sound Blaster line of sound cards, developed the SoundFont format. Most recent Sound Blaster sound cards are SoundFont compatible. For more information about Sound Blaster sound cards, check out http://www.soundblaster.com. For more information about SoundFonts (as well as free SoundFont downloads), check out the following Web sites:

▶ http://www.computermusic.co.uk/tutorial/soundfont/soundfont.asp

▶ http://www.soundfonts.com

▶ http://atlas.hemmet.chalmers.se/livecenter/showpage.php?name=soundfonts

Using the LiveSynth Pro DXi

To use the LiveSynth Pro DXi to play SoundFonts, follow these steps:

1. Create a new project or open a pre-existing project.

2. Choose Insert > DXi Synth > LiveSynth Pro SE.

3. In the Insert DXi Synth Options dialog box, activate the First Synth Output and Synth Property page options.

4. Click on OK. The LiveSynth Pro window will open (see Figure 10.39).

Figure 10.39
Use the LiveSynth Pro
DXi to play SoundFonts
with any sound card.

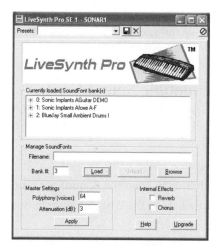

5. In the LiveSynth Pro window, click on the Browse button and choose the SoundFont file you want to use. Click on Open. The name of the SoundFont file will appear in the Filename field.

SONAR SOUNDFONTS

SONAR includes a selection of SoundFont files, which are located in the following folder on your hard drive: C:\Program Files\Cakewalk\SONAR 3\Sample Content\Soundfonts.

6. Choose an unused bank number and type it into the Bank # field.

7. Click on the Load button. LiveSynth Pro will load your selected SoundFont into the selected bank. The Bank and SoundFont are listed in the Currently Loaded SoundFont Bank(s) list.

8. Repeat steps 5 through 7 to load additional SoundFonts. If you want to remove a SoundFont from the list, select the SoundFont and click on the Unload button.

9. When you're finished loading SoundFonts, close the LiveSynth Pro window.

10. If you opened a pre-existing project that already contains MIDI tracks, you can skip this step. Otherwise, right-click in the Track pane of the Track view and choose Insert MIDI Track to create a new MIDI track. Then widen the track to display its parameters.

11. Set the Input parameter to the MIDI channel that is being used to receive data from your MIDI keyboard and set the Output parameter to LiveSynth Pro.

12. Set the Channel parameter to the same MIDI channel as your MIDI keyboard. Set the Bank parameter to the same bank that contains the SoundFont you want to use for this MIDI track. Set the Patch parameter to one of the patches available in the SoundFont. You'll see a list of available patches.

13. Repeat steps 10 through 12 to set up any additional new or pre-existing MIDI tracks.

After you record some data in your MIDI tracks (or if the tracks already contained data), when you play the project, your MIDI tracks will drive the LiveSynth Pro, which in turn will play the appropriate sounds from the SoundFonts you have loaded.

Using SoundFonts with a Compatible Sound Card

If you have a SoundFont-compatible sound card (like the Sound Blaster Live!), you can play SoundFonts with your sound card instead of the LiveSynth Pro DXi. The procedure for using a sound card to play SoundFonts is as follows:

1. Create a new project or open a pre-existing project.

2. Choose Options > SoundFonts to open the SoundFont Banks dialog box.

3. Select an empty bank and click on the Attach button to open the SoundFont File dialog box.

4. Choose the SoundFont file you want to load and click on Open. The SoundFont you chose will be loaded into the bank you selected.

5. Repeat steps 3 and 4 to load any additional SoundFonts.

6. To remove a SoundFont from your project, just select it in the list and click on Detach.

7. Click on Close when you're finished loading SoundFonts.

8. If you opened a pre-existing project that already contains MIDI tracks, you can skip this step. Otherwise, right-click in the Track pane of the Track view and choose Insert MIDI Track to create a new MIDI track. Then widen the track to display its parameters.

9. Set the Input parameter to the MIDI channel that is being used to receive data from your MIDI keyboard and set the Output parameter to SoundFont Device.

10. Set the Channel parameter to the same MIDI channel as your MIDI keyboard. Set the Bank parameter to the same bank that contains the SoundFont you want to use for this MIDI track. Set the Patch parameter to one of the patches available in the SoundFont. You'll see a list of available patches.

11. Repeat steps 8 through 10 to set up any additional new or pre-existing MIDI tracks.

After you record some data into your MIDI tracks (or if the tracks already contained data), when you play the project, your MIDI tracks will drive your SoundFont-compatible sound card, which in turn will play the appropriate sounds from the SoundFonts you have loaded.

SHARE SOUNDFONT PROJECTS

If you want to share your project with someone, and the project uses SoundFonts, be sure to send copies of the SoundFonts along with the project file. Of course, if you purchased the SoundFonts and they are copyrighted, the other person will have to purchase them as well. Sending copies of copyrighted SoundFonts to friends is a no-no. Thanks for respecting the rights of all the hard-working musicians out there.

11

Exploring Effects

Just as adding spices to a recipe makes it taste better, adding effects to your music data makes it sound better. Effects can make the difference between a dull, lifeless recording and a recording that really rocks. For example, you can apply echoes and background ambience to give the illusion that your song was recorded in a certain environment, such as a concert hall. You also can use effects to make your vocals sound rich and full. And the list goes on.... SONAR provides a number of different Effects features that you can use to spice up both your MIDI and audio tracks. Although applying these effects to your data isn't overly complicated, understanding what they do and how to use them can sometimes be confusing. This chapter will do the following:

▶ Explain plug-ins

▶ Discuss offline and real-time processing

▶ Introduce audio effects, including chorus, equalization, reverb, delay, flanging, pitch shifting, time/pitch stretching, and more

▶ Introduce MIDI effects, including quantization, delay, filtering, arpeggio, chord analyzing, transposition, and velocity

▶ Discuss the Session Drummer

Offline or Real-Time?

SONAR's Effects features are very similar to its editing features (which you learned about in Chapter 8), but there are a couple of differences. One difference is that, although the Effects features are included with SONAR, they are not actually part of the main application. Instead, they come in the form of plug-ins.

PLUG-INS

In basic terms, a plug-in is a small computer program that by itself does nothing, but when used together with a larger application, provides added functionality to the larger program. You therefore can use plug-ins to easily add new features to a program. In SONAR's case, plug-ins provide you with additional ways to process your MIDI and audio data. As a matter of fact, Cakewalk offers additional plug-in products for sale (Audio FX 3) so you can add even more power to your copy of SONAR.

What's more, Cakewalk isn't the only vendor that can sell plug-ins for SONAR. You can use plug-ins from a number of different third-party vendors because many plug-ins are programmed using standard computer code. SONAR enables you to use any audio plug-ins that are in the DirectX or VST formats.

Because the Effects features are plug-ins, not only do they add functionality to SONAR, but they also add more flexibility. Unlike the editing features, you can use the Effects features to process your data in two different ways—offline and real-time.

Offline Processing

You already know what offline processing is because you used it when you used SONAR's editing features. With offline processing, the MIDI and audio data in your clips and tracks is permanently changed. Therefore, offline processing is also called *destructive processing* because it "destroys" the original data by modifying (or overwriting) it according to any processing you apply.

UNDO OFFLINE PROCESSING

As you know, you can remove any offline processing done to your data by using SONAR's Undo feature. You also can load a saved copy of your project that contains the original data. But neither of these restoration methods is as convenient as using real-time processing, which I'll explain shortly.

The basic procedure for using effects in offline mode is essentially the same as when you use any of SONAR's editing features. You just follow these steps:

1. Select the data you want to change.

2. Choose the MIDI or audio Effects feature you want to use by choosing either Process > Audio Effects or Process > MIDI Effects.

3. Make the appropriate parameter adjustments in the dialog box that appears.

4. Click on the Audition button to test the current parameter settings. Make further adjustments if necessary.

5. If you're using an audio effect, click on the Mixing tab (see Figure 11.1). These parameters determine how your data will be processed. If you select the Process In-Place, Mono Result option, SONAR will take your originally selected data, process it with the chosen effect, and then replace it with the processed data. This means your original data will be overwritten. If your original data was in stereo, it will be converted to *mono* (or *monophonic*, meaning only one channel, whereas stereo has two channels, left and right). If you select the Process In-Place, Stereo Result option, SONAR will take your originally selected data, process it with the chosen effect, and then replace it with the processed data. Again, this means your original data will be overwritten. Also, if your original data was in mono, it will be converted to stereo. If you select the Create a Send Submix option, SONAR will take your selected data, mix it all together into a stereo signal, process it with the chosen effect, and then place it into a new stereo track, which you designate by setting the Return Track parameter. In addition, if you activate the Keep Original Data option, your original data will be left untouched. If you deactivate the Keep Original Data option, your original data will be deleted.

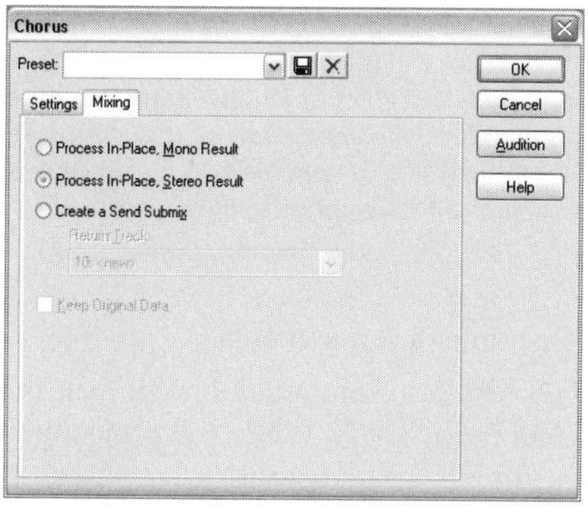

Figure 11.1
The Mixing parameters are available only when you're using an audio effect in offline mode.

Chorus
Preset: [_____] ⌄ 🖫 ✕   [OK]
[Settings] [Mixing]   [Cancel]
○ Process In-Place, Mono Result   [Audition]
◉ Process In-Place, Stereo Result   [Help]
○ Create a Send Submix
☐ Return Track
10 Views   ⌄
☐ Keep Original Data

   6.   Click on OK to close the dialog box.

SONAR will process the data by applying the effect according to the parameter settings you specified. It's very simple. Don't worry; I'll go over each individual effect and its corresponding parameters later in the chapter.

Real-Time Processing

On the other hand, real-time processing doesn't change the actual data in your clips and tracks. Instead, the Effects features are applied only during playback, which lets you hear the results while leaving your original data intact. Therefore, real-time processing is also called *nondestructive* because it doesn't apply any permanent changes to your data. By simply turning off the Effects features, you can listen to your data as it was originally recorded.

The basic procedure for using effects in real-time mode isn't any more difficult than using them in offline mode, although it is a little different, as you can see here:

   1.   In the Track view, right-click in the Fx bin of the track to which you want to add an effect. A drop-down menu will appear.

USE THE CONSOLE VIEW
You also can apply effects in real-time by using the Console view, but I'll talk about that approach in Chapter 12, "Mixing It Down."

   2.   Choose the effect you want to use from the drop-down menu. Depending on whether the track is for MIDI or audio, the list of effects will be different. The effect you choose will be added to the list in the Fx bin.

   3.   The corresponding window for the effect will be opened automatically. You also can open an effect window by double-clicking on it in the Fx bin.

EFFECTS WINDOWS

In real-time mode, the parameters of an effect are displayed in a window instead of a dialog box. You therefore can access any of the other features in SONAR while still having access to the effect parameters. You also can use more than one effect at the same time, which I'll talk about in a moment.

4. Make the appropriate parameter adjustments.

5. Start playback of the project. You immediately will hear the results of the effect being applied to the data in the track. While the project plays, you can make further parameter adjustments if necessary.

THE BYPASS BUTTON

If you want to make a quick comparison between how the original data sounds and how it sounds with the effect applied, some of the effects provide a Bypass button. This button (located in the effect window) is available only when you're applying effects to audio tracks.

When you activate the button, it bypasses (or turns off) the effect so you can hear how the original data sounds. When you deactivate the button, you can hear how the data sounds with the effect applied. You also can bypass an effect by clicking on the green box next to the name of the effect in Fx bin.

NO AUDITION OR MIXING

Notice that there is no Audition button shown in the effect window. It isn't needed because in real-time mode you can hear the results as the project plays. Also, notice there is no Mixing tab shown. In real-time mode, all mixing is handled via the Console view, which I'll talk about in Chapter 12. In addition, effects used in real-time mode don't provide a Cancel button. Instead, they provide a Reset and Cancel button, which still applies the effect to the track but with the default parameter settings. Any parameter settings that you changed are removed.

6. If you want to add another effect to the same track (or add some effects to different tracks), go back to Step 1. You can leave the effects windows open or you can close them; it doesn't matter. You also can let the project continue to play as you add new effects. As soon as you add an effect to the Fx bin, you will hear the results according to the current parameter settings.

7. If you want to remove an effect, right-click on the effect you want to remove and select Delete from the drop-down menu.

ORDER OF EFFECTS

If you apply more than one effect to a track, the order in which the effects appear in the Fx bin will determine the order in which they are applied to the data in the track. For example, if you have the Chorus and Reverb effects added (in that order) to the Fx bin of an audio track, SONAR will apply the Chorus effect to the data, and then take the result of that application and apply the Reverb effect to it. This means that the order in which you apply effects to a track matters. If you apply effects in a different order, you will get different results. This makes for some interesting experimentation. To change the order of the effects listed in the Fx bin, simply drag and drop the name of an effect within the list.

You can simply continue using SONAR with the real-time effects in place. Remember that you will be aware of the results only during playback. The original data looks the same even if you examine it in the various views. Also, editing your original data doesn't change how the effects are applied to it. For example, if you have a track set up with some effects applied and you transpose the pitch of one of the clips within that track, during playback SONAR still will apply the effects to the track in the same way. When the Now time reaches the point in the track containing the transposed clip, you simply will hear the effect applied to the transposed data. This is one of the features that makes real-time effects so flexible.

APPLY EFFECTS DURING RECORDING

You also can apply real-time effects during recording. For example, this allows you to add some reverberation (which I'll explain later) to a vocal part to make it sound more appealing to the performer while his or her part is being recorded. This helps a performer get more "in the groove," so to speak. To apply real-time effects during recording, you have to activate input monitoring, which I talked about in Chapter 6.

Advantages and Disadvantages to Real-Time Processing

You might be asking yourself, "Why don't I just use real-time processing all the time; it's so much more flexible?" Well, applying effects in real-time is very flexible, but in a couple of instances you need to apply them offline. The first instance deals with your computer's processing power. Most of SONAR's effects need to perform complex mathematical calculations to achieve their results. Applying effects in real-time means that not only does your computer have to deal with these calculations, but it also has to deal with SONAR playing back your MIDI and audio data. All these things going on at once can put a lot of strain on your computer's CPU. If you use too many effects in real-time at once, your computer might not be able to keep up. You might hear skips in playback or SONAR might stop playing altogether. If this ever happens, you need to apply some of the effects offline and keep only a few of them going in real-time. You lose a bit of flexibility in terms of being able to make changes to your data, but there's no limit to the number of effects you can apply to your data offline.

CREATE A SEND SUBMIX

One thing you can do to make applying effects offline a little more flexible is to select the Create a Send Submix option and activate the Keep Original Data option under the Mixing tab when you're applying an effect. Also be sure to set the Wet parameter to 100%. This way, you can keep your original data intact and place only the output from the effect in another track. Although this approach doesn't allow you to change the way the effect is applied, you can adjust how much of the effect you want to hear by adjusting the volumes of the two tracks. If you want to hear more of the original data, increase the volume on the original data track and decrease the volume on the track that contains the processed data (and vice versa if you want to hear more of the processed data).

Applying effects offline also comes in handy when you want to process some specifically selected data. For example, if you want to process a short segment of data within a track or clip, you have to do it offline. In real-time, you can apply effects only to whole tracks.

USE AUTOMATION

Actually, you can apply real-time effects to specific parts of a track by using automation, but it's a bit more complicated that simply applying an effect offline. I'll explain automation in Chapter 12.

Audio Effects

SONAR provides more than 30 different audio effects. If you choose either Process > Audio Effects or Process > Audio Effects > Cakewalk, you'll notice that some of these effects cover the same type of processing. Why would Cakewalk include multiple effects that accomplish the same task?

Well, some of the effects are designed to work with mono audio signals, and others are designed to work with stereo audio. They include parameters for both the left and right stereo channels. In addition, some of the effects process audio with a lower level of quality, and they include fewer parameter settings. So why include them? Because they provide one advantage: They don't take up as much computer-processing power. This means you can apply more of the lower-quality effects to your tracks in real-time, especially if you have a slow computer system.

You also might have noticed that some of the effects mimic some of SONAR's editing features (as is the case of EQ). They mimic these effects so you can process your data with these features in real-time. You can't use SONAR's editing features in real-time because they aren't plug-ins. The Effects features, however, come with their own sets of parameters, so I'll go over them here step by step.

BASIC OFFLINE STEPS

Because I've already covered how to apply effects offline and in real-time, I'll only include the basic offline steps (along with parameter descriptions) in each of the following explanations. For detailed step-by-step procedures for applying effects offline and in real-time, refer to the previous sections in this chapter.

Equalization

I talked about the how, what, and why of equalization back in Chapter 8. In addition to the two EQ editing features, SONAR provides four EQ effects (actually, there are five if you have SONAR Producer Edition). These are similar to the Parametric EQ editing feature.

2-Band EQ

As a matter of fact, the 2-Band EQ effect has the same parameters available as the Parametric EQ editing feature, but instead of one set of parameters, it has two. With these two parameters, you can apply two different types of equalization to your data at once. You use it as follows:

1. Select the audio data you want to process.

2. Choose Process > Audio Effects > Cakewalk > 2-Band EQ to open the 2-Band EQ dialog box (see Figure 11.2).

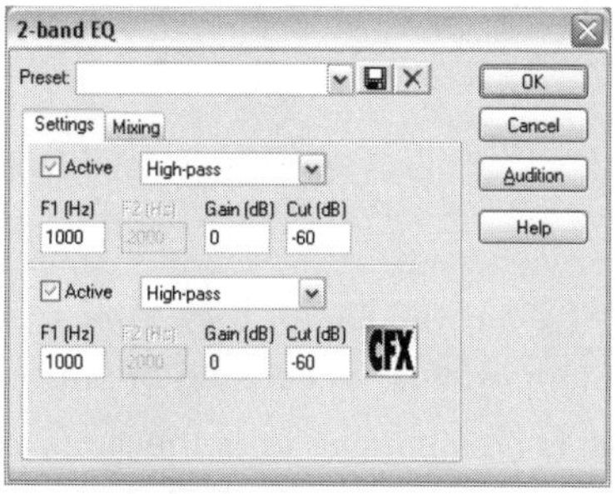

Figure 11.2
You can use the 2-Band
EQ effect to apply two
different types of
equalization to your data
at once.

3. Under the Settings tab, activate one or both of the Active options to turn on each type of EQ.

4. Set the F1, F2, Gain, and Cut parameters. I explained these parameters in the "Equalization (EQ)" section of Chapter 8.

NO QUALITY PARAMETER

You've probably noticed that one parameter setting is missing—the Q (or Quality) parameter. It isn't here because the 2-Band EQ effect has a permanent Q parameter setting of 2. This is one of the factors that keeps this effect from taking up too much computer-processing power. If you need more flexibility, use the Parametric EQ or FxEq effects, which I will explain in a moment.

5. Click on the Audition button to test the current parameter settings. Make further adjustments if necessary.

6. Set the appropriate options under the Mixing tab.

7. If you want to use the current settings at a later time, save them as a preset.

8. Click on OK.

SONAR will process the data by applying the effect according to the parameter settings you specified.

CHAPTER 11

ParamEq

The ParamEq effect provides only one band of EQ and only three parameter settings, but it also requires the least CPU processing power, although this doesn't really make much difference because it can't be used in real-time. Here's how it works:

1. Select the audio data you want to process.

2. Choose Process > Audio Effects > ParamEq to open the ParamEq dialog box (see Figure 11.3).

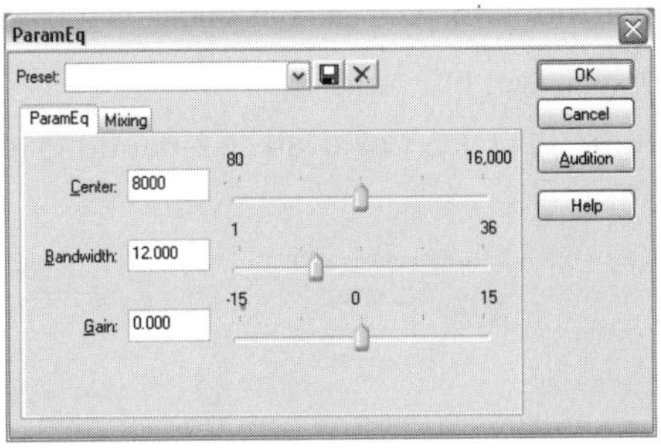

Figure 11.3
The ParamEq effect provides a single band of parametric EQ.

3. Set the Center parameter. This sets the center frequency (80 Hz to 16 kHz) for the EQ, around which the frequencies will be boosted or cut.

4. Set the Bandwidth parameter. This parameter is the same as the Q parameter I mentioned earlier. It influences how many other frequencies around the center frequency will be affected. A low value means fewer frequencies around the center frequency will be affected; a high value means more frequencies around the center frequency will be affected.

5. Set the Gain parameter. This parameter determines whether the frequencies will be cut (use a negative value) or boosted (use a positive value), and by how much (−15dB to +15dB).

6. Click on the Audition button to test the current parameter settings. Make further adjustments if necessary.

7. Set the appropriate options under the Mixing tab.

8. If you want to use the current settings at a later time, save them as a preset.

9. Click on OK.

SONAR will process the data by applying the effect according to the parameter settings you specified.

Parametric EQ

Even though the Parametric EQ effect also provides parametric equalization, its parameters are a bit different from those previously mentioned. You use it like this:

1. Select the audio data you want to process.

2. Select Process > Audio Effects > Cakewalk > Parametric EQ to open the Parametric EQ dialog box (see Figure 11.4).

Figure 11.4

The Parametric EQ effect also provides parametric equalization, but with slightly different parameter settings.

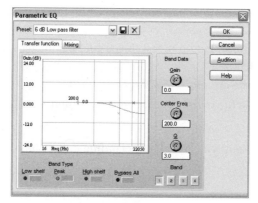

3. In the Band section under the Transfer Function tab, select the number of the EQ band you want to modify. Like the 2-Band EQ effect, the Parametric EQ effect enables you to set up more than one equalization type at once. In this case, you can have up to four different equalization types set up to process your data at the same time. This way, you can do some very complex equalization processing.

4. You'll notice a couple of familiar parameters in the Band Data section—Gain and Q. They work just as they do in all the other EQ features. You can set the Gain from −24 to +24dB, and you can set the Q from 0.1 to 30. The Center Freq (short for frequency) parameter works a bit differently depending on what type of equalization you choose in the Band Type section. Essentially, it determines the frequency below which other frequencies will be cut or boosted, above which other frequencies will be cut or boosted, or exactly where boosting or cutting will occur. You can set the Center Freq parameter from 16 to 22050 Hz. Choose the settings that you want to use for these parameters.

5. In the Band Type section, choose the type of equalization you want to use. If you choose the Low Shelf option, any frequencies below the Center Freq will be boosted or cut depending on how you set the Gain parameter. If you choose the High Shelf option, any frequencies above the Center Freq will be boosted or cut depending on how you set the Gain parameter. If you choose the Peak option, the exact frequency designated by the Center Freq parameter will be the frequency that is boosted or cut depending on how you set the Gain parameter.

EQ GRAPH DISPLAY

You've probably noticed that in addition to the parameter settings, the Parametric EQ dialog box contains a graph display. This graph shows all the current equalization settings for all four types (bands). Along the left, it shows the amplitudes (gain), and along the bottom it shows the frequencies. The shape of the line drawn on the graph shows you what frequencies in the audio spectrum are either boosted or cut, but that's not all. Four colored points on the graph represent each EQ band. Red is for band 1, blue is for band 2, green is for band 3, and purple is for band 4. By clicking and dragging on these points, you can change the Gain and Center Freq settings graphically for each of the EQ types (bands), essentially "drawing" the EQ settings. You still have to set the Band Type and Q settings manually, though.

CHAPTER 11

6. If you want to set up more than one equalization type, go through steps 3 through 5 again.

7. Click on the Audition button to test the current parameter settings. Make further adjustments if necessary.

8. Set the appropriate options under the Mixing tab.

9. If you want to use the current settings at a later time, save them as a preset.

10. Click on OK.

SONAR will process the data by applying the effect according to the parameter settings you specified.

FxEq

Like Parametric EQ, the FxEq effect provides multiple EQ bands (with many of the same parameters) for you to adjust, but instead of four, you now have eight bands at your disposal, plus hi-shelf and lo-shelf filters. Here is how it works:

1. Select the audio data you want to process.

2. Choose Process > Audio Effects > Cakewalk > FxEq to open the FxEq dialog box (see Figure 11.5).

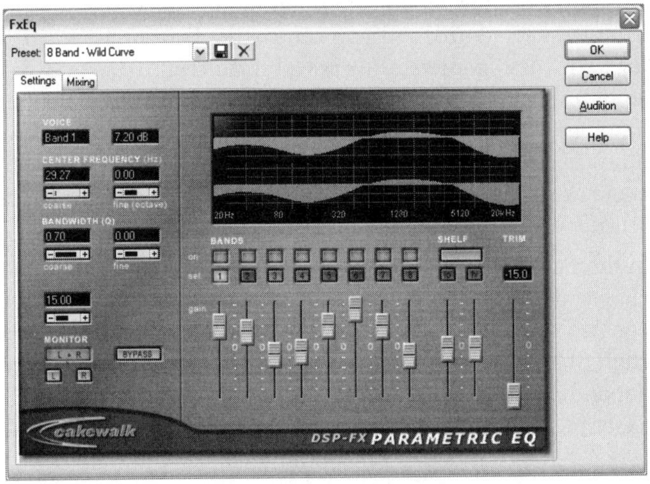

Figure 11.5
The FxEq effect provides eight bands of parametric EQ plus single hi-shelf and lo-shelf filters.

3. In the Bands section, click on the number of the EQ band you want to modify to select it. To turn a band on or off, click on the green button located just above the band number.

4. When you select a band, you'll notice that the Voice section displays the name of the selected band as well as the Gain setting for that band. To adjust the Gain, just drag the appropriate slider for the selected band up or down.

ADJUST THE AMPLITUDE RANGE

You can adjust the amplitude range for all the EQ bands by setting the dB Scale control, which is located just above the Monitor section. Setting the dB Scale control limits the Gain range for each of EQ bands. For example, setting the dB Scale to 15 dB means that the gain for each EQ band can only be adjusted from −15 dB to +15 dB.

5. Selecting a band also displays the Center Frequency and Bandwidth (Q) for that band in the sections of the same names. The Center Frequency and Bandwidth parameters work the same as they do for the Parametric EQ effect, which I explained earlier.

6. If you want to set up more than one EQ band, go through steps 3 through 5 again.

7. You also can set up a hi-shelf and/or a lo-shelf filter using the controls in the Shelf section. These parameters work just like the High Shelf and Low Shelf band types in the Parametric EQ effect, which I explained earlier.

8. To adjust the final output volume of the FxEq effect, use the Trim control.

9. You also can determine whether the FxEq effect will process the left, right, or both channels of a stereo signal by using the controls in the Monitor section.

10. Click on the Audition button to test the current parameter settings. Make further adjustments if necessary.

11. Set the appropriate options under the Mixing tab.

12. If you want to use the current settings at a later time, save them as a preset.

13. Click on OK.

SONAR will process the data by applying the effect according to the parameter settings you specified.

Sonitus:fx Equalizer (SONAR Producer Edition)

If you purchase the Producer Edition of SONAR, you'll have one additional EQ effect at your disposal. This is the Equalizer effect from the Sonitus:fx collection. Like the FxEq, the Equalizer provides multiple EQ bands for you to adjust; in this case, it's six bands. Here is how it works:

1. Select the audio data you want to process.

2. Choose Process > Audio Effects > Sonitus:fx > Equalizer to open the Equalizer dialog box (see Figure 11.6).

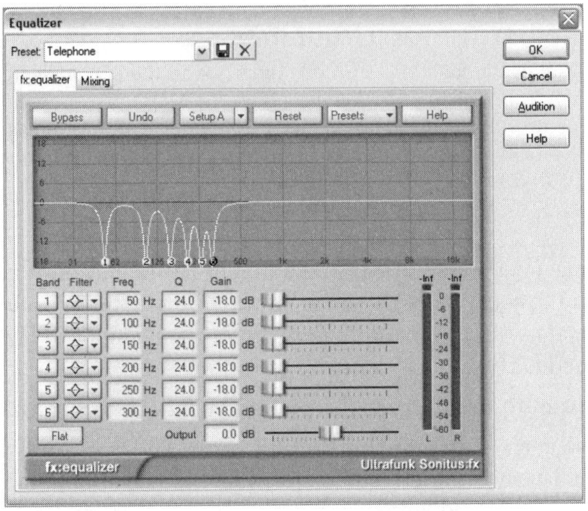

Figure 11.6
The Equalizer effect
provides six bands of
parametric EQ.

3.   In the lower section of the dialog box, there are six EQ bands. You need to activate bands in order for their parameters to be adjusted. To activate a band, click on its number button. You also can turn the entire Equalizer effect on or off by clicking on the Bypass button in the upper section of the dialog box.

4.   To adjust the gain for a band, just drag its Gain slider left or right.

PRECISE ADJUSTMENTS
To make precise parameter adjustments, double-click on the Gain number parameter and then enter a new value using your computer keyboard.

5.   There are also Center Frequency (Freq) and Bandwidth (Q) parameters available for each band. These parameters work the same as they do for the Parametric EQ effect, which I talked about earlier.

6.   To set the type of equalization a band will use, click on the Filter button. If you choose the Peak/Dip option, the exact frequency designated by the Freq parameter will be boosted or cut depending on how you set the Gain parameter. If you choose the Shelving Low option, any frequencies below the Freq setting will be boosted or cut depending on how you set the Gain parameter. If you choose the Shelving High option, any frequencies above the Freq setting will be boosted or cut depending on how you set the Gain parameter. If you choose the Lowpass option, all the frequencies above the Freq setting will be cut, and all the frequencies below it will be boosted, depending on how you set the Gain parameter. If you choose the Highpass option, all the frequencies below the Freq setting will be cut, and all the frequencies above it will be boosted, depending on how you set the Gain parameter.

7. To reset a band to its default parameter values, right-click on the band's number button and choose Set Band Defaults from the drop-down menu. You also can reset the parameters for all the bands by clicking on the Reset button in the upper section of the dialog box.

8. If you want to set up more than one EQ band, repeat steps 3 through 7.

THE EQ GRAPH

You've probably noticed that in addition to the parameter settings, the Equalizer dialog box provides an equalization graph. This graph shows all the current equalization settings. The vertical part of the graph represents amplitude (gain), and the bottom of the graph shows the frequency measurements. The shape of the line drawn on the graph shows you what frequencies in the audio spectrum are either boosted or cut, but that's not all. The six colored balls on the graph represent each EQ band. By clicking and dragging on these balls, you can change the Gain and Frequency settings graphically for each band, essentially "drawing" the EQ settings. You still have to adjust the Q and Filter settings manually.

9. To adjust the final output volume of the Equalizer effect, use the Output parameter in the lower section of the dialog box.

10. Click on the Audition button to test the current parameter settings. Make further adjustments if necessary.

11. Set the appropriate options under the Mixing tab.

12. If you want to use the current settings at a later time, save them as a preset.

SAVE YOUR SETTINGS

You can save Equalizer presets using the standard method for all SONAR effects, or you can use a special method by clicking on the Presets button in the upper section of the dialog box. This will bring up a menu that will allow you to load and save presets to separate files that you can share with friends. Another advantage to saving presets this way is that if you use another program to access the Equalizer effect, your presets will be available in that program too—not just in SONAR.

13. Click on OK.

SONAR will process the data by applying the effect according to the parameter settings you specified.

Delay

You know what an echo is, right? It's a repeating sound that mimics an initial sound. For example, if you yell the word *hello* in a large enclosed area (such as a concert hall or a canyon), you will hear that word repeated (or echoed) over and over until it fades away. This is exactly what the Delay effect allows you to do to your audio data. You can create echoes that vary in the number of repeats and the time between each repeat. SONAR includes four delay effects (five if you have SONAR Producer Edition).

Delay/Echo (Mono)

The Delay/Echo (Mono) effect is pretty straightforward in terms of operation. This effect is intended to be used with monophonic audio rather than stereo. It works like this:

1. Select the audio data you want to process.

2. Select Process > Audio Effects > Cakewalk > Delay/Echo (Mono) to open the Delay/Echo (Mono) dialog box (see Figure 11.7).

Figure 11.7
Using the Delay/Echo (Mono) effect, you can add echoes to your audio data.

3. Under the Settings tab, set the Delay Time parameter. This parameter determines the time (in milliseconds) that occurs between each echo. You can set the Delay Time from 0.02 to 5000 milliseconds (which is equal to 5 seconds).

SYNCHRONIZE ECHOES

Many professional musicians use delay to synchronize the echoes with the music. For instance, you can have the echoes play in time with each quarter note, eighth note, sixteenth note, and so on. All that's required for this cool trick is a little simple math.

Begin by figuring the Delay Time needed to synchronize the echoes to each quarter note. To do so, simply divide 60,000 (the number of milliseconds in one minute) by the current tempo (measured in beats per minute) of your project. So, for a tempo of 120 bpm, you get 500 milliseconds. If you set the Delay Time to 500, the resulting echoes sound at the same time as each quarter note.

To figure out the Delay Time for other note values, you just need to divide or multiply. Because an eighth note is half the value of a quarter note, you simply divide 500 by 2 to get 250 milliseconds. A sixteenth note is half the value of an eighth note, so 250 divided by 2 is 125. See how it works? If you want to find out larger note values, just multiply by 2. Because a half note is twice as long as a quarter note, you multiply 500 by 2 to get 1,000 milliseconds, and so on.

4. Set the Dry Mix and Wet Mix parameters. When you apply an effect to your original data, you can determine how much of the effect and how much of the original data will end up in the final sound. This way, you can add a certain amount of effect without drowning out all the original data. The Dry Mix parameter determines how much of the original data you will hear in the final signal, and the Wet Mix parameter determines how much of the effect you will hear in the final signal. You can set both of these parameters anywhere from 0 to 100 percent.

5. Set the Feedback Mix parameter. With some effects, you can take their resulting signals and send them back through to have the effect applied multiple times. That's what the Feedback Mix parameter does. The resulting sound can differ depending on the effect. For delay effects, the Feedback Mix controls the number of echoes that occur. You can set it anywhere from 0 to 100 percent. The lower the value, the fewer the number of echoes; the higher the value, the more echoes. Unfortunately, there's no way to determine exactly how many echoes will occur according to the percentage. You have to experiment with this one.

6. Set the Mod Rate and Mod Depth parameters. These parameters are a bit difficult to describe. They enable you to add a "warble" type of effect to your audio data along with the echoes. The sound is also similar to that of the tremolo you hear on an electronic organ. To hear what I mean, check out the Fast Tremolo Delay preset. The Mod Rate determines the speed (in Hz or cycles per second) of the warble, and the Mod Depth determines how much your audio data will be affected by it. This is just another one of those features that you have to experiment with to understand.

7. Click on the Audition button to test the current parameter settings. Make further adjustments if necessary.

8. Set the appropriate options under the Mixing tab.

9. If you want to use the current settings at a later time, save them as a preset.

10. Click on OK.

SONAR will process the data by applying the effect according to the parameter settings you specified.

Echo

The Echo effect is similar to the Delay/Echo (Mono) effect except that it works with stereo audio and some of its parameters are slightly different. Here is how it works:

1. Select the audio data you want to process.

2. Choose Process > Audio Effects > Echo to open the Echo dialog box (see Figure 11.8).

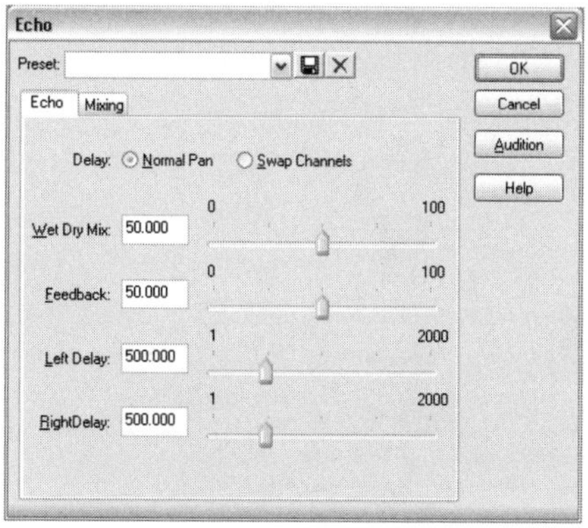

Figure 11.8
The Echo effect is similar to the Delay/Echo (Mono) effect except that it works with stereo audio.

3. If you want the echoes from each stereo channel added to themselves, choose the Normal Pan option for the Delay parameter. If you want the echoes from the left stereo channel to be heard in the right stereo channel and vice versa, choose the Swap Channels option for the Delay parameter.

4. I've explained the Wet Dry Mix parameter before, but in this case there is only one parameter rather than two. Setting the Wet Dry Mix parameter to 50 percent gives you an equal balance between the original audio signal and the effect audio signal. Setting the Wet Dry Mix parameter to 0 percent means you'll hear only the original audio signal. Setting the Wet Dry Mix to 100 percent means you will hear only the effect audio signal.

5. Set the Feedback parameter. This parameter works just like the Feedback parameter in the Delay/Echo (Mono) effect.

6. Set the Left Delay and Right Delay parameters. These parameters work just like the Delay Time parameter in the Delay/Echo (Mono) effect, except that here you get a separate setting for each stereo channel.

7. Click on the Audition button to test the current parameter settings. Make further adjustments if necessary.

8. Set the appropriate options under the Mixing tab.

9. If you want to use the current settings at a later time, save them as a preset.

10. Click on OK.

SONAR will process the data by applying the effect according to the parameter settings you specified.

Delay

Very similar to Delay/Echo (Mono), the Delay effect has most of the same parameters. Because it works with stereo audio, however, there are two sets, plus a few extras. It works like this:

1. Select the audio data that you want to process.

2. Select Process > Audio Effects > Cakewalk > Delay to open the Delay dialog box (see Figure 11.9).

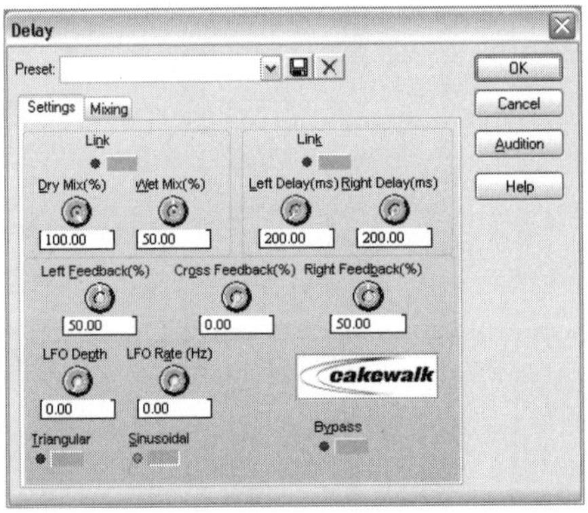

Figure 11.9
The Delay effect has a few additional parameters because it is designed to work with stereo audio.

3.   Set the Left Delay and Right Delay parameters. These parameters work the same way as the Delay Time parameter in the Delay/Echo (Mono) effect. In this case, separate controls are available for the left and right stereo channels. A Link option is also available. Activating this option links the Left Delay and Right Delay parameters together so if you change the value of one, the other will be set to the same value. Most of the time, you should keep the Link option activated so both stereo channels have the same amount of delay. However, setting different values for each channel can sometimes yield interesting results. Don't be afraid to experiment.

4.   Set the Dry Mix and Wet Mix parameters. These parameters work the same way as their counterparts in the Delay/Echo (Mono) effect. Separate controls are not available for each stereo channel in this case, but a Link option is available. Activating this option links the Dry Mix and Wet Mix parameters together so if you increase the value of the Wet Mix, the value of the Dry Mix will decrease and vice versa. This feature enables you to achieve a perfect balance between the original data and the effect.

5.   Set the Left Feedback and Right Feedback parameters. These parameters work the same way as the Feedback Mix parameter in the Delay/Echo (Mono) effect. In this case, separate controls are available for the left and right stereo channels. A Cross Feedback parameter also is available. Using this parameter, you can take the resulting signal from the left channel and send it back through the right channel, and you can take the resulting signal from the right channel and send it back through the left channel. Essentially, this means that this parameter provides control over the number of echoes that will occur and, at the same time, helps to make the stereo field sound "fuller."

6.   Set the LFO Depth and LFO Rate parameters. These parameters work the same way as the Mod Depth and Mod Rate parameters in the Delay/Echo (Mono) effect. In addition, two other options called Triangular and Sinusoidal are available. They determine the type of warble that will be applied. The Triangular option creates a coarse or sharp sound, and the Sinusoidal option creates a smooth or flowing sound. You'll have to try them out to hear what I mean.

7.   Click on the Audition button to test the current parameter settings. Make further adjustments if necessary.

8.   Set the appropriate options under the Mixing tab.

9.   If you want to use the current settings at a later time, save them as a preset.

10. Click on OK.

SONAR will process the data by applying the effect according to the parameter settings you specified.

CHAPTER 11

FxDelay

The FxDelay effect allows you to create very complex echo effects by letting you set up multiple delays at once, such as setting up multiple Delay/Echo (Mono) effects at the same time to process your audio data. Here is how the FxDelay effect works:

1. Select the audio data you want to process.

2. Choose Process > Audio Effects > Cakewalk > FxDelay to open the FxDelay dialog box (see Figure 11.10).

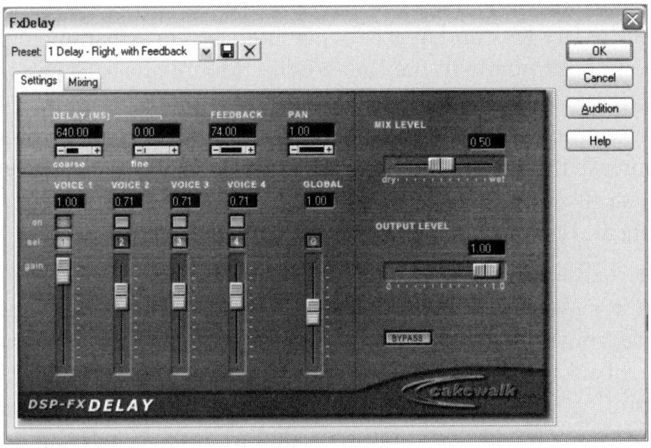

Figure 11.10
The FxDelay effect lets you create complex echo effects.

3. Set the Mix Level parameter. This parameter works just like the Wet Dry Mix parameter in the Echo effect.

4. Set the On options for each of the Voice parameters (1, 2, 3, and 4). The On options let you determine how many different delays you want to set up in your effect. You can have up to four different delays.

5. Each Voice (delay) comes with its own Gain, Delay, Pan, and Feedback parameters. This means you can control the initial volume, echo time, panning in the stereo field, and feedback (number of echoes) for each voice. To adjust the parameters for a voice, select the number of the voice via the Sel options. Then, adjust the Gain, Delay, Feedback, and Pan parameters for that voice. You can do this for all four voices individually.

6. To adjust the gain for all four voices simultaneously, use the Global parameter.

7. Set the Output Level parameter, which controls the overall volume level of the effect output.

8. Click on the Audition button to test the current parameter settings. Make further adjustments if necessary.

9. Set the appropriate options under the Mixing tab.

10. If you want to use the current settings at a later time, save them as a preset.

11. Click on OK.

SONAR will process the data by applying the effect according to the parameter settings you specified.

Sonitus:fx Delay (SONAR Producer Edition)

Similar to the Delay effect, the Sonitus:fx Delay effect provides a single stereo delay with separate controls for both the left and right channels. It works like this:

1. Select the audio data you want to process.

2. Choose Process > Audio Effects > Sonitus:fx > Delay to open the Delay dialog box (see Figure 11.11).

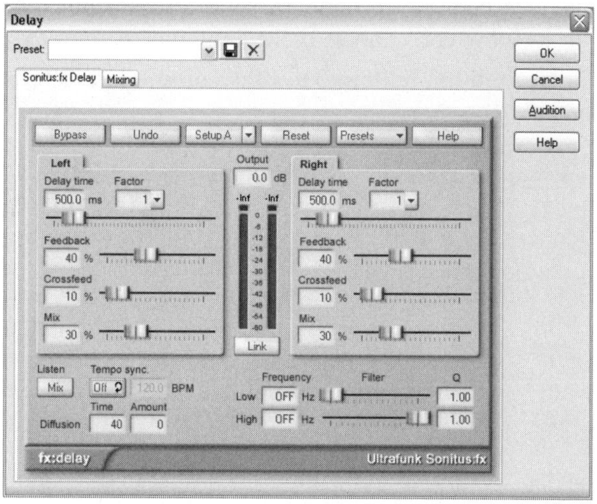

Figure 11.11
The Sonitus:fx Delay effect provides stereo operation with separate controls for each channel.

3. If you want to specify a delay using a time value, set the Delay Time parameters for each channel. These parameters work the same way as the Delay Time parameter in the Delay/Echo (Mono) effect. In this case, separate controls are available for the left and right stereo channels. A Link option is also available. Activating this option links the Delay parameters together so if you change the value of one, the other will be set to the same value.

4. If you want to specify a delay that will be synchronized to a specific musical tempo, activate the Tempo Sync option. If you choose Manual mode, you can type in a tempo. If you choose Host mode, the tempo of your current project will be used. Now instead of using the Delay Time parameters, set the Factor parameters for each channel. These parameters allow you to set the delay using musical values based on the tempo. A Factor of 1 equals a quarter-note delay. A Factor of 1/2 equals an eighth-note delay, and so on.

5. Set the Mix parameters. A value of 0% equals a totally dry signal, a value of 50% equals a 50/50 mix of the dry and wet signal, and a value of 100% equals a totally wet signal.

6. Set the Feedback and Crossfeed parameters. These parameters work the same way as the Feedback Mix and Cross Feedback parameters of the Delay effect.

7. The Diffusion parameter allows you to simulate environments more precisely. Instead of hearing distinct echoes, you hear a large number of echoes that sound together very quickly, giving you the illusion of your audio being played in an

CHAPTER 11

irregularly-shaped environment. The higher the Time value, the farther apart the echoes will sound, simulating a larger environment. The higher the Amount value, the more pronounced the effect will be.

8. If you want to apply some low-pass and high-pass EQ to your Delay effect, use the High Filter and Low Filter functions. You can set frequency and Q for both functions. There's no gain control because they both simply cut out frequencies. Use High Filter to cut frequencies above its Frequency setting; use Low Filter to cut frequencies below its Frequency setting. Check out some of the supplied presets to see how you can use these functions to simulate different effects.

9. Click on the Audition button to test the current parameter settings. Make further adjustments if necessary.

LISTEN MODE

Click on the Listen button to set it to either Mix or Delay. When it is set to Mix, you will hear both the original audio signal and the Delay effect. When it is set to Delay, you will hear only the Delay effect.

10. Set the appropriate options under the Mixing tab.

11. If you want to use the current settings at a later time, save them as a preset.

12. Click on OK.

SONAR will process the data by applying the effect according to the parameter settings you specified.

Chorus

Believe it or not, you'll find that SONAR's chorus effects (of which there are four) have many of the same parameters as its delay effects. Why? Because technically, chorus is a form of delay. Chorus uses delay and detuning to achieve its results. You don't hear echoes when using chorus, though, because the delay is extremely short. Instead, chorus makes your audio data sound fatter or fuller. The name *chorus* comes from the fact that people singing in a chorus produce a full sound because each person sings slightly out of tune and out of time—not enough to make the music sound bad, but enough to actually make it sound better. You can use SONAR's chorus effects to achieve similar results with your audio data. The following sections describe how to use them.

Chorus (Mono)

The Chorus (Mono) effect is designed to work with monophonic audio rather than stereo. To apply the Chorus (Mono) effect, follow these steps:

1. Select the audio data you want to process.

2. Select Process > Audio Effects > Cakewalk > Chorus (Mono) to open the Chorus (Mono) dialog box (see Figure 11.12).

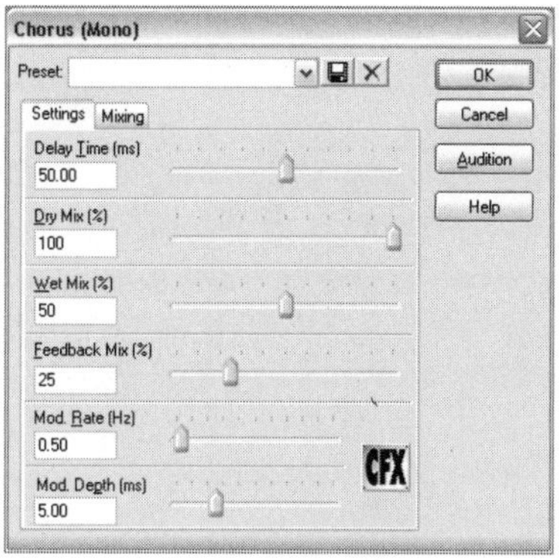

Figure 11.12
The Chorus (Mono) effect
has the same parameters
as the Delay/Echo (Mono)
effect, although they
provide different results.

3. Under the Settings tab, set the Delay Time parameter. The only difference between this Delay Time parameter and the same parameter in the Delay/Echo (Mono) effect is that this one has a range of only 20 to 80 milliseconds. If you set this parameter high enough, you actually can get some quick repeating echoes out of it. For adding chorus to your audio though, you should keep it set somewhere between 20 and 35.

4. Set the Dry Mix and Wet Mix parameters. I explained these parameters earlier.

5. Set the Feedback Mix parameter. Instead of setting the number of echoes to occur (as in the Delay/Echo (Mono) effect), this parameter determines the thickness of the chorus. The higher the value, the thicker the chorus.

6. Set the Mod Rate and Mod Depth parameters. Instead of adding a warble to your audio (as in the Delay/Echo (Mono) effect), these parameters determine how detuning is added to the chorus. The Mod Rate determines how quickly the detuning occurs, and the Mod Depth determines the amount of detuning. A high Mod Depth setting makes your audio sound really out of tune (which isn't usually desirable), but a lower setting produces a nice chorusing.

7. Click on the Audition button to test the current parameter settings. Make further adjustments if necessary.

8. Set the appropriate options under the Mixing tab.

9. If you want to use the current settings at a later time, save them as a preset.

10. Click on OK.

SONAR will process the data by applying the effect according to the parameter settings you specified.

Chorus

Very similar to Chorus (Mono), the Chorus effect has most of the same parameters. Because it works with stereo audio, however, there are a couple differences. It works like this:

1. Select the audio data you want to process.

2. Choose Process > Audio Effects > Chorus to open the Chorus dialog box (see Figure 11.13).

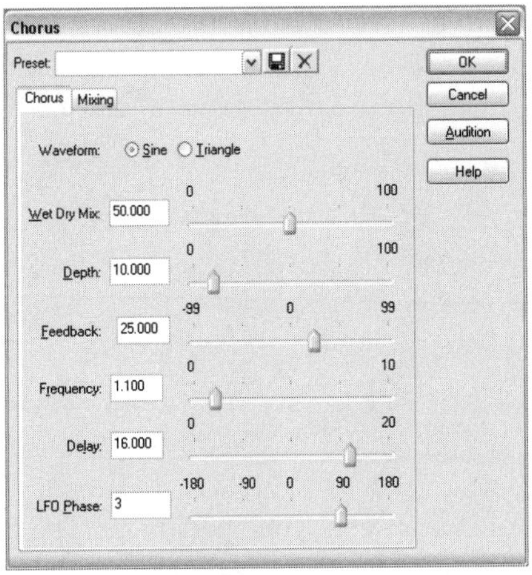

Figure 11.13
The Chorus effect is
similar to the Chorus
(Mono) effect except that
it works with stereo
audio.

3. Set the Delay parameter. This parameter provides the same chorusing results as the Delay Time parameter in the Chorus (Mono) effect, but for stereo audio (of course).

4. Set the Wet Dry Mix parameter. Set the value of the parameter low to hear more of the original audio data. Set the value of the parameter high to hear more of the effect audio data. Set the value of the parameter at 50 percent to hear an equal mix of the original and effect audio data.

5. Set the Feedback parameter. This parameter provides the same chorusing results as the Feedback Mix parameter in the Chorus (Mono) effect, but for stereo audio (of course).

6. Set the Depth and Frequency parameters. They provide the same results as the Mod Depth and Mod Rate parameters in the Chorus (Mono) effect.

7. Set the Waveform parameter. The Sine and Triangle parameters determine the type of warble to be applied to the Chorus effect. The Triangle option creates a coarse or sharp sound, and the Sine option creates a smooth or flowing sound. You'll have to try them out to hear what I mean.

8. Set the LFO Phase parameter. This parameter allows you to change the sound of the warble (mentioned earlier) to give it a sort of hollow sound. You'll need to experiment to hear what I mean.

9. Click on the Audition button to test the current parameter settings. Make further adjustments if necessary.

10. Set the appropriate options under the Mixing tab.

11. If you want to use the current settings at a later time, save them as a preset.

12. Click on OK.

SONAR will process the data by applying the effect according to the parameter settings you specified.

Chorus

Yes, there are actually two chorus effects with the same exact name, but they are accessed and operated differently. To apply this Chorus effect (which provides more features and better-sounding output), follow these steps:

1. Select the audio data you want to process.

2. Select Process > Audio Effects > Cakewalk > Chorus to open the Chorus dialog box (see Figure 11.14).

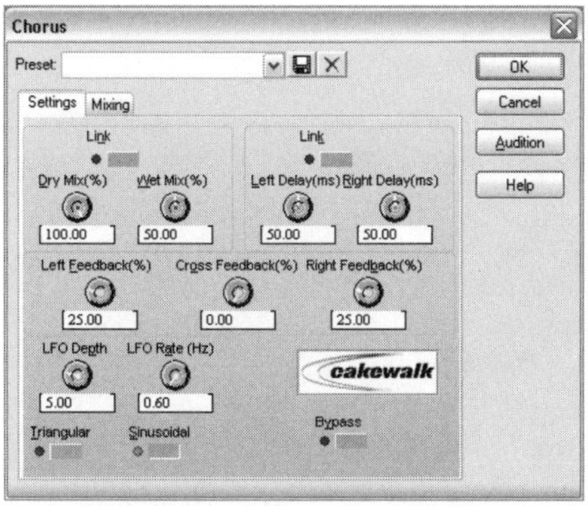

Figure 11.14
The Chorus effect has the same parameters as the Delay effect, although they provide different results.

3. Set the Left Delay and Right Delay parameters. They provide the same chorusing results as the Delay Time parameter in the Chorus (Mono) effect, but for the separate left and right stereo channels (of course). You also can link these parameters by activating the Link option.

4. Set the Dry Mix and Wet Mix parameters. I explained these parameters earlier.

5. Set the Left Feedback and Right Feedback parameters. They provide the same chorusing results as the Feedback Mix parameter in the Chorus (Mono) effect, but for the separate left and right stereo channels, of course. Also, just as the Cross Feedback parameter in the Delay effect enhances the delay, this Cross Feedback parameter enhances the chorus.

6. Set the LFO Depth and LFO Rate parameters. They provide the same results as the Mod Depth and Mod Rate parameters in the Chorus (Mono) effect. I explained the Triangular and Sinusoidal parameters earlier in the "Delay" section.

7. Click on the Audition button to test the current parameter settings. Make further adjustments if necessary.

8. Set the appropriate options under the Mixing tab.

9. If you want to use the current settings at a later time, save them as a preset.

10. Click on OK.

SONAR will process the data by applying the effect according to the parameter settings you specified.

CHAPTER 11

FxChorus

The FxChorus effect allows you to create very complex chorus effects by letting you set up multiple choruses at once, such as setting up multiple Chorus (Mono) effects at the same time to process your audio data. Here is how the FxChorus effect works:

1. Select the audio data you want to process.

2. Choose Process > Audio Effects > Cakewalk > FxChorus to open the FxChorus dialog box (see Figure 11.15).

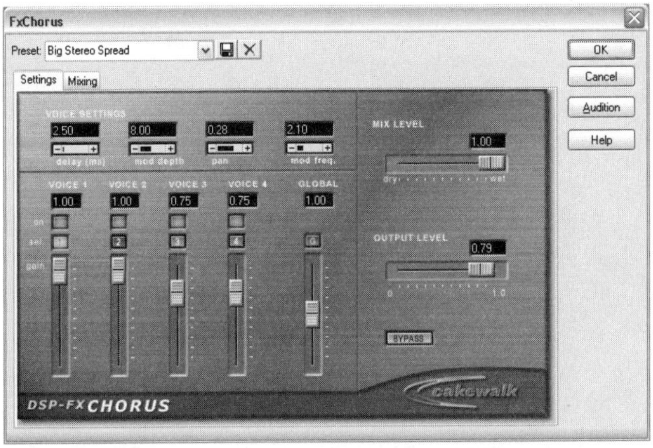

Figure 11.15

The FxChorus effect lets you create complex chorus effects.

3. Set the Mix Level parameter. This parameter works just like the Wet Dry Mix parameter in the Echo effect.

4. Set the On options for each of the Voice parameters (1, 2, 3, and 4). The On options let you determine the number of different choruses you want to set up in your effect. You can have up to four different choruses.

5. Each voice (chorus) comes with its own Gain, Delay, Pan, Mod Depth, and Mod Freq parameters. This means that you can control the initial volume, chorus strength, panning in the stereo field, and depth and speed of the warble for each voice. To adjust the parameters for a voice, select the number of the voice via the Sel options. Then, adjust the Gain, Delay, Pan, Mod Depth, and Mod Freq parameters for that voice. You can do this for all four voices individually.

6. To adjust the Gain for all four voices simultaneously, use the Global parameter.

7. Set the Output Level parameter, which controls the overall volume level of the effect output.

8. Click on the Audition button to test the current parameter settings. Make further adjustments if necessary.

9. Set the appropriate options under the Mixing tab.

10. If you want to use the current settings at a later time, save them as a preset.

11. Click on OK.

SONAR will process the data by applying the effect according to the parameter settings you specified.

Flanging

Guess what? As with SONAR's chorus effects, you'll find that the program's flanger effects have many of the same parameters as its delay effects because (yep, that's right) flanging is also a form of delay. Flanging produces a kind of spacy or whooshy type of sound by mixing a slightly delayed version of the original data with itself. As with chorus, you don't hear echoes because the delay occurs so quickly. It's difficult to describe what flanging sounds like, so you'll have to hear it for yourself. You can apply SONAR's flanging effects as described in the following sections.

Flanger (Mono)

The Flanger (Mono) effect is designed to work with monophonic audio, rather than stereo. To apply the Flanger (Mono) effect, follow these steps:

1. Select the audio data you want to process.

2. Select Process > Audio Effects > Cakewalk > Flanger (Mono) to open the Flanger (Mono) dialog box (see Figure 11.16).

Figure 11.16

The Flanger (Mono) effect has the same parameters as the Delay/Echo (Mono) effect, although they provide different results.

3. Under the Settings tab, set the Delay Time parameter. The only difference between this Delay Time parameter and the same parameter in the Delay/Echo (Mono) effect is that this one has a range of only 1 to 20 milliseconds. If you set this parameter high enough, you can actually get some chorusing out of it. To add flanging to your audio, though, you should keep it set somewhere between 1 and 11.

4. Set the Dry Mix and Wet Mix parameters. I explained these parameters earlier.

5. Set the Feedback Mix parameter. Instead of setting the number of echoes to occur (as in the Delay/Echo (Mono) effect), this parameter determines the thickness of the flanging. The higher the value, the thicker the flanger.

6. Set the Mod Rate and Mod Depth parameters. Instead of adding a warble to your audio (as in the Delay/Echo (Mono) effect), these parameters determine the speed and amount of the flanging. The Mod Rate determines the speed at which the flanging occurs, and the Mod Depth determines the amount of flanging. Check out some of the included presets to get an idea of what values to use for these parameters.

7. Click on the Audition button to test the current parameter settings. Make further adjustments if necessary.

8. Set the appropriate options under the Mixing tab.

9. If you want to use the current settings at a later time, save them as a preset.

10. Click on OK.

SONAR will process the data by applying the effect according to the parameter settings you specified.

Flanger

Very similar to Flanger (Mono), the Flanger effect has most of the same parameters. Because it works with stereo audio, however, there are a couple differences. It works like this:

1. Select the audio data you want to process.

2. Choose Process > Audio Effects > Flanger to open the Flanger dialog box (see Figure 11.17).

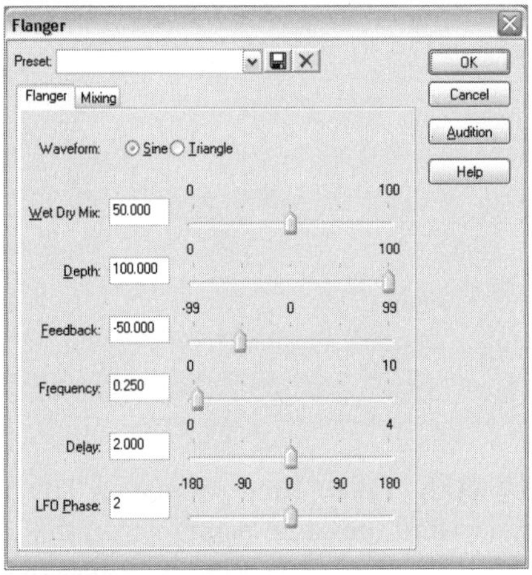

Figure 11.17
The Flanger effect is similar to the Flanger (Mono) effect, except that it works with stereo audio.

3. Set the Delay parameter. This parameter provides the same flanging results as the Delay Time parameter in the Flanger (Mono) effect, but for stereo audio, of course.

4. Set the Wet Dry Mix parameter. Set the value of the parameter low to hear more of the original audio data. Set the value of the parameter high to hear more of the effect audio data. Set the value of the parameter at 50 percent to hear an equal mix of the original and effect audio data.

5. Set the Feedback parameter. This parameter provides the same flanging results as the Feedback Mix parameter in the Flanger (Mono) effect, but for stereo audio, of course.

6. Set the Depth and Frequency parameters. They provide the same results as the Mod Depth and Mod Rate parameters in the Flanger (Mono) effect.

7. Set the Waveform parameter. The Sine and Triangle parameters determine the type of warble applied to the Chorus effect. The Triangle option creates a coarse or

sharp sound, and the Sine option creates a smooth or flowing sound. You'll have to try them out to hear what I mean.

8. Set the LFO Phase parameter. This parameter allows you to change the sound of the warble (mentioned earlier) to give it a sort of a hollow sound. You'll need to experiment to hear what I mean.

9. Click on the Audition button to test the current parameter settings. Make further adjustments if necessary.

10. Set the appropriate options under the Mixing tab.

11. If you want to use the current settings at a later time, save them as a preset.

12. Click on OK.

SONAR will process the data by applying the effect according to the parameter settings you specified.

Flanger

Yes, there are actually two flanger effects with the same exact name, but they are accessed and operated differently. To apply this Flanger effect, follow these steps:

1. Select the audio data you want to process.

2. Select Process > Audio Effects > Cakewalk > Flanger to open the Flanger dialog box (see Figure 11.18).

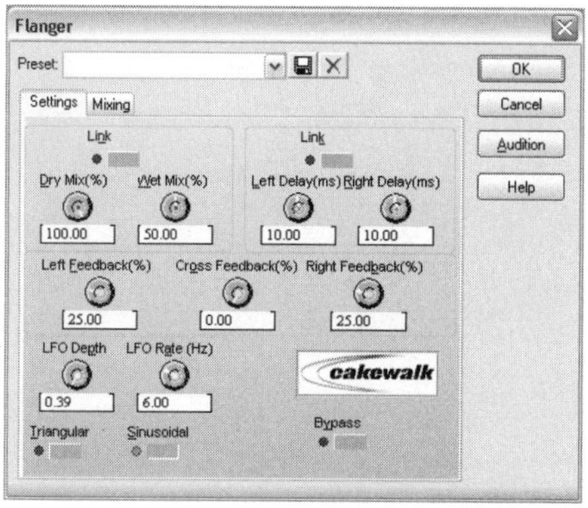

Figure 11.18
The Flanger effect has the same parameters as the Delay effect, although they provide different results.

3. Set the Left Delay and Right Delay parameters. They provide the same flanging results as the Delay Time parameter in the Flanger (Mono) effect, but for the separate left and right stereo channels. You also can link these parameters together by activating the Link option.

4. Set the Dry Mix and Wet Mix parameters. I explained these parameters earlier.

5. Set the Left Feedback and Right Feedback parameters. They provide the same flanging results as the Feedback Mix parameter in the Flanger (Mono) effect, but for the separate left and right stereo channels. Also, just like the Cross Feedback parameter in the Delay effect enhances the delay, this Cross Feedback parameter enhances the flanging.

6. Set the LFO Depth and LFO Rate parameters. They provide the same results as the Mod Depth and Mod Rate parameters in the Flanger (Mono) effect. I explained the Triangular and Sinusoidal parameters earlier in the "Delay" section.

7. Click on the Audition button to test the current parameter settings. Make further adjustments if necessary.

8. Set the appropriate options under the Mixing tab.

9. If you want to use the current settings at a later time, save them as a preset.

10. Click on OK.

SONAR will process the data by applying the effect according to the parameter settings you specified.

FxFlange

The FxFlange effect allows you to create complex flange effects by letting you set up multiple flanges at once, such as setting up multiple Flanger (Mono) effects at the same time to process your audio data. Here is how the FxFlange effect works:

1. Select the audio data you want to process.

2. Choose Process > Audio Effects > Cakewalk > FxFlange to open the FxFlange dialog box (see Figure 11.19).

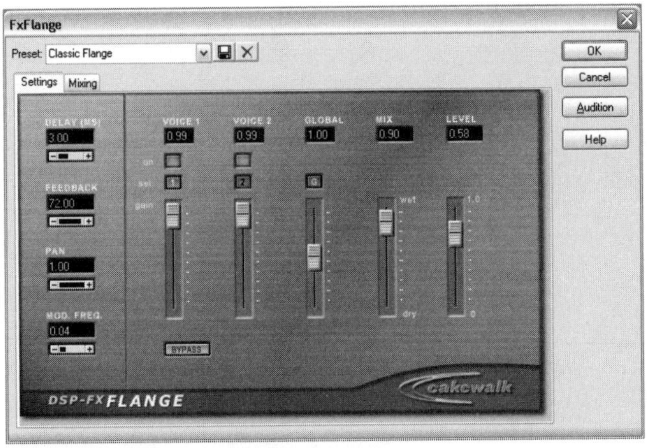

Figure 11.19
The FxFlange effect lets you create complex flanging effects.

3. Set the Mix parameter. This parameter works just like the Wet Dry Mix parameter in the Echo effect.

4. Set the On options for each of the Voice parameters (1 and 2). The On options let you determine how many different flanges you want to set up in your effect. You can have up to two different flanges.

5. Each voice (flange) comes with its own Gain, Delay, Pan, Feedback, and Mod Freq parameters. This means you can control the initial volume, flanging strength, panning in the stereo field, and depth and speed of the flanging of each voice. To adjust the parameters for a voice, select the number of the voice via the Sel option.

Then adjust the Gain, Delay, Pan, Feedback, and Mod Freq parameters for that voice. You can do this for both voices individually.

6. To adjust the gain for both voices simultaneously, use the Global parameter.

7. Set the Level parameter, which controls the overall volume level of the effect output.

8. Click on the Audition button to test the current parameter settings. Make further adjustments if necessary.

9. Set the appropriate options under the Mixing tab.

10. If you want to use the current settings at a later time, save them as a preset.

11. Click on OK.

SONAR will process the data by applying the effect according to the parameter settings you specified.

Reverberation

Reverb (short for reverberation) is also a form of delay, but it's special because instead of distinct echoes, reverb adds a complex series of very small echoes that simulate artificial ambience. In other words, reverb produces a dense collection of echoes that are so close together that they create a wash of sound, making the original audio data sound like it's being played in another environment, such as a large concert hall. Using SONAR's reverb effects, you can make your music sound like it's being played in all kinds of different places, such as in an arena, a club, or even on a live stage. SONAR includes four reverb effects (six if you have SONAR Producer Edition).

Reverb (Mono)

The Reverb (Mono) effect is designed to work with monophonic audio, rather than stereo. To apply the Reverb (Mono) effect to your data, follow these steps:

1. Select the audio data you want to process.

2. Select Process > Audio Effects > Cakewalk > Reverb (Mono) to open the Reverb (Mono) dialog box (see Figure 11.20).

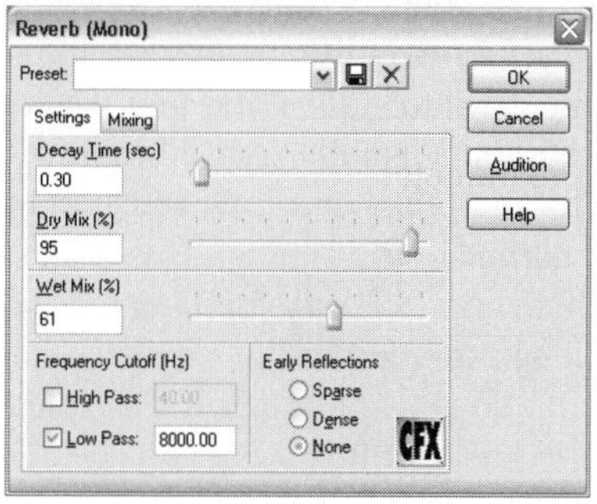

Figure 11.20
Using the Reverb (Mono) effect, you can add reverberation to your audio data.

3. Under the Settings tab, set the Decay Time parameter. When you're applying reverb to your data, you should imagine the type of environment you want to

create. Doing so will help you set the effect parameters. Technically, the Decay Time determines how long it takes for the reverberation to fade away, but you can think of it as controlling how large the artificial environment will be. The lower the Decay Time, the smaller the environment; the higher the Decay Time, the larger the environment. You can set the Decay Time from 0.20 to 5 seconds. If you want to make your music sound like it's playing in a small room, a good Decay Time might be about 0.25. If you want to make your music sound like it's being played on a live stage, a good Decay Time might be about 1.50. Be sure to check out some of the included presets for more sample parameter settings.

4. Set the Dry Mix and Wet Mix parameters. I explained these parameters earlier in this chapter. One point you should note, however, is that in the case of Reverb, the Dry Mix and Wet Mix parameters also make a difference on how the effect sounds. If you set the Dry Mix high and the Wet Mix low, your audio data will sound like it's positioned closer to the front of the imaginary environment. If you set the Dry Mix low and the Wet Mix high, your audio data will sound like it's positioned farther away. For example, if you want to simulate what it sounds like to be seated in the very back row of a music concert, you can set the Dry Mix low and the Wet Mix high. You need to experiment to get the exact parameter settings.

5. In the Early Reflections section, choose one of the following options: None, Dense, or Sparse. When you make a sound in any enclosed environment, some very quick echoes always occur because of the reflective surfaces (such as walls) that you are standing next to. These echoes are known as *early reflections*. To make your reverb simulations sound more authentic, SONAR provides this parameter so you can control the density of the early reflections. If you select None, no early reflections are added to the effect. The Sparse option makes the reflections sound more like distinct echoes, and the Dense option makes the reverb effect sound thicker. Early reflections are more pronounced in larger spaces, so if you want to simulate a really large space, you'll probably want to use the Sparse option. If you want to simulate a moderately sized space, you'll probably want to use the Dense option. And if you want to simulate a small space (such as a room), you should use the None option.

6. In the Frequency Cutoff section, set the High Pass and Low Pass parameters. If you think these parameters look like equalization settings, you're right. Using these parameters also helps to create more authentic environment simulations because smaller, closed environments tend to stifle some frequencies of the audio spectrum, and larger environments usually sound brighter, meaning they promote more of the frequencies. The High Pass and Low Pass parameters work just like the EQ parameters I described earlier in the chapter. If you activate the High Pass parameter and set its frequency (in Hz), any frequencies above that frequency will be allowed to pass and will be included in the Effect, and any frequencies below that frequency will be cut. If you activate the Low Pass parameter and set its frequency, any frequencies below that frequency will be allowed to pass, and any frequencies above that frequency will be cut. If you want to simulate a small room, you can leave the High Pass parameter deactivated, activate the Low Pass parameter, and set its frequency to around 8000 Hz. This setting would cut out any really high frequencies, making the room sound small and enclosed. For more

examples on how to set these parameters, be sure to take a look at some of the included presets.

7. Click on the Audition button to test the current parameter settings. Make further adjustments if necessary.

8. Set the appropriate options under the Mixing tab.

9. If you want to use the current settings at a later time, save them as a preset.

10. Click on OK.

SONAR will process the data by applying the effect according to the parameter settings you specified.

Reverb

To apply the Reverb effect to your data, follow these steps:

1. Select the audio data you want to process.

2. Select Process > Audio Effects > Cakewalk > Reverb to open the Reverb dialog box (see Figure 11.21).

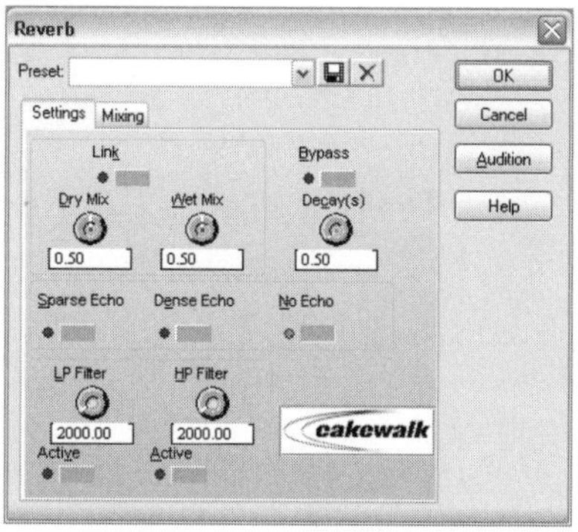

Figure 11.21
The Reverb effect parameters are exactly the same as for the Reverb (Mono) effect except that they control both the left and right channels of the signal if your audio is in stereo.

3. Under the Settings tab, set the Decay(s) parameter. It is exactly the same as the Decay Time parameter in the Reverb (Mono) effect except that it controls both the left and right channels of the signal if your audio is in stereo.

4. Set the Dry Mix and Wet Mix parameters. They are exactly the same as the Dry Mix and Wet Mix parameters in the Reverb (Mono) effect except that they control both the left and right channels of the signal if your audio is in stereo. A Link option is also available, which I explained previously.

5. Choose an early reflections option. The No Echo, Dense Echo, and Sparse Echo options are exactly the same as the None, Dense, and Sparse options in the Reverb (Mono) effect, respectively.

6. Activate and set the frequency cutoff parameters. The LP Filter and HP Filter parameters are exactly the same as the Low Pass and High Pass filters in the Reverb (Mono) effect, respectively.

7. Click on the Audition button to test the current parameter settings. Make further adjustments if necessary.

8. Set the appropriate options under the Mixing tab.

9. If you want to use the current settings at a later time, save them as a preset.

10. Click on OK.

SONAR will process the data by applying the effect according to the parameter settings you specified.

WavesReverb

The WavesReverb effect is a simplified reverb effect that provides only four adjustable parameters. Because of this, it also takes up the least CPU processing power, although this doesn't really matter because it can't be used in real-time. Here is how the WavesReverb effect works:

1. Select the audio data you want to process.

2. Choose Process > Audio Effects > WavesReverb to open the WavesReverb dialog box (see Figure 11.22).

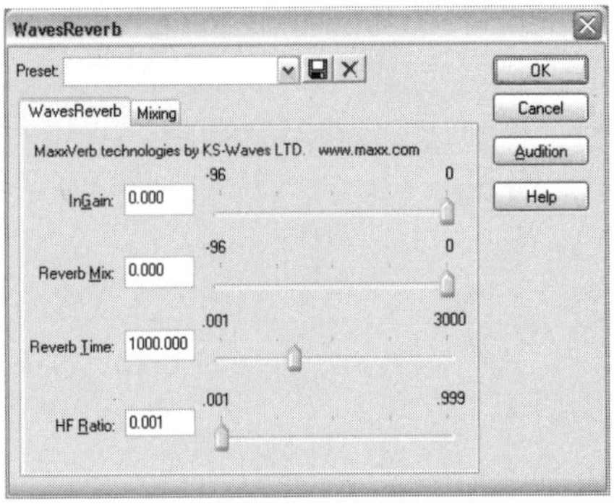

Figure 11.22
The WavesReverb effect provides reverb without taking up a lot of CPU processing power.

3. Set the InGain parameter. This parameter determines how loud the audio signal coming into the effect will be. More often than not, you'll want to keep this set at 0.

4. Set the Reverb Mix parameter. This parameter determines the balance between the original audio signal and the effect audio signal. Set it to 0 to hear the full reverberation effect.

5. Set the Reverb Time parameter. This parameter works just like the Decay Time parameter in the Reverb (Mono) effect, except that it is limited to 3 seconds.

6. Set the HF Ratio. This parameter is similar to the Low Pass parameter in the Reverb (Mono) effect. Using a low value cuts out the high frequencies in the effect, and using a high value boosts the high frequencies in the effect.

7. Click on the Audition button to test the current parameter settings. Make further adjustments if necessary.

8. Set the appropriate options under the Mixing tab.

9. If you want to use the current settings at a later time, save them as a preset.

10. Click on OK.

SONAR will process the data by applying the effect according to the parameter settings you specified.

FxReverb

In contrast to the WavesReverb effect (as well as the previous reverberation effects), the FxReverb effect provides a high-quality sound as well as more adjustable parameters. Here is how it works:

1. Select the audio data you want to process.
2. Choose Process > Audio Effects > Cakewalk > FxReverb to open the FxReverb dialog box (see Figure 11.23).

Figure 11.23
The FxReverb effect provides better quality than the previously mentioned effects.

3. Set the Room Size parameter. This parameter determines the size of the environment you are trying to simulate.
4. Set the Mix parameter. I explained this parameter earlier in the chapter. It is similar to the Wet Dry Mix parameter used in other effects. One point you should note, however, is that in the case of reverb, the Mix parameter also makes a difference in how the effect sounds. If you set the Mix parameter low, your audio data will sound like it's positioned closer to the front of the imaginary environment. If you set the Mix parameter high, your audio data will sound like it's positioned farther away. For example, if you want to simulate what it sounds like to be seated in the very back row of a music concert, you can set the Mix parameter high. You need to experiment to get the exact parameter settings you desire.
5. Set the Decay Time parameter. When you're applying reverb to your data, you should imagine the type of environment you want to create. Doing so will help you set the parameters. Technically, the Decay Time determines how long it takes for the reverberation to fade away, but you can also think of it as controlling how large the artificial environment will be. It works in conjunction with the Room Size parameter. The lower the Decay Time, the smaller the environment, and vice versa. If you want to make your audio sound like it's playing in a small room, a good Decay Time might be about 0.5 seconds. If you want to make your audio sound like it's playing in a large area, a good Decay Time might be about 3 seconds.

CHAPTER 11

6. Set the Predelay parameter. This parameter is similar to the Decay Time parameter, except that the Predelay determines the time between when your audio is first heard and when the reverb effect begins. This gives you even more control in determining your artificial environment. For small spaces, use a low setting (such as 1 millisecond). For large spaces, use a high setting (such as 70 milliseconds).

7. Set the High Frequency Rolloff and High Frequency Decay parameters. If you think these parameters look like equalization settings, you're right. Using these parameters also helps to create more authentic environment simulations because smaller, closed environments tend to stifle some frequencies of the audio spectrum, and larger environments usually sound brighter, meaning they promote more of the frequencies. When you set the High Frequency Rolloff parameter (in Hz), any frequencies below that frequency are allowed to pass and any frequencies above that frequency are cut. Setting the High Frequency Decay parameter determines how quickly the high frequencies above the High Frequency Rolloff are cut as the reverberation sounds. For examples on how to set these parameters, be sure to take a look at some of the included presets.

8. Set the Density parameter. This parameter determines the thickness of the reverberation. Experiment with it to hear what I mean.

9. Set the Motion Depth and Motion Rate parameters. In a real environment, reverberation is constantly changing as it sounds; it isn't static at all. The reverberant echoes actually move around the environment, which is what gives the environment a distinct sound. You can simulate this movement using the Motion Depth and Motion Rate parameters. The Motion Depth parameter determines how much movement there is and the Motion Rate parameter determines the speed of that movement. For examples on how to set these parameters, be sure to take a look at some of the included presets.

10. Set the Level parameter, which controls the overall volume level of the effect output.

11. Click on the Audition button to test the current parameter settings. Make further adjustments if necessary.

12. Set the appropriate options under the Mixing tab.

13. If you want to use the current settings at a later time, save them as a preset.

14. Click on OK.

SONAR will process the data by applying the effect according to the parameter settings you specified.

Sonitus:fx Reverb (SONAR Producer Edition)

If you purchased the Producer Edition of SONAR, you have access to an additional reverb effect called Sonitus:fx Reverb. Here is how it works:

1. Select the audio data you want to process.

2. Choose Process > Audio Effects > Sonitus:fx > Reverb to open the Reverb dialog box (see Figure 11.24).

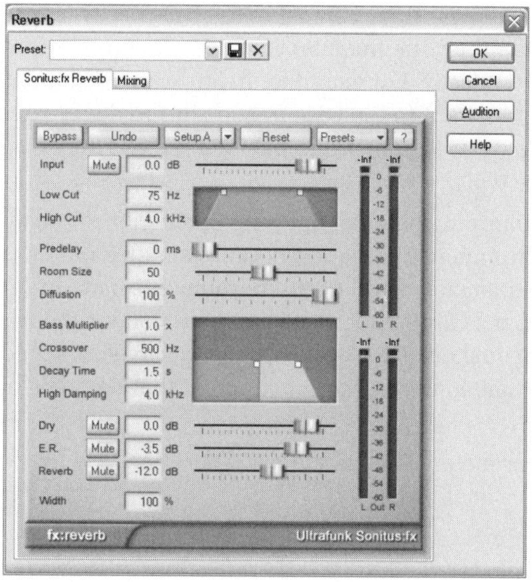

Figure 11.24
The Sonitus:fx Reverb effect provides some additional parameters not found in the other reverb effects.

3. Set the Input parameter. This parameter lets you set the level of the signal coming into the Reverb effect.

4. Set the Low Cut and High Cut parameters. These are EQ parameters that allow you to define the frequencies for different types of environments. The Low Cut parameter cuts out low frequencies below the frequency you specify. The High Cut parameter cuts out frequencies above the frequency you specify.

5. Set the Predelay parameter. This parameter determines the time between when your audio is first heard and when the reverb effect begins. To simulate small spaces, use a low setting (such as 1 millisecond). For large spaces, use a higher setting (such as 45 to 70 milliseconds).

6. Set the Room Size parameter. This parameter determines the size of the environment you are trying to simulate. For small spaces, use a low value (such as 20). For large spaces, use a high value (such as 70).

7. Set the Diffusion parameter. This parameter determines the thickness of the reverberation. Experiment with it to hear what I mean.

8. Set the Decay Time parameter. When you're applying reverb to your data, you should imagine the type of environment you want to create. Doing so will help you set the parameters. Technically, the Decay Time determines how long it takes for the reverberation to fade away, but you can also think of it as controlling how large the environment will be. It works in conjunction with the Room Size parameter. The lower the Decay Time, the smaller the environment, and vice versa.

9. Set the Crossover and Bass Multiplier parameters. There may be times when you want to simulate an environment that has more or less bass sound to it. The Bass Multiplier parameter allows you to specify how much longer or shorter the Decay Time of the bass frequencies in your environment will last (compared to the other frequencies). Setting the Bass Multiplier higher than 1.0 makes the bass decay

longer; setting it lower than 1.0 makes the bass decay shorter. The Crossover parameter determines the frequency below which other frequencies will have a longer or shorter decay. For example, if you want to simulate a bright-sounding room, you would want to the bass frequencies to decay faster. So you might set the Crossover parameter to something like 500 Hz and the Bass Multiplier to something like 0.5.

10. Set the High Damping parameter. Using this parameter also helps to create a more authentic environment simulation because smaller, closed environments tend to stifle some frequencies, and larger environments usually sound brighter, meaning they promote more of the frequencies. When you set the High Damping parameter (in Hz), any frequencies above that frequency are slowly reduced (dampened) to simulate the same high-frequency reduction that happens as the reverb effect fades.

11. Set the Dry parameter. This parameter determines the level of the original non-effected audio signal.

12. Set the E.R. parameter. This parameter determines the level of the early reflections in the reverb effect. I discussed early reflections previously in this chapter.

13. Set the Reverb parameter. This parameter determines the level of the affected audio signal, also known as the *wet signal*. It works the same as the Wet Mix parameter discussed earlier in this chapter, in the previous reverberation sections.

14. Set the Width parameter. This parameter allows you to adjust the stereo width of the reverberation effect. Use a setting of 0 to create a monophonic signal; use a setting of 100 to create a regular stereo signal. Use a setting of more than 100 for a simulated wide stereo signal.

15. Click on the Audition button to test the current parameter settings. Make further adjustments if necessary.

16. Set the appropriate options under the Mixing tab.

17. If you want to use the current settings at a later time, save them as a preset.

18. Click on OK.

SONAR will process the data by applying the effect according to the parameter settings you specified.

Lexicon Pantheon (SONAR Producer Edition)

In addition to the Sonitus:fx Reverb effect, SONAR Producer Edition users get a very high-quality reverb effect called the Lexicon Pantheon. Here is how it works:

1. Select the audio data you want to process.

2. Choose Process > Audio Effects > Lexicon Pantheon to open the Lexicon Pantheon dialog box (see Figure 11.25).

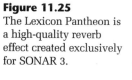

Figure 11.25
The Lexicon Pantheon is a high-quality reverb effect created exclusively for SONAR 3.

3. Set the Reverb Type parameter. This parameter determines the type of environment you are trying to simulate. The available options are self-explanatory.

4. Set the Mix and Level parameters. These parameters work the same as the Mix and Level parameters of the FxReverb effect.

5. Set the Pre-Delay parameter. This parameter works the same as the Pre Delay parameter for the FxReverb effect.

6. Set the Room Size parameter. This parameter works the same as the Room Size parameter for the FxReverb effect.

7. Set the RT 60 parameter. This parameter allows you to set the reverberation time and it works the same as the Decay Time parameter for the FxReverb effect.

8. Set the Damping parameter. This parameter works the same as the High Damping parameter for the Sonitus:fx Reverb effect.

9. Set the Density Regen and Delay parameters. These parameters work the same as the Density parameter for the FxReverb effect, except that here you have more control over the thickness of the reverberation. Lower Regen and Delay values provide a more natural reverb effect.

10. Set the Echo Level and Time values. Together, these parameters allow you to introduce echo effects into both the left and right stereo channels of your reverb effect. It's similar to applying a delay effect to your audio data and then applying a reverb effect after that. Refer to the section on Delay in this chapter for more information about echo effects.

11. Set the Bass Boost and Bass Freq parameters. These parameters work the same as the Bass Multiplier and Crossover parameters for the Sonitus:fx Reverb effect.

12. Set the Diffusion parameter. This parameter works the same as the Diffusion parameter for the Sonitus:fx Reverb effect.

13. Set the Spread parameter. This parameter works the same as the Width parameter for the Sonitus:fx Reverb effect.

CHAPTER 11

14. Click on the Audition button to test the current parameter settings. Make further adjustments if necessary.

15. Set the appropriate options under the Mixing tab.

16. If you want to use the current settings at a later time, save them as a preset.

17. Click on OK.

SONAR will process the data by applying the effect according to the parameter settings you specified.

Dynamics

SONAR includes a number of effects that allow you to apply dynamic processing to your audio data, including compression and limiting. What does that mean? Well, one way to explain it would be to talk about taming vocal recordings. Suppose you recorded this vocalist who can really belt out a tune but doesn't have a very good microphone technique. When he sings, he just stays in one place in front of the mike. Professional singers know that during the quiet parts of the song, they need to sing up close to the mike, and during the loud parts, they need to back away so that an even amplitude level is recorded. If a singer doesn't do this, the amplitude of the recorded audio will be very uneven. That's where compression and limiting comes in. Compression allows you to squash the audio signal so the amplitude levels are more even. Limiting allows you to stop the amplitude of the audio signal from rising past a certain level to prevent clipping. This can happen if the performer sings too loudly. I'll talk about each of the available effects one at a time.

Compressor

The Compressor effect allows you to apply compression to your audio data. The effect works as follows:

1. Select the audio data you want to process.

2. Choose Process > Audio Effects > Compressor to open the Compressor dialog box (see Figure 11.26).

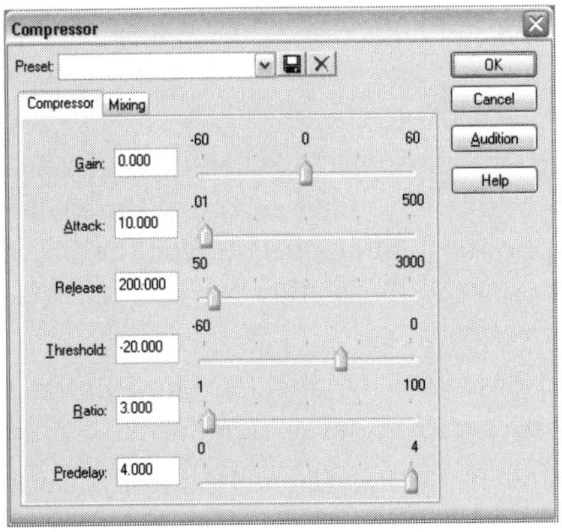

Figure 11.26
Use the Compressor effect to apply compression to your audio data.

3. Set the Threshold parameter. The Compressor effect uses a digital noise gate to identify the parts of your audio data that should be processed. The Threshold parameter determines at what amplitude level your audio data will start being compressed. When the amplitude of your audio data reaches the Threshold level, processing will begin.

4. Set the Ratio parameter. This parameter determines how much processing is done to your audio data. A ratio of 1 means no processing is done; a ratio of 100 means the audio is fully processed.

5. Set the Attack parameter. This parameter determines how quickly after the input level has reached the threshold that processing is applied. For example, if the input level reaches the threshold, it doesn't have to be compressed right away. A slow attack means the signal won't be compressed unless it lasts for a while. This is a good way to make sure fast, percussive parts are left alone, but long, drawn-out parts are compressed. The Predelay parameter works in conjunction with the Attack parameter by delaying the processing when the input signal is first detected.

6. Set the Release parameter. This parameter determines how quickly after the input level goes below the threshold that processing is stopped (or the digital noise gate is closed). If you set the Release parameter too low, your audio could be cut off. A longer release allows processing to sound more natural. You'll have to experiment to get to the right setting.

7. Set the Gain parameter. This parameter allows you to adjust the overall amplitude of your audio after it is processed.

8. Click on the Audition button to test the current parameter settings. Make further adjustments if necessary.

9. Set the appropriate options under the Mixing tab.

10. If you want to use the current settings at a later time, save them as a preset.

11. Click on OK.

SONAR will process the data by applying the effect according to the parameter settings you specified.

FX Compressor/Gate

The FX Compressor/Gate effect is similar to the Compressor effect, but it provides better-quality processing and more features. Here is how it works:

1. Select the audio data you want to process.

2. Choose Process > Audio Effects > Cakewalk > FX Compressor/Gate to open the FX Compressor/Gate dialog box (see Figure 11.27). The dialog box displays a graph. The right side of the graph shows output amplitude, and the bottom of the graph shows input amplitude. Inside the graph is a line representing the input amplitude and output amplitude as they relate to each other. Initially, the line is drawn diagonally, and you read it from left to right. This shows a 1:1 ratio between input and output amplitudes, meaning as the input level goes up 1 dB, the output level also goes up 1 dB.

Figure 11.27
The FX Compressor/Gate effect provides high-quality compression with some extra features.

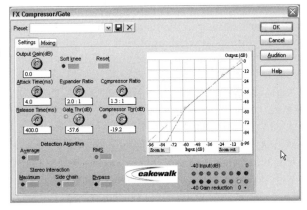

3. Set the Compressor Thr (threshold) parameter. This parameter works the same as the Threshold parameter in the Compressor effect.

4. Set the Compressor Ratio parameter. This parameter works the same as the Ratio parameter in the Compressor effect, except the values are numbered differently. A ratio of 1:1 means no processing is done. A ratio of 2:1 means that for every 2-dB increase in input amplitude, there is only a 1-dB increase in output amplitude. Thus, the amplitude is being compressed. If you set the Ratio parameter to its highest value (Inf:1), that causes limiting, so no matter how loud the input amplitude gets, it is limited to the level set by the Threshold parameter. I'll talk more about limiting later.

5. Set the Attack Time parameter. This parameter works the same way as the Attack parameter in the Compressor effect.

6. Set the Release Time parameter. This parameter works the same way as the Release parameter in the Compressor effect.

7. In addition to being able to compress audio data, the FX Compressor/Gate effect can cut out noises using a special noise gate (hence the name Compressor/Gate). By setting the Gate Thr (threshold) parameter, you can remove any unwanted noises that have an amplitude level that falls below the threshold. This is great for removing bad notes or string noise on guitar parts, for instance. Setting the Expander Ratio determines how soft the amplitudes below the Gate Thr will be made. For example, if you set the Expander Ratio to 100:1, then any sounds that fall below the Gate Thr will be cut out completely.

8. Set the Detection Algorithm parameter. This parameter establishes how the FX Compressor/Gate effect will determine the amplitude level of the incoming audio signal. Choosing the Average option tells the effect to determine the average value of the input signal and use that to apply compression appropriately. Choosing the RMS (root mean square) option tells the effect to determine the perceived loudness (as a listener would hear it over a period of time) of the input signal and use that to apply compression appropriately. The best method to use depends on the material being processed. You'll need to experiment to see which one works best.

9. Set the Stereo Interaction parameter. Choose the Maximum option to apply compression to both stereo channels equally. Choose the Side Chain option to apply compression only to the right channel of the stereo signal, while using the left channel signal to activate the threshold. You can use this option as a *ducking* effect, which can come in handy if you have music playing in the right channel and a voiceover playing in the left channel. As the voice comes in, the music will be lowered so listeners can hear the voice over the background music. For most applications, you'll want to use the Maximum option.

10. Activate the Soft Knee option to give a smoother transition as the input signal starts to be compressed.

11. Set the Output Gain parameter. This parameter allows you to adjust the overall amplitude of your audio after it is processed.

12. Click on the Audition button to test the current parameter settings. Make further adjustments if necessary.

13. Set the appropriate options under the Mixing tab.

14. If you want to use the current settings at a later time, save them as a preset.

15. Click on OK.

SONAR will process the data by applying the effect according to the parameter settings you specified.

FX Expander/Gate

Like the special noise gate option in the FX Compressor/Gate effect, the FX Expander/Gate effect allows you to cut out unwanted noises below a certain amplitude threshold. This effect takes less CPU processing power for those times when you don't need compression. Here is how it works:

1. Select the audio data you want to process.

2. Choose Process > Audio Effects > Cakewalk > FX Expander/Gate to open the FX Expander/Gate dialog box (see Figure 11.28). The dialog box displays a graph. This graph is the same as the one in the FX Compressor/Gate effect.

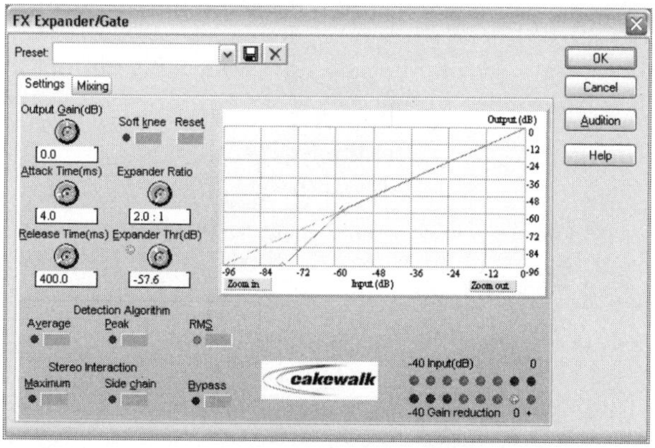

Figure 11.28
Use the FX Expander/Gate effect to remove low-volume noises from your audio data.

3. Set the Expander Thr (threshold) parameter. This parameter works the same as the Gate Thr parameter in the FX Compressor/Gate effect.

4. Set the Expander Ratio parameter. This parameter works the same as the Expander Ratio parameter in the FX Compressor/Gate effect.

5. Set the Attack Time parameter. This parameter works the same as the Attack Time parameter in the FX Compressor/Gate effect.

6. Set the Release Time parameter. This parameter works the same as the Release Time parameter in the FX Compressor/Gate effect.

7. Set the Detection Algorithm parameter. This parameter works the same as the Detection Algorithm parameter in the FX Compressor/Gate effect, except there is one additional option. Choosing the Peak option tells the effect to determine the peak value of the input signal and use that to apply processing appropriately.

8. Set the Stereo Interaction parameter. This parameter works the same as the Stereo Interaction parameter in the FX Compressor/Gate effect.

9. Activate the Soft Knee option to give a smoother transition as the input signal starts to be processed.

10. Set the Output Gain parameter. This parameter allows you to adjust the overall amplitude of your audio after it is processed.

11. Click on the Audition button to test the current parameter settings. Make further adjustments if necessary.

12. Set the appropriate options under the Mixing tab.

13. If you want to use the current settings at a later time, save them as a preset.

14. Click on OK.

SONAR will process the data by applying the effect according to the parameter settings you specified.

FX Limiter

The FX Limiter effect allows you to stop an audio signal from getting any louder than a specified amplitude level. You can put this effect to good use during recording to prevent your input signal from getting too high and causing distortion or clipping. Here is how the effect works:

1. Select the audio you want to process.

2. Choose Process > Audio Effects > Cakewalk > FX Limiter to open the FX Limiter dialog box (see Figure 11.29).

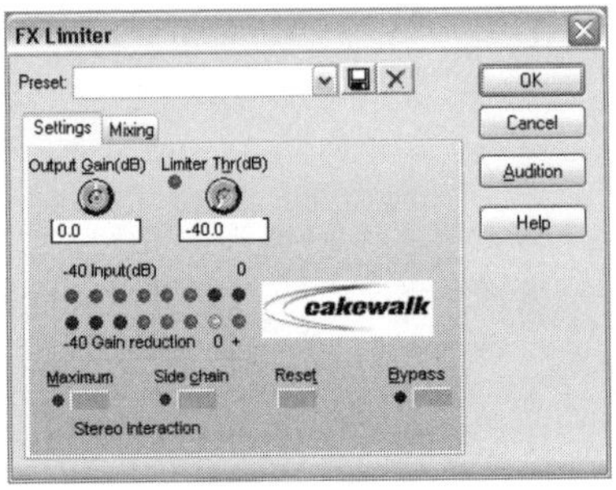

Figure 11.29
Use the FX Limiter effect to prevent an audio signal from getting too loud.

3. Set the Limiter Thr (threshold) parameter. This is the level above which you don't want your audio signal level to go. This means the amplitude of the audio won't be able to get any higher than this value.

4. Set the Stereo Interaction parameter. I explained this parameter earlier.

5. Set the Output Gain parameter. This parameter allows you to adjust the overall amplitude of your audio after it is processed.

6. Click on the Audition button to test the current parameter settings. Make further adjustments if necessary.

7. Set the appropriate options under the Mixing tab.

8. If you want to use the current settings at a later time, save them as a preset.

9. Click on OK.

SONAR will process the data by applying the effect according to the parameter settings you specified.

FX Dynamics Processor

The FX Dynamics Processor effect (see Figure 11.30) combines all of the features of the previous dynamics effects into one. This means that this one effect can perform all of the functions of the FX Compressor/Gate, FX Expander/Gate, and FX Limiter effects. It also has the same parameter settings, which all work the same as in the previously described effects. Please review the previous sections to learn how to operate the parameters of this effect.

Figure 11.30
The FX Dynamics Processor combines all of the features of the other dynamics effects.

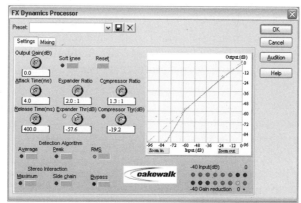

Sonitus: fx Compressor

If you purchased the Producer Edition of SONAR, you'll have three additional dynamics effects at your disposal. The first is the Sonitus:fx Compressor, which provides pretty much the same functionality as FX Compressor/Gate effect. Here is how it works:

1. Select the audio data you want to process.

2. Choose Process > Audio Effects > Sonitus:fx > Compressor to open the Compressor dialog box (see Figure 11.31).

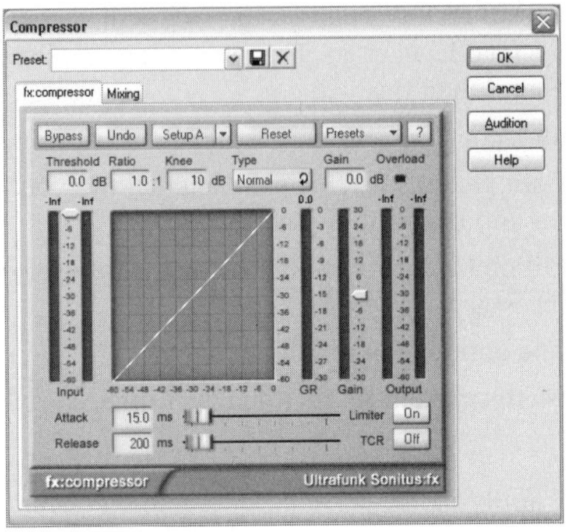

Figure 11.31

The Compressor effect provides similar functionality to the FX Compressor/Gate effect.

3. To adjust the input signal level, just drag the Input slider up or down.

4. Set the Threshold parameter. This parameter works the same as the Threshold parameter for the FX Compressor/Gate effect.

5. Set the Ratio parameter. This parameter works the same as the Ratio parameter for the FX Compressor/Gate effect.

6. Set the Attack parameter. This parameter works the same as the Attack parameter for the FX Compressor/Gate effect.

7. Set the Release parameter. This parameter works the same as the Release parameter for the FX Compressor/Gate effect, with one exception. Just to the right of the Release parameter is a button labeled TCR. Activating this button tells the Compressor effect to try to determine the release time automatically during processing. This may or may not work well, depending on the material you are processing.

8. In addition to being able to compress audio data, the Compressor effect can apply limiting to your data. To turn limiting on or off, use the Limiter button located to the right of the Attack parameter.

9. Set the Type parameter by clicking on the Type button. A setting of Normal provides the operation of a normal compressor effect. A setting of Vintage emulates the compression characteristics of a classic analog-based compressor like the Teletronix LA2A. This might give your audio data more warmth and punch.

10. Set the Knee parameter. Choosing a soft setting (10 dB or greater) will give you a warmer quality to the compression. Choosing a hard setting (below 10 dB) will give you a harsher quality to the compression.

11. Set the Gain parameter. This parameter works the same as the Output Gain parameter in the FX Compressor/Gate effect.

12. Click on the Audition button to test the current parameter settings. Make further adjustments if necessary.

13. Set the appropriate options under the Mixing tab.

14. If you want to use the current settings at a later time, save them as a preset.

15. Click on OK.

SONAR will process the data by applying the effect according to the parameter settings you specified.

Sonitus:fx Gate

The second extra dynamics effect that you receive with the SONAR Producer Edition is the Sonitus:fx Gate effect. I've talked about digital noise gates before as they pertain to other functions, but you also can use digital noise gates independently to remove (or reduce the level of) parts of your audio data. For example, if you want the quiet sections in a vocal dialogue recording to be turned to silence, you can use a noise gate. The Sonitus:fx Gate effect can do this, and here is how it works:

1. Select the audio data you want to process.

2. Choose Process > Audio Effects > Sonitus:fx > Gate to open the Gate dialog box (see Figure 11.32).

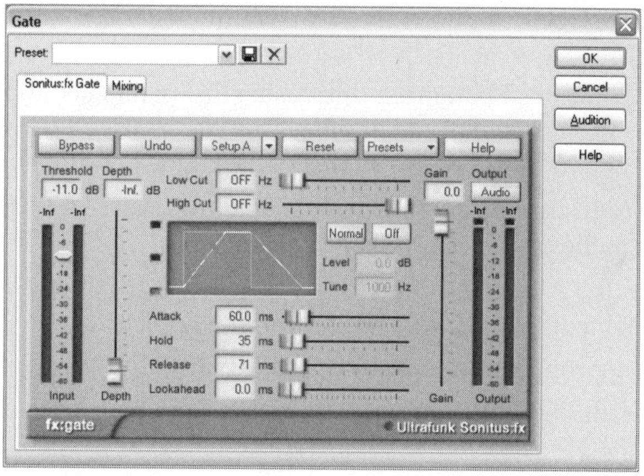

Figure 11.32
The Gate effect provides similar functionality to the FX Expander/Gate effect.

3. To adjust the input signal level, just drag the Input slider up or down.

4. Set the Threshold parameter. This parameter determines at what amplitude audio is allowed to pass through the gate unaffected. Anything below the threshold will have its level reduced.

5. Set the Depth parameter. This parameter determines how soft the input signal level will be made after the gate is closed. Most of the time this parameter is set to −Inf, making the signal completely silent.

6. Set the Low Cut and High Cut parameters. These are EQ parameters that allow you to gate an audio signal according to frequency. Any frequencies below the Low Cut frequency are reduced; any frequencies above the High Cut frequency are reduced.

7. Set the Gate Mode parameter using the Gate Mode button (which is located below the High Cut parameter). Initially, the button displays a Normal setting. Click on the button to toggle it to Duck mode and vice versa. In Duck mode, the gate is

inverted so signals below the threshold are allowed to pass and signals above the threshold are attenuated.

8. Set the Punch Mode, Punch Level, and Punch Tune parameters (which are located next to the Gate Mode button). The Punch feature allows you to add gain to the signal as it starts to pass through the gate. This can be useful to add punch to percussion sounds. Setting the mode to Wide adds punch to a wide signal range. Setting the mode to Tuned allows you to add punch to a specific frequency. The Level and Tune parameters let you specify the amount of gain added and the frequency used.

9. Set the Attack parameter. This parameter determines how quickly after the input level has reached the threshold that the noise gate opens and allows audio through. A low setting keeps any quick, percussive sound intact.

10. Set the Hold parameter. This parameter determines how long the gate stays open after the input signal has gone below the threshold.

11. Set the Release parameter. This parameter determines how quickly after the input level goes below the threshold and the hold time ends that the noise gate is closed. A low setting makes the noise gate close quickly. Again, this is good for percussive sounds.

12. Set the Lookahead parameter. Increasing this parameter allows the Gate effect to scan the input signal ahead of time. This can be useful if you have percussive sounds but you want to use a longer attack time and not chop off part of the signal.

13. Set the Gain parameter. This parameter allows you to adjust the overall amplitude of your audio after it is processed.

14. Click on the Audition button to test the current parameter settings. Make further adjustments if necessary.

15. Set the appropriate options under the Mixing tab.

16. If you want to use the current settings at a later time, save them as a preset.

17. Click on OK.

SONAR will process the data by applying the effect according to the parameter settings you specified.

Sonitus:fx Multiband

Like the Sonitus:fx Compressor effect, the Multiband effect allows you to apply compression to your audio data. This effect has one important difference though; it allows you to process different frequency ranges in your audio independently. Why is that important? Well, one way to explain it is to talk about *de-essing*. You might have noticed while doing vocal recordings that some singers produce a sort of hissing sound whenever they pronounce words with the letter "s" in them. That hissing sound is called *sibilance*, and you usually don't want it in your audio. The process of removing sibilance is called de-essing, and it is done by compressing certain frequencies in the audio spectrum. To use the Multiband effect, follow these steps:

1. Select the audio data you want to process.

2. Choose Process > Audio Effects > Sonitus:fx > Multiband to open the Multiband dialog box (see Figure 11.33).

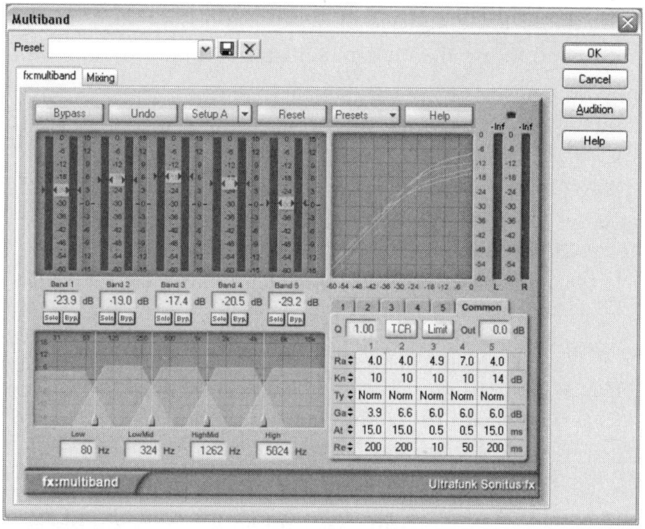

Figure 11.33
Use the Sonitus:fx
Multiband effect to
compress different
frequency ranges.

3. The Multiband effect actually provides five compression effects in one. It's basically like having five of the Sonitus:fx Compressor effects together in one effect. You'll find five sets of controls called *bands* in the upper-left section of the dialog box. You can turn each band on or off using the Byp (bypass) buttons, and you can solo a band using the Solo buttons. All the bands are identical.

4. To set the Threshold parameter for each band, use the vertical sliders or type in a value. The Threshold parameters work the same as for the Sonitus:fx Compressor effect.

5. In the lower-right section of the dialog box, you'll find a tabbed area. Clicking on a numbered tab displays the compression settings for each band.

6. Set the Ratio, Knee, Type, Gain, Attack, and Release parameters for each band. All of these parameters work the same as the corresponding parameters for the Sonitus:fx Compressor effect.

7. Clicking on the Common tab displays all the band settings in a grid, as well as some global effect settings.

8. Set the TCR, Limit, and Out parameters. These also work the same as they do for the Sonitus:fx Compressor effect.

9. The lower-left portion of the dialog box contains the frequency graph. This graph displays the frequency ranges for each band. You can adjust the ranges by clicking and dragging the four separators on the graph or you can type in new values for the Low, LowMid, HighMid, and High parameters. These parameters determine the range of frequencies that will be affected by each band.

10. There is also a global Q parameter that affects all the bands located in the Common panel. The Q parameter works the same as the previously mentioned Q parameter in the "Equalization" section of this chapter.

11. Click on the Audition button to test the current parameter settings. Make further adjustments if necessary.

CHAPTER 11

12. Set the appropriate options under the Mixing tab.

13. If you want to use the current settings at a later time, save them as a preset.

14. Click on OK.

SONAR will process the data by applying the Multiband effect according to your parameter settings.

MASTERING

In addition to regular compression/limiting tasks, the high quality of the Multiband effect allows you to use it for mastering. *Mastering* is the procedure during which the final mixed-down stereo audio for a song is processed with various effects (such as EQ, compression, and limiting) to give the song that final professional touch before it is burned to CD. There have been entire books written on the topic of mastering, but you can also find some good information on the Internet at these sites:

▶ **iZotope, Inc.**
http://www.izotope.com/products/audio/ozone/ozoneguide.html

▶ **ProRec.com.**
http://www.prorec.com/prorec/articles.nsf/files/F717F79532C9067386256688001A7623

▶ **Digital Domain.**
http://www.digido.com/portal/pmodule_id=11/pmdmode=fullscreen/pageadder_page_id=18

Also, be sure to sign up for my free DigiFreq music technology newsletter so you don't miss the mastering information I will be providing in future issues. To sign up, go to http://www.digifreq.com/digifreq.

Distortion

Most of the time, bad-sounding audio isn't something that you want. Distortion is something you usually try to avoid when recording audio data. But sometimes distortion can be a good thing (as Martha Stewart would say). For example, if you want to dress up a guitar part for a rock song, adding a bit of distortion can make it sound really cool. Or maybe you want to add a bit of grit to a vocal part. Using the Distortion effect, you can achieve these sounds; here's how:

1. Select the audio data you want to process.

2. Choose Process > Audio Effects > Distortion to open the Distortion dialog box (see Figure 11.34).

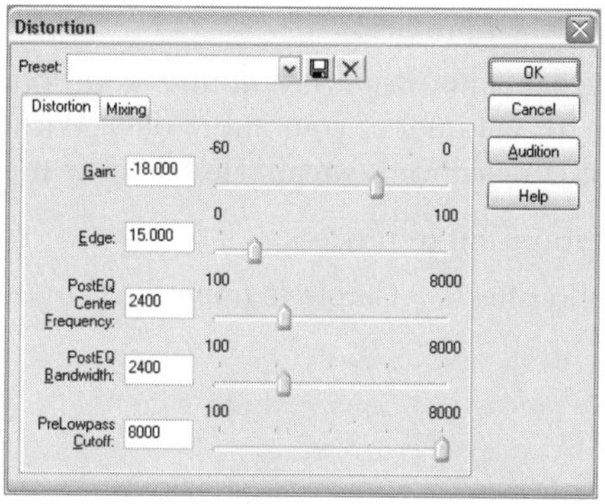

Figure 11.34
Use the Distortion effect to add distortion to your audio data.

Distortion	☒

Preset: [_____] ▾ 🖫 ✕   [OK]

[Distortion | Mixing]   [Cancel]

     -60   0   [Audition]
Gain: [-18.000]   [Help]

    0   100
Edge: [15.000]

PostEQ
Center [2400] 100   8000
Frequency:

PostEQ [2400] 100   8000
Bandwidth:

PreLowpass [8000] 100   8000
Cutoff:

3. Set the Edge parameter. This parameter determines by how much your audio data will be distorted. A low level means less distortion; a high level means more distortion.

4. Set the PostEQ Center Frequency and PostEQ Bandwidth parameters. These parameters allow you to apply equalization to the output signal of the Distortion effect. Using these parameters, you can achieve different-sounding distortion effects. You'll need to experiment with them.

5. Set the PreLowpass Cutoff parameter. Any frequencies above the frequency you set for this parameter will be cut from the audio signal. You can use this to reduce the harshness that sometimes accompanies distorted audio so you can achieve more of an effect rather than noise.

6. Set the Gain parameter. This controls the overall volume of the effect.

START WITH A LOW LEVEL

Don't set the gain too high, because the distortion might damage your speakers (or your ears, if you're using headphones). Start off with a nice low level when you are auditioning this effect.

7. Click on the Audition button to test the current parameter settings. Make further adjustments if necessary.

8. Set the appropriate options under the Mixing tab.

9. If you want to use the current settings at a later time, save them as a preset.

10. Click on OK.

SONAR will process the data by applying the effect according to the parameter settings you specified.

CHAPTER 11

Gargle

The Gargle effect provides something that is known as *amplitude modulation*. The effect modulates (or vibrates) the amplitude (or volume) of your audio data. With this effect, you can achieve sounds such as the tremolo on an electronic organ. Here is how the Gargle effect works:

1. Select the audio data you want to process.

2. Choose Process > Audio Effects > Gargle to open the Gargle dialog box (see Figure 11.35).

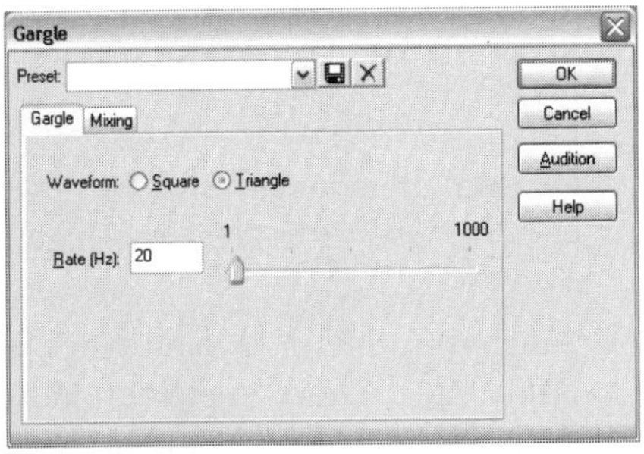

Figure 11.35
The Gargle effect lets you modulate the amplitude of your audio data.

3. Set the Waveform parameter. Choose the Square option for a harsh-sounding amplitude modulation. Choose the Triangle option for a smooth-sounding amplitude modulation.

4. Set the Rate parameter. For a tremolo effect, use a low value, such as 7. For a very weird ringing effect, use a high value, such as 800.

5. Click on the Audition button to test the current parameter settings. Make further adjustments if necessary.

6. Set the appropriate options under the Mixing tab.

7. If you want to use the current settings at a later time, save them as a preset.

8. Click on OK.

SONAR will process the data by applying the effect according to the parameter settings you specified.

Changing Time and Pitch

In addition to the Length and Transpose editing features, SONAR provides the Pitch Shifter and Time/Pitch Stretch effects, which you also can use to change the length and pitch of your audio data. The effects, however, are more powerful and flexible. This is especially true of the Time/Pitch Stretch effect.

Pitch Shifter

The Pitch Shifter effect provides low quality, but it doesn't take up as much CPU processing power. If you want to try out the Cakewalk FX Pitch Shifter, here's how it works:

1. Select the audio data you want to process.

2. Select Process > Audio Effects > Cakewalk > Pitch Shifter to open the Pitch Shifter dialog box (see Figure 11.36).

Figure 11.36
The Pitch Shifter effect doesn't provide very good sound quality. For better quality, use the Time/Pitch Stretch effect.

3. Under the Settings tab, set the Pitch Shift parameter. It is exactly the same as the Amount parameter in the Transpose editing function. You can use it to transpose the pitch of your audio data from -12 to $+12$ semitones (an entire octave down or up).

UNWANTED ARTIFACTS

Normally when you change the pitch of audio data, the length is altered, too. Raise the pitch and the data gets shorter; lower the pitch and the data gets longer. When this happens, the processed audio no longer plays in sync with the other data in your project. Luckily, you can use SONAR's pitch-shifting effects to change pitch without changing the length of the audio data. The only problem to be leery of is that pitch shifting can

produce unwanted artifacts if you use too great an interval. The famous Alvin & the Chipmunks were a product of this phenomenon. It's best to stay within an interval of a major third (four semitones) up or down if possible.

4. Set the Dry Mix and Wet Mix parameters. I explained these parameters earlier in the chapter, but in reference to pitch shifting, you should almost always keep the Dry Mix set to 0 percent and the Wet Mix set to 100 percent.

5. As far as the Feedback Mix, Delay Time, and Mod Depth parameters are concerned, they don't seem to have anything to do with the Cakewalk FX Pitch Shifter effect. Changing these parameters only introduces unwanted artifacts into the sound. My advice is to simply leave them set at their default values: Feedback Mix = 0, Delay Time = 0, and Mod Depth = 35.

6. Click on the Audition button to test the current parameter settings. Make further adjustments if necessary.

7. Set the appropriate options under the Mixing tab.

8. If you want to use the current settings at a later time, save them as a preset.

9. Click on OK.

SONAR will process the data by applying the effect according to the parameter settings you specified.

Time/Pitch Stretch

The Time/Pitch Stretch effect is much more advanced and flexible, and it provides better quality than the Pitch Shifter effect. However, that doesn't mean it's difficult to use. Some of the more advanced parameters can be a bit confusing, but I'll go over them one at a time. The effect works like this:

1. Select the audio data you want to process.

2. Select Process > Audio Effects > Cakewalk > Time/Pitch Stretch to open the Time/Pitch Stretch dialog box (see Figure 11.37).

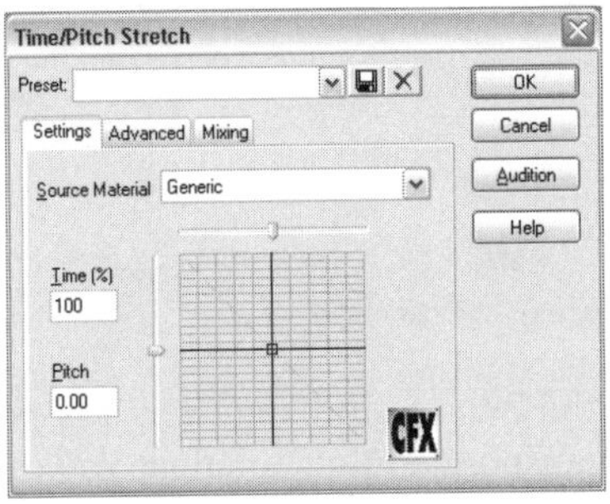

Figure 11.37
The Time/Pitch Stretch effect provides advanced time-stretching and pitch-shifting capabilities.

3. Under the Settings tab, set the Source Material parameter. One of the reasons the Time/Pitch Stretch effect provides better quality than the Pitch Shifter effect is that it takes into account the type of audio data you are processing. You should select the appropriate value for the Source Material parameter according to the type of data you want to process. For instance, if you are processing percussion data, you should set the Source Material parameter to Drums. If you can't find an appropriate setting in the supplied list, just set the Source Material parameter to Generic. This setting usually still provides good results.

4. Set the Time parameter. Using the Time parameter, you can change the length of your audio data as a percentage. If you want to make the data shorter, set the Time parameter to a percentage less than 100. For example, to make the data half of its original length, use a setting of 50 percent. If you want to make the data longer, set the Time parameter to a percentage greater than 100. For example, if you want to make data the twice its original length, use a setting of 200 percent. To change the Time parameter, just type a value or use the horizontal slider.

STAY WITHIN 10 PERCENT

I mentioned earlier that when you're transposing audio, it's best to stay within a major third (four semitones) up or down if possible, because audio doesn't react well to higher values. Well, the same concept applies when you're changing the length of audio data. You should try to stay within 10 percent longer or shorter if possible; otherwise, the results might not sound very good. This is another feature with which you have to experiment.

5. Set the Pitch parameter. Using the Pitch parameter, you can transpose your audio data up or down one octave (in semitones). To change the Pitch parameter, just type a value or use the vertical slider.

TIME/PITCH GRAPH

Notice that a graph is shown in the Time/Pitch Stretch dialog box. Using this graph, you can change the Time and Pitch parameters by dragging the small blue square. Drag the square up or down to change the Pitch parameter. Drag the square left or right to change the Time parameter. If you hold down the Shift key on your computer keyboard at the same time, the square automatically will snap to the exact grid points on the graph.

6. Under the Advanced tab, you'll see three parameters called Block Rate, Overlap Ratio, and Crossfade Ratio. These very advanced settings are used by the Time/Pitch Stretch effect to determine how your data will be processed. Luckily, you don't have to deal with them because they are set to the appropriate values automatically, according to the setting you use for the Source Material parameter. Basically, don't worry about them.

7. You'll also notice two other parameters under the Advanced tab—Accuracy and Algorithm. You *do* need to deal with these parameters. The Accuracy parameter determines the quality of the effect processing. If you set the Accuracy parameter to High, you'll get better quality out of the effect, but it will also take longer to process your data. The Algorithm parameter is strictly for use when you're processing audio data containing vocals. If you're processing any other kind of material, you should leave the Algorithm parameter set to Normal. In the case of vocal material, though, setting the Algorithm parameter to Formant Preserving tells the effect to preserve the original vocal characteristics when transposing the pitch up or down. Without the Algorithm parameter set to Formant Preserving, transposing your vocal material up can make it sound like Alvin & the Chipmunks, and transposing it down can make it sound like Fat Albert.

8. Click on the Audition button to test the current parameter settings. Make further adjustments if necessary.

9. Set the appropriate options under the Mixing tab.

10. If you want to use the current settings at a later time, save them as a preset.

11. Click on OK.

SONAR will process the data by applying the effect according to the parameter settings you specified.

Amplifier Simulation

For all you electric guitar players out there, SONAR provides the Amp Sim effect. Using this effect, you can simulate the sound of real-life guitar amplifiers, making your recorded guitar audio data sound like it's being played through different kinds of amps. To achieve this sound, the effect uses technology called *physical modeling*. In this technology, the characteristics of a real instrument or device are converted into a mathematical algorithm (called a *model*). You can use the model to apply those same characteristics to your audio data to achieve more authentic-sounding recordings. This explanation of the process is simplified, of course, but that's the gist of it. The Amp Sim effect works like this:

1. Select the audio data you want to process.

USEFUL FOR VOCALS

Even though the Amp Sim effect was designed for guitar amplifiers, that doesn't mean you can't use it on other types of data. The distorted sounds the effect produces also work well on vocals, especially if you're looking for that hard rock sound. Check out some of the music by Kid Rock to hear what I mean.

2. Select Process > Audio Effects > Cakewalk > Amp Sim to open the Amp Sim dialog box (see Figure 11.38).

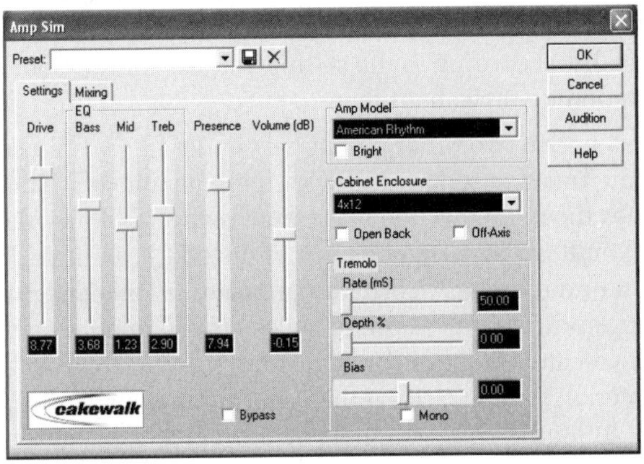

Figure 11.38
Using the Amp Sim effect, you can simulate your music being played through different kinds of guitar amplifiers.

3. Under the Settings tab in the Amp Model section, select the type of guitar amplifier you want to simulate. An additional parameter called Bright also is available in this section. It is similar to the Brightness switch found on many guitar amplifiers. It makes the effect sound brighter by boosting the high frequencies (everything above 500 Hz) of the audio spectrum.

4. In the Cabinet Enclosure section, select the type of cabinet you want to use for your virtual guitar amplifier. By setting this parameter, you can simulate different types of speaker enclosures. You have five options to choose from—No Speaker, 1×12, 2×12, 4×10, and 4×12. If you choose the No Speaker option, the effect will sound as though you plugged your guitar directly into the output of the amplifier and recorded the sound without using a microphone or the amplifier speakers. If you choose any of the other options, the effect will sound as though you played your guitar through an amplifier that has a certain number of speakers of a certain size and recorded the output by placing a microphone in front of the amp. For example, if you choose 4×12, the simulated amp will contain four speakers each at 12 inches in size. Also, when you select the other options, two other parameters become available—Open Back and Off-Axis. Activating the Open Back parameter makes the effect simulate a guitar amplifier that has a cabinet

enclosure with an open (rather than a closed) back. Activating the Off-Axis parameter makes the effect sound as though you placed the virtual microphone (mentioned earlier) off to the side of the amplifier speaker rather than directly in front of it.

5. In the Tremolo section, set the Rate and Depth parameters. Setting these parameters allows you to add a warble type of sound to the effect. The Rate parameter controls the speed of the tremolo, and the Depth parameter controls the amount of tremolo added. There is also a bias control (like that found on most guitar amps) that lets you determine whether the tremolo will add to or subtract from the volume level of the effect. In addition, by activating the Mono option, the tremolo will produce a mono output rather than stereo.

6. Set the Bass, Mid, and Treb parameters in the EQ section. These parameters act similarly to the parameters in SONAR's Graphic EQ editing feature (which I discussed in Chapter 8). Each parameter enables you to cut or boost a specific frequency by −10 or +10dB. The Bass parameter is set to 60 Hz, the Mid parameter is set to 600 kHz, and the Treb parameter is set to 6000 kHz.

7. Set the Drive parameter. This parameter basically controls the amount of distortion added to the audio data being processing.

8. Set the Presence parameter. This parameter acts like a high-pass EQ with a permanent frequency of 750 Hz. You can use it to boost some of the higher frequencies of the effect, giving it more presence.

9. Set the Volume parameter. This parameter controls the overall volume of the effect. No Dry Mix or Wet Mix parameters are available for this effect, so you hear only the totally processed signal through this one.

10. Click on the Audition button to test the current parameter settings. Make further adjustments if necessary.

11. Set the appropriate options under the Mixing tab.

12. If you want to use the current settings at a later time, save them as a preset.

13. Click on OK.

SONAR will process the data by applying the effect according to the parameter settings you specified.

Analog Tape Simulation

Similar to the Amp Sim effect, the FX2 Tape Sim effect uses physical modeling to simulate a realistic audio situation. But instead of simulating the sound of a guitar amplifier, the FX2 Tape Sim effect simulates the sound of your audio data being played off an analog tape deck. Why would you want to simulate old recording technology, especially when you have the clean and crisp sound of digital recording? Well, analog tape recording provides a sort of warm sound that can't be produced with digital recording, and you can use that sound to create authentic jazz or blues recordings. And some musicians just prefer the warm sound of analog as opposed to the crisp sound of digital. The FX2 Tape Sim effect lets you achieve that warm sound, and here is how it works:

1. Select the audio data you want to process.
2. Choose Process > Audio Effects > Cakewalk > FX2 Tape Sim to open the FX2 Tape Sim dialog box (see Figure 11.39).

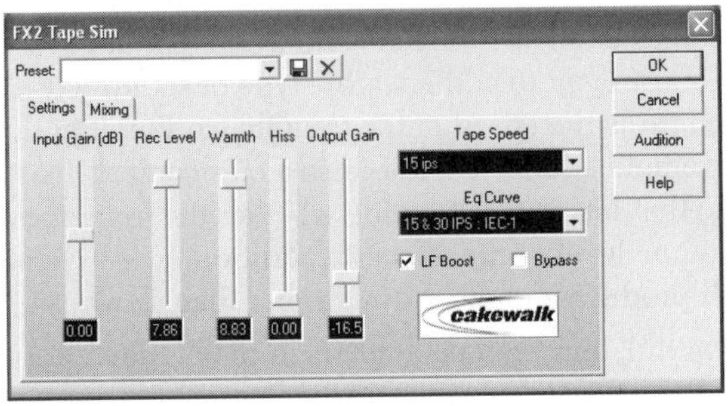

Figure 11.39
Use the FX2 Tape Sim effect to simulate the warm sound of analog tape recordings.

3. Choose the type of tape machine you want to simulate by setting the Tape Speed and Eq Curve parameters. An additional parameter called LF Boost lets you add a small increase to the lower frequencies of the audio data, giving it an even warmer sound.
4. Set the Input Gain parameter. This parameter controls the volume of the input signal into the effect. Usually, you'll just want to keep it set at 0 dB.
5. Set the Rec (short for Record) Level parameter. This parameter lets you control the level of the audio that would be recorded in an actual tape-recording situation. Setting this parameter too high will cause distortion.
6. Set the Warmth parameter. This parameter controls that warmth sound I talked about earlier.
7. Set the Hiss parameter. As in an actual tape-recording situation, you usually get tape hiss. If you want to be totally authentic in your simulation, you can use this parameter to add hiss to your audio data. A setting of 0 will turn off the Hiss parameter.
8. Set the Output Gain parameter. This parameter controls the overall volume of the effect. No Dry Mix or Wet Mix parameters are available for this effect, so you hear only the totally processed signal through this one.
9. Click on the Audition button to test the current parameter settings. Make further adjustments if necessary.
10. Set the appropriate options under the Mixing tab.
11. If you want to use the current settings at a later time, save them as a preset.
12. Click on OK.

SONAR will process the data by applying the effect according to the parameter settings you specified.

Other Effects (SONAR Producer Edition)

SONAR Producer Edition users also have four additional effects—Sonitus:fx Phase, Sonitus:fx Modulator, Sonitus:fx Wahwah, and Sonitus:fx Surround. These effects didn't fit into the previously mentioned categories, so instead I will cover them separately here.

Sonitus:fx Phase (SONAR Producer Edition)

When you mix certain sound files together, phase cancellation can occur. Phase cancellation occurs when one audio waveform increases in volume and the other decreases in volume at exactly the same time and by the same amount. Because of this phenomenon, they cancel each other out, making the mixed audio sound hollow. You can use the Sonitus:fx Phase effect to change the phase of audio data either for correction or for many different kinds of effects. Here is how it works:

1. Select the audio data you want to process.

2. Choose Process > Audio Effects > Sonitus:fx > Phase to open the Phase dialog box (see Figure 11.40).

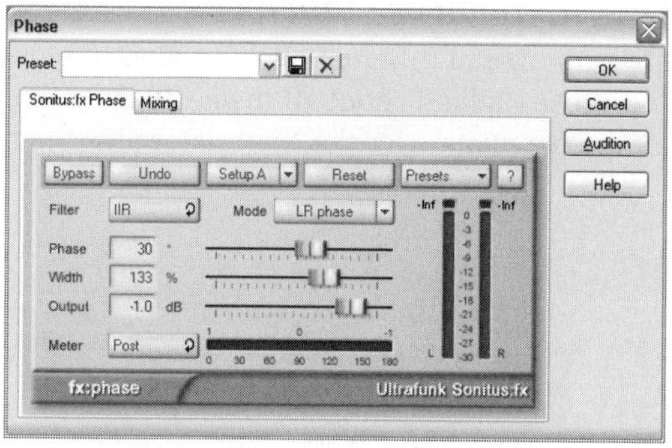

Figure 11.40
Change the phase of
audio data with the
Sonitus:fx Phase effect.

3. Set the Filter parameter. Use the IIR (*Infinite Impulse Response*) filter type for more accurate phase shift of low-frequency material. Use the FIR (*Finite Impulse Response*) filter type for more accurate phase shift of high-frequency material.

4. Set the Mode parameter. The LR Phase mode allows you to adjust the phase of the left and right channels of a stereo signal. The MS Phase mode allows you to adjust the phase of the middle (mono) and side (stereo difference) signals. The CS Encode mode allows you to adjust the phase of a stereo signal by placing the center part of the signal in the left channel and the surrounding material in the right channel. The SC Encode mode allows you to adjust the phase of a stereo signal by placing the center part of the signal in the right channel and the surrounding material in the left channel.

5. Set the Phase parameter. This parameter allows you specify the amount of phase shift that will occur. A value of 0 means no phase shift. To make the left and right channels of a stereo signal completely out of phase with one another, you can use a value of −180 degrees or +180 degrees.

6. Set the Width parameter. This parameter allows you to control the width of the stereo signal. A value of 100 percent means no change to the incoming stereo

signal. A value of 0 percent converts the stereo signal into a mono signal. A value of 200 percent makes is sound like the stereo signal is spread beyond the positions of your stereo speakers.

7. Set the Output parameter. This parameter allows you to adjust the overall amplitude of your audio after it is processed.

8. Click on the Audition button to test the current parameter settings. Make further adjustments if necessary.

9. Set the appropriate options under the Mixing tab.

10. If you want to use the current settings at a later time, save them as a preset.

11. Click on OK.

SONAR will process the data by applying the Phase effect according to your parameter settings. Be sure to check out the presets supplied with the Phase effect. This effect has many uses, including converting a mono signal to a stereo signal, widening a stereo signal, and even removing vocals from a song.

Sonitus:fx Modulator (SONAR Producer Edition)

The Modulator effect is actually a number of different effects rolled into one. It provides flanging, phasing, and chorus effects. I've already talked about all these effects in previous sections of this chapter, and you'll find most of the parameters for the Modulator effect to be familiar (see Figure 11.41).

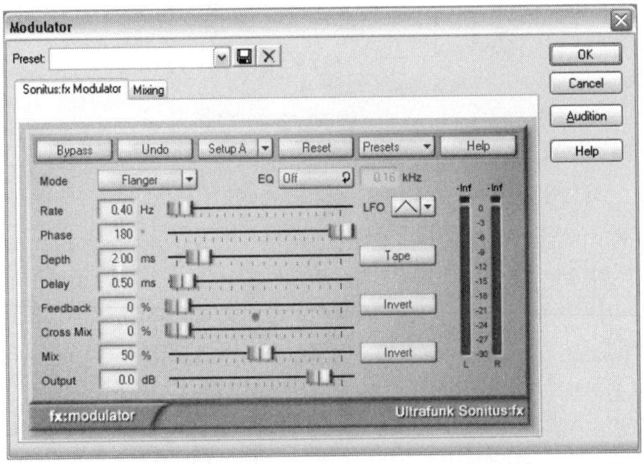

Figure 11.41
The Modulator effect provides flanging, phasing, and chorus effects.

The main differences are the Mode and Tape parameters. The Mode parameter allows you to set the type of effect you want to use. The Flanger setting allows you to create a flanging effect (see the "Flanging" section of this chapter). The Ensemble setting allows you to create a chorus effect (see the "Chorus" section of this chapter). The String Phaser, Phaser 6, and Phaser 12 settings allow you to create phasing effects. Phasing effects let you change the phase of stereo data in real time for some very interesting sounds (see the "Sonitus:fx Phase" section of the chapter for a description of phase). The Tremolo setting allows you to create warble effects by modulating the amplitude of your audio data, similar to the tremolo effect you hear on an electronic organ. Use the Tape parameter to create an effect similar to the old type of analog tape-recorder flanging. This effect ships with a large number of presets. Be sure to try them out for demonstrations of what it can do.

Sonitus:fx Wahwah (SONAR Producer Edition)

The Sonitus:fx Wahwah effect allows you to simulate the classic guitar wahwah stomp box effect. Here is how it works:

1. Select the audio data you want to process.

2. Choose Process > Audio Effects > Sonitus:fx > Wahwah to open the Wahwah dialog box (see Figure 11.42).

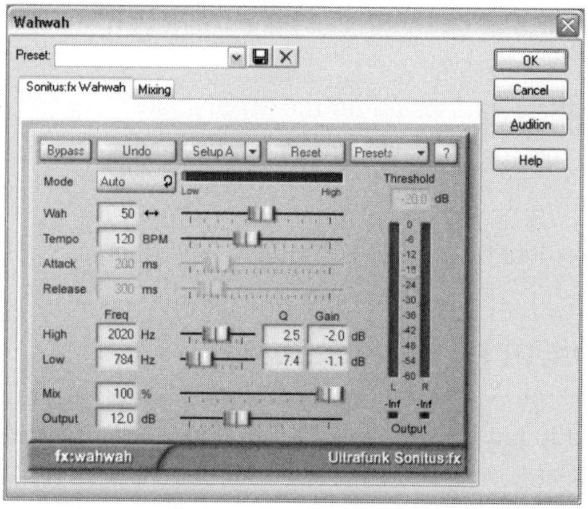

Figure 11.42

Use the Sonitus:fx Wahwah effect to simulate the classic guitar wahwah effect.

3. Set the Mode parameter. The Wahwah effect uses the up and down movement of an envelope to apply itself to your audio data. The Mode parameter determines how that envelope is controlled. Use the Auto mode to control the up and down speed of the envelope using a tempo setting. Use the Triggered mode to control the envelope using a threshold setting. Use the Manual mode to control the envelope manually using the Wah slider.

4. Set the Wah parameter. If you chose the Auto mode, the Wah parameter will determine the starting point of the envelope as it's applied to the audio. If you chose the Triggered mode, the Wah parameter will determine the range of the envelope and thus how much of the effect will be applied to the audio after the amplitude of the audio goes above the threshold. If you chose the Manual mode, you can use the Wah parameter slider to control the up and down motion of the envelope.

5. If you chose the Auto mode, set the Tempo parameter. This parameter determines the cycling speed (meaning the speed of one up-and-down motion) of the envelope and thus the wah effect.

6. If you chose the Triggered mode, set the Threshold parameter. If the level of your audio stays below the threshold, the wah effect will not be applied. If the level of your audio goes above the threshold, the wah effect will be applied, and the amount above the threshold determines how the amount of the effect applied.

7. If you chose the Triggered mode, also set the Attack and Release parameters. These parameters determine the up and down speed of the envelope, respectively.

8. You also can apply some EQ to the effect using the High and Low Freq, Q , and Gain parameters. These parameters work just like the all the other similarly named EQ parameters I've described in this chapter.

9. Set the Mix parameter to determine how much of the original audio signal and how much of the affected signal will be heard.

10. Set the Output parameter to determine the overall volume level of the effect output.

11. Click on the Audition button to test the current parameter settings. Make further adjustments if necessary.

12. Set the appropriate options under the Mixing tab.

13. If you want to use the current settings at a later time, save them as a preset.

14. Click on OK.

SONAR will process the audio data by applying the Wahwah effect according to your parameter settings.

Sonitus:fx Surround (SONAR Producer Edition)

The Sonitus:fx Surround effect allows you to create surround sound panning for your audio data. To get the full effect, you need to have a surround sound decoder and speaker system, but even with only a pair of stereo speakers, you can hear some of the effect. Here is how it works:

1. Select the audio data you want to process.

2. Choose Process > Audio Effects > Sonitus:fx > Surround to open the Surround dialog box (see Figure 11.43).

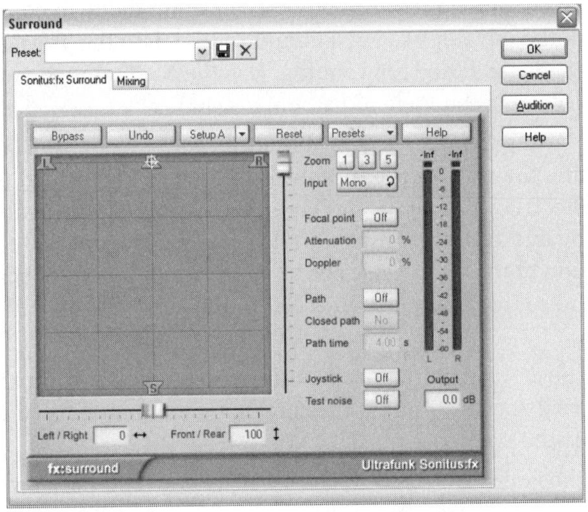

Figure 11.43
Create surround panning effects using the Sonitus:fx Surround effect.

3. In the left portion of the dialog box, you will see a graph with four speaker icons and a crosshair icon. The four speakers represent the locations of the Left, Center, Right, and Surround speakers, thus designating the listening field. The crosshair icon represents the position of your audio data being played in the listening field. You can click and drag the crosshair to move the playing position of your audio data.

4. If you want to move your audio data position outside of the listening field (so it sounds like the audio is being played from a point beyond the speaker positions), use the Zoom parameter. A setting of 1 designates a normal listening field. Settings of 3 or 5 designate larger listening fields outside of the speaker range.

5. Set the Input parameter. Choose Mono to process your audio as a mono signal. Choose stereo to process your audio as a stereo signal. Choose Left to process the left channel of a stereo signal. Choose Right to process the right channel of a stereo signal.

6. Set the Focal Point parameter to On or Off. If you turn the parameter on, a yellow cross will appear on the graph, designating the position of a virtual listener in the listening field. You can click and drag the cross to change the position of the virtual listener. This allows you to create attenuation and Doppler shift effects.

7. If you turn the Focal Point parameter on, you also need to set the Attenuation and Doppler parameters. The Attenuation parameter determines how soft your audio data will get when its position is moved away from the virtual listener. This allows you to create more realistic surround effects because as audio moves away from a listener in real life, its volume gets lower. The Doppler parameter determines how much of a pitch change will be applied to your audio data as it gets closer or farther away from the virtual listener. In real life, a sound seems to get higher in pitch as it moves toward you and lower in pitch as it moves away from you. The Doppler parameter lets you simulate that effect.

8. In addition to manually setting the playing position of your audio data in the listening field, you can have the playing position move in real time according to a path that you draw on the listening field. To create this automatic panning effect, set the Path parameter to On. When you do this, the crosshair icon will turn into a white square, designating the starting position of the path. Click on the white square and drag your mouse to a new position. This will drag the first line in the path. To create additional lines, double-click anywhere on the path to create a node. You can drag this node to another position. You can keep creating nodes and dragging them to new positions to create a complex path.

9. With the Path parameter on, you also can determine whether the path will be open or closed by setting the Closed Path parameter.

10. With the Path parameter on, use the Path Time parameter to determine how long it will take for the audio position to move along the path.

11. If you have the Path parameter off, you can control the audio position using a joystick (the same type of joystick used for computer games). If you have a joystick attached to your computer, set the Joystick parameter to On to use the joystick to control the audio panning position.

12. Click on the Audition button to test the current parameter settings. Make further adjustments if necessary.

13. Set the appropriate options under the Mixing tab.

14. If you want to use the current settings at a later time, save them as a preset.

15. Click on OK.

SONAR will process the data by applying the Surround effect according to your parameter settings.

CHAPTER 11

MIDI Effects

SONAR provides one set of eight MIDI effects, a couple of which (Chord Analyzer and Session Drummer) are not really effects (but I'll get into that later). Like the audio effects, some of the MIDI effects mimic some of SONAR's editing features. Again, they have this capability so you can process your data with these features in real time. You cannot use SONAR's editing features in real time because they aren't plug-ins. In addition, the effects provide more power and flexibility, and they include additional parameters not found in the editing features, so I'll go over them here step by step.

BASIC OFFLINE STEPS

As I mentioned earlier, because I've already covered how to apply effects offline and in real time, I'm just going to include the basic offline steps (along with parameter descriptions) in each of the following explanations. For detailed step-by-step procedures for applying effects offline and in real time, refer to the previous sections in this chapter.

Automatic Arpeggios

In music, you can play the notes of a chord in a number of different ways. Most often, the notes are played all at once. You also can play them one at a time in sequence; this is called an *arpeggio*. SONAR's Arpeggiator effect automatically creates arpeggios for each note or chord in your selected MIDI data. Depending on how you set the parameters, however, you can achieve some very strange and interesting "melodies." This feature works as follows:

1. Select the MIDI data you want to process.

2. Choose Process > MIDI Effects > Cakewalk FX > Arpeggiator to open the Arpeggiator dialog box (see Figure 11.44).

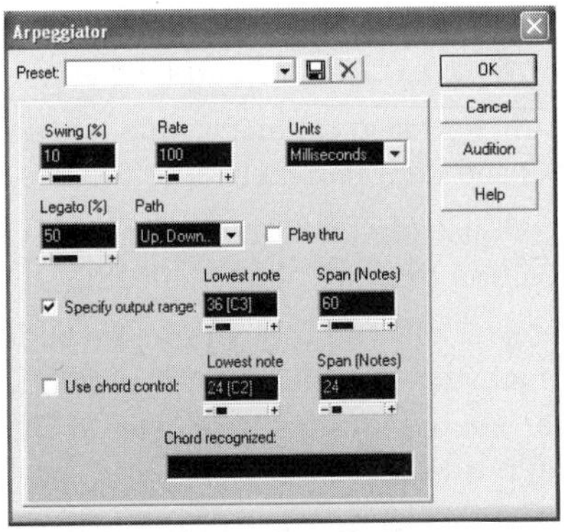

Figure 11.44
The Arpeggiator effect automatically converts your selected MIDI data into arpeggios.

3. Set the Swing parameter. This parameter works the same as the Swing parameter in the Quantize editing feature (which I talked about in Chapter 8). The only difference is that 50 percent is the normal setting (meaning no swing is applied) in the Quantize editing feature; in this case, 0 percent is the normal setting. And you can set this Swing parameter from −100 to +100 percent. More often than not, you'll want to keep it set to 0 percent.

4. Set the Rate and Units parameters. These two parameters work together. The Rate parameter determines the amount of time between each note in the arpeggio, and the Units parameter determines what units you want to use to set the Rate parameter. You can set the Rate parameter in notes, ticks, or milliseconds. By setting the Units parameter to Notes, you can easily synchronize the notes in the arpeggio to a certain note value so you know they will play in sync with the rest of the music in your project.

5. Set the Legato parameter. This parameter determines the duration of the notes in the arpeggio. If you set the Legato parameter to 1 percent (the lowest value), the notes in the arpeggio will be played with a very short duration (as in a staccato fashion, in which the note is played and let go very quickly). If you set the Legato parameter to 99 percent (the highest value), the notes in the arpeggio will be played with a very long duration. To be exact, each note plays until the start of the next note in the arpeggio.

6. Set the Path parameter. This parameter determines the direction in which the notes in the arpeggio will be played. If you select Up, Up, the notes in the arpeggio will go up consecutively in pitch. If you select Up, Down, the notes in the arpeggio will go up in pitch first, and then come back down. If you select Down, Down, the notes in the arpeggio will go down consecutively in pitch. If you select Down, Up, the notes in the arpeggio will go down in pitch first, and then come back up.

7. Set the Play Thru option. If you activate the Play Thru option, your original data will remain intact and play along with the new arpeggio data. If you deactivate the Play Thru option, only the arpeggio data will remain, and your original data will be removed.

8. Set the Specify Output Range option, along with the Lowest Note and Span (Notes) parameters. If you activate the Specify Output Range option, additional notes will be added so the arpeggio will play smoothly over each octave in the range you specify. Otherwise, only your original will be used to create the arpeggio. The Lowest Note parameter determines the lowest note that will be included in the arpeggio. The Span (Notes) parameter determines the number of half-steps in the range (from 12 to 127).

9. Set the Use Chord Control option, along with the Lowest Note and Span (Notes) parameters. If you activate the Use Chord Control option, the Arpeggiator effect will analyzes the original data that falls in the range you specify, and then guess at what chord is being played. If you use the effect in real-time mode, the name of the chord that is guessed will be shown in the Chord Recognized field. The effect uses the recognized chord to create the notes for the arpeggio (meaning the notes in the arpeggio are based on the recognized chord).

10. Click on the Audition button to test the current parameter settings. Make further adjustments if necessary.

11. If you want to use the current settings at a later time, save them as a preset.

12. Click on OK.

SONAR will process the data by applying the effect according to the parameter settings you specified.

I know the parameter settings for the Arpeggiator effect can be a bit confusing. Sometimes it's difficult to tell what the results will be after you apply the effect. Basically, they'll be different depending on the data you process. You'll have to experiment. By the way, this effect usually works best on slow, chord-based data. Of course, you can try it out on faster, different kinds of data. Like I said, be sure to experiment with it.

Chord Analysis

Earlier, I mentioned that a couple of the MIDI effects aren't really effects at all. The Chord Analyzer is one of them. This effect doesn't do anything to your data, meaning it doesn't make any changes. The Chord Analyzer simply looks at your data and guesses what kind of chord is being played. Personally, I haven't found much use for it. If you don't already know the chords used in your song, how are you writing the music?

But just in case you're interested, here's how the effect works:

BEST IN REAL-TIME

Although you can use the Chord Analyzer effect offline, it works best in real time as your project is playing. Therefore, I'll go through the real-time procedure here instead of the offline procedure.

1. In the Track view, right-click in the Fx bin of the track to which you want to add an effect.

2. Choose MIDI Effects > Cakewalk FX > Chord Analyzer to add the Chord Analyzer to the list.

3. The Chord Analyzer window will open (see Figure 11.45).

Figure 11.45
The Chord Analyzer is best used in real time.

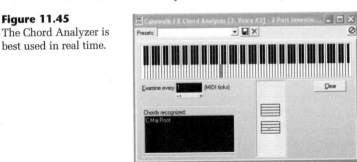

4. Set the Examine Every parameter. Using this parameter, you can control how often the Chord Analyzer effect analyzes your data. The lower the number, the more accurate it is at guessing the names of the chords being played. This feature also requires more processing power from your computer, but I've never had any problems keeping this parameter set at 1 (the lowest setting). Unless you have trouble with playback, I recommend that you just leave this setting at its default value.

5. Start playback of the project. As the project plays, the effect will analyze your data and display the name of the chord it thinks is being played, along with how the chord looks in music notation and on a piano keyboard.

Actually, I stand corrected. This effect is useful as a learning tool because it displays the chords being played on a piano keyboard and as music notation. Plus, it lists (in the Chord Recognized section) some possible alternatives you might want to try in place of the chord you are using currently.

Echo Delay

Just as the delay effects enable you to add echoes to your audio data, the Echo Delay effect enables you to add echoes to your MIDI data. But because this effect works on MIDI data, some of the parameters are different, and some additional parameters are available as well. This feature works as follows:

1. Select the MIDI data you want to process.

2. Choose Process > MIDI Effects > Cakewalk FX > Echo Delay to open the Echo Delay dialog box (see Figure 11.46).

Figure 11.46
You can use the Echo Delay effect to add echoes to your MIDI data.

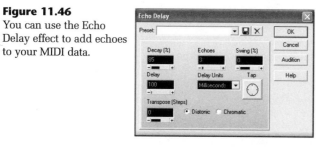

3. Set the Delay and Delay Units parameters. These two parameters work together. The Delay parameter determines the amount of time between each echo. The Delay Units parameter determines the units you want to use to set the Delay parameter. You can set the Delay parameter in notes, ticks, and milliseconds. By setting the Delay Units parameter to Notes, you can easily synchronize the echoes to a certain note value so you know they will play in sync with the rest of the music in your project.

THE TAP BUTTON
You also can set the Delay parameter by clicking on the Tap button in the Echo Delay dialog box. Clicking on the button at a certain tempo sets the Delay parameter to that tempo.

4. Set the Decay parameter. This parameter determines whether the echoes get softer or louder (and by how much). If you set the Decay parameter to a value below 100 percent, the echoes will get softer. If you set the Decay parameter to a value above 100 percent, the echoes will get louder.

5. Set the Echoes parameter. This parameter determines how many echoes you will have.

6. Set the Swing parameter. This parameter works the same way as the Swing parameter in the Quantize editing feature (which I talked about in Chapter 8). The only difference is that 50 percent is the normal setting (meaning no swing is applied) in the Quantize editing feature; 0 percent is the normal setting in this feature. And you can set this Swing parameter from −100 to +100 percent. More often than not, you'll want to keep it set to 0 percent.

7. Set the Transpose (Steps) parameter. If you want, you can have each echo transposed to a different pitch value, which allows you to create some interesting sounds. You can set the Transpose (Steps) parameter from −12 to +12 steps. You determine the types of steps by choosing either the Diatonic (the pitches follow the diatonic musical scale) or Chromatic (the pitches follow the chromatic musical scale) options.

8. Click on the Audition button to test the current parameter settings. Make further adjustments if necessary.

9. If you want to use the current settings at a later time, save them as a preset.

10. Click on OK.

SONAR will process the data by applying the effect according to the parameter settings you specified.

The Echo Delay effect is fairly easy to use, but just to give you a quick idea of what you can do with it, try the following example:

1. Select File > Open, select the file called 2-Part Invention #13 in A minor.cwp, and click on Open to open that sample project.

2. Close all the windows except for the Track view.

3. Play the project to hear what the original data sounds like.

4. Select Track 1.

5. Choose Process > MIDI Effects > Cakewalk FX > Echo Delay.

6. Choose the preset called 16th Note.

7. Click on OK.

8. Play the project again.

Hear that echo? You can achieve some pretty cool sounds by using this effect. As always, don't be afraid to experiment.

MIDI Event Filter

The MIDI Event Filter effect works almost the same as the Select By Filter editing feature (which I talked about in Chapter 8). The only difference is that instead of simply selecting the specified events, it deletes them. This feature gives you a quick way to remove specific kinds of MIDI data from your clips or tracks. It works like this:

1. Select the MIDI data you want to process.

2. Choose Process > MIDI Effects > Cakewalk FX > MIDI Event Filter to open the MIDI Event Filter dialog box (see Figure 11.47).

Figure 11.47
Using the MIDI Event Filter effect, you can remove specific kinds of MIDI data from your clips and tracks easily.

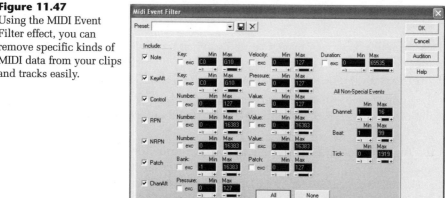

3. Set the appropriate parameters for the types of MIDI data you want to remove. These settings are the same as the settings for the Event Filter - Select Some dialog box (which I explained in Chapter 8).

4. Click on the Audition button to test the current parameter settings. Make further adjustments if necessary.

5. If you want to use the current settings at a later time, save them as a preset.

6. Click on OK.

SONAR will process the selected data and remove the types of MIDI data you specified via the effect parameter settings.

Quantize

The Quantize effect works almost exactly the same as the Quantize editing feature (which I talked about in Chapter 8). The only difference is that the effect provides a couple of additional parameters. It works like this:

1. Select the MIDI data you want to process.

2. Choose Process > MIDI Effects > Cakewalk FX > Quantize to open the Quantize dialog box (see Figure 11.48).

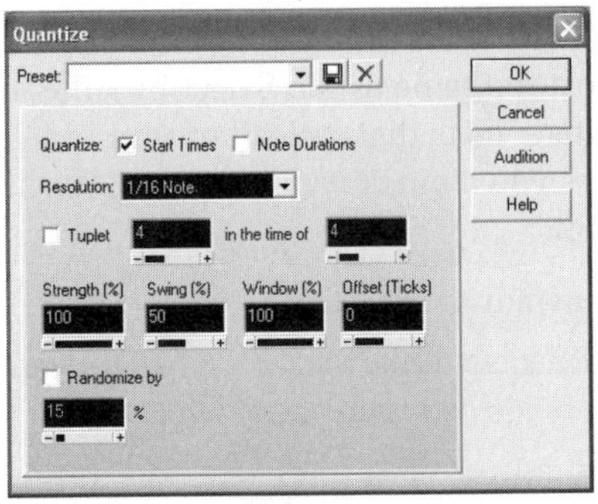

Figure 11.48
The Quantize effect
works almost exactly the
same as the Quantize
editing feature.

3.   Set the Quantize parameter by activating/deactivating the Start Times and Note Durations options. These settings simply tell SONAR whether you want to quantize the start times and/or durations of each selected MIDI event.

4.   Set the Resolution parameter. This parameter works exactly the same as the Resolution parameter in the Quantize editing feature (which I talked about in Chapter 8).

5.   Set the Tuplet option. Using this option, you can further define the Resolution parameter. For example, if you want to quantize your data according to an odd note value, activate the Tuplet option and set its related parameters to 5 and 4 (which would mean you want to quantize your data to the value of five notes occurring in the time of four notes).

6.   Set the Strength, Swing, Window, and Offset parameters. These parameters work exactly the same as the Strength, Swing, Window, and Offset parameters in the Quantize editing feature (which I talked about in Chapter 8).

7.   Set the Randomize By option. If you activate this option, a random time offset will be applied to the timing of each quantized event. You can use this option to achieve some very strange sounds. Do a little experimenting to hear what I mean.

8.   Click on the Audition button to test the current parameter settings. Make further adjustments if necessary.

9.   If you want to use the current settings at a later time, save them as a preset.

10. Click on OK.

SONAR will process the data by applying the effect according to the parameter settings you specified.

Transpose

Like the Transpose editing feature, the Transpose effect enables you to transpose your MIDI note data up or down by a number of half-steps either chromatically or diatonically. However, the Transpose effect also provides some more advanced transposition methods. It works like this:

1.   Select the MIDI data you want to process.

2.   Choose Process > MIDI Effects > Cakewalk FX > Transpose to open the Transpose dialog box (see Figure 11.49).

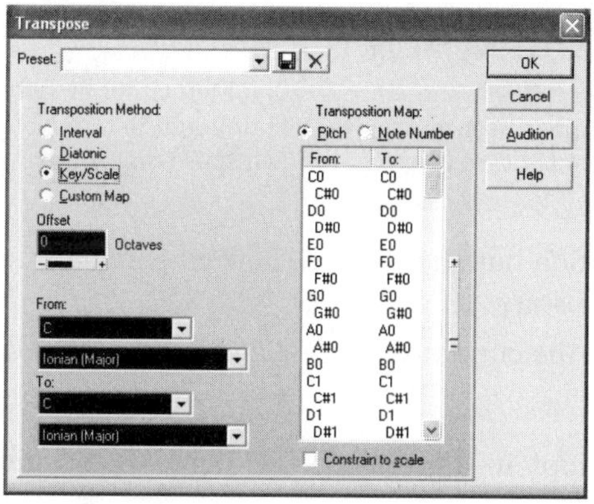

Figure 11.49
Using the Transpose
effect, you can transpose
your MIDI note data in a
number of different ways.

3. If you want to transpose your data by a simple musical interval, choose the Interval option for the Transposition Method parameter. Then enter the number of half steps (−127 to +127) into the Offset parameter by which you want to transpose the data.

4. If you want to transpose your data diatonically so that the notes are changed according to degrees of a certain musical scale, choose the Diatonic option for the Transposition Method parameter. Then enter the number of scale degrees (−24 to +24) into the Offset parameter by which you want to transpose the data. Also, choose the musical scale you want to use by setting the Key parameter.

CONSTRAIN TO SCALE

If you want any of the notes in your data that don't fit within the chosen musical scale to be transposed so they will fit, activate the Constrain to Scale option. This feature works well for pop music. For something like jazz, though, in which many different non-scale notes are used in the music, it's best to keep this option deactivated. This option works for both the Diatonic and Key/Scale Transposition Methods.

5. If you want to transpose your data from one musical key and scale to another, choose the Key/Scale option for the Transposition Method parameter. In the From and To parameters, choose the musical keys and scales by which you want to transpose your data. You also can transpose the data up or down by a number of octaves at the same time by setting the Offset parameter.

6. To specify exactly how each note in the musical scale will be transposed, choose the Custom Map option for the Transposition Method parameter. Using this option, you can define your own transposition map. This means you can set the note to which each note in the musical scale will be transposed. To change the transposition value of a note in the musical scale, select the note in the From column of the Transposition Map, and then click on the plus or minus button to transpose that note up or down. This option is pretty tedious, but it gives you precise control over every musical note.

CHAPTER 11

PITCH OR NOTE NUMBER
You can view notes in the Transposition Map either by note name or by MIDI note number. Simply select the appropriate option (Pitch or Note Number) located above the Transposition Map in the Transpose dialog box.

7. Click on the Audition button to test the current parameter settings. Make further adjustments if necessary.

8. If you want to use the current settings at a later time, save them as a preset.

9. Click on OK.

SONAR will process the data by applying the effect according to the parameter settings you specified.

Velocity

I'm tempted to compare the Velocity effect to the Scale Velocity editing feature (which I talked about in Chapter 8), but the effect not only enables you to scale MIDI velocity data, it also enables you to change it in many more advanced ways. As a matter of fact, you'll probably stop using the Scale Velocity editing feature when you get the hang of the Velocity effect, because you can use this effect as an editing tool as well. It works like this:

1. Select the MIDI data you want to process.

2. Choose Process > MIDI Effects > Cakewalk FX > Velocity to open the Velocity dialog box (see Figure 11.50).

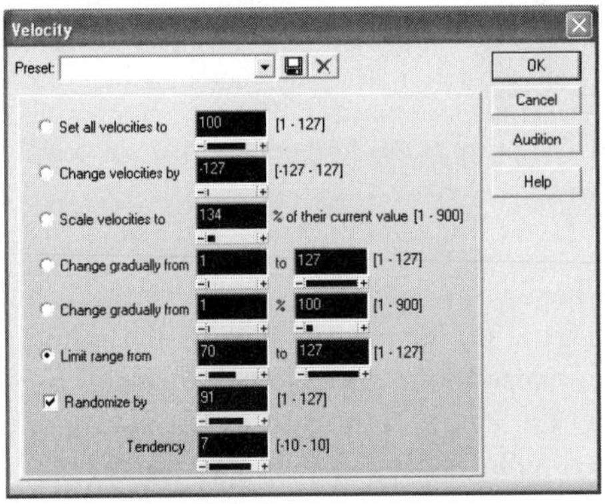

Figure 11.50
Using the Velocity effect, you can change your MIDI velocity data in many more ways than you can using the Scale Velocity editing feature.

3. To change all MIDI velocity values to an exact number, choose the Set All Velocities To parameter, and then type the value (1 to 127) you want to use.

4. To add or subtract a certain amount from each MIDI velocity in your selected data, choose the Change Velocities By option and type the value (−127 to +127) you want to use.

5. To scale all MIDI velocity values by a certain percentage, choose the Scale Velocities To option and type the value (1 to 900 percent) that you want to use.

6. The next two options also enable you to scale MIDI velocities, but from one value to another. If you choose the first Change Gradually From option, you can scale MIDI velocities by exact values (1 to 127). If you choose the second Change Gradually From option, you can scale MIDI velocities by a percentage (1 to 900 percent).

7. If you choose the Limit Range From option, all the MIDI velocities in your selected data will be changed to fit within the range of velocity values (1 to 127) you specify.

8. In addition to choosing one of the previous options, you can choose the Velocity effect's Randomize By option, which works in tandem with the others. By activating this option, you can add or subtract a random offset to or from each MIDI velocity in your selected data. You can enter a maximum value (1 to 127) to be used, and you can give priority over whether the random offset will be lower or higher (− 10 to +10) than the maximum value that you specify.

9. Click on the Audition button to test the current parameter settings. Make further adjustments if necessary.

10. If you want to use the current settings at a later time, save them as a preset.

11. Click on OK.

SONAR will process the data by applying the effect according to the parameter settings you specified.

Session Drummer

Even though the Session Drummer is listed along with all the other MIDI effects, technically it is not an effect because it doesn't process existing data. Instead, it actually generates new MIDI data. You can think of the Session Drummer like a drum machine (a programmable MIDI instrument used to create drum parts). With the Session Drummer, you can compose your own MIDI drum tracks by combining existing rhythmic patterns into songs. You can even create your own patterns for use with the Session Drummer.

Using the Session Drummer consists of a number of multi-step processes, so I'll provide you with step-by-step procedures for each part of the process.

Opening and Setting Up the Session Drummer

The best way to use the Session Drummer is in real time because you can use it to compose a drum track while listening to the existing tracks in your project. You can get started by following these steps:

1. Create a new project or open an existing one.

2. In the Track view, create a new MIDI track.

3. Set the Output and Channel parameters for the new track. The Channel should probably be set to 10 because that is the standard channel for General MIDI drums on most sound cards and synthesizers. Click on OK.

4. Add the Session Drummer effect to the Fx bin of the new track by right-clicking in the Fx bin and choosing MIDI Effects > Cakewalk FX > Session Drummer.

5. The Session Drummer window will open (see Figure 11.51).

Figure 11.51
The Session Drummer window allows you to compose your own MIDI drum tracks by combining existing rhythmic patterns.

6. You'll see three different sections in the window—Style, Pattern, and Song. Just below the Style section is a row of buttons. These buttons control the different Session Drummer features. Click on the Plugin Settings button (the one with the picture of the yellow sprocket on it) to open the Settings dialog box (see Figure 11.52). Don't worry; I'll go over all the other Session Drummer features shortly.

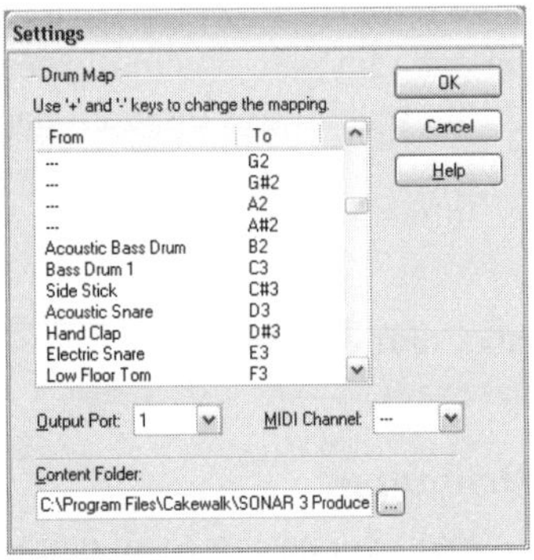

Figure 11.52
In the Settings dialog box, you can set the Session Drummer's Drum Map, Output Port, MIDI Channel, and Content Folder parameters.

7. All the drum patterns and styles included with SONAR are programmed to work with General MIDI. So if you're using a General MIDI-compatible synthesizer, you should be all set. If not, you can change the Drum Map parameter so each drum instrument is mapped to a different MIDI pitch. To do so, click on the name of the drum instrument you want to change in the From column of the Drum Map. Then, to raise or lower the pitch for that instrument, press the plus or minus keys on the numeric keypad of your computer's keyboard, respectively.

8. Set the Output Port and MIDI Channel parameters to the same settings you used for the Out and Ch parameters you entered earlier.

9. All the drum styles and patterns included with SONAR are contained in special MIDI files. These files are initially located in the C:\Program Files\Cakewalk SONAR 3\Drum Styles folder on your hard drive. If you want to change the location of the files, enter a new location in the Content Folder parameter. Be sure to move any existing files from the old folder to the new folder.

10. Click on OK to close the Settings dialog box.

SAVE SETTINGS

If you want to use these same settings again in the future, you can save them as a preset. The Presets parameter in the Session Drummer window saves only the parameter values from the Settings dialog box. Saving your Session Drummer songs requires a different procedure, which I'll talk about later, in the "Saving and Loading Song Files" section.

Creating a Song

As I mentioned earlier, the Session Drummer window is divided into three sections—Style, Pattern, and Song. The Style section lists all the available drum style files currently in the content folder. Each file contains a number of different drum patterns. When you select a style from the list in the Style section, all the patterns contained in that style are listed in the Pattern section. By selecting patterns from the Pattern section, you can piece together a song. A song is an entire percussion performance that spans a certain number of measures, depending on how many patterns it contains and the length of each pattern used. The basic procedure for creating a song is as follows. (I'm assuming you've already gone through the setup procedure, and the Session Drummer window is open and waiting to be used.)

1. Select a style from the Style section.

2. In the Pattern section, you'll see all the patterns within the selected style. The name of each pattern and its length in measures are shown. To hear what a pattern sounds like, click on it to select it and then start your project playing. You can keep the project playing while you select different patterns. When you find a pattern you like, double-click on it (or click on the Add Pattern to Song button— the one with the picture of a plus sign on it) to add the pattern to the Song section.

3. In the Song section, the name, length, and the time (in measures, beats, and ticks) of when the pattern will be played within the project is shown. You'll also see a Loop Count parameter for the pattern. It tells the Session Drummer how many times to play that pattern before moving on to the next pattern in the song. Set the Loop Count by double-clicking on it and typing a number.

4. Go back to Step 2 to add more patterns to the song.

5. If you want to remove a pattern from the song, select the pattern from the list in the Song section, and then click on the Remove Pattern from Song button (the one with the picture of a minus sign on it). You also can remove all the patterns from the song by clicking on the Clear Song button (the one with the picture of a red X on it).

6. If you want to change the order of a pattern within the song, select the pattern. Then click on the Move Down button (the one with the picture of a downward-pointing arrow on it) to move the pattern toward the end of the song. Alternatively, click on the Move Up button (the one with the picture of an upward-pointing arrow on it) to move the pattern toward the beginning of the song.

7. To listen to the song, select the first pattern in the list and then start your project playing.

Saving and Loading Song Files

After you've finished creating your song, you can save it as a special Session Drummer Song file. This file type has an .SDX extension, and the files are stored in the same disk location as the styles. To save your song, follow these steps:

1. Click on the Save Song to File button (the one with the picture of a floppy disk on it) to open the Save As dialog box.

2. Type a name for the file and use an .SDX extension.

3. Click on Save.

To load your song for use in the Session Drummer at a later date, follow these steps:

1. Click on the Load Song from File button (the one with the picture of a yellow folder on it) to open the Open dialog box.

2. Select the file you want to load.

3. Click on Open.

SAVE YOUR SONG
If you don't save your song, you'll lose it when you close the current project.

Applying the Song to Your Project

When you save a song, only the information that makes up the song is saved. In other words, only the names of each pattern, their locations in the song, and their number of loops are saved. The actual MIDI data is not saved. To save the MIDI data that is generated from a song into a track, follow these steps. (I'm assuming you've already gone through the setup procedure, you've created a song, and the Session Drummer window is still open.)

1. Go to the Track view and select the track you set up previously by clicking on its number.

2. Choose Process > Apply MIDI Effects.

3. In the Apply MIDI Effects dialog box, activate the Delete the Effects from the Track Inserts option.

4. Click on OK.

SONAR will place the song data in the selected track. No matter where the Now time is currently set, the song data is always placed at the beginning of the project.

Creating Your Own Session Drummer Styles

Styles are stored as standard MIDI files. Therefore, you can easily create your own styles for use in the Session Drummer. If you open one of the existing style files as a project in SONAR, you'll notice that a style is made up of nothing more than a single track containing MIDI data composed specifically to be played by General MIDI drum sounds. The track is separated into sections with markers; each marker designates a different drum pattern. The name of the style file shows up in the Style section of the Session Drummer, and the names of the markers show up in the Pattern section.

After you've recorded your own drum patterns, you can create your own Session Drummer style easily by following these steps:

1. Open the project that contains the existing drum patterns you recorded.

2. Create a new project and set a tempo for the project.

3. In the Track view of the original project, copy one of the drum patterns by using Edit > Copy.

4. Create 10 new MIDI tracks in the new project.

5. In the Track view of the new project, paste the drum pattern at the very beginning of Track 10. Track 10 is the standard track used for MIDI drum parts.

6. Set the Now time to the beginning of the project.

7. Choose Insert > Marker to open the Marker dialog box. Type a name. This is the name of the pattern, and it will appear in the Pattern section of the Session Drummer. Click on OK.

8. If you want to add more patterns, be sure to paste each new pattern at the end of the previous one. Each pattern should start at the beginning of a measure and should be at least one measure long.

9. Save the project as a style by choosing File > Save As to open the Save As dialog box. Type a name for the file. This is the name that will appear in the Style section of the Session Drummer. Also, be sure to choose MIDI Format 0 for the Save as Type parameter, and be sure to save the file to the same directory you set in the Content Folder parameter of the Session Drummer Settings dialog box. Click on Save.

The next time you open the Session Drummer, your new style should be listed in the Style section.

Session Drummer Song Example

To give you a quick idea of the results you can get from the Session Drummer, I've put together this short demonstration:

1. Choose File > Open, select the file called 2-Part Invention #13 in A minor.cwp, and click on Open to open the sample project.

2. Close the File Info window, along with the Staff and Big Time views. You don't need them for this example.

3. In the Track view, create a new MIDI track (Track 3).

4. Set the Output and Channel parameters for Track 3. You should probably set the Channel to 10. Click on OK.

5. Add the Session Drummer effect to the Fx bin of Track 3 by right-clicking in the Fx bin and choosing MIDI Effects > Cakewalk FX > Session Drummer.

6. The Session Drummer window will open.

7. Select the style named Alternative 080 - Straight 16ths.

8. Add the following patterns to the song in the order listed:

▶ Crash/Kick/SN/Hat/Tamb: 1 loop

▶ SN/Tom fill1: 2 loops

▶ var1/Crash/Kick/SN/Hat/Tamb: 1 loop

▶ SN/Tom fill2: 2 loops

▶ Crash/Kick/SN/Hat: 1 loop

▶ SN/Tom fill3: 2 loops

▶ var1/Crash/Kick/SN/Hat: 1 loop

▶ SN fill1: 2 loops

▶ var2/Crash/Kick/SN/Hat: 1 loop

▶ SN fill3: 2 loops

9. At this point, you can save the song and apply it to the track if you want, but because this is just a demonstration, it's up to you.

10. Before you play the project, change the tempo to 100. The original tempo sounds too slow.

11. Play the project.

Sounds like one of those rearranged classical recordings like the ones on Don Dorsey's *BachBusters* CD, doesn't it? Have fun!

12
Mixing It Down

After you've recorded, edited, and added effects to your MIDI and audio data, it's time to mix down your project. This is called the *mixdown process* because you are taking all the MIDI and audio tracks in your project and mixing them together into a single stereo audio track. From there, you can put your music on CD, distribute it over the Internet, or record it onto tape. SONAR provides a number of different features that make the mixdown process as simple and intuitive as possible. This chapter will do the following:

▶ Show you how to use the Console view and Track view for mixing

▶ Explain the Module and Track Managers

▶ Demonstrate how to take a Snapshot

▶ Show you how to record and edit automation

▶ Explain grouping

▶ Demonstrate working with envelopes

The Console View

For mixing down the MIDI and audio tracks in your project, you can use either the Console view or the Track view. I've already covered many of the Track view features in earlier chapters, so in this chapter I'll tell you about the Console view and also let you know how the Track view fits into the mixdown process.

The Console view enables you to adjust the main parameters for each track in your project via onscreen buttons, knobs, sliders, and faders (vertical sliders). Similar in appearance to a hardware-based mixing board found in most recording studios, the Console view displays tracks as a collection of modules, each with its own set of adjustable controls.

More precisely, the Console view consists of four major sections (starting from left to right)—the toolbar (containing some of the view's related controls); the MIDI and audio track modules (displaying the controls for each MIDI and audio track in the project); the buses (containing additional mixing controls, which I'll explain later); and the mains (also containing additional mixing controls, which I'll explain later).

Opening the Console View

To open the Console view, simply choose View > Console. The Console view will open, displaying modules for every track in the current project. To see how it works, follow these steps:

1. Choose File > Open. In the Open dialog box that appears, select one of the bundle (.cwb) files that ships with SONAR and click on Open to open that sample project file.

2. Choose View > Console to open the Console view.

The Console view should look similar to Figure 12.1.

Figure 12.1
When you open the Console view, it automatically displays a module for every track in the current project.

The MIDI Track Modules

Each MIDI track module contains a number of different controls that enable you to manipulate many of its corresponding track parameters (see Figure 12.2).

As matter of fact, all the controls are the equivalent of the track parameters shown in the Track pane of the Track view (all of which I have described in previous chapters). This means that if you change the value of a control in the Console view, the equivalent track parameter is also changed in the Track view. From top to bottom, the controls in a MIDI track module correspond to the controls described in the following sections.

Figure 12.2
A MIDI track module contains controls for adjusting the parameters of its corresponding track.

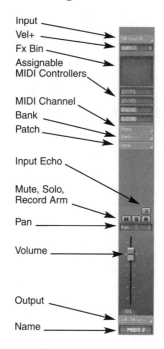

Input
Vel+
Fx Bin
Assignable
MIDI Controllers

MIDI Channel
Bank
Patch

Input Echo

Mute, Solo,
Record Arm

Pan

Volume

Output

Name

Input

The Input parameter enables you to set the MIDI input of the track represented by the MIDI track module. It is the equivalent of the Input parameter in the Track view. You can change the input by clicking on the control and selecting a new input from the drop-down menu.

Vel+

The Vel+ parameter enables you to raise or lower the MIDI velocity of each note in a track by adding or subtracting a number from −127 to +127. It is the equivalent of the Velocity Trim parameter in the Track view. You can change the Vel+ parameter by clicking and dragging your mouse over the parameter. Click and drag left to lower the value; click and drag right to increase the value.

SET DEFAULT VALUES

When you're adjusting sliders, knobs, or faders in the Console view or parameters in the Track view, a quick way to return them to their original positions is to double-click on them. When you do, the control snaps back to its default value. You also can change the default value for a control. To do so, set the control to the value you want to use as its default. Then right-click on the control and choose Set Snap-To = Current from the drop-down menu.

Fx Bin

You can use the Fx bin to assign effects to the track represented by the MIDI track module. These effects are applied only in real-time. The Fx bin works exactly the same as the Fx bin in the Track view (which I described in Chapter 11).

Assignable MIDI Controllers

The assignable MIDI controllers are similar to the Chorus and Reverb parameters found in the Track view, but here you can reassign these parameters to transmit any MIDI controller you want—not just Chorus and Reverb. In addition, you get four parameters here instead of just two. By default, these four parameters are assigned to MIDI controller numbers 91, 93, 11, and 74. To reassign a parameter to a different MIDI controller, right-click on the parameter and choose Reassign Control from the drop-down menu. In the MIDI Envelope dialog box, choose a new type, value, and channel for the parameter.

Channel

The Channel parameter enables you to set the MIDI channel of the track represented by the MIDI track module. It is the equivalent of the Channel parameter in the Track view. You can change the channel by clicking on the parameter and selecting a new MIDI channel from the drop-down menu.

Bank

You can use the Bank parameter to set the MIDI patch bank of the track represented by the MIDI track module. It is the equivalent of the Bank parameter in the Track view. You can change the bank by clicking on the parameter and selecting a new MIDI patch bank from the drop-down menu.

Patch

You can use the Patch parameter to set the MIDI patch of the track represented by the MIDI track module. It is the equivalent of the Patch parameter in the Track view. You can change the patch by clicking on the parameter and selecting a new MIDI patch from the drop-down menu.

Input Echo

You can use the Input Echo parameter to turn MIDI echo on or off for the track represented by the MIDI track module. It is the equivalent of the Input Echo parameter in the Track view. Just click on the button to change the parameter. I talked about MIDI echo in Chapter 6.

Mute, Solo, and Record Arm

The Mute, Solo, and Record Arm parameters enable you to turn the mute, solo, and record arm (for recording) options on or off for the track represented by the MIDI track module. They are the equivalents of the Mute, Solo, and Record options in the Track view (which I described in Chapter 6). You can toggle these options on and off by clicking on them.

CONSOLE VIEW RECORDING

The Record Arm parameter is available in the Console view because you can actually use the view during recording instead of the Track view if you want. You can even create new tracks in the Console view. To do so, simply right-click in any blank space and choose Insert Audio Track or Insert MIDI Track from the drop-down menu. A new MIDI or audio track module will be added, representing the new track. You'll notice that the new track will be added to the Track view as well.

Pan

You can use the Pan parameter to set the MIDI panning of the track represented by the MIDI track module. It is the equivalent of the Pan parameter in the Track view. You can change the pan by clicking and dragging the slider left or right.

Volume

Using the Volume parameter, you can set the MIDI volume of the track represented by the MIDI track module. It is the equivalent of the Volume parameter in the Track view. You can change the volume by clicking and dragging the fader (vertical slider) up or down. As you drag the fader, the number box located below the slider will display the current value of the parameter. The value can range from 0 (the lowest volume level) to 127 (the highest volume level).

Output

Using the Output parameter, you can set the MIDI output of the track represented by the MIDI track module. It is the equivalent of the Output parameter in the Track view. You can change the output by clicking on the parameter and selecting a new MIDI port from the drop-down menu.

Name

The Name parameter displays the name of the track represented by the MIDI track module. It is the equivalent of the Name parameter in the Track view. You can change the name by double-clicking on the parameter, typing some new text, and pressing the Enter key on your computer keyboard.

The Audio Track Modules

Like the MIDI track modules, the audio track modules contain a number of different controls you can use to manipulate their corresponding track parameters (see Figure 12.3).

Figure 12.3
The audio track modules are very similar to the MIDI track modules in terms of the controls they provide.

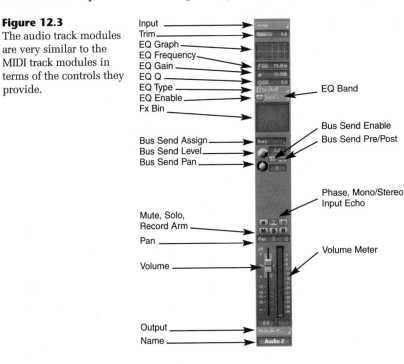

Input
Trim
EQ Graph
EQ Frequency
EQ Gain
EQ Q
EQ Type
EQ Enable
Fx Bin

Bus Send Assign
Bus Send Level
Bus Send Pan

Mute, Solo,
Record Arm
Pan

Volume

Output
Name

EQ Band

Bus Send Enable
Bus Send Pre/Post

Phase, Mono/Stereo
Input Echo

Volume Meter

As a matter of fact, many of the controls are the same as those on the MIDI track modules. Included are the Input, Fx Bin, Mute, Solo, Record Arm, Pan, Volume, and Name parameters. They all work in exactly the same manner as they do on the MIDI track modules, except, of course, they are controlling audio data instead of MIDI data. The one difference is with the Volume control. Instead of displaying its value as a MIDI volume controller number, its value is shown as decibels (dB).

Some of the parameters, however, are unique to audio track modules.

Trim

The Trim parameter allows you to adjust the volume of a track before the signal gets to the regular Volume parameter. This can be helpful for adjusting the relative volume of one track to another without having to change the final mix positions of your Volume parameters. It is the equivalent of the Volume Trim parameter in the Track view. Click and drag your mouse left or right over the parameter to adjust it.

EQ Parameters (SONAR Producer Edition)

This section of the audio track module provides built-in EQ effects that you can apply to your tracks. It provides four bands of EQ, each with the following parameters: EQ Graph, Frequency, Gain, Q, Type, and Enable (Bypass). To adjust a certain band, use the EQ Band parameter. This EQ effect provides the same parameters as the Sonitus:fx Equalizer, which I talked about in Chapter 11. To display the Equalizer dialog box, double-click on the EQ Graph.

Phase

Sometimes phase cancellation can occur between the audio data of two different tracks. Phase cancellation occurs when one audio waveform increases in volume and the other decreases in volume at exactly the same time and by the same amount. Because of this phenomenon, they cancel each other out, making the mixed audio sound hollow. The Phase parameter allows you to invert the audio waveform of the data in an audio track around the zero axis. This can help eliminate phase cancellation sometimes. To invert the data in an audio track, just click on the Phase button in the Console view. The Phase parameter is the equivalent of the Phase parameter in the Track view.

Mono/Stereo

There might be times when you want to hear a stereo track play in mono (via one channel) or a mono track play in stereo (if stereo effects are applied). Using the Mono/Stereo parameter in the Console view or the Mono/Stereo parameter in the Track view, you can determine how the data in a track will be played. To adjust the parameter, just click on the Mono/Stereo button. A single left-speaker symbol means mono, and a double-speaker symbol means stereo.

Input Echo

When you record an audio track, you usually want to listen to your performance as it's being recorded. In the past, due to the limitations of sound card drivers, you were able to listen only to the "dry" version of your performance. This means you had to listen to your performance without any effects applied. With the input monitoring feature, however, SONAR allows you to listen to your performance with effects applied as it's being recorded. This can be especially useful, for example, when you are recording vocals, when it's customary to let the singer hear a little echo or reverberation during his or her performance. Similar to MIDI tracks, audio tracks provide an Input Echo button. This button can be turned on or off, and it activates or deactivates the input monitoring feature.

Output

The Output parameter enables you to route the data from the track represented by the audio track module to one of the available buses or mains (which I'll explain later). This parameter is the equivalent of the Output parameter in the Track view. You can change the output by clicking on the parameter and selecting a new bus or main from the drop-down menu.

Bus Send Parameters

The Bus Send parameters enable you to route (send) the audio data from the track represented by the audio track module to one of the available buses or mains (which I'll explain later). You can have as many sends as you want for each audio track module. (I'll show you how to change this later.) Each send has a number, which corresponds to the number of the bus to which its data will

CHAPTER 12

be sent (although you can change this too). Each send also has four controls within it—an on/off button (Bus Send Enable), a level slider (Bus Send Level), a pan slider (Bus Send Pan), and a pre/post button (Bus Send Pre/Post).

To toggle a send on or off, just click on its Bus Send Enable button. The Bus Send Level slider controls the volume (or level) of the audio data that will be sent to the bus. To adjust the slider, simply drag it left or right. If you drag the slider left, the value gets lower. If you drag the slider right, the value gets higher. You can adjust the send level from −INF (infinity, the lowest level setting) to +6 dB (the highest level setting). The Bus Send Pan slider controls the panning of the audio data that will be sent to the bus. Adjust it the same way as the Bus Send Level slider. The Bus Send Pre/Post button determines from what point in the audio track module the audio data will be taken and sent to the bus. You can toggle the Bus Send Pre/Post button by clicking on it. Initially, the button is set to Post. (You can see this because the button says Post on it.) When you click on the button, it changes its name to Pre. When you click on it again, it changes its name back to Post.

AUDIO SIGNAL FLOW

As SONAR plays a project, it reads the data for each audio track from your hard drive. It then routes the data through the appropriate sections of the Console view, until it is finally sent to your sound card, and then to your speakers so you can hear it. The routing works as follows: The data for an audio track is read from your hard drive and routed through the corresponding audio track module. Within the module, the data first passes through the Fx bin, where any assigned effects are applied. The data is then sent through the Volume parameter (where its level can be adjusted), then the Pan parameter, and finally to the Output parameter. From here, it is sent out of the module and into the assigned bus or main (which I'll talk about shortly). During this routing process, the data can be sent to a bus either before or after it reaches the Volume parameter. If the Bus Send Pre/Post button is set to Pre, the data is routed to the bus after it goes through the Fx bin but before it reaches the Volume parameter. This means the Volume parameter will have no effect on the level of the signal being sent to the bus. If the Bus Send Pre/Post button is set to Post, the data is routed to the bus after it goes through the Volume parameter. This means the Volume parameter does affect the level of the signal being sent to the bus. For a graphical view of how audio signals are routed in SONAR, take a look at the following topic in the SONAR Help file: Mixing and Effects Patching > Routing and Mixing Digital Audio.

The Buses

The buses provide additional mixing control for your audio signals (see Figure 12.4). Buses provide most of the same parameters as the audio track modules including Input, EQ Parameters, Fx Bin, Mono/Stereo button, Mute, Solo, Pan, Volume, Output, and Name. A bus provides one parameter not found in an audio track module, which is Input Pan. This parameter allows you to adjust the panning of the signal coming into the bus.

Figure 12.4

Shown here in the Console view, the buses provide some of the same controls as the audio track modules.

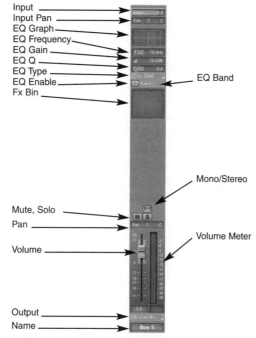

Input
Input Pan
EQ Graph
EQ Frequency
EQ Gain
EQ Q
EQ Type
EQ Enable
Fx Bin

EQ Band

Mono/Stereo

Mute, Solo
Pan

Volume Meter

Volume

Output
Name

You can also access the buses in the Track view by clicking on the Show/Hide Bus Pane button located at the bottom of the Track view (see Figure 12.5).

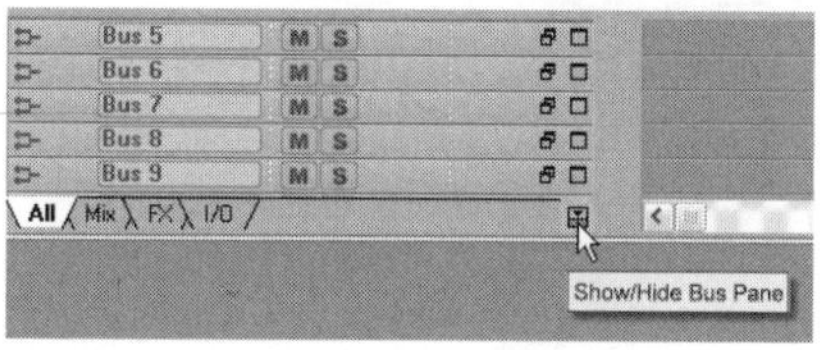

Figure 12.5

Access the buses in the Track view by clicking on the Show/Hide Bus Pane button.

What Are the Buses Good For?

One good use for the buses is to add the same effects to a number of different tracks. For example, suppose you have four audio tracks (1, 2, 3, and 4) containing the background vocals for your project, and you want to add some nice chorus to them. Without using a bus, you would have to set up a Chorus effect in the Fx bin of each of the audio track modules for tracks 1, 2, 3, and 4 (each with identical parameter settings). Not only is this approach cumbersome and tedious, it also puts extra strain on your computer because it has to process each of the four effects at the same time.

CHAPTER 12

Using a bus, however, the process becomes much more streamlined. First you create a send in track 1 by right-clicking in track 1 and choosing Insert Send > New Bus from the drop-down menu. This creates a new send in track 1 and also a new bus in the Bus pane (call it Bus 1 for this example). Then you create new sends for tracks 2, 3, and 4. But this time instead of choosing Insert Send > New Bus, you choose Insert Send > Bus 1. This ensures that each send in each track is set to Bus 1. Also make sure to click on the Bus Enable button for each send since it is off by default. Then you set the Bus Send Level for each of the sends. In the Fx bin for Bus 1, you set up the Chorus effect. You only need to set up one effect because all four tracks are being sent to the bus. You then set the Input Gain, Input Pan, Output Gain, and Output Pan parameters for Bus 1. Finally, you set the Bus Send Pre/Post buttons to Pre or Post. If you set the buttons to Pre, the data in each audio track module is sent to the bus before it's routed through each Volume parameter. This means you can control the level of the effect (with the Bus Send Levels) and the level of the original data (with the Volume parameter) independently. If you set the buttons to Post, the level of the effect goes up and down with the level of the original data via the Volume parameters.

The Mains

For every individual output on your sound card, a main will be displayed in the Console view (see Figure 12.6).

Figure 12.6
A main looks similar to an audio track module.

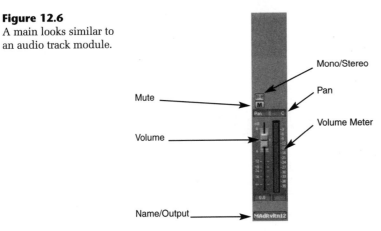

If your sound card has only one output, only one main is displayed and all the audio data from the audio track modules and buses is sent to it. If your sound card has more than one output, more than one main is shown, and you can choose to which main the data from each audio track module and bus will be sent.

A main provides five different parameters: Mono/Stereo, Mute, Pan, Volume, and Name/Output. These parameters all work the same way as the same parameters in an audio track module. The only difference is the Name/Output parameter, which simply displays the name of the sound card output assigned to that main. It cannot be changed.

Configuring the Console and Track Views

Earlier, I mentioned that you can change the number of buses shown in the Console view. Along with these changes, you can customize how the Console view looks and works in many other ways. These methods are described in the following sections.

Number of Buses

To add a new bus, simply right-click on a blank area of the Bus pane in the Console view and choose Insert Bus from the drop-down menu (see Figure 12.7).

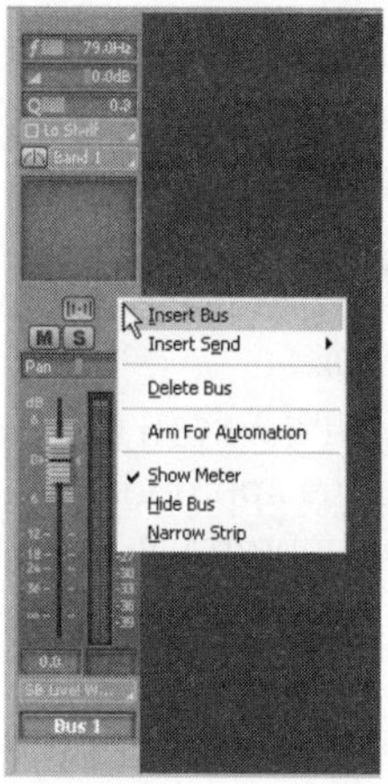

Figure 12.7
You can adjust the number of buses by right-clicking in the Bus pane.

To delete a bus, right-click on a blank part of the bus and choose Delete Bus from the drop-down menu. When you adjust the number of buses, it also affects the number of buses displayed in the Bus pane of the Track view.

The Track Managers

SONAR provides Track Managers for the both the Console view and the Track view, which allow you to hide modules, buses, and mains. What might be a bit confusing, however, is that the Track Managers in the Console view and Track view work independently of one another. This means if you hide a track in the Track view, its corresponding track module in the Console view will *not* be hidden. Instead, you would have to hide the track module using the Track Manager in the Console view. In a way, this might seem a bit awkward at first, but it provides you with the flexibility to have the Track view and Console view set up differently.

The Track Managers work as follows:

1. To open the Track view Track Manager, make sure the Track view is the active window and then press the M key on your computer keyboard.

2. To open the Console view Track Manager, make sure the Console view is the active window and then press the M key on your computer keyboard.

334   Mixing It Down — Chapter 12

3. The Track Manager dialog box will open (see Figure 12.8). The Track Managers are identical, so the remaining instructions apply to both. The only difference is that the mains are not displayed in the Track view Track Manager.

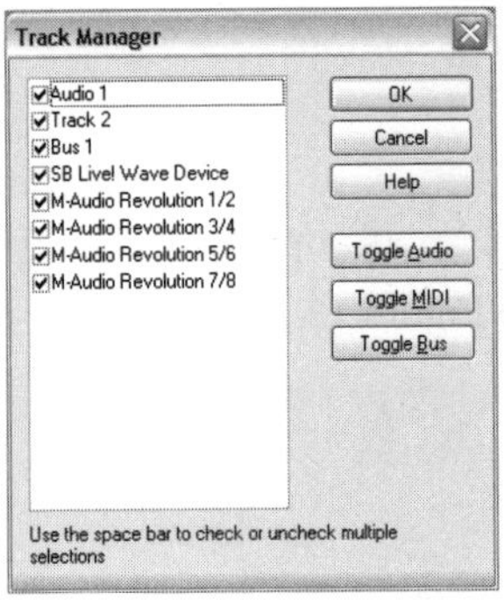

Figure 12.8
The Track Managers are identical except for displaying mains.

Track Manager

☑ Audio 1
☑ Track 2
☑ Bus 1
☑ SB Live! Wave Device
☑ M-Audio Revolution 1/2
☑ M-Audio Revolution 3/4
☑ M-Audio Revolution 5/6
☑ M-Audio Revolution 7/8

OK
Cancel
Help

Toggle Audio
Toggle MIDI
Toggle Bus

Use the space bar to check or uncheck multiple selections

4. To hide an individual component, click to remove the check mark next to that component in the list, and then click on OK.

5. To hide a group of components (such as all the MIDI track modules, all the audio track modules, or all the buses), click on the appropriate button—Toggle Audio, Toggle MIDI, or Toggle Bus—to select the appropriate group, and then press the spacebar on your computer keyboard to remove the check marks. Finally, click on OK.

Of course, you also can make the components reappear by doing the opposite of the preceding procedures. These changes to the Console view and Track view are in appearance only; they don't affect what you hear during playback. For example, if you hide an audio track module that outputs data during playback, you still hear that data even if you hide the module. Hiding components of the Console view or Track view can come in handy when you want to work only on a certain group of tracks and you don't want to be distracted or overwhelmed by the number of controls displayed.

ADDITIONAL TRACK MANAGEMENT
The Track view actually provides some additional features when it comes to managing tracks, which are not available in the Console view. I covered these features in Chapter 7.

Changing the Meters

You can change how the meters in the Console and Track views behave. Use the Show/Hide All Meters button to turn all meters on or off in the Console view. Or use the Meter Options button to turn groups of meters on and off using the Track Record Meters, Track Playback Meters, Bus Meters, and Mains Meters options.

In the Track view, click on the down arrow next to the Show/Hide All Meters button to access the meter options (see Figure 12.9).

Figure 12.9
Access meter options in
the Track view using the
Show/Hide All Meters
down arrow.

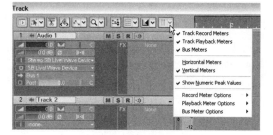

METER INDEPENDENCE

Like the Track Managers, the meters in the Console view and Track view work
independently. For instance, if you turn off the record meters in the Track view,
the record meters in the Console view are *not* turned off, and vice versa.

METER PERFORMANCE

If you ever need to lighten the load on your computer during recording or
playback, you might want to try turning off some or all of the meters. The meters
can take up quite a bit of your computer's processing power and affect SONAR's
performance.

In addition to being able to turn the meters on and off, you can set various options to determine
how the meters will work. If you click on the down arrow next to the Show/Hide All Meters
button in the Console view or the Track view, you'll see a drop-down menu with a number of
options available. These options let you set the way the meters will display the audio signal, the
audio signal measurement, the range of measurement, and various cosmetic options such as
whether or not the decibel markings are shown. For detailed descriptions of each option, take a
look at the following section the SONAR Help file: Mixing and Effects Patching > Metering >
Changing the Meters' Display.

Taking Snapshots

SONAR provides a number of different methods of mixdown, one of which is called Snapshots.
Using Snapshots, you can take a "picture" of all the current control values in the Console and
Track views and then store those values in your project at a specified Now time. For example, if
your project is a pop song with a number of different sections (such as the intro, verse, chorus, and
so on), you might want to change the mix each time a new section is reached by the Now time
during playback. You can do so easily by creating a different Snapshot at the beginning of each
section of the song. During playback, as the Now time passes a point in the project where a
Snapshot is stored, the values for all the recorded controls are changed to reflect the Snapshot
automatically.

LINKED AUTOMATION

For automation purposes, the controls in the Console view and the parameters in the Track view work together rather than independently. This means if you automate a control in the Console view, its corresponding parameter in the Track view will be automated as well and vice versa.

To create a Snapshot, just follow these steps:

1. Set the Now time to the point in the project where you want the Snapshot to be stored.

2. Adjust the controls in the Console or Track view to the values at which you want them to be set during that part of the project.

3. Right-click on each control you adjusted and choose Arm for Automation from the drop-down menu.

MULTIPLE ARMING

Instead of arming each control one-by-one, you can arm all the controls in a track by first selecting the track (by clicking on the track number to select it), and then choosing Track > Arm for Automation. You also can arm the controls in multiple tracks at once. Just select all the tracks whose controls you want to arm (use Ctrl-click to select more than one track) and again choose Track > Arm for Automation.

ARMING UNAVAILABLE

You'll notice that not all the parameters can be automated. If a parameter cannot be automated, the Arm for Automation option in the drop-down menu will be grayed out. Also, after a parameter in the Track view is armed for automation, it will have a red outline displayed around it.

4. Make sure the Automation toolbar is visible by choosing View > Toolbars, activating the Automation option, and clicking on Close. The Automation toolbar will be displayed (see Figure 12.10).

Figure 12.10
Use the Automation
toolbar to take Snapshots.

5. Click on the Snapshot button (the one with the picture of a camera on it) on the Automation toolbar.

6. Repeat steps 1 through 5 until you've created all the Snapshots you need for your project.

7. When you're finished, click on the Disarm All Automation Controls button (the first button to the right of the Snapshot button) on the Automation toolbar to disarm all of the previously armed parameters.

When you play your project, you'll notice that the Snapshots take effect as the Now time passes each Snapshot point.

ENABLE/DISABLE AUTOMATION

If you want to disable automation temporarily without changing or deleting any of the Snapshots in your project, click on the Enable/Disable Automation Playback button (the second button to the right of the Snapshot button) on the Automation toolbar.

Snapshot control values for each of the MIDI and audio track modules, as well as the buses, are stored as nodes on individual envelopes in the individual tracks represented by those modules. These envelope nodes can be edited, allowing you to change your recorded Snapshot data. I'll talk more about envelopes later in the chapter, in the "Working with Envelopes" section.

Automating the Mix

Snapshots are great if you need quick control for changing values at certain points in your project, but most of the time you'll want the controls to change smoothly over time as the project plays. To achieve this effect, you need to use SONAR's Record Automation feature. Using Record Automation, you can record the movements of any of the parameters in the Console or Track views. You do so in real time as your project plays.

You can record the values of the parameters in the Console and Track views into your project by activating the Record Automation feature and manipulating the controls with your mouse as the project plays. This feature works as follows:

1. Make sure the Automation toolbar is visible by choosing View > Toolbars, and then activate the Automation option and click on Close.

2. Right-click on each parameter you want to automate and choose Arm for Automation from the drop-down menu. You can arm multiple parameters at the same time, as explained earlier.

3. Set the Now time to just before the point in the project where you want to start recording control changes.

4. Choose Transport > Record Automation to start the project playing and to start recording automation data.

5. When the Now time gets to the point in the project at which you want to begin recording parameter changes, adjust the parameters with your mouse.

6. When you're finished, choose Transport > Stop to stop playback of the project.

7. Because you're manipulating onscreen parameters with your mouse, you can make only one change at a time. What if you want to have two different controls change at the same time? For every parameter that you want to change in the same time frame, you must repeat steps 2 through 6.

LOOP RECORDING

Instead of starting and stopping playback each time you want to record additional control changes, try setting up a loop so SONAR will play the project (or the section of the project) over and over again. I described loop recording in Chapter 6.

8.   After you've finished recording all the control changes you need for your mix, click on the Disarm All Automation Controls button (the first button to the right of the Snapshot button) in the Automation toolbar to disarm all of the previously armed controls/parameters.

When you play your project, you'll notice the automation taking effect as the Now time passes the sections in which you recorded data.

Just as with Snapshots, the parameter values for each of the MIDI and audio track modules (as well as the buses) are stored as envelopes in the individual tracks represented by those modules. These envelopes can be edited, allowing you to change your recorded automation data.

Grouping

As I mentioned earlier, to change more than one parameter at the same time while you're recording automation data, you have to play through your project several times. To make things easier, you can connect a number of parameters together so if you move one, the others will move with it. You do so by using SONAR's Grouping feature. With the Grouping feature, you can create groups of parameters whose changes are linked to one another.

Creating Groups

You can create up to 24 different groups, each of which is designated by a letter of the alphabet (A through X) and a color. The number of parameters that can belong to a group is unlimited. To create a group, follow these steps:

1.   Right-click on a parameter in the Console view or the Track view and choose Group > A–X. Depending on what letter you choose, that parameter takes on the associated color.

2.   Right-click on another parameter and choose Group > A–X. This time, choose the same letter for this parameter as you did for the previous parameter. This other parameter will take on the same color.

3.   Continue to add as many other parameters to the group as you want. You can even create other groups. The same parameter, however, cannot belong to more than one group.

Now if you change the first parameter, the second parameter will change as well, and vice versa. The values of both of these parameters will be recorded if you have them grouped while you are recording automation data.

Ungrouping

To remove a parameter from a group, right-click on the parameter and then select Ungroup from the drop-down menu. The color of the parameter will return to normal.

Group Properties

In addition to simple groups, in which you link different parameters so they change identically, you can create some advanced parameter groups by manipulating the properties of a group. To change the properties of a group, right-click on one of the parameters in the group and select Group Properties from the drop-down menu to open the Group Properties dialog box (see Figure 12.11).

Figure 12.11
You can use the Group Properties dialog box to change the properties of a group.

By changing the properties of a group, you can change the way the parameters in the group are related to one another in terms of the way they change. Parameters in groups can be related absolutely, relatively, or via a custom definition.

Absolute

To make the parameters in a group related absolutely, select the Absolute option (which is the default setting when you create a new group) in the Group Properties dialog box and click on OK. Parameters in a group that are related absolutely have the same range of change. This means if you change one parameter in the group, the others will change by the same amount. This is true even if one parameter starts at one value and another parameter starts at a different value. For example, suppose you have two Volume parameters on two different MIDI track modules linked together, and one of the Volume parameters has a value of 10 and the other has a value of 20. If you increase the value of the first parameter by 10, the other parameter value will increase by 10 too. Now the first parameter has a value of 20, and the second parameter has a value of 30.

Relative

To link the parameters in a group relatively, select the Relative option in the Group Properties dialog box and click on OK. Parameters in a group that are linked relatively do not have the same range of change. This means if you change one parameter in the group, the others can change by different amounts. For example, suppose you have two Pan parameters linked, and one has a value of 100% Left and the other has a value of C (centered in the middle). If you change the first parameter so it has a value of C (centered in the middle), the other will change so that it has a value of 100% Right. Now if you change the first parameter to a value of 100% Right, the second parameter will remain at 100% Right. The second parameter can't go any higher so it stays at that value, while the first parameter continues to increase in value. I know this concept is a bit confusing, but if you try it for a while you'll begin to understand it.

Custom

To relate the parameters in a group according to your own custom definition, select the Custom option in the Group Properties dialog box. All the parameters in the group will be listed in the dialog box (see Figure 12.12).

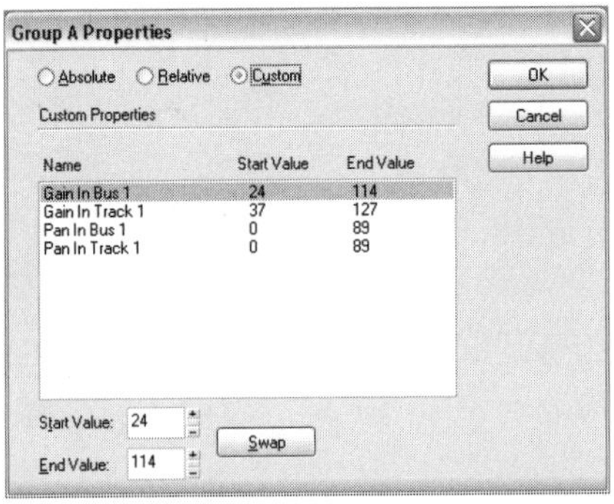

Figure 12.12
You can create complex relationships between parameters in a group by using the Custom option.

Along with the names of each parameter, the Start and End values are also listed. By changing the Start and End values for each parameter, you can define some complex value changes. For example, one good use of the Custom option is to create a crossfade between two Volume parameters. Suppose you have one Volume parameter in a group with a Start value of 0 and an End value of 127, and another Volume parameter in the same group with a Start value of 127 and an End value of 0. As you increase the value of the first parameter, the second parameter value will decrease, and vice versa. You also can set up more complex relationships simply by assigning different Start and End values to each parameter in a group.

To change the Start or End value of a parameter in the list in the Group Properties dialog box, select the parameter and then type a value for either the Start Value or End Value parameter located at the bottom of the box. If you want to exchange the current Start and End values, click on the Swap button. After you've finished creating your custom definition, click on OK.

QUICKLY SET START AND END
You also can change the Start and End values of a parameter without opening the Group Properties dialog box. Just set the parameter to the value you want to set as the start or end, right-click on the parameter, and select either Set Start = Current or Set End = Current.

Remote Control

Even with grouping, you still might find it cumbersome to adjust onscreen parameters with your mouse. To remedy this situation, SONAR provides a Remote Control feature. With the Remote Control feature, you can use an external MIDI device to control the changes to the onscreen parameters in the Console view or Track view. For example, if you have a MIDI keyboard, you can use a key on the keyboard to manipulate one of the button parameters. Or if you have a pitch bend wheel on your keyboard, you can use it to manipulate one of the knob or slider parameters.

By assigning different types of MIDI controller messages to the parameters in the Console view or Track view, you no longer have to use your mouse to change the value of the parameters; you can use the actual buttons and keys or levers and sliders on your MIDI instrument or device. To activate the Remote Control feature for a parameter, just follow these steps:

1. Right-click on the parameter and select Remote Control from the drop-down menu to open the Remote Control dialog box (see Figure 12.13).

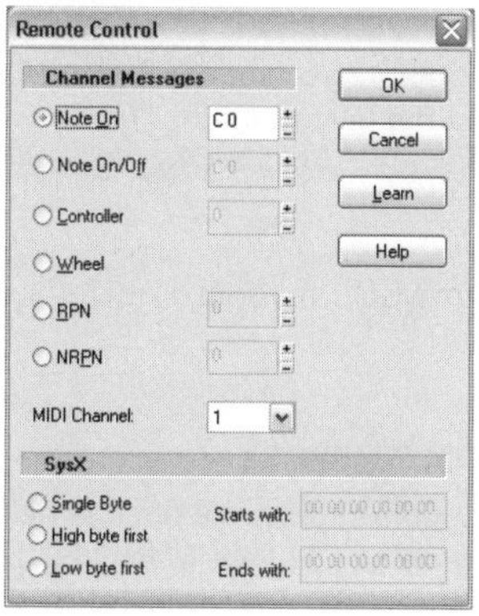

Figure 12.13
You can use the Remote Control dialog box to assign MIDI controller messages to parameters in the Console view so they can be changed via an external MIDI device.

2. If you want to use a key on your MIDI keyboard to manipulate this parameter, select either the Note On option or the Note On/Off option, and then enter the pitch of the key that you want to use. If you choose Note On, the value of the parameter will be toggled on or off (for a button parameter) or set to minimum or maximum value (for knobs and sliders) each time you press the key. If you select the Note On/Off option, the value of the parameter will be toggled on when you press the key and off when you release the key.

3. If you want to use a lever or slider on your MIDI keyboard to manipulate this parameter, select the Controller option, and then enter the value of the MIDI controller you want to use. You can use this option only to manipulate knob and slider parameters.

4. If you want to use the pitch bend wheel on your MIDI keyboard to manipulate this parameter, select the Wheel option.

5. If you want to use the special registered parameter number or non-registered parameter number MIDI messages to manipulate this parameter, choose either the RPN or NRPN option, and then enter the number of the RPN or NRPN that you want to use.

6. If you want to use a Sysx message to manipulate this parameter, choose a byte option. If the message contains a single byte of data that changes while the rest of the bytes in the message remain static, choose the Single Byte option. If the changing data contains two bytes, with the first being the high byte, choose the High Byte First option. If the changing data contains two bytes with the first being the low byte, choose the Low Byte First option. Then enter into the Starts With field the bytes in the Sysx message that come before the changing data and enter into the Ends With field the bytes in the Sysx message that come after the changing data.

7. Set the MIDI channel your MIDI keyboard or device is using.

8. Click on OK.

THE LEARN FEATURE

Instead of having to figure out how you need to set the parameters for Remote Control, you can use the Learn feature to have it done for you automatically. First, move a control on your external MIDI device. Right-click on the parameter in SONAR that you want to manipulate and choose Remote Control from the drop-down menu, and then click on the Learn button. The Remote Control parameters will be set up for you automatically. Click on OK.

Now you can manipulate the parameter from your MIDI keyboard or device—even while you are recording automation.

SPECIAL REMOTE CONTROL SUPPORT

SONAR 3 provides special support for external devices designed specifically for remote control purposes, such as the CM Labs MotorMix, the Tascam US-428, the Roland U-8, and the Peavey StudioMix. For more information on how to use each of these devices, look in the SONAR Help file under the topic Working with External Devices.

Working with Envelopes

In addition to the Snapshot and Record Automation features, SONAR provides one more method of automating its parameters. I'm talking about the Envelope feature. Using this feature, you can "draw" parameter changes into individual clips or entire tracks in the Track view. In the following sections, I'll cover how to create and edit parameter changes using the Envelope feature.

Creating and Editing Envelopes

Earlier I mentioned that whenever you use the Snapshot or Record Automation features, SONAR stores the automation data as envelopes in the Track view. Well, you can also create (as well as edit) envelopes manually using the Envelope tool and your mouse.

Audio Envelopes

SONAR allows you to create envelopes for both audio and MIDI tracks, as well as the buses in the Track view. Since the buses deal with audio data, you automate them using audio envelopes. MIDI and audio envelopes are basically the same, but they have enough differences to require separate step-by-step procedures. To create and/or edit an audio envelope, follow these steps:

1. Activate the Envelope tool by clicking on the Envelope Tool button in the Track view (see Figure 12.14).

Figure 12.14
Use the Envelope tool to create a new envelope.

2. If you want to create an envelope for an individual clip, right-click on that clip and choose Envelopes > Clip > [*name of the parameter you want to automate*]. For individual clips, you can automate the gain (volume) or panning.

3. If you want to create an envelope for an entire track (including the buses), right-click on that track in the Clips pane and choose Envelopes > Create Track Envelope (or Create Bus Envelopes) > [*name of the parameter you want to automate*]. For tracks, you can automate the Mute, Volume, Pan, Bus Send Level/Pan, and EQ parameters. The buses provide different parameters for automation (see the list in the drop-down menu).

MERGED ENVELOPES

If you create an envelope for a clip inside a track that already has an envelope for the same parameter, the clip envelope will be merged into the track envelope.

4. Initially, the envelope is shown as a straight dotted line that runs from left to right in the clip or track. If it's a clip envelope, it will stop at the end of the clip. If it's a track envelope, it will continue past the right side of the Track view (see Figure 12.15). The vertical position of the envelope inside the clip or track indicates the current value for its associated parameter. For example, if you're automating the Volume parameter and its current value is 0, the envelope will be shown at the very bottom of the clip or track. If the Volume parameter value is 127, the envelope will be shown at the very top of the clip or track. And other values will be shown somewhere between the top and bottom of the clip or track.

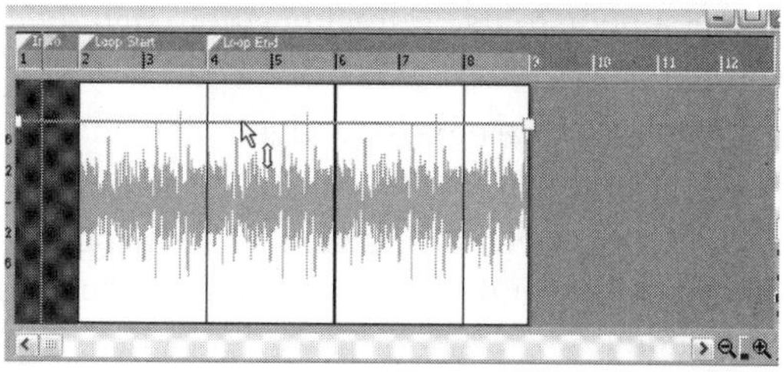

Figure 12.15
A straight line in a clip or track represents a new envelope.

CHAPTER 12

SHOW/HIDE ENVELOPES

You can show and hide envelopes for easier editing. If you don't see your new envelope, click on the down arrow next to the Envelope Tool button and choose one of the options (such as Show All Envelopes) from the drop-down menu.

5. At the beginning of the envelope is a small square (called a *node*). To change the value of the envelope, click and drag the node up or down. As you drag the node, you will see the value of the parameter represented by an envelope displayed alongside your mouse cursor.

6. To make things more interesting, you can add more nodes to the envelope either by double-clicking anywhere on the envelope or by right-clicking on the envelope and selecting Add Node from the drop-down menu. You can add as many nodes as you need, which enables you to create some very complex parameter value changes. In addition to dragging them up or down, you can also drag nodes left or right (to change their time/location within the project), so you can create any envelope shape you want (see Figure 12.16). You also can change the time and value of a node more precisely by right-clicking on it, choosing Properties from the drop-down menu, and then entering the new values in the Edit Node dialog box.

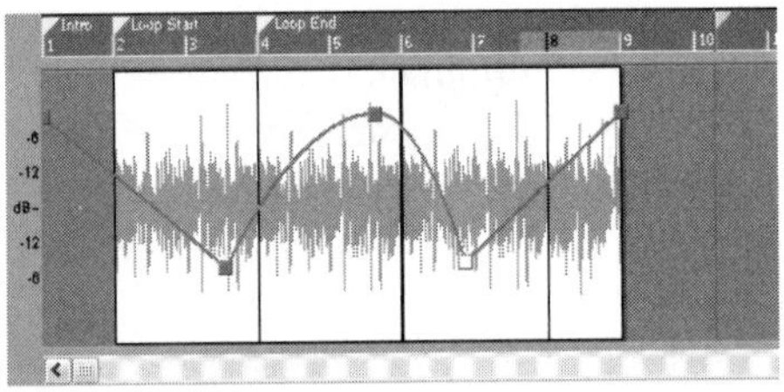

Figure 12.16

You can create complex envelopes by adding more nodes.

7. To make things even more interesting, you can change the shape of the line segments between two nodes. Right-click on a line segment and choose one of the following options from the drop-down menu: Jump, Linear, Fast Curve, or Slow Curve. If you want abrupt changes in the parameter values, choose Jump. For straight changes in the values, choose Linear. For fast but smooth changes in the values, choose Fast Curve. For slow and smooth changes in the values, choose Slow Curve. Depending on the option you choose, the shape of the line segment will change accordingly.

8. If you need to delete a node, right-click on it and select Delete Node from the drop-down menu. To delete all nodes, just right-click on the envelope and select Clear All from the drop-down menu.

9. If you need to reset a node to its original position, right-click on it and select Reset Node from the drop-down menu.

10. If you want to delete an entire envelope, right-click on it and select Delete Envelope from the drop-down menu.

11. If you want to change an envelope assignment so it controls a different parameter, right-click on the envelope and choose Assign Envelope > [*name of the new parameter to automate*].

MIDI Envelopes

To create and/or edit a MIDI envelope, follow these steps:

1. Activate the Envelope tool by clicking on the Envelope Tool button in the Track view.

2. If you want to create an envelope for an individual clip, right-click on that clip and choose Envelopes > Clip > [*name of the parameter you want to automate*]. For individual MIDI clips, you can automate the velocity.

3. If you want to create an envelope for an entire track, right-click on that track in the Clips pane and choose Envelopes > Create Track Envelope > [*name of the parameter you want to automate*]. For MIDI tracks, you can automate the Mute, Volume, Pan, Chorus, and Reverb parameters. In addition, you can automate any other MIDI controller messages by choosing the Envelopes > Create Track Envelope > MIDI option, which opens the MIDI Envelope dialog box (see Figure 12.17). In the dialog box, choose the type of controller, the value of that controller, and the MIDI channel you want to use for the controller. Then click on OK to create the new envelope.

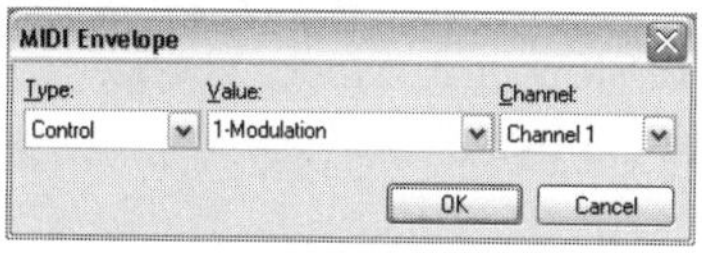

Figure 12.17
For MIDI tracks, you can create envelopes for any kind of MIDI controller messages.

MIDI Envelope		
Type:	Value:	Channel:
Control	1-Modulation	Channel 1
	OK	Cancel

CONVERT MIDI TO SHAPES

If you think the parameters in the MIDI Envelope dialog box look familiar, you're right. They are the same parameters found in the Controller pane at the bottom of the Piano Roll view, which are used to choose MIDI controllers for editing in the Controller pane. If a track contains MIDI controller messages and you create an envelope for that track with the same controller, they will contradict one another. In this case, you should select the track and choose Edit > Convert MIDI to Shapes. You'll see the Convert MIDI to Shapes dialog box, which is exactly the same as the MIDI Envelope dialog box. Choose the controller you want to convert and click on OK. The controller messages in that track will be converted to envelopes.

4. Initially, the envelope is shown as a straight line that runs from left to right in the clip or track. If it's a clip envelope, it will stop at the end of the clip. If it's a track envelope, it will continue past the right side of the Track view. The vertical position of the envelope inside the clip or track indicates the current value for its associated parameter. For example, if you're automating the Volume parameter and its current value is 0, the envelope will be shown at the very bottom of the clip or track. If the Volume parameter value is 127, the envelope will be shown at the very top of the clip or track. And other values will be shown somewhere between the top and bottom of the clip or track.

5. At the beginning of the envelope is a small square (called a *node*). To change the value of the envelope, click and drag the node up or down. As you drag the node, you will see the value of the parameter represented by the envelope displayed alongside your mouse cursor.

6. To make things more interesting, you can add more nodes to the envelope either by double-clicking anywhere on the envelope or by right-clicking on the envelope and selecting Add Node from the drop-down menu. You can add as many nodes as you need, which enables you to create some very complex parameter value changes. In addition to dragging them up or down, you can also drag nodes left or right (to change their time/location within the project), so you can create any envelope shape you want. You also can change the time and value of a node more precisely by right-clicking on it, choosing Properties from the drop-down menu, and then entering the new values in the Edit Node dialog box.

7. To make things even more interesting, you can change the shape of the line segments between two nodes. Right-click on a line segment and choose one of the following options from the drop-down menu: Jump, Linear, Fast Curve, or Slow Curve. If you want abrupt changes in the parameter values, choose Jump. For straight changes in the values, choose Linear. For fast but smooth changes in the values, choose Fast Curve. For slow and smooth changes in the values, choose Slow Curve. Depending on the option you choose, the shape of the line segment will change accordingly.

8. If you need to delete a node, right-click on it and select Delete Node from the drop-down menu. And to delete all nodes, just right-click on the envelope and select Clear All from the drop-down menu.

9. If you need to reset a node to its original position, right-click on it and select Reset Node from the drop-down menu.

10. If you want to delete an entire envelope, right-click on it and select Delete Envelope from the drop-down menu.

11. If you want to change an envelope assignment so it controls a different parameter, right-click on the envelope and choose Assign Envelope > [*name of the new parameter to automate*].

Now when you play your project, the parameter values you edited will follow the shape of the envelopes.

ENABLE/DISABLE ENVELOPES

If you want to temporarily turn off all envelopes in your tracks to hear how your project sounds without the automation, click on the Enable/Disable Automation Playback button on the Automation toolbar.

ENVELOPE/OFFSET MODE

Normally during playback, if you have an envelope assigned to a track parameter, you cannot change that parameter because the envelope is controlling it. But SONAR provides a special mode in which you can add an offset to envelope values by changing parameters during playback. This is called Offset mode, and you can activate it by clicking on the Envelope/Offset Mode button on the Track view toolbar (see Figure 12.18). This button toggles between Envelope mode and Offset mode. Also be aware that when you return to Envelope mode, your last parameter offset settings are still in effect. So if you change a parameter in Offset mode and leave it, the parameter will still be offset even if you return to Envelope mode. A good use for this feature is when you have an envelope that's just about perfect, but you want to make an adjustment to the entire envelope without having to change all the nodes in it.

Figure 12.18
Use the Envelope/Offset Mode button to toggle between Envelope and Offset modes.

Additional Envelope Editing

Even though I've covered most of the editing procedures for envelopes in the previous sections, there are some additional ways in which you can edit envelopes.

Deleting Envelopes

Earlier I mentioned that to delete an envelope, you just need to right-click on it and choose Delete Envelope from the drop-down menu. But if you want to delete more than one envelope or only part of an envelope, the procedure is a bit different.

1. Make sure the Select tool is activated by clicking on the Select tool button in the Track view (see Figure 12.19).

Figure 12.19
For normal data selection, use the Select tool.

2. Select the data containing the envelope data you want to delete. This can be a single clip, an entire track, multiple tracks, or even part of a clip or track. To refresh your memory on how to select data in the Track view, review Chapter 7.
3. Choose Edit > Delete to open the Delete dialog box.
4. Depending on the data you selected in Step 2, either the Track/Bus Automation option or the Clip Automation option will be available (or maybe both). Activate one or both options.

ENVELOPES ONLY

If you don't want to delete any other data along with the envelope data, make sure to deactivate all other options in the Delete dialog box.

5. Click on OK.

SONAR will delete your selected envelope/automation data.

Copying and Pasting Envelopes

You can also copy and paste an envelope (or part of an envelope) from one track to another. Why would you want to do that? Well, you might want the volume of one instrument in your project to follow the volume of another instrument. You can do this by copying and pasting the volume envelope from the first instrument track to the other. Here is how it works:

1. Make sure the Select tool is activated by clicking on the Select tool button in the Track view.

2. Select the data containing the envelope data you want to copy. This can be a single clip, an entire track, multiple tracks, or even part of a clip or track. To refresh your memory on how to select data in the Track view, go back to Chapter 7.

SELECT TRACK ENVELOPES OPTION

If you are selecting clips in the Clips pane and you want to select the track envelope data for the track in which the clips reside, be sure to choose Edit > Select > Select Track Envelopes with Selected Clips.

3. Choose Edit > Copy to open the Copy dialog box.

4. Depending on the data you selected in Step 2, either the Track/Bus Automation option or the Clip Automation option will be available (or maybe both). Activate one or both options.

ENVELOPES ONLY

If you don't want to copy any other data along with the envelope data, make sure to deactivate all other options in the Copy dialog box.

5. Click on OK.

6. Select the tracks and change the Now time to the position in the project at which you want to paste the envelope data.

7. Choose Edit > Paste to open the Paste dialog box. Then click on the Advanced button to expand the Paste dialog box to its full size.

8. Make sure the Blend Old and New option is activated in the What to Do with Existing Material section.

9. Make sure the Track/Bus Automation and/or Clip Automation options are activated in the What to Paste section.

10. Click on OK.

SONAR will copy your selected envelope data and paste it at the new location in the project.

Automating Effects and DXis

In addition to automating track parameters, SONAR lets you automate individual audio effect and DXi parameters. I talked about effects in Chapter 11 and about DXis in Chapter 10. The procedures for automating audio effects and DXis are essentially the same as for track parameters, but arming the parameters is a bit different.

Automating Effects Parameters

To automate effects parameters, you can follow the same procedures outlined in the "Taking Snapshots" and "Automating the Mix" sections of this chapter, which I discussed earlier. But when you get to the part of the procedure where you need to arm the parameter that you want to automate, follow these steps instead:

1. Right-click in the Fx bin of the audio track to which you want to apply the real-time effect and choose Audio Effects > [*the name of the effect you want to use*].

2. After the window for the effect appears, right-click on the name of the effect in the Fx bin and choose Arm Parameter.

3. In the dialog box that appears, put a check mark next to each of the parameters you want to automate in the Param Armed list.

4. Click on OK.

Now just follow the procedures in the "Taking Snapshots" or "Automating the Mix" sections of this chapter to record automation for your effect parameters.

As with track parameters, you can use envelopes to automate effects parameters. The procedure is basically the same as outlined in the "Audio Envelopes" section of this chapter, which I discussed earlier. But you can use only track envelopes to automate effects parameters, and the procedure for initially creating the envelope is a bit different. To create an envelope to automate an effect parameter, follow these steps:

1. Right-click in the Fx bin of the audio track to which you want to apply the real-time effect and choose Audio Effects > [*the name of the effect you want to use*].

2. When the window for the effect appears, close it. Then right-click in the Clips pane of the track to which you applied the effect and choose Envelopes > Create Track Envelope > [*the name of the effect to be automated*].

3. In the dialog box that appears, put a check mark next to each of the parameters you want to automate in the Envelope Exists list.

4. Click on OK.

Now just follow the procedures in the "Audio Envelopes" section of this chapter to finish creating the envelopes for your effect parameters.

CHAPTER 12

Automating DXi Parameters

Unlike effects, some DXis can be automated only by using envelopes. It depends on the DXi. In addition, the procedure for recording DXi parameter movements is different from what I described earlier, so I'll go through each procedure step by step.

Recording Parameter Movements

If you want to record automation for a DXi by directly manipulating its onscreen parameters, follow these steps:

1. If you haven't done so already, set up a DXi in the Track view of your project. I went over this procedure in Chapter 10. Be sure to keep the DXi's window open.

2. Arm for recording the MIDI track to which you want to record the automation data.

3. Choose Transport > Record Options to set the recording mode. I explained this feature in Chapter 6; it works the same way here. More than likely, you'll want to keep the recording mode set to Sound On Sound. This will allow you to record new data to the track without overwriting any of the existing data.

4. Set up the DXi to enable automation recording. This procedure is different for every DXi so you will have to refer to the DXi's documentation for instructions.

SONAR DX INSTRUMENTS

Although automation setup for each DXi is different, SONAR ships with a number of DXis, so I can at least show you how to work with those particular products. Here's how to set up each of the DXis included with SONAR:

▶ **Alien Connection's ReValver SE.** This DXi can be automated only by using envelopes, so please refer to the next section of this chapter to learn how to automate it.

▶ **Cyclone.** This DXi doesn't provide any kind of automation. It cannot be automated via recording its control movements or via envelopes.

▶ **DreamStation DXi2.** This DXi doesn't require any setup procedure. Just follow the step-by-step instructions to record automation. As you move the DreamStation's onscreen controls, they will be recorded.

▶ **Edirol VSC.** To activate automation for the Edirol Virtual Sound Canvas, click on its Setup button to open the VSC Settings dialog box. Then click on the Misc tab and activate the Record VSC Panel Operations option.

▶ **LiveSynth Pro SE.** This DXi doesn't provide any kind of automation. It cannot be automated via recording its control movements or via envelopes.

5. Set the Now time to the point in the project at which you want to start recording automation.

6. Choose Transport > Record (or press the R key on your computer keyboard) to start recording.

7. Move the DXi's controls to record their movements.

8. Choose Transport > Stop (or press the spacebar on your computer keyboard) to stop recording.

9. If you want to record more automation, repeat steps 5 through 8.

CONVERT MIDI TO SHAPES

When you record automation data from a DXi, it is saved to the MIDI track as MIDI controller data. There's nothing wrong with this. You can edit the data easily using the Controller pane in the Piano Roll view. But if you would rather edit the data as envelopes in the Track view, use the Edit > Convert MIDI to Shapes feature to convert the MIDI controller data to envelopes.

Using Envelopes

You'll find that using envelopes to automate DXi parameters is more accurate, since you can actually "draw" the control movements. To use envelopes to automate DXi parameters, follow these steps:

1. Set up a DXi in the Track view of your project. I went over this procedure in Chapter 10.

2. In the MIDI track that drives the DXi, right-click in the Clips pane and choose Envelopes > Create Track Envelope > MIDI to open the MIDI Envelope dialog box.

3. In the Type drop-down list, choose the Control, RPN, or NRPN option.

4. The Value drop-down list will show all of the parameters that the DXi offers for automation. Choose a parameter from the list.

5. In the Channel drop-down list, choose the MIDI channel of the current patch (program) being used in the DXi.

6. Click on OK.

Now follow the procedures in the "MIDI Envelopes" section of this chapter to automate the DXi parameters.

The Next Steps

After you've finished mixing all the data in your tracks at just the right settings, it's time to create a final stereo track, which you can use to burn your project onto CD or get it ready for distribution in a multimedia project or on the Internet. Instead of including the information on how to do that here in this chapter, I've decided to break things up a bit. The next few chapters deal with some other important features found in SONAR, such as music notation and using StudioWare and CAL. If you would prefer to read these chapters later, you can skip to Chapter 17, "Taking Your SONAR 3 Project to CD," to learn how to finish the mixing process and burn your music to a compact disc. For information on converting your project to a compatible format for multimedia or the Internet, read Appendix C, "Producing for Multimedia and the Web."

CHAPTER 12

13

Making Sheet Music

In Chapter 7, I described how you can edit the data in your MIDI tracks graphically by using the Piano Roll view. SONAR also provides tools so you can edit your MIDI data as standard music notation and guitar tablature. As a matter of fact, you can compose new music while working with notation by graphically adding, editing, and deleting notes. You can also add many of the symbols used in music notation, such as chord symbols, expression markings, and lyrics. When you're ready, you can print your music as sheet music, complete with title, copyright notice, page numbers, and more by using the printer attached to your computer. To give you an idea of how to use all these wonderful features, this chapter will do the following:

▶ Show you how to use the Staff view

▶ Explain how to edit music as notes and tablature

▶ Demonstrate applying musical symbols

▶ Teach you how to handle percussion

▶ Show you how to use the Lyrics view

▶ Explain how to print your music

The Staff View

SONAR provides three different tools for editing MIDI data: the Event view, the Piano Roll view, and the Staff view. For really precise numerical editing, the Event view can't be beat. For precise graphical editing of both MIDI note and controller data, the Piano Roll view is the tool you'll want to use. (I described the Event and Piano Roll views in Chapter 7.) Many musicians, however, are used to composing and editing in standard music notation. The Staff view comes into play at this point.

Using the Staff view (see Figure 13.1), you can add, edit, and delete MIDI note data within your MIDI tracks. The Staff view looks similar to sheet music on a piece of paper and represents notes as standard music notation and guitar tablature on musical staves with clefs, key signatures, time signatures, and many of the other symbols you might expect to see on a sheet of music.

Figure 13.1
Working in the Staff view is just like composing music on paper, but a lot easier.

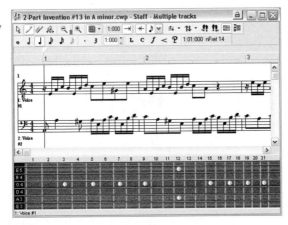

More precisely, the Staff view consists of three major sections: the toolbars (located at the top of the view, containing all the related controls), the Staff pane (located in the center of the view, displaying the notes in the currently selected tracks), and the Fretboard pane (located at the bottom of the view, displaying the notes currently being played as they would appear on a six-string guitar neck that uses standard tuning).

You'll also notice that the Staff view has scroll bars. They work just as they do in the other views. In addition, this view has a Snap to Grid function, which is represented by the Grid button in the first toolbar. Other similarities are the Marker area and the Time Ruler, which are located just above the Staff pane. The Staff view also has zoom tools, but they are located in the first toolbar rather than in the lower-right corner of the view. They are placed this way because when you're zooming in on the Staff view, the notation grows larger both horizontally and vertically in equal proportions, so you don't need multiple zoom tools.

You can open the Staff view in two different ways.

▶ In the Track view, select the MIDI track(s) you want to edit and then choose View > Staff.

▶ In the Track view, right-click on a track or clip and choose View > Staff from the drop-down menu.

Whatever method you choose, SONAR will open the Staff view and display the data from the track(s) you selected.

Changing the Layout

If you select more than one track to be displayed, the Staff view will show the data from each track on a separate stave.

PICK TRACKS
Just like the other views, the Staff view provides a Pick Tracks button in the first toolbar. You can use it to change the tracks that are displayed.

SONAR picks the clef (treble or bass) for each stave automatically by looking at the range of notes contained in the data. If a track has notes that fall into both clefs, it shows the data on two connected staves, one with a treble clef and one with a bass clef.

UP TO 24 STAVES

You can display up to 24 staves of notation in the Staff view at once. This does not necessarily mean you can display 24 tracks, though. If the data from each track is shown on a single stave, then you can display 24 tracks at once. If, however, the data from each track is shown on a pair of staves (as previously mentioned), you can display only 12 tracks at once. Of course, you can show some tracks with one stave and some with two, so the number of tracks will vary.

If you want, you can override these automatic stave settings by adjusting the Staff View Layout parameters. To adjust the way the data from your MIDI tracks is displayed in the Staff view, just follow these steps:

1. Right-click anywhere in the Staff pane and choose Layout from the drop-down menu to open the Staff View Layout dialog box (see Figure 13.2).

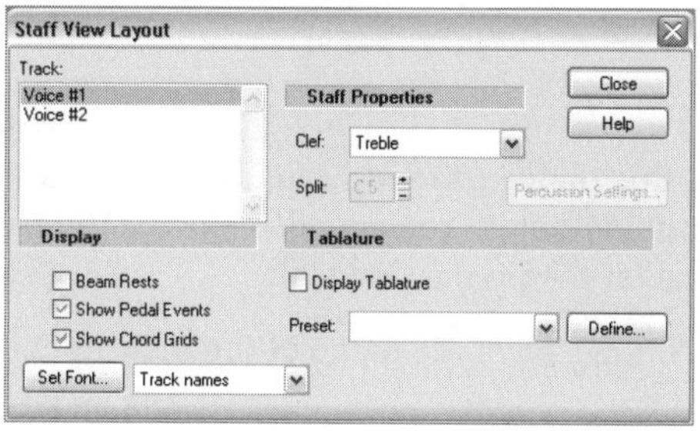

Figure 13.2
You can use the Staff View Layout dialog box to change the way your data is displayed in the Staff view.

2. From the Track list, select the name of the track that you want to change.

3. In the Staff Properties section, set the Clef parameter to the type of clef you want to use for that track. If you choose the Treble/Bass option, the track will be displayed on two staves. To determine the notes that will be shown on each stave, enter a note value for the Split parameter. Notes that are at or higher than the pitch you enter are shown on the treble clef staff, and notes that are lower than the pitch you enter are shown on the bass clef staff.

4. Click on Close.

The track will be shown with the stave settings you specified.

Percussion Tracks

If you open in the Staff view a MIDI track that has its Channel parameter set to 10, and you had previously set up your sound card ports to use the General MIDI instrument definitions (which you learned about in Chapter 3), the Staff view will display that track automatically as percussion notation in a percussion staff. It displays the track this way because when you're using General

MIDI, it is standard practice to put all percussion instruments on MIDI channel 10. If you want to override this automatic setting, you can do so as explained previously.

You can also change a number of other settings to customize the way your percussion staves appear. If you select your percussion track in the Staff View Layout dialog box, a new button (called Percussion Settings) will become active. If you click on this button, the Percussion Notation Key dialog box will appear (see Figure 13.3).

Figure 13.3
You can use the Percussion Notation Key dialog box to further adjust how your percussion tracks appear.

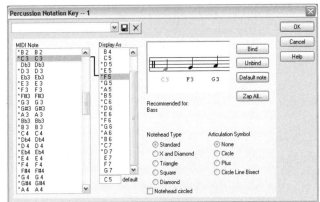

By manipulating the parameters in this dialog box, you can change the noteheads and articulation symbols used to display your percussion notes. You can also change the percussion sounds that correspond to the different positions on the percussion staff.

1. In the MIDI Note section, select the name of the instrument you want to change.

2. If you want to change the position on the percussion staff where that instrument will be shown, select the appropriate pitch in the Display As section. Then click on the Bind button to assign that staff position to the selected instrument.

3. If you don't want an instrument to have a specific staff position assignment, select the instrument and click on either the Unbind button or the Default Note button. To remove all instrument assignments, click on the Zap All button.

DEFAULT PITCH POSITION

Any instruments that don't have a specific assigned staff position automatically use the default position, shown at the bottom of the Display As section. This means that those instruments are shown at that pitch position on the percussion staff. You can change the default position by typing in a new pitch value.

4. After you've bound an instrument to a position on the staff, you can designate the notehead type and articulation symbol it will use. Just select the appropriate options in those sections of the dialog box. When you set the notehead type, you can also opt to have the notehead circled or not by setting the Notehead Circled parameter.

5. If you want to use these settings again later, save them as a preset.

6. Click on OK to close the Percussion Notation Key dialog box.

7. Click on Close to close the Staff View Layout dialog box.

Now the data in your percussion tracks will be shown using the settings you specified.

GHOST STROKES

SONAR displays *ghost strokes* (percussion notes played very softly for ornamentation) using the standard method of parentheses around the percussion notehead. It determines ghost strokes by testing to see whether the note velocity is lower than 32. This number is a fixed value that can't be changed. You can, however, change the note velocities of your data and then use the Velocity Trim track parameter to trick SONAR into using a different determining value. For example, to stop notes from being shown as ghost notes, simply raise their velocity values. Then, so the sound of the data isn't changed, set the Velocity Trim parameter so it lowers the velocities to their original values during playback. Do the opposite to have notes shown as ghost notes.

Showing Pedal Events and Chord Grids

You also can control whether or not the Staff view will display pedal events or guitar chord grids. (I'll talk more about both of these symbols later.) To do so, in the Display section of the Staff View Layout dialog box, set the Show Pedal Events and Show Chord Grids options.

Changing Text Fonts

You can also change how any of the text used in your data will be displayed. For example, you can change track names, measure numbers, lyric text, expression text, chord text, triplet numbers, and tablature fret numbers. To do so, just follow these steps:

1. Right-click anywhere in the Staff pane and choose Layout from the drop-down menu to open the Staff View Layout dialog box.

2. In the Display section, choose the type of text you want to change by picking its designation from the Set Font drop-down list. For example, if you want to change how the track names look in your sheet music, select Track Names from the list.

3. Click on the Set Font button to open the Font dialog box (see Figure 13.4).

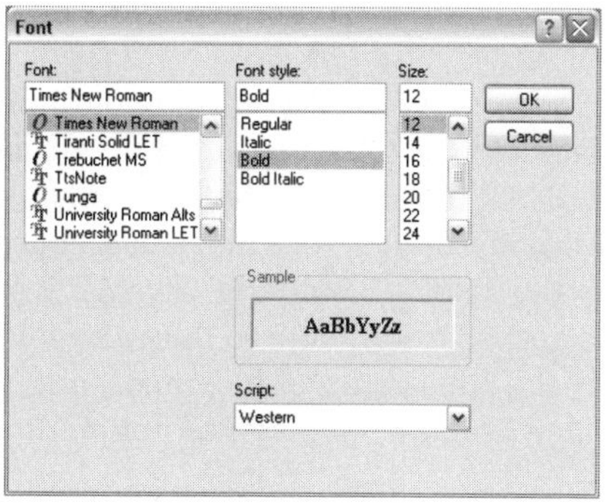

Figure 13.4
Using the Font dialog box, you can set how you want the text in your sheet music to appear.

4.   In the Font section, choose the font you want to use.

5.   In the Font Style section, choose a style for your text, such as Bold or Italic.

6.   In the Size section, choose the size of the text you want to use.

TEXT PREVIEW

As you are changing these parameters, you can see a preview of how the text will look in the Sample section of the Font dialog box.

7.   Click on OK to close the Font dialog box.

8.   Click on Close to close the Staff View Layout dialog box.

Your text will be displayed according to the settings you specified.

Rhythmic Appearance

When converting your MIDI data into music notation, SONAR has to make some educated guesses about how to display the rhythmic values of the notes. It does so because when you record your musical performance in real time, instead of playing notes with perfect timing, you'll more than likely play some of them either a little ahead or a little behind the beat. You might also hold some notes a little longer than they should be held. Most often, these slight timing errors are desirable because they give your music a more human feel.

SONAR doesn't understand these slight rhythmic variations, however; it knows only exact note timing and duration. So when SONAR displays your data in the Staff view, the data might not always look like it should. That's why SONAR provides a number of parameters you can adjust to give it a better idea of how the music should be displayed.

Using Beaming Rests

When you're notating music with very complex rhythms, it's standard practice to lengthen the beams on beamed groups of notes to also include rests. Lengthening the beams makes it much easier for the person reading the music to pick out the correct rhythms. For rhythmically simple music, however, it's usually best not to beam rests. If you need this feature, you can turn it on and off by opening the Staff View Layout dialog box and setting the Beam Rests option in the Display section.

Setting the Display Resolution

For SONAR to make an educated guess about how the rhythms in your music should be displayed, you have to give it a point of reference, which is called the *display resolution*. By setting this parameter, you are telling SONAR the smallest rhythmic note value used in your music. For example, if the smallest rhythmic value in your music is a sixteenth note, you would set a sixteenth-note value to be used for the display resolution. SONAR would then round any start times and note durations to the nearest sixteenth note so that your music would look more like it should. This setting changes only the appearance of the music, not how it sounds. To set the display resolution, select a rhythmic value from the Display Resolution drop-down list located in the first toolbar (see Figure 13.5).

Figure 13.5
You can set the display
resolution so that SONAR
can make a better guess
as to how your data
should be displayed.

Filling and Trimming Durations

In addition to the Display Resolution parameter, SONAR provides two other options you can set to help it better understand how to display your music. The Fill Durations option rounds note durations up to the next beat or note (whichever comes first). For example, instead of showing two quarter notes tied together in the same measure, SONAR simply shows a single half note.

The Trim Durations option rounds note durations down so that they do not overlap. For example, if you have a note with a duration that extends past the start of the next note, the first note's duration will be shortened so that you don't end up with something like a half note tied to a quarter note with an eighth note sitting between the two.

Neither of these options changes the music in any way—just how it's displayed. The results will vary depending on the music you are trying to display as notation, so you'll have to try either or both of these options to see whether they help clean up the rhythmic notation values. To turn the options on or off, just click on the Fill Durations and Trim Durations buttons (located to the immediate left of the Display Resolution parameter in the first toolbar) or press F and M on your computer keyboard, respectively.

Dealing with Notes

As you know, when you open a MIDI track in the Staff view, the notes in that track are displayed in the Staff pane as standard music notation. In addition to simply displaying the notes, the Staff view also enables you to edit and delete them, as well as add new ones.

You can add new notes to a track or edit the existing ones by using the tools represented by the first four buttons in the first toolbar (going from left to right on the left side of the Staff view).

Selecting

The first button in the toolbar represents the Select tool. Using this tool, you can select the notes for further manipulation, such as deleting, copying, moving, and so on. Essentially, you select notes the same way you would in the Piano Roll view. To select a single note, click on it. To select more than one note, hold down the Ctrl key on your computer keyboard while you click on the notes you want to select. You know the rest. For more information, check out Chapter 7.

TIED NOTES

When you select a note that is tied to another note, both notes are selected automatically because they are essentially the same MIDI note with its duration shown as two tied notes rather than as one note with a larger rhythmic value.

Editing

After you've made a selection, you can copy, cut, paste, move, and delete the notes the same way you would in the Piano Roll view. You can also edit notes individually using the Draw tool. The second button in the toolbar represents the Draw tool. Using this tool, you can add (which I'll talk about shortly) and edit the notes in the Staff pane.

To move a note to a different location within a staff, simply click on its notehead and drag it left or right. This action moves the note to a different horizontal location on the staff and along the Time Ruler.

SNAP TO GRID

If you have the Snap to Grid feature activated, the note will snap to the nearest note value set in the Snap to Grid dialog box.

To change the pitch of a note, simply click on its notehead and drag it up or down in the same staff or drag it into another staff. As you move the note, SONAR will play the different pitches so you can hear what they sound like.

CHROMATIC NOTE CHANGES

By default, SONAR uses note pitches that match the current diatonic key signature of the music. This means that as you drag a note to a new pitch, it automatically remains in the correct musical key. If you don't want the note to stay within the key, however, press the right mouse button after you've begun to drag the note to a new pitch. This allows you to change the pitch of the note chromatically in half steps.

Of course, sometimes you might want to make more precise changes to a note or change its duration. You can do so by using the Note Properties dialog box. With the Draw tool, just right-click on a note to open the Note Properties dialog box (see Figure 13.6).

Figure 13.6
Using the Note Properties dialog box, you can make precise changes to a note in the Staff view.

Note Properties	
Time:	2:02:000
Pitch:	B 2
Velocity:	127
Duration:	1
Channel:	10
Fret:	0
String:	0

OK
Cancel
Help

In the Note Properties dialog box, you can make precise changes to the time, pitch, velocity, duration, and MIDI channel of an individual note by typing in numerical values. You can also specify the fret and string upon which the note will be played in the Fretboard pane (which I'll talk about later).

THE EVENT INSPECTOR

You can get quicker access to the properties of a note using the Event Inspector toolbar. To activate it, choose View > Toolbars. Select Event Inspector so that there is a checkmark next to it, and then click on Close. Now whenever you use the Select tool to select a note in the Staff view, the note's properties will be displayed in the Event Inspector toolbar. You can also change the note's properties using the toolbar. Just click on a property in the toolbar and either type in a new value or use the spin controls to increase or decrease the value.

Drawing (or Adding)

In addition to editing, the Draw tool enables you to add notes to a staff by literally drawing them. To do so, follow these steps:

1. Select the Draw tool by clicking on its toolbar button.

2. Select a duration for the new note(s). If you look at the second toolbar (just below the first one), you'll notice a number of buttons with note values shown on them. Clicking on these buttons determines the duration for your new notes. For example, if you click on the Quarter Note button, the duration will be set to a quarter note. This toolbar also contains two additional buttons—one representing a dotted note and another representing a triplet. If you want your notes to be dotted or part of a triplet, click on one of these buttons as well.

TRIPLET QUIRKS

When you create a triplet, SONAR places all three notes on the staff with the same pitch. Triplets have to be created with a full set of three notes without rests or ties. After you add the triplet, you can change the pitches of the notes to whatever you desire.

3. Click anywhere on a staff in the Staff pane to place the new notes at the start times and pitches you want.

DISABLE FILL AND TRIM

It's a good idea to turn off the Fill Durations and Trim Durations options when you're entering new notes in the Staff pane. When you add notes, SONAR will try to change the way they are displayed, and you might find this confusing when you're trying to read the music.

Erasing

Even though you can select and delete notes (as described earlier), the Staff view includes an Erase tool for added convenience. To use it, just select the Erase tool and then click on any notes in the Staff pane that you want to delete. You can also click and drag the Erase tool over a number of notes to erase them all at once. The Erase tool is represented by the button on the toolbar with the picture of an eraser on it, located right next to the Draw tool.

Scrub and Step Play

When you're editing the data in a track, the procedure usually involves making your edits and then playing back the project to hear how the changes sound. But playing back very small sections can be a bit difficult, especially when you're working with a fast tempo. To remedy this situation, you can use the Scrub tool and the Step Play feature in the Staff view.

Scrub

Using the Scrub tool, you can drag over the notes in the Staff view to hear what they sound like. To use it, simply select the Scrub tool by clicking on its button in the first toolbar. (The Scrub tool is the one with the small yellow speaker on it, located right next to the Erase tool.) Then click and drag over the notes in the Staff pane. Dragging left to right plays the data forward (what would normally happen during playback), and dragging right to left enables you to hear the data played in reverse. This feature can be useful for testing very short (one or two measure) sections.

Step Play

The Step Play feature enables you to step through (play) the notes in the Staff view note by note. To use it, follow these steps:

1. Set the Now time to the point in the music where you want to begin stepping through the notes. You can do so by simply clicking in the Time Ruler.

2. To step forward through the notes, click on the Play Next button on the first toolbar (the third-to-last button, going from left to right). You can also press Ctrl plus the right arrow key on your computer keyboard.

USE LOOPING FOR EDITING

Instead of using the Scrub tool or the Step Play feature, you might want to try another useful technique for hearing what your changes sound like. Did you know that you can edit the data in your project as it's being played back? Of course, it's a bit difficult to edit anything while SONAR is scrolling the display as the project plays. What I like to do is work on a small section of a project. I set up a section of the project to loop over and over, and as SONAR is playing the data, I make any changes I think might be needed. Because the data is being played back while I edit, I can instantly hear what the changes sound like. Using this approach is much easier than going back and forth, making changes and manually starting and stopping playback. I described looping in Chapter 6.

3. To step backward through the notes, click on the Play Previous button on the first toolbar (the fourth-to-last button, going from left to right). You can also press Ctrl plus the left arrow key on your computer keyboard.

SONAR will move the Now time cursor one set of notes at a time either to the right or left and play the notes on which it lands.

Dealing with Symbols and Lyrics

In addition to notes, SONAR lets you add other markings to your notated music, including chord symbols, guitar chord grids, expression marks, and pedal marks. These markings, however, are ornamental in nature; they have nothing to do with the data in your MIDI tracks. They also do not affect your music in any way (although there is one exception, which I'll explain later).

Essentially, SONAR provides these features so you can create sheet music with a more professional look, but you have to enter the marks manually. The procedures are basically the same as when you're working with notes. You use the Draw tool to add the markings, and you can select, copy, cut, paste, delete, and move them. To give you an idea of how to utilize the markings, I'll go through them one at a time.

Chord Symbols and Grids

Most sheet music sold to the public includes chord symbols with simple chord names or with both names and guitar grids. SONAR gives you the flexibility to enter one or both.

Adding and Editing

To add a chord symbol to your music, follow these steps:

1. Select the Draw tool.

2. Select the Chord tool by clicking on the Chord button in the second toolbar. (The Chord button has the letter *C* on it.)

3. Position your mouse pointer above the staff to which you want to add the symbol.

CHORD SYMBOL POSITIONING

You can add chord symbols only in certain positions in your music. If a track is displayed as a single staff, you can place symbols above that staff. If a track is shown using a pair of staves (treble and bass clefs), you can place symbols above the top (treble clef) staff only.

Also, chord symbols in music are usually lined up with the notes in the staff. SONAR allows you to place chord symbols in the same horizontal location above a note along the staff only (although there is an exception, which I'll explain later). As you move your mouse pointer along the top of the staff, the pointer changes to look like a pencil when you find a "legal" position to place a chord symbol.

4. Click to place the symbol above the staff. SONAR will add a copy of the most recently added chord (the default is C).

5. To change the name of the chord symbol, right-click on it to open the Chord Properties dialog box (see Figure 13.7).

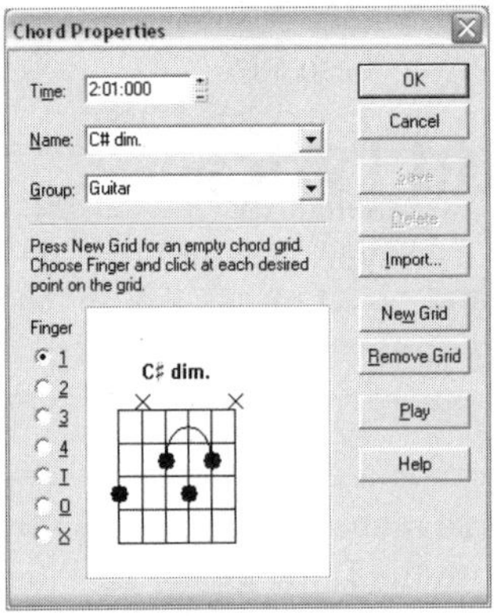

Figure 13.7
You can change the name (and other assets) of a chord symbol by using the Chord Properties dialog box.

6. Select the types of chords from which you want to choose by selecting a group from the Group drop-down list. SONAR includes only a single group of chords, called Guitar. You can, however, create your own groups and chord symbols, which I'll talk about shortly.

7. For the Name parameter, select a new name from the drop-down list. You'll notice that multiple chords in the list have the same name. They're named the same because some chords have guitar chord grids associated with them and some don't. If a chord includes a grid, the grid is shown in the Grid section of the dialog box. You'll also find multiple chords with grids that have the same name. This is to accommodate the different fingerings that you can use to play each chord on a guitar.

QUICK CHORD SELECTION
The list of chords is very long, and sometimes it can be tedious to scroll through it all just to find the chord you want. For a quicker way to navigate through the list, type the name of the chord you want to find in the Name field. Then click on the up or down arrow key (depending on which way you want to move through the list) on your computer keyboard.

8. Earlier I mentioned that SONAR allows you to place chords only at certain horizontal locations along the top of a staff. Although this is true when you are initially adding a chord, you can change the position of the chord by changing its start time. Just enter a new time (in measures, beats, and ticks) in the Time field of the Chord Properties dialog box. This way, you can place chord symbols anywhere along the top of a staff—they don't have to line up with the notes.

9. Click on OK.

SONAR will change the name and position of the chord symbol and add a grid to it according to the new properties you specified.

The Chord Library

SONAR includes a large number of predefined chord symbols, which it stores as a Chord Library in a file named CHORDS.LIW. (This file is located on your hard drive in the folder named C:\Program Files\Cakewalk\SONAR 3.) You can edit these chords or add your own by using the Chord Properties dialog box.

To add a chord into a new or existing group, follow these steps:

1. Right-click on a chord symbol to open the Chord Properties dialog box.

2. To add a chord to an existing group, select the group from the Group drop-down list. To add a chord to a new group, type the name of the new group in the Group field.

3. Type the name of the new chord in the Name field.

4. To add a grid to the new chord, click on the New Grid button. An empty grid will be displayed in the Grid area (see Figure 13.8).

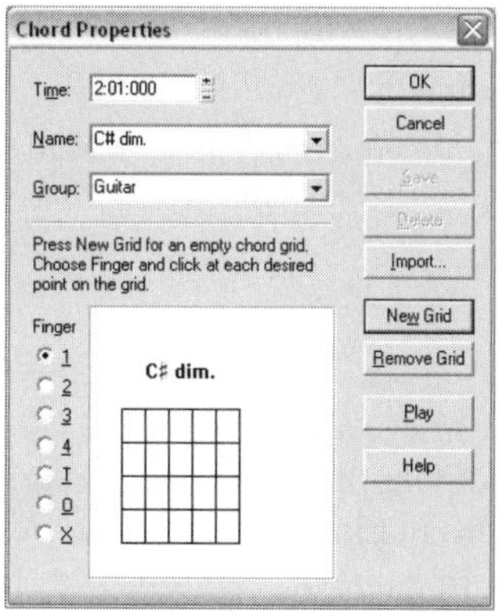

Figure 13.8
You can add a grid to a chord symbol by clicking on the New Grid button.

5. To place a dot on the grid, first choose a finger number from the Finger options, and then click on the appropriate string and fret location on the grid. To assign an open string, select O for the finger number. To assign a muted string, select X for the finger number.

6. To insert a fret designation for the grid, click just to the right of the grid in the Grid section to open the Chord Fret Number dialog box. Then type a fret number and click on OK.

7. To hear what the chord sounds like, click on the Play button.

8. When you're satisfied with the new chord, click on the Save button to save it to the Chord Library.

9. Click on OK.

To edit a chord or group in the Chord Library, follow these steps:

1. Right-click on a chord symbol to open the Chord Properties dialog box.

2. To delete a group, select it from the Group drop-down list and click on the Delete button.

3. To edit a chord in an existing group, select the group from the Group drop-down list.

4. To delete a chord, select the chord from the Name drop-down list and click on the Delete button.

5. To edit a chord, select the chord from the Name drop-down list and then type a new name.

6. If the chord has an accompanying chord grid, you can either delete it or edit it. To delete it, click on the Remove Grid button.

7. To edit the grid, change the finger assignment for a dot by clicking on the dot repeatedly to cycle through the finger options.

8. To hear what the chord sounds like, click on the Play button.

9. When you're satisfied with the edited chord, click on the Save button to save it to the Chord Library.

10. Click on OK.

IMPORT CHORD DEFINITIONS

You can also import new chord definitions into the Chord Library by clicking on the Import button and selecting an .LIW file.

Expression Marks

Expression marks in music designate any kind of text that provides instructions on how the music should be played during different passages. These marks include tempo designations (such as *allegro*), musical characteristics (such as *play with feeling*), and dynamics instructions (such as *cresc.*, *ppp*, or *fff*). Essentially, expression marks are just simple text added to the sheet music.

Adding an Expression Mark

To add an expression mark to your music, follow these steps:

1. Select the Draw tool.

2. Select the Expression tool by clicking on the Expression button in the second toolbar. (The Expression tool has a letter *f* on it.)

3. Position your mouse pointer below the staff to which you want to add the mark.

EXPRESSION MARKS POSITIONING

As with chord symbols, you can place expression marks only at certain positions in your music. If a track is displayed as a single staff, you can place a mark below that staff. If a track is shown using a pair of staves (treble and bass clefs), you can place marks below the top (treble clef) staff only.

Also, as with chord symbols, marks are initially lined up with the notes in the staff (although you can change the way they're lined up by editing the marks and altering their start times). As you move your mouse pointer below the staff, the pointer will change to look like a pencil when you find a "legal" position to place a mark.

4. Click to place the mark below the staff. SONAR will open an insertion box.

5. Type the text you want to use for the mark (see Figure 13.9).

Figure 13.9
Expression marks are just simple text that you type into the Staff pane.

DANGLING HYPHENS

To leave a dangling hyphen at the end of an expression mark, type a space and a single hyphen after the text in the insertion box. Dangling hyphens are often used with expression marks in sheet music to show that the expression should be continued over a range of notes or measures until the next expression mark appears.

6. Press the Enter key on your computer keyboard.

USE TAB TO MOVE

You can also press the Tab or Shift+Tab keys on your computer keyboard to move to the next or previous expression mark location, respectively.

SONAR will add the expression mark to your music.

Editing an Expression Mark

To edit an expression mark, follow these steps:

1. Right-click on the expression mark to open the Expression Text Properties dialog box (see Figure 13.10).

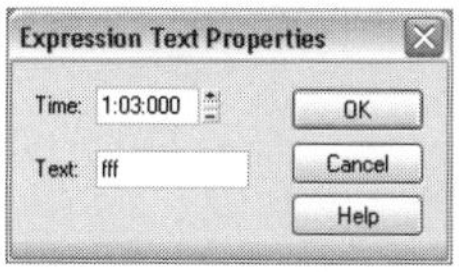

Figure 13.10
Using the Expression Text Properties dialog box, you can edit expression marks.

2. To change the position of the expression mark, enter a new start time (in measures, beats, and ticks) in the Time field.

3. To change the text of the expression mark, enter the new text in the Text field.

4. Click on OK.

The expression mark will be displayed in the new position and will show the new text according to your settings.

EDIT WITH THE DRAW TOOL

You can also edit the text of an expression mark by clicking on it with the Draw tool to reopen the insertion box.

Hairpin Symbols

In addition to showing crescendos and decrescendos as text via expression marks, you can show them graphically via hairpin symbols. These symbols look like large greater than and less than signs (see Figure 13.11).

Figure 13.11

You can designate crescendos and decrescendos via hairpin symbols.

Adding a Hairpin Symbol

To add a hairpin symbol to your music, follow these steps:

1. Select the Draw tool.

2. Select the Hairpin tool by clicking on the Hairpin button on the second toolbar. (The Hairpin button has a less than sign on it.)

3. Position your mouse pointer below the staff to which you want to add the symbol.

SYMBOL PLACEMENT

As with expression marks, if a track is displayed as a single staff, you can place the symbol below that staff. If a track is shown using a pair of staves (treble and bass clefs), you can place the symbol below the top (treble clef) staff only.

4. Click to place the symbol below the staff.

SONAR will add a copy of the most recently added hairpin symbol. To change the symbol, you can edit it by using the Hairpin Properties dialog box.

Editing a Hairpin Symbol

To edit a hairpin symbol, follow these steps:

1. Right-click on the hairpin symbol to open the Hairpin Properties dialog box (see Figure 13.12).

Figure 13.12
Using the Hairpin
Properties dialog box,
you can edit hairpin
symbols.

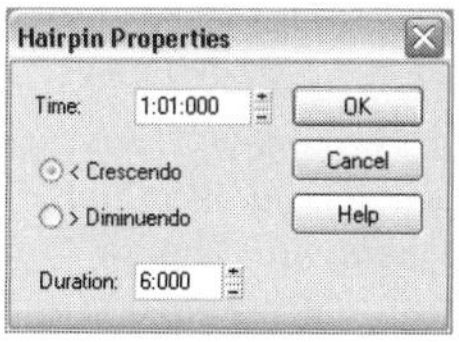

2. To change the position of the hairpin symbol, enter a new start time (in measures, beats, and ticks) in the Time field.

> **DRAG TO A NEW POSITION**
> You can also change the position of the hairpin symbol by dragging it.

3. To change the type of the hairpin symbol, choose either the Crescendo option or the Diminuendo (same as decrescendo) option.

4. To change the length of the hairpin symbol, enter a new value (in beats and ticks) in the Duration field.

5. Click on OK.

The hairpin symbol will be displayed in the new position with the new type and duration according to your settings.

Pedal Marks

Earlier, I mentioned that there was one exception to the rule that markings do not affect the data in your MIDI tracks; that exception is pedal marks. On a sheet of music, pedal marks usually designate when the performer is supposed to press and release the sustain pedal on a piano. In SONAR, they mean essentially the same thing, but they refer to the sustain pedal attached to your MIDI keyboard (if it has one). More precisely, pedal marks in the Staff view designate MIDI controller number 64 (pedal-sustain) messages in your MIDI tracks (which you can also edit in the Controller pane of the Piano Roll view). So whenever you add or edit pedal marks in the Staff view, you are also editing the MIDI controller number 64 messages in that track.

Adding a Pedal Mark

To add a pedal mark to your music, follow these steps:

1. Select the Draw tool.

2. Select the Pedal tool by clicking on the Pedal button in the second toolbar. (The Pedal button has a letter *P* on it.)

3. Position your mouse pointer below the staff to which you want to add the mark.

PEDAL SYMBOL PLACEMENT

Similar to expression marks, if a track is displayed as a single staff, you can place the symbol below that staff. If, however, a track is shown using a pair of staves (treble and bass clefs), you can place the symbol below the bottom (bass clef) staff only.

4.   Click to place the mark below the staff.

SONAR will add a pair of pedal marks (pedal down, which looks like an asterisk, and pedal up, which looks like a *P*) to your music. To edit the marks, you can use the Pedal Properties dialog box.

Editing a Pedal Mark

To edit a pedal mark, follow these steps:

1.   Right-click on the pedal mark (either a pedal down mark or a pedal up mark; you can't edit them both at once) to open the Pedal Properties dialog box (see Figure 13.13).

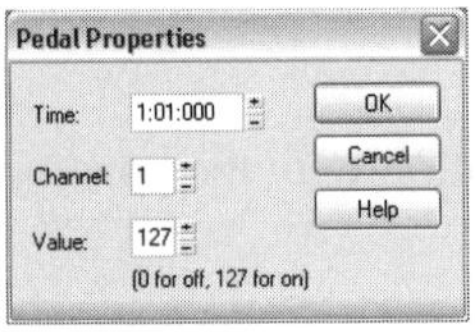

Figure 13.13
You can use the Pedal Properties dialog box to edit pedal marks.

2.   To change the position of the pedal mark, enter a new start time (in measures, beats, and ticks) in the Time field.

DRAG TO A NEW POSITION

You can also change the position of the pedal mark by dragging it.

3.   To change the MIDI channel for the pedal mark, type a new channel number in the Channel field.

4.   To change the type of pedal mark, enter a new number in the Value field. Enter 0 to make it a pedal up mark; enter 127 to make it a pedal down mark. Entering any numbers between that range produces no effect.

5.   Click on OK.

The pedal mark will be displayed in the new position with the new type and MIDI channel according to your settings.

Lyrics

Just like any good notation software, SONAR enables you to add lyrics to your sheet music. Lyrics (like expression marks) are represented by simple text displayed below a staff. You can add lyrics to a track by using the Lyrics tool or the Lyrics view.

The Lyrics Tool

Follow these steps to add lyrics to your music using the Lyrics tool:

1. In the Staff view, select the Draw tool.

2. Select the Lyric tool by clicking on the Lyric button in the second toolbar. (The Lyric button has a letter *L* on it.)

3. Position your mouse pointer below the staff, underneath the first note to which you want to add lyrics.

LYRIC PLACEMENT

If a track is displayed as a single staff, you can place the lyrics below that staff. If a track is shown using a pair of staves (treble and bass clefs), you can place marks below the top (treble clef) staff only.

Also, each word or syllable in the lyrics must be aligned with a note. SONAR automatically aligns the lyrics to the notes in the staff.

4. Click to place the lyric below the staff. SONAR will open an insertion box, just like when you add expression marks.

5. Type a word or syllable to be aligned with the current note.

6. To move forward and add a lyric to the next note, enter a space, type a hyphen, or press the Tab key on your computer keyboard. The insertion box will move to the next note and wait for you to enter text.

7. To skip over a note, don't type any text in the insertion box. Enter a space or type a hyphen.

8. To move back to the previous note, press the Shift+Tab keys on your computer keyboard.

9. When you're finished entering lyrics, press the Enter key on your computer keyboard.

To edit lyrics using the Lyric tool, follow these steps:

1. Select the Draw tool.

2. Select the Lyric tool.

3. Click on the word you want to change.

4. Edit the word.

5. Press the Enter key on your computer keyboard.

The Lyrics View

After you've entered some lyrics in the Staff view, you can display them in a separate window called the Lyrics view. This view is useful for providing a cue for performers who are recording vocal tracks because you can make the lyrics appear in any size font you like (see Figure 13.14).

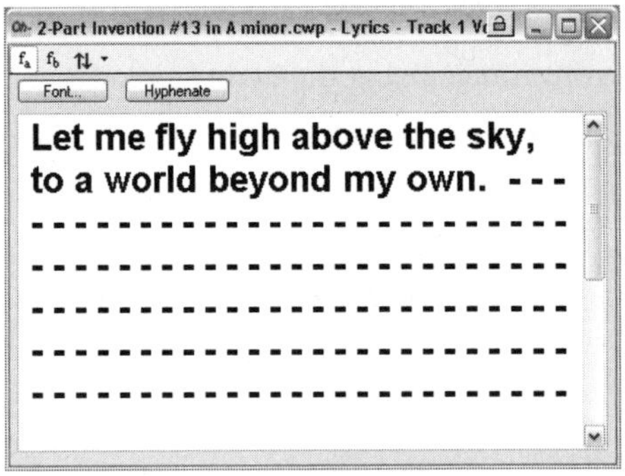

Figure 13.14
The Lyrics view is useful as a cue for vocal performers.

To open the Lyrics view, select a track in the Track view, and then choose View > Lyric. To change the size of the text, click on the fa or fb buttons, which provide two different preset font sizes. You can use more specific font settings by clicking on the Font button to open the Font dialog box (which I described earlier). In this dialog box, you can change the font, style, and size of the text. The Lyrics view also has a Pick Tracks button that works just as in the other views.

Of course, you can also add and edit lyrics in the Lyrics view, but I don't recommend it. The process is not very intuitive because you can't see the notes to which the words and syllables are being aligned. If you want to use the Lyrics view for adding and editing, you can do so just as you would enter and edit text in Windows Notepad. Each word you type is aligned automatically to a note in the current track, and you can split words into syllables by clicking on the Hyphenate button to enter hyphens manually or automatically. That's all there is to it.

COPY AND PASTE LYRICS

In addition to typing and editing lyrics in the Lyrics view, you can also select, cut, copy, paste, and delete text. Again, this procedure works just like in Windows Notepad. What's nice about the Lyrics view is that if you already have some text saved in a text file, you can copy and paste it into this view to quickly add lyrics to a track. When you look at the lyrics in the Staff view, the words are aligned automatically to the notes in the staff. And if you want all or some of the words to be hyphenated automatically, just select all or some of the text in the Lyrics view and then click on the Hyphenate button. It's very quick and simple.

The Fretboard and Tablature

For all the guitar players out there, SONAR provides a couple of nice notation-related features just for you. The first one I'll describe is the Fretboard pane.

The Fretboard Pane

The Fretboard pane, located at the bottom of the Staff view, is both a visual aid and an editing tool. During playback, the Fretboard displays the notes at the current Now time in a selected track as they would be played on a six-string guitar using standard tuning. This makes the Fretboard a cool learning tool when you're trying to learn to play a new piece of music. It also displays notes when you use the Scrub tool or Step Play feature, which makes it even easier to pick out the fingerings. The color of the notes matches the color of the clip (from the Track view) in which they are stored.

Fretboard Properties

You can configure certain aspects of the Fretboard, such as its background style and the orientation of the strings. You can also turn it on or off. To toggle the Fretboard on and off, click on the Fret View button located in the first toolbar. It's the second-to-last button, going from left to right. You can also press V on your computer keyboard.

To change the background style, right-click on the Fretboard and choose one of the following from the drop-down list: Rosewood Hi, Rosewood Lo, Ebony Hi, Ebony Lo, Maple Hi, or Maple Lo. The Hi and Lo designations deal with the screen resolution you are using on your computer monitor. If you're using a high screen resolution, use one of the styles marked Hi. If you're using a low screen resolution, use one of the styles marked Lo. To be honest, the resolution you choose really doesn't make that much of a difference.

To change the orientation of the strings, right-click on the Fretboard and select Mirror Fretboard from the drop-down menu to invert the Fretboard so that the highest-sounding string appears at the bottom. To change it back, just select Mirror Fretboard again.

Adding Notes

In addition to using the Fretboard to display notes, you can add new notes to a track (staff) by clicking on the Fretboard. Just follow these steps:

1. Set the Now time so that the cursor rests at the point in the staff where you want to add the note(s). You can do so quickly by clicking in the Time Ruler.
2. Select the Draw tool.
3. Select a note duration by clicking on one of the appropriate buttons in the second toolbar.
4. Click on the guitar strings in the Fretboard to enter notes on the staff. You can enter up to six notes (one per string).
5. Make the Now time cursor move forward by the same amount as the current note duration setting by pressing the Shift and right arrow keys on your computer keyboard.
6. Repeat steps 3 through 5 to continue adding more notes.

Editing Notes

You can also edit existing notes in a track (staff) by using the Fretboard. You can change only the pitch of the notes, though. To do so, just follow these steps:

1. Set the Now time so the cursor rests on top of the note(s) that you want to edit. You can do so quickly by clicking in the Time Ruler. You can also use the Step Play feature.

2. Select the Draw tool.

3. Drag the notes along the strings to a new fret (thus changing the pitch).

After you release the mouse button, SONAR will change the pitch of the notes in the staff.

Tablature

As a guitar or bass player, you might be more comfortable reading and working with tablature than standard notation. If that's the case, you're in luck because SONAR includes a number of features that enable you to display and edit your music as tablature.

Displaying Tablature

To display tablature for a track (staff), follow these steps:

1. Right-click in the Staff pane and select Layout from the drop-down menu to open the Staff View Layout dialog box.

2. Select from the list the name of the track for which you want to display tablature.

3. In the Tablature section, activate the Display Tablature option.

4. Select a tablature style from the Preset drop-down list.

5. Click on OK.

SONAR will display a tablature staff below the current staff, complete with tablature for each note in the track (see Figure 13.15).

Figure 13.15

Adding tablature to a track in the Staff view is very easy with SONAR.

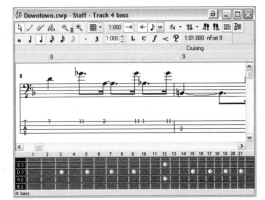

THE QUICKTAB FEATURE

SONAR also offers a feature called QuickTab that lets you quickly generate tablature for a track, but it works only when you're displaying a single track in the Staff view. I recommend you simply use the previously mentioned method.

Defining a Tablature Style

When you're setting up a track to display tablature, you might not find a preset style that fits your needs. If that's the case, you can always create your own tablature style by following these steps:

1. Right-click in the Staff pane and select Layout from the drop-down menu to open the Staff View Layout dialog box.

2. Select from the list the name of the track for which you want to display tablature.

3. In the Tablature section, activate the Display Tablature option.

4. Click on the Define button to open the Tablature Settings dialog box (see Figure 13.16).

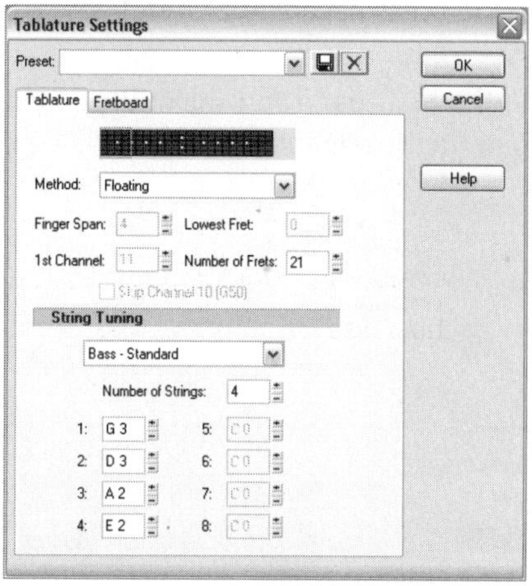

Figure 13.16
You can create your own tablature styles by using the Tablature Settings dialog box.

5. Under the Tablature tab, set the Method parameter. This parameter determines how the tablature will be displayed. If you select Floating, the notes can be shown anywhere on the Fretboard. If you select Fixed, notes are limited to a specific area on the neck of the guitar. To determine the size and position of that area, you must set the Finger Span and Lowest Fret parameters. The Finger Span parameter sets the size of the area in a number of frets. The Lowest Fret parameter sets the position of the area on the neck of the guitar by specifying the first fret upon which the area is based. The last tablature method (MIDI Channel) is useful if you record your guitar parts using a MIDI guitar and you use Mono mode so that each string is recorded using its own MIDI channel. If this is your situation, then select the MIDI Channel method and set the 1st Channel parameter to the lowest number channel used by your MIDI guitar.

6. In the Number of Frets field, enter the number of frets on which the tablature should be based.

7. In the String Tuning section, choose an instrument/tuning upon which to base the tablature.

8. Set the Number of Strings parameter to the number of strings the instrument provides.

9. The pitch of each string for the instrument appears in the parameters below the Number of Strings field. You can either leave them as is, or you can customize the pitches to your liking.

10. Save your settings as a preset.

11. Click on OK to close the Tablature Settings dialog box.

Your new tablature style should appear in the Preset drop-down list in the Tablature section of the Staff View Layout dialog box.

Regenerating Tablature

You can use different tablature styles for different sections of the same tablature staff by following these steps:

1. In the Staff pane, select the notes or tablature numbers for which you want to use a different tablature style.

2. Right-click anywhere in the Staff pane and select Regenerate Tablature from the drop-down menu to open the Regenerate Tablature dialog box (see Figure 13.17).

Figure 13.17
You can define different tablature styles for selected notes by using the Regenerate Tablature feature.

3. Set the Method, Finger Span, Lowest Fret, and 1st Channel parameters, if applicable. These parameters work the same way as described previously.

4. Click on OK.

SONAR will change the tablature style of the selected notes based on your parameter settings.

Adding Notes via Tablature

In addition to displaying tablature, you can use a tablature staff to add notes to a track by following these steps:

1. Select the Draw tool.

2. Choose a note duration by clicking on the appropriate note duration button in the second toolbar.

3. Move the mouse pointer over the tablature staff. It will change its shape to a crosshair.

4. Position the crosshair within any measure and over a line in the tablature staff.

5. Click and hold the left mouse button, and then drag your mouse pointer up and down to select a fret number.

6. Release the mouse button to enter the note.

Editing Notes via Tablature

You can also edit notes via a tablature staff. To do so, just follow these steps:

1. Select the Draw tool.

2. To change the fret number of a note, right-click on it and select a new number from the drop-down menu.

3. To move a note to a different string (line) on the tablature staff, click and drag the note while pressing the Alt key on your computer keyboard. Drag the note up or down to move it. If the note is not supposed to play on a certain string, it will not be allowed to move there.

Exporting Tablature to a Text File

One last tablature feature that you might find useful is being able to save the tablature as a text file either for printing or distribution over the Internet. By saving the tablature this way, you can share it with other guitarists—even if they don't own SONAR. You use this feature as follows:

1. Select a MIDI track in the Track view.

2. In the Staff view, right-click anywhere in the Staff pane and select Export to ASCII TAB. The Save As dialog box will open.

3. Type a name for the file.

4. Click on Save.

SONAR will save the data in the MIDI track as tablature in a text file.

QUANTIZE FOR ACCURACY

You might want to try quantizing the track before you save it as tablature. Doing so usually produces more accurate results.

Printing Your Music

After all is notated and done, you can print your music to paper if you have a printer connected to your computer. SONAR automatically sets up your music on separate pages, including the song title, composer, and other information, along with the notation. You can print your musical score by following these steps:

1. Choose File > Info to open the File Info window, and then fill out all the information you want to include on your sheet music. You can use the Title, Subtitle, Instructions, Author, and Copyright parameters. For more information about the File Info window, refer to Chapter 4.

2. With the Staff view open, choose File > Print Preview. SONAR will go into Print Preview mode (see Figure 13.18) and display your music on virtual pages, letting you see how it will look before you print it.

Figure 13.18

You can use Print Preview mode to see how your music will look on paper before you print it.

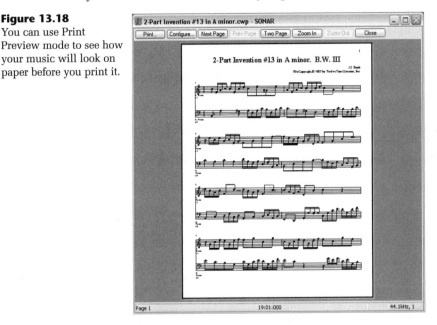

3. To zoom the display in or out, click on the Zoom In or Zoom Out button.

4. Depending on the length of your song, SONAR usually shows two pages at once on the screen. If you would rather view only one page at a time, click on the One Page button.

5. If your song takes up more than two pages, you can navigate through them by using the Next Page and Prev Page buttons.

6. Before you print your music, you need to select a size for your score. To do so, click on the Configure button to open the Staff View Print Configure dialog box.

7. From the single drop-down list, choose the size you want to use. SONAR provides nine different standard music-engraving sizes used by professional music publishers. Each size is used for a different purpose. Size 0 (Commercial or Public) usually is used for wire-bound manuscripts. Size 1 (Giant or English) usually is used for school band music books or instructional books. Sizes 2 and 3 (Regular, Common, or Ordinary) usually are used for printing classical music. Size 4 (Peter) usually is used for folios or organ music. Size 5 (Large Middle) usually is used for ensemble music. Size 6 (Small Middle) usually is used for condensed sheet music. Size 7 (Cadenza) usually is used for pocket music editions. And Size 8 (Pearl) usually is used for thematic advertisement.

8. Click on OK. The music will be redrawn using the new size.

9. Click on the Print button.

When the standard Windows Print dialog box opens, you can set up your printer and print your music.

COMPOSE WITH THE STAFF VIEW

Here's one final tip: If you like to compose your music from scratch using the Staff view, you can use one of the included templates listed in the New Project File dialog box when you create your new project. For example, if you want to compose for a string quartet, select the Classical String Quartet template.

The templates come with all the track parameters preset, but you might need to change a few of them to match your studio setup. After that, select all the tracks in the Track view and then choose View > Staff to open them in the Staff view. Everything will be set up with the proper clefs, staff names, and more; the only settings you might need to adjust are the meter and key. Other than that, you will have a blank slate ready and waiting to be filled with the music notation for your latest masterpiece.

14

Studio Control with StudioWare and Sysx

Most of today's modern appliances are computer-controlled. Need to cook a meal? Push a few buttons on the stove, and it automatically sets the right time and temperature for your recipe. Need to wash your clothes? Yada, yada, yada…. It's the same thing with modern recording-studio gear—almost everything is computer-controlled, and the gear supports MIDI, too. I'm not just talking about MIDI instruments (such as synthesizer keyboards), but audio processing equipment and mixing boards as well.

Why would these products include support for MIDI? Because, like MIDI instruments, they have internal parameters that you can change and store. Because these products provide support for MIDI, their parameters become accessible to other MIDI devices, such as your computer. This means it is now possible to control almost every piece of equipment in your studio via your computer, provided the equipment supports MIDI and you have the right software. Lucky for you, you don't need to buy any additional software because SONAR has some built-in features for controlling and storing the parameters for any outboard MIDI gear. All you have to do is connect your MIDI devices to your computer (just as you would any MIDI instrument), and they can "talk" to each other. This chapter will do the following:

▶ Show you how to work with System Exclusive data

▶ Teach you how to use the Sysx view

▶ Introduce StudioWare

▶ Explain how to take Snapshots with StudioWare

▶ Teach you to record control movements in StudioWare

System Exclusive

MIDI devices (other than MIDI instruments) usually don't provide standard musical functions, so their internal parameters are not compatible with standard MIDI messages, such as Note On messages. Instead, they have to communicate using special MIDI messages called *System Exclusive messages*. I talked a little about System Exclusive messages in Chapter 3. They give you access to any special functions that a manufacturer includes in a MIDI instrument or device.

Not only do you have access to these functions, but also by utilizing System Exclusive messages, you can send all the data from the MIDI instruments and devices in your studio to SONAR to be stored in your projects. Why is this capability important? Because you can set up all your equipment with specific settings for a project, store the data in the project, and then send the data back to the devices at the beginning of your next recording session. This means that the next time you open the project, you can have all the equipment in your studio set up automatically, and you won't have to touch a single knob. Cool, no?

The Sysx View

SONAR gives you access to System Exclusive data via the Sysx view (see Figure 14.1). Using the Sysx view, you can store up to 8,191 banks, each of which can contain any number of System Exclusive messages (limited only by the amount of memory in your computer system). For example, you could dedicate a different bank to store the data for each separate piece of equipment in your studio. You could also store different sets of patch data for a single MIDI instrument in separate banks. Then, at different times in your project, you could send specific patch data to change the sounds in the instrument for that part of the song. (You'll learn more about this topic later, in the "Sending System Exclusive Data" section.)

Figure 14.1
The Sysx view lets you store System Exclusive data within the current project.

Receiving System Exclusive Data

To store System Exclusive data in a bank in the Sysx view, you need to do a *data dump*. Essentially, the MIDI device from which you want to grab data dumps (or sends) it to your computer to be stored in one of the Sysx view banks.

THE RECORD SYSTEM EXCLUSIVE SETTING

Be sure to check SONAR's global MIDI options to see whether the Record System Exclusive Data setting is activated. To do so, choose Options > Global to open the Global Options dialog box, and then select the MIDI tab. In the Record section, click on System Exclusive to place a check mark next to it. If this setting isn't turned on, SONAR will block all incoming System Exclusive data.

To do a data dump, follow these steps:

1. Choose View > Sysx to open the Sysx view, and then click on a bank to highlight it for incoming System Exclusive data.

2. Click on the Receive Bank button (the one with the downward-pointing red arrow) or press C on your computer keyboard to open the Receive System Exclusive dialog box (see Figure 14.2).

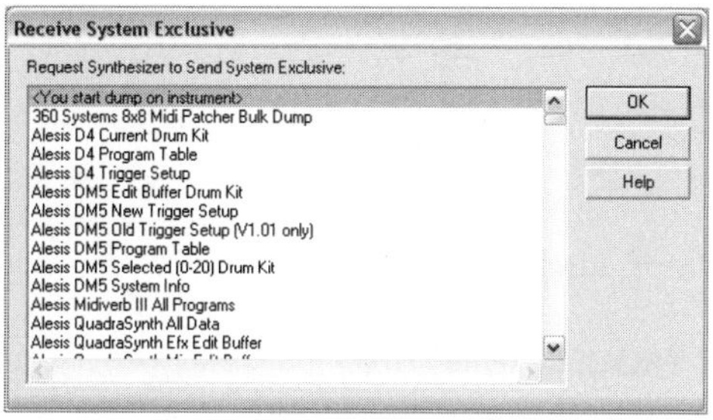

Figure 14.2
You use the Receive
System Exclusive dialog
box to request a data
dump from your MIDI
device.

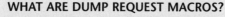

3. Choose a DRM (*Dump Request Macro*) from the list. If you don't see your MIDI device listed, select the very first option: <You start dump on instrument>. Click on OK. Then start the data dump using the control panel on your device. (See the device's user manual for more information on how to use the control panel.)

WHAT ARE DUMP REQUEST MACROS?

DRMs are special System Exclusive messages. Some MIDI devices support them and some don't. If you have a MIDI device that supports DRMs, SONAR can send a DRM to the device, asking it to send back its parameter data. If you have a MIDI device that doesn't support DRMs, you have to initiate the data dump manually from the control panel on the device.

ADD NEW DUMP REQUEST MACROS

If your MIDI device isn't listed in the Receive System Exclusive dialog box, it doesn't necessarily mean the device doesn't support DRMs. You need to look in the device's user manual to see whether it has DRMs available. If it does, you can set them up to be used within SONAR. To do so, open the file C:\Program Files\Cakewalk\SONAR 3\cakewalk.ini using Windows Notepad. Inside that file, you'll find instructions for how to add new DRMs to the list in the Receive System Exclusive dialog box.

4. If you see your device listed, select the appropriate DRM and click on OK. The DRM might ask you for additional information. For instance, if the DRM requests that the device send the data for a single sound patch, you need to input the patch number you want it to send. This process is pretty straightforward; you can simply follow the prompts.

5. Whichever method you use to initiate the data dump, SONAR ultimately displays the Sysx Receive dialog box when it's ready to receive the data (see Figure 14.3). The dialog box shows the number of bytes of data being received as the dump takes place.

CHAPTER 14

Figure 14.3
The Sysx Receive dialog box displays a count of the System Exclusive data.

6.   When the count stops, click on Done.

TRANSFER TROUBLESHOOTING

If the number of bytes stays at zero for more than a few seconds, most likely something is wrong. Your MIDI device might not be hooked up properly, or you could have given the wrong answers for the additional DRM questions. Those answers differ depending on the MIDI device, so you'll need to consult its user manual. In any event, if you have this problem, click on Cancel and then check your connections and try the procedure again.

After the dump is complete, the Sysx view will show the bank you selected with a new name and length (in bytes).

Changing the Name of a Bank

If you want to change the name of a bank, follow these steps:

1.   Select the bank.

2.   Click on the Name button (the one with the lowercase *abc* on it) or press N on your computer keyboard to open the Sysx Bank Name dialog box (see Figure 14.4).

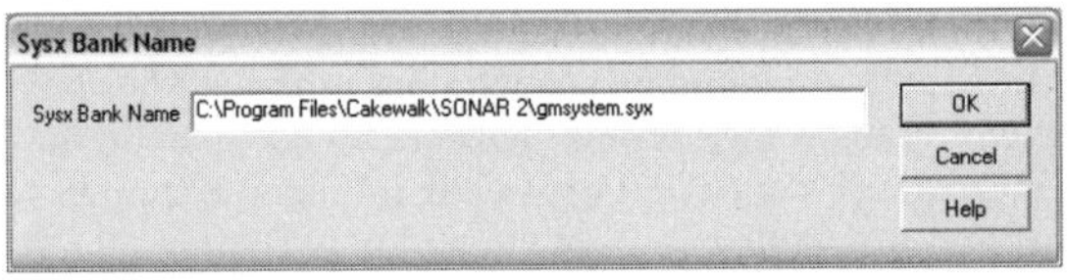

Figure 14.4
In the Sysx Bank Name dialog box, you can change the name of a bank.

3.   Type a new name in the Sysx Bank Name field.

4.   Click on OK.

RECORD SYSTEM EXCLUSIVE DATA

You can also record System Exclusive data directly to a track, just as you would any other MIDI data. To do so, just set up your track parameters, start SONAR recording, and then manually initiate a data dump from your MIDI device. You should be aware of some limitations, though. When you're recording directly to a track, SONAR stores the data in Sysx Data Events instead of banks. Each Sysx Data Event can hold a single System Exclusive message of only 255 bytes in length. This means that if your MIDI device sends a message longer than 255 bytes, the message will be cut off and it won't work when you try to send back the data. Plus, you won't get any warning that this has happened—it just won't work. Essentially, you're better off using the Sysx view and banks to handle System Exclusive data. It's much easier, more efficient, and you can still send data back to a device during playback. (I'll talk more about that in the next section.)

Sending System Exclusive Data

After you set up your banks in a project, you can send the data back to your MIDI devices. Before you do, though, you should be sure that each bank being sent is first set to the appropriate MIDI output. Just as you can set each track in the Track view to send data to a particular MIDI output on your MIDI interface, you can set each bank in the Sysx view to a specific output as well. To do so, follow these steps:

1. Select the bank.

2. Click on the Output button (the one with the picture of a MIDI connection on it) or press P on your computer keyboard to open the Sysx Bank Output dialog box (see Figure 14.5).

Figure 14.5
In the Sysx Bank Output dialog box, you can change the MIDI output assigned to a bank.

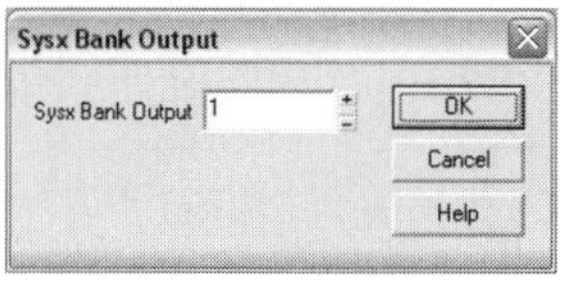

3. Type a new output number. Remember that the data in this bank will be sent only to this MIDI output, so be sure the number is the same as the output number to which your device is connected.

4. Click on OK.

After you assign the right output numbers to each of your banks, you can easily transmit the data to the appropriate MIDI devices in one of three ways.

Sending Data Manually

To send the data in a bank manually, just select the bank and click on the Send Bank button (the one with the single black upward-pointing arrow on it) or press S on your computer keyboard. That's all there is to it—no muss, no fuss. You also can send all the data in every bank at once. You don't need to make any selections; just click on the Send All Banks button (the one with three upward-pointing arrows on it) or press L on your computer keyboard.

Sending Data Automatically

Each bank in the Sysx view has an option called Auto. If you activate this option for a bank, that bank will be sent automatically every time you open the project. For example, if you store all the parameter data from all your MIDI devices in a number of banks using the Sysx view and you set the Auto option on each of those banks, the next time you open your project, SONAR will send the System Exclusive data to your MIDI devices automatically. Your studio will then be ready to go with all the correct settings for your project, without your having to do anything manually. To set the Auto option for a bank, just select the bank and click on the Auto Send Bank button (the one with the black upward-pointing arrow and yellow star on it) or press A on your computer keyboard.

Sending Data during Playback

Although using the Auto option is a very convenient way to send System Exclusive data, sometimes you might want to send a bank at a specific time during the playback of your project. For this purpose, SONAR provides a special Sysx Bank Event that you can place in any MIDI track in your project. Whenever SONAR encounters a Sysx Bank Event, it looks up the event's associated bank number in the Sysx view and then sends that bank.

You have to add a Sysx Bank Event to a MIDI track manually by using the Event view. Here's how:

1. Select a MIDI track in your project and choose View > Event List to open the Event List view for that track (see Figure 14.6).

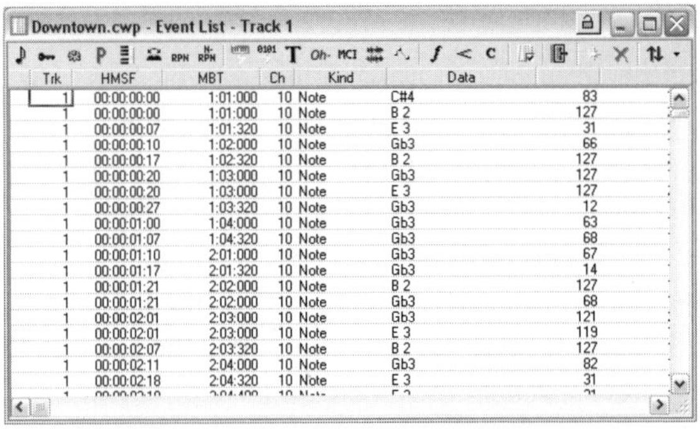

Figure 14.6

Using the Event List view, you can add Sysx Bank Events to your MIDI tracks.

2. Move the Now time cursor to the point within the list where you want to insert the new Sysx Bank Event.

3. Click on the Insert Event button (the one with the yellow star on it) or press Insert on your computer keyboard to insert a new event. Initially, the event will take on the characteristics of the event at which the Now time cursor was placed.

4. To change the event to a Sysx Bank Event, move the Now time cursor over to the Kind column and press the Enter key on your computer keyboard to open the Kind of Event dialog box (see Figure 14.7).

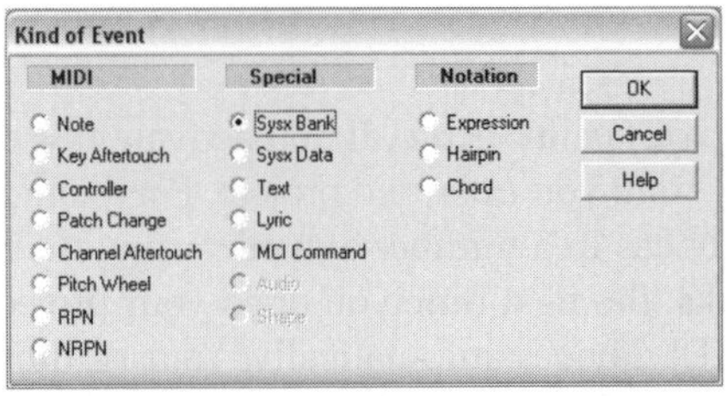

Figure 14.7

In the Kind of Event dialog box, you can change the type of the current event.

5. Select the Sysx Bank option in the Special section and click on OK.

6. Move the Now time cursor over to the Data column and press the Enter key on your computer keyboard. The number in the Data column will be highlighted. Here, you enter the number of the bank you want to send.

7. Type a bank number and press the Enter key on your computer keyboard.

Now, when SONAR encounters that Sysx Bank Event during playback, it will send the appropriate System Exclusive data to your MIDI device.

TOO MUCH INFORMATION

MIDI is meant to transmit only one piece of data at a time. Of course, it transmits the data so fast that it sounds as if all the data in the tracks is playing simultaneously. But MIDI does have its limits, and if you try to transmit huge amounts of data in a short amount of time, playback will be interrupted. This happens quite often with System Exclusive data, so if you're going to send banks of data during playback, try to send only one bank at a time throughout your project and also try to keep each bank short. You'll have to do a little experimenting, but if you keep each bank between 100 and 255 bytes, you shouldn't have any problems.

Editing Bank Data

The Sysx view provides a feature that allows you to edit the data in a bank. To edit this data, select a bank and click on the Edit Data button (the one with a hand pointing to a piece of paper on it) or press E on your computer keyboard. Clicking on this button opens the Edit System Exclusive Bytes dialog box (see Figure 14.8).

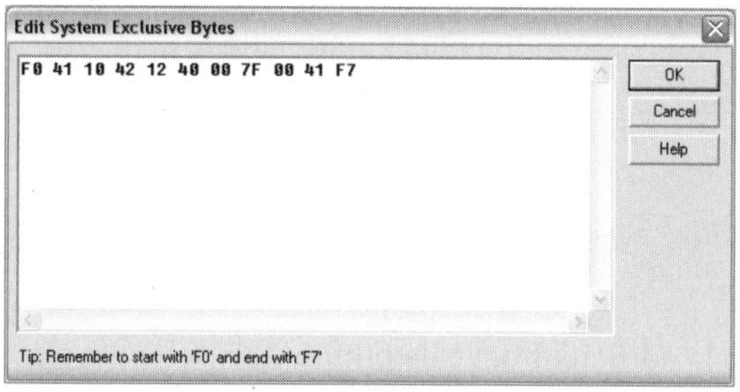

Figure 14.8
In the Edit System Exclusive Bytes dialog box, you can edit the data in a bank.

Edit System Exclusive Bytes	
F0 41 10 42 12 40 00 7F 00 41 F7	OK Cancel Help

Tip: Remember to start with 'F0' and end with 'F7'

In the dialog box, you'll see a list of numbers. Each number represents one byte of System Exclusive data in hexadecimal format. You can change the numbers just as you would text in a word processor. If the bank contains more than one System Exclusive message, the beginning of each message is designated by the number F0 and the end of each message is designated by the number F7. This way, System Exclusive data stays compatible with standard data in the MIDI language.

Whenever a MIDI device sees the number F0, it automatically knows that this number designates the beginning of a System Exclusive message. But that's as far as it goes in terms of identifying the data. All the bytes in a System Exclusive message that fall between the F0 and F7 are different depending on which MIDI device they are associated with, so there's really not much else I can explain about this feature. If you want to learn more about the System Exclusive messages your MIDI device supports, consult the user manual for the device.

If you want to delete a bank in the Sysx view, just select the bank and click on the Clear Bank button (the one with the big red X on it) or press D on your computer keyboard. SONAR will ask whether you really want to delete. Be careful, because you cannot undo this procedure. When a bank is deleted, you cannot get it back without doing a data dump all over again.

Sharing with Friends

Even though all the data in the banks of the Sysx view is stored along with the data in your current project, you also can load and save banks individually in a special System Exclusive data file format. This file format is the same one used by the public-domain System Exclusive data dump software utility called MIDIEX. MIDIEX is such a popular program that its file format has become a standard for storing System Exclusive data on disk. What's great about the file format is that SONAR and many other sequencers support it, so you can easily share your System Exclusive data with your friends. Of course, being able to share won't matter much if you don't own the same MIDI devices, but if you do, you can easily share sound patch data for your MIDI instruments and so on.

Saving

To save the data in a bank, follow these steps:

1. Select the bank.
2. Click on the Save Bank to File button (the one with the floppy disk on it) or press V on your computer keyboard to open the Save As dialog box.
3. Type a name for the file. The file should have an .SYX extension; SONAR should append this extension to the name automatically.
4. Click on Save.

Loading

To load data into a bank, follow these steps:

1. Select a bank.
2. Click on the Load Bank from File button (the one with the yellow folder on it) or press O on your computer keyboard.
3. If the bank you selected already has some data in it, SONAR will ask whether you want to append the data from the file to the existing data. Click on Yes to append the data, or click on No to replace the data. SONAR will display the Open dialog box.
4. Select an .SYX file to load and click on Open.

The data from the file will be loaded into the bank you selected, and the bank will be named after the file. You can change the name of the bank, as you learned earlier.

COPY A BANK

There's no easy method for copying a bank either within the same project or from one project to another, but you can copy using the Save Bank and Load Bank features. Just save a bank to an .SYX file from the current project. If you want to have a copy of that bank in the current project, just load it into another bank. If you want to have a copy of that bank in another project, open the other project and then load the bank into the Sysx view of that project.

Introducing StudioWare

Being able to store all the parameter settings for your MIDI gear within a project is great. You can have your entire studio set up in a matter of seconds. But to set those parameters initially, you still have to fiddle with the knobs and controls on the MIDI gear. Because some MIDI devices have a limited number of controls, the only way to change their parameters is to wade through an endless maze of menus on a small (and sometimes cryptic) LCD screen. SONAR provides a feature called StudioWare that lets you adjust all the parameters in your MIDI devices without ever leaving your computer. More important, it lets you access those less-than-accessible parameters in a very intuitive and easy manner.

Using StudioWare, you can adjust the parameters for any of your MIDI devices remotely from your computer. Basically, you can have virtual buttons, knobs, and faders on your computer screen that represent each of the adjustable parameters in your MIDI devices. When you move a knob or fader on your computer screen, it changes the value of an assigned parameter in a MIDI device. Now, not only can you store MIDI device parameters, you also can adjust them. Using the Sysx view and StudioWare, you may never have to touch your MIDI gear again (except maybe to turn it on). Plus, you can record the adjustments you make to any onscreen controls and then play them back in real-time, which means you can automate parameter changes for a MIDI device as well.

The StudioWare View

StudioWare uses what are known as *panels* to represent your external MIDI devices. A panel can contain any number of controls (such as buttons, knobs, and faders) depending on the number of parameters your MIDI device provides. To start using StudioWare, you need to open a StudioWare panel file, which is displayed in the StudioWare view.

Opening a StudioWare Panel

A StudioWare panel is stored either as part of a project file or as a separate StudioWare file with the extension .CakewalkStudioWare. If a project file contains a panel, the panel is automatically opened when you open the project. To open a StudioWare file, just follow these steps:

1. Choose File > Open to display the Open dialog box.
2. Select StudioWare from the Files of Type drop-down list to display only StudioWare files.
3. Choose a file.
4. Click on Open.

SONAR will display the StudioWare view containing the panel from the file you just opened (see Figure 14.9).

Figure 14.9

The StudioWare view displays your chosen panel.

Because all panels are different, I can't really explain how each one works. Usually a panel mimics the controls of a MIDI device, so if you own the corresponding MIDI device, you shouldn't have any trouble figuring out how to use its StudioWare panel.

After you've opened a panel, you can adjust the controls, take a Snapshot, record your control movements, and so on. Adjusting the controls is straightforward. The buttons, knobs, and faders in a StudioWare panel work the same way they do in the Console view (which you learned about in Chapter 12).

Unfortuantely, SONAR 3 doesn't allow you to create your own StudioWare panels, but SONAR does include a number of predesigned panels that you can use in your own projects.

DESIGN STUDIOWARE PANELS

If you upgraded from SONAR 1 or 2 and you still want to design your own StudioWare panels, be sure to keep your previous version of the software. Using a previous version of SONAR is the only way you can access the StudioWare design mode, which has been removed from SONAR 3.

If you can't find a panel for your MIDI device, Cakewalk also provides a nice library of additional StudioWare panels on its Web site; you can download them for free. You even can find other places on the Internet where you can download free panels written by other users (see Appendix D, "SONAR Resources on the Web").

Taking a Snapshot

The Snapshot function works almost the same as with the Console view, but there are a few differences. Instead of recording the control data in separate tracks, the control data from a StudioWare panel is recorded into a single track. Most StudioWare panels include a knob control that allows you to set the track into which the control data will be recorded. As an example, take a look at the General MIDI.CakewalkStudioWare panel, shown in Figure 14.10.

Figure 14.10
The General MIDI.
CakewalkStudioWare
panel provides a track
control.

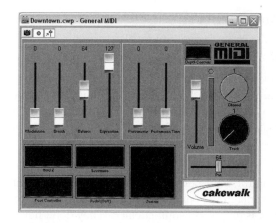

You'll see a knob labeled Track. Adjusting that knob changes the track number for the panel. If you open some of the other sample panels, you'll notice the same type of track control. It might look a little different, but it functions in the same way. By the way, if a panel doesn't have a track control knob, either the panel wasn't designed to record data to a track (some of them don't) or the panel will automatically record its data to Track 1. When you're working with this kind of panel, it's a good idea to leave Track 1 dedicated to recording MIDI control data.

To take a Snapshot of the controls in a StudioWare panel, follow these steps:

1. Set the Now time to the point in the project where you want the Snapshot to be stored.

2. Adjust the controls in the StudioWare panel to the desired values for that part of the project.

3. Click on the Snapshot button (the one with the picture of a camera on it) in the toolbar at the top of the StudioWave view (see Figure 14.11).

Figure 14.11
Click on the Snapshot
button to take a Snapshot
in the StudioWare view.

4. Repeat Steps 1 through 3 until you've created all the Snapshots you need for your project.

Recording Control Movements

Recording the movements of the controls on a StudioWare panel is also similar to the same procedure in the Console view, but as with taking a Snapshot, there are a few differences.

The first difference is the track number procedure I described in the preceding section. The second difference is in grouping controls together. Just as you can do in the Console view, you can group multiple controls together in a StudioWare panel so you can easily change more than one control simultaneously. The differences here are in how controls are grouped and how single controls in a group are adjusted.

For grouping controls, instead of right-clicking on a control and assigning it to a colored group, you simply select an initial control, hold down the Ctrl key on your computer keyboard, and click on one or more additional controls in the panel. Those controls are then grouped. Grouping controls in a StudioWare panel is much less sophisticated. They don't have any grouping properties like exist in the Console view either.

To adjust a single control that belongs to a group, just hold down the Shift key on your computer keyboard and then adjust the control. In the Console view, the procedure is the same except that you hold down the Ctrl key.

All these techniques work with any StudioWare panel. However, there are also differences in the actual recording of the control movements. The procedure for recording control movements in the StudioWare view is as follows:

1. Turn on the Record Widget Movements function by clicking on the Record Widget Movements button (the button with the big red dot on it), located just to the right of the Snapshot button at the top of the StudioWare view (see Figure 14.12).

Figure 14.12
Click on the Record Widget Movements button to activate the Record Widget Movements function.

2. Set the Now time to just before the point in the project where you want to start recording control changes.

3. Start the project playing.

4. When the Now time gets to the point in the project where you want to begin recording control changes, adjust the controls in the StudioWare panel with your mouse.

5. When you're finished, stop the playback of the project.

6. Because you're manipulating onscreen controls with your mouse, you can make only one change at a time. What if you want to have two different controls change at the same time? For every control that you want to change in the same timeframe, you must repeat Steps 2 through 5.

TRY LOOPING INSTEAD

Instead of starting and stopping playback each time you want to record additional control changes, try setting up a loop so SONAR will just play the project (or section of the project) over and over again. I described looping in Chapter 6.

7. After you've finished recording all the control changes that you need, be sure to turn off the Record Widget Movements function.

UPDATE WIDGET VALUES

If you want the controls in your StudioWare panel to move according to the changes you recorded, activate the Update Widget Values function by clicking on the Update Widget Values button (the button with the picture of a slider on it), located just to the right of the Record Widget Movements button at the top of the StudioWare view.

CHAPTER 14

15

CAL 101

One advantage that SONAR has over any other music-sequencing product I've worked with is that it enables you to extend its functionality. If you find yourself in a situation in which you need to edit your MIDI or audio data in some way that is not possible with any of the current SONAR features (which is not a common occurrence, but it can happen), you can create a new editing function to take care of the task by using CAL. What is CAL, and how do you use it? Well, that's exactly what you'll learn in this chapter. This chapter will do the following:

▶ Define CAL

▶ Show you how to run an existing CAL program

▶ Explain prewritten CAL programs

▶ Demonstrate how to view CAL programs

What Is CAL?

CAL (*Cakewalk Application Language*) is a computer-programming language that exists within the SONAR environment. You can extend the functionality of SONAR by creating your own custom MIDI and audio data editing commands using CAL programs (also called *scripts*). A CAL program is a set of instructions written in the Cakewalk Application Language that tells SONAR how to perform a certain task. For example, if you want to change the volume of every other MIDI note in Track 1 to a certain value automatically, you can write a CAL program to do just that. And for future use, you can save CAL programs to disk as files with a .CAL extension.

PROGRAMMING LANGUAGES

A *programming language* is a set of commands, symbols, and rules that are used to "teach" a computer how to perform tasks. By combining these language elements in different ways, you can teach a computer to perform any number of tasks, such as recording and playing music. The combination of elements for a certain task or set of tasks is called a computer *program*. For example, SONAR is a computer program, albeit a very complex one.

A number of different kinds of programming languages exist, including BASIC, FORTRAN, C, LISP, and many others. Each has unique characteristics. If you are familiar with C and LISP, you'll feel right at home with CAL; it derives many of its characteristics from these two languages.

You might be saying to yourself, "Um, well, that's nice, but I know nothing about computer programming, so what good is CAL going to do me?" Not to worry. Yes, CAL is a very complex feature of SONAR. If you really want to take full advantage of it, you have to learn how to use the language, but that doesn't mean CAL isn't accessible if you're a beginning user.

There are a number of prewritten CAL programs included with SONAR that you can use in your own projects. Cakewalk also provides a nice library of additional CAL programs on its Web site that you can download for free. You even can find other places on the Internet where you can download free CAL programs that have been written by other users (see Appendix D, "SONAR Resources on the Web"). Next I want to talk about how you can use the existing CAL programs included with SONAR and any others that you might download from the Internet.

Running a CAL Program

Because all CAL programs are different, I can't explain how to use them in one all-encompassing way. When you run a CAL program, it usually asks you for some kind of input, depending on what the program is supposed to do and how it is supposed to manipulate your music data. But you can still follow this basic procedure to run a CAL program:

1. Select the track(s) (or data within the tracks) in the Track view that you want the CAL program to edit. This first step is not always necessary; it depends on the task the CAL program is supposed to perform. It also depends on whether the CAL program was written to process only selected data in a project or all the tracks in a project. The only way to determine the function of a CAL program is to view it with Windows Notepad, which you'll learn about later in this chapter.

2. Choose Process > Run CAL to display the Open dialog box.

3. Choose the CAL program you want to run and click on Open.

That's all there is to it. Some CAL programs immediately carry out their tasks, whereas others first display additional dialog boxes if you need to input any values. The best way to begin using CAL (and to see how it works) is to try out some of the sample programs included with SONAR.

RUN CAL PROGRAMS DURING PLAYBACK

You can run CAL programs while a project is being played back. This means you can hear the results of the editing the CAL program applies to your data at the same time your music is being played. If you don't like what the CAL program does, just choose Edit > Undo to remove any changes the program makes to your data. If you then decide that you actually like the changes, instead of running the CAL program again, just choose Edit > Redo to put the changes back in place.

The CAL Files

To give you a better understanding of how CAL works and how you can benefit from it, I'll describe the prewritten CAL programs included with SONAR in the following sections. I'll give you a brief description of what each program does and how to use it.

Dominant 7th Chord.CAL

The Dominant 7th Chord.CAL program builds dominant seventh chords by adding three notes with the same time, velocity, and duration to each selected MIDI note in a track. In other words, if you select a note within a track and you run Dominant 7th Chord.CAL, the program treats the selected note as the root of a dominant seventh chord and adds a minor third, a perfect fifth, and a minor seventh on top of it, thus creating a dominant seventh chord automatically.

Of course, if you know how to compose music, you probably won't get much use out of this CAL program. However, you might find it useful while working in the Staff view. While you're editing a MIDI data track in the Staff view, try highlighting a note and then running Dominant 7th Chord.CAL. It's cool to see those additional notes just appear as if by magic. This program can save you some time while you're inputting notes by hand too.

Other Chord.CAL Programs

SONAR includes a number of other chord-building CAL programs that work the same way as Dominant 7th Chord.CAL, except they build different kinds of chords:

▶ **Major 7th Chord.CAL.** This builds major seventh chords by adding the major third, perfect fifth, and major seventh intervals to the selected root note or notes.

▶ **Major Chord.CAL.** This builds major chords by adding the major third and perfect fifth intervals to the selected root note or notes.

▶ **Minor 7th Chord.CAL.** This builds minor seventh chords by adding the minor third, perfect fifth, and minor seventh intervals to the selected root note or notes.

▶ **Minor Chord.CAL.** This builds minor chords by adding the minor third and perfect fifth intervals to the selected root note or notes.

Random Time.CAL

If you overindulge yourself while using SONAR's quantizing features (see Chapter 8), your music can sometimes sound like computer music, with a robotic or machine-like feel to it. In some cases this sound is desirable, but when you're working on a jazz or rhythm and blues piece you don't want the drums (or any of the other instruments, for that matter) to sound like a robot played them. In this case, Random Time.CAL may be of some help.

This CAL program takes the start times of each selected event in a track and adds a random number of ticks to them. To give you some control over this randomization, the program first asks you for a number of ticks on which to base its changes. It then adds a random number to each event time that is between plus or minus one-half the number of ticks that you input. For instance, if you tell the program to use six ticks, each event time will have one of the following numbers (chosen at random) added to it: $-3, -2, -1, 0, 1, 2,$ or 3. Using this program is a great way to add a little bit of "human" feel back into those robotic-sounding tracks. To use Random Time.CAL, just follow these steps:

1. Select the track(s) in the Track view that you want to process. Alternatively, you can select a single clip within a track or a specific range of events in one of the other views, such as the Piano Roll view or the Staff view.

2. Choose Process > Run CAL to display the Open dialog box.

3. Choose the Random Time.CAL file and click on Open. The Random Time.CAL program will display a CAL dialog box (see Figure 15.1).

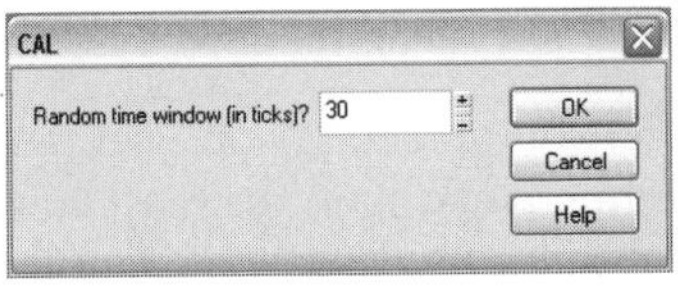

Figure 15.1
The Random Time.CAL program asks for the number of ticks upon which to base its event time processing.

4. Enter the number of ticks you want to use and click on OK.

You'll probably need to experiment a little bit with the number of ticks that you use because a number that is too large can make your music sound sloppy or too far off the beat.

Scale Velocity.CAL

The Scale Velocity.CAL program is included with SONAR just to serve as a programming example; other than that, you don't really need it. SONAR already includes a Scale Velocity editing function, which provides even more features than Scale Velocity.CAL. For more information about Scale Velocity, see Chapter 8.

Split Channel to Tracks.CAL

If you ever need to share your music data with someone who owns a sequencing program other than SONAR, you can save your project as an .SMF file (*Standard MIDI File*). Most computer music software products on the market support Standard MIDI Files; thus, they allow musicians to work together on the same song without having to own the same software.

However, not all Standard MIDI Files are created equal. Actually, several types of files are available; one in particular is called Type 0. A Type 0 MIDI file stores all its data—which is all the MIDI data from all 16 MIDI channels—on one track. Type 0 files are used sometimes for video game composing, but hardly ever when composing for any other medium. Still, you might run across a Type 0 MIDI file, and if you open the file in SONAR, all the data shows up on one track in the Track view. Editing the data is rather difficult, so Split Channel to Tracks.CAL is a useful tool in this situation.

Split Channel to Tracks.CAL takes the selected track and separates the data from it by MIDI channel into 16 new tracks. For example, if the track contains data on MIDI channels 1, 4, 5, and 6, Split Channel to Tracks.CAL creates 16 new tracks (from the initial track), with the first track containing data from channel 1, the fourth track containing data from channel 4, and so on. The remaining tracks that don't have corresponding channel data are just blank. You use Split Channel to Tracks.CAL like this:

1. Select a track in the Track view.

2. If you want to split only a portion of the track, set the From and Thru markers to the appropriate time values.

3. Choose Process > Run CAL to open the Open dialog box.

4. Choose the Split Channel to Tracks.CAL file and click on Open. The Split Channel to Tracks.CAL program will display a CAL dialog box (see Figure 15.2).

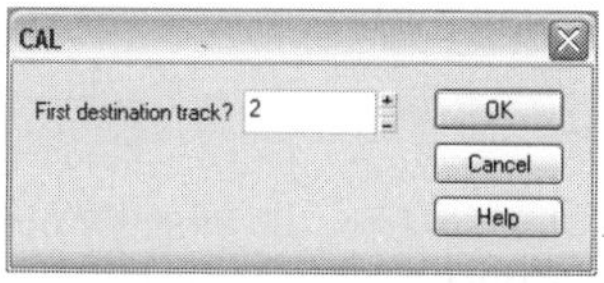

Figure 15.2
The Split Channel to Tracks.CAL program asks for the number of the track to start with when you're creating the new tracks.

5. Enter the number of the first track that you want Split Channel to Tracks.CAL to use when it creates the new tracks, and then click on OK.

OVERWRITE TRACKS
Be sure to enter the number of the last track in your project plus one, so the newly created tracks don't overwrite any existing ones. For example, if the number of the last track in your project is 16, then enter 17.

After it's finished processing the original track, Split Channel to Tracks.CAL will create 16 new tracks starting with the track number you selected, each containing data from the 16 corresponding MIDI channels. Now you can access and edit the music data more easily.

Split Note to Tracks.CAL

The Split Note to Tracks.CAL program is similar to Split Channel to Tracks.CAL, except that instead of separating the MIDI data from a selected track by channel, it separates the data by note. For example, if you select a track that contains notes with values of C4, A2, and G3, Split Note to Tracks.CAL separates that track into three new tracks, each containing all notes with only one of the available note values. In this example, a new track containing only notes with a value of C4 would be created, another new track containing only A2 notes would be created, and another new track containing only G3 notes would be created.

This CAL program can be useful if you're working with a single drum track that contains the data for a number of different drum instruments. In MIDI, different drum instruments are represented by different note values because drums can't play melodies. So if you want to edit a single drum instrument at a time, having each instrument on its own track would be easier. In that case, Split Note to Tracks.CAL can be put to good use. To apply Split Note to Tracks.CAL to your music data, follow these steps:

1. Choose Process > Run CAL to open the Open dialog box.

2. Choose the Split Note to Tracks.CAL file and click on Open.

3. The Split Note to Tracks.CAL program will ask for the number of your source track (see Figure 15.3). This is the track you want to split into new tracks. Enter a track number and click on OK.

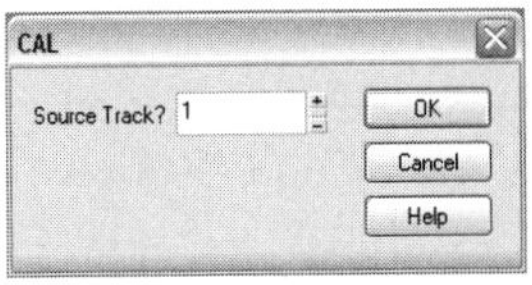

Figure 15.3
Here you can enter the source track for the Split Note to Tracks.CAL program.

CAL

Source Track? 1   OK
Cancel
Help

DIFFERENT OPERATION

You'll notice this program is different from the other CAL programs in which you had to select a track first in the Track view. It's different because the person who wrote this CAL program did it differently from the rest. Why? I have no idea.

4. The program will ask you for the number of the first destination track (see Figure 15.4). This is the number of the first new track that will be created. Enter a number and click on OK.

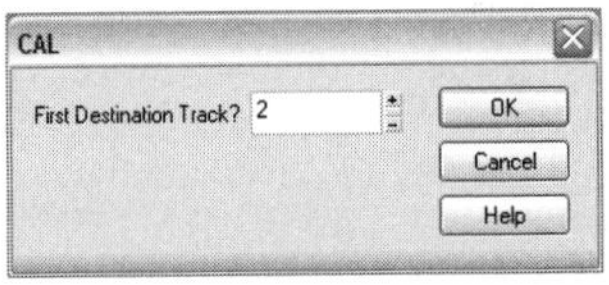

Figure 15.4
Here you can enter the first destination track for the Split Note to Tracks.CAL program.

CAL

First Destination Track? 2   OK
Cancel
Help

OVERWRITE TRACKS

Be sure to enter the number of the last track in your project plus one, so the newly created tracks don't overwrite any existing ones. For example, if the number of the last track in your project is 16, then enter 17.

5. The program will ask you for the number of the destination channel (see Figure 15.5). This is the MIDI channel to which you want all the new tracks to be set. Unless you want to change the channel, you should simply select the same channel that the source track is using. Enter a number from 1 to 16 and click on OK.

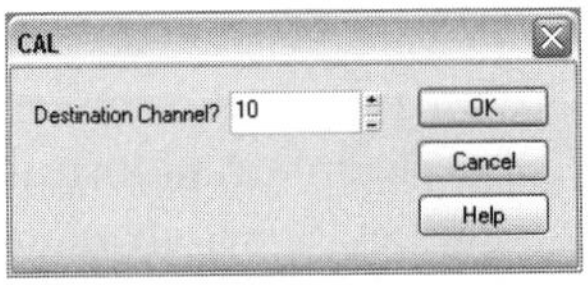

Figure 15.5
Here you can enter the destination channel for the Split Note to Tracks.CAL program.

CAL

Destination Channel? 10   OK
Cancel
Help

6. Finally, the program will ask you for the number of the destination port (see Figure 15.6). This is the MIDI output to which you want all the new tracks to be set. Again, you should simply select the same output that the source track is using. Enter a number from 1 to 16 and click on OK.

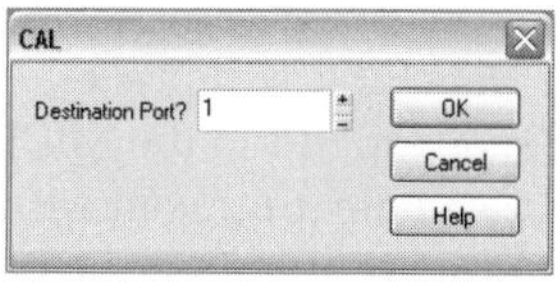

Figure 15.6
Here you can enter the destination port for the Split Note to Tracks.CAL program.

After you answer the last question, Split Note to Tracks.CAL will process the original track and create a number of new tracks (depending on how many different note values are present in the original track), each containing all the notes for each corresponding note value.

Thin Controller Data.CAL

You use MIDI controller data to add expressive qualities to your MIDI music tracks. For example, you can make a certain passage of music get gradually louder or softer (crescendo or decrescendo) by adding MIDI controller number 7 (Volume) to your MIDI tracks. Sometimes, though, an overabundance of MIDI data can overload your MIDI instruments and cause anomalies such as stuck notes and delays in playback. If you have this problem, you can try thinning out the MIDI controller data in your tracks by using Thin Controller Data.CAL. This program allows you to decrease the amount of data being sent to your MIDI instruments by deleting only a select number of controller events—enough to reduce the amount of data without adversely affecting the music performance. It works like this:

1. Select the track(s) in the Track view that you want to process. You also can select a single clip within a track, or you can select a specific range of events within one of the other views, such as the Piano Roll view or the Staff view.

2. Choose Process > Run CAL to display the Open dialog box.

3. Choose the Thin Controller Data.CAL file and click on Open.

4. The Thin Controller Data.CAL program will ask you for the number of the MIDI controller you want to process (see Figure 15.7). For example, if you want to remove some of the volume data from a track, use MIDI controller number 7. Enter a number from 0 to 127 and click on OK.

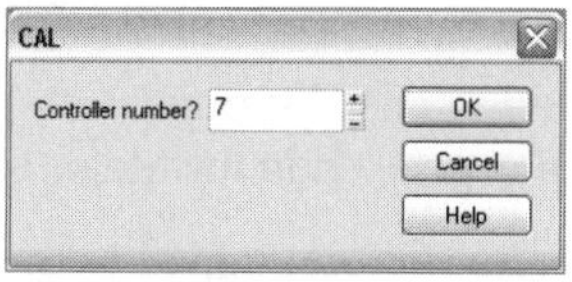

Figure 15.7
Here you can enter the controller number for the Thin Controller Data.CAL program.

5. The program will ask you for the thinning factor (see Figure 15.8). For example, if you enter a value of 4, the program will delete every fourth volume event it finds in the selected track or tracks. Enter a number from 1 to 100 and click on OK.

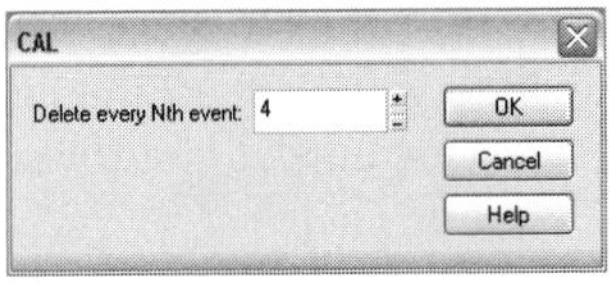

Figure 15.8

Here you can enter the thinning factor for the Thin Controller Data.CAL program.

CAL	☒
Delete every Nth event: 4 ⬍	OK
	Cancel
	Help

After you answer the last question, Thin Controller Data.CAL will process the selected track or tracks and delete all the MIDI controller events that correspond to the MIDI controller number and the thinning factor you entered. If this procedure doesn't clear up your MIDI playback problems you can try thinning the data some more, but be careful not to thin it too much; otherwise, your crescendos and decrescendos (or other controller-influenced music passages) will start to sound choppy rather than smooth.

Other Thin.CAL Programs

SONAR also includes two other controller-thinning CAL programs. These programs work almost the same way as Thin Controller Data.CAL, but each is targeted toward one specific type of controller. Thin Channel Aftertouch.CAL thins out channel aftertouch MIDI controller data, and Thin Pitch Wheel.CAL thins out pitch wheel (or pitch bend) MIDI controller data. To run these programs, you use the same procedure as you do with Thin Controller Data.CAL, but with one exception. The programs don't ask you to input the number of a MIDI controller because each is already targeted toward a specific controller. Other than that, they work in the same manner.

Viewing CAL Programs

Unless a CAL program comes with some written instructions, you won't know what it is designed to do to the data in your project. This is especially true if you download CAL programs from the Internet. Many come with documentation, but many don't. However, most programs do come with a brief description (as well as instructions for use) within their source code.

WHAT IS SOURCE CODE?

Source code (or *program code*) is the text of the programming language commands used for a particular program. You create a program by first writing its source code. Then a computer can run the program by reading the source code and executing the commands in the appropriate manner, thus carrying out the intended task.

To read the source code of a CAL program, you need to use Windows Notepad (or some other plain text editor). As an example, take a look at the source code for Major Chord.CAL:

1. Choose Start > All Programs > Accessories > Notepad to open Windows Notepad.

2. Choose File > Open and select the Major Chord.CAL file from the SONAR directory on your hard drive (or some other directory where your CAL files are stored). Click on Open. Windows Notepad will open Major Chord.CAL and display its source code (see Figure 15.9).

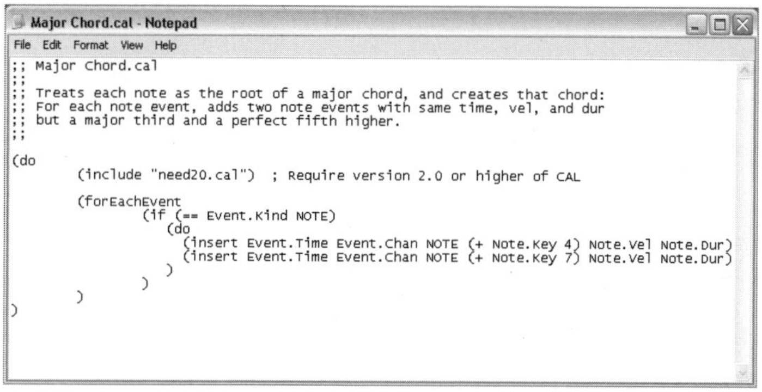

```
Major Chord.cal - Notepad
File Edit Format View Help
;; Major Chord.cal
;;
;; Treats each note as the root of a major chord, and creates that chord:
;; For each note event, adds two note events with same time, vel, and dur
;; but a major third and a perfect fifth higher.
;;

(do
	(include "need20.cal")  ; Require version 2.0 or higher of CAL

	(forEachEvent
		(if (== Event.Kind NOTE)
			(do
				(insert Event.Time Event.Chan NOTE (+ Note.Key 4) Note.Vel Note.Dur)
				(insert Event.Time Event.Chan NOTE (+ Note.Key 7) Note.Vel Note.Dur)
			)
		)
	)
)
```

Figure 15.9
You can use Windows Notepad to examine and edit the source code of a CAL program.

As you can see in Figure 15.9, Windows Notepad allows you to see the source code of Major Chord.CAL and also to read the brief description included there. You can do the same thing with any other CAL program to find out how you can use it and what task it's supposed to perform. But that's not all! Using Windows Notepad, you can edit the source code for a CAL program, as well as create a CAL program from scratch. Because CAL programs are just plain text, you can use the same editing techniques you do with any other text, such as cut, copy, and paste text-editing procedures. I'll cover creating your own CAL programs in Chapter 16, "Advanced CAL Techniques."

16

Advanced CAL Techniques

In Chapter 15, you learned about the Cakewalk Application Language—what it is, what it does, and how you can run prewritten CAL programs to tackle some of the editing tasks that the built-in SONAR functions can't handle. I briefly touched on the topic of creating your own CAL programs. This chapter continues the CAL discussion and will do the following:

 Teach you the Cakewalk Application Language programming basics

 Explain the anatomy of a CAL program

Introduction to CAL Programming

Unfortunately, there is no easy way to create your own CAL programs. To tap the full power of its functionality, you need to learn how to create programs from scratch using the Cakewalk Application Language. The problem is that teaching a course in CAL programming would take up an entire book. So instead, I'll just get you started by providing a brief introduction to the language. The best way to do that is to walk you through the code of one of the CAL programs that comes included with SONAR.

To get started, open the Scale Velocity.CAL program (see Figure 16.1). The first thing you'll see is a bunch of lines that start with semicolons and contain some text describing the CAL program. These lines are called *comments*. Whenever you insert a semicolon into the code of a CAL program, SONAR ignores that part of the code when you run the program. This way, you can mark the code with descriptive notes. When you come back to the program at a later date, you will understand what certain parts of the program are supposed to accomplish.

Figure 16.1
The code for the Scale
Velocity.CAL program
provides a nice example
for an explanation of the
Cakewalk Application
Language.

```
Scale Velocity.cal - Notepad
File  Edit  Format  View  Help
;;  Scale Velocity.cal
;;
;;  This is a sample CAL program that implements an editing command to
;;  scale note velocities by a certain percentage.
;;
;;  Demonstrates:
;;
;;    (forEachEvent)
;;    Getting input from the user
;;    Arithmetic operators
;;    Event kind and parameter variables

(do
        (include "need20.cal")  ; Require version 2.0 or higher of CAL

        (int percent 100)
        (getInt percent "Percentage?" 1 1000)

        (forEachEvent
                (if (== Event.Kind NOTE)
                    (do
                            (*= Note.Vel percent)
                            (/= Note.Vel 100)
                    )
                )
        )
)
```

A little further down, you'll notice the first line of the actual code used when the program is run. The line reads (do. All CAL programs start with this code. The parenthesis designates the start of a function, and the do code designates the start of a group of code. As a matter of fact, a CAL program is just one big function with a number of other functions in it. You'll notice that for every left parenthesis, you'll have a corresponding right parenthesis. CAL programs use parentheses to show where a function begins and ends.

The Include Function

The next line in Scale Velocity.CAL reads (include "need20.cal"). This is the Include function, and it allows you to run a CAL program within a CAL program. You might want to do this for a number of reasons. For instance, if you're creating a very large program, you might want to break it down into different parts to make it easier to use. Then you could have one master program that runs all the different parts. You can also combine CAL programs. For example, you could combine the Thin Channel Aftertouch.CAL, Thin Controller Data.CAL, and Thin Pitch Wheel.CAL programs that come with SONAR by using the Include function in a new CAL program. Then when you run the new program, it will run each of the included programs, one right after another, so you can thin all the types of MIDI controller data from your project in one fell swoop.

In Scale Velocity.CAL, the Include function is used to run the need20.CAL program. This program simply checks the version of CAL and makes sure it is version 2.0 or higher. Some CAL programs check the version to avoid an error in case a very old version of CAL is being used.

Variables

After the Include function, the code for Scale Velocity.CAL shows (int percent 100). This is a variable function. In CAL programs, you can define variables to hold any values you might need while the program is running. In this instance, the variable percent is defined as an integer and given a value of 100. You can use variables to store both number and text information. After you define a variable, you can refer to its value later in your code by simply using the variable name. That's what you see in the next line of code in Scale Velocity.CAL.

User Input

This next line reads (getInt percent "Percentage?" 1 1000). Here, the program asks for input from the user. In plain English, this line of code translates to, "Get an integer between 1 and 1000 from the user by having the user type a value into the displayed dialog box. Then store the value in the variable named percent." Basically, when SONAR reaches this line of code in the program, it pauses and displays a dialog box (see Figure 16.2) and waits for the user to input a value and click on the OK button. It then assigns the input value to the variable percent and continues running the rest of the program.

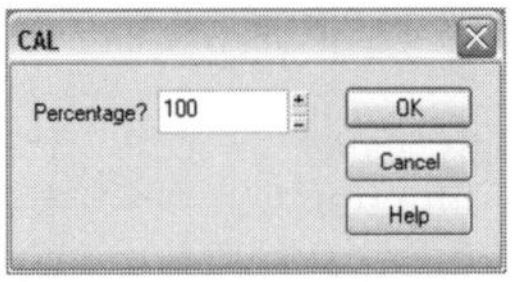

Figure 16.2
A CAL program gets input from the user by displaying dialog boxes.

The ForEachEvent Function

The main part of the Scale Velocity.CAL program begins with the line of code that reads (forEachEvent. This is known as an *iterating* function. In this type of function, a certain portion of code is run (or cycled through) a specific number of times. In this case, for every event in the selected track(s), the code enclosed within the forEachEvent function is cycled through one time. So in Scale Velocity.CAL, the following block of code is run through once for every event in the selected track(s):

```
(if (== Event.Kind NOTE)
    (do
            (*= Note.Vel percent)
            (/= Note.Vel 100)
    )
)
```

What does this code do? Well, I'll talk about it in the following sections.

Conditions

Within the forEachEvent function in Scale Velocity.CAL, every event in the selected track is tested using the if function. This function is known as a *conditional* function. Depending on whether certain conditions are met, the code enclosed within the if function may or may not run. In Scale Velocity.CAL, every event is tested to see whether it is a MIDI note event. This test is performed with the line of code that reads (= = Event.Kind NOTE). In plain English, this line translates to "Check to see whether the current event being tested is a MIDI note event." If the current event is a MIDI note event, then the next block of code is run. If the current event is not a MIDI note event, then the next block of code is skipped and the forEachEvent function moves on to the next event in the selected track until it reaches the last selected event; then the CAL program stops running.

Arithmetic

The final part of Scale Velocity.CAL is just some simple arithmetic code. If the current event is a MIDI note event, the velocity value of the note is multiplied by the value of the percent variable, and the resulting value is assigned as the note velocity. Then the new velocity value of the note is divided by 100, and the resulting value is assigned to be the final value of the note velocity. This way, the program scales the velocities of the notes in the selected track(s).

Master Presets

One of the most effective uses I've found for CAL is in creating what I like to call *Master Presets*. As I mentioned in Chapter 8, SONAR lets you save the settings for some of its editing functions as presets. This way, you can use the same editing parameters you created simply by calling them up by name, instead of having to figure out the settings every time you use a function.

Presets are a real timesaver, but unfortunately, you can save presets only for each of the individual functions. What if you want to combine a few of the functions to create a certain editing process? For example, suppose you like to shorten your MIDI tracks before you quantize them. To do so, you need to select the tracks, use the Length function, and then use the Quantize function to process your tracks. For each of the editing functions, you have to make the appropriate setting adjustments. If you create a CAL program to automatically run through the process for you, though, all you need to do is select your tracks and run the CAL program.

To show you what I mean, I've cooked up a sample Master Preset you can run as a CAL program and use in your projects. You need to complete the following steps:

1. Open Windows Notepad.

2. Type in the first few lines of code, as shown in Figure 16.3.

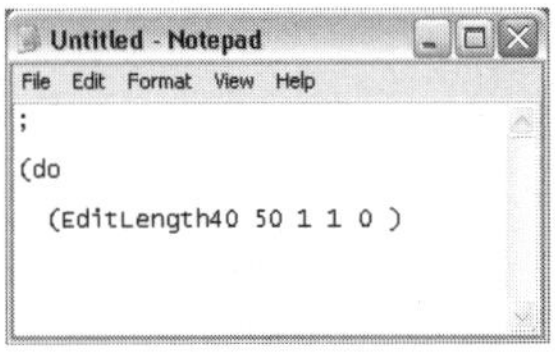

Figure 16.3
These are the first few lines of code in your new Master Preset.

3. Examine the code. The first line is just a blank comment. The second line designates the beginning of the program. The third line tells SONAR to activate the Length function using the parameters shown in Figure 16.4. In the source code, the command EditLength40 tells SONAR to activate the Length function. The number 50 corresponds to the Percent parameter in the Length dialog box. The numbers 1, 1, and 0 correspond to the Start Times, Durations, and Stretch Audio options, respectively. A 1 indicates that the option is activated; a 0 indicates that it is not.

Figure 16.4
The first part of the CAL program shortens the selected MIDI tracks by 50 percent with the Length editing function.

4. Now type in the last two lines of code, as shown in Figure 16.5.

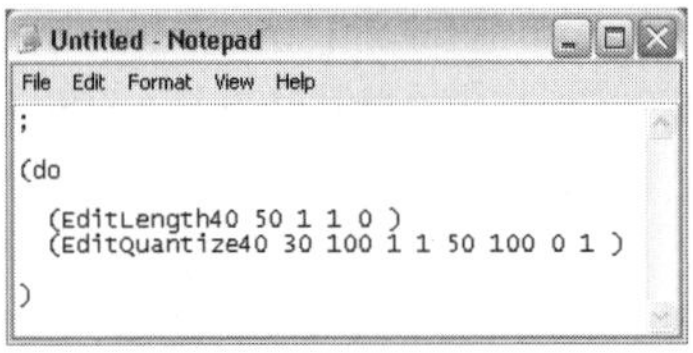

Figure 16.5
The final source code should look like this after you edit it.

5. Examine the code. The command EditQuantize40 tells SONAR to activate the Quantize function using the parameters shown in Figure 16.6. The numbers following that command designate the following parameter settings: Resolution, Strength Percent, Start Times (on/off), Note Durations (on/off), Swing Percent, Window Percent, Offset, and Notes/Lyrics/Audio (on/off).

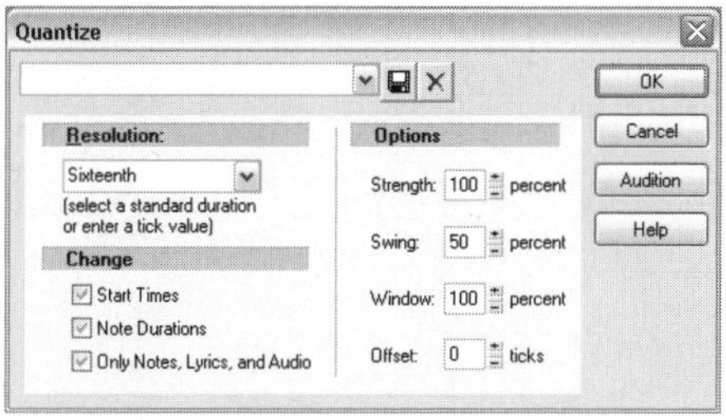

Figure 16.6
The second part of the
CAL program quantizes
the notes in the selected
MIDI tracks with the
`Quantize` editing
function.

CHAPTER 16

6.   Save the new program with a file extension of .CAL.

Now when you run this CAL program, it performs all the editing functions for you automatically,
with the same settings you used. It's too bad CAL doesn't support SONAR's MIDI or audio effects
functions. I really wish it did, because then you could create Master Presets to process your audio
tracks, too. That capability would make CAL a hundred times more powerful than it already is. I
hope Cakewalk will add this functionality in a future version. In the meantime, you can still find
plenty of uses for CAL.

CAL References

So are you totally confused yet? If you've had some previous programming experience, you should
have no trouble picking up the Cakewalk Application Language. If you're familiar with the C or
LISP computer programming language, CAL is just a stone's throw away in terms of functionality.

Really, the best way to learn about CAL is to study the code of existing CAL programs. If you still
find yourself lost in all this technical jargon even after this discussion, you can utilize CAL by
using prewritten programs. As I mentioned before, this part of SONAR has a lot of power, and it
would be a shame if you let it go to waste. CAL can save you time and even let you manipulate
your music data in ways you might never have considered. Don't be afraid to experiment. Just be
sure to back up your data in case things get a bit messed up in the process.

MORE CAL INFORMATION
For more information about programming with CAL, check out some of the Web
sites I've listed in Appendix D, "SONAR Resources on the Web."

17

Taking Your SONAR Project to CD

Congratulations! You've made it to the final chapter of the book. Your project has been recorded, edited, and mixed, and now you can share it with the rest of the world. To be able to share it, you need to create your very own CD. This chapter will cover the basics of creating a custom audio CD and will do the following:

▶ Show you how to prepare your project for CD audio

▶ Explain how to use Cakewalk's Pyro 2003 CD-burning software

▶ Demonstrate how to use the built-in Windows XP CD burning functions

Preparing a Project for CD Audio

A project can't be laid down as audio tracks on a CD as is. Instead, you have to convert all your MIDI tracks in a project to audio tracks. Then you have to export those audio tracks to a WAV file so that your CD recording software can write the file to your CD. To do so, you need to follow a number of steps, which the following sections will detail.

Converting Your MIDI Tracks

As I explained in Chapter 2, you really shouldn't use Sound Blaster and other similar consumer-level sound cards for serious music making. But if you happen to have one of these cards that provides a built-in synthesizer, the first step is to convert any MIDI tracks that use your sound card's built-in synthesizer for playback to audio tracks as follows:

1. Insert a new audio track and assign the input for the track to your sound card's stereo input. For instance, if you have a Sound Blaster Live! card, set the track to the Stereo SB Live Wave Device input.

2. Mute all the tracks in your project except the one you just created and the MIDI tracks you're going to convert.

3. Open your sound card's mixer controls (see Figure 17.1) by double-clicking on the small speaker icon in the Windows taskbar.

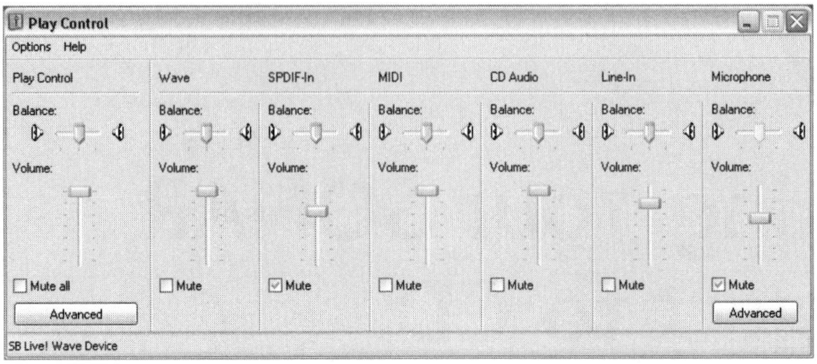

Figure 17.1
This window shows the sound card mixer controls for the Sound Blaster Live! sound card.

4. Choose Options > Properties and click on Recording in the Adjust Volume For section of the resulting Properties dialog box. Then click on OK to bring up the recording mixer controls, as shown in Figure 17.2.

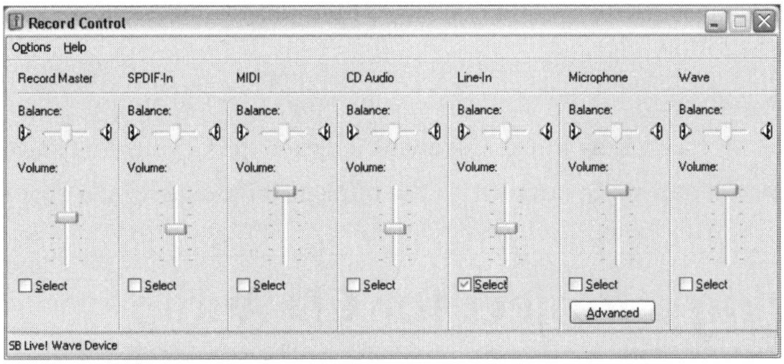

Figure 17.2
This window shows the recording mixer controls for the Sound Blaster Live! sound card.

5. Activate the recording source for your sound card's synth by clicking on the appropriate Select option (see Figure 17.3).

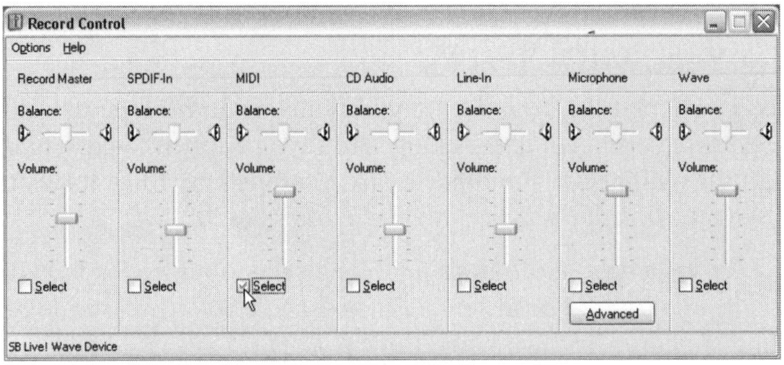

Figure 17.3
You need to activate your sound card's synth before you can record its output.

6. Click on the Record button on the toolbar in SONAR, and your MIDI tracks will be recorded to the stereo audio track.

Next you need to convert any MIDI tracks that use external MIDI instruments for playback to audio tracks, as shown in the following steps. If you don't have any MIDI tracks of this kind, you can skip this section.

1. Insert a new audio track and assign the input for the track to your sound card's stereo input. For instance, if you have a Sound Blaster Live! card, set the track to the Stereo SB Live Wave Device input.

2. Mute all the tracks in your project except the one you just created and the MIDI tracks you're going to convert.

3. Open your sound card's mixer controls by double-clicking on the small speaker icon in the Windows taskbar.

4. Choose Options > Properties, and then click on Recording in the Adjust Volume For section of the resulting Properties dialog box. Then click on OK to bring up the recording mixer controls.

5. Activate the recording source for your sound card's line input(s) by clicking on the appropriate Select option (see Figure 17.4).

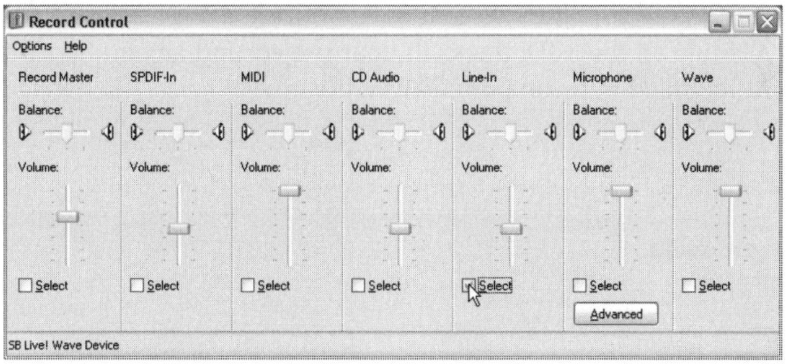

Figure 17.4
You need to activate your sound card's line input(s) before you can record any external MIDI instruments.

6. Be sure the audio outputs from your external MIDI instrument are connected to the line inputs of your sound card. If you have more than one MIDI instrument and you're using a mixing board, connect the stereo outputs of your mixing board to the line inputs of your sound card.

7. Click on the Rewind button on the toolbar in SONAR so that recording will start at the beginning of the song. Then click on the Record button on the toolbar in SONAR, and your MIDI tracks will be recorded to the stereo audio track.

After you're finished, you should have two new audio tracks representing your sound card's built-in synthesizer and your external MIDI instruments.

Converting Your DXi Tracks

You also need to convert any MIDI tracks that use DXis for playback. To do so, just follow these steps:

1. Mute all the tracks in your project except the MIDI and audio tracks pertaining to your DXis.

2. Choose Edit > Bounce to Tracks to open the Bounce to Tracks dialog box. I talked about the Bounce to Tracks function in Chapter 7.

3. Choose New Track in the drop-down list for the Destination field.

4.   Choose Mix to Single Track Stereo Event(s) in the drop-down list for the Format field.

5.   For the Separation field, choose the All Main Out's to Single Mix option.

6.   In the Mix Enables section, make sure all the options are activated.

7.   Click OK.

SONAR will create a new stereo audio track containing all the music from your DXis.

Converting Your Audio Tracks

After all your MIDI tracks are converted to audio tracks, you need to mix and export all your audio tracks down to a WAV file. SONAR provides a very convenient feature expressly for this purpose, called Export Audio. This feature takes any number of original audio tracks (preserving their volume, pan, and effects settings) and mixes them into a single stereo WAV file. Here's how to use it:

1.   Mute all the MIDI tracks in your project and any audio tracks that you don't want included in the exported WAV file.

2.   Choose File > Export > Audio to open the Export Audio dialog box, as shown in Figure 17.5.

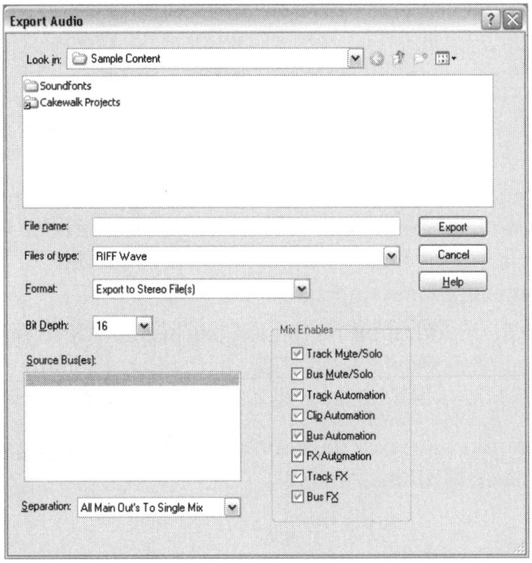

Figure 17.5
You use the Export Audio dialog box to mix and export your tracks.

3.   From the Look In list, select the folder into which you want to save the WAV file. Then type a name for the file in the File Name field.

4.   Choose the file type from the Files of Type drop-down list. In this case, use the RIFF Wave option.

5.   Select the format you want to use. You can mix your audio tracks to a single stereo file, two mono files (that, when combined, create a stereo file), or a single mono file. You can also set the bit depth using the Bit Depth parameter. I explained bit depth in Chapter 6.

BURN TO CD

If you plan to burn your project to CD, then choose the Export to Stereo File(s) option for the Format parameter, and choose the 16 Bit option for the Bit Depth parameter. This will give you a single stereo WAV file with a bit depth of 16, which is what you need for audio CD burning.

6. For the Separation field, choose the All Main Out's to Single Mix option.

7. Leave all the Mix Enables options activated to ensure that your new WAV file will sound exactly the same when played back as the original audio tracks.

8. Click on the Export button, and SONAR will mix all your audio tracks down to a new WAV file.

When you're done, you should have a WAV file that you can use along with your CD-recording software to create an audio CD.

Using Cakewalk Pyro 2003

To burn your WAV file to an audio CD, you'll need a CD-burning application such as Cakewalk's Pyro 2003. Pyro is very easy to use and provides a number of useful CD-burning features. To burn an audio WAV file to CD using Pyro 2003, follow these basic steps:

1. Start Pyro 2003 and click on the Make Audio CD tab to display the audio CD burning screen, as shown in Figure 17.6. The bottom half of the screen shows all of the resources available on your PC. This includes your Windows desktop, the hard drives, and all the files stored on your computer. The left pane is the Folders view, and the right pane is the Files view. The top half of the screen represents your new audio CD. Initially you'll see only blank white space.

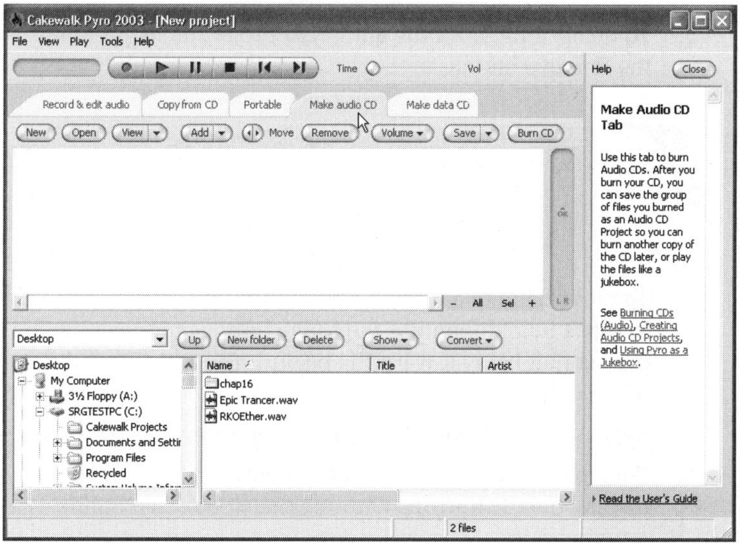

Figure 17.6
Click on the Make Audio CD tab to access Pyro's audio CD functions.

2. In the Folders view, choose the resource or disk drive containing the audio files you want to burn to CD. For example, if you have some files on your Windows desktop that you want to burn, click on Desktop in the Folders view. The Files view will then display a list of all the folders and files available on the desktop.

3. In the Files view, select the audio files you want to burn to CD. To select multiple files, hold down the Ctrl key on your computer keyboard as you click on the files with your mouse.

4. Click on the Add button in the top half of the screen to add the selected files to your audio CD project. The files will be added to the audio CD project area, as shown in Figure 17.7.

Figure 17.7
Click on the Add button
to add files to your audio
CD project.

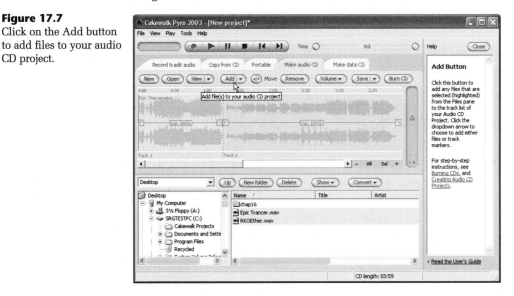

5. To delete a file from the audio CD project, click on it to select it, and then click on the Remove button.

LIST VIEW
You can also view the tracks on your audio CD project as a list by clicking on the View button.

6. To move a file to a different track location in the audio CD project, click on the file to select it, and then use the Move buttons to move the file left or right in the project (left being toward the beginning of the CD and right being toward the end of the CD).

7. Repeat steps 2 through 6 until you've finished adding all your files to the project.

8. Put a blank CD-R disc in your CD burner and then click on the Burn CD button to display the CD Burning Options dialog box (see Figure 17.8).

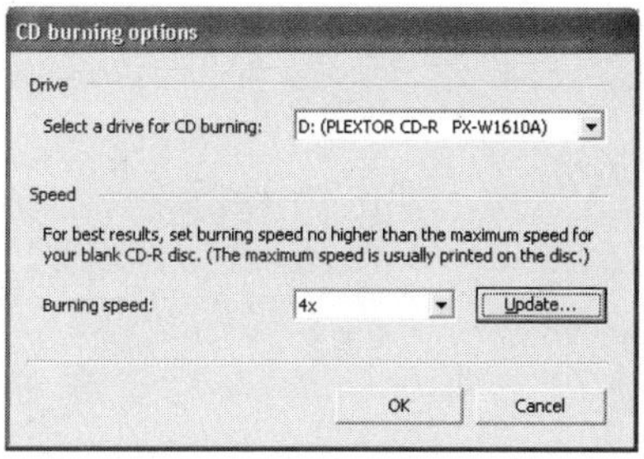

Figure 17.8
Use the CD Burning
Options dialog box to
choose the drive and the
burning speed you want
to use.

CD burning options
Drive
Select a drive for CD burning: D: (PLEXTOR CD-R PX-W1610A)   ▼
Speed
For best results, set burning speed no higher than the maximum speed for your blank CD-R disc. (The maximum speed is usually printed on the disc.)
Burning speed: 4x   ▼   Update...
OK   Cancel

9. Choose the drive you want to use from the Select a Drive for CD Burning drop-down list. If you have only one CD burner attached to your computer, it should be chosen automatically.

10. Choose the burning speed you want to use from the Burning Speed drop-down list. If the list doesn't look accurate, you can have Pyro scan your drive by clicking on the Update button.

CD BURNING SPEEDS

When choosing a burning speed, be sure to read the label on the blank disc you are using to determine its maximum speed rating. Some CDs are created to withstand high burning speeds and some are not. If you choose a speed that is higher than what your disc can withstand, it might not burn correctly.

11. Click on OK. Pyro 2003 will display the Burning CD dialog box and show you its progress as it burns your new audio CD.

AVOID GLITCHES

To avoid glitches in the burning process—especially for audio CDs—you should leave your computer alone until the process is complete. If it gets bogged down while burning, you could end up with a ruined CD. Of course, you can just go ahead and burn another one, but then you'll be wasting both your time and money.

Burning CDs with Windows XP

If you are running SONAR under Windows XP, then you don't need any third-party CD burning software because Windows XP provides built-in burning capabilities. By utilizing the new version of Windows Media Player (included with Windows XP), you can burn audio CDs and data CDs (which I'll talk about in Appendix B, "Backing Up Your Project Files") by following a few simple steps.

1. In Windows XP, click on Start > Windows Media Player to open Windows Media Player.

2. If the Player is not displayed in full mode (as a normal window with a menu bar), click on the Show Menu Bar button (see Figure 17.9).

Figure 17.9
Click on the Show Menu
Bar button to display
Windows Media Player in
a full window.

3. Click on the Media Library button (located on the left side of the Player window) to display the Media Library (see Figure 17.10).

Figure 17.10
Access the Media Library
using the Media Library
button.

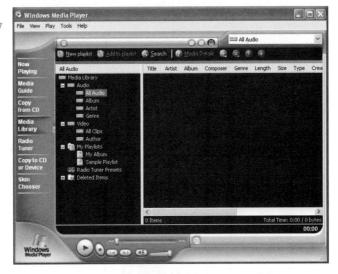

4. In the list on the left side of the Media Library, select All Audio.

5. Choose File > Add to Media Library > Add File to display the Open dialog box.

6. In the Look In drop-down list, choose the location of the WAV files you want to burn to CD.

7. In the file list below the Look In drop-down list, select the WAV files you want to burn to CD. To select multiple files, hold down the Ctrl key on your computer keyboard as you select files with your mouse.

8. When you are finished selecting files, click on Open. Your selected files will be displayed as a list on the right side of the Media Library.

9. If you want to remove a file from the list, right-click on the file and choose Delete from Library.

10. To change the title of a file, right-click on the file and choose Properties to open the Properties dialog box (see Figure 17.11). In addition to the title, you can also specify the file's artist, author, album, and genre. Click on OK.

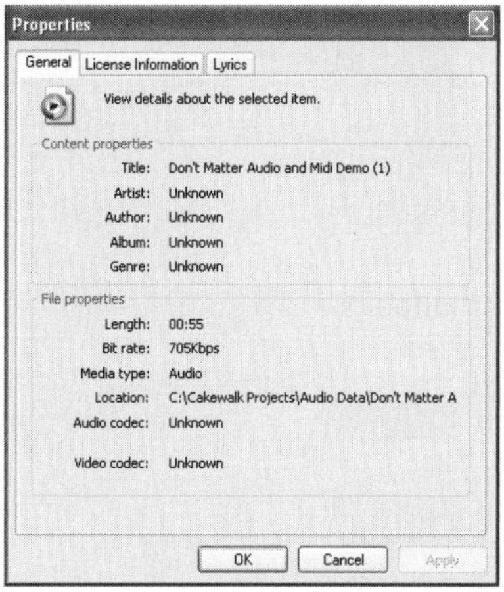

Figure 17.11
Use the Properties dialog box to specify a title, artist, and other attributes for your files.

11. Click on the Copy to CD or Device button (located on the left side of the Player window) to display the CD Copier (see Figure 17.12).

Figure 17.12
Use the CD Copier to burn your audio to CD.

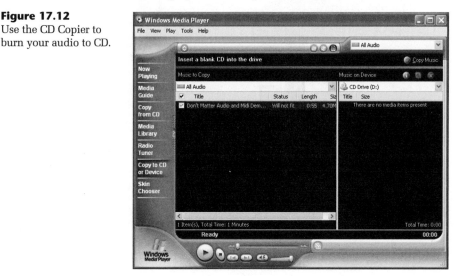

12. Insert a blank CD-R disc into your CD-R drive. The CD Copier will recognize the blank disc and display the message Copy "All Audio" to "CD Drive".

13. To burn your CD, click on the Copy Music button (located on the top right of the CD Copier).

AVOID GLITCHES

To avoid glitches in the burning process—especially for audio CDs—you should leave your computer alone until the process is complete. If it gets bogged down while burning, you could end up with a ruined CD. Of course, you can just go ahead and burn another one, but then you'll be wasting both your time and money.

Appendix A
Sample Project Outline: From Recording to Mixdown

Throughout this book, you've learned about everything you need to know to create a project from start to finish in SONAR. This information includes how to set up a project, record your tracks, edit your MIDI and audio data, mix your tracks down to stereo, and burn the final recording to CD. But just to give you a brief overview of the whole process, I've put together this outline of all the steps you need to take to record a song using SONAR.

Setting Up Your Project

1. Create a new project. If you use a template other than Normal to automatically set the parameters for your project, you can skip the rest of this section. Otherwise, move on to Step 2.

2. Add a title and other descriptive information to your project using the File Info window.

3. Set the types of MIDI data to be recorded on the MIDI tab of the Global Options dialog box.

4. Set the Clock, Metronome, and MIDI Out parameters in the Project Options dialog box.

5. Set the tempo for the project by using the Tempo toolbar.

6. Set the Meter and Key for the project by using the Meter/Key view.

7. Set the bit depth and sampling rate (if you're going to record audio) for the project under the General tab in the Audio Options dialog box.

For more information, refer to Chapter 4.

Recording Your Tracks

1. Create a new track and set it up, typing in a name and choosing an input and output in the Track view.

2. Enter initial values for the Volume and Pan parameters, if needed.

3. If the track is for audio, you can skip this step; otherwise, for a MIDI track, choose values for the Channel, Bank, and Patch parameters.

4.   Set the record mode using the Record Options dialog box.

5.   Arm the track and set your input signal level.

6.   Click on the Record button and start your performance.

7.   If you need to add data to only a certain part of the track, use the Auto Punch Record mode and set the Punch In and Punch Out times. You can also use the Loop toolbar to set loop points and have SONAR loop a certain section of the song for recording in only that section.

8.   Repeat steps 1 through 7 for every track you need to complete your song.

9.   Save your project.

For more information, refer to Chapter 6.

Editing Your Data

1.   Use the Track view to make any arrangement changes to your song. For example, you can move clips from one part of the song to another part. You can also mute any tracks that you don't want to use in the final mix. Also, adjust the Key+, Velocity Trim, and Time+ parameters at this time.

2.   If you need to do any precise editing to your MIDI tracks, use the Piano Roll and Event views. You use these views for tasks such as changing the pitch and velocity of different notes or correcting the timing of your performance using quantizing. You also can use the Staff view for certain tasks if you feel more comfortable using standard music notation. If you want to add any permanent MIDI effects to your data, do so at this time. Otherwise, you can add effects in real time during mixdown.

3.   For precise editing of your audio tracks, use the Track view. Cut, copy, or paste sections of audio and make adjustments to the volume if necessary. Add any EQ or permanent effects at this point, too. Otherwise, you can wait to add effects in real time during mixdown, if your computer system can handle it.

4.   Save your project.

For more information, refer to Chapters 7 and 8.

Mixing Down Your Project

1.   Using the Track view or the Console view, set initial values for the volume and panning for each track in the project.

2.   Set the chorus and reverb settings for the MIDI tracks.

3.   Set the Send settings for the audio tracks.

4.   Add any real-time effects you want to use for the individual MIDI and/or audio tracks.

5.   Add any real-time effects you want to use on the buses.

6. Arm any of the parameters that you might adjust during mixdown, and then take a Snapshot of the current setup in case you want to come back to it later.

7. Perform a test run of the mix by playing the song and adjusting the parameters during playback.

8. Record your mix movements using the Record Automation feature. If you find that you need to make two different value changes at once during a mix, just make multiple Record Automation passes. You can also use envelopes for automation if you prefer that method.

9. Save your project.

For more information, refer to Chapters 11 and 12.

Burning to CD

1. Export your project to a stereo audio WAV file.

2. Use Cakewalk's Pyro 2003 or Windows XP to record your WAV file to CD.

For more information, refer to Chapter 17.

Appendix B

Backing Up Your Project Files

At the end of every recording session, I back up my project files. It doesn't matter whether I'm running late or whether I'm so tired that I can barely keep my eyes open; I always back up my files. Why? Because there once was a time when I didn't think much of making backups. I would do it occasionally—just to be safe—but I never thought I'd run into any trouble. Then one day I went to boot up my PC, and *poof*! My hard drive crashed, taking a lot of important files with it, including a project that I had spent weeks working on. Believe me, after that experience I never took file backups for granted again, and you shouldn't either.

Backing up your files really isn't difficult, and it doesn't take much extra time. This is especially true if your project includes only MIDI data. Project files containing only MIDI data are usually very small, and you can back them up by simply copying them to a floppy disk, just like you would any other small files. On the other hand, you might need to handle project files that contain audio data a little differently because of their possibly large size. Some larger project files might fit on a floppy disk, but if not, you can use an Iomega Zip disk drive (or a similar "super floppy" drive) and make a quick backup copy that way.

Backing Up with Pyro 2003

If you have a bunch of files to back up, you might need a much larger storage format, such as a CD-R. In Chapter 16, you learned about using Cakewalk's Pyro 2003 to create an audio CD from your SONAR project. In case you didn't know it, you can also use Pyro 2003 along with your CD-R drive to back up data files. The procedure is a bit different from creating an audio CD, but it's not difficult. To create a data CD with Pyro 2003, follow these steps:

1. Start Pyro 2003 and click on the Make Data CD tab to display the data CD burning screen, as shown in Figure B.1. The bottom half of the screen shows all of the resources available on your PC. This includes your Windows desktop, the hard drives, and all the files stored on your computer. The left pane is the Folders view, and the right pane is the Files view. The top half of the screen represents your new data CD. The left pane is the Data CD Folders view, and the right pane is the Data CD Files view.

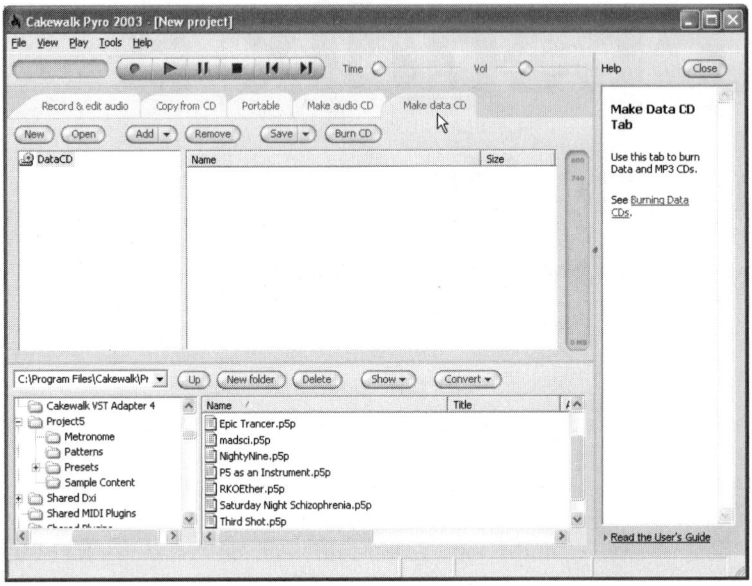

Figure B.1
Click the Make Data CD
tab to access Pyro's data
CD functions.

2. In the Folders view, choose the resource or disk drive that contains the files you
    want to burn to CD. For example, if you have some files or a folder of files on your
    Windows desktop that you want to save, click on Desktop in the Folders view.
    The Files view will then display a list of all the folders and files available on the
    desktop.

3. In the Files view, select the files and/or folders you want to burn to CD. To select
    multiple files, hold down the Ctrl key on your computer keyboard as you click on
    the files with your mouse.

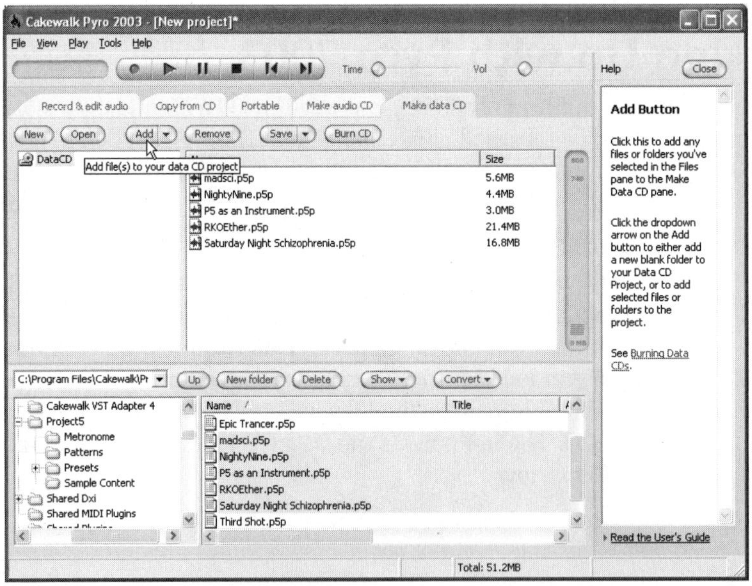

Figure B.2
Click on the Add button
to add files and/or folders
to your data CD project.

4. Click on the Add button in the top half of the screen to add the selected files to your data CD project. The files and/or folders will be added to the Data CD Folders view and the Data CD Files view respectively, as shown in Figure B.2.

5. To delete a file or folder from the data CD project, click on it to select it, and then click on the Remove button.

CD STORAGE CAPACITY

As you add or remove files and folders from your data CD project, be sure to keep an eye on the blue gauge located to the right of the Data CD Files view. This gauge shows you how much room you have left on the current data CD. Most CDs can store up to 740 MB, but some can go as high as 800 MB. You need to read the label on your blank CD to determine how much it can store.

6. Repeat steps 2 through 5 until you've finished adding all your files and/or folders to the project.

7. To give your data CD a name, click on DataCD in the Data CD Folders view to select it. Click on it again to make it editable, and then type a new name for the CD. The name for a data CD can be up to 11 characters and can only contain letters, numbers, or underscore characters.

8. Put a blank CD-R disc in your CD burner and then click on the Burn CD button located above the Data CD Files view to display the CD Burning Options dialog box (see Figure B.3).

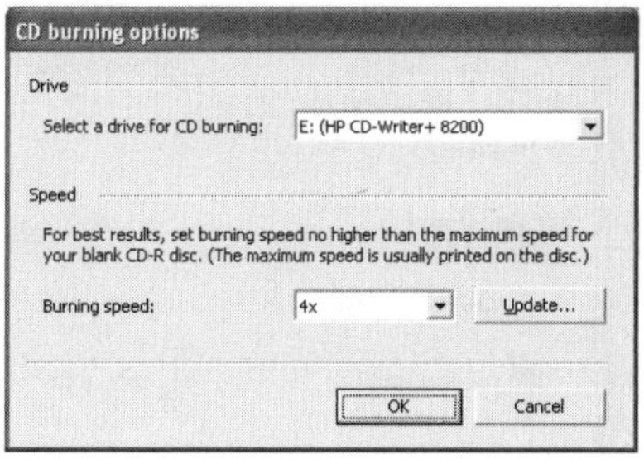

Figure B.3
Use the CD Burning Options dialog box to choose the drive and the burning speed you want to use.

9. Choose the drive you want to use from the Select a Drive for CD Burning drop-down list. If you have only one CD burner attached to your computer, it should already be selected.

10. Choose the burning speed you want to use from the Burning Speed drop-down list. If the list doesn't look accurate, you can have Pyro scan your drive; simply click on the Update button.

CD BURNING SPEEDS
When you choose a burning speed, be sure to read the label on the blank disc you are using to determine its maximum speed rating. Some CDs are created to withstand high burning speeds and some are not. If you choose a speed that is higher than what your disc can withstand, it might not burn correctly.

11. Click on OK. Pyro 2003 will display the Burning CD dialog box and show you its progress as it burns your new data CD.

Backing Up with Windows XP

As I mentioned in Chapter 16, Windows XP provides built-in CD burning capabilities for data CDs as well as audio CDs. If you are using Windows XP, you can back up your project files to CD using the following procedure:

1. Insert a blank CD-R or CD-RW disc into your CD recording drive. If Windows XP opens a CD Drive window, just click on Cancel.

2. In Windows XP, choose Start > My Computer to open My Computer (see Figure B.4).

Figure B.4
Use My Computer in Windows XP to select your project files.

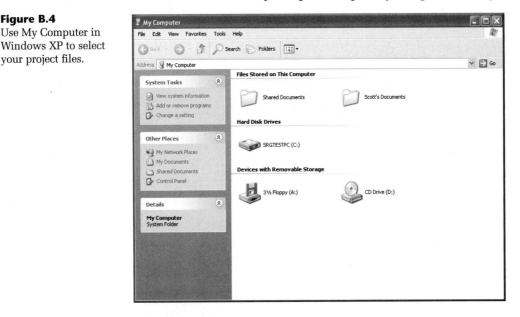

3. Double-click on the hard disk icon and navigate to the location of your project files. Then select the files that you want to back up.

4. On the left side of the window, you'll see a section called File and Folder Tasks (see Figure B.5). Click on Copy This File (for single files) or Copy the Selected Items (for multiple files).

Figure B.5
Choose the appropriate option in the File and Folder Tasks section.

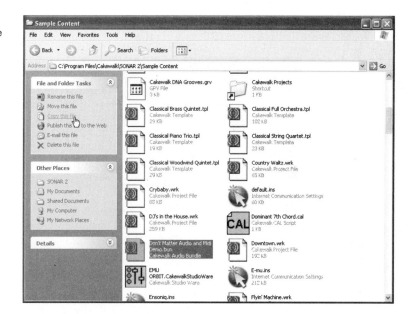

5. In the Copy Items dialog box, select your CD recording drive and click on the Copy button.

6. A balloon message will pop up in the Windows XP taskbar with the message "You have files waiting to be written to the CD." Click on the balloon to open a new window for your CD recording drive (see Figure B.6). The right side of the window will list the files to be burned.

Figure B.6
The CD Drive window lists the files to be burned.

7. On the left side of the window, you'll see a section called CD Writing Tasks. Click on Write These Files to CD to open the CD Writing Wizard (see Figure B.7).

Figure B.7
Use the CD Writing
Wizard to burn your files
to CD.

Welcome to the CD Writing
Wizard

This wizard helps you write, or record, your files to a CD
recording drive.

Type the name you want to give to this CD, or just click Next
to use the name below.

CD name:

BackUp1

New files being written to the CD will replace any files
already on the CD if they have the same name.

☐ Close the wizard after the files have been written

< Back   Next >   Cancel

8. Enter a name for the CD in the CD Name field, and then click on Next. Windows XP will burn your file to the CD.

9. Follow the remaining prompts and click on Finish when you are done.

FILE SPLITTING

Sometimes you might find that you have a project file that is too big to fit on a single CD. Project files containing audio can get quite large, especially if they contain many audio tracks or you are using a high bit depth (such as 24-bit) or a high sampling rate (such as 96 kHz). In this case, it would seem that you have no way of storing your file on a data CD. Well, if you use a file-splitting utility, you can get around this limitation.

A file-splitting utility will take your file and divide it into smaller files that can be burned to multiple CDs. These smaller files represent different sections of your one large file. If you ever need to access the file again, you can copy the smaller files from the CDs to your hard drive, and then use the utility to combine them into the large file.

Take a look at the following Internet site for a list of some of the available file splitting utilities:

http://download.com.com/3120-20-0.html?qt=file+splitter&tg=dl-20.

Now, don't you feel better already? You can rest easy knowing that all your difficult recording work won't be lost even if your computer decides to give up on you one of these days. Believe me, it's not a fun experience.

Appendix C
Producing for Multimedia and the Web

In addition to enabling regular music production, SONAR includes a number of features to help you create music for multimedia and the Internet. You can import a video file into a SONAR project and then compose music for it. You can also export video files along with your synchronized music. And you can export your music files to a number of popular Internet audio file formats, including RealAudio, Windows Media Format, and MP3. In essence, these capabilities round out SONAR's full set of features, allowing you to use the program for most (if not all) of your music production needs.

Importing Video Files

If you're ever asked to compose music for film, video games, or some other visually-based task, SONAR's File > Import > Video File command will come in very handy. Using this command, you can include an AVI, MPEG, or QuickTime video in your project and edit the existing audio tracks or add new ones.

VIDEO FILE FORMATS
AVI, MPEG, and QuickTime are special digital video file formats specifically designed for working with video on computers. Each format uses its own unique compression scheme to achieve the highest possible video quality in the smallest possible file size. AVI (*Audio Video Interleaved*) is a Windows-based format, which means that any computer running Windows can play AVI files. QuickTime is a Mac-based format, which means that any Macintosh computer can play QuickTime files. With special player software, a computer running Windows can play QuickTime files too, which is why SONAR supports the format. MPEG (*Motion Pictures Expert Group*) is a more advanced format that sometimes requires special hardware for playback. Therefore, MPEG video files are usually much better quality than AVI or QuickTime files, and they are also smaller in size.

To add a video file to your project, follow these steps:

1. Choose File > Import > Video File to open the Video File dialog box (see Figure C.1).

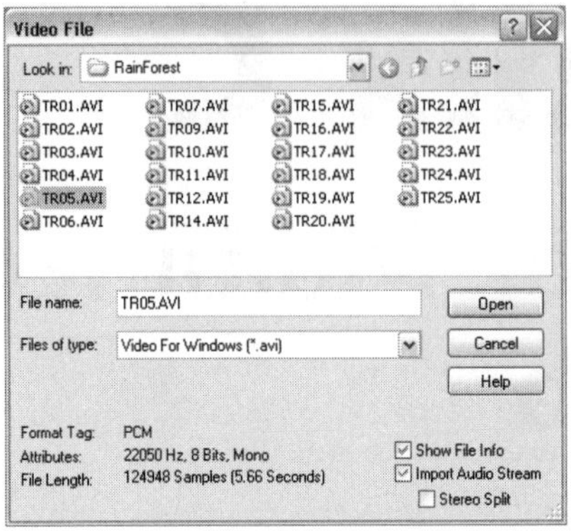

Figure C.1

Here you can select a video file to add to your project.

2. Choose the type of video file (AVI, MPEG, or QuickTime) you want to add from the Files of Type drop-down list, and then select a file.

3. If the video file contains audio data, you can import that data by activating the Import Audio Stream option at the bottom of the dialog box. If the audio is in stereo, you can import it as a single stereo audio track or a pair of audio tracks containing the left and right channels of the stereo signal by deactivating or activating the Stereo Split option, respectively.

4. Click on Open.

SONAR will load the video file and display the first video frame along with the current Now time in the Video view (see Figure C.2). If you imported audio along with the video, the new audio tracks will be inserted into the project above the currently selected track.

Figure C.2

The Video view displays the video along with the current Now time.

When you initially play the project, the video will start playing back at the beginning, but you can change where the video starts by adjusting the start time, as well as the trim-in and trim-out times. Using these parameters, you can adjust when the video will start and end playback. To change the parameters, follow these steps:

1. Right-click in the Video view and select Video Properties from the drop-down menu to open the Video Properties dialog box.

2. On the Video Settings tab, input the new values for the start time, trim-in time, and trim-out time. The start time uses measures, beats, and frames for its value; and the trim-in and trim-out times use hours, minutes, seconds, and frames, just as with SMPTE time code.

3. Click on OK.

The video will start and stop playing back within the project at the times you specified. You can adjust a number of other parameters for the Video view, and you access all of them via the right-click menu. For instance, if you want to remove the video from your project, just select the Delete command. If you want to temporarily disable video playback, select the Animate command. You can even change the size of the video display by using the Stretch Options command.

EXITING FROM FULL-SCREEN MODE

If you choose Full Screen under the Stretch Options command, the video display will cover the entire computer screen and you will not be able to access SONAR with the mouse (although the keyboard commands will still work). To get back to the normal display, just press the Esc (Escape) key on your computer keyboard.

SONAR 3 provides some additional settings on the Render Quality tab of the Video Properties dialog box. These include Preview Mode, Frame Rate, and Video Size. Basically, these parameters allow you to choose how you will view the video during playback in SONAR; they do not alter the video data itself. If you activate the Preview Mode option, SONAR will display the video using slightly lower quality. This lets SONAR use more processing power for audio playback and less for video playback, and it comes in handy if your PC is having a hard time playing both data formats at once. The Frame Rate parameter provides a similar functionality. Enter a lower frame rate for lower-quality video and to ease the strain on your PC. Using the Video Size parameters, you can adjust the size of the video during playback in SONAR. This essentially lets you preview how your video would look at a different size, but it doesn't actually change the size of the video when you export it.

Exporting Video Files

After you've imported a video file into your project and either edited its existing audio or added new audio tracks to it, you can export the file so other people can see and hear your work. Follow these steps to export the file:

1. Choose File > Export > Video to AVI to open the Video to AVI dialog box (see Figure C.3).

2. Type a name for the file in the File Name field. You don't need to select a file type because SONAR allows you to save your video in the AVI (Video for Windows) format only. You can't save it as MPEG or QuickTime.

3. Click on Save, and the video file will be saved with its original parameter settings. If you want to dabble with the method of compression used for the file or with other video-related parameters, you can set them in the lower half of the dialog box.

APPENDIX C

Figure C.3
You can use the Video to AVI dialog box to export video files.

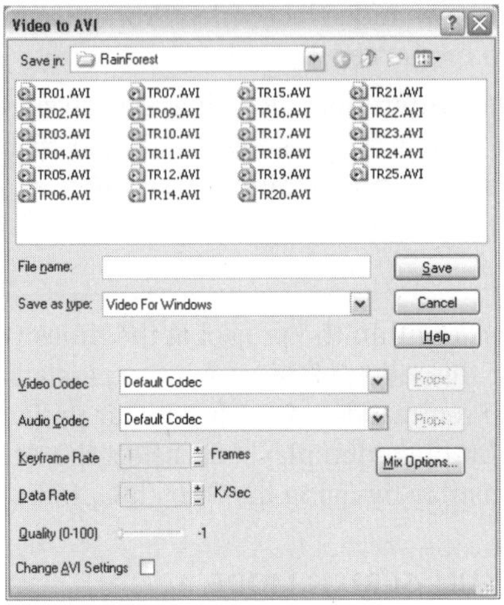

Video to AVI

Save in:	RainForest		
TR01.AVI	TR07.AVI	TR15.AVI	TR21.AVI
TR02.AVI	TR09.AVI	TR16.AVI	TR22.AVI
TR03.AVI	TR10.AVI	TR17.AVI	TR23.AVI
TR04.AVI	TR11.AVI	TR18.AVI	TR24.AVI
TR05.AVI	TR12.AVI	TR19.AVI	TR25.AVI
TR06.AVI	TR14.AVI	TR20.AVI	

File name:
Save as type: Video For Windows
Save
Cancel
Help

Video Codec: Default Codec   Prope...
Audio Codec: Default Codec   Prop2...
Keyframe Rate: 1 Frames   Mix Options...
Data Rate: 1 K/Sec
Quality (0-100): -1
Change AVI Settings ☐

MULTIMEDIA: MAKING IT WORK

For more information about multimedia and video-related parameters, you should consult a book dedicated to the subject. I've found *Multimedia: Making It Work, Fifth Edition* (McGraw-Hill Osborne Media, 2001) to be very informative.

When you save your video file, any audio tracks in your project will be mixed down and saved along with the video.

Exporting Audio Files

In addition to exporting your audio tracks as WAV files for the purpose of burning to CD (as you learned in Chapter 17), you can also export them as RealAudio, Windows Media Format, and MP3 files for distribution over the Internet.

AUDIO FILE FORMATS

Just as AVI, MPEG, and QuickTime are special digital video file formats, RealAudio, Windows Media, and MP3 are special audio file formats specifically designed for distributing audio over the Internet. Each format uses its own unique compression scheme to achieve the best possible sound quality in the smallest possible file size. All three formats are very popular, and all three support streaming audio as well. This means you can listen to the audio as you download it rather than waiting for the entire audio file to download before you can play it.

In terms of quality, the order from highest to lowest is Windows Media, MP3, RealAudio. However, this order depends on who's listening, because every person has his or her own opinions on the subject. For more information about RealAudio, visit http://www.realnetworks.com/resources. For more information about Windows Media, visit http://www.microsoft.com/windows/windowsmedia. For more information about MP3, visit http://www.mpeg.org/MPEG/mp3.html.

Preparing Audio for the Internet

Because the RealAudio, MP3, and Windows Media formats all use compression to reduce the size of audio data so it's easier to download over the Internet, they sometimes affect the sound of your audio. You can compensate for these unwanted changes in quality by following a few simple processing procedures before you convert your files.

▶ **Mix down tracks first.** Instead of processing your existing tracks, it is a good idea to mix down all your tracks to a single stereo audio track. That way you can keep all your original tracks intact and just process the single stereo track for exporting as RealAudio, MP3, or Windows Media.

▶ **Remove DC offset.** Before you process your audio data, you should remove any DC offset that might be present in it. What is DC offset? Well, depending on the quality of your sound card, your audio might not be recorded as accurately as it should. Many times an electrical mismatch can occur between a sound card and the input device (especially with less-expensive sound cards, such as the Sound Blaster). When this happens, an excess of current is added to the incoming signal, and the resulting audio waveform is offset from the zero axis (a line running horizontally through the center of a waveform that represents no sound or zero amplitude). This is known as DC offset. Unfortunately, SONAR doesn't provide a DC offset removal function, but you can download a free DirectX effects plug-in to use for this purpose. The plug-in is called DCOffset, and you can download it from http://www.analogx.com/contents/download/audio/dcoffset.htm.

Applying Equalization

Equalize your audio but keep in mind that you might lose most of the high-end and extreme low-end content when you export the audio to one of the compressed file formats. It might take some experimentation, but cutting the low frequencies (below 60 Hz) and the high frequencies (above 10 kHz) is a good place to start. This will help reduce any of the anomalies that can occur during the file format compression. To compensate for the frequencies being cut, you can boost some of the low frequencies that are still intact, around 200 Hz. You can also boost the important content in your audio, such as vocals (if there are any). Here's how it's done:

1. Select the stereo audio track that you created from bouncing down all the other existing tracks (mentioned earlier).

2. Choose Process > Audio Effects > Cakewalk > FxEq to open the FxEq dialog box.

3. Choose the None preset to assign all the parameter settings to their default values.

4. Activate the Lo Shelf option. Set its Center Frequency (Coarse) to around 60 Hz, and then set its gain to −15 dB (the lowest setting). Doing this will cut out most frequencies below 60 Hz, as I mentioned earlier.

5. Activate the Hi Shelf option. Set its Center Frequency (Coarse) to around 10,000 Hz, and then set its gain to −15 dB (the lowest setting). Doing this will cut out most frequencies above 10 kHz, as I mentioned earlier.

6. Set the Gain on the first parametric band to +3.0 dB, and then set its Center Frequency (Coarse) to around 200 Hz. Also, set its Bandwidth (Coarse) to 1.00. You can experiment with how much the frequencies are boosted, but I wouldn't go any higher than +6.0 dB.

7. Set the Gain on the second parametric band to +3.0 dB, and then set its Center Frequency (Coarse) to around 2,500 Hz. Also, set its Bandwidth (Coarse) to 1.00. This will boost the mid-range frequencies around 2,500 Hz. You can experiment with how much the frequencies are boosted, but I wouldn't go any higher than +6.0 dB.

8. Leave all the other parameters set to their defaults. When you're finished, the FxEq dialog box should look similar to Figure C.4.

Figure C.4
Use the FxEq function to equalize your audio in a single process.

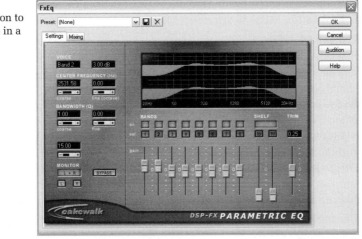

9. Click on the Audition button to preview your audio before you make any changes. If you hear any clipping or distortion, try lowering the gain on one or both of the parametric bands.

10. Click on OK.

Applying Dynamic Processing

In addition to altering the frequency content of your audio, converting to RealAudio, MP3, or Windows Media can reduce the dynamic (amplitude) range, making your audio sound flat or dull. Adding a bit of dynamic processing before conversion will give you some control over your final signal levels, rather than leaving them to chance. To accomplish this, you need to use SONAR's FX Compressor/Gate effect.

1. Select the stereo audio track that you created from bouncing down all the other existing tracks (mentioned earlier).

2. Choose Process > Audio Effects > Cakewalk > FX Compressor/Gate to open the FX Compressor/Gate dialog box.

3. Choose the Flat preset to assign all the parameter settings to their default values.

4. Set the Attack Time parameter to 1 ms (millisecond).

5. Set the Compressor Ratio parameter to 2.0:1. You can experiment with the Compressor Ratio if you'd like. A good ratio range is between 2.0:1 and 4.0:1, but it might vary with some audio material so you'll have to use your own judgment. But

be careful—too much dynamic processing can sometimes add unwanted artifacts and make your audio sound dull and lifeless.

6. Set the Release Time parameter to 500 ms.

7. Set the Compressor Thr (Threshold) parameter to −18 dB.

8. Leave all the other parameters set to their defaults. When you're finished, the FX Compressor/Gate dialog box should look similar to Figure C.5.

Figure C.5
Use the FX Compressor/Gate effect to apply dynamic processing to your audio.

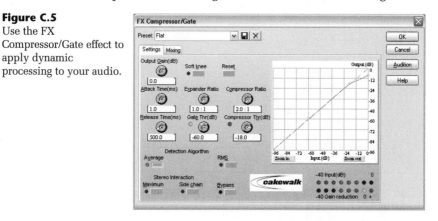

9. Click on the Audition button to preview your audio before you make any changes.

10. Click on OK.

Normalizing Your Audio

The last step is to normalize your audio. As I discussed in Chapter 8, normalization raises the amplitude of an audio signal as high as it can go without causing clipping or distortion. This guarantees that your file will use the maximum amount of digital resolution and amplitude available. It also ensures that you'll be using the highest possible volume when exporting your audio for the Internet, which helps mask low-level noise and possible compression artifacts. But keep in mind that normalization is not always necessary, so you might want to try exporting your audio with and without normalization. To normalize your audio:

1. Select the stereo audio track that you created from bouncing down all the other existing tracks (mentioned earlier).

2. Choose Process > Audio > Normalize.

Now your audio is ready to be exported to RealAudio, MP3, or Windows Media.

Exporting to RealAudio

Follow these steps to mix and save your audio tracks as a RealAudio file:

1. Select the tracks you want to export in the Track view.

2. Choose File > Export Audio to open the Export Audio dialog box (see Figure C.6).

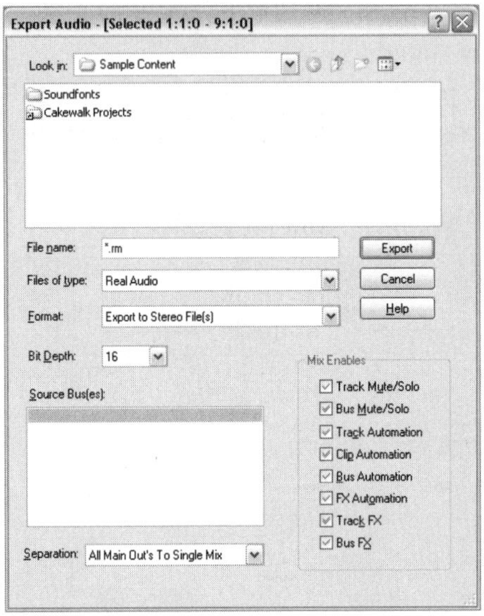

Figure C.6
You can use the Export Audio dialog box to export to RealAudio.

3. From the Look In list, select the folder in which you want to save the RealAudio file. Then type a name for the file in the File Name text box.

4. Choose a file type from the Files of Type list. In this case, use the RealAudio option.

5. Select the Format you want to use. You can mix your audio tracks to a single stereo file, two mono files (that, when combined, create a stereo file), or a single mono file.

6. For the Separation parameter, choose the All Main Out's to Single Mix option.

7. Leave all the Mix Enables options activated to ensure that your new RealAudio file will include the same effects and mix automation that you used on the original audio tracks.

8. Click on Export to open the RealAudio Settings dialog box (see Figure C.7).

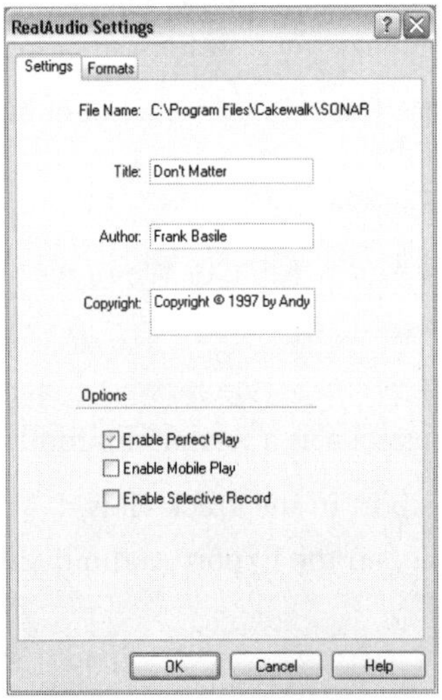

Figure C.7
In the RealAudio Settings dialog box, you can adjust specific parameters for the RealAudio file.

9. On the Settings tab, you can enter title, author, and copyright information for the RealAudio file.

10. Choose from the three options at the bottom of the dialog box: Enable Perfect Play, Enable Mobile Play, and Enable Selective Record. Enable Perfect Play requires listeners to download the entire RealAudio file before hearing it, rather than allowing them to stream the file. This option ensures uninterrupted playback, but your listeners will also have to wait for the download. Enable Mobile Play gives listeners a choice between downloading and streaming a file. Enable Selective Record lets listeners save the file to their hard drive for later. If you don't want people to be able to keep a copy of the file, make sure Enable Mobile Play and Enable Selective Record are not activated.

11. On the Formats tab (see Figure C.8), you can select the modem speeds for which you want your RealAudio file to be optimized. It's really best to select them all so your listeners can hear the best quality at their own specific modem speed. For example, someone using a 56 Kbps modem will hear a better version of your file than someone listening with a 28 Kbps modem. Otherwise, everyone would hear the same low-quality file.

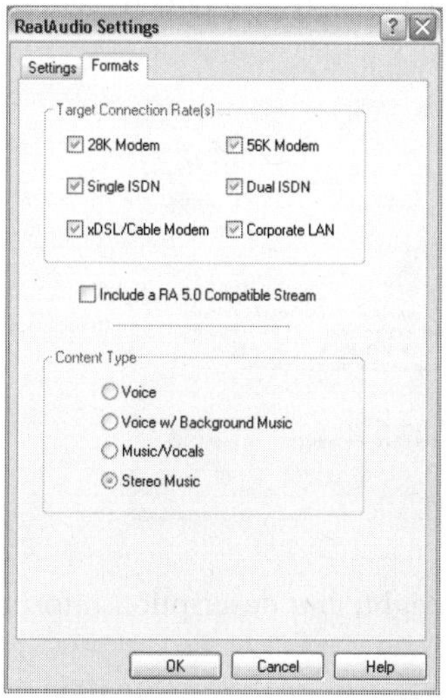

Figure C.8
You can set modem speeds on the Formats tab of the RealAudio Settings dialog box.

12. If you want your file to be compatible with the older 5.0 version of RealAudio, select the Include a RA 5.0 Compatible Stream option. This option makes your file a little bigger, but it's worth the extra size in case someone using the old RealAudio Player software tries to listen to your file.

13. If you want to optimize the RealAudio file for certain types of content, select the type of music you've recorded in your project in the Content Type section. Most of the time, you'll probably use the Stereo Music option.

14. Click on OK, and your audio will be saved as a RealAudio file with an .RM extension.

Exporting to Windows Media

To mix and save your audio tracks as a Windows Media file, just follow these steps:

1. Select the tracks you want to export in the Track view.

2. Choose File > Export Audio to open the Export Audio dialog box.

3. From the Look In list, select the folder in which you want to save the Windows Media file. Then type a name for the file in the File Name text box.

4. Choose the type of file from the Files of Type list. In this case, use the Windows Media option.

5. Select the format you want to use. You can mix your audio tracks to a single stereo file, two mono files (that, when combined, create a stereo file), or a single mono file.

6. For the Separation parameter, choose the All Main Out's to Single Mix option.

7. Leave all the Mix Enables options activated to ensure that your new Windows Media file will include the same effects and mix automation as you used on the original audio tracks.

8. Click on Export to open the Microsoft Audio Encode Options dialog box (see Figure C.9).

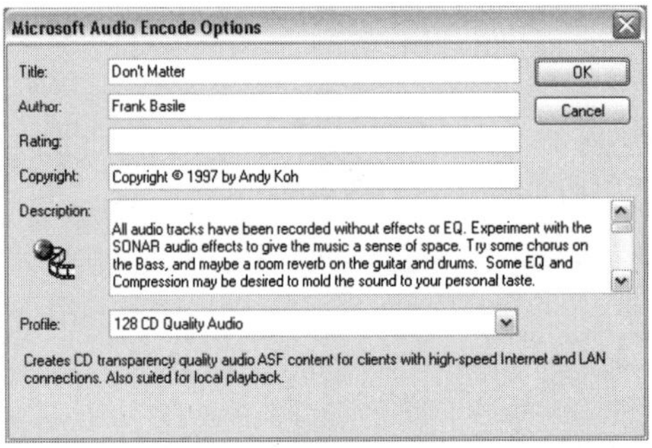

Figure C.9
In the Microsoft Audio Encode Options dialog box, you can adjust specific parameters for the Windows Media file.

9. Enter title, author, rating, copyright, and description information for the Windows Media file.

10. Choose a profile for your Windows Media file. The Profile parameter allows you to choose the audio quality for your file. The higher the quality, the better the file will sound, but the bigger the file size will be. The profile also lets you target the modem speed for the Windows Media file. For example, if you want the file to be able to play over a 28.8 Kbps modem, select the 28.8 FM Radio Stereo option. If you want to produce a higher-quality file, such as a CD-quality file, you can choose the 128 CD Quality Audio option, but the file won't play on a 28.8 Kbps modem. (The listener will have to download the file first.)

11. Click on OK, and your audio will be saved as a Windows Media file with a .WMA extension.

Exporting to MP3

To mix and save your audio tracks as an MP3 file, follow these steps:

1. Select the tracks you want to export in the Track view.

2. Choose File > Export Audio to open the Export Audio dialog box.

3. From the Look In list, select the folder in which you want to save the MP3 file. Then type a name for the file in the File Name text box.

4. Choose the type of file from the Files of Type list. In this case, use the MP3 option.

5. Select the format you want to use. You can mix your audio tracks to a single stereo file, two mono files (that, when combined, create a stereo file), or a single mono file.

6. For the Separation parameter, choose the All Main Out's to Single Mix option.

7. Leave all the Mix Enables options activated to ensure that your new MP3 file will include the same effects and mix automation as you used on the original audio tracks.

8. Click on Export to open the Cakewalk MP3 Encoder dialog box (see Figure C.10).

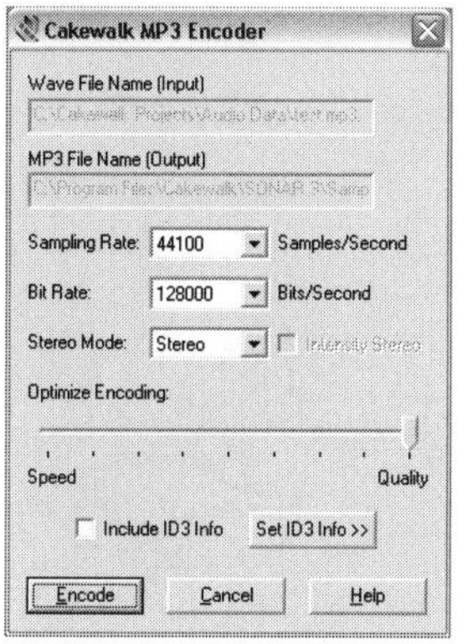

Figure C.10
In the Cakewalk MP3 Encoder dialog box, you can adjust specific parameters for the MP3 file.

9. Here you can select a sampling rate, bit rate, and stereo mode for your file. You learned about sampling rates in Chapter 1; they let you set the sampling rate for the MP3 file. The higher the rate, the better the file will sound, but the bigger the file size will be.

    Bit rate lets you target the modem speed for the MP3 file. For example, if you want the file to be able to play over a 56 Kbps modem, select the 56000 bit rate. This bit rate should play over any modem speed 56 Kbps or higher. However, you might want to choose the 48000 or even the 40000 bit rate instead because the Internet can be slow at times. If you want to produce a higher-quality file, you can choose a higher bit rate, but the file won't play over a 56 Kbps modem. For example, to produce a near CD-quality file, the standard rate to choose would be 128000.

    The Stereo Mode parameter is pretty straightforward. Choose Stereo to produce a stereo file; choose Mono to produce a mono file. There is also a Joint Stereo mode, which lets you create smaller MP3 files by comparing the left and right audio signals and eliminating any material that is the same in both channels. Using this option usually degrades the audio quality, though, so I advise against it unless you really need smaller MP3 files.

10. Use the Optimize Encoding setting to adjust the time it takes to encode your MP3 file. If you set the slider toward the left, encoding will go faster; set it to the right, and encoding will go slower. But the more time you spend on encoding, the better the quality of the file. I recommend you leave the slider set all the way to the right. Encoding a file doesn't take very long anyway.

11. If you want to include some information about the file, select the Include ID3 Info option. To enter the information, click on Set ID3 Info to open the ID3 Info dialog box. There you can enter title, artist, album, year, track number, comment, and genre information. Click on OK when you're finished.

12. Click on Encode, and your audio will be saved as an MP3 file with an .MP3 extension.

CONVERT YOUR MIDI TRACKS

If you want to include the music from the MIDI tracks of your project in your RealAudio, Windows Media, or MP3 files, read the "Converting Your MIDI Tracks" section of Chapter 17.

Appendix D
SONAR Resources
on the Web

Although I've made every effort to include as much information as possible about SONAR within this book, someone will always have that one question that goes unanswered. And, as I mentioned earlier in the book, some of the topics could fill up tomes all on their own. But that doesn't mean I'm going to leave you out in the cold with nowhere to turn.

I spent some time searching the Internet and found that it provides a number of resources you can use to locate any additional information you might need. I've tried to be sure to list all the quality sites that are available, but I might have missed a few. If you know of a great Cakewalk-related Web site that's not on this list, please drop me a note at http://www.garrigus.com so I can be sure to include the site in the next edition of this book.

DigiFreq

http://www.digifreq.com/digifreq

This is one of the first sites you should visit. I have created a site called DigiFreq that provides free news, reviews, and tips and techniques for music technology users. There is a discussion area where you can post your questions and get them answered directly by me. There is also a live chat area where I hold scheduled chat sessions. You can get a free subscription to the *DigiFreq* monthly music technology newsletter, which includes articles, tips, and all kinds of information about music technology, including SONAR. Plus, as a subscriber you are eligible to win free music products each month, and you also have access to all of the newsletter back issues. Be sure to stop by to sign up for the free newsletter and to meet all of the other *SONAR 3 Power!* readers out there!

SONAR Support Home Page

http://www.cakewalk.com/Support/SONAR/default.asp

The SONAR Support Home Page is also one of the first places you should look for answers. Cakewalk provides a large selection of materials, including answers to the most frequently asked questions (FAQs), product updates, and technical documents. You also can find lessons, tips, and tricks, as well as additional helpful publications and resources. And, of course, you can get in touch with Cakewalk's Tech Support people.

Official Cakewalk Newsgroups

http://www.cakewalk.com/Support/newsgroups.asp

Another place you can look for help is the official Cakewalk Newsgroups page. The Cakewalk newsgroups not only provide you with direct access to Cakewalk Technical Support, but also to other users. You can find specific topics on SONAR, as well as other Cakewalk products.

AudioForums SONAR Forum

http://www.audioforums.com/cgi-bin/ubbcgi/forumdisplay.cgi?action=topics&forum=Sonar&number=24

AudioForums is yet another Web site where you can find discussions about Cakewalk products. You won't find anything overly special about this site, but you can find some good information here.

Homerecording.com BBS Cakewalk Forum

http://www.homerecording.com/bbs/forumdisplay.php?forumid=10

The Homerecording.com BBS Cakewalk forum also provides a discussion area with a good amount of activity for Cakewalk products.

Li'l Chips Systems

http://www.lilchips.com/store/index.asp

Li'l Chips Systems provides free Instrument Definition files and free StudioWare panels for download. Most of them pertain to Roland MIDI products, but you still can find a nice collection that could be useful to you.

Synth Zone

http://www.synthzone.com

Although not a dedicated Cakewalk site, the Synth Zone is an excellent MIDI, synthesizer, and electronic music production resource guide. You can find links to a ton of information, such as patches and associated software, for almost any synthesizer product from almost any manufacturer. In addition, you can find links to discussion groups, classifieds ads and auctions, music and audio software downloads, and more.

Harmony Central

http://www.harmony-central.com

Another excellent non-dedicated Cakewalk site, Harmony Central is one of the best Internet resources for musicians. Updated on a daily basis, the site provides industry news and separate "departments" for Guitar, Bass, Effects, Software, Recording, MIDI, Keyboard and Synths, Drums and Percussion, and Computers and Music, as well as a Bands page. Sifting through all the information on this site will take a while, but it's definitely worth the time and effort.

ProRec

http://www.prorec.com

An additional non-dedicated Cakewalk site, ProRec is one of the best audio recording resources for musicians. Updated regularly, the site provides industry news, articles, and reviews. Like on Harmony Central, sifting through all the information on this site will take a while, but it's definitely worth the time and effort.

Index

INDEX